NEUE HORIZONTE

NEUE HORIZONTE

A First Course in German Language and Culture

Second Edition

David B. Dollenmayer

Massachusetts Institute of Technology

Thomas S. Hansen

Wellesley College

D. C. HEATH AND COMPANY

Lexington, Massachusetts   Toronto

About the Authors

David B. Dollenmayer received his B.A. and Ph.D. from Princeton University, and was a Fulbright Fellow at the University of Munich. He wrote his doctoral dissertation on the idea of history in the novels of the Austrian writers Joseph Roth, Heimito von Doderer, and Robert Musil. He has published articles on Alfred Döblin, Joseph Roth, and Christa Wolf. His book on the Berlin novels of Alfred Döblin will appear in 1988. He is an Assistant Professor of German at the Massachusetts Institute of Technology.

Thomas S. Hansen received his A.B. from Tufts University and his Ph.D. from Harvard University. As a child he attended school in Innsbruck, Austria, and as a student spent six semesters at the University of Tübingen, FRG. After writing his doctoral dissertation on the literature of the German exiles (1933–45), he published several articles on the culture and fictional works of these emigrés. He has received research grants from the Woodrow Wilson Foundation, DAAD, and the NEH. His current research focusses on the 20th century writer Arno Schmidt. He is the chairman of the German Department at Wellesley College in Wellesley, Massachusetts.

Preface

Neue Horizonte, Second Edition, is a complete first-year German program for colleges and universities. It presents the basic grammar of German in the context of the four skills of speaking, listening, reading, and writing, and introduces the culture of contemporary West Germany, East Germany, Austria, and Switzerland as an integral part of the learning process.

Our goal is to help learners achieve linguistic proficiency as a preparation for further study of German language and culture. Special emphasis is therefore placed on communicative competency. We also hope to excite students' curiosity, to help them view their own culture more critically, and to broaden their intellectual horizons in the spirit of Wittgenstein's maxim, "Die Grenzen meiner Sprache sind die Grenzen meiner Welt" (The borders of my language are the borders of my world).

Neue Horizonte has a flexible structure, consisting of an introductory chapter on pronunciation and useful classroom expressions, sixteen regular chapters, and grammar summaries with self-correcting review tests after every four chapters. Each regular chapter contains the following features:

Dialoge and Neue Kombinationen (Dialogues and New Combinations)
The dialogues introduce new grammatical structures and vocabulary through idiomatic German conversations in everyday situations. There are two or three dialogues per chapter, all short enough to be memorized if the teacher desires. Idiomatic English translations are printed on the following page. The *Neue Kombinationen* vary sentences from the dialogues by means of replacement exercises. They are meant to be done in class with books closed. They give students an inductive sense of some of the new grammar before they study it.

Übung zur Aussprache (Pronunciation Practice)
In the first eight chapters, this section reviews phonetic points already presented in the introductory chapter, but which pose special difficulties for English speakers. In the final eight chapters, the *Übung zur Aussprache* presents a German poem to be read aloud in class. These are primarily contemporary poems related to the cultural topic presented in the reading. Most are short enough to be memorized.

Grammatik and Üben wir! (Grammar and Let's Practice!)
Grammar explanations are brief but complete. Important topics such as the passive voice, adjectival nouns, impersonal passive, the endings of unpreceded adjectives, and the double-infinitive construction receive full coverage for active use by the student. No previous familiarity with grammatical terminology is presupposed, and no new vocabulary is introduced in this section. After each step in a grammar explanation, the *Üben wir!* sections present reinforcement drills. These range from simple replacements to transformations to drills calling for a free response from the student. Ninety percent of the drills in *Üben wir!* are designed to be done with books closed. As

often as possible, they require interaction among students, since it is our conviction that language is best learned through interpersonal communication.

Wortschatz 1 & 2 (Vocabulary 1 & 2)

Each chapter contains two groups of words and phrases to be learned for active use. *Wortschatz 1* follows the dialogues, and *Wortschatz 2* immediately precedes the reading selection. Words are arranged alphabetically by parts of speech, and nouns are arranged by gender to facilitate learning. Each *Wortschatz* ends with a list of antonyms (*Gegensätze*—Opposites) for newly introduced adjectives, adverbs, and verbs. By the end of *Neue Horizonte* the student will have acquired a total active lexicon of about 1500 words and phrases. Easily recognized cognates are presented without English equivalents in a special section called *Leicht zu merken* (Easy to Remember) at the end of the *Grammatik* section. These cognates are recognition vocabulary and will not be glossed in the readings. Their English equivalents are, however, given for reference in the final glossaries.

Lesestücke (Readings)

The *Lesestücke* are the core of the presentation of culture in *Neue Horizonte*. The *Lesestücke* of chapters 1–9 provide basic information on daily life in Germany. Topics include the family, geography, secondary schools, the working world, travel, and university and urban life. The readings of chapters 10–16 address more specific issues in twentieth-century German culture and history, for example: divided Germany, foreign workers, women's issues, the Weimar era, and the legacy of World War II. The readings in chapters 11, 13, and 14 are devoted to the German Democratic Republic, Switzerland, and Austria, respectively. The readings in chapters 12 and 15 are authentic, unedited nonfiction texts by the modern writers Anna Seghers and Max von der Grün.

Vom Lesen zum Sprechen (From Reading to Speaking)

This section leads students from the receptive skill of reading back to the communicative skill of speaking. After a brief presentation of additional vocabulary relevant to a specific cultural topic or conversational situation, students are offered a variety of activities—interviews, role-playing, guided dialogues—that stress student-to-student communication. The topical vocabulary of this section is not considered active nor recycled in subsequent chapters, leaving the teacher free to decide whether to have students learn it or not.

Mündliche Übungen and Schriftliche Übungen (Oral and Written Exercises)

These exercises close each chapter by integrating and combining the grammatical and cultural material that has been covered. Oral exercises emphasize student interaction, while written exercises encourage increasing freedom in self-expression. The final written exercise, *Wie sagt man das auf deutsch?* (How do you say that in German?), stresses accuracy in translation from English to German.

Almanach (Almanac)

The final section of each chapter provides either more detailed information in

English on the cultural topic of the chapter, or presents an authentic document related to the theme of the chapter, for example, help-wanted ads in chapter 5.

Photo Essays
The two photo essays on German places and German faces convey a vivid visual impression of the German-speaking countries today. They are meant to pique students' curiosity and whet their appetite for further study of German.

Appendices
The appendices include a reference list of all the strong and irregular verbs introduced in *Neue Horizonte,* a table of equivalent weights and measures, and a comprehensive index to grammatical topics. Both the German-English and the English-German vocabularies list not only all active vocabulary, but also the cognates from *Leicht zu merken* and the optional vocabulary from *Vom Lesen zum Sprechen.*

Finally, we have made a consistent effort in *Neue Horizonte* to eliminate stereotyped sexual roles throughout the book. This effort is itself a reflection of the realities of contemporary life in the German-speaking countries.

Supplementary Materials

Annotated Edition

New to the second edition, the *Annotated Edition* of *Neue Horizonte* contains a detailed description of the program, suggestions for its use, and sample lesson plans. Its main section consists of the student text with overprinted annotations containing a variety of suggestions for implementing and supplementing it. These include variations on exercises, tips on classroom presentation, and etymological and cultural notes.

Workbook/Laboratory Manual

The *Workbook/Laboratory Manual for Neue Horizonte* has been extensively revised. It consists of two sections: the workbook section contains a wide variety of exercises and writing activities that provide additional practice and reinforcement of material covered in the textbook, the laboratory manual contains material to be used in conjunction with the listening comprehension, pronunciation, and dictation exercises of the audio program.

The *Workbook/Laboratory Manual* has answer keys for both sections. To a great extent, students can thus correct the exercises themselves.

Audio Program

A complete audio program accompanies *Neue Horizonte*. The program consists of dual-track cassettes and a tapescript. Each chapter cassette contains the *Dialoge, Neue Kombinationen, Übung zur Aussprache*, and selected *Üben wir!* exercises from the textbook. In addition, each chapter cassette has the following new material for sharpening listening comprehension: multiple choice and true/false questions on the textbook dialogues, a *new* dialogue followed by content and interpretive questions (*Hören Sie gut zu*—Listen Carefully), an *Übung zur Betonung* (Stress Practice) emphasizing cognates and loan words, and a 10-sentence *Diktat* (Dictation). Both the new dialogue and the dictation contain only vocabulary and grammar the students have already learned. A cassette symbol next to an exercise in the text means that it has been recorded.

Software Testing Program and Test Item File

Also new to the second edition, the Archive test bank is a fund of approximately 50 test questions for each chapter of *Neue Horizonte*. The questions test primarily grammar and vocabulary. Archive can be run on an IBM PC® with one or 2 disk drives and a printer. Instructors may both modify the questions already on the disk and add more questions of their own. They can either choose the questions they want to use, or ask Archive to give them a random selection of questions. The program automatically provides an answer key for the questions chosen. Archive is accompanied by a 20-page *User Booklet* and a printed *Test Item File* that contains all of the test questions and answers.

Acknowledgments

We wish to express special thanks to Ms. Gabriele Koch for her painstaking reading of the manuscript and her many valuable suggestions for improvements to the second edition. Thanks are also due to Mr. John Servideo of D. C. Heath and Company for his unfailing patience and generosity.

We also wish to thank the following colleagues for their advice and help.

Ms. Ellen Crocker (Massachusetts Institute of Technology)
Prof. John Hoberman (University of Texas, Austin)
Prof. Michael Knittel (Massachusetts Institute of Technology)
Dr. Wighart von Koenigswald and the Hessisches Landesmuseum (Darmstadt, FRG)
Prof. Claire Kramsch (Massachusetts Institute of Technology)
Prof. Jens Kruse (Wellesley College)
Prof. Margaret Ward (Wellesley College)
Prof. Christiane Zehl-Romero (Tufts University)

David B. Dollenmayer
Thomas S. Hansen

Contents

Introduction 2

The Sounds of German 3
Vowels ◆ Vowels with Umlaut: **ä, ö, ü** ◆ Unstressed **-e** and **-er** ◆ Diphthongs ◆ Consonants ◆ Consonant Clusters: **gn, kn, pf, ps** ◆ Glottal Stop

Spelling and Punctuation 11
The Alphabet ◆ Capitalization ◆ Punctuation ◆ Syllabication

Classroom Expressions 12
For the First Day ◆ Expressions Useful in Class ◆ Pronunciation Practice

Almanach 14
Where is German spoken?

1 Wie geht es Ihnen? 16

Dialoge 17
Im Büro ◆ In der Mensa ◆ Auf der Straße

Wortschatz 1 18

Grammatik 21
1. Personal Pronouns 21
2. Verbs: The Infinitive and the Present Tense 21
   The Infinitive ◆ The Present Tense ◆ Regular Variations in Personal Endings ◆ English and German Present Tenses Compared ◆ Present Tense with Future Meaning
3. The Verb **sein** (to be) 24
4. Noun Gender 25
5. Noun Plurals 26
6. The Nominative Case 27
   Formation ◆ Use
7. The Sentence: German Word Order 29
   Statement: Verb-Second Word Order ◆ Questions
8. Expanding Your Vocabulary 31
   Months of the Year ◆ Leicht zu merken (Easy to remember)

Wortschatz 2 32

Lesestück 33
Wie sagt man "you" auf deutsch?

Vom Lesen zum Sprechen   34
„Sie" oder „Du"?

Almanach   38
Profile of West Germany

2   Familie und Freunde   **40**

Dialoge   41
Ich habe eine Frage ♦ Wer liest die Zeitung? ♦ Georg sucht ein
Zimmer

Wortschatz 1   42

Grammatik   44
1. Contraction of **du**-Form: **heißen**   44
2. Verbs with Stem Vowel Change: **e** to **i(e)**   44
3. The Verb **wissen** (to know)   46
4. The Verb **haben** (to have)   46
5. The Accusative Case   47
     Accusative of Definite and Indefinite Articles ♦ Accusative
     of Interrogative Pronoun: **wen** ♦ Accusative of the Personal
     Pronouns
6. The Possessive Adjective   49
7. The Flavoring Particle **denn**   50
8. Expanding Your Vocabulary   52
     Cardinal Numbers 0–20 ♦ Leicht zu merken

Wortschatz 2   53

Lesestück   54
Die Familie heute

Vom Lesen zum Sprechen   56
Die Familie

Almanach   60
Der Stammbaum–The Family Tree

3   Jugend und Schule   **62**

Dialoge   63
Zwei Freundinnen ♦ In den Bergen ♦ Ich habe keinen Wagen

Wortschatz 1   64

Grammatik   66
1. Verbs with Stem Vowel Change: **a** to **ä; au** to **äu**   66
2. The Predicate   67
3. Modal Verbs   67
4. Negation with **nicht** (not)   71
5. Negation with **kein** (not a, not any, no)   73
6. Expecting an Affirmative Answer: **nicht wahr?**   74

7. Contradicting a Negative Statement or Question: **doch**   74
8. Expanding Your Vocabulary   75
Cardinal Numbers above 20 ◆ Die Deutsche Mark (DM)
◆ Compound Nouns ◆ Leicht zu merken

Wortschatz 2   77

Lesestück   78
Eine Klassendiskussion

Vom Lesen zum Sprechen   80
Die Kleidung (*clothing*) ◆ Farben (*colors*)

Almanach   84
A Word About German Schools

4   Land und Leute   **86**

Dialoge   87
Am See ◆ Winterurlaub ◆ Es wird dunkel

Wortschatz 1   88

Grammatik   90
1. Commands   90
The **Sie**-Imperative ◆ The **wir**-Imperative (*Let's do something*) ◆ The **ihr**-Imperative ◆ The **du**-Imperative ◆ Imperative of **sein**
2. The Verb **werden** (to become)   94
3. Negating **müssen**   94
4. Negating **schon** and **noch**   95
5. Prepositions with the Accusative Case   96
6. Equivalents of English "like"   98
To like something: **mögen** ◆ To like to do something: verb + **gern(e)**
7. The Impersonal Pronoun **man**   100
8. Sentence Adverbs   101
9. **gehen** + Infinitive   102
10. Expanding Your Vocabulary   102
Leicht zu merken

Wortschatz 2   103

Lesestück   104
Deutschland: Ein bißchen Geographie

Vom Lesen zum Sprechen   106
Das Wetter und das Klima

Almanach   110
The Common Origin of English and German

Summary and Review I   **111**

5   **Arbeit und Freizeit**   **122**

Dialoge   123
Schule oder Beruf? ◆ Der neue Lehrling

Wortschatz 1   124

Grammatik   126
1. Verbs with Separable and Inseparable Prefixes   126
2. Dative Case   129
     Indirect Object ◆ Forms of the Dative Case
     ◆ Dative Personal Pronouns
3. Word Order   132
     Sentences with Two Objects ◆ Pronoun Word Order
4. Prepositions With Dative Case   135
5. **Der**-Words   137
     der-Words versus **ein**-Words
6. Omission of Article with Professions, Nationalities,
     Religions, etc.   139
7. Expanding Your Vocabulary   139
     Agent Nouns Ending in **-er** and **-erin** ◆ Leicht zu merken

Wortschatz 2   141

Lesestück   142
Drei Deutsche bei der Arbeit

Vom Lesen zum Sprechen   144
Berufe

Almanach   148
Stellenangebote

6   **An der Universität**   **150**

Dialoge   151
In der Mensa ◆ Im Studentenwohnheim ◆ An der Uni
in Tübingen

Wortschatz 1   152

Grammatik   154
1. The Perfect Tense   154
     Formation ◆ Conjugation with **haben** ◆ Past Participle
     of Weak Verbs ◆ Past Participle of Strong Verbs
     ◆ Conjugation with **sein** ◆ Past Participles of
     Separable-Prefix Verbs ◆ Past Participles of Verbs
     with Inseparable Prefixes ◆ Use of Perfect Tense
2. The Question Words **wohin** and **woher**   160
3. Two-Way Prepositions   161
4. Masculine N-Nouns   164
5. Expanding Your Vocabulary   165
     Verbal Nouns ◆ The Prefix **Haupt-** ◆ Leicht zu merken

Wortschatz 2   166
A Note on Letter Writing

Lesestück   168
Ein Brief aus Freiburg

Vom Lesen zum Sprechen   170
Das Studium (University Studies)
Das Studentenzimmer

Almanach   176
Mark Twain Visits Heidelberg

7   **Auf Reisen**   **178**

Dialoge   179
Am Bahnhof   ◆   Vor der Reise   ◆   Nach dem Mittagessen

Wortschatz 1   180

Grammatik   182
1. Perfect Tense of Irregular Weak Verbs   182
2. Perfect Tense of Modal Verbs   182
3. Coordinating Conjunctions   183
   aber versus **sondern**   ◆   Position of **nicht** before **sondern**
4. Verbs with Dative Objects   187
5. Personal Dative   189
6. More on Two-Way Prepositions   190
7. Expanding Your Vocabulary   192
   Identifying Noun Gender   ◆   Leicht zu merken

Wortschatz 2   193

Lesestück   194
Unterwegs per Autostop oder mit der Bahn

Vom Lesen zum Sprechen   196
Reisen und Verkehr

Almanach   200
Youth Hostels

8   **Das Leben in der Stadt**   **202**

Dialoge   203
„Brauchen wir noch etwas?"   ◆   Der Stadtbummel
◆   „Zahlen bitte!"

Wortschatz 1   204

Grammatik   206

1. Subordinating Conjunctions   206
Verb Last Word Order in the Subordinate Clause
   - Question Words as Subordinating Conjunctions
   - Verbs with Separable Prefixes in Subordinate Clauses
   - Order of Clauses in the Sentence
2. Infinitive Constructions with **zu**   210
Infinitives with **um . . . zu** and **ohne . . . zu**
3. Genitive Case   213
Formation • Use of the Genitive • Prepositions
with the Genitive
4. Telling Time   217
Asking for the Time • Asking What Time Something
Occurred • Official Time-Telling
5. Nouns of Measure, Weight, and Number   221
6. Translating English *to:* **nach, zu, in**   222
7. Expanding Your Vocabulary   222
Leicht zu merken

Wortschatz 2   223

Lesestück   224
Aspekte der Großstadt

Vom Lesen zum Sprechen   226
In der Stadt • Essen im Restaurant

Almanach   232
Das Kulturleben einer Stadt

Color Photo Essay   German-speaking Countries of Europe   follows 232
Summary and Review II   233

9   **Der Sport**   **244**

Dialoge   245
Das neue Fahrrad • „Treibst du Sport?" • „Wo warst du?"

Wortschatz 1   246

Grammatik   249

1. Attributive Adjectives   249
Predicate Adjectives vs. Attributive Adjectives • The
Noun Phrase • Attributive Adjectives after **der**-Words
 • Attributive Adjectives after **ein**-Words
2. Simple Past of **sein** and **haben**   255
3. Word Order: Time-Manner-Place   256
4. Expanding Your Vocabulary   258
Ordinal Numbers and Dates • Leicht zu merken

Wortschatz 2   261

Lesestück 262

Sport für alle

Vom Lesen zum Sprechen 264

Der Sport

Almanach 268

Sport Culture in the Two Germanies

10 Deutschland im 20. Jahrhundert 270

Dialoge 271

◆ „Was ist los?" ◆ Damals ◆ Schlimme Zeiten

Wortschatz 1 272

Grammatik 275

1. Unpreceded Adjectives 275
2. Simple Past Tense ◆ Formation ◆ Use 276
3. German Equivalents for English "when": **als, wenn, wann** 284
4. Past Perfect Tense ◆ Formation ◆ Use 285
5. Some Time Expressions 286
   vor + dative = ago ◆ Expressing Duration
6. Expanding Your Vocabulary 290
   The Noun Suffix **-ismus** ◆ City Names as Adjectives
   ◆ Leicht zu merken

Wortschatz 2 292

Lesestück 293

Besuch einer Ausstellung historischer Plakate

Vom Lesen zum Sprechen 296

Die Politik

Almanach 301

Political Parties in West Germany

11 Die Deutsche Demokratische Republik 302

Dialoge 303

Die Abiturientenreise ◆ Ein Unfall

Wortschatz 1 304

Grammatik 307

1. Adjectival Nouns 307
   Adjectival Nouns Referring to People ◆ Adjectival Nouns
   Referring to Concepts
2. Adjectives of Indefinite Number 310
3. Reflexive Verbs 311
   Reflexive Verbs and Pronouns ◆ Verbs with Accusative Reflexive
   Pronouns ◆ Verbs with Dative Reflexive Pronouns

4. Dative Pronouns with Parts of the Body and Clothing   317
5. More on **bei**   319
6. Expanding Your Vocabulary   320
Country Names, Nouns and Adjectives of Nationality
◆ Leicht zu merken

Wortschatz 2   322

Lesestück   323
Die Deutsche Demokratische Republik

Vom Lesen zum Sprechen   326
An der Grenze

Almanach   330
Profile of the German Democratic Republic

12   Erinnerungen   **332**

Dialoge   333
Das Referat ◆ Rita hat sich verlobt ◆ Vor der Wohnungstür

Wortschatz 1   334

Grammatik   337
1. Comparison of Adjectives and Adverbs   337
Formation of the Comparative ◆ Formation of the
Superlative ◆ Umlaut in Comparative and Superlative
◆ Irregular Comparatives and Superlatives ◆ Comparisons
2. Relative Clauses   346
Relative Pronouns ◆ The Relative Pronoun **was**
◆ The Indefinite Pronouns **wer** and **was**
3. The Verb **lassen**   352
4. **Mal** and its Use   354
5. Questions with **was für?** (What kind of?)   355
6. Parts of the Day   356
7. Expanding Your Vocabulary   357
The Prefix **irgend-**

Wortschatz 2   358

Lesestück   359
Zwei Denkmäler

Vom Lesen zum Sprechen   361
„Das geht mir nicht aus dem Kopf"

Almanach   365
Five Modern Women Writers

Summary and Review III   **367**

13   Die Schweiz   380

Dialoge   381
Schilaufen in der Schweiz   ◆   Am Informationsschalter im
Bahnhof   ◆   In einer Wohngemeinschaft

Wortschatz 1   382

Grammatik   385
1. Verbs with Prepositional Complements   385
2. Pronouns as Objects of Prepositions   388
    da-Compounds   ◆   **wo**-Compounds
3. Future Tense   391
4. Wanting X to Do Y   393
5. Past Participles as Adjectives   394
6. Expanding Your Vocabulary   394
    Leicht zu merken

Wortschatz 2   395

Lesestück   396
Zwei Schweizer stellen ihre Heimat vor

Vom Lesen zum Sprechen   400
Klischees

Almanach   404
Profile of Switzerland

14   Österreich   406

Dialoge   407
An der Rezeption   ◆   Zwei Studentinnen in Wien
  ◆   Auf Urlaub in Österreich

Wortschatz 1   408

Grammatik   411
1. Present Tense of the General Subjunctive   411
2. More Time Expressions   421
3. Expanding Your Vocabulary   422
    The Suffix **-lang** and the Adverbs **montags, dienstags,** etc.
    Leicht zu merken

Wortschatz 2   425

Lesestück   426
Zwei Österreicher stellen sich vor

Vom Lesen zum Sprechen   430
Wie stellt man sich vor?

Almanach   434
Profile of Austria

15 Gastarbeiter in Deutschland 436

Dialoge 437
Wo liegt die Heimat? ◆ Die verpaßte Geburtstagsfeier
◆ Vor der Post

Wortschatz 1 438

Grammatik 441
1. Past Tense of the General Subjunctive 441
   Formation ◆ Use
2. Passive Voice 445
   Formation ◆ Use
3. The Present Participle 449
   Formation ◆ Use
4. Equivalents for English "think" 451
5. Directional Prefixes: **hin-** and **her-** 452
6. Expanding Your Vocabulary 453
   Leicht zu merken

Wortschatz 2 454

Lesestück 455
Leben im gelobten Land

Vom Lesen zum Sprechen 457
Wohnen und Wohnungen

Almanach 461
Foreign Workers in German-Speaking Countries

16 Die Frau 462

Dialoge 463
Goldene Hochzeit ◆ Kind oder Beruf?

Wortschatz 1 464

Grammatik 467
1. Impersonal Passive 467
2. Subjective Use of Modal Verbs 468
3. Indirect Quotation and Special Subjunctive 470
   Direct Versus Indirect Quotation ◆ Special Subjunctive
   ◆ Tenses in Indirect Quotation ◆ Questions and Commands
   in Indirect Quotation
4. Subjunctive with **als ob** (as if, as though) 475
5. Extended Modifiers 476
6. Expanding Your Vocabulary 478
   Leicht zu merken

Wortschatz 2 479

Lesestück   480
Gedanken über die Emanzipation der Frau

Vom Lesen zum Sprechen   483
Unterschiede und Ähnlichkeiten

Almanach   488
Women, Pregnancy, and West German Law

Color Photo Essay   Wer sprecht Deutsch?   follows **488**
Summary and Review IV   **489**

Answers to *Check Your Progress*   **502**

Appendix 1 Strong and Irregular Verbs   **507**

Appendix 2 Table of Equivalent Weights and Measures   **509**

German-English Vocabulary   **510**

English-German Vocabulary   **526**

Index   **540**

Credits   **544**

Maps

The Federal Republic of Germany   39
German-speaking Countries of Europe   follows 232
The German Democratic Republic   331
Language Areas of Switzerland   404
Austria   435

Introduction

The Sounds of German
Vowels ♦ Vowels with Umlaut: **ä, ö, ü** ♦ Unstressed **-e** and **-er** ♦ Diphthongs ♦ Consonants ♦ Consonant Clusters: **gn, kn, pf, ps** ♦ Glottal Stop

Spelling and Punctuation
The Alphabet ♦ Capitalization ♦ Punctuation ♦ Syllabication

Classroom Expressions
For the First Day ♦ Expressions Useful in Class ♦ Pronunciation Practice

Almanach
Where is German spoken?

The Sounds of German

The following descriptions are meant as an introduction to the sounds of German. The English equivalents given here can only be approximate. You should practice German phonetics by listening carefully to and then imitating your teacher and the tapes.

◆ Vowels

German vowels, unlike English vowels, are "pure," that is, they do not glide off into another sound at the end. The English **o** in "flow," for instance, glides off to **u.** The **a** in "bait" glides off to **ee.** Compare:

English	*German*
flow	Floh
bait	Beet

German has both long and short vowels. Short vowels are tenser and of much shorter duration than long vowels.

German spelling is a much better indication of pronunciation than is English spelling. German vowels are long when they are:

1. followed by an unpronounced **h: Sohn, lehnen**
2. doubled: **Beet, Saat**
3. followed by a single consonant (in most cases): **Wesen, Blume**

German vowels are generally short if they are followed by double or multiple consonants: **bitte, offen, links.**

a

Long **a** sounds like English **a** in **Ma** and **Pa.**
Short **a** sounds the same, but is tenser and shorter. Notice that the following pairs of words are identical except for the length of the vowels.

long a	*short a*
Wahn	wann
Bahn	Bann
Kahn	kann
Schafe	schaffe

e

Long **e** sounds like English **ay** in **hay,** but without gliding off to **ee.**
Short **e** sounds like English **e** in **let.**

long e	*short e*
den	denn
wen	wenn
Beet	Bett
stehlen	stellen

i

Long **i** (usually spelled **ie**) sounds like English **ee** in **free**.
Short **i** sounds like English **i** in **fit**, but is shorter and tenser.

long i	short i
bieten	bitten
Miete	Mitte
ihn	in
Bienen	binnen

o

Long **o** sounds like English **o** in **so**, but without gliding off to **u**.
Short **o** sounds like English **au** in **caught**, but is tenser and shorter. Short **o** is a difficult sound for English speakers and will need lots of practice.

long o	short o
wohne	Wonne
Ofen	offen
Sohle	solle
Ton	Tonne
Sohn	Sonne

Be sure to distinguish among long **a**, short **a**, and short **o**.

long a	short a	short o
Bahn	Bann	Bonn
kam	Kamm	komm
fahl	Fall	voll
Haken	hacken	hocken
Gas	Gassen	gossen

u

Long **u** sounds like English **oo** in **soon**, but the lips are more rounded and there is no off-glide.
Short **u** sounds like English **u** in **put**.

long u	short u
Mus	muß
Ruhm	Rum
Buhle	Bulle
Huhn	Hunne

◆ Vowels with Umlaut: *ä, ö, ü* 🔲

German spelling adds a diacritical mark called an umlaut to three vowels: **ä**, **ö**, and **ü**. In the speech of most Germans, **ä** is the equivalent of **e**, both long and short, but **ö** and **ü** represent different sounds from **o** and **u**.

ö

The sound represented by **ö** has no English equivalent. To make long **ö**, round your lips to say German long **o**, freeze them in that position, and say German long **e** instead. Short **ö** is pronounced in the same way, except that it is shorter and tenser.

long o	long ö	short o	short ö
Ton	Töne	Gott	Götter
Sohn	Söhne	konnte	könnte
Lohn	Löhne	Topf	Töpfe
Floh	Flöhe	Bock	Böcke
Bogen	Bögen	Dorf	Dörfer

ü

The sound represented by **ü** (also spelled **y**) has no English equivalent. To make long **ü**, round your lips to say German long **u**, freeze them in that position, and say German long **i** instead. Short **ü** is pronounced in the same way, except that it is shorter and tenser.

long u	long ü	short u	short ü
gut	Güte	Mutter	Mütter
Mut	Mythos	Kunst	Künste
Fuß	Füße	Bund	Bünde
Zug	Züge	Kuß	Küsse
Schub	Schübe	Busch	Büsche

◆ Unstressed -e and -er

It is important to distinguish between two unstressed vowel sounds occurring at the end of words and syllables.

Unstressed **-e** sounds like English **a** in **sofa** (the so-called "schwa"). Unstressed **-er** is a vowel sound which resembles the **u** in English **but.** The difference between **träge** and **Träger,** for instance, is that in the latter, the tongue is quickly retracted at the end of the word.

unstressed -e	unstressed -er
träge	Träger
Liebe	lieber
lese	Leser
bitte	bitter
Wunde	Wunder

Neue Mode: Alte Häuser

♦ Diphthongs

Diphthongs are combinations of two vowel sounds. There are three of them in German: The diphthong **au** sounds like English **ow** in **cow: Haus.** The diphthong **ei** (also spelled **ai**) sounds like English **ei** in **height: leid.** The diphthong **eu** (also spelled **äu**) sounds like English **oi** in **oily: Leute, läuten.**

au	*ei (ai)*	*eu (äu)*
Laus	leise	Läuse
aus	Eis	äußern
Frau	frei	Freude
laut	leiten	läuten
baut	beide	Beute

The sound spelled **ie** is not a diphthong, but simply a long **i.**

♦ Consonants

ch

After the "back" vowels **a, o, u,** and **au,** the sound represented by **ch** sounds like Scots **ch** in **Loch Ness.**

Bach	Tuch
Loch	auch

After other vowels and consonants, **ch** sounds like English **h** in **Hugh** or **huge,** if you draw out this sound before saying the **u.**

echt	Löcher
Bäche	Furcht
ich	Teich

Contrast back **ch** and front **ch:**

back ch	*front ch*
Bach	Bäche
Loch	Löcher
Buch	Bücher
Brauch	Bräuche

-ig

When **-ig** ends a word, it is pronounced as if it were spelled **-ich.** When it is followed by an ending, it is pronounced **-ig-.**

-ich	*-ig-*
König	Könige
Pfennig	Pfennige
fertig	fertige
artig	artige

chs

The combination **chs** is pronounced **ks.**

sechs	Fuchs
Wachs	wuchs

l

German **l** is pronounced with the top of the tongue against the upper gum ridge and with the tongue flat from front to back, not dipped in the middle and raised at the back, like an American **l.** The American **l** in initial position is closer to the German **l** than is the American **l** when it comes in the middle or at the end of a word. Listen carefully to your teacher and the tapes.

English	*German*
leaf	lief
light	Leid
late	lädt
built	Bild
plots	Platz
feel	fiel
hell	hell
pole	Pol

r

German never uses the American **r,** in which the tip of the tongue curves backward. Some Germans tongue-trill the **r,** but most use the uvular **r** (the back of the tongue is raised toward the uvula, the small flap of tissue hanging down at the back of your mouth) and it is the one you should learn. Uvular **r** is similar to the back **ch,** except that the **r** is voiced (the vocal cords vibrate). Pronounce the following sequence of words. With **waren,** keep your vocal cords vibrating: **wach, wachen, waren.**

Beere	Frau	Rede
ihre	frei	rot
Ohren	Trauer	richtig
lehren	grün	Raum

When **r** is not followed by a vowel, it usually becomes a vowel sound like English **u** in **but.**

consonantal r	*vocalic r*
Tore	Tor
führe	für
studiere	studiert
bittere	bitter
höre	hört

b, d, g

The letters **b, d,** and **g** are pronounced as in English. The German **g** is always "hard" as in English **go: gehen.**

Bube	Bude	Tage
leben	leiden	legen

When **b, d,** and **g** come at the end of a word or syllable, or before **s** or **t,** they become "unvoiced," that is, the vocal cords do not vibrate and **b** thus sounds like **p, d** sounds like **t,** and **g** like **k.**

voiced (b, d, g)	unvoiced (p, t, k)
Diebe	Dieb
leben	lebt
schieben	schiebst
Lieder	Lied
Fäden	fad
Kriege	Krieg
legen	legt
liegen	liegst

j

The letter **j** is pronounced like English **y.**

ja	jagen
jung	je

qu

The letters **qu** stand for the consonant combination **kv.**

quick	Qualität
quer	Quatsch
Quark	

s

Before vowels, **s** is voiced like English **z** in **zeal.** In all other positions, **s** is unvoiced like English **s** in **seal.**

voiced s	unvoiced s
so	es
lesen	ist
Gänse	Thomas

ss, ß

The letters **ss** and **ß** (the latter called "ess-tsett" in German and "digraph s" in English) stand for unvoiced **s** (as in English **seal**).

essen	ißt
müssen	muß
messen	Maß

v

The letter **v** usually stands for the same sound as **f.** In words of foreign origin, however, it is pronounced like English **v** (i.e., voiced).

v = f	voiced v
Vetter	Vera
vier	Vase
voll	Universität

w

The letter **w** stands for the sound spelled **v** in English.

wir	Wetter
Wasser	Wagen

y

The letter **y** occurs only in words of foreign origin and is most commonly pronounced like **ü.**

Physik
Gymnasium
Symphonie

z, tz

Both **z** and **tz** are pronounced like **ts** in English **its.** This sound can come at the beginning of a word in German, not just in the middle and at the end as in English.

Zoo
zehn
sitzen
Zug
Satz

◆ Consonant Clusters: *gn, kn, pf, ps*   ⬚

Be careful to pronounce both elements of the following consonant clusters, especially when they occur at the beginning of a word or syllable.

gn	*kn*	*pf*	*ps*
Gnade	Knie	Apfel	Psalm
Vergnügen	Knabe	Pfanne	Psychologie
Gnom	Knall	Pferd	Psychiater

ng

In German, the letters **ng** always stand for the sound in English **singer,** never for the sound in English **finger.**

Sänger	Achtung
Finger	Hunger
Ring	

sch, st-, sp-

The German sound spelled **sch** is like the English sound spelled **sh,** but with more pronounced lip-rounding:

Schiff	Schule
Asche	schön
rasch	

The combinations **st-** and **sp-** at the beginning of a word or syllable are pronounced "scht-" or "schp-."

spielen   spüren
Stein   versprechen
aufstehen

-tion

This combination is always pronounced "-tsión," with the primary word stress on the last syllable.

Nation
Zivilisation
Tradition

♦ Glottal stop

The glottal stop is used more frequently in German than in English. It is the brief closing of the vocal cords one hears between the words of the phrase "Utica Avenue." It is the way we distinguish between "a nice man" and "an ice man." In German, it occurs before all words and syllables beginning with a vowel.

er ist es   ich arbeite oft
eine alte Adresse   in einer Oper

Studenten in einer Vorlesung (*students in a lecture*).

Spelling and Punctuation

◆ The Alphabet   *(das Alphabet)*

Since the name of almost every letter in German contains the sound ordinarily represented by that letter, it will be useful to memorize the German alphabet.

a	ah	**j**	jot	**s**	ess
b	beh	**k**	kah	**t**	teh
c	tseh	**l**	ell	**u**	uh
d	deh	**m**	emm	**v**	fau
e	eh	**n**	enn	**w**	weh
f	eff	**o**	oh	**x**	iks
g	geh	**p**	peh	**y**	üppsilon
h	hah	**q**	kuh	**z**	tsett
i	ih	**r**	err	**ß**	ess-tsett

◆ Capitalization

1. All nouns are capitalized, wherever they occur in the sentence.
2. Adjectives denoting nationality are not capitalized: **deutsch, amerikanisch, kanadisch** (German, American, Canadian).

◆ Punctuation

German punctuation is quite similar to English. The most important difference is that all subordinate clauses must be set off by commas.

◆ Syllabication

Note the following divisions at the end of a line in German:

1. A single consonant goes with the following syllable: **sa-gen**—to say.
2. The last of two or more consonants is carried over to the following syllable: **Ar-beit**—work, **brann-ten**—burned.
3. The letter combinations **ch, sch,** and initial **st** and **sp** are never separated: **Dä-cher**—roofs, **Bü-sche**—bushes, **ge-spielt**—played.
4. **ck** (as in **Deckel**—lid) is separated into **k-k: Dek-kel.**
5. Compound words are divided between their component parts: **Klassen-zimmer**—classroom.

◆ Classroom Expressions

1. der **Professor**
   (der **Lehrer**)
2. die **Professorin**
   (die **Lehrerin**)
3. der **Student**
   (der **Schüler**)
4. die **Studentin**
   (die **Schülerin**)
5. die **Tafel**
6. der **Tisch**
7. die **Uhr**
8. die **Wand**
9. das **Fenster**
10. der **Stuhl**
11. die **Tür**
12. die **Landkarte**

1. das **Buch**
2. das **Heft**
3. das **Papier**
4. der **Bleistift**
5. der **Kugelschreiber**
6. der **Radiergummi**

◆ For the First Day

Guten Morgen!	*Good morning! (before 10:00 a.m.)*
Guten Tag!	*Hello! (after 10:00 a.m.)*
Wie heißen Sie?	*What's your name?*
Ich heiße Thomas Hartmann.	*My name is Thomas Hartman.*

Ich bin Frau Keller.	*I'm Mrs. Keller.*
Ich bin Herr Keller.	*I'm Mr. Keller.*
Ich bin Professor Hauser.	*I'm Professor Hauser.*
Wie heißt sie?	*What's her name?*
Sie heißt Monika Richter.	*Her name is Monika Richter.*
Wie heißt er?	*What's his name?*
Er heißt Thomas Hartmann.	*His name is Thomas Hartmann.*
Wie geht es Ihnen heute?	*How are you today?*
Gut, danke. Und Ihnen?	*Fine thanks, and you?*
Welcher Tag ist heute?	*What day is today?*
Heute ist Montag.	*Today is Monday.*
Morgen ist Dienstag.	*Tomorrow is Tuesday.*
Mittwoch	*Wednesday*
Donnerstag	*Thursday*
Freitag	*Friday*
Samstag (or:	*Saturday*
Sonnabend)	
Sonntag	*Sunday*
Auf Wiedersehen!	*Good-bye!*

◆ Expressions Useful in Class 🔲

Wie sagt man "the book" auf deutsch?	*How do you say "the book" in German?*
Man sagt „das Buch."	*You say „das Buch."*
Was ist das?	*What is that?*
Das ist das Buch.	*That's the book.*
Wie schreibt man das?	*How do you spell that?*
„Buch" schreibt man B-u-c-h.	*You spell „Buch" B-u-c-h.*
Übersetzen Sie bitte.	*Please translate.*
Wiederholen Sie bitte.	*Please repeat.*
Üben wir!	*Let's practice!*
Machen Sie Nummer drei, bitte.	*Please do number three.*
Alle zusammen, bitte.	*All together, please.*
Sie sprechen zu leise.	*You're speaking too softly.*
Sprechen Sie lauter, bitte.	*Please speak more loudly.*
Das ist richtig.	*That's correct.*
Das ist falsch.	*That's incorrect.*

◆ Pronunciation Practice

Here are some German loan-words in English. Pronounce them in German and see if you know what they mean.

Angst	Kindergarten	Strudel
Ersatz	Kitsch	Wanderlust
Gestalt	Rucksack	Weltanschauung
Gesundheit	Sauerkraut	Zeitgeist
Hinterland	Spiel	Zwieback

Almanach

Where is German spoken?

Today the word Germany is largely a conversational convenience that no longer defines a single political entity. Germany as an individual state has not existed since 1945 and the Germans, politically divided as they were in the earliest times, now populate two countries. When speaking of Germany, one carefully distinguishes between West Germany (the Federal Republic of Germany—*Die Bundesrepublik Deutschland*), and East Germany (the German Democratic Republic—*Die Deutsche Demokratische Republik*). Almost 80 million German-speakers live in these two countries. Yet German is also the language of

Augsburg in Bayern, Blick auf St. Ulrich.

Austria, parts of Switzerland and Luxembourg, and Liechtenstein. Scattered linguistic enclaves of German speakers in the U.S.A. (notably in Pennsylvania), Canada, Brazil, South Africa, Australia and the South Tirol (now in Italy) bring the number of German-speakers up around 118 million. Here are some comparative statistics on the world's major languages, showing numbers of native speakers in 1986.

Chinese	976 Million
English	420 Million
Spanish	296 Million
Russian	285 Million
Arabic	177 Million
Portuguese	164 Million
Japanese	122 Million
German	118 Million
French	114 Million
Italian	63 Million

Wie geht es Ihnen?

Dialoge
Im Büro ◆ In der Mensa ◆ Auf der Straße

Wortschatz 1

Grammatik
1. Personal Pronouns
2. Verbs: The Infinitive and the Present Tense
   The Infinitive ◆ The Present Tense ◆ Regular Variations in Personal Endings ◆ English and German Present Tenses Compared ◆ Present Tense with Future Meaning
3. The Verb **sein** (to be)
4. Noun Gender
5. Noun Plurals
6. The Nominative Case
   Formation ◆ Use
7. The Sentence: German Word Order
   Statement: Verb-Second Word Order ◆ Forming Questions
8. Expanding Your Vocabulary
   Months of the Year ◆ Leicht zu merken (Easy to remember)

Wortschatz 2

Lesestück
Wie sagt man "you" auf deutsch?

Vom Lesen zum Sprechen
„Sie" oder „Du"?

Almanach
Profile of West Germany

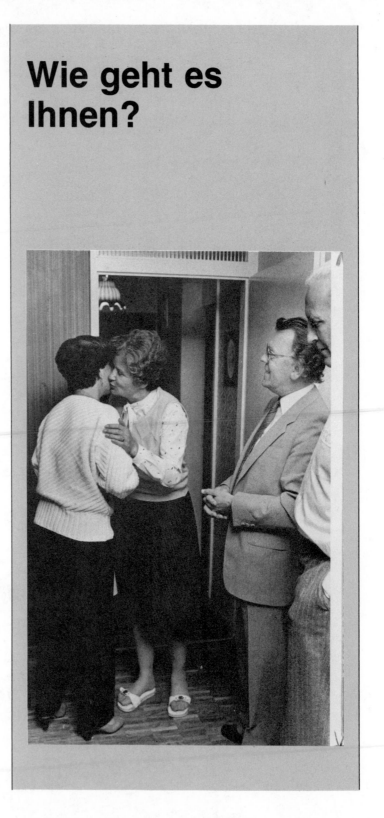

Dialoge

Im Büro[1]

HERR LEHMANN: Guten Morgen, Frau Hauser!

FRAU HAUSER: Morgen, Herr Lehmann. Entschuldigung, aber ich bin in Eile. Ich fliege um elf nach Wien.

HERR LEHMANN: Wann kommen Sie wieder zurück?

FRAU HAUSER: Am Mittwoch bin ich wieder zurück. Auf Wiedersehen!

HERR LEHMANN: Auf Wiedersehen! Gute Reise!

In der Mensa[1]

KARIN: Tag, Michael! Wie ist die Suppe heute?

MICHAEL: Tag, Karin! Sie ist ganz gut. . . . Übrigens, arbeitest du viel im Moment?

KARIN: Nein, nicht sehr viel. Warum, was machst du heute abend?

MICHAEL: Heute abend gehe ich zu Horst. Du auch?

KARIN: Ja, natürlich.

MICHAEL: Also tschüs, bis dann.

Auf der Straße[1]

FRAU BACHMANN: Guten Tag, Frau Kuhn! Wie geht's?

FRAU KUHN: Tag, Frau Bachmann! Sehr gut, danke, und Ihnen?

FRAU BACHMANN: Danke, auch gut. Was machen die Kinder?

FRAU KUHN: Sie spielen draußen, das Wetter ist heute so schön.

FRAU BACHMANN: Ja, endlich scheint die Sonne. Aber vielleicht regnet es morgen wieder.

FRAU KUHN: Typisch für September.

„Das Wetter ist heute so schön"

[1] The form of the definite article in these prepositional phrases indicates that the following noun is in the dative case. See pp. 130 and 161–163.

Wortschatz 1
(Vocabulary 1)

In the Office

MR. LEHMANN: Good morning, Mrs. Hauser.

MS. HAUSER: Morning, Mr. Lehmann. Forgive me, but I'm in a hurry. I'm flying to Vienna at eleven.

MR. LEHMANN: When are you coming back?

MS. HAUSER: I'll be back on Wednesday. Good-bye!

MR. LEHMANN: Good-bye, have a good trip.

In the University Cafeteria

KARIN: Hi, Michael! How's the soup today?

MICHAEL: Hi, Karin! It's pretty good. . . . By the way, are you studying a lot at the moment?

KARIN: No, not very much. Why? What are you doing this evening?

MICHAEL: I'm going to Horst's tonight. You too?

KARIN: Yes, of course.

MICHAEL: Okay. So long, until then.

On the Street

MRS. BACHMANN: Hello Mrs. Kuhn. How are you?

MRS. KUHN: Hi, Mrs. Bachmann. Very well, thanks, and you?

MRS. BACHMANN: Thanks, I'm fine too. What are your children up to?

MRS. KUHN: They're playing outside, the weather is so nice today.

MRS. BACHMANN: Yes, the sun is finally shining. But maybe it will rain again tomorrow.

MRS. KUHN: Typical for September.

Verben (Verbs)

arbeiten to work; study (for a class)
fliegen to fly
gehen to go; walk
kommen to come
machen to make; do
regnen to rain
scheinen to shine; seem
sein to be
spielen to play

Substantive (Nouns)

der[1] **Herr, -en**[2] gentleman
  Herr Lehmann Mr. Lehmann
der **Morgen, -** morning
der **September** September
der **Tag, -e** day

das **Büro, -s** office
das **Kind, -er** child
das **Wetter** weather
(das) **Wien** Vienna

die **Frau, -en** woman
  Frau Kuhn Mrs./Ms. Kuhn
die **Mensa** university cafeteria
die **Sonne** sun
die **Straße, -n** street; road
die **Suppe, -n** soup

Andere Vokabeln
(Other words)

aber but
also well . . .
auch also, too

bis until; by
  bis dann until then; by then
danke thanks
dann then
draußen outside
elf eleven
endlich finally
für for
gut[3] good, well
  ganz gut pretty good
heute abend this evening, tonight
in in
ja yes
nach to (with cities and countries)
natürlich[3] natural(ly)
nein no
nicht not
schön beautiful; nice
sehr very
typisch typical
übrigens by the way
um at (with expressions of time)
und and
viel much, a lot
vielleicht maybe, perhaps
wann when
warum why
was what
wer who
wie how; like, as
wieder again
wo where
zu to (with people); too (as in "too much")
zurück back

---

[1] See p. 25 for an explanation of the form of the definite article.

[2] The endings after a hyphen are plural endings. See p. 26.

[3] In German, there is no special adverb ending like the *-ly* ending that makes an English adjective into an adverb (natural - naturally). The German word **natürlich** can mean "natural" or "naturally," depending on the context. Similarly, **gut** means both "good" and "well."

Studenten in der Mensa.

Nützliche Ausdrücke (*Useful Expressions*)

am Mittwoch (Donnerstag, usw.) on Wednesday (Thursday, etc.)

Entschuldigung! Pardon me!, Excuse me!

Guten Morgen! Good morning!

Morgen! Morning!

Guten Tag! Hello! (*literally* "Good Day")

Tag! Hi! (*short for* **Guten Tag**)

Gute Reise! (Have a) good trip!

im Moment at the moment

in Eile in a hurry

Tschüs! So long! (*informal, among friends*)

Wie geht's? How are you? (*informal*)

Gegensätze[1] (*Opposites*)

gut ≠ schlecht	good; well ≠ bad; badly
schön ≠ häßlich	beautiful ≠ ugly

[1] Frequently used antonyms will be presented in this special section at the end of each **Wortschatz**.

Neue Kombinationen *(New Combinations)*

A. Substitute the elements provided for those in italics.

> EXAMPLE: *Mittwoch* bin ich wieder zurück. (morgen)
> Morgen bin ich wieder zurück.

1. Ich fliege *um elf* nach Wien.
   (morgen, heute abend, am Dienstag, am Mittwoch, am Montag)
2. *Kommst* du auch?
   (arbeitest, fliegst, gehst)
3. *Endlich* scheint die Sonne wieder.
   (natürlich, vielleicht, morgen, übrigens, am Freitag)
4. Ich *fliege* um elf. (gehe, arbeite, komme)

B. Respond to the following greetings and farewells:

1. Guten Morgen!
2. Wie geht es Ihnen?
3. Guten Tag!
4. Auf Wiedersehen!
5. Gute Reise!
6. Tschüs, bis dann!

◻▬◻ **Übung zur Aussprache** *(Pronunciation Practice)*

Practice the difference between the front **ch** that follows **e, i, ie, ei, ö, ü, eu,** and **äu** and the back **ch** after **a, o, u,** and **au** (see Introduction, p. 6).
  When a noun with **ch** takes an umlaut in the plural, the sound of **ch** automatically shifts from back to front:

back **ch** *(singular)*	*front* **ch** *(plural)*
Buch (book)	Bücher
Bach (brook)	Bäche
Loch (hole)	Löcher
Brauch (custom)	Bräuche
Tuch (cloth)	Tücher
Dach (roof)	Dächer
Koch (cook)	Köche
Schlauch (hose)	Schläuche

Read these sentences aloud, paying attention to the difference between front and back **ch.** Remember that final **-ig** is pronounced as though it were spelled **-ich.**

1. Was machst du heute abend?
2. Ich gehe zu Friedrich. Du auch?
3. Natürlich!
4. Fliegst du am Mittwoch nach Zürich?
5. Vielleicht.
6. Ich nicht. Das Wetter ist zu schlecht.

Grammatik *(Grammar)*

1 ◆ Personal Pronouns

Personal pronouns as the subject of a sentence:

		Singular		*Plural*
1st person	**ich**	I	**wir**	we
2nd person	**du**	you (familiar)	**ihr**	you (familiar)
	Sie	you (formal)	**Sie**	you (formal)
3rd person	**er**	he		
	es	it	**sie**	they
	sie	she		

- German has three words for the personal pronoun "you": **du, ihr,** and **Sie.**
- The familiar pronouns **du** (singular) and **ihr** (plural) are used when addressing children, family members, close friends, and the deity. Members of certain groups (students, blue-collar workers, soldiers, athletes) converse among themselves almost exclusively with **du** and **ihr.**
- **Sie** is used when addressing one or more adults who are not close friends of the speaker. In writing, **Sie** meaning *you* is distinguished from **sie** meaning *they* by always beginning with a capital letter.
- The pronoun **ich** is not capitalized except when it is the first word in a sentence.

2 ◆ Verbs: Infinitive and Present Tense

The Infinitive

German verbs are found in a dictionary in the *infinitive* form. In English, the infinitive is usually preceded by *to: to go, to say.*

In German, the infinitive is expressed by the ending **-en** or **-n** attached to the stem of the verb: geh**en** (*to go*); arbeit**en** (*to work*), sein (*to be*).

Present Tense

The verb must indicate *tense* (present, past, or future), *person* (first, second, or third), the *number* (singular or plural) when it is used with a subject. The subject is the person or thing that performs the action denoted by the verb. A German verb conveys tense, person, and number by adding endings to a verb stem, a process known as verb inflection.

In English, the only inflectional ending of the present tense occurs in the third person singular, as an *-s:* she sing*s*, work*s*, put*s*, or an *-es:* he miss*es*, fix*es*, push*es*. In German, *each* person has an ending.

In order to form the present tense of a German verb, find the stem by eliminating the infinitive ending **-en** or **-n**:

komm- ~~en~~

and add the personal endings:

Singular

stem + ending			present tense		
ich	komm-	e	ich	komme	I come
du	komm-	st	du	kommst	} you come
(Sie	komm-	en)[1]	(Sie	kommen)[1]	
er, es, sie	komm-	t	er, es, sie	kommt	he, it, she comes

Plural

stem + ending			present tense		
wir	komm-	en	wir	kommen	we come
ihr	komm-	t	ihr	kommt	} you come
(Sie	komm-	en)[1]	(Sie	kommen)[1]	
sie	komm-	en	sie	kommen	they come

Üben wir!

(Let's Practice)

A. Tell who is coming tomorrow.

EXAMPLE: ich
Ich komme morgen.

1. er
2. Sie, Frau Bachmann
3. wir
4. sie (they)

5. sie (she)
6. du, Michael
7. ich
8. ihr

B. Tell who is doing that.

EXAMPLE: ich
Ich mache das.

1. sie (she)
2. ihr
3. er
4. du, Stefan

5. Sie, Herr Hauser
6. wir
7. sie (they)
8. ich

---

[1] The third person plural **sie kommen** (they come) is also the polite form of address: **Sie kommen** (*you come*—singular and plural). These forms are always identical except for capitalization. From now on, the **Sie**-form will be given with the third person plural in verb paradigms: **sie, Sie kommen.**

Regular Variations in Personal Endings

Verbs with stems ending in **-d, -t,** or a consonant cluster such as **-gn** insert an **-e-** before the **du, er,** and **ihr** endings to make them pronounceable:

---

arbeiten   stem: **arbeit-**

ich	arbeite	wir	arbeiten
du	arbeitest	ihr	arbeitet
er, es, sie	arbeitet	sie, Sie	arbeiten

---

regnen   stem: **regn-**
es regnet

Üben wir!

A. Tell who is working a lot.

> EXAMPLE: wir
> Wir arbeiten viel.

1. ich
2. Herr Lehmann
3. sie (they)
4. du

5. ihr
6. Frau Kuhn
7. wir
8. Michael

Was studieren die Studenten?

English and German Present Tense Compared

German present tense is equivalent to three English forms:

$$\text{sie geht} \begin{cases} \text{she goes} \\ \text{she is going} \\ \text{she does go} \end{cases}$$

Present Tense with Future Meaning

In German the present tense often expresses future meaning, especially when another element in the sentence makes the future meaning clear:

Ich fliege um elf nach Wien.	*I'm flying to Vienna at eleven.*
Heute abend gehe ich zu Horst.	*I'm going to Horst's tonight.*
Mittwoch bin ich wieder zurück.	*I'll be back Wednesday.*

Note that English often uses the present progressive (I'm flying, I'm going) for the same purpose.

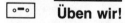

Üben wir!

A. Contradict these statements, substituting **morgen** for **heute.**

> EXAMPLE: Wir gehen heute zu Horst.
> Nein, wir gehen morgen zu Horst.

1. Herr Lehmann kommt heute zurück.
2. Stefan fliegt heute nach Wien.
3. Sie arbeiten heute.
4. Frau Bachmann macht das heute.
5. Wir gehen heute zu Frau Kuhn.
6. Horst arbeitet heute in der Mensa.

3 ♦ The Verb *sein* (to be)

The verb **sein** is irregular and its forms must be memorized:

ich	**bin**	I am	wir	**sind**	we are
du	**bist**	you are	ihr	**seid**	you are
er, es, sie	**ist**	he, it, she is	sie, Sie	**sind**	they, you are

Üben wir!

A. Substitute the new subjects given.

> EXAMPLE: *Er* ist in Eile. (ich)
> Ich bin in Eile.

1. *Wir* sind in Eile.
   (du, ich, Frau Kuhn und Frau Bachmann, ihr, Sie, er)
2. Am Mittwoch bin *ich* wieder zurück.
   (Herr Hauser, du, Sie, ihr, wir, Frau Kuhn, Stefan und Michael)

4 ◆ Noun Gender

Unlike English, each German noun has a *gender*, that is, it is masculine, neuter, or feminine. English has *natural gender*, that is, in English one refers to a man as "he," a woman as "she," and chair as "it." German nouns have *grammatical gender* which does not necessarily correspond to natural gender.

The article indicates the gender of the German noun. When learning a noun, also memorize its definite article (**der, das,** or **die**). For example, learn **der Stuhl** and not simply **Stuhl.**

masculine:	**der** Mann (the man)	**der** Stuhl (the chair)
neuter:	**das** Kind (the child)	**das** Buch (the book)
feminine:	**die** Frau (the woman)	**die** Tafel (the blackboard)

The pronoun agrees in gender with the noun it replaces. **Er, es,** and **sie** can all mean "it."

Wo ist **der** Stuhl?	**Er** ist hier.	*It's here.*
Wo ist **das** Buch?	**Es** ist hier.	*It's here.*
Wo ist **die** Tafel?	**Sie** ist hier.	*It's here.*

Gender distinctions disappear in the plural. The definite article **die** is used with all nouns:

die Stühle[1]	*the chairs*
die Bücher	*the books*
die Tafeln	*the blackboards*

Remember that the plural pronoun is **sie** for all nouns:

| Wo sind **die** Bücher? | **Sie** sind hier. | *They are here.* |

___

Üben wir!

A. Answer with the appropriate pronoun.

EXAMPLE: Ist das die Tafel?   Is that the blackboard?
         Ja, das ist **sie.**   Yes, that's it.

1. Ist das der Stuhl?
2. Ist das die Suppe?
3. Ist das das Kind?
4. Ist das Michael?

5. Ist das Frau Kuhn?
6. Ist das das Buch?
7. Ist das die Mensa?
8. Ist das die Straße?

___

[1] For plural endings, see page 26.

The most common plural ending for English nouns is **-s** or **-es**: *chair, chairs; dish, dishes.* A handful of nouns have irregular plurals: *man, men; mouse, mice; child, children; sheep, sheep.*

German has a much greater variety of plural forms. There is no one basic rule, nor is any one form the most common. The following table gives examples of all the plural forms:

	Singular	Plural
1. no change	der Lehrer	die Lehrer
2. umlaut added to stem vowel	die Mutter	die Mütter
3. -e	der Tisch	die Tische
4. umlaut + -e	der Stuhl	die Stühle
5. -er	das Kind	die Kinder
6. umlaut + -er	das Buch	die Bücher
7. -en	die Frau	die Frauen
8. -n	die Straße	die Straßen
9. -s	das Büro	die Büros

It is customary in dictionaries and vocabulary lists to indicate the plural by an abbreviation. An umlaut above the hyphen indicates that the stem (stressed) vowel is umlauted in the plural:

Dictionary Entry	You Must Learn
der **Lehrer, -**	der **Lehrer,** die **Lehrer**
die **Mutter, ⁝**	die **Mutter,** die **Mütter**
der **Tag, -e**	der **Tag,** die **Tage**
der **Stuhl, ⁝e**	der **Stuhl,** die **Stühle**
usw.	etc.

Üben wir!

A. Look at the following vocabulary and say aloud both the singular and plural forms with their articles:

1. das **Kind, -er**
2. das **Büro, -s**
3. der **Tisch, -e**
4. die **Mutter, ⁝**

5. die **Tafel, -n**
6. die **Straße, -n**
7. der **Stuhl, ⁝e**
8. die **Frau, -en**

B. Give the plural forms of the following nouns.

EXAMPLE: die Straße
die Straßen

1. der Morgen
2. der Tag
3. das Büro
4. die Frau

5. das Kind
6. der Lehrer
7. der Herr
8. die Suppe

C. Now substitute plural for singular and change the verb accordingly.

> EXAMPLE: **Der Herr kommt** um elf.
> **Die Herren kommen** um elf.

1. Das Büro ist sehr schön.
2. Die Frau fliegt nach Wien.
3. Das Kind kommt zu Horst.
4. Die Straße ist sehr schön.
5. Das Buch ist gut.
6. Der Lehrer arbeitet morgen im Büro.

6 ◆ Nominative Case

German nouns can occur in four different cases. These cases are indicated by changes in the form of the article preceding the noun, and sometimes in the form of the noun itself. Cases signal different relationships between the noun and the verb of the sentence, or between two nouns. For example, they show whether the noun is the subject (*The student* eats soup.) or object (The student eats *soup*.) of the verb, or they may show possession (*the student's* soup). In this chapter, you will learn the formation and use of the *nominative* case.

Formation

The article signals the case of the noun. You have already learned the definite article in the nominative:

Masculine	Neuter	Feminine	Plural	
der Mann	**das** Kind	**die** Frau	**die**	Männer Kinder Frauen

Here is the indefinite article (English: a, an) in the nominative:

Masculine	Neuter	Feminine
ein Mann	**ein** Kind	**eine** Frau

■ Note that masculine and neuter singular are identical in the nominative: **ein** Mann, **ein** Kind.

Use

1. The subject of the sentence is always in the nominative case:

Der Herr ist in Eile.	*The gentleman is in a hurry.*
Endlich kommt **die Suppe.**	*The soup is finally coming.*
Morgen fliegt **sie** zurück.	*She's flying back tomorrow.*

2. A predicate nominative is a noun that refers to the same person or thing as the subject of the sentence. It follows the subject and the verb **sein**.[1]

Das ist **Frau Schmidt.**   *That is Mrs. Schmidt.*
Paul ist **ein Kind.**   *Paul is a child.*

Üben wir!

A. Substitute new subjects or predicate nominatives with the proper article:

1. Wie ist *die Suppe* heute? (Wetter, Mensa)
2. Wann kommen *die Herren* zurück? (Frauen, Kinder, Studenten, Lehrer)
3. Das ist *die Mensa.* (Büro, Fenster, Tisch, Sonne, Herr, Stuhl, Tafel)
4. Das ist *eine Uhr.* (Büro, Stuhl, Tisch, Tafel, Straße, Fenster, Student, Studentin)

„Wie geht's dir, Stephanie?" „Danke gut, und Ihnen?"

[1] A few other verbs (**bleiben,** *to remain;* **heißen,** *to be called;* **werden,** *to become*) also take the predicate nominative. You will learn them later.

Statements: Verb-Second Word Order

In sentences that make a statement (rather than ask a question or give a command), the subject must precede the verb in English:

> Subject   Verb
> **We**   **are going** to Horst's tonight.

Other elements may precede the subject-verb combination:

> Tonight **we are going** to Horst's.

In German statements, only the verb has a fixed position. It is *always the second element* in the sentence:

> 1   2   3   4
> Wir **gehen** heute abend zu Horst.

This is an ironclad rule and one that you must get used to. If an element other than the subject begins the sentence, the verb *remains* in second position and the subject then *follows* the verb. Note the difference from English, where the subject always precedes the verb:

> 1   2   3   4
> Heute abend **gehen** wir zu Horst.
> Zu Horst   **gehen** wir heute abend.

■ A time phrase (**heute abend**) or a prepositional phrase (**zu Horst**) may consist of two or more words, but counts as *one* grammatical element.

■ First position is usually used to restate what's being talked about. A new element with informational value—the answer to a question, for instance— is usually placed at the end of the statement:

> What are we doing?   Wir gehen **zu Horst.**
> What are we doing tonight?   Heute abend gehen wir **zu Horst.**
> When are we going to Horst's? Zu Horst gehen wir **heute abend.**

Üben wir!

A. Restate the sentences, beginning with the word or phrase in italics.

> EXAMPLE: Ich arbeite *übrigens* viel.
> *Übrigens* arbeite ich viel.

1. Die Lehrerin geht *morgen* zu Frau Bachmann.
2. Die Sonne scheint *endlich* wieder!
3. Es ist *schön* heute.
4. Wir fliegen *um elf* nach Wien.
5. Das ist *vielleicht* die Straße.
6. Ich arbeite viel *im Moment.*
7. Die Suppe ist *heute* ganz gut.
8. Es regnet *natürlich* viel.

Questions

There are two main types of questions in German: yes/no questions and informational questions.

1. Yes/no questions are answered by **ja** or **nein,** and the verb is always the first element:

Ist	Andrea hier?	*Is Andrea here?*
Arbeitet	sie in Berlin?	*Does she work in Berlin?*
Kommst	du wieder zurück?	*Are you coming back again?*

2. Questions asking for information start with a question word (what, how, when, etc.) and have the same verb-second word order as statements:

1	**2**		
Was	macht	er?	*What is he doing?*
Wie	geht	es Ihnen?	*How are you?*
Wann	kommen	Sie wieder zurück?	*When are you coming back again?*

Here are the most commonly used question words:

wann	when	**wer**	who
warum	why	**wie**	how
was	what	**wo**	where

■ Do not confuse **wer** (who) and **wo** (where)!

`o━o` **Üben wir!**	**A.** Change these statements to yes/no questions.

> EXAMPLE: Stefan arbeitet in Stuttgart.
> Arbeitet Stefan in Stuttgart?

1. Das ist typisch für September.
2. Ihr geht wieder zu Karin.
3. Es regnet.
4. Herr Hauser fliegt nach Berlin.
5. Frau Kuhn kommt auch.
6. Im Moment arbeitest du viel.
7. Er ist sehr in Eile.
8. Der Herr kommt am Mittwoch zurück.

B. Ask the questions for which the following statements are answers.

> EXAMPLE: Das ist der Professor.
> Wer ist das?

1. Er fliegt um elf.
2. Sehr gut, danke, und Ihnen?

3. Sie sind im Büro.

4. Das ist Frau Bachmann.

5. Das ist die Mensa.

6. Die Suppe ist gut, danke.

8 ◆ Expanding Your Vocabulary

Months of the Year

The months of the year are all masculine in German:

(der) Januar	im Januar	*in January*
Februar	im Februar	*in February*
März	usw.	*etc.*
April (Ap*ril*)[1]		
Mai		
Juni		
Juli		
August (Au*gust*)		
September		
Oktober		
November		
Dezember		

Üben wir!

A. Tell in what months these things are going to happen.

> EXAMPLE: Wann fliegt sie nach Wien?
> Im Januar.

1. Wann fliegen wir nach Deutschland?

2. Wann arbeiten Sie in Wien?

3. Wann regnet es viel?

4. Wann kommt Herr Hauser zurück?

5. Wann scheint die Sonne viel?

6. Wann spielen die Kinder draußen?

Leicht zu merken (*Easy to Remember*)

German has many words that look so much like their English equivalents that you can easily guess their meanings. Both languages have borrowed many of these words from Latin or French. When such words occur in the reading, we will preview them in this special section called „**Leicht zu merken.**" See if you can guess their meanings.

> formell (for*mell*)
> die Solidarität (Solidar*ität*)

■ Note that the stress of the German word can be different from its English equivalent.

---

[1] When the stress of a German cognate is different from its English equivalent, the German stress will be given in parentheses.

Wortschatz 2

Verben

bedeuten to mean, signify

  Was bedeutet das? What does that mean?

fragen to ask

grüßen to greet, say hello to

meinen to be of the opinion, think

sagen to say; tell

stimmen to be right (*cannot have a person as subject*)

  das stimmt that's right, that's true

studieren to attend a university

wohnen to live, dwell

Substantive

der **Amerikaner, -** American (*m.*)[1]

der **Deutsche, -n** German (*m.*)

der **Schüler, -** secondary school pupil (*m.*)

der **Student, -en** university student (*m.*)

der **Tourist, -en** tourist (*m.*)

(das) **Deutschland** Germany

das **Haus, ¨er** house

die **Amerikanerin, -nen** American (*f.*)

die **Deutsche, -n** German (*f.*)

die **Gruppe, -n** group

die **Klasse, -n** class; grade

die **Schülerin, -nen** secondary school pupil (*f.*)

die **Studentin, -nen** university student (*f.*)

die **Touristin, -nen** tourist (*f.*)

Andere Vokabeln

eins one

freundlich friendly

hier here

höflich polite

immer always

man one (*impersonal pronoun*)

oder or

oft often

so so; like this

sogar even, in fact

viele many

wahrscheinlich probably

zehn ten

ziemlich fairly, quite

Nützliche Ausdrücke

zum Beispiel for example

auf deutsch in German

Wie geht es dir? How are you? (*to someone whom you address as* **du**)

Gegensätze

immer ≠ nie	always ≠ never
oft ≠ selten	often ≠ seldom

[1] See list of abbreviations in the Appendix.

Wie sagt man „you" auf deutsch?

Touristen in Deutschland sagen oft, die Deutschen sind sehr freundlich und höflich. Das stimmt, aber wahrscheinlich meinen viele Amerikaner, die Deutschen sind auch ziemlich formell.

5 Frau Bachmann und Frau Kuhn sind zum Beispiel Nachbarinnen.° Sie wohnen im selben° Haus und sind sogar befreundet,° aber Frau Bachmann fragt nicht: „Wie geht es dir, Gisela?" Nein, sie sagt: „Wie geht es Ihnen, Frau Kuhn?" Sie grüßen einander° formell.

10 Die Lehrer duzen° die Schüler von Klasse eins bis Klasse zehn. Aber ab° Klasse elf sagen sie „Sie". Die Schüler siezen° die Lehrer natürlich immer.

Heute ist das „Du" auch ein Ausdruck der° Solidarität. Für die Studenten bedeutet es: wir sind eine Gruppe. Karin 15 und Michael, zum Beispiel, studieren[1]. Sie sagen von Anfang an° „Du" zueinander.°

*neighbors / **im selben** = in the same on friendly terms*

each other
*address with **du***
*beginning in / address with **Sie***

***Ausdruck der** = expression of*

***von . . . an** = from the beginning to each other*

Das Wetter ist schön, und wir sitzen draußen.

---

[1] Note that **studieren** means to attend college or university and is not used to describe the student's daily activity of studying. Thus, "I'm studying tonight" is translated as "Ich **arbeite** heute abend."

Fragen zum Lesestück (*Questions on the Reading*)

1. Wer meint, die Deutschen sind ziemlich formell?
2. Was sagt Frau Bachmann zu Frau Kuhn?
3. Sagen Lehrer und Schüler „Du"?
4. Was sind Karin und Michael?
5. Sagen Karin und Michael „Sie"?
6. Was bedeutet das „Du" für die Studenten?

Vom Lesen zum Sprechen (*From Reading to Speaking*)

„Sie" oder „Du"?

A. Conduct the following dialogues in German:

MRS. MÜLLER: Where do you live?
MRS. BRAUN: In Berlin. And you?

KARIN: Are you studying this evening?
MICHAEL: No. Why do you ask?

MOTHER: What are you doing today, children?
CHILD: We're playing outside.

B. Now ask your classmates where they live. Use the **du**-form.

Lehrer und Schüler

Mündliche Übungen (*Oral Exercises*)

A. Persönliche Fragen

  1. Wie geht es Ihnen?
  2. Scheint die Sonne heute oder regnet es?
  3. Sind Sie oft in Eile?
  4. Welcher Tag ist heute?
  5. Arbeiten Sie viel im Moment?
  6. Was machen Sie heute abend?

B. Answer the questions, beginning with the cue you will hear.

> EXAMPLE: Machst du das heute? (natürlich)
> Natürlich mache ich das heute.

  1. Wann fliegst du nach Berlin? (am Montag)
  2. Wann kommst du wieder zurück? (am Donnerstag)
  3. Wann geht ihr zu Marion? (um zehn)
  4. Studiert sie in Berlin? (natürlich)
  5. Ist das Herr Hauser? (wahrscheinlich)
  6. Kommt er morgen? (ja, vielleicht)
  7. Wann regnet es wieder? (heute abend)
  8. Arbeiten Sie? (ja, im Moment)

C. Replace the definite article with the indefinite article in these sentences.

> EXAMPLE: Der Tourist sagt das oft.
> Ein Tourist sagt das oft.

  1. Die Gruppe arbeitet heute.
  2. Das Buch ist hier.
  3. Der Schüler fragt immer warum.
  4. Die Deutsche wohnt hier.
  5. Hier ist die Straße.
  6. Wo ist das Kind?
  7. Ist das das Haus?

D. Replace the subject with a pronoun as you answer.

> EXAMPLE: Ist der Lehrer freundlich?
> Ja, er ist freundlich.

  1. Ist das Buch gut?
  2. Ist Frau Schmidt sehr freundlich?
  3. Ist das Wetter typisch für September?

4. Scheint die Sonne endlich?

5. Sind Karin und Michael in der Mensa?

6. Ist die Suppe gut?

7. Ist der Tag schön?

E. Your teacher asks you what you are doing. Respond using the cue given in English.

> EXAMPLE: Was machst du? (flying to Vienna)
> Ich fliege nach Wien.

1. Was macht ihr? (going to Stefan's)

2. Was machst du, Richard? (working a lot at the moment)

3. Was machen Sie, Frau Gruber? (finally studying)

4. Was machst du heute, Regina? (playing outside)

5. Was macht ihr, Rolf und Helene? (flying to Hamburg)

6. Was machen Sie, Frau Bachmann? (greeting Mrs. Kuhn)

Schriftliche Übungen (*Written Exercises*)

F. Write sentences using the verb **sein** and the cues below.

> EXAMPLE: wir / Amerikaner
> Wir sind Amerikaner.

1. Richard / freundlich

2. du / ziemlich formell

3. Michael und Karin / Touristen

4. ihr / Studenten

5. wir / Amerikaner

6. du / schön

7. ich / oft in Eile

8. der August / schön

G. Answer the following questions. Answer the yes/no questions positively.

1. Was machst du heute abend?

2. Bist du in Eile?

3. Fliegt er nach New York?

4. Wer wohnt hier?

5. Regnet es wieder?

6. Was machen wir im Moment?

7. Arbeitest du vielleicht morgen?

8. Ist das typisch?

H. Write a dialogue using the following cues:

> ULLI: Tag / Horst! du / arbeiten / morgen?
> HORST: nein warum / du / fragen?
> ULLI: morgen / wir / gehen / zu Hans du / kommen / auch?
> HORST: natürlich / ich / kommen

I. Write the following conversation in German:

Good morning, Mrs. Huber.
Good morning. How are you?
Fine thanks, and you?
Pretty good. At the moment I'm working a lot.

J. Wie sagt man das auf deutsch?

1. When are you coming back, Jürgen and Katrin?

2. We are coming back tomorrow.

3. Excuse me, are you in a hurry?

4. Yes, I'm going to Helene's.
   Ja, ich gehe zu Helene.

5. She says the Germans are friendly.
   Sie saget der deutscher freundlich sind

6. Yes, that's right.
   Ja, da ist richtig

7. How are you, Herr Beck?
   Wie geht es Ihnen

8. Fine thanks, and you?
   Gut Danke, und Ihnen

9. The sun is shining again.
   Die Sonne scheint wieder?

10. Good! We'll work outside.
    Gut! Wir abeiten draußen.

„Heute arbeite ich draußen."

Almanach

**Profile of West Germany
(The Federal Republic of Germany)**

Area: 248,717 square kilometers; 96,030 square miles
Population: 60.8 million or 245 people per square kilometer
West Germany consists of 10 states (**Bundesländer**) plus West Berlin.
Currency: German mark = **Deutsche Mark**
             1 DM = 100 Pfennig

Major cities: Bonn, capital (pop. 292,600);
                West Berlin (pop. almost 2 million);
                Hamburg, München (Munich),
                Köln (Cologne), Essen, Düsseldorf, Frankfurt

Volkszählung '87
Zehn Minuten, die allen helfen.

After the United States and Japan, West Germany ranks third as an industrial power in the western world. It depends to a large extent on the export of its industrial products and the import of natural resources. Its total foreign trade is surpassed only by the US. The per capita income of $10,500 (1980) is among the highest in the world, and its birth rate of less than 10 per 1,000 of population is the lowest in the world.

It is a member of the European Common Market and of NATO. Since 1972 it has also been a member of the UN.

Lübeck: Das
Holstentor (1477).

Familie und Freunde

Dialoge
Ich habe eine Frage ♦ Wer liest die Zeitung? ♦ Georg sucht ein Zimmer

Wortschatz 1

Grammatik
1. Contraction of **du**-Form: **heißen**
2. Verbs with Stem Vowel Change: **e** to **i(e)**
3. The Verb **wissen** (to know)
4. The Verb **haben** (to have)
5. The Accusative Case
   Accusative of Definite and Indefinite Articles. ♦
   Accusative of Interrogative Pronoun: **wen** ♦ Accusative of the Personal Pronouns
6. The Possessive Adjective
7. The Flavoring Particle **denn**
8. Expanding Your Vocabulary
   Cardinal Numbers 0–20 ♦
   Leicht zu merken

Wortschatz 2

Lesestück
Die Familie heute

Vom Lesen zum Sprechen
Die Familie

Almanach
Der Stammbaum–The Family Tree

Dialoge

Ich habe eine Frage

ANNETTE: Katrin, ich habe eine Frage. Wie heißt der Mann?
KATRIN: Wen meinst du denn?
ANNETTE: Den Mann da drüben. Er spricht mit Stefan. Ich sehe, er kennt dich.
KATRIN: Und ich kenne ihn—sehr gut sogar! Das ist mein Bruder Max.
ANNETTE: Ach, du hast auch einen Bruder! Ich kenne nur deine Schwester.

Wer liest die Zeitung?

VATER: Tobias, ich suche meine Zeitung. Weißt du, wo sie ist?
SOHN: Wieso *deine* Zeitung? Ist sie nicht für uns alle da? Ich lese sie im Moment.
VATER: Gut, *unsere* Zeitung. Was liest du denn?
SOHN: Ich lese den Artikel über unsere Schule.

Georg sucht ein Zimmer

GEORG: Wen kennst du in München?
STEFAN: Viele Leute. Meine Familie wohnt da. Warum fragst du?
GEORG: Ich studiere nächstes Semester in München und brauche ein Zimmer.
STEFAN: Unser Haus ist ziemlich groß. Sicher haben meine Eltern ein Zimmer frei.
GEORG: Phantastisch! Vielen Dank!
STEFAN: Bitte, bitte. Nichts zu danken.

Wohnungsmarkt

3-ZIMMER-WOHNUNG zu vermieten, frisch gestrichen, moderne Küche, nahe Universität. Tel. 09 11/35 24 03

HAUS ZU VERMIETEN 4 Schlafzimmer, Möbel, Moltkestr. 66/Ecke Engelstr., Tel. 02 41/52 31 22

Wortschatz 1

I Have a Question

ANNETTE: Katrin, I have a question. What's that man's name?

KATRIN: Whom do you mean?

ANNETTE: That man over there. He's talking to Stefan. I see he knows you.

KATRIN: And I know him—very well, in fact! That's my brother Max.

ANNETTE: Oh, you have a brother too! I only know your sister.

Who's Reading the Newspaper?

FATHER: Tobias, I'm looking for my newspaper. Do you know where it is?

SON: What do you mean *your* newspaper? Isn't it here for all of us? I'm reading it at the moment.

FATHER: Okay, *our* newspaper. So what are you reading?

SON: I'm reading the article about our school.

Georg Looks for a Room

GEORG: Whom do you know in Munich?

STEFAN: A lot of people. My family lives there. Why do you ask?

GEORG: I'm going to study in Munich next semester and I need a room.

STEFAN: Our house is fairly large. My parents surely have a room free.

GEORG: Fantastic! Thanks a lot!

STEFAN: You're welcome. Don't mention it.

Verben

brauchen   to need
essen (ißt)   to eat
haben   to have
heißen   to be called
  Er heißt Max.   His name is Max.
kennen   to know, to be acquainted with
lesen (liest)   to read
  lesen über (+ *acc.*)   to read about
meinen   to mean
nehmen (nimmt)   to take
sehen (sieht)   to see
sprechen (spricht)   to speak, talk
  sprechen über (+ *acc.*)   to talk about
suchen   to look for, seek
wissen (weiß)   to know (a fact)

Substantive

der **Artikel, -**   article
der **Bruder, ⸚**   brother
der **Freund, -e**   friend
der **Mann, ⸚er**   man; husband
der **Sohn, ⸚e**   son
der **Vater, ⸚**   father

das **Semester, -**   semester
das **Zimmer, -**   room

die **Frage, -n**   question
die **Schule, -n**   school
die **Schwester, -n**   sister

die **Zeitung, -en**   newspaper
die **Leute** (*pl.*)   people
die **Eltern** (*pl.*)   parents

Andere Vokabeln

ach   oh; ah
alle (*pl.*)   all; everybody
bitte   you're welcome
da   there; here; then
(da) drüben   over there
dein (*fam. sing.*)   your
denn (*flavoring particle, see p. 50*)
frei   free; unoccupied
groß   big
mein   my
mit   with
nur   only
sicher   certain, sure
über (+ *acc.*)   about
unser   our
wen?   whom?
wieso?   How come? How's that? What do you mean?
wie viele?   how many?

Nützliche Ausdrücke

Phantastisch!   Fantastic!
vielen Dank   many thanks
nächstes Semester   next semester
Nichts zu danken!   Don't mention it!

Gegensätze

danke ≠ bitte	thank you ≠ you're welcome
groß ≠ klein	big ≠ little

Neue Kombinationen

A. Your friend asks you the names of various people. Answer with names from the dialogues: Georg, Stefan, Katrin, Frau Bachmann, Herr Hauser, etc.

> EXAMPLE: Weißt du, wie **der Mann** heißt?
> Ja, er heißt Georg.

Weißt du, wie *der Mann* heißt? (die Frau, der Sohn, das Kind, der Lehrer, die Lehrerin, der Student)

B. Replace **deine Schwester** with the new phrases.

Ich kenne nur *deine Schwester*. (deinen Bruder, deinen Vater, dein Kind, deine Frau)

Now replace **unseren Bruder** with the new phrases.

Wir suchen *unseren Bruder*. (unseren Sohn, unser Kind, unsere Schwester, unsere Eltern)

C. You friend is looking for various things and people and you say that they're not here.

> EXAMPLE: Ich suche **meine Zeitung.**
> Sie ist nicht hier.

Ich suche *mein Buch*. (meine Eltern, meinen Bruder, meine Schwester, meine Lehrerin, meine Schüler)

D. Herr Beck has just moved to Aachen. Tell all the things he needs.

Er braucht *ein Zimmer*. (ein Büro, einen Stuhl, eine Zeitung, ein Haus, eine Uhr, einen Tisch)

⊡ **Übung zur Aussprache**

Practice the sound of German **z** (see Introduction, p. 9). Do not confuse **z** with voiced **s** preceding a vowel:

Zone	Sohn	zagen	sagen
Zeit	seit	Ziege	Siege
zog	Sog	Zoo	so

Read these sentences aloud, watching out for the difference between **z** and **s**.

1. Ist meine **Z**eitung hier im **Z**immer? Ich suche sie.
2. Du sagst, du siehst die **Z**eitung nicht? Ich lese sie.
3. Das ist **z**iemlich typisch.
4. Sie gibt die **Z**eitung **z**urück.

Grammatik

1 ◆ Contraction of *du*-form: *heißen*

Verbs with stems ending in a sibilant (a hissing sound: **-s, -ß,** or **-z**) contract the **du**-form ending **-st** to **-t.**

In these verbs, the **du**-form and the **er**-form are identical.

heißen to be called		stem: **heiß-**	
ich	heiße	wir	heißen
du	**heißt**	ihr	heißt
er, es, sie	heißt	sie, Sie	heißen

Üben wir!

A. A teacher is learning names on the first day of class. Figure out his questions from the answers given.

> EXAMPLE: Ich heiße Christl.   Question: Wie heißt du?

1. Ich heiße Andreas.
2. Ich heiße Ursula.
3. Nein, sie heißt Marie.
4. Er heißt Ulrich.
5. Ich heiße Otto.
6. Wir heißen Anna und Jan Müller.
7. Sie heißen Ziegler.
8. Sie heißt Susanne.

2 ◆ Verbs with Stem Vowel Change: *e* to *i(e)*

Some German verbs change their stem vowel in the **du-** and **er**-forms of the present tense.

e → ie **sehen** to see			
ich	sehe	wir	sehen
du	**siehst**	ihr	seht
er, es, sie	**sieht**	sie, Sie	sehen

■ Another verb in this group is **lesen** (er **liest**), to read.[1]

e → i **sprechen** to speak			
ich	spreche	wir	sprechen
du	**sprichst**	ihr	sprecht
er, es, sie	**spricht**	sie, Sie	sprechen

[1] Stem vowel change will be indicated in the vocabulary by inclusion of the **er**-form: **sehen (sieht)** to **see.**

■ Two other verbs in this group are **essen,** to eat; and **nehmen,** to take. They change not only their stem vowel, but also some consonants:

essen to eat		**nehmen** to take	
ich	esse	ich	nehme
du	**ißt**	du	**nimmst**
er, es, sie	**ißt**	er, es, sie	**nimmt**

A. Restate the sentences, using the new subjects indicated.

1. *Ich* sehe das Haus. (Katrin, wir, die Leute, du, mein Bruder, die Schüler, ihr)
2. *Tobias* liest die Zeitung. (ich, die Studenten, du, wir, Georg, Annette, ihr, unsere Eltern)
3. *Wir* sprechen mit Stefan. (Georg, ich, ihr, der Lehrer, die Kinder, du, wir, die Leute)
4. Was eßt *ihr*? (wir, der Mann, ich, du, die Touristen, der Tourist, Marie, ihr, er)
5. *Karin* nimmt das Zimmer. (ich, die Freunde, du, wir, die Lehrerin, Michael, ihr)

Was ißt die Familie heute abend?

3 ◆ The Verb *wissen* (to know)

The verb **wissen** (*to know*) is irregular in the singular present. Its forms must be memorized:

ich	**weiß**	wir	wissen
du	**weißt**	ihr	wißt
er, es, sie	**weiß**	sie, Sie	wissen

■ Both the first person singular and the third person singular lack endings: **ich weiß, er weiß.**

■ wissen *vs.* kennen
Both **wissen** and **kennen** may be translated as "to know," but **wissen** means "to know a fact" and **kennen** means "to be familiar, acquainted with," and is used when the direct object (see below, p. 47) is a person or place:

Weißt du, wer das ist?   *Do you know who that is?*
Ja, ich **kenne** ihn sehr gut.   *Yes, I know him very well.*

Kennen Sie Berlin, Herr Brandt?   *Do you know Berlin, Mr. Brandt?*
Nein, nicht sehr gut.   *No, not very well.*

Üben wir!   **A.** Form sentences with the cues you will hear, using either **wissen** or **kennen** as required.

EXAMPLE: ich / Georg   Ich kenne Georg.

1. er / Michael
2. wir / Berlin
3. Katrin / wo ich wohne
4. ihr / was sie macht
5. ich / Stefan und Annette
6. du / München
7. ich / wer das ist
8. die Schüler / was der Lehrer meint

4 ◆ The Verb *haben* (to have)

The verb **haben** (*to have*) is irregular in the present singular:

ich	habe	wir	haben
du	**hast**	ihr	habt
er, es, sie	**hat**	sie, Sie	haben

A. Your teacher is looking for the newspaper. Tell who has it, using the subjects you will hear.

> EXAMPLE: Wer hat die Zeitung? (Michael)
> Michael hat sie.

1. Agnes
2. wir
3. die Kinder
4. du
5. ich
6. ihr

5 ♦ The Accusative Case

In German, the accusative case is used for the direct object of a verb. The direct object is the thing or person acted upon, known, or possessed by the subject.

Subject (*nominative*)		Direct Object (*accusative*)
Sie	lesen	**das Buch.**
Anna	kennt	**meine Eltern.**
Horst	hat	**einen Bruder.**

Accusative of Definite and Indefinite Articles

Like the nominative case, the accusative case is signaled by the form of the article which accompanies the noun:

		Singular			Plural
definite article	**nom:**	der Stuhl	das Buch	die Tafel	die Stühle
	acc:	**den** Stuhl	das Buch	die Tafel	die Stühle
indefinite article	**nom:**	ein Stuhl	ein Buch	eine Tafel	meine Stühle[1]
	acc:	**einen** Stuhl	ein Buch	eine Tafel	meine Stühle

Only the masculine singular article has different forms for the nominative and accusative.

Üben wir!

A. Change the sentences according to the example, supplying the accusative form of the article:

> EXAMPLE: Wo ist das Buch?
> Ich suche **das Buch.**

1. Wo ist der Stuhl? Ich suche . . .
2. Wo sind die Kinder?
3. Wo ist ein Zimmer?
4. Wo ist ein Tisch?
5. Wo ist die Zeitung?
6. Wo ist eine Uhr?
7. Wo sind die Leute?
8. Wo ist der Lehrer?

---

[1] Because the indefinite article **ein** has no plural, the possessive adjective **mein** (*my*) has been used to show the plural endings.

Accusative of Interrogative Pronoun: wen

The accusative form of the question word **wer** is **wen:**

> **Wen** kennst du in München?
> ***Whom*** *do you know in Munich?*

Üben wir!

A. Ask your neighbor these questions in German:

> EXAMPLE: Whom do you know?
> Wen kennst du?

1. Whom do you see?
2. Whom are you looking for?
3. Whom are you asking?
4. Whom do you know?

Accusative of the Personal Pronouns

	Singular			Plural		
nom.	*acc.*		*nom.*	*acc.*		
ich	**mich**	me	wir	**uns**	us
du	**dich**	you	ihr	**euch**	you
er	**ihn**	him, it			
es	**es**	it	sie	**sie**	they
sie	**sie**	she, it	(Sie	**Sie**	you)

 Üben wir!

A. Expand each sentence as in the examples, substituting an accusative pronoun for the noun direct object.

> EXAMPLE: TEACHER: Vater kennt **Katrin.**
> STUDENT: Ich kenne **sie** auch.

1. Vater kennt den Lehrer.
2. Vater kennt Frau Braun.
3. Vater kennt die Leute.
4. Vater kennt Stefan.
5. Vater kennt die Schüler.
6. Vater kennt das Kind.

> EXAMPLE: TEACHER: Mutter braucht **den Stuhl.**
> STUDENT: Mutter braucht **den Stuhl.** Has du **ihn?**

7. Mutter braucht das Buch.
8. Mutter braucht die Zeitung.
9. Mutter braucht die Uhr.
10. Mutter braucht den Bleistift.
11. Mutter braucht die Stühle.
12. Mutter braucht die Bücher.

B. Expand the following sentences as in the example, reversing the subject and direct object.

> EXAMPLE: Ich kenne ihn.
> Ich kenne ihn, **und er kennt mich.**

1. Du suchst mich.
2. Ich sehe es.
3. Sie kennt uns.
4. Sie brauchen ihn.

5. Wir fragen euch.
6. Er sucht dich.
7. Ihr seht sie (her).
8. Er kennt uns.

6 ♦ The Possessive Adjective

Personal Pronoun	Possessive Adjective	
ich	**mein**	my
du	**dein**	your
er	**sein**	his; its
es	**sein**	its
sie	**ihr**	her; its
wir	**unser**	our
ihr	**euer**	your *pl*
sie	**ihr**	their
(Sie)	**(Ihr)**	(your)

■ Just as **er** and **sie** can mean "it" when they replace masculine and feminine nouns like **der Tisch** and **die Straße** (see page 25), so **sein** and **ihr** can mean "its."
■ Note that **Ihr** (your), like **Sie** (you), is always capitalized.

The possessive adjectives must agree with the nouns they modify in gender, number, and case. This agreement is shown by endings that are the same as those of **ein**. Possessive adjectives are therefore called **ein**-words.

In the following table, the possessive adjective **mein** is used with nouns of different gender, number and case. Note the endings of **mein**; they are the same as those of **ein** (see page 47).

	masculine	neuter	feminine	plural
nom.	mein Bruder	mein Kind	meine Schwester	meine Eltern
acc.	**meinen** Bruder	mein Kind	meine Schwester	meine Eltern

■ Only the masculine singular has different forms for the nominative and accusative.

EXAMPLES:
Mein Bruder wohnt in Mannheim.
Ich suche **meinen** Bruder.

My brother lives in Mannheim.
I'm looking for my brother.

■ *The* **-er** on **unser** and **euer** is not an ending, but part of the stem. When **euer** and **unser** take endings, the second **-e-** of the stem may be dropped.

> EXAMPLES: **Unser** Vater liest die Zeitung.
> Wir suchen **unsren** Vater.
> Das ist **euer** Buch.
> **Eure** Bücher sind hier.

Üben wir!

A. Answer the following questions according to the example.

> EXAMPLE: Kennst du meinen Bruder?
> Ja, ich kenne deinen Bruder.

1. Sieht er seine Schwester?
2. Liest sie ihr Buch?
3. Kennst du mein Haus?
4. Suchst du dein Heft?
5. Kennst du unsere Schule?
6. Sehen Sie meine Eltern?
7. Wiederholen Sie meine Frage?
8. Habt ihr eure Bücher?

B. Student A forms a question from the statement given and student B responds as in the example:

> EXAMPLE: Das sind[1] meine Eltern.
> Student A: Kennst du meine Eltern?
> Student B: Ja, ich kenne deine Eltern.

1. Das sind seine Schüler. Kennst du . . .
2. Das ist ihr Sohn.
3. Das ist ihr Bruder.
4. Das ist mein Bruder.
5. Das ist unser Lehrer.
6. Das ist unser Kind.
7. Das sind unsre Kinder.
8. Das ist meine Lehrerin.

7 ♦ The Flavoring Particle *denn*

German adds various kinds of emphasis with words known as intensifying or "flavoring" particles. They are used especially in the spoken language to add emotional flavor, and cannot be directly translated into English. Probably the most frequently used flavoring particle is **denn**. **Denn** makes a question more emphatic by indicating mild surprise, impatience or genuine interest in the answer.

Denn is never stressed. Read the following examples, stressing the word in italics.

Wo *ist* er denn?
Wer ist denn *das*?
Was *liest* du denn da?

Where can he be?
Who in the world is that?
What are you reading?

Denn usually comes immediately after the subject and verb.

---
[1] **das sind** = *these are, those are* (plural of **das ist**).

ICH SCHREIB VON FERNE
ICH HAB DICH GERNE
DENK AUCH AN MICH
SO WIE ICH HEUT AN DICH

ALLES GUTE
ZUM GEBURTSTAG

Üben wir!

A. Add **denn** to make these questions more emphatic:

1. Wie heißt der Junge?
2. Wen meinst du?
3. Kommt ihr heute abend?
4. Wann essen wir?
5. Was hat sie?
6. Wie machst du das?
7. Kennt ihr meine Schwester?
8. Ißt du heute in der Mensa?

Cardinal Numbers 0–20

Here are the German cardinal numbers (numbers expressing amount: one, two, three, etc.) from zero to twenty:

	0 null		
1	eins	11	elf
2	zwei	12	zwölf
3	drei	13	dreizehn
4	vier	14	vierzehn
5	fünf	15	fünfzehn
6	sechs	16	sechzehn
7	sieben	17	siebzehn
8	acht	18	achtzehn
9	neun	19	neunzehn
10	zehn	20	zwanzig

The form **eins** is used when counting. When used with a noun (**eine** Zeitung = *one* newspaper), the number **ein** takes the endings of the indefinite article. The other numbers do not take endings. When **ein** means "one," it is stressed when speaking; when it means "a, an," it is unstressed:

Ich lese eine Zeitung.   *I'm reading a newspaper.*
Ich lese nur **eine** Zeitung.   *I only read one newspaper.*

Learn the question words: **wie viele?**—how many?

Üben wir!

A. (books open) Tell how many of the following you have.

> EXAMPLE: Wie viele Brüder haben Sie?
> Ich habe zwei Brüder.

1. Uhren (5)
2. Söhne (3)
3. Schwestern (6)
4. Kinder (7)
5. Häuser (1)

6. Freunde (4)
7. Zimmer (8)
8. Büros (2)
9. Brüder (1)
10. Bücher (20)

Leicht zu merken

die **Alternative, -n**	Alternati*ve*
der **Konflikt, -e**	Kon*flikt*
(das) **Nordamerika**	*Nord*amerika
relativ	rela*tiv*
sozial	so*zial*
traditionell	tradi*tionell*

Wortschatz 2

Verben

besitzen to own
bleiben to stay, remain
finden to find
geben (gibt) to give
kochen to cook
verdienen to earn

Substantive

der **Beruf, -e** profession, vocation
der **Großvater, ⁚** grandfather
der **Onkel, -** uncle

das **Auto, -s** car
das **Essen** food
das **Geld** money
das **Klischee, -s** cliché
das **Problem, -e** problem

die **Arbeit** work
  die **Hausarbeit** housework
die **Bundesrepublik (Deutschland)** the Federal Republic (*of Germany*)
  die **BRD** the FRG
die **Diskussion, -en** discussion
  die **Familiendiskussion** family discussion
die **Familie, -n** family
die **Großmutter, ⁚** grandmother
die **Hausfrau, -en** housewife

die **Mutter, ⁚** mother
die **Rolle, -n** role
die **Stelle, -n** job, position
die **Tante, -n** aunt
die **Tochter, ⁚** daughter

die **Großeltern** (*pl.*) grandparents

Andere Vokabeln

anders different
deutsch (*adj.*) German
dort there
fast almost
jung young
manchmal sometimes
mehr more
  nicht mehr no longer, not any more
niemand nobody, no one
noch still
  noch ein another, an additional
normal normal
überall everywhere
wenigstens at least
wichtig important
zwischen between

Nützliche Ausdrücke

es gibt (+ *acc.*) there is, there are
das sind (*pl. of* **das ist**) those are
zu Hause at home

Oma und Opa fahren Rad.

Gegensätze

jung ≠ alt	young ≠ old
niemand ≠ jemand	no one ≠ someone
wichtig ≠ unwichtig	important ≠ unimportant

Die Familie heute

„Der Vater arbeitet und verdient das Geld, die Mutter ist Hausfrau. Sie bleibt zu Hause, kocht das Essen und versorgt° die Kinder." Wir kennen die Klischees. Heute stimmen sie aber nicht mehr, wenigstens nicht für junge[1] Familien in Deutschland. Dort ist die Rollenverteilung° oft anders. Viele Frauen haben einen Beruf oder suchen eine Stelle. Tagsüber° ist manchmal niemand zu Hause. Oft teilen° der Mann und die Frau die Hausarbeit, und in Familiendiskussionen haben die Kinder heute auch eine Stimme.°

Die typische[1] Familie ist relativ klein: ein oder zwei Kinder, das ist normal. Viele Familien in der Bundesrepublik haben ein Haus oder eine Eigentumswohnung.°

takes care of

assignment of roles

during the day
share

voice

condominium

[1] When German adjectives are used attributively (before nouns), they receive endings, most often -e or -en. You will learn how to use these endings actively in Chapters 9 and 10.

Eine Geburtstagsfeier.

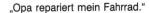
„Opa repariert mein Fahrrad."

15 Fast alle Familien besitzen ein Auto und einen Fernseher.° *TV*
Der Lebensstandard° ist heute sogar höher als° in Nord- *standard of living* / **höher**
amerika. **als** = *higher than*
Aber gibt es denn keine° Probleme? Natürlich! Man *no*
findet in Deutschland, wie überall, Konflikte zwischen Eltern und Kindern. Viele junge Leute suchen Alternativen.
20 Sie wohnen manchmal in Wohngemeinschaften° oder Land- *living groups*
kommunen.° Aber für die Mehrheit° bleibt die traditionelle *rural communes* / *majority*
Familie—Mutter, Vater und Kinder—noch die wichtigste° *most important*
soziale Gruppe.

Fragen zum Lesestück

1. Was sind die Klischees über die traditionelle Familie?
2. Was tun heute viele Frauen?
3. Haben Familien in Deutschland viele Kinder?
4. Besitzen alle Familien in der Bundesrepublik ein Haus?
5. Wer hat oft Konflikte?
6. Ist die Familie auch heute noch wichtig?

Vom Lesen zum Sprechen

Here is some useful vocabulary for talking about your family. You already know some of these words.

Die Familie

die **Großeltern**	
die **Großmutter,** ¨	
die **Oma, -s**	grandma
der **Großvater,** ¨	
der **Opa, -s**	grandpa
die **Eltern**	
die **Mutter,** ¨	
die **Mutti, -s**	mama, mom
der **Vater,** ¨	
der **Vati, -s**	papa, dad
der **Sohn,** ¨e	
die **Tochter,** ¨	
die **Geschwister** (*pl.*)	siblings
der **Bruder,** ¨	
die **Schwester, -n**	
der **Onkel, -**	
die **Tante, -n**	
die **Kusine, -n**	cousin (*f.*)
der **Vetter, -n**	cousin (*m.*)

A. Sprechen Sie über Ihre Familie.

EXAMPLE: Haben Sie Geschwister?
Ja, ich habe zwei Brüder und eine Schwester.

1. Wer verdient das Geld?
2. Ist Ihre Familie klein?
3. Wer kocht das Essen?
4. Wer bleibt zu Hause?
5. Besitzt Ihre Familie ein Auto oder zwei?

Mündliche Übungen

A. Persönliche Fragen

1. Wie heißen Sie?
2. Wie heißen Ihre Eltern?
3. Wo wohnt Ihre Familie?
4. Ist Ihre Familie groß oder klein?
5. Lesen Sie eine Zeitung?
6. Lesen Sie oft Zeitungen, oder nur manchmal?

München, Marienplatz
mit Rathaus.

B. Was gibt es hier?
Use **es gibt** to tell what is in your classroom. Your teacher will give you a cue in English.

> EXAMPLE: table
> Hier gibt es einen Tisch.

1. chairs
2. a window
3. a door
4. students
5. a clock

6. a wall
7. a professor
8. a blackboard
9. a map
10. a ball-point pen

Use the same vocabulary to ask your neighbor if there are certain things in the classroom.

> EXAMPLE: Student A: Gibt es hier einen Tisch?
> Student B: Ja, dort gibt es einen Tisch.

C. Student A asks who someone is. Student B answers, using the cue.

> EXAMPLE: Michael = Bruder
> Student A: Wer ist denn Michael?
> Student B: Michael ist mein Bruder.

1. Maria = Schwester
2. Heinrich = Onkel
3. die Leute = Großeltern
4. Katrin = Kusine
5. der Junge = Freund
6. Marlene und Udo = Geschwister

D. Answer these questions, using pronouns.

> 1. EXAMPLE: Kennen Sie Rolf?
> Natürlich kenne ich **ihn.**

Kennen Sie Professor Beck?
(Frau Weiß, Richard und Anna, uns, mich,
meine Schwester, das Kind, meinen Onkel)

> 2. EXAMPLE: Ich suche meine Zeitung.
> Ich habe **sie.**

Ich suche meinen Artikel.
(mein Auto, mein Geld, meinen Stuhl, meine Uhr, mein Buch)

E. Using the cue, student A asks student B if he/she needs something. Student B answers no, as in the example.

> EXAMPLE: das Buch
> Student A: Brauchst du das Buch?
> Student B: Nein danke, ich habe ein Buch.

1. den Stuhl
2. die Uhr
3. die Zeitung
4. das Heft
5. den Tisch

F. Ask a classmate for the following information. He/she responds.

> EXAMPLE: Ask where she lives.
> Student A: Wo wohnst du?
> Student B: Ich wohne in New York.

Ask:

1. where his books are
2. when he is going to Germany
3. what her mother's name is
4. who her teacher is
5. if it's raining
6. if he practices often
7. whom he knows here
8. if she has a brother

Schriftliche Übungen

G. Create short sentences using the items provided. Add any necessary verb endings, articles, etc.

> EXAMPLE: ich / suchen / morgen / Stelle
> Ich suche morgen eine Stelle.

1. du / kennen / natürlich / mein Bruder
2. Frau Huber / lesen / Artikel
3. Max / verdienen / viel Geld / im August
4. er / finden / Stelle / in München
5. ihr / besitzen / Haus / in Deutschland?
6. er / suchen / mein / Bruder
7. du / sehen / Mann / da?
8. du / kochen / Suppe / und / ich / essen / sie

H. Construct dialogues from the following cues (a double slash means a comma).

1. Sie / kennen / Berlin?
   ja // mein / Familie / wohnen / dort. warum / Sie / fragen?
   ich / studieren / im Oktober / da / und / suchen / Zimmer
2. wie / du / heißen?
   ich / heißen / Klaus
   wen / du / suchen / denn?
   mein / Bruder. du / wissen // wo / er / sein?

I. Wie sagt man das auf deutsch?

1. Her family is rather typical.
2. Their name is Schölz and they live in Munich.
3. Does her brother work, or is he looking for a job?
4. He's studying in Heidelberg.

5. I'm looking for my newspaper.
6. Fritz has it.
7. He's reading an article.

8. Where are your children now, Mr. Asch?
9. They're living at home.

10. When are you eating, children?
11. Probably at six.

Almanach

Die ganze Familie

Der Vater, der heißt Daniel,
der kleine Sohn heißt Michael,
die Mutter heißt Regine
die Tochter heißt Rosine,
der Bruder, der heißt Kristian,
der Onkel heißt Sebastian,
die Schwester heißt Johanna,
die Tante heißt Susanna,
der Vetter, der heißt Benjamin,
die Kusine, die heißt Katharin,
die Oma heißt Ottilie—
nun kennst du die Familie.

Most popular first names for children born in the Federal Republic are currently:

Girls: **Christine, Stefanie, Julia, Sabrina, Melanie, Nadine, Kathrin, Katharina, Nicole, Anna**

Boys: **Christian, Michael, Daniel, Stefan, Andreas, Sebastian, Matthias, Markus, Alexander, Thomas**

The use of English names, like **Sarah, Jessica, Jennifer, Vanessa; Dennis, Oliver, Patrick,** is on the increase.

Geburtsanzeige

Sabrina hat ein Brüderchen bekommen,

Stefan

geboren am 3.2. 1988
Die glücklichen Eltern:
Ludwig und Anna Beck

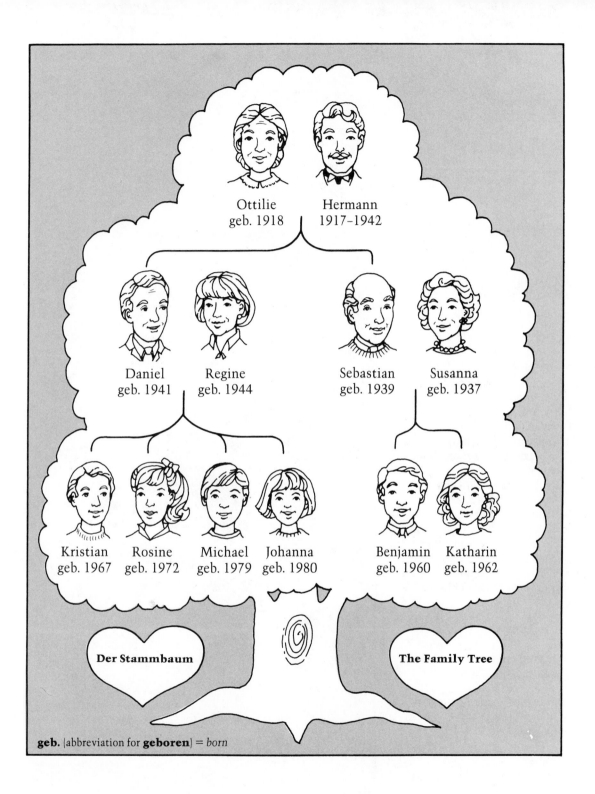

Ottilie
geb. 1918

Hermann
1917–1942

Daniel
geb. 1941

Regine
geb. 1944

Sebastian
geb. 1939

Susanna
geb. 1937

Kristian
geb. 1967

Rosine
geb. 1972

Michael
geb. 1979

Johanna
geb. 1980

Benjamin
geb. 1960

Katharin
geb. 1962

Der Stammbaum

The Family Tree

geb. (abbreviation for **geboren**) = *born*

Kapitel **3**

Jugend und Schule

Dialoge
Zwei Freundinnen
In den Bergen
Ich habe keinen Wagen

Wortschatz 1

Grammatik
1. Verbs with Stem Vowel Change: **a** to **ä; au** to **äu**
2. The Predicate
3. Modal Verbs
4. Negation with **nicht** (not)
5. Negation with **kein** (not a, not any, no)
6. Expecting an Affirmative Answer: **nicht wahr?**
7. Contradicting a Negative Statement or Question: **doch**
8. Expanding Your Vocabulary Cardinal Numbers Above 20
   ♦ Die Deutsche Mark (DM) ♦ Compound Nouns ♦ Leicht zu merken

Wortschatz 2

Lesestück
Eine Klassendiskussion

Vom Lesen zum Sprechen
Die Kleidung (*clothing*)
Farben (*colors*)

Almanach
A Word About German Schools

Zwei Freundinnen

MONIKA: Du hast es gut, Renate. Es gibt so viel zu tun in Frankfurt. Hier in Hinterwalden ist es so langweilig.

RENATE: Dann sollst du mich bald besuchen. Oder willst du nicht?

MONIKA: Doch, ich möchte schon nach Frankfurt, aber ich habe leider im Moment kein Geld.

RENATE: Ich verstehe dich nicht. Bis Juni kannst du sicher genug verdienen.

In den Bergen

KURT: Wir müssen noch eine Stunde fahren.

STEFAN: Wollen wir nicht hier halten und eine Pause machen? Ich möchte ein bißchen laufen.

KURT: Ich auch. Wir können da drüben parken. Es ist schön hier, nicht?

STEFAN: Ja. Aber der Berg ist sehr steil.

KURT: Was ist denn los? Bist du nicht fit?

STEFAN: Wer sagt denn das?

Ich habe keinen Wagen

CAROLA: Es ist schon spät. Fährst du jetzt nach Hause?

KLAUS: Nein, heute muß ich laufen. Ich habe leider keinen Wagen.

CAROLA: Warum denn nicht?

KLAUS: Mein Bruder braucht ihn heute abend.

Kinder am ersten Schultag

Wortschatz 1

Two Friends

MONIKA: You've got it good, Renate. There's so much to do in Frankfurt. It's so boring here in Hinterwalden.

RENATE: Then you should visit me soon. Or don't you want to?

MONIKA: Yes I do. I really would like to go to Frankfurt, but unfortunately I have no money at the moment.

RENATE: I don't understand you. You can certainly earn enough by June.

In the Mountains

KURT: We still have an hour to drive.

STEFAN: Why don't we stop here and take a break? I'd like to walk a bit.

KURT: Me too. We can park over there. It's nice here, isn't it?

STEFAN: Yes. But the mountain is very steep.

KURT: What's the matter? Aren't you in shape?

STEFAN: Who says?

I Don't Have a Car

CAROLA: It's late already. Are you driving home now?

KLAUS: No, I have to walk today. Unfortunately, I don't have a car.

CAROLA: Why not?

KLAUS: My brother needs it tonight.

Verben

besuchen to visit
fahren (fährt) to drive, go (by vehicle)
halten (hält) to stop (*intrans.*); hold
können (kann) can, be able to
laufen (läuft) to run; to go on foot, walk (*colloq.*)
ich möchte I would like to [1]
müssen (muß) must, have to
parken to park
schlafen (schläft) to sleep
sollen (soll) should, be supposed to
tun to do
verstehen to understand
wollen (will) to want to

Substantive

der **Berg, -e** mountain
der **Wagen, -** car

die **Freundin, -nen** friend (*f.*)
die **Pause, -n** break; intermission **eine Pause machen** to take a break
die **Stunde, -n** hour; class hour

Gegensätze

spät ≠ früh	late ≠ early
langweilig ≠ interessant	boring ≠ interesting
nichts ≠ etwas	nothing ≠ something

die **Deutschstunde** German class

Andere Vokabeln

bald soon
doch yes I *do*, I *am*, etc. (*contradictory*, see p. 74)
fit in snape
genug enough
jetzt now
kein[2] not a, not any, no
langweilig boring
leider unfortunately
nichts nothing
schon already
spät late
steil steep

Nützliche Ausdrücke

ein bißchen a little; a little bit; a little while
nicht (wahr)? isn't it?, can't you?, doesn't he?, etc. (see p. 74.)
nach Hause home (*as destination of motion*) **Ich fahre nach Hause.** I'm driving home.
Was ist los? What's the matter?; What's going on?

---

[1] For an explanation of **möchte**, see pp. 69 and 413.
[2] For the endings of **kein**, see, p. 73.

Neue Kombinationen

A. Replace the word or phrase in italics with the cues you will hear.

1. Hier ist es so *langweilig*! (schön, interessant, steil, häßlich)
2. Ich habe leider im Moment *kein Geld*. (keinen Wagen, keinen Freund, kein Zimmer, keine Freundin, keine Freunde)
3. Ich möchte ein bißchen *laufen*. (arbeiten, lesen, sprechen, fahren, bleiben)
4. Heute *muß* ich arbeiten. (will, kann, soll, möchte)
5. Können wir da drüben *parken*? (lesen, arbeiten, fragen, bleiben)
6. Wir können *genug verdienen*. (Klaus fragen, euch besuchen, eine Pause machen, nach Hause gehen)

B. Answer the following negative questions affirmatively, using *doch* to contradict.

> EXAMPLE: Besuchst du mich nicht?
> Doch, ich besuche dich.

1. Bist du nicht fit?
2. Fährst du nicht nach Deutschland?
3. Haben wir nicht genug zu tun?
4. Arbeitest du nicht?
5. Gehen wir nicht nach Hause?
6. Verstehen Sie mich nicht?

Übung zur Aussprache

See the Introduction, p. 4, for the pronunciation of the sound represented by **ö**. Practice the difference between long **o** and long **ö**, short **o** and short **ö**. (In some proper names, **ö** is spelled **oe**.)

Long o	Long ö	Short o	Short ö
Gote	Goethe	Gott	Götter
Ton	Töne	konnte	könnte
Sohn	Söhne	Bock	Böcke
schon	schön	Kopf	Köpfe
Ostern	Österreich	Stock	Stöcke

Now read the following exchanges aloud, paying particular attention to **ö**:

1. Hatte Goethe viele Söhne?
2. Das möchte ich auch wissen. Ich weiß nur, er hatte keine Töchter.
3. Können wir im Oktober Köln besuchen?
4. Hoffentlich. Im Oktober ist es in Köln sehr schön.

Grammatik

1 ◆ Verbs with Stem Vowel Change: *a* to *ä*; *au* to *äu*

a → ä	fahren	to drive; go by vehicle	
ich	fahre	wir	fahren
du	**fährst**	ihr	fahrt
er, es, sie	**fährt**	sie, Sie	fahren

■ Other verbs in this group: **halten (hält),**[1] to stop or hold; **schlafen (schläft),** to sleep; **tragen (trägt),** to carry or wear.

au → äu	laufen	to run	
ich	laufe	wir	laufen
du	**läufst**	ihr	lauft
er, es, sie	**läuft**	sie, Sie	laufen

Üben wir!

A. Supply the new subject indicated and change the verb accordingly.

1. *Ich fahre* heute nach Frankfurt. (Birgit, du, wir, ihr, sie)
2. *Laufen Sie* nach Hause? (ihr, Robert, wir, du, er, die Kinder)
3. *Ich trage* die Bücher. (du, wir, Frau Kuhn, ihr, er)
4. *Das Auto hält* da drüben. (wir, ihr, die Leute, Robert, du, Renate)
5. *Schlafen Sie* noch? (du, ihr, Konrad, die Kinder, Herr Braun)

B. Respond according to the pattern:

EXAMPLE: Fährst du nach Hause? Ja, ich fahre nach Hause.

1. Hältst du hier?
2. Trägst du meine Bücher?
3. Läufst du oft?
4. Fährst du nach Bremen?
5. Schläfst du bis zehn?

EXAMPLE: Wir halten hier. Anna hält auch hier.

6. Wir tragen Jeans.
7. Wir laufen nach Hause.
8. Wir fahren schnell.
9. Wir halten dort drüben.
10. Wir schlafen bis acht.

[1] Stem-changing verbs whose stem ends in **-t** do *not* insert **-e-** between stem and personal ending: **du hältst, er hält** (in the latter form, the ending **-t** merges with the **-t** of the stem).

2 ◆ The Predicate

At this point, it is important to say a few more words about the structure of sentences. In both German and English, all statements and questions contain a subject (S) and an inflected verb (V):

S V	S V
Ich arbeite viel.	*I work a lot.*

V S	V S
Schläfst du?	*Are you sleeping?*

The verb by itself, however, is not always adequate to express the entire action or condition in which the subject is involved. For example, consider the simple English statement

John is young.

"John" is the subject and "is" is the verb. When taken by themselves, however—

John is

—they are not a meaningful utterance in English.[1] The verb "is" must be completed by a *complement*, in this case, the adjective "young." The verb and its complement together make up the entire verbal idea, or *predicate*. In the example sentence, "young" is called a *predicate adjective* because it is used together with the verb "is" to form the entire predicate.

Similarly, in the sentence

Herr Beck ist unser Lehrer.   *Mr. Beck is our teacher.*

unser Lehrer—a noun in the nominative case—is the complement of the verb **sein**; it is therefore called a *predicate nominative*.[2]

In both German and English, various kinds of words and phrases can complement the verb to form the complete predicate. In the sentence

She can ski.

the verb "can" is complemented by a second verb "ski" to form the predicate "can ski." You will learn about verbs like "can" in the following section.

3 ◆ Modal Verbs

The six modal verbs are different from other verbs in German. They do not express an action or condition by themselves, but rather an attitude toward the action expressed by another verb.

---

[1]Except as an abbreviated answer to a question, with repetitious elements omitted but understood: "Who is playing the harmonica?" "John is (playing it)."
[2]See p. 28.

Wir **müssen** noch eine Stunde
fahren.

We still have to drive for an hour.

The modal verb **müssen** (have to) indicates that it is *necessary* for the subject
(**wir**) to perform the action of driving (**fahren**). **Müssen** is the first part of the
predicate, and the infinitive **fahren** is the second part of the predicate. The
German modals are:

infinitive	*expresses*	
dürfen	permission	to be allowed to, may
können	ability	to be able to, can
mögen[1]		
ich möchte	inclination, desire	I would like to
müssen	necessity	to have to, must
sollen	obligation	to be supposed to, should
wollen	desire, intention	to want to

[1] The form **möchte** (would like to) is a subjunctive form of **mögen**. **Mögen** will be treated later.

Kloster Ettal bei Oberam-
mergau (Bayern), heute
ein Internat (das Kloster:
monastery; das Internat:
private boarding school)

The modal auxiliaries take no endings in the *ich-* and *er-* forms, and most have a changed stem vowel in the singular.

dürfen	to be allowed to		
ich	darf	wir	dürfen
du	darfst	ihr	dürft
er, es, sie	darf	sie, Sie	dürfen

können	to be able to		
ich	kann	wir	können
du	kannst	ihr	könnt
er, es, sie	kann	sie, Sie	können

müssen	to have to		
ich	muß	wir	müssen
du	mußt	ihr	müßt
er, es, sie	muß	sie, Sie	müssen

sollen	to be supposed to[1]		
ich	soll	wir	sollen
du	sollst	ihr	sollt
er, es, sie	soll	sie, Sie	sollen

wollen	to want to		
ich	will	wir	wollen
du	willst	ihr	wollt
er, es, sie	will	sie, Sie	wollen

mögen (ich möchte[2]	I would like to)		
ich	möchte	wir	möchten
du	möchtest	ihr	möchtet
er, es, sie	möchte	sie, Sie	möchten

[1] Notice that only **sollen** does not have a stem-vowel change in the singular.
[2] **Möchte** has endings different from the other modals.

The modal verb is always the inflected verb. The infinitive, which is the second part of the predicate, is in sentence-final position. Note carefully the difference from English, where the dependent infinitive immediately *follows* the modal verb:

Wir **können** da drüben **parken.**   *We **can park** over there.*
Ich **muß** das für morgen **lesen.**   *I **have to read** that for tomorrow.*
Marie **soll** ihre Eltern **besuchen.**   *Marie **is supposed to visit** her parents.*

This word order is typical not just for the infinitive used with a modal verb, but for the second part of the German predicate in general. *It is important that you get used to this two-part predicate, since it is the central structural feature of the German sentence.*

Üben wir!

A. Restate the sentence, using the modal auxiliaries indicated (use **möchte** form of **mögen**).

> EXAMPLE: Ich lerne Deutsch. (wollen)
> Ich will Deutsch lernen.

1. Wir verdienen genug Geld. (sollen, wollen, müssen, können, mögen)
2. Heute arbeitet sie. (können, mögen, wollen, müssen, sollen)
3. Man tut das nicht. (dürfen, können, sollen)
4. Fahrt ihr nach Amerika? (wollen, mögen, können, dürfen, müssen)
5. Wann kommen Sie nach Berlin? (können, müssen, wollen, mögen)
6. Schläfst du nicht? (können, wollen, mögen)

Omission of the Infinitive

The infinitive used with a modal may be omitted, but only when it is clearly understood as **haben, tun, machen,** or a verb of motion such as **gehen, fahren,** or **fliegen.**

		Modal	*Infinitive*	
	Möchten	Sie ein Zimmer für heute abend	**(haben)?**	*Would you like (to have) a room for tonight?*
Ich	**kann**	das leider nicht	**(tun).**	*Unfortunately, I can't do that.*
Wir	**müssen**	bald wieder nach Deutschland	**(fahren).**	*We've got to go to Germany again soon.*
Ich	**will**	jetzt nach Hause	**(gehen).**	*I want to go home now.*

- A verb of motion (**gehen, fahren**) can only be omitted when the sentence includes an indication of destination (**nach Deutschland, nach Hause**).
- The infinitive **sprechen** is also omitted in this idiom:

Ich **kann** Deutsch (Englisch).　　　*I can speak German (English).*

Üben wir!

A. Give the English equivalent of these sentences:

1. Wollen Sie jetzt nach Hause?
2. Er kann das noch nicht.
3. Willst du meinen Bleistift?
4. Mein Vater will das nicht.
5. Können Sie schon gut Deutsch?
6. Möchten Sie das Geld?
7. Darf man denn das?
8. Wann wollen Sie nach Amerika?

4 ◆ Negation with *nicht* (not)

Nicht is used to negate a sentence:

Karin ist meine Schwester.   *Karin is my sister.*
Karin ist *nicht* meine Schwester.   *Karin is not my sister.*

In the example above, the position of **nicht** is exactly parallel to the position of **not** in English. In most German sentences, however, this will not be the case. Here are some preliminary guidelines for the position of **nicht**.

1. Nicht usually *follows* the subject, verb, and direct object:

Ich kenne deinen Freund **nicht**.   *I don't know your friend.*
Er sagt das **nicht**.   *He doesn't say that.*
Wir besitzen das Auto **nicht**.   *We don't own the car.*

2. **Nicht** also usually *follows* expressions of definite time:

Sie kommen heute abend **nicht**.   *They're not coming tonight.*
Hans arbeitet jetzt **nicht**.   *Hans isn't working now.*

Üben wir!

A. Negate these sentences by adding **nicht**:

1. Kurt besucht seinen Bruder.
2. Ich kenne eure Mutter.
3. Frau Schmidt besucht uns morgen.
4. Monika macht das heute abend.

3. **Nicht** *precedes* complements that constitute the second part of the predicate. These include:

■ Predicate adjectives:

Der Berg ist *steil.*   *The mountain is steep.*
Der Berg ist *nicht* steil.   *The mountain is not steep.*

■ Predicate nominatives:[1]

Das ist *Herr Böhm.*   *That is Mr. Böhm.*
Das ist *nicht* Herr Böhm.   *That is not Mr. Böhm.*

■ Adverbs modifying the verb:

Margit läuft *gut.*   *Margit runs well.*
Margit läuft *nicht* gut.   *Margit doesn't run well.*

---

[1] See page 67.

In der Deutschstunde (DDR): Was lesen die Schüler?

■ Prepositional phrases that show destination (**nach Wien, nach Hause**) or location (**in Berlin, zu Hause**):

Sie geht *nach Hause.*	*She's going home.*
Sie geht *nicht* nach Hause.	*She's not going home.*
Er arbeitet *in Berlin.*	*He works in Berlin.*
Er arbeitet *nicht* in Berlin.	*He doesn't work in Berlin.*

■ Infinitives complementing modal verbs:

Er kann mich *sehen.*	*He can see me.*
Er kann mich *nicht* sehen.	*He can't see me.*

Üben wir!

A. Negate these sentences by adding **nicht.**

1. Das Wetter ist schön.
2. Du sollst mich besuchen.
3. Unsere Freunde kommen morgen.
4. Ich möchte Berlin sehen.
5. Der Berg ist steil.
6. Wir wollen halten.
7. Frau Kramsch ist unsere Lehrerin.
8. Ich muß nach Hause gehen.
9. Margit läuft gut.
10. Er kann mich sehen.

B. Answer these questions in the negative.

> EXAMPLE: Kennen Sie Berlin?
> Nein, ich kenne Berlin nicht.

1. Müssen Sie nach Hause?
2. Wollen wir parken?
3. Kennt er deinen Freund?
4. Ist das der Berg?
5. Können Sie das machen?
6. Darf sie nach München fahren?
7. Kommt Carola heute abend?
8. Sind deine Eltern alt?
9. Ist es heute schön?
10. Fahren wir heute abend?

5 ◆ Negation with *kein*

Kein (not a, not any, no) is the negative of **ein.** It negates nouns preceded by **ein** or nouns not preceded by any article.

Morgen will ich ein Buch lesen.
Morgen will ich **kein** Buch lesen. *I don't want to read a book tomorrow.*

Hier wohnen Studenten.
Hier wohnen **keine** Studenten. *No students live here.*

Kein is an **ein**-word and takes the same endings as **ein** and the possessive adjectives. **Nicht** and **kein** are mutually exclusive. In any given situation, only one will be correct. If a noun is preceded by the definite article or by a possessive adjective, use **nicht** rather than **kein:**

Ist das die Frau? *Is that the woman?*
  Nein, das ist **nicht** die Frau. *No, that's not the woman.*
Ist das seine Frau? *Is that his wife?*
  Nein, das ist **nicht** seine Frau. *No, that's not his wife.*

Üben wir!

A. Negate these sentences with the correct form of **kein.**

1. Meine Familie besitzt einen Wagen.
2. Maria hat heute Geld.
3. Es gibt hier ein Problem.
4. Hier wohnen Studenten.
5. Morgen gibt es eine Diskussion.
6. Herr Meyer hat Kinder.

B. Answer the following questions in the negative, using **kein** or **nicht** as appropriate.

> EXAMPLE: Hat Barbara einen Freund? Nein, sie hat **keinen** Freund.
> Ist das ihr Freund? Nein, das ist **nicht** ihr Freund.

1. Haben Sie einen Freund in Amerika?
2. Haben Sie Freunde in Washington?
3. Ist das der Lehrer?
4. Verdient er Geld?

5. Siehst du das Haus?
6. Ist das seine Freundin?
7. Suchst du das Buch?
8. Suchst du ein Buch?

6 ◆ Expecting an Affirmative Answer: *nicht wahr?*

Nicht wahr? (literally "not true?"), when added to a positive statement, anticipates confirmation (English: doesn't he? wasn't it? didn't you? etc). In spoken German, it is often shortened to **nicht?**

Heute ist es schön, **nicht wahr?**	*It's beautiful today, isn't it?*
Sie studieren in Freiburg, **nicht wahr?**	*You're studying in Freiburg, aren't you?*
Gisela kennst du, **nicht?**	*You know Gisela, don't you?*

Üben wir!

A. Give the German equivalents for these sentences:

1. You have a car, don't you?
2. You're learning German, aren't you?
3. You'll visit me soon, won't you?
4. He's in good shape, isn't he?
5. We can work today, can't we?

7 ◆ Contradicting a Negative Statement or Question: *doch*

Stressed **doch** must be used instead of **ja** to contradict a negative statement or question:

Ich spreche nicht gut Deutsch.	*I don't speak German well.*
Doch, Sie sprechen sehr gut Deutsch!	*Yes you do, you speak German very well.*
Kennst du Ursula nicht?	*Don't you know Ursula?*
Doch, ich kenne sie sehr gut!	*Sure, I know her very well.*

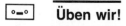 **Üben wir!**

A. Contradict the following negative statements and questions, beginning your answer with a stressed **doch.**

> EXAMPLE: Bist du nicht fit?
> Doch, ich bin fit.

1. Wir wollen nicht hier halten.
2. Wir haben nicht genug Geld.
3. Hast du keinen Bruder?
4. Es ist nicht sehr spät.
5. Kannst du kein Deutsch?
6. Eure Kinder möchten nicht laufen.

8 ◆ Expanding Your Vocabulary

Cardinal Numbers Above 20

German forms the cardinal numbers above twenty as in the English nursery rhyme "Four-and-twenty blackbirds"

21	einundzwanzig	30	dreißig
22	zweiundzwanzig	31	einunddreißig
23	dreiundzwanzig	40	vierzig
24	vierundzwanzig	50	fünfzig
25	fünfundzwanzig	60	sechzig
26	sechsundzwanzig	70	siebzig
27	siebenundzwanzig	80	achtzig
28	achtundzwanzig	90	neunzig
29	neunundzwanzig	100	hundert

1 000 tausend

German numbers are written out as one word:

1980 neunzehnhundertachtzig
3.526 dreitausendfünfhundertsechsundzwanzig

German uses a period or a space to divide thousands from hundreds:

German		*English*
4.982 or 4 982	=	4,982

(viertausendneunhundertzweiundachtzig)

German uses a comma where English uses a decimal point. The comma is read as **Komma:**

0,5	=	0.5
(null Komma fünf)		(zero point five)

Üben wir!

A. Say the following numbers and years aloud:

26	1.066	3.001
69	533	0,22
153	985	3,45
4.772,08	48	71
1984	90	

Die Deutsche Mark (DM)

The abbreviation DM (Deutsche Mark) is spoken simply as **Mark**, e.g.:
DM 5,80 is pronounced **fünf Mark achtzig.**

Üben wir!

You and your friends are pooling your savings to buy a used car. Say what each person has and the total.

EXAMPLE: Marie / DM 250
Marie hat zweihundertfünfzig Mark.

1. ich / DM 729
2. Engelbert / DM 1.347
3. Jutta / DM 228
4. Herbert / DM 850

5. Thomas / DM 1.517
6. Karl / DM 512
7. alle zusammen / DM 5.183

Compound Nouns

A characteristic feature of German is its formation of compound nouns from two or more nouns. Get used to analyzing these words and learn to identify their component parts.

Sometimes the only difference between the formation of English and German compound nouns is that in German they are written as one word:

die Rockmusik[1]   *rock music*

Often a connecting **-(e)s-** or **-(e)n-** is inserted between the components:

der Bund (*federation*) + die Republik = die Bund**es**republik
die Klasse + die Diskussion = die Klasse**n**diskussion

The gender of the *last* component noun is *always* the gender of the entire compound:

die Klasse + **die** Diskussion = die Klassendiskussion
die Klasse + **das** Zimmer = das Klassenzimmer
das Amerika + **die** Reise = die Amerikareise (*trip to America*)
das Atom + **der** Krieg = der Atomkrieg (*nuclear war*)
das Wort (*word*) + **der** Schatz (*treasure*) = der Wortschatz (*vocabulary*)

Leicht zu merken

international   intern*atio*nal
die **Jeans** *pl.*
optimistisch   opti*mis*tisch
pessimistisch   pess*imis*tisch
das **System, -e**   *Sys*tem
das **Schulsystem**   *Schul*system

---

[1] In German, the first element is stressed.

Wortschatz 2

Verben

besprechen (bespricht) to discuss
fürchten to fear
hassen to hate
hören to hear
lachen to laugh
  lachen über (+ *acc.*) to laugh about
lernen to learn
schreiben to write
  schreiben über (+ *acc.*) to write about
singen to sing
tragen (trägt) to carry; wear

Substantive

der **Krieg, -e** war
der **Mantel, ¨** coat
der **Pullover, -** pullover, jersey
  also: der **Pulli, -s**
der **Schuh, -e** shoe
  der **Turnschuh** sneaker, gym shoe

(das) **Amerika** America
(das) **Deutsch** German (*language*)
(das) **Englisch** English (*language*)
das **Gymnasium**, die **Gymnasien** secondary school (*prepares pupils for university*)
das **Hemd, -en** shirt
das **Kleid, -er** dress; *pl.* = dresses *or* clothes

die **Angst, ¨e** fear
  Angst haben to be afraid
  Ich habe Angst. I am afraid.
die **Bluse, -n** blouse
die **Hausaufgabe, -n** homework assignment
die **Hose, -n** trousers, pants
die **Jacke, -n** jacket
die **Musik** music
die **Reise, -n** trip, journey
  eine Reise machen to take a trip

die **Sprache, -n** language
die **Fremdsprache** foreign language

die **Pommes frites** (*pl.*, *pronounced "Pomm fritt"*) French fries

Andere Vokabeln

ähnlich similar
amerikanisch American
besser better
bitte please
darum therefore, for that reason
ehrlich honest
eigentlich actually, in fact
fremd strange; foreign
neu new
schnell fast
toll (*colloq.*) great; terrific

Nützlicher Ausdruck

gar nicht not at all

Gegensätze

hassen ≠ **lieben**	to hate ≠ to love
lachen ≠ **weinen**	to laugh ≠ to cry
neu ≠ **alt**	new ≠ old
schnell ≠ **langsam**	fast ≠ slow

Eine Klassendiskussion

(Last spring class 10a from the Kepler-Gymnasium in Hannover visited a high school in Maryland. Now they are discussing their experiences and impressions of the States with their teacher, Herr Beck.)

HERR BECK: Können wir jetzt unsere Amerikareise ein
bißchen besprechen? Rolf, möchtest du etwas
sagen? . . . Ach, er schläft wieder. *(Alle lachen)*

ROLF: Meinen Sie mich? Entschuldigung! Unsere
Reise? Sie war° toll.   *was*

KIRSTEN: Für mich auch. Und ich weiß jetzt, die Schüler
in Amerika sind eigentlich gar nicht so anders.
Dort trägt man auch Jeans und Turnschuhe,
hört Rockmusik, singt dieselben Schlager° und   ***dieselben Schlager** = the same hits*
ißt Pommes frites.

HERR BECK: Interessant, aber haben die Schüler in Amerika
auch ähnliche Probleme wie ihr?

ANDREAS: Ach, wissen Sie, alle Schüler hassen ihre Haus-
aufgaben. *(Alle lachen)* Nein, aber im Ernst,° wir   ***im Ernst** = seriously*
sind alle manchmal pessimistisch: man meint,
man kann später° keine Arbeit finden, oder man   *later*
fürchtet den Atomkrieg. Diese Ängste haben die
amerikanischen Schüler auch.

HERR BECK: Ich habe auch Angst, muß ich ehrlich sagen.
Aber gibt es denn keine Unterschiede° zwischen   *differences*
hier und dort?

KIRSTEN: Doch, natürlich! Dort gehen alle Schüler in die
high school, bis sie 18 Jahre sind. Mit zehn Jahren kommen wir ins Gymnasium oder in die
Realschule[1] oder Hauptschule,[1] je nach unserer
Leistung.° Das Schulsystem ist in Amerika also   ***je . . . Leistung** = according to our achievement*
ganz anders.

CHRISTA: Das ist aber nicht unbedingt° gut. Ich finde, wir   ***nicht unbedingt** = not necessarily*
müssen hier mehr und schneller° lernen.   *faster*
Deutschland ist relativ klein und hat viele
Nachbarländer.° Wir müssen darum Fremd-   *neighboring countries*
sprachen lernen. Wir können besser Englisch
als° die Amerikaner Deutsch.   *than*
                                                  over

HERR BECK: Die Stunde ist leider um.° Morgen können wir
einen Artikel über unsere Reise für die Schülerzeitung schreiben.

---

[1] See Almanach, p. 84.

Eine Klassendiskussion: „Möchtest du etwas sagen?"

Fragen zum Lesestück

1. Wer bespricht die Amerikareise?
2. Wie war die Reise?
3. Sind die Schüler in Amerika sehr anders, oder sind sie ähnlich?
4. Was trägt man auch in Amerika?
5. Was ißt man auch dort?
6. Was hassen alle Schüler?
7. Was fürchten viele Schüler?
8. Warum müssen die Deutschen mehr Fremdsprachen lernen?
9. Was ist in Amerika ganz anders?
10. Was schreibt die Klasse für ihre Schülerzeitung?

Vom Lesen zum Sprechen

You already know some of this vocabulary.

Die Kleidung—Clothing

das Kostüm   suit – women

1. der **Anzug**, ⸚e   suit – men
2. die **Bluse**, -n   *blouse*
3. die **Brille** (*sing.*)   glasses
4. der **Handschuh**, -e   glove
5. das **Hemd**, -en   *shirt*
6. die **Hose**, -n   *pants*
7. der **Hut**, ⸚e   hat
8. die **Jacke**, -n   *jacket*
9. das **Kleid**, -er   *dress*
10. die **Krawatte**, -n   tie
11. der **Mantel**, ⸚   *coat*
12. der **Pulli**, -s   *sweater*
13. der **Rock**, ⸚e   skirt
14. die **Tasche**, -n   pocket; handbag, shoulder-bag
15. das **T-Shirt**, -s   T-shirt

der schuh -e
der Turnschuh -- e

A. Sprechen wir über Kleider. Was tragen Sie heute?

EXAMPLE: Ich trage heute eine Bluse, einen Rock und eine Jacke.

B. Was trägt Ihr Freund heute?

EXAMPLE: Heute trägt Fred ein Hemd, Jeans und Turnschuhe.

Farben—Colors

die **Farbe, -n**	color
blau	blue
braun	brown
gelb	yellow
grau	gray
grün	green
rot	red
schwarz	black
weiß	white

C. Describe the clothing of your classmates, using the possessive adjectives **sein** and **ihr.**

EXAMPLE: (You're describing Fred's clothing) Sein Hemd ist blau.
(You're describing Mary's clothing) Ihre Bluse ist rot.

D. *Expressing your opinion.* In discussions like the one in the reading, speakers often begin by saying „**Ich finde . . .**" Express your opinion on the following questions. Begin your answer with „**Ja, ich finde . . .**" or „**Nein, ich finde . . .**"

EXAMPLE: Ist New York interessant?
Ja, ich finde, New York ist sehr interessant *or* Nein, ich finde, New York ist nicht interessant.

1. Sind die Schulen in Amerika gut?
2. Sind die Schulen in Deutschland besser?
3. Sollen die Amerikaner mehr Fremdsprachen lernen?
4. Haben die Schüler in Amerika Probleme?
5. Sind sie manchmal pessimistisch?
6. Haben die Schüler in Amerika Angst?
7. Ist Rockmusik schön?

Mündliche Übungen

A. Persönliche Fragen

1. Wo sind Sie zu Hause?
2. Gibt es da viel zu tun oder ist es langweilig?
3. Möchten Sie eine Deutschlandreise machen?
4. Haben Sie genug Geld für eine Reise?
5. Sind Sie fit?
6. Können Sie schnell laufen?
7. Müssen Sie Geld verdienen?
8. Können Sie Auto fahren?

B. Substitute the new elements you will hear.

> EXAMPLE: Ich möchte morgen nach Berlin.
> (wollen)
> Ich will morgen nach Berlin.

1. Ich möchte morgen nach Berlin.
   wollen.
   nach München
   müssen
   wir
   nach Kopenhagen

2. Bis Juni kannst du Geld verdienen.
   müssen
   September
   viel Geld
   ich
   haben

3. Wir können da drüben parken.
   sollen
   halten
   da
   können
   arbeiten
   zu Hause

4. Er geht später nach Hause.
   fahren
   jetzt
   Max
   laufen
   bald
   ihr

C. Answer each of your teacher's questions in the negative, making sure to use **nicht** or **kein** correctly.

1. Möchten Sie Deutsch lernen?
2. Wollen wir nach Deutschland fahren?
3. Möchten Sie da eine Schule besuchen?
4. Tragen die Schüler in Deutschland Jeans?
5. Sind die Schüler anders?
6. Wollen Sie Bücher über Deutschland lesen?
7. Müssen Schüler in Amerika Hausaufgaben machen?
8. Wollen Sie für morgen Hausaufgaben machen?

Lehrer Lämpel aus „Max und Moritz" (1858)
von Wilhelm Busch (1832–1908)

D. An acquaintance from the big city is asking you about life in your small town. Respond to these questions in the negative.

1. Sind die Menschen in Hinterwalden ehrlich?
2. Tragen die Schüler Turnschuhe?
3. Kann man in Hinterwalden Geld verdienen?
4. Ist das Leben langweilig?
5. Es gibt Berge dort, nicht wahr?
6. Hört man in Hinterwalden Rockmusik?

Schriftliche Übungen

E. Udo is throwing a party but nobody can come. Write him a note explaining why, using the cues below.

> EXAMPLE: leider / Monika / müssen / zu Hause bleiben
> Leider muß Monika zu Hause bleiben.

1. Klaus / müssen / für morgen / machen / seine Hausaufgaben
2. Ruth / möchten / fliegen / nach Berlin
3. Peter und Ute / wollen / besuchen / ihre Tante / in Wien
4. Herr Beck / können / leider / finden / seinen Anzug / nicht
5. Andreas / dürfen / nicht / so spät / kommen / nach Hause
6. ich / gar nicht / wollen / kommen

F. Answer the following questions affirmatively. Omit the infinitive wherever possible.

1. Soll ich meine Eltern fragen?
2. Können wir jetzt gehen?
3. Mußt du nach München fahren?
4. Möchten Sie den Mantel haben?
5. Willst du in Heidelberg studieren?
6. Kannst du das machen?

G. Wie sagt man das auf deutsch?

1. Wouldn't you like to stay a bit?
2. Yes, but unfortunately I have to work this evening.

3. Don't you have any friends in Hinterwalden?
4. Yes I do, but they're quite boring.
5. Then you have to visit us soon.

6. You want to come to Berlin, don't you?
7. Yes. I can't stay in Hinterwalden.
8. Why not? Aren't there any jobs there?
9. Yes, but I would like to earn more money.

Almanach

A Word About German Schools

In the Federal Republic of Germany, all children attend four years of elementary school (*die Grundschule*). In the fourth grade, when they are ten years old, they take placement tests whose results, along with their grades, determine how they will continue their education.

There are three possibilities: The *Hauptschule*, the *Realschule*, or the *Gymnasium*. The first two are oriented respectively toward trades and business and prepare the pupils for various forms of apprenticeship and job training. The *Gymnasium* is the traditional preparation for university study. After passing their final examination, called the *Abitur* in Germany and the *Matura* in Austria, the pupils may apply to a university.

In the German Democratic Republic, all pupils attend the *Oberschule*, a unified school, for the first ten grades. Those who will go on to a university then continue their secondary studies for two more years and must also pass the *Abitur* examination.

Since 1971 there have also been *Gesamtschulen* (unified schools) in the Federal Republic comprising all three kinds of secondary school. Here pupils do not need to make their important decision at the age of ten, but can wait until they are sixteen. In 1981, there were about 270 *Gesamtschulen* with approximately 2.4% of all pupils.

The university library in Frankfurt am Main.

Land und Leute

Dialoge
Am See ♦ Winterurlaub
♦ Es wird dunkel

Wortschatz 1

Grammatik
1. Commands
   The **Sie**-Imperative ♦ The
   wir-Imperative (*Let's* do something) ♦ The **ihr**-Imperative
   ♦ The **du**-Imperative
   ♦ Imperative of **sein**
2. The Verb **werden** (to become)
3. Negating **müssen**
4. Negating **schon** and **noch**
5. Prepositions with the
   Accusative Case
6. Equivalents of English "like"
   To like something: **mögen**
   ♦ To like to do something:
   verb + **gern(e)**
7. The Impersonal Pronoun **man**
8. Sentence Adverbs
9. **gehen** + Infinitive
10. Expanding Your Vocabulary
    Leicht zu merken

Wortschatz 2

Lesestück
Deutschland: Ein bißchen
Geographie

Vom Lesen zum Sprechen
Das Wetter und das Klima

Almanach
The Common Origin of English and
German

Dialoge

Am See

FRAU MÜLLER: Gehen wir noch einmal schwimmen?

FRAU BRINKMANN: Nein, das Wasser ist zu kalt. Gehen Sie ohne mich.

FRAU MÜLLER: Oder wir können zusammen Karten spielen.

FRAU BRINKMANN: Ja, warum nicht? Ich spiele gern Karten.

Winterurlaub

RICHARD: Möchtest du im Winter nach Österreich?

EVA: Ja, gern! Fahren wir doch im Januar nach Innsbruck![1]

RICHARD: Meinst du, wir können noch ein Hotelzimmer bekommen?

EVA: Ich weiß nicht. Hoffentlich ist es noch nicht zu spät.

Es wird dunkel

ANDREA: Hoffentlich brauchst du nicht mehr lange zu arbeiten. Wirst du denn nicht müde?

NINA: Doch, aber ich muß noch etwas für das Seminar lesen.

ANDREA: Aber es wird schon dunkel, und ich gehe nicht gern allein durch die Stadt.

NINA: Geh nicht ohne mich! Warte noch ein bißchen. Dann können wir zusammen gehen.

[1] A city on the Inn River, capital of the Austrian state of Tyrol. See map, p. 435.

München: Stadtmitte

At the Lake

MRS. MÜLLER: Shall we go swimming once more?

MRS. BRINKMANN: No, the water is too cold. You go without me.

MRS. MÜLLER: Or we can play cards together.

MRS. BRINKMANN: Yes, why not? I like to play cards.

Winter Vacation

RICHARD: Would you like to go to Austria this winter?

EVA: Yes, very much! Let's go to Innsbruck in January!

RICHARD: Do you think we can still get a hotel room?

EVA: I don't know. I hope it isn't already too late.

It's Getting Dark

ANDREA: I hope you don't need to work much longer. Aren't you getting tired?

NINA: Yes I am, but I still have to read something for the seminar.

ANDREA: But it's already getting dark, and I don't like to walk through the city alone.

NINA: Don't go without me! Just wait a little bit longer. Then we can go together.

Verben

bekommen to receive, get

mögen (mag) to like

schwimmen to swim

warten to wait

werden (wird) to become, get (*in the sense of* "become")

Substantive

der **Baum, ¨e** tree

der **See, -n** lake
am See at the lake

der **Urlaub** vacation (*from a job*)

der **Winter, -** winter
im Winter in the winter

das **Hotel, -s** hotel

(das) **Österreich** Austria

das **Seminar, -e** (*university*) seminar

das **Wasser** water

die **Karte, -n** card; ticket; map

die **Stadt, ¨e** city

Gegensätze

allein ≠ **zusammen**	alone ≠ together
dunkel ≠ **hell**	dark ≠ bright, light
kalt ≠ **heiß**	cold ≠ hot

Andere Vokabeln

allein alone

doch (*unstressed*) flavoring particle (See p. 90)

dunkel dark

durch through

einmal once
noch einmal once again, once more

gern gladly, with pleasure
gern (+ *verb*) = like to
Ich gehe gern durch die Stadt. I like to walk through the city.

hoffentlich I hope

kalt cold

lang(e) long; for a long time

müde tired, weary

noch nicht not yet

ohne without

zusammen together

Neue Kombinationen

A. Replace the words in italics with the new word or phrase you will hear.

1. *Hoffentlich* können wir heute schwimmen.
   (vielleicht, sicher, natürlich)
2. Ich muß etwas für *das Seminar* schreiben.
   (meinen Freund, ihn, Andrea, sie, meine Freunde)
3. Ich *spiele* gern *Karten*.
   (trage . . . Jeans; esse . . . Pommes frites; gehe . . . schwimmen;
   lerne . . . Deutsch; fahre . . . Auto)
4. Es ist noch nicht *spät*.
   (dunkel, kalt, interessant, alt)
5. Es wird langsam *dunkel*.
   (kalt, heiß, spät, steil)
6. *Gehen* Sie ohne mich!
   (fahren, schwimmen, kochen, arbeiten, warten)

B. Answer affirmatively these questions about what you like to do, repeating the word **gern**. Then repeat the exercise, giving negative responses.

> EXAMPLE: Spielen Sie **gern** Karten?
> Ja, ich spiele **gern** Karten.
> Nein, ich spiele nicht **gern** Karten.

1. Gehst du gern schwimmen?
2. Fahren Sie gern nach Österreich?
3. Geht ihr gern durch die Stadt?
4. Besuchst du mich gern?
5. Bleiben Sie gern zu Hause?

⊡━⊡ **Übung zur Aussprache**

Practice the difference between the German uvular **r** before a vowel and the vocalic **r** at the end of a word or syllable, or before a consonant (*see* Introduction, p. 7).

rieb	Bier	führt
Rat	Haar	Fahrt
rot	Tor	bohrt
Ruhm	fuhr	Furcht
Reh	er	ehrt

Read these sentences aloud.

1. Was macht ihr morgen?
2. Wir machen eine Reise in die Berge.
3. Ist der Pullover für mich?
4. Natürlich ist er für dich!
5. Wir brauchen eine Straßenkarte von Österreich.
6. Dürfen wir im Winter nach Innsbruck fahren?

Grammatik

1 ♦ Commands

Imperative forms are used to give commands.

The Sie-*imperative*

To give a command or order to someone you address as **Sie,** use verb-first word order and place **Sie** after the verb:

Kommen Sie bald wieder! *Come again soon!*

Although commands have the same word order as yes/no questions, the voice rises at the end of a question, whereas it drops at the end of a command. Compare the following intonation curves:

Kommen Sie bald wieder?   Kommen Sie bald wieder!

The wir-*imperative* = Let's *do something!*

Commands for **wir** also have verb-first word order. The **wir**-imperative is really a suggestion:

Fahren wir im Januar. *Let's go in January.*

The unstressed flavoring particle **doch** softens any command to a suggestion:

Gehen Sie nach Hause!   *Go home!*
Gehen Sie doch nach Hause. *Why don't you go home.*

 Üben wir!

A. Encourage acquaintances to carry out their plans. Use the **Sie**-imperative and the flavoring particle **doch.**

> EXAMPLE: Ich möchte eine Reise machen.
> Machen Sie doch eine Reise!

1. Ich möchte morgen schwimmen.
2. Ich will nach Rom fahren.
3. Ich muß nach Hause gehen.
4. Ich möchte bis Donnerstag warten.
5. Ich möchte Karten spielen.
6. Ich muß Frau Klein besuchen.
7. Ich möchte eine Pause machen.

B. Now use the **wir**-imperative to suggest that you both do these things.

> EXAMPLE: Ich möchte eine Reise machen.
> Ich auch! Machen wir doch eine Reise!

C. Now tell your acquaintance *not* to do certain things:

> EXAMPLE: Soll ich eine Reise machen?
> Nein, machen Sie keine Reise!

1. Soll ich zu Hause bleiben?
2. Soll ich eine Fremdsprache lernen?
3. Soll ich Turnschuhe kaufen?
4. Soll ich wieder schwimmen gehen?
5. Soll ich bis Donnerstag warten?
6. Soll ich ein Hotel suchen?
7. Soll ich eine Pause machen?

The **ihr**-imperative

The **ihr**-imperative is identical to the present-tense **ihr**-form of the verb, but without the pronoun **ihr.**

Besucht uns bald, Fritz und Willy.   *Visit us soon, Fritz and Willy.*

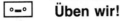

Üben wir!

A. Tell the children what to do.

> EXAMPLE: Sollen wir bald nach Hause kommen?
> Ja, kommt bald nach Hause.

1. Dürfen wir Karten spielen?
2. Sollen wir Tante Hildegard besuchen?
3. Dürfen wir das Buch lesen?
4. Sollen wir nach Hause laufen?

B. Now tell them what *not* to do.

> EXAMPLE: Sollen wir nach Hause kommen?
> Nein, kommt nicht nach Hause.

1. Sollen wir Jeans tragen?
2. Sollen wir heute kommen?
3. Sollen wir hier bleiben?
4. Sollen wir das sagen?

Die Spitze des Doldenhorns mit Bergsteigern (Schweiz)

The du-imperative

The **du**-imperative is expressed by the verb stem without ending. The pronoun **du** is not used.

Geh ohne mich.	*Go without me.*
Frag mich nicht.	*Don't ask me.*
Lauf schnell nach Hause!	*Run home quickly!*

If the verb changes its stem vowel from **e → i(e)**, the *changed* stem is used:

	statement	*du-imperative*
lesen	Du **liest** das für morgen.	**Lies** das für morgen.
geben	Du **gibst** Peter das Buch.	**Gib** Peter das Buch!

Verb stems ending in **-d** or **-t** add an **-e** to the stem:

Arbeite nicht so viel.	*Don't work so hard.*
Warte hier.	*Wait here.*

Üben wir!

A. Your friend Beate wonders if she should do certain things. Tell her to go ahead.

> EXAMPLE: Soll ich drüben parken?
> Ja, park drüben.

1. Soll ich das tun?
2. Soll ich mit Hans sprechen?
3. Soll ich Peter das Buch geben?
4. Soll ich schnell laufen?
5. Soll ich hier warten?
6. Soll ich Pommes frites essen?
7. Soll ich etwas singen?
8. Soll ich nach Rom fahren?
9. Soll ich eine Zeitung lesen?
10. Soll ich Deutsch lernen?
11. Soll ich den Professor fragen?

B. Now tell Beate *not* to do the same things.

> EXAMPLE: Soll ich drüben parken?
> Nein, park nicht drüben.

Imperative of sein

The verb **sein** is irregular in the **Sie, wir,** and **du**-imperatives:

Seien Sie	bitte freundlich, Herr Kaiser.	*Please be friendly, Mr. Kaiser.*
Seien wir	freundlich.	*Let's be friendly.*
Seid	freundlich, Kinder.	*Be friendly, children.*
Sei	freundlich, Rolf.	*Be friendly, Rolf.*

Üben wir!

A. Tell the following people to be honest.

> EXAMPLE: Richard
> Sei doch ehrlich, Richard!

1. Kinder
2. Herr und Frau Bachmann
3. wir
4. Barbara

B. Now tell them not to be so boring.

> EXAMPLE: Herr Stolze
> Seien Sie doch nicht so langweilig, Herr Stolze!

1. Ute
2. Frau Klein
3. Thomas und Beate
4. wir

2 ◆ The Verb *werden* (to become)

The verb **werden** is irregular in the **du-** and **er-**forms of the present tense:

ich	werde	wir	werden
du	**wirst**	ihr	werdet
er, es, sie	**wird**	sie, Sie	werden

Werden, like **sein** and **bleiben,** is followed by either a predicate nominative or a predicate adjective. Depending on the context, **werden** can be translated with various English equivalents:

Es wird langsam dunkel.	*It's gradually becoming dark.*
Ihre Kinder werden groß.	*Your children are getting big.*
Meine Schwester will Professorin werden.	*My sister wants to be a professor.*
Am Montag werde ich 21.	*I'm turning 21 on Monday.*

Üben wir!

A. Say who is getting tired.

EXAMPLE: Barbara
Barbara wird müde.

1. wir	3. meine Mutter	5. du
2. die Kinder	4. ihr	6. ich

B. Wie sagt man das auf englisch?

1. Morgen wird es heiß.
2. Wann wirst du denn zwanzig?
3. Draußen wird es kalt.
4. Das Buch wird langsam interessant.
5. Meine zwei Freunde wollen Professoren werden.

3 ◆ Negating *müssen*

There are two ways to negate the modal verb **müssen:**

1. **muß nicht = *don't have to***

Ich muß nicht zu Hause bleiben.	*I don't have to stay home (but I will anyway).*

2. **brauche nicht zu = *don't need to, don't have to***

Ich brauche nicht zu Hause zu bleiben.	*I don't need to stay at home (i.e., I can go out tonight).*

Brauche nicht zu is the more common way of negating müssen.

Üben wir!

A. Answer in the negative using **brauchen nicht zu.**

> EXAMPLE: Muß er warten?
> Nein, er braucht nicht zu warten.

1. Muß Hans Englisch lernen?
2. Müssen wir in Gelsenkirchen wohnen?
3. Müßt ihr denn nach Österreich fahren?
4. Muß ich die Lehrerin fragen?
5. Muß man das Buch lesen?
6. Müssen wir die Reise machen?

B. Say you don't *have* to do the following, but you *want* to.

> EXAMPLE: Müssen Sie denn so ehrlich sein?
> Nein, ich muß nicht so ehrlich sein, aber ich will ehrlich sein.

1. Müssen Sie denn Karten spielen?
2. Müssen Sie denn nach Hause?
3. Müssen Sie denn im Winter schwimmen?
4. Müssen Sie denn so schnell sprechen?
5. Müssen Sie denn Suppe kochen?
6. Müssen Sie denn bis sieben arbeiten?

4 ♦ Negating *schon* and *noch*

schon ≠ noch nicht, noch kein

The negation of **schon** (already) is **noch nicht** (not yet) or **noch kein** (not a . . . yet; not any . . . yet):

Wollen Sie **schon** gehen?	*Do you want to leave already?*
Nein, ich will **noch nicht** gehen.	*No, I don't want to leave yet.*
Habt ihr **schon** Karten?	*Do you have tickets yet?*
Nein, wir haben **noch keine** Karten.	*No, we don't have any tickets yet.*

Üben wir!

A. Answer the questions negatively:

1. Habt ihr schon Kinder?
2. Ist Rolf schon da?
3. Studiert sie schon in Berlin?
4. Haben wir schon Probleme?
5. Ist es schon zu spät?
6. Verdienst du schon genug?
7. Mußt du schon gehen?
8. Hast du schon eine Karte?

noch ≠ nicht mehr, kein . . . mehr

The negation of **noch** (still) is **nicht mehr** (no longer) or **kein . . . mehr** (no more):

Ich glaube, sie studiert **noch**.	*I think she's still in college.*
Nein, sie studiert **nicht mehr**, sie arbeitet..	*No, she's no longer in college, she's working.*
Entschuldigung! Können wir **noch** Karten bekommen?	*Pardon me! Can we still get tickets?*
Leider habe ich **keine** Karten **mehr**.	*I'm sorry, but I have no more tickets.*

Note that in the **kein . . . mehr** pattern, **mehr** follows the noun.

A. Answer the questions negatively, using **nicht mehr** or **kein . . . mehr** as appropriate.

1. Sind deine Eltern noch jung?
2. Wohnen Sie noch in Innsbruck?
3. Hat er noch Arbeit für uns?
4. Können Sie noch warten?
5. Geht die Uhr noch?
6. Hat deine Großmutter noch einen Bruder?
7. Kannst du uns noch besuchen?
8. Hassen Sie ihn noch?
9. Ist er noch ein Kind?

5 ◆ Prepositions with the Accusative Case

The following prepositions are always used with the accusative:

~~bis~~	until, by	Wir warten **bis Dienstag**.
		Ich muß es **bis morgen** lesen.
durch	through	Er fährt **durch die Berge**.
für	for	Sie arbeitet **für ihren Vater**.
gegen	against	Was hast du **gegen mich**?
ohne	without	Wir gehen **ohne dich**.
um	around *(the outside of)*	Das Auto fährt **um das Hotel**.

In time expressions, **um** means "at" (*not* "around"!):

Ute kommt **um drei**.	*Ute is coming at 3:00.*

"Around three" is **gegen drei**.

Ute kommt **gegen drei**.	*Ute is coming around three.*

Ein Sommertag am Meer

In spoken German, **durch**, **für**, and **um** often contract with the article **das**:

durch das → **durchs**	Sie läuft **durchs Zimmer.**
für das → **fürs**	Ich habe etwas **fürs Kind.**
um das → **ums**	Er fährt **ums Haus.**

Üben wir!

A. Supply the correct accusative form.

1. Tu das bitte für *mich.*
   (him, her, us, them, your friend, the group, the family, your brother, your sister)
2. Lisa geht durch *das Hotel.*
   (the house, the school, the office, the *Mensa*)
3. Bist du denn gegen *uns?*
   (me, her, them, him, the teacher (m.), the teacher (f.))
4. Das Auto fährt um *das Haus.*
   (the hotel, our house, the mountain, our school)
5. Ohne *dich* ist es langweilig.
   (him, her, you (pl. fam.), them, my sister, his brother, my friends, the music)

To like something: mögen

Mögen is a modal verb. Its present-tense forms are

mögen	to like (something)		
ich	**mag**	wir	mögen
du	**magst**	ihr	mögt
er, es, sie	**mag**	sie, Sie	mögen

Mögen means "to like (something.)" Unlike the other modals, it is used without an infinitive.

Ich **mag** Maria.	*I like Maria.*
Mögen Sie die Suppe nicht?	*Don't you like the soup?*

Remember that the form **möchte** means "would like to (do something)" and *is* used with an infinitive:

Ich **möchte** Maria **besuchen.**	*I would like to visit Maria.*

Üben wir!

A. Tell who likes Frau Brandt.

> EXAMPLE: die Schüler
> Die Schüler mögen Frau Brandt.

1. du
2. wir
3. Franz

4. meine Eltern
5. ich
6. ihr

To like to do something: verb + gern(e)

Gern(e) plus a verb corresponds to English "to like to (do something)":

Ich **schwimme gern.**	*I like to swim.*
Sie **läuft gern** durch die Stadt.	*She likes to walk through the city.*
Hören Sie **gerne** Musik?	*Do you like to listen to music?*

Gern(e) generally comes immediately after the subject and verb. The negation of **gern** is **nicht gern:**

Ich schwimme **nicht gern.**	*I don't like to swim.*

A. An acquaintance suggests some activities. Answer yes, you'd *like* to do them.

> EXAMPLE: Wollen wir schwimmen?
> O ja, ich schwimme gern.

1. Wollen wir Karten spielen?
2. Wollen wir Pommes frites essen?
3. Wollen wir Deutsch sprechen?
4. Wollen wir Musik hören?
5. Wollen wir eine Pause machen?
6. Wollen wir durch die Stadt gehen?

Distinguish carefully among the three German equivalents for English "like:"

1. **Mögen** means "to like" people or things and is used with a noun or pronoun:

   > Ich **mag** Professor Jäger.
   > Ich **mag** ihn.

2. **Möchte** means "would like to" do something and is used with a complementary infinitive (which may sometimes be omitted, see above, p. 70):

   > Ich **möchte** Innsbruck **besuchen.**
   > Ich **möchte** nach Innsbruck (fahren).

3. A verb + **gern** means "to like to" do something.

   > Ich **spiele gern** Karten.

Möchte expresses a wish for something, while a verb + **gern** makes a general statement about your likes or dislikes:

Ich **möchte** Karten spielen.   *I would like to play cards.*
Ich **spiele gern** Karten.   *I like to play cards.*

Üben wir!

A. Wie sagt man das auf deutsch?

1. I like the soup.
2. I like to eat soup.
3. I would like the soup.
4. They would like to study in Germany.
5. Karl doesn't like to wait.
6. Do you like Professor Lange?
7. Our children like to play outside.
8. We would like to take a trip.

7 ◆ The Impersonal Pronoun *man*

The impersonal pronoun **man** is the equivalent of English "one," which may sound somewhat formal in everyday English speech. In German, however, **man** is used in all styles, both literary and colloquial. It can also be translated as "people," "they," "you," or even "we." **Man** is third person singular and may *only* be used as the subject of a sentence:

In Deutschland sagt **man** das oft.	*They often say that in Germany.*
Das muß **man** lernen.	*You've got to learn that.*
Das weiß **man** nie.	*One never knows.*

Do not confuse **man** with **der Mann** (the man).

Üben wir!

A. Change the subject to **man.**

> EXAMPLE: In Deutschland tragen viele Leute Jeans.
> In Deutschland trägt man Jeans.

1. In Hinterwalden können die Leute genug verdienen.
2. In Deutschland lernen viele Leute Fremdsprachen.
3. Hoffentlich können wir noch ein Hotelzimmer bekommen.
4. Hier können Sie gut essen.
5. Dürfen wir hier Karten spielen?
6. Dort haben die Schüler auch Angst.

B. Wie sagt man das auf deutsch? (Use **man** as the subject)

1. In America we don't learn that.
2. You've got to stop here.
3. One has to do that.
4. People say there are a lot of problems here.
5. Can one get a newspaper here?
6. You don't need to read that.

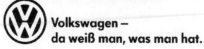

Volkswagen —
da weiß man, was man hat.

8 ◆ Sentence Adverbs

Adverbs are normally words that modify a verb, an adjective, or another adverb and answer the question **Wie?**:

modifying a verb:	Wie spielt sie?	Sie spielt **schön.**
modifying an adjective:	Wie müde bist du?	Ich bin **sehr** müde.
modifying an adverb:	Wie gut kann er Deutsch?	Er kann **ziemlich** gut Deutsch.

Certain adverbs, however, can modify entire sentences and express the speaker's attitude toward the content of the whole:

Natürlich bin ich kein Tourist.	*Of course I'm not a tourist.*
Du hast **sicher** genug Geld.	*You surely have enough money.*

Learn these important German sentence adverbs:

Gott sei Dank	*thank goodness*
hoffentlich	*"Let's hope that . . . "*
leider	*unfortunately*
natürlich	*naturally, of course*
selbstverständlich	*"It goes without saying that . . . ," of course*
sicher	*certainly, surely*
übrigens	*by the way, incidentally*

Note on punctuation: When sentence adverbs come at the beginning of a sentence, they are *not* followed by a comma, as they are in English:

Übrigens studiert sie noch.	*Incidentally, she's still a student.*

Üben wir!

A. Begin these sentences with the adverb given in parentheses.

1. Er ist noch nicht da. (sicher)
2. Sie können Deutsch. (hoffentlich)
3. Ich habe Geld. (selbstverständlich)
4. Ich muß heute abend arbeiten. (übrigens)
5. Der Berg ist gar nicht so steil. (Gott sei Dank)
6. Er ist kein Amerikaner. (natürlich)
7. Wir können die Reise nicht mehr machen. (leider)
8. Sie brauchen einen Mantel. (sicher)

9 ♦ *gehen* + infinitive

The verb **gehen** is sometimes used with an infinitive as its complement. English **go** functions in a similar way, but with a present participle (**-ing**) as its complement:

Sie **geht** oft **schwimmen.**   *She often **goes swimming.***

The complementary infinitive (**schwimmen**) functions like the infinitive following a modal verb.

Gehen wir noch einmal **schwimmen!**   *Let's go swimming again!*

Ich **gehe** mit Dieter **schwimmen.**   *I'm going swimming with Dieter.*

Note what happens when **schwimmen gehen** (to go swimming) as a whole is used as an infinitive with a modal verb:

Wollen wir heute **schwimmen gehen?**   *Shall we go swimming today?*

10 ♦ Expanding Your Vocabulary

Leicht zu merken

die **Alpen**
barbarisch   bar*bar*isch
zirka
die **Geographie**   Geogra*phie*
die **Kolonie, -n**   Kolo*nie*
der **Kontrast, -e**   Kon*trast*
die **Kultur**   Kul*tur*
mild
der **Rhein**
wild

ERHOLUNG AUF DEM RHEIN.
DIE BAHN BRINGT SIE ZUM SCHIFF.

K͞D Köln-Düsseldorfer ☐☐ **Deutsche Bundesbahn**

Wortschatz 2

Verben
beschreiben to describe
liegen to lie; be situated
schneien to snow
  Es schneit. It's snow-
  ing.
trinken to drink
wandern to hike

Substantive
der **Frühling** spring
der **Herbst** fall, autumn
der **Norden** the North
der **Osten** the East
der **Schnee** snow
der **Sommer** summer
der **Süden** the South
der **Wald, ⸚er** forest
der **Wein, -e** wine
der **Westen** the West

das **Bier, -e** beer
(das) **Europa** Europe
das **Klima** climate
das **Land, ⸚er** country
das **Leben** life
das **Märchen, -** fairy tale
das **Meer, -e** sea

die **Landschaft, -en**
  landscape
die **Rolle, -n** role, part
  eine Rolle spielen to
  play a part; be important
die **Schweiz** Switzerland

Andere Vokabeln
also (*here* =) thus
immer noch (or **noch**
  immer) still
  (intensification of **noch**)
kühl cool
modern modern
naß wet, damp
schrecklich terrible
sonnig sunny
trocken dry
von from
warm warm

Nützliche Ausdrücke
im Süden (**Norden, Osten,**
  Westen) in the South
  (North, East, West)
im Winter (**Frühling, Som-**
  mer, Herbst) in the winter (spring, summer, fall)
Gott sei Dank! Thank
  goodness!

Gegensätze

kühl ≠ warm	cool ≠ warm
naß ≠ trocken	wet ≠ dry

LIENZER HÜTTENWANDERUNGEN

Deutschland:
Ein bißchen Geographie

Für die alten Römer° war° das Leben in der Kolonie *Germania* nicht sehr schön. Der Historiker° Tacitus (zirka 55–115 n. Chr.°) beschreibt das Land als° kalt und neblig.° Über die Germanen° schreibt er: „Sie sind ohne Kultur, haben keine Städte und leben im Wald. Sie sind wild und barbarisch, wie ihr Land."

Das moderne Deutschland liegt in der Mitte Europas°, und die „wilden Germanen" wohnen heute zum größten Teil° in der Stadt. Es gibt keinen Urwald° mehr, aber der Wald ist immer noch typisch und wichtig für die Landschaft in Deutschland, Österreich und der Schweiz. Am Sonntag wandert man gern durch die Wälder, und die Kinder hören auch heute noch gern Märchen wie „Hänsel und Gretel" oder „Schneewittchen", in denen° der Wald eine große Rolle spielt.

Romans / was
historian
nach Christo = *A.D. / as / foggy*
Germanic tribesmen

in ... Europas = *in the middle of Europe*
zum ... Teil = *for the most part / primeval forest*

which

Weinberge und Burgen (*vineyards and castles*) am Rhein

An der Ostsee

Auch das Wetter in Deutschland ist Gott sei Dank nicht so schrecklich, wie° Tacitus meint. Selbstverständlich ist es nicht so warm und sonnig wie in Italien,° aber das deutsche Klima ist eigentlich ziemlich mild. Im Süden, wo die Alpen liegen, gibt es natürlich viel Schnee im Winter, aber in den großen Flußtälern° wird es im Winter nicht sehr kalt. Der Rhein, die Weser, die Elbe und die Oder[1] fließen° durch das Land von Süden nach Norden. Nur die Donau[1] fließt von Westen nach Osten. Am° Rhein und an der° Donau trinkt man gern Wein; die Römer brachten° den Weinbau° nach Deutschland. Die Deutschen trinken also nicht nur Bier!

Im Norden ist das Land flach° und fruchtbar.° Hier beeinflußt° das Meer—die Nordsee und die Ostsee[1]—Landschaft und Klima. Man sieht also, in Deutschland gibt es viele Kontraste: Wald und Feld,° Stadt und Land, Berge und Meer.

so . . . wie = *as . . . as*
Italy

river valleys
flow

am and *an der* = *on the*
brought
viniculture

flat / fertile
influences

field

Fragen zum Lesestück

1. Wie beschreibt Tacitus die Kolonie *Germania*?
2. Was ist noch immer typisch für die Landschaft in Deutschland?
3. Was macht man gern am Sonntag?
4. Was spielt eine große Rolle in „Hänsel und Gretel"?
5. Wie ist das Klima in Deutschland?
6. Ist es so warm und sonnig wie in Italien?
7. Wo gibt es viel Schnee im Winter?
8. Wo trinkt man viel Wein?
9. Wie ist das Land im Norden?

[1] See map in color insert.

Vom Lesen zum Sprechen

You already know most of these words:

Das Wetter und das Klima

die **Jahreszeit, -en**	season of the year
der **Frühling**	
der **Sommer**	
der **Herbst**	
der **Winter**	
die **Luft**	air
der **Regen**	rain
Es regnet.	
der **Schnee**	
Es schneit.	
die **Wolke, -n**	cloud
wolkig	cloudy
der **Nebel**	fog, mist
neblig	foggy
heiß	
kalt	
warm	
kühl	
trocken	
mild	
naß	

A. Read this traditional poem aloud.

Es war° eine Mutter,	*there was*
Die hatte° vier Kinder:	*who had*
Den Frühling, den Sommer,	
Den Herbst und den Winter.	
Der Frühling bringt Blumen,°	*flowers*
Der Sommer bringt Klee,°	*clover*
Der Herbst, der° bringt Trauben,°	*it / grapes*
Der Winter bringt Schnee.	

B. Sprechen wir über das Wetter!

EXAMPLE: Wie ist das Wetter heute?
Ich finde das Wetter heute schön. Es ist warm, und die Sonne scheint.

1. Wie ist das Wetter hier im Frühling? im Sommer? im Herbst? im Winter?
2. Wo wohnt Ihre Familie? Können Sie das Klima dort beschreiben?
3. Gibt es viel Regen dort? Wann?
4. Wann scheint die Sonne?
5. Wann schneit es?
6. Ist der Winter mild?
7. Ist der Sommer sehr heiß?

„Der Herbst, der bringt Trauben."

Mündliche Übungen

A. Persönliche Fragen

1. Was machen Sie morgen?
2. Wie viele Märchen kennen Sie?
3. Wie heißen die Märchen?
4. Spielen Sie manchmal Karten?
5. Möchten Sie im Winter nach Innsbruck?
6. Machen Sie im Sommer eine Reise, oder müssen Sie arbeiten?

B. Student A is indecisive and asks if he/she should do certain things. Student B tells him/her to do them.

> EXAMPLE: Teacher: die Suppe kochen?
> Student A: Soll ich die Suppe kochen?
> Student B: Ja, koch bitte die Suppe.

1. das Buch lesen?
2. hier parken?
3. einen Mantel tragen?
4. nach Hause kommen?

5. Deutsch sprechen?
6. Wein trinken?
7. höflich sein?
8. nicht mehr fragen?

Now play the same scene with *two* indecisive friends.

> EXAMPLE: Teacher: die Suppe kochen?
> Student A: Sollen wir die Suppe kochen?
> Student B: Ja, kocht bitte die Suppe.

C. Your teacher plays a relative visiting from Germany. You're a morose child and answer all questions in the negative.

> EXAMPLE: Bist du schon acht?
> Nein, ich bin noch nicht acht.

1. Kannst du schon Deutsch?
2. Kannst du schon schwimmen?
3. Liest du schon Märchen?

4. Darfst du schon Karten spielen?
5. Trägst du schon eine Uhr?
6. Darfst du schon allein wandern?

D. Your teacher plays a friend who has been away for a while, and is asking if things are still the same. You answer negatively.

> EXAMPLE: Hast du noch ein Auto?
> Nein, ich habe kein Auto mehr.

1. Trinkst du noch viel Wein?
2. Wohnt Jutta noch hier?
3. Trägst du noch Jeans?

4. Bist du noch fit?
5. Kannst du noch Englisch?
6. Suchst du noch ein Haus?

E. You've met a group of German students and are asking them what they like. Use the cue from your teacher to form question and answer.

> EXAMPLE: Teacher: die Suppe?
> Student A: Mögt ihr die Suppe?
> Student B: Ja, wir mögen die Suppe.

1. euren Lehrer?
2. das Wetter hier?

3. den Winter?
4. Bier?

5. Wein?
6. Amerikaner?

F. Complete the sentence with a word that fits, either a preposition, personal pronoun, or article. (books open)

1. Der Wald ist noch immer typisch _____ die Landschaft.
2. Für _____ ist der Winter oft zu kalt.
3. Fahren Sie nicht so schnell _____ die Stadt!
4. Gehen wir zusammen durch _____ Wald.
5. Wir müssen _____ vier Uhr dort sein.
6. Soll ich um _____ Hotel fahren?
7. Ich finde den Professor langweilig. Ihr könnt _____ mich gehen.
8. Nein, ohne _____ wollen wir nicht gehen.
9. Ich mag deine Freundin und sage nichts _____ sie.

Schriftliche Übungen

G. *Tacitus modern:* You are the Roman historian Tacitus. You have miraculously returned to contemporary Germany to update your first impressions. Write in German about the country. What do the people still (**noch**) do? What do they no longer (**nicht mehr**) do? What plays a role in modern life? How do you find things nowadays, such as the cities, the wine, etc.?

H. Write complete sentences using the elements provided. You may have to add words.

1. wer / wollen / wandern / durch / Berge?
2. er / möchten / fahren / ohne / sein / Freund
3. wann / schneien / viel?
4. wir / kennen / kein / mehr / Märchen (*plural*)
5. mein / Bruder / arbeiten / für / unser / Onkel

I. Wie sagt man das auf deutsch?

1. The sun is shining and the water is warm. Let's go swimming.
2. I don't want to go swimming yet. Go without me.
3. But I don't like to swim alone.

4. Do you like the winter, Mr. Müller?
5. No, I don't like it any more.
6. I don't like to walk through the snow.

7. Wait here, Eva and Andrea.
8. We don't need to wait.

9. I hope that you still have money.
10. Unfortunately, I don't have any more money.

11. Can you do something for me?
12. Unfortunately, I have to go home now.

Almanach

The Common Origin of English and German

Although Tacitus thought the Germanic tribes had "always been there," they in fact originated in the Baltic region around the second millenium B.C. In the fourth century A.D., the Germanic peoples began to migrate south, a movement that continued through the early middle ages. The *Germani* (as they were called by the Romans) displaced the Celts from the heart of the European continent, pushing them as far west as Ireland. The Romans halted their expansion to the south by establishing their own northern frontier, a series of fortifications called the *limes*, literally the "limits" or boundaries of their empire. Eventually the Germanic tribes settled in the area known today as Germany. Contemporary German dialects and regional differences have their origins in these various tribes.

Thanks to the migration of the Angles and Saxons to the British Isles in the fifth century, the Germanic language that was to evolve into modern English was introduced there. German and English thus share common origins. Some other languages included in the Germanic family are Yiddish, Dutch, Flemish, Norwegian, Swedish, Danish, and Icelandic. You will easily recognize cognates in English and German (words that have the same etymological root) although the meanings may be different. These words can be identified by some regularly alternating consonants:

German **z** and English **t:**	zehn = ten
	Herz = heart
German **ss** and English **t:**	Wasser = water
	groß = great
German **pf** and English **p:**	Pflanze = plant
	Pflug = plough
German **f** or **ff** and English **p:**	Schiff = ship
	Pfeffer = pepper
German **ch** and English **k:**	machen = make
	Milch = milk
German **t** and English **d:**	Tag = day
	Tür = door
German **d** and English **th:**	du = thou
	drei = three

Summary and Review

FORMS

1 ◆ Verbs

A. Infinitive (ends in **-en** or **-n**)

komm**en**	to come
tu**n**	to do
arbeit**en**	to work

B. Stem (infinitive minus **-en** or **-n**)

komm-
tu-
arbeit-

C. Present Tense.

1. Personal Endings (added to stem)

Basic Paradigms

ich	komme	wir	kommen	ich	tue	wir	tun
du	komm**st**	ihr	kommt	du	tust	ihr	tut
er, es, sie	kommt	sie, Sie	kommen	er, es, sie	tut	sie, Sie	tun

---

Stems Ending in **-t** or **-d**

ich	arbeite	wir	arbeiten
du	arbeit**est**	ihr	arbeit**et**
er, es, sie	arbeit**et**	sie, Sie	arbeiten

Stems Ending in **-s, -ß, -z**

ich	heiße	wir	heißen
du	hei**ßt**	ihr	heißt
er, es, sie	heißt	sie, Sie	heißen

2. Stem-Vowel Change (in **du-** and **er-**forms)

sehen $e \rightarrow ie$	**sprechen** $e \rightarrow i$	**tragen** $a \rightarrow \ddot{a}$	**laufen** $au \rightarrow \ddot{a}u$
ich sehe	spreche	trage	laufe
du **siehst**	**sprichst**	**trägst**	**läufst**
er, es, sie **sieht**	**spricht**	**trägt**	**läuft**

3. Verbs With Irregular Present Tense

sein to be

ich bin	wir sind
du bist	ihr seid
er, es, sie ist	sie, Sie sind

haben to have

ich habe	wir haben
du hast	ihr habt
er, es, sie hat	sie, Sie haben

werden to become

ich werde	wir werden
du wirst	ihr werdet
er, es, sie wird	sie, Sie werden

wissen to know (facts)

ich weiß	wir wissen
du weißt	ihr wißt
er, es, sie weiß	sie, Sie wissen

■ Note that **wissen** is structurally similar to the modal verbs in the present tense (see next section).

4. Modal Verbs

a. Basic Conjugation (changed stem in singular, no ending for **ich-** and **er-**forms)

dürfen to be allowed to, may

ich darf	wir dürfen
du darfst	ihr dürft
er, es, sie darf	sie, Sie dürfen

similarly:

können (ich kann)	to be able to, can
mögen (ich mag)	to like
müssen (ich muß)	to have to, must
sollen (ich soll)	to be supposed to, should
wollen (ich will)	to want to

Mögen occurs most often in the form:

---

ich möchte   I would like to

ich	möchte	wir	möchten
du	möchtest	ihr	möchtet
er, es, sie	möchte	sie, Sie	möchten

---

b. Modal Verb + Infinitive (in final position)

	Modal		*Infinitive*
Ich	**darf**	heute abend nicht	**mitkommen.**
	Willst	du denn gar nichts	**trinken?**
Robert	**möchte**	Lehrer	**werden.**

c. Infinitive Omitted (implicit **fahren, gehen, haben, machen, tun**)

	Modal	
Ich	**muß**	in die Schule.
	Dürfen	wir denn das?
Hannah	**möchte**	ein Bier.

2 ♦ Pronouns and Noun Phrases

A. Personal Pronouns

	Singular		Plural	
	nom.	*acc.*	*nom.*	*acc.*
first person	ich	mich	wir	uns
second person	du	dich	ihr	euch
third person	er	ihn		
	es	es	sie	sie
	sie	sie	(Sie	Sie)

B. Noun Phrases (= the noun + all words associated with it)

1. Definite Article

Definite Article + Noun

		Singular				*Plural*	
masculine	nom.	**der**	Mann				
	acc.	**den**	Mann				
neuter	nom.	**das**	Kind	nom.	**die**	Männer, Kinder, Frauen	
	acc.	**das**	Kind	acc.	**die**	Männer, Kinder, Frauen	
feminine	nom.	**die**	Frau				
	acc.	**die**	Frau				

---

2. Indefinite Article and Other **ein**-words

ein	a, an (unstressed); one (stressed)
kein	not a, no

possessive adjectives	mein	my
	dein	your
	sein	his (its)
	sein	its
	ihr	her (its)
	unser	our
	euer	your
	ihr (Ihr)	their (your)

---

ein-Word + Noun

		Singular				*Plural*	
masculine	nom.	kein	Mann				
	acc.	keinen	Mann				
neuter	nom.	kein	Kind	nom.	keine	Männer, Kinder, Frauen	
	acc.	kein	Kind	acc.	keine	Männer, Kinder, Frauen	
feminine	nom.	keine	Frau				
	acc.	keine	Frau				

---

3 ◆ Prepositions

Prepositions with Accusative

bis	until, by
durch	through
für	for
gegen	against
ohne	without
um	around (something), at (time)

FUNCTIONS

1 ◆ Making Statements

first element	+	*inflected verb*	→	(*rest of sentence*)
Heute abend		**kommt**		Richard.
Seit April		**wohnt**		sie bei ihrer Tante.
Diese Studenten		**haben**		keine Zeit gehabt.
Ich		**kann**		meine Schuhe nicht finden.

2 ◆ Asking Questions

A. Yes/No Questions:

verb	+	*subject*	→	(*rest of sentence*)
Kommt		**er?**		
Wohnen		**Sie**		in Berlin?
Müßt		**ihr**		gehen?

B. Information Questions:

(*preposition*)	+	*question word*	+	*verb*	→	(*rest of sentence*)
		Was		**trinkst**		du gern?
		Warum		**sagen**		Sie das?
Für		**wen**		**arbeiten**		Sie denn?

Question words: **wann, warum, was, wie, wo, wer, wen**

3 ◆ Giving Commands and Suggestions

A. **Sie**-Imperative:

verb	+	*Sie*	→	(*rest of sentence*)
Warten		**Sie**		ein bißchen.
Lesen		**Sie**		das Buch.

B. **wir**-Imperative (suggestion: Let's do something):

verb	+	*wir*	→	(*rest of sentence*)
Sprechen		**wir**		über unsere Probleme.
Gehen		**wir**		nach Hause.

C. **ihr**-Imperative (no pronoun!):

verb	→	(*rest of sentence*)
Wartet		noch ein bißchen.
Kommt		doch um neun.

D. du-Imperative (no pronoun!):

1. Basic Form:

verb stem	→	*(rest of sentence)*
Komm		doch um neun.
Frag		mich nicht.
Lauf		schnell, Konrad!

2. Present-Tense Stem-Vowel Change **e → i (ie)**:

	changed stem	→	*(rest of sentence)*
lesen:	**Lies**		das für morgen bitte.
sprechen:	**Sprich**		doch nicht so schnell.

3. Stems Ending in **-t** or **-d:**

	stem + e	→	*(rest of sentence)*
arbeiten:	**Arbeite**		nicht so viel!
warten:	**Warte**		bis sieben!

E. sein (irregular in the **Sie-, wir-,** and **du**-form):

Seien Sie	freundlich!
Seien wir	freundlich!
Seid	freundlich!
Sei	freundlich!

4 ◆ Negating

A. kein

1. **kein** negates **ein** + noun:

> Hast du **einen Bruder?**
> Nein, ich habe **keinen Bruder.**

2. **kein** negates nouns without articles:

> Braucht sie **Geld?**
> Nein, sie braucht **kein Geld.**

B. nicht

1. **nicht** follows:

   a. the subject and the inflected verb:

> Ich esse.
> Ich esse **nicht.**

   b. the direct object:

> Sie liest das Buch.
> Sie liest das Buch **nicht.**

c. expressions of definite time:

> Sie kommen morgen.
> Sie kommen morgen **nicht.**

2. **nicht** precedes verbal complements (the second part of the predicate)

   a. adverbs:

   > Der Lehrer spricht schnell.
   > Der Lehrer spricht **nicht** schnell.

   b. predicate adjectives:

   > Der Wald ist dunkel.
   > Der Wald ist **nicht** dunkel.

   c. predicate nominatives:

   > Er ist der Chef.
   > Er ist **nicht** der Chef.

   d. prepositional phrases showing destination or location:

   > Sie fliegt nach Wien.
   > Sie fliegt **nicht** nach Wien.

   e. infinitives complementing verbs:

   > Du sollst es kaufen.
   > Du sollst es **nicht** kaufen.

C. Negating **schon** and **noch**

1. **schon ≠ noch nicht, noch kein**

   > Ist Peter **schon** hier?
   > Nein, Peter ist **noch nicht** hier.

2. **noch ≠ nicht mehr, kein . . . mehr**

   > Wohnen Sie **noch** hier?
   > Nein, ich wohne **nicht mehr** hier.

   > Hast du **noch** Zeit?
   > Nein, ich habe **keine** Zeit **mehr.**

5 ◆ Translating English "like"

A. mögen + direct object = to like something or some one

> Ich **mag** dich sehr.
> Die Suppe **mag** ich nicht.

B. verb + **gern(e)** = to like to (do something)

> Ich schwimme **gern.**
> Machen Sie das **gern?**

C. möchten + infinitive = would like to

    Ich **möchte** etwas sagen.
    Das **möchte** ich auch.

6 ◆ Review of Useful Expressions

A. Greeting and Parting

Guten Tag!
Tag!
Guten Morgen!
Morgen!
Gute Reise!

Bis dann.
Bis Montag.
Wie geht es Ihnen (dir, euch)?
Wie geht's?

B. Polite Expressions

Danke!
Vielen Dank.
Nichts zu danken!

Bitte!
Entschuldigung.

C. Reactions and Opinions

Gott sei Dank!
Phantastisch!
Was ist los?
Hoffentlich!

Das mache ich gern.
Du hast es gut.
Das spielt keine Rolle.

D. Time and Place

Was machst du am Mittwoch?
Im Moment bin ich in Eile.
Bist du morgen zu Hause?
Nächstes Semester studiere ich in Deutschland.
Fährst du bald nach Hause?
Im Norden ist es im Sommer kühl.

CHECK YOUR PROGRESS 1

You will find the answer key to these exercises on page 503.

A. Rewrite each sentence with the new subject provided.

1. Ich möchte schon nach Berlin. (Barbara)
2. Ich will noch ein bißchen bleiben. (die Studenten)
3. Was tragen die Kinder am Freitag? (du)
4. Nehmen Sie die Suppe? (Karin)

5. Lesen alle Menschen die Zeitung? (du)
6. Schlaft ihr bis neun? (er)
7. Wißt ihr, wie er heißt? (Gisela)
8. Warten wir bis zehn? (er)

B. Provide the verb form to agree with the German subject. Then give the English infinitive.

1. scheinen: es _____ ; to _____ .
2. spielen: die Kinder _____ ; to _____ .
3. gehen: ihr _____ ; to _____ .
4. bedeuten: es _____ ; to _____ .
5. meinen: ich _____ ; to _____ .
6. laufen: er _____ ; to _____ .
7. stimmen: es _____ ; to _____ .
8. schlafen: du _____ ; to _____ .
9. fahren: wir _____ ; to _____ .
10. besuchen: ihr _____ ; to _____ .
11. wollen: sie (*sing.*) _____ ; to _____ .
12. dürfen: ich _____ ; to _____ .
13. werden: du _____ ; to _____ .
14. schneien: es _____ ; to _____ .
15. bekommen: Sie _____ ; to _____ .
16. lesen: du _____ ; to _____ .
17. tragen: ihr _____ ; to _____ .
18. können: er _____ ; to _____ .
19. warten: ich _____ ; to _____ .
20. sollen: er _____ ; to _____ .

C. Give the definite article and plural forms of the following nouns:

EXAMPLE: _____ Buch / die _____
das Buch / die Bücher

1. _____ Schule / die _____
2. _____ Hemd / die _____
3. _____ Mutter / die _____
4. _____ Schuh / die _____
5. _____ Sprache / die _____
6. _____ Freund / die _____
7. _____ Freundin / die _____
8. _____ Bruder / die _____
9. _____ Schwester / die _____
10. _____ Klischee / die _____
11. _____ Sohn / die _____
12. _____ Tochter / die _____
13. _____ Haus / die _____
14. _____ Zeitung / die _____
15. _____ Beruf / die _____
16. _____ Land / die _____
17. _____ Stuhl / die _____
18. _____ Frau / die _____
19. _____ Lehrer / die _____
20. _____ Lehrerin / die _____

D. Answer the following questions according to the cues provided.

1. Ist die Stunde nicht langweilig? Nein, sie _____ .
2. Müssen Sie heute abend arbeiten? Nein, heute abend _____ .
3. Wollen Sie die Zeitung kaufen? Nein, ich _____ .
4. Mußt du schon um acht zu Hause sein? Nein, um acht _____ .
5. Hat er noch Geld? Nein, leider _____ .
6. Haben Sie dort Freunde? Nein, dort _____ .

E. Answer the following questions negatively.

1. Bist du schon müde?
2. Wohnt ihr noch zu Hause?
3. Ist sie noch Studentin?
4. Kennst du schon meine Schwester?
5. Habt ihr schon Kinder?
6. Schreibst du noch Briefe?
7. Muß ich immer noch hier bleiben?
8. Haben Sie noch Angst?

F. Fill in the blank with the correct article or correct ending. Some blanks may need to be left empty.

1. Mein _____ Freunde haben morgen leider kein _____ Zeit.
2. Für _____ Hemd habe ich heute leider kein _____ Geld.
3. Ihr _____ Sohn mag ich sehr.
4. Hoffentlich hast du nichts gegen mein _____ Bruder.
5. Kaufst du etwas für unser _____ Essen morgen?
6. Leider muß ich ohne mein _____ Freunde gehen.
7. _____ Studenten müssen schnell laufen.
8. Ich kenne Ihr _____ Familie nicht.
9. Mein _____ Vater und mein _____ Mutter sind jetzt zu Hause.
10. _____ Klima ist oft sehr kalt, aber das spielt kein _____ Rolle.

G. Fill in the blanks with the correct pronouns.

1. Das ist nicht _____ Buch.
   (her)
2. Kennst du _____ gut?
   (her)
3. Geht _____ jetzt nach Hause?
   (you)
4. Ich möchte _____ Freunde besuchen.
   (his)
5. Das kann nicht _____ Vater sein.
   (her)
6. _____ Vater kenne ich leider noch nicht.
   (Her)

7. Kinder, ich kann _____ sehen.
   (you)

8. Sind das _____ Kinder, Frau Overholzer?
   (your)

9. Ist _____ Freund Amerikaner, Frau König?
   (your)

10. Ich will _____ morgen sehen.
    (them)

H. Wie sagt man das auf deutsch?

1. I like you a lot.
2. Don't you like my friends?
3. I'd like to be alone.
4. I like to be alone.
5. Would you like to go swimming?
6. I like to hike.
7. I do not like the climate here.

Arbeit und Freizeit

Dialoge
Schule oder Beruf? ◆ Der neue Lehrling

Wortschatz 1

Grammatik
1. Verbs with Separable and Inseparable Prefixes
2. Dative Case
   Indirect Object ◆ Forms of the Dative Case
3. Word Order
   Sentences with Two Objects ◆ Pronoun Word Order
4. Prepositions With Dative Case
5. **Der**-Words
   der-Words versus **ein**-Words
6. Omission of Article with Professions, Nationalities, Religions, etc.
7. Expanding Your Vocabulary
   Agent Nouns Ending in **-er** and **-erin** ◆ Leicht zu merken

Wortschatz 2

Lesestück
Drei Deutsche bei der Arbeit

Vom Lesen zum Sprechen
Berufe

Almanach
Stellenangebote

Dialoge

Schule oder Beruf?

VATER: Warum willst du denn jetzt die Schule verlassen? Du hast nur noch ein Jahr bis zum Abitur, und dann bist du fertig.

KURT: Ich brauche das Abitur nicht. Ich möchte Automechaniker werden und mit meinen Händen arbeiten.

VATER: Sei nicht so dumm! Ein Lehrling arbeitet drei Jahre und verdient wenig.

KURT: Aber ich mag die Schule einfach nicht mehr.

VATER: Quatsch! Hör auf mit diesem Unsinn! Ich kaufe dir ein Moped und du machst das Abitur.

Der neue Lehrling

MARTIN: Morgen. Ich heiße Martin Niedermeyer. Ich fange heute bei euch an.

GEORG: Morgen. Ich bin Georg. Den Chef lernst du erst um 9 Uhr kennen.

MARTIN: Seit wann arbeitest du hier?

GEORG: Seit fünf Jahren. Komm jetzt mit. Wir machen die Fenster auf und dann zeige ich dir den Laden.

In einer Autofabrik

Wortschatz 1

School or Work?

FATHER: Why do you want to leave school now? You've only got one more year until your *Abitur* and then you're done.

KURT: I don't need the *Abitur*. I want to be a car mechanic and work with my hands.

FATHER: Don't be so stupid! An apprentice works for three years and doesn't earn much.

KURT: But I simply don't like school any more.

FATHER: Rubbish! Stop this nonsense! I'll buy you a moped and you'll take your exam.

The New Apprentice

MARTIN: Morning. I'm Martin Niedermeyer. I'm starting work here today.

GEORG: Morning. I'm Georg. You won't meet the boss until 9 o'clock.

MARTIN: How long have you worked here?

GEORG: For five years. Come along now. We'll open the windows and then I'll show you the store.

Verben

an·fangen (fängt an)[1] to begin, start
an·rufen to call up
auf·hören (mit etwas) to cease, stop (doing something)
auf·machen to open
auf·stehen to stand up; get out of bed
kaufen to buy
kennen·lernen to get to know; meet
mit·kommen to come along
schenken to give (*as a gift*)
stehen to stand
verlassen (verläßt) (*trans.*) to leave (*a person or place*)
zeigen to show

Substantive

der **Automechaniker, -** auto mechanic
der **Chef, -s** boss (*m.*)
der **Laden, ̈** shop, store
der **Lehrling, -e** apprentice
der **Unsinn** nonsense, foolishness

das **Abitur** final secondary school examination
das **Jahr, -e** year
das **Moped, -s** moped

die **Chefin, -nen** boss (*f.*)
die **Hand, ̈e** hand

die **Zeit, -en** time
die **Freizeit** free time

Andere Vokabeln

dieser, dieses, diese; *pl.*: **diese** this; these
bei at, near
bei euch = with you (where you work or live)
dir (*dat. form of* **du**) you
dumm dumb
einfach simple, easy
erst not until; only
euch (*dat. form of* **ihr**) you (*pl.*)
fertig (mit) done, finished (with); ready
Mit den Hausaufgaben bin ich bald fertig. I'll be done with my homework soon.
Das Essen ist fertig. The meal is ready.
seit since
seit 5 Jahren for 5 years
Ich arbeite seit 5 Jahren hier. I've been working here for 5 years.
wenig small amount, little, not much

Nützliche Ausdrücke

bis zu until, up to
Quatsch! Rubbish! Baloney! Nonsense!
9 Uhr 9 o'clock

Gegensätze

an·fangen ≠ auf·hören	to start ≠ to stop
dumm ≠ klug	dumb ≠ smart, bright
einfach ≠ schwierig	simple ≠ difficult
wenig ≠ viel	little ≠ much

[1] See below, p. 127, for an explanation of the raised period.

Neue Kombinationen

A. Replace the word in italics with the new word or phrase you will hear.

1. Ich mag *die Schule* einfach nicht mehr.
   (dieses Moped, die Chefin, diesen Beruf)
2. Den Chef lernst du *um neun* kennen.
   (morgen, bald, heute)
3. Ich fange heute *bei euch* an.
   (bei Ihnen, bei ihm, bei dir)
4. Er arbeitet *seit fünf Jahren* hier.
   (seit 3 Tagen, seit Mittwoch, seit dem Winter)
5. Ich möchte *Automechaniker* werden.
   (Professor, Lehrer, Lehrerin)
6. Machen wir *das Fenster* auf.
   (das Buch, die Tür, den Laden)
7. Bist du *mit der Schule* bald fertig?
   (mit der Arbeit, mit meinem Buch, mit den Hausaufgaben)
8. Hoffentlich lerne ich *den Chef* bald kennen.
   (deine Schwester, die Studenten, den Lehrling, die Stadt)

Übung zur Aussprache

Review the German l. (See Introduction, p. 7). Remember that the sound represented by English l varies according to the vowels that precede or follow it. The l in "leaf" is different from the l in "wool." The German l always has a quality similar to the l in "leaf."

Repeat the following words after your teacher:

laut	bald
Lied	Zoll
Lob	Zahl
hilft	wohl
half	Wolle

Read these sentences aloud:

1. Lina, warum willst du nicht in der Schule bleiben?
2. Ich finde die Schule langweilig. Ich will in einem Laden arbeiten.
3. Verlaß die Schule nicht, Lina! Du hast noch viel zu lernen!

Grammatik

1 ◆ Verbs with Separable Prefixes

Some verbs in English can be complemented by another word to change their meaning: to find *out*, to look *up*, to burn *down*, to hang *around*. The meanings of many German verbs are modified or changed by a similar process, the addition of a prefix:

fangen	to catch	hören	to hear
anfangen	to begin	**auf**hören	to cease, stop
stehen	to stand		
aufstehen	to stand up; get out of bed		

similarly:

anrufen	to call up
aufmachen	to open
kennenlernen	to get to know, meet
mitkommen	to come along
zurückkommen	to come back

These prefixes are most frequently identical in form to prepositions like **an** and **auf,** but they can also derive from other parts of speech like **kennen** (to know) or **zurück** (back). In the infinitive the prefix is attached to the verb. This infinitive is the dictionary form of the verb: (**anfangen** will be found in the dictionary under *A*)

In the present tense and the imperative, the prefix is separated and placed in final position. It is the second part of the predicate:

		verb		*prefix*	
statement:	Ich	**stehe** morgen sehr früh		**auf.**	*I'm getting up very early tomorrow.*
information question:	Wann	**stehst** du		**auf?**	*When are you getting up?*
imperative:		**Stehen** Sie bitte		**auf!**	*Please get up.*
yes / no question:		**Steht** ihr denn bald		**auf?**	*Are you getting up soon?*

When a verb with separable prefix complements a modal verb, the separable prefix is again attached to the stem, i.e., the verb appears in its infinitive form.

	without modal				*with a modal*		
Er	**fängt**	morgen	**an.**	Er	**soll**	morgen	**anfangen.**
Ich	**lerne**	sie	**kennen.**	Ich	**möchte**	sie	**kennenlernen.**

- Separable prefixes will be indicated in the *Wortschatz* sections by a raised period between prefix and verb stem: **an·fangen.** This period is *not* used in German spelling.

- Separable prefixes are *always* stressed in pronunciation.

- There are also *inseparable* prefixes in German. They *never* separate from the verb stem. You can tell them from separable prefixes in the following ways:

  1. Inseparable prefixes are *not* stressed.
  2. Inseparable prefixes have no independent meaning of their own, while separable prefixes resemble in their form other parts of speech such as prepositions and adverbs.

The inseparable prefixes are: **be-, ent-, er-, ge-, ver-,** and **zer-.** Here are the verbs with inseparable prefixes you already know: **bedeuten, bekommen, beschreiben, besitzen, besprechen, besuchen, verdienen, verlassen** and **verstehen.**

Üben wir!

A. Substitute the new subjects you will hear.

> EXAMPLE: Er steht bald auf. (ich)
> Ich stehe bald auf.

1. *Wir* fangen sehr früh an. (du, Gabi, ihr, ich, er, die Studenten)
2. Heute abend lerne *ich* Frau Berger kennen. (wir, die Kinder, du, ihr, Michael)
3. *Sie* machen den Laden um sieben Uhr auf. (ich, meine Frau, wir, der Lehrling, ihr, du)
4. Wann hören *wir* denn auf? (ihr, du, die Musik, die Schüler)

B. Substitute the new verb you will hear.

1. Ich *fange* heute abend *an.* (aufhören, aufmachen, aufstehen, anrufen)
2. Wann *steht* Richard am Samstag *auf?* (aufhören, anfangen, aufmachen, zurückkommen)

C. Use the appropriate command for the person named.

> EXAMPLE: Stehen Sie bitte bald auf! (du)
> Steh bitte bald auf!

1. Kommen Sie doch mit! (ihr, du)
2. Hör doch bitte auf! (Sie, wir, ihr)
3. Fangen wir noch nicht an! (du, ihr, Sie)
4. Macht den Laden um sieben auf! (du, wir, Sie)
5. Rufen Sie bitte morgen an! (du, ihr)

Schweizer Holzschnitzer
(*wood carver*)

 D. Restate the sentence without the modal verb.

> EXAMPLE: Anton muß um sieben Uhr aufstehen.
> Anton steht um sieben Uhr auf.

1. Wir dürfen noch nicht anfangen.
2. Ich will früh aufstehen.
3. Er möchte heute Frau Huber kennenlernen.
4. Der Lehrling muß früh aufmachen.
5. Wann willst du morgen anrufen?
6. Wolf kann nicht aufhören.

E. Say that you cannot do what you are told to do.

> EXAMPLE: Fang am Mittwoch an!
> Ich kann nicht am Mittwoch anfangen.

1. Komm am Mittwoch zurück!
2. Mach den Laden auf!
3. Hör doch auf!
4. Ruf doch deine Mutter an!
5. Steh bitte morgen um 6 Uhr auf!
6. Komm doch mit!

F. Add the following elements one by one to these short sentences. Start by inserting them right after the verb.

> EXAMPLE: Du stehst auf. (morgen)
> Du stehst morgen auf. (um zehn Uhr)
> Du stehst morgen um zehn Uhr auf.

1. Frank kommt mit. (sicher)(am Donnerstag)
2. Du lernst meinen Freund kennen. (hoffentlich)(morgen)
3. Wir kommen zurück. (selbstverständlich)(sehr früh)
4. Greta fängt an. (schon) (am Donnerstag)

2 ♦ Dative Case

Indirect Object

The dative case is used for the indirect object of a verb, that is, the person or thing *for* whom an action is performed or *to* whom it is directed:

Ich kaufe **dir** das Moped.	*I'll buy the moped* **for you.**
Sag **dem Lehrer** guten Morgen!	*Say good morning* **to the teacher.**
Sie gibt **ihrer Tochter** das Geld.	*She's giving the money* **to her daughter.**

Indirect objects in English are shown either by their position in the sentence or by the use of a preposition:

> She's giving **her daughter** the money.
> or: She's giving the money **to her daughter.**

German does not use a preposition. The dative case alone signals the indirect object. When both objects are nouns, their usual order in German is indirect object, direct object:

	i. o.	*d. o.*	
Sie gibt	**ihrer Tochter**	**das Geld.**	*She gives her daughter the money.*
Ich kaufe	**meinem Sohn**	**ein Moped.**	*I'm buying my son a moped.*

In negative sentences, **nicht** follows both the indirect and the direct object, unless one of them is already negated by **kein.** The sentences above are negated like this:

> Sie gibt ihrer Tochter das Geld **nicht.**
> Ich kaufe meinem Sohn **kein** Moped.

Üben wir!

A. Identify the direct object and the indirect object in the following sentences:

1. We owe our friends a debt of gratitude.
2. Give me one good reason.
3. I'm buying my father a necktie.
4. Tell me what you think.
5. We're cooking spaghetti for the kids.
6. Write her a letter!
7. To whom did you say that?

Forms of the Dative Case

1. Dative of definite article and **ein**-words

	masc.	neut.	fem.	plural
nom.	der Vater	das Kind	die Mutter	die Leute
acc.	den Vater	das Kind	die Mutter	die Leute
dat.	**dem** Vater	**dem** Kind	**der** Mutter	**den** Leuten
	einem Vater	einem Kind	einer Mutter	keinen Leuten
	unserem Vater	ihrem Kind	eurer Mutter	meinen Leuten

■ All nouns add an **-n** in the dative plural except those already ending in **-n** (den Frauen) and those ending in **-s** (den Hotels).

2. Dative of Interrogative Pronoun: **wem**
   The dative form of the question word **wer** is **wem:**

Wem geben Sie das Geld?   *To whom are you giving the money?*

Üben wir!

A. Beate has some extra money. Use the cue you will hear to tell her whom to give it to.

> EXAMPLE: der Lehrer
> Gib es dem Lehrer.

1. der Automechaniker
2. die Lehrerin
3. das Kind

4. die Kinder
5. die Frauen
6. der Chef

B. Tell your friend whom you are buying a moped for.

> EXAMPLE: Wem kaufst du das Moped? (Mutter)
> Ich kaufe es meiner Mutter.

1. Bruder
2. Tante
3. Eltern

4. Freundin
5. Großvater
6. Kinder

C. Wie sagt man das auf deutsch?

1. I'm buying my sister a book.
2. Give my parents the money.
3. Describe the problem to the mechanic.
4. Write your mother a card.
5. Cook the food for your friends.
6. Show my friend the city.

Dative Personal Pronouns[1]

singular			plural		
nom.	acc.	**dat.**	nom.	acc.	**dat.**
ich	mich	**mir**	wir	uns	**uns**
du	dich	**dir**	ihr	euch	**euch**
er	ihn	**ihm**			
es	es	**ihm**	sie, Sie	sie, Sie	**ihnen, Ihnen**
sie	sie	**ihr**			

Üben wir!

A. You're buying a book. Your friend asks whom you're buying it for. Use the dative form of the pronoun in your answer.

> EXAMPLE: Wem kaufst du das Buch? (sie, singular)
> Ich kaufe **ihr** das Buch.

1. er
2. du
3. ihr
4. sie (plural)

5. ich
6. wir
7. sie (singular)

[1] Note that English pronouns do not distinguish between the direct object and the indirect object, whereas German pronouns (except **uns** and **euch**) do:

| I see *him*. | Ich sehe **ihn.** |
| I'm giving *him* the book. | Ich gebe **ihm** das Buch. |

B. People are asking you to do various things and you agree to do them. Use dative pronouns in your answer.

> EXAMPLE: Kannst du Christine das Buch geben?
> Ja, ich kann ihr das Buch geben.

1. Kannst du Georg ein Moped kaufen?
2. Kannst du den Kindern das Bild zeigen?
3. Kannst du Frau Klein dein Zimmer beschreiben?
4. Kannst du deiner Schwester das Geld schenken?
5. Kannst du uns Karten kaufen?
6. Kannst du meinem Freund etwas sagen?

3 ◆ Word Order

Sentences with Two Objects

Verbs like **geben, schenken, kaufen** and **zeigen** often have both a direct object in the accusative (usually a thing) and an indirect object in the dative (usually a person). The usual order of these objects is 1) indirect object, 2) direct object:

	i. o.	**d. o.**	
Ich schenke	**meiner Freundin**	**eine Uhr.**	*I'm giving my girlfriend a watch.*
Ich schenke	**ihr**	**eine Uhr.**	*I'm giving her a watch.*

When the direct object is a pronoun, however, the order *must* be 1) direct object, 2) indirect object:

	d. o.	**i. o.**	
Ich schenke	**sie**	**meiner Freundin.**	*I'm giving it to my girlfriend.*
Ich schenke	**sie**	**ihr.**	*I'm giving it to her.*

Üben wir!

A. Replace the *indirect* object with a pronoun.

> EXAMPLE: Schenkst du deiner Schwester ein Moped?
> Ja, ich schenke ihr ein Moped.

1. Kochst du den Kindern eine Suppe?
2. Schreibst du deinem Bruder eine Karte?
3. Machst du den Schülern das Fenster auf?
4. Kaufst du deiner Freundin einen Pulli?
5. Zeigst du den Amerikanern den See?

B. Now replace the *direct* object with a pronoun.

> EXAMPLE: Schenkst du deiner Schwester das Moped?
> Ja, ich schenke es meiner Schwester.

1. Zeigst du deinem Freund das Buch?
2. Kaufst du deinen Eltern diesen Wein?
3. Schreibst du deiner Freundin die Karte?
4. Gibst du deinem Bruder das Geld?
5. Machst du der Studentin die Tür auf?

C. Your neighbor tells you to do something and you comply. Replace all nouns with pronouns.

> EXAMPLE: Schenke deiner Mutter die Uhr!
> Gut, ich schenke sie ihr.

1. Kauf deiner Mutter diese Zeitungen!
2. Beschreib den Freunden deine Reise!
3. Gib deinem Vater das Geld!
4. Schenke mir deinen Bleistift!
5. Mach dem Kind das Fenster auf!

Diese Frauen kaufen in der Apotheke ein (Hamburg, BRD)

Pronoun Word Order

When they are not in first position, German personal pronouns are placed *immediately after the inflected verb*:

> Ich gebe **ihm** mein Buch.
> Ich gebe **es** meinem Bruder.

If more than one personal pronoun follows the verb, they come in this order: *nominative, accusative, dative.*

		nom.	*acc.*	*dat.*	
Ich	gebe		**es**	**ihm**	heute.
Heute	gebe	**ich**	**es**	**ihm.**	

Üben wir!

A. Your teacher asks when you're going to do certain things. Say that you'll do them tomorrow. Use pronouns in your answer.

> EXAMPLE: Wann gibst du Hermann das Buch?
> Ich gebe es ihm morgen.

1. Wann kaufst du deiner Mutter den Mantel?
2. Wann kochst du den Kindern das Essen?
3. Wann zeigst du Frau Klein die Altstadt?
4. Wann schreibst du deiner Schwester eine Karte?
5. Wann machst du dem Chef das Büro auf?
6. Wann beschreibst du uns dein Zimmer?

Alle reden vom Wetter.

Wir nicht.

The following prepositions always have a dative object:

aus	out of from (native country or region)	Sie geht **aus dem** Zimmer. Ich komme **aus** Amerika.	*She's leaving the room.* *I'm from America.*
außer	except for besides, in addition to	**Außer ihm** sind wir alle hier. **Außer ihm** wohnt auch sein Bruder hier.	*We're all here except for him.* *Besides him, his brother lives here too.*
bei	in the home of near at	Ich wohne **bei meiner** Tante. Das Kind spielt **beim** Fenster. Er ist **bei der** Arbeit.	*I live at my aunt's.* *The child is playing near the window.* *He's at work.*
mit	with	Ich will **mit den** Händen arbeiten.	*I want to work with my hands.*
nach	after to (with country and city names)	**Nach** der Deutschstunde bin ich manchmal müde. Wir fahren im August **nach** Österreich.	*After German class I'm sometimes tired.* *We're going to Austria in August.*
seit	since (temporal)	**Seit dem** Tag mag ich ihn nicht mehr.[1]	*Since that day I haven't liked him.*
von	from of by	Das Buch habe ich **von meiner** Mutter. Er ist ein Freund **von mir.** Das Buch ist **von** Hermann Hesse.	*I have that book from my mother.* *He is a friend of mine.* *The book is by Hermann Hesse.*
zu	to (with people and some locations)	Ich gehe **zur** Schule und dann **zu meinen** Freunden.	*I'm going to school and then to my friends' house.*

■ The following contractions of prepositions with the dative of the definitive article are common:

bei dem → **beim**	Das Kind spielt **beim** Fenster
von dem → **vom**	Ich komme gerade **vom** Chef.
zu dem → **zum**	Ich muß schnell **zum** Professor.
zu der → **zur**	Wie kommt man **zur** Stadt?

[1] Notice that for an action or situation beginning in the past and continuing in the present, English uses perfect tense (**haven't liked**) while German uses present (**mag . . . nicht**). See pp. 288–289.

■ You have learned **bis** (until, by) as a preposition followed by accusative case and used in time phrases:

> Wir bleiben **bis** Dienstag.   *We're staying until Tuesday.*
>
> Ich muß es **bis** morgen lesen.   *I've got to read it by tomorrow.*

However, **bis** is often used in combination with the dative preposition **zu**. **Bis zu** means "up until" or "as far as." The **zu** governs the case of the following noun, which must be in the dative:

> Der Bus fährt **bis zu meiner** Straße.   *The bus goes as far as my street.*

Üben wir!

A. Substitute the new prepositional objects you will hear. Put them in the dative case.

> EXAMPLE: Wir sehen ihn nach *der Schule.* (das Essen)
> Wir sehen ihn nach *dem Essen.*

1. Karla kommt gerade aus *dem Laden.* (das Haus, die Schule, das Büro, das Zimmer)
2. Gehen wir doch mit *den Kindern.* (die Tante, meine Schwester, deine Freunde, die Studenten)
3. Er hat das Geld von *seiner Freundin.* (sein Freund, sein Vater, seine Eltern, meine Mutter)
4. Seit *dem Tag* arbeite ich hier. (das Abitur, September, der Herbst)
5. Ich wohne bei *meinem Großvater.* (meine Tante, seine Familie, ihr Onkel, eure Freunde)
6. Außer *Ihnen* wollen alle schon nach Hause. (er, ich, mein Bruder, Ihre Freunde)
7. Was machst du nach *dem Essen?* (die Schule, die Arbeit, die Deutschstunde)
8. Gehen wir heute abend zu *Rolf!* (deine Familie, unser Lehrer, Frau König, die Studentinnen, unsere Freunde)

B. Ask your classmates whom they live with. Use the following model:

> EXAMPLE: Teacher: Eltern
> Student A: Wohnst du bei deinen Eltern?
> Student B: Ja, ich wohne bei meinen Eltern.
>   *or*:   Nein, ich wohne nicht bei meinen Eltern.

1. Tante
2. Familie
3. Bruder
4. Großeltern

5. Freundin
6. Freund
7. Vater

C. Now ask your classmates whom they're going to see.

> EXAMPLE: Teacher: Freund
> Student A: Gehst du zu deinem Freund?
> Student B: Ja, ich gehe zu meinem Freund.
> *or:* Nein, ich gehe nicht zu meinem Freund.

1. Professor
2. Professorin
3. Großmutter

4. Chef
5. Freunde
6. Schwester

5 ♦ *Der*-Words

The **der**-words are a group of words that modify nouns and share a common set of endings. The most common **der**-words are:

der, das, die	the; that (when stressed)
dieser, -es, -e	this, these
jeder, -es, -e	each, every (singular only, plural: **alle**)
~~**solcher, -es, -e**~~	~~such~~ solche (plural only)
welcher, -es, -e	which (interrogative)

We use **dieser** to show the endings of the **der**-words:[1]

	masc.		*neut.*		*fem.*		*plural*	
nom.	dieser	Stuhl	dieses	Buch	diese	Uhr	diese	Bücher
acc.	diesen	Stuhl	dieses	Buch	diese	Uhr	diese	Bücher
dat.	diesem	Stuhl	diesem	Buch	dieser	Uhr	diesen	Büchern

der-*words versus* ein-*words*

Note the cases (boxed in the table above) where the **der**-words have endings while the **ein**-words[2] lack them:

Masc sing. nom.:	Ein Student wohnt hier.
	Welch**er** Student wohnt hier?
Neuter sing. nom.:	Mein Kind lernt Englisch.
	Dies**es** Kind lernt Englisch.
Neuter sing. acc.:	Kennst du sein Buch?
	Kennst du dies**es** Buch?

---

[1] The endings of the definite article, **der, das, die,** are slightly irregular and we therefore do not use it as a model for the full declension.
[2] For *ein*-words, see p. 49.

„Die Arbeit ist schwer, aber gut bezahlt." (siehe Seite 143)

Üben wir!

A. Follow the example.

EXAMPLE: Das Bier ist kalt.
Welches Bier ist kalt?
Dieses Bier ist kalt.

1. Die Hausaufgaben sind interessant.
2. Das Hemd ist viel besser.
3. Die Turnschuhe sind neu.
4. Der Lehrling heißt Martin.
5. Die Gruppe fährt nach Österreich.
6. Das Problem ist schwierig.
7. Der Pulli ist häßlich.
8. Die Kleider sind alt.

B. Expand the sentence you will hear.

EXAMPLE: Dieser Berg ist steil.
Dieser Berg ist steil, aber nicht **jeder** Berg ist steil.

1. Diese Stadt ist langweilig.
2. Dieses Hemd ist schön.
3. Dieser Tourist kann Deutsch.
4. Diese Arbeit macht mich müde.
5. Dieser Laden macht früh auf.
6. Diese Deutschstunde ist interessant.
7. Dieses Semester fängt am Montag an.

6 ♦ Omission of Article with Professions, Nationalities, Religions, etc.

When stating affiliation with a group (political, religious, professional, national), German omits the **ein** before the noun:

Mein Sohn möchte Auto- mechaniker werden.	*My son wants to become **an** auto mechanic.*
Frau Gerhard ist Lehrerin.	*Mrs. Gerhard is **a** teacher.*
Hugh ist Amerikaner.	*Hugh is **an** American.*
Ich bin Katholik.	*I am **a** Catholic.*

To negate such sentences, use either **nicht** or **kein.**

Rolf, bist du Student?	Nein, ich bin **nicht** Student.
	Nein, ich bin **kein** Student.

Üben wir!

A. Ask your neighbors if they are the following things.

EXAMPLE: Teacher: Amerikaner(in)
           Student A: Sind Sie Amerikaner(in)?
           Student B: Nein, ich bin kein(e) Amerikaner(in).
              or: Nein, ich bin nicht Amerikaner(in).

1. Lehrling
2. Student(in)
3. Amerikaner(in)

4. Automechaniker(in)
5. Lehrer(in)
6. Professor(in)

7 ♦ Expanding Your Vocabulary

Agent Nouns Ending in -er and -erin.

Both English and German add the suffix **-er** to a verb stem to form a noun denoting a personal agent (someone who performs the action):

work	→ the worker	read	→ the reader
arbeiten	→ **der Arbeiter**	lesen	→ **der Leser**

In German, however, the suffix **-er** labels a man. The suffix **-erin** labels a woman:

die Arbeiterin	the (female) worker
die Leserin	the (female) reader

To form the plural of these nouns, add -**nen:**

die Arbeiterin	**die Arbeiterinnen**

The masculine plural is *always* identical to its singular except in the dative:

der Arbeiter	**die Arbeiter**	dative plural: den Arbeitern

Sometimes the verb stem is umlauted in the noun. These must be learned for each individual noun:

anfangen → **der Anfänger**	beginner
tragen → **der Briefträger**	mailman (*literally:* letter carrier)
handeln (to trade, deal) → **der Händler**	tradesman, dealer
der Buchhändler	book seller

Üben wir!

A. Say what the following people do.

EXAMPLE: Mein Onkel ist Weintrinker.
Er trinkt Wein.

1. Herr Kropf ist Trinker.
2. Frau Baumann ist Zeitungsleserin.
3. Wir sind alle Biertrinker.
4. Albert ist bei uns Anfänger.
5. Martin ist Frühaufsteher.

Leicht zu merken

die **Industrie, -n**	Indus*trie*
(das) **Kanada**	
der **Korrespondent, -en**	Korrespon*dent*
kritisch	
die **Universität, -en**	Universi*tät*

(**Noten** = *grades*   **Straßenkehrer** = *street sweeper*)

Wortschatz 2

Verben

aus·sehen (sieht aus) to appear, look (like)
Du siehst schrecklich aus. You look terrible.
berichten to report
ein·kaufen to shop for; go shopping
leben to live, be alive
schließen to close
spazieren·gehen to go for a walk
vergessen (vergißt) to forget
verkaufen to sell
vorbei·kommen to come by, drop by
zu·machen to close

Substantive

der **Arbeiter, -** worker
der **Fußball** soccer; soccer ball
Fußball spielen to play soccer

der **Journalist, -en** journalist
der **Lohn, ⁝e** wages
der **Roman, -e** novel

das **Bild, -er** picture; image
das **Geschäft, -e** business; store
(das) **Jugoslawien** Yugoslavia
das **Mittagessen** midday meal (*traditionally the main meal*), lunch
das **Schaufenster, -** store window
das **Wochenende, -n** weekend
am Wochenende on the weekend
das **Wörterbuch, ⁝er** dictionary

die **Buchhandlung, -en** bookstore
die **Fabrik, -en** factory

die **Muttersprache, -n** native language
die **Postkarte, -n** postcard
die **Stimme, -n** voice
die **Woche, -n** week

die **Lebensmittel** (*pl.*) groceries
die **USA** (*pl.*) the USA

Andere Vokabeln

abends (in the) evenings
besonders especially
bunt colorful
meistens mostly, usually
schwer heavy; hard, difficult

Nützliche Ausdrücke

jeden Tag (*acc.*) every day
Urlaub machen to take a vacation (*from a job*)

Gegensätze

schwer ≠ leicht heavy; difficult ≠ light (in weight); easy

**Die Wälder sterben—
nach den Wäldern
sterben die Menschen.**

Drei Deutsche
bei der Arbeit

Man sagt über die Deutschen, sie „leben um zu° arbeiten.''   um zu° = in order to
Stimmt das heute noch? Unsere Beispiele zeigen ein anderes
Bild.

Christine Sauermann, Buchhändlerin

Christine Sauermann ist 35 Jahre alt, geschieden° und   divorced
hat einen jungen Sohn. Sie besitzt seit fünf Jahren eine
Buchhandlung in der Altstadt°¹ von Tübingen.² Mit den   old city
5   neuesten° Romanen sieht ihr Schaufenster immer bunt und   newest
interessant aus.

Das Geschäft geht gut, denn° viele Touristen gehen   because
durch die Altstadt spazieren, und Studenten kommen auch
jeden Tag vorbei. Den Studenten verkauft sie Wörterbücher
10   und Nachschlagewerke,° aber die Touristen kaufen mei-   reference works
stens Reiseführer° und Postkarten von der Stadt.   guide books

In der Buchhandlung

Sie macht um 9 Uhr auf und um 6 Uhr abends zu. Von 1 Uhr bis 3 Uhr macht sie Mittagspause.° Sie schließt den Laden, geht nach Hause, kocht ihrem Sohn das Mittagessen und kauft dann noch Lebensmittel ein.

midday break[3]

Jörg Krolow (19 Jahre alt), Fabrikarbeiter

Jörg Krolow arbeitet seit einem Jahr als Mechaniker in einer Autofabrik in Dortmund.[4] Die Arbeit ist schwer, aber gut bezahlt.° Nach der Arbeit trinkt er oft ein Bier mit Freunden zusammen, und am Wochenende spielt er mit ihnen Fußball.

paid

Wie° alle deutschen Arbeiter in der Schwerindustrie ist Jörg in einer Gewerkschaft.° Sie sichert° jedem Mitglied° einen guten Lohn und gibt den Arbeitern eine Stimme im Aufsichtsrat.°

(here) like
trade union / ensures / member

board of directors[5]
wie . . . Deutschen = *like most Germans*

Jörg hat wie die meisten Deutschen° fünf Wochen Urlaub im Jahr. Dieses Jahr will er im Sommer mit seiner Freundin nach Jugoslawien fahren. Im Oktober macht er noch einmal Urlaub. Wahrscheinlich besucht er dann Freunde in Süddeutschland.

Klaus Ostendorff (53 Jahre alt), Journalist

Klaus Ostendorff ist Korrespondent bei der Deutschen Presseagentur° in Nordamerika. Seit fünfzehn Jahren berichtet er über die USA und Kanada für Zeitungen und Zeitschriften° in Westdeutschland. Seine Artikel geben den Lesern ein kritisches Bild von Amerika.

wire service

magazines

Zur Zeit° schreibt Ostendorff einen Artikel über das Waldsterben° in Nordamerika. Dieses Problem ist in Deutschland besonders aktuell,° denn der saure° Regen bedroht° auch die Wälder in Europa.

zur Zeit = *currently*
death of the forests
topical / acid
threatens

Ostendorff lebt mit seiner Frau Martine und den drei Kindern in Washington. Die Kinder sollen ihre Muttersprache nicht vergessen, und darum spricht die Familie meistens Deutsch zu Hause.

---

[1] Most German cities and towns have an *Altstadt* ("old city") in their centers. This is the original core of the city, which may date from the Middle Ages. Many of these old city centers have been renovated and closed to traffic.

[2] A famous university town on the Neckar River in Baden-Württemberg about twenty miles south of Stuttgart. The university was founded in 1477.

[3] Many small shops and businesses close from one to two-thirty or three p.m. This is less true nowadays in large cities.

[4] An industrial city in the Ruhr area in the state of Nordrhein-Westfalen.

[5] West German workers in large companies elect up to 50% of the board of directors. This has meant a high degree of cooperation between management and labor and has resulted in fewer strikes than in other industrial nations.

Fragen zum Lesestück

1. Beschreiben Sie Christine Sauermanns Geschäft.
2. Wie geht das Geschäft?
3. Wann macht sie das Geschäft auf und wann macht sie es zu?
4. Was macht sie jeden Tag nach 1 Uhr?

5. Welchen Beruf hat Jörg Krolow?
6. Wie ist seine Arbeit?
7. Wo macht er dieses Jahr Urlaub?
8. Warum fährt er nach Süddeutschland?

9. Seit wann ist Herr Ostendorff in den USA?
10. Wer liest seine Artikel?
11. Was wissen Sie über seine Familie?
12. Warum spricht die Familie Ostendorff meistens Deutsch zusammen?

Vom Lesen zum Sprechen

Berufe

der **Beruf, -e**	profession, vocation
der **Arzt, ̈e** / die **Ärztin, -nen**	doctor
der **Elektrotechniker, -** / die **Elektrotechnikerin, -nen**	electrician or electrical engineer
der **Geschäftsmann**, die **Geschäftsleute**	businessman
die **Geschäftsfrau, -en**	businesswoman
der **Ingenieur, -e** / die **Ingenieurin, -nen**	engineer
der **Landwirt, -e** / die **Landwirtin, -nen**	farmer
der **Programmierer, -** / die **Programmiererin, -nen**	programmer
der **Rechtsanwalt, ̈e** / die **Rechtsanwältin, -nen**	lawyer
der **Schriftsteller, -** / die **Schriftstellerin, -nen**	writer, author
der **Sekretär, -e** / die **Sekretärin, -nen**	secretary

You already know:

die **Hausfrau, -en**
der **Lehrer, -** / die **Lehrerin, -nen**
der **Mechaniker, -** / die **Mechanikerin, -nen**
der **Professor, -en** / die **Professorin, -nen**
der **Journalist, -en, -en** / die **Journalistin, -nen**

Was sind Sie von Beruf?	What is your profession?

A. Here are some statements about where people work and what they do. Can you guess their professions?

1. Herr Schneider ist Chef in einer Fabrik.
2. Gabriele besitzt ein Kleidergeschäft.
3. Rolf schreibt für eine Zeitung.
4. Frau Waldstein arbeitet an der Universität.
5. Jörg Schölz arbeitet mit Schülern.
6. Hanna Wendling arbeitet im Computerzentrum.
7. Johann repariert Autos.
8. Frau Overholzer ist Mutter von vier Kindern und macht die Hausarbeit.

B. Guided Conversation. Ask each other what you would like to do after college.

> EXAMPLE: A. Was möchtest du werden?
> B. Ich möchte Elektrotechniker werden, und du?
> A. Ich möchte Lehrerin werden.

C. Now go into more detail. One person asks as many questions as possible about the career plans of the other, who answers. Then switch roles.

> EXAMPLE: Warum willst du Lehrer werden?
> Verdient ein Lehrer viel oder wenig?
> Sind deine Eltern auch Lehrer?
> usw.

Mündliche Übungen

A. Persönliche Fragen.

1. Arbeiten Sie gern mit Ihren Händen?
2. Kauft Ihnen Ihr Vater ein Moped?
3. Stehen Sie immer früh auf?
4. Gehen Sie gern durch die Stadt spazieren?
5. Lesen Sie jeden Tag eine Zeitung? Welche?
6. Spielen Sie Fußball?

B. You are a manager in a firm. The boss tells you what should happen and you must give the direct orders, using **bitte.**

> EXAMPLE: Boss: Herr Schneider soll mit diesem Unsinn aufhören!
> you: Herr Schneider, hören Sie bitte mit diesem Unsinn auf!

1. Frau Blumenstiel soll um acht Uhr den Laden aufmachen.
2. Herr Pohl soll zurückkommen.

3. Frau Fischer kann morgen anfangen.

4. Herr Hinrich soll um sieben zumachen.

5. Frau von Polenz soll Mittwoch vorbeikommen.

6. Johannes soll Frau Professor Jäger anrufen.

C. Contradict the statement you will hear.

> EXAMPLE: Dieser Wagen ist *neu*.
> Nein, dieser Wagen ist alt.

1. Die Kinder kommen heute *früh* nach Hause.
2. Hamburg liegt *im Süden.*
3. Jetzt *fängt* der Unsinn *an.*
4. Hans *schließt* den Laden.
5. Der Chef möchte *etwas* sagen.
6. Wir essen *viel.*

D. Der Arbeitstag. (Books open) You have started a new job. Call a friend and describe your day. (Use the cues to help you.)

1. aufstehen / meistens / um sechs Uhr
2. Arbeit / anfangen / sieben Uhr
3. ich / arbeiten / mit / ein Freund / zusammen
4. Fabrik / zumachen / um vier Uhr
5. ich / gehen / nach / Arbeit / Bier trinken
6. am Abend / ich / sein / oft / müde

E. Answer the questions below using words from the list provided.

das Geld	eine Postkarte
die Reise nach Österreich	das Mittagessen
das Bilderbuch	der Wagen
das Haus	

> EXAMPLE: Was willst du deinem Freund zeigen?
> Ich will ich ihm meinen Wagen zeigen.

1. Was willst du Susanne schenken?
2. Was schreibst du deinem Großvater?
3. Was kannst du mir geben?
4. Was willst du uns morgen kochen?
5. Was möchtest du den Kindern zeigen?
6. Was wollen Sie uns beschreiben?

Schriftliche Übungen

F. Complete the sentences with the prepositional phrase cued in English.

1. In Freiburg wohne ich (at my aunt's).
2. Besuchen Sie mich (after school).
3. Ich bin jetzt fertig. Gehen wir also (to your grandparents').
4. Herbert ist ein Freund (of my sister's).
5. (Except for the girls) sind wir alle da.
6. Kannst du nicht (with me) bleiben?
7. (Since the seminar) bin ich immer noch müde.
8. Meine Freundin geht schnell (out of the shop).
9. Könnt ihr denn nicht (until the weekend) warten?
10. Bleibt ihr im Sommer hier? Nein, wir wollen (to Stuttgart).

G. Essay: Was ist in Deutschland anders?

You have read about the lives of working Germans. Write a paragraph or two in German about their schedules and routines and how they differ from workers in North America.

H. Wie sagt man das auf deutsch?

1. When are you getting up tomorrow?
2. At six. I have to leave the house early.
3. Why? What are you doing?
4. I'm driving my girl friend to Munich.

5. What are you doing this weekend?
6. I don't know yet. Why do you ask?
7. Can you come by? A student from Germany is visiting me.
8. Gladly. I'd like to meet him.
9. Can you come along after the seminar?
10. Of course. We can show him the city.
11. So long, until then.

Arbeit Mensch Maschine

Der Weg in die Industriegesellschaft
Oberösterreichische
Landesausstellung
30. April bis 2. November 1987
Steyr, Wehrgraben

Almanach

Karrieren beginnen hier.

Here is a selection of help-wanted ads (**Stellenangebote**) from the West German press. They range from unskilled labor (**Zeitungsträger/in**) to highly-specialized professionals (**Statistiker/in**). Note the amount of English business and computer jargon in the technical fields.

148

Stellen-Angebote

An der Universität

Dialoge
In der Mensa ◆ Im Studentenwohnheim ◆ An der Uni in Tübingen

Wortschatz 1

Grammatik
1. The Perfect Tense
   Formation ◆ Conjugation with **haben** ◆ Past Participle of Weak Verbs ◆ Past Participle of Strong Verbs ◆ Conjugation with **sein** ◆ Past Participles of Separable-Prefix Verbs ◆ Past Participles of Verbs with Inseparable Prefixes ◆ Use of Perfect Tense
2. The Question Words **wohin** and **woher**
3. Two-Way Prepositions
4. Masculine N-Nouns
5. Expanding Your Vocabulary Verbal Nouns ◆ The Prefix **Haupt-** ◆ Leicht zu merken

Wortschatz 2
A Note on Letter Writing

Lesestück
Ein Brief aus Freiburg

Vom Lesen zum Sprechen
Das Studium (University Studies)

Almanach
Mark Twain Visits Heidelberg

Dialoge

In der Mensa

STEFAN: Hat Karin endlich ein Zimmer gefunden?

MICHAEL: Noch nicht. Gestern hat sie mir gesagt, sie hat keinen Platz mehr im Studentenwohnheim bekommen.

STEFAN: Will sie jetzt in eine Wohngemeinschaft?[1]

MICHAEL: Nein, sie will allein wohnen, wenn möglich.

Im Studentenwohnheim

CLARA: Wo bist du denn gewesen?

EVA: In der Buchhandlung.

CLARA: Hast du mir ein Vorlesungsverzeichnis mitgebracht?

EVA: Ja, ich habe es auf deinen Schreibtisch gelegt.

CLARA: Ach ja, hier liegt es unter der Zeitung. Wieviel hat es denn gekostet?[2]

EVA: Vier Mark fünfzig.

An der Uni in Tübingen

TOBIAS: Ich kenne jetzt fast jeden Studenten im Studentenwohnheim.

HEINZ: Ich habe Carl noch nicht kennengelernt. Woher kommt er denn?

TOBIAS: Ich glaube, er kommt aus Kanada.

HEINZ: Wirklich? Aber er kann sehr gut Deutsch.

TOBIAS: Ja, er hat schon zwei Semester in Konstanz studiert.

[1] Because dormitory space is scarce in Germany, many students share houses or apartments in communal living arrangements called *Wohngemeinschaften* (abbreviated *WG*).

[2] At German universities students buy their course catalogues. These go on sale at the start of each semester at local bookstores.

Wortschatz 1

Verben

bringen, hat gebracht[1] to bring
glauben to believe; think
kosten to cost
legen to lay, put down
mit·bringen, hat mitgebracht[1] to bring along, take along

Substantive

der **Mensch, -en** person, human being
der **Platz, ⁓** place; space; city square
der **Schreibtisch, -e** desk

(das) **Kanada** Canada
das **Studentenwohnheim, -e** student dormitory
das **Vorlesungsverzeichnis, -se** university catalogue, list of lectures and courses

die **Deutsche Mark (DM)** the German Mark
DM 4,50 (spoken: **vier Mark fünfzig**) four Marks fifty
die **Universität, -en** university
die **Uni, -s** (colloq.) university
an der Uni(versität) at the university
die **Vorlesung, -en** university lecture
die **Wohngemeinschaft, -en** communal living group
die **WG, -s = Wohngemeinschaft**

Andere Vokabeln

gestern yesterday
möglich possible
unter under, beneath; among
wirklich real; really
woher from where

Gegensätze

möglich ≠ unmöglich	possible ≠ impossible
woher ≠ wohin	from where ≠ to where

[1] For an explanation of this form, see p. 182.

Neue Kombinationen

A. Replace the last word in each sentence with the new word you will hear.

1. Das hat sie gestern *gesagt.* (gesehen, gelesen, gehabt, gesucht)
2. Mein Freund hat dort *studiert.* (gewohnt, gewartet, gearbeitet, gespielt)
3. Hast du es schon *gefunden*? (gehört, gemacht, getrunken)
4. Ich bin gestern nach München *gekommen.* (gefahren, geflogen, gegangen)

B. Your teacher tells you what he or she has done. Respond that you would like to do the same.

> EXAMPLE: Ich habe in Berlin gewohnt.
> Ich möchte auch in Berlin wohnen.

1. Ich habe Deutsch gelernt.
2. Ich habe in Konstanz studiert.
3. Ich habe Professor Brandt kennengelernt.
4. Wir haben Karten gespielt.

C. Ask each other where various people come from. Answer with a city or country you know.

> EXAMPLE: Teacher: die Studenten?
> Student A: Woher kommen die Studenten?
> Student B: Sie kommen aus Kanada.

1. euer Lehrer / eure Lehrerin?   3. der Journalist / die Journalistin?
2. die Arbeiter?   4. deine Mutter?

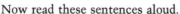 **Übung zur Aussprache**

Remember that when **b, d** and **g** come at the end of a word or syllable, or before **s** or **t,** they are pronounced unvoiced as (**p**), (**t**) and (**k**)—(see Introduction, pp. 7–8). Practice these sounds by pronouncing these pairs of words.

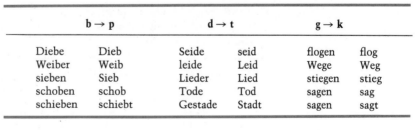

b → p		d → t		g → k	
Diebe	Dieb	Seide	seid	flogen	flog
Weiber	Weib	leide	Leid	Wege	Weg
sieben	Sieb	Lieder	Lied	stiegen	stieg
schoben	schob	Tode	Tod	sagen	sag
schieben	schiebt	Gestade	Stadt	sagen	sagt

Now read these sentences aloud.

1. Wann sei**d** ihr en**d**lich gefahren?
2. Im Herb**st**, un**d** ihr?
3. Wir sin**d** im Winter gefahren, wir un**d** unsere Freunde.
4. Was hat dein Freun**d** gesagt?
5. Er fragt, o**b** ihr das Kin**d** gesehen ha**bt**.
6. Sag ihm, wir haben es leider nicht gesehen.

Grammatik

1 ◆ The Perfect Tense

Formation

The perfect tense is used to refer to an action that happened in the past. It is a compound tense, that is, it consists of a conjugated auxiliary or "helping" verb, and a form of the main verb called a "past participle." The participle is the second part of the predicate and is in final position. Past participles in German usually begin with the prefix **ge-**.

	auxiliary		*past participle*	
Sie	**hat**	das Buch	**gekauft.**	*She has bought the book.*
				or: *She bought the book.*

Conjugation with haben

Most German verbs use **haben** as their auxiliary verb. Here is a sample conjugation:

	aux.		*past participle*	
Ich	**habe**	es	**gekauft.**	*I bought it.*
Du	**hast**	es	**gekauft.**	*You bought it.*
Sie	**hat**	es	**gekauft.**	*She bought it.*
Wir	**haben**	es	**gekauft.**	*We bought it.*
Ihr	**habt**	es	**gekauft.**	*You bought it.*
Sie	**haben**	es	**gekauft.**	*They bought it.*

Past Participle of Weak Verbs

There are two basic classes of verbs in German: the weak verbs and the strong verbs. They are distinguished by the way they form their past participle.

The weak verbs form their past participle by adding the unstressed prefix **ge-** and the ending **-t** or **-et**[1] to the verb stem. Here are some examples:

infinitive	*stem*	*auxiliary and past participle*
arbeiten	arbeit-	hat gearbeitet
kaufen	kauf-	hat gekauft
kosten	kost-	hat gekostet
legen	leg-	hat gelegt
meinen	mein-	hat gemeint

■ Verbs ending in **-ieren** do *not* add the prefix **ge-** in the past participle:

studieren → studier- → hat **studiert**
Er hat in Freiburg **studiert**.   *He studied in Freiburg.*

---

[1] Stems ending in **-d** or **-t** add **-et**.

Weak verbs with inseparable (unstressed) prefixes also do *not* add the prefix **ge-** in the past participle:

> berichten → bericht- → hat **berichtet**
> Sie hat uns über Amerika **berichtet.**   *She reported to us about America.*

 Üben wir!

A. Restate the sentences with the new subjects provided.

1. *Ich* habe gestern einen Schreibtisch gekauft.
   (Clara, wir, du, ihr, meine Freunde, Stefan, ich)
2. *Eva* hat zwei Jahre in Freiburg studiert.
   (die Amerikaner, du, ich, wir, Michael, ihr)
3. *Tobias* hat das Buch auf den Tisch gelegt.
   (ich, ihr, Sie, du, Anna, wir)
4. *Meine Freundin* hat über Deutschland berichtet.
   (du, meine Eltern, ihr, Jörg)
5. *Franz* hat gestern gearbeitet.
   (ich, du, die Studenten, Eva, wir, ihr)

Past Participle of Strong Verbs

The strong verbs form their past participle by adding the prefix **ge-** and the suffix **-n** or **-en** to the verb stem. In addition, many strong verbs change their stem vowel and occasionally some consonants in the stem. For this reason, the past participle of each strong verb must be memorized.[1] Here are some examples:

infinitive	*auxiliary and past participle*
geben	**hat gegeben**
sehen	**hat gesehen**
stehen	**hat gestanden**
trinken	**hat getrunken**
tun	**hat getan**

 Üben wir!

A. Restate the sentences with the new subjects provided.

1. *Ich* habe ihnen Geld gegeben.
   (Richard, wir, ihr, du, diese Leute)
2. *Barbara* hat dort gestanden.
   (ich, der Lehrer, wir, ihr, du, diese Studenten)
3. *Ich* habe das Studentenwohnheim noch nicht gesehen.
   (er, wir, meine Freunde, ihr, du, Tobias)
4. Abends haben *wir* immer Wein getrunken.
   (er, ich, ihr, die Arbeiter, du, Helga)
5. Was habt *ihr* gestern getan?
   (du, Sie, Renate, Konrad, wir, ich, die Frauen)

---

[1] From now on, the past participle of each new strong verb will be given in the **Wortschatz** following the infinitive (and stem-vowel change, when applicable).

Conjugation with sein

Some German verbs use **sein** rather than **haben** as their auxiliary verb in the perfect tense:

Herr Hauser **ist** nach Wien **geflogen.**   *Mr. Hauser flew to Vienna.*

These verbs fulfill two conditions:

1. They are intransitive (do not take a direct object).
2. They indicate change of location or condition.

There are two common verbs that are exceptions to the rule: they do not show motion or change of condition but take **sein** in the perfect nevertheless: **sein** (to be) and **bleiben** (to stay, remain).

Verbs with **sein** as auxiliary may be either weak or strong. The ones you already know are all strong except for **wandern.** Here are some of them:

infinitive	auxiliary and past participle	shows
fliegen	**ist geflogen**	change of location
gehen	**ist gegangen**	change of location
wandern	**ist gewandert**	change of location
werden	**ist geworden**	change of condition
bleiben	**ist geblieben** ⎱	
sein	**ist gewesen** ⎰	(exceptions)

Üben wir!

A. Restate the sentences with the new subjects provided.

1. *Wir* sind gestern nach Berlin geflogen.
   (diese Herren, Luise, ich, du, Rolf, ihr)
2. Wann bist *du* endlich nach Hause gegangen?
   (deine Freunde, er, ihr, wir, ich)

Nach dem Seminar: „Wohin geht ihr denn essen?" (Uni in Frankfurt/M.)

3. *Er* ist in Österreich gewandert.
   (wir, ihr, ich, meine Schwester, du, die Kinder)
4. *Rolf* ist gerade einundzwanzig geworden.
   (ich, diese Studentinnen, wir, ihr, du)
5. Wo bist *du* denn gestern gewesen? (ihr, Sie, er, ich, wir)
6. Wie lange ist *Jutta* geblieben? (du, wir, die Schüler, ich, ihr)

The following table contains all the strong verbs with which you are already familiar.[1] Review your knowledge of the infinitives and stem-vowel changes in the present tense (the verbs that change their stem vowels in the **du-** and **er-** form are *always* strong verbs), and memorize the past participles.

infinitive	present-tense stem-vowel change	auxiliary + past participle	English
anfangen	fängt an	hat **angefangen**	to begin
anrufen		hat **angerufen**	to call up
besitzen		hat **besessen**	to possess
bleiben		*ist* **geblieben**	to stay
essen	ißt	hat **gegessen**	to eat
fahren	fährt	*ist* **gefahren**	to travel; drive
finden		hat **gefunden**	to find
fliegen		*ist* **geflogen**	to fly
geben	gibt	hat **gegeben**	to give
gehen		*ist* **gegangen**	to go; walk
halten	hält	hat **gehalten**	to hold; stop
heißen		hat **geheißen**	to be called
kommen		*ist* **gekommen**	to come
laufen	läuft	*ist* **gelaufen**	to run
lesen	liest	hat **gelesen**	to read
liegen		hat **gelegen**	to lie
nehmen	nimmt	hat **genommen**	to take
scheinen		hat **geschienen**	to shine; seem
schlafen	schläft	hat **geschlafen**	to sleep
schließen		hat **geschlossen**	to close
schreiben		hat **geschrieben**	to write
schwimmen		*ist* **geschwommen**	to swim
sehen	sieht	hat **gesehen**	to see
sein	ist	*ist* **gewesen**	to be
singen		hat **gesungen**	to sing
sprechen	spricht	hat **gesprochen**	to speak
stehen		hat **gestanden**	to stand
tragen	trägt	hat **getragen**	to carry; wear
trinken		hat **getrunken**	to drink
tun		hat **getan**	to do
vergessen	vergißt	hat **vergessen**	to forget
verlassen	verläßt	hat **verlassen**	to leave (a person or place)
werden	wird	*ist* **geworden**	to become

[1] Except for **anfangen, anrufen, besitzen,** and **vergessen,** this list includes only the basic verb (e.g. **stehen,** but not **aufstehen** or **verstehen**). See pp. 158–159 below for formation of past participles of verbs with separable and inseparable prefixes.

A. Restate the following sentences in the perfect.

> EXAMPLE: Emma beschreibt mir die Stadt.
> Emma hat mir die Stadt beschrieben.

1. Leider scheint die Sonne nicht oft.
2. Abends trage ich einen Pulli.
3. Das Kind heißt Daniel.
4. Die Zeitung liegt nicht da.
5. Findest du die Vorlesungen gut?
6. Fahrt ihr im Sommer nach Österreich?
7. Er singt laut.
8. Vater nimmt heute den Wagen.
9. Um eins schließt Christine den Laden.
10. Er kommt heute um zehn nach Hause.
11. Der Professor spricht zu lange.
12. Tobias steht lange dort.
13. Was liest du denn?
14. Im Sommer essen wir um acht.
15. Elke wird heute achtzehn.
16. Das tut man nie.

Past Participles of Separable-Prefix Verbs

Verbs with separable (stressed) prefixes form their past participles by inserting **-ge-** between the prefix and the verb stem:

Der Film hat um acht Uhr **angefangen.**	*The film began at eight o'clock.*
Wann bist du denn **aufgestanden?**	*When did you get up?*
Wann hat er den Laden **aufgemacht?**	*When did he open the shop?*

The root verb may be either weak or strong.

Üben wir!

A. Repeat the sentence with the new subject you will hear.

1. *Ich* habe um drei Uhr aufgehört. (wir, der Regen, er, ihr)
2. *Robert* ist um vier Uhr vorbeigekommen. (die Studenten, du, mein Freund)
3. *Ich* habe ihn in Wien kennengelernt. (wir, meine Mutter, die Schüler)

B. Now restate the following sentences in the perfect tense.

1. Sie macht die Tür auf.
2. Wir gehen oft abends spazieren.
3. Ich kaufe heute für meine Großmutter ein.

4. Wann fangt ihr mit der Arbeit an?

5. Trude steht um elf auf.

6. Die Frau macht das Geschäft zu.

Past Participles of Verbs with Inseparable Prefixes

Verbs with inseparable (unstressed) prefixes do *not* add a **ge-** to their past participle. Some are weak verbs and some are strong.

Was hast du von deinem Onkel **bekommen?**	*What did you get from your uncle?*
Ich habe die Vorlesung nicht **verstanden.**	*I didn't understand the lecture.*

Üben wir!

A. Repeat the sentence with the new subject you will hear.

1. *Christian* hat alles vergessen. ← *forgot*
(Toni, ihr, wir, die Kinder, ich, du)

2. *Christine* hat über Amerika berichtet. ← *reported*
(meine Eltern, ich, Johannes, ihr, du)

B. Now restate the following sentences in the perfect tense.

1. Ich besuche die Vorlesung von Professor Klein.

2. Warum verkaufst du deinen Wagen?

3. Er berichtet über Amerika.

4. Sie beschreibt mir ihr Haus.

5. Was verdient ihr im Geschäft?

"The Germans have an inhuman way of cutting up their verbs. Now a verb has a hard enough time of it in this world when it's all together. It's downright inhuman to split it up. But that's just what those Germans do. They take part of a verb and put it down here, like a stake, and they take the other part of it and put it away over yonder like another stake, and between these two limits they just shovel in German."

Mark Twain

Use of Perfect Tense

The perfect tense is used much more frequently in German than it is in English. In spoken German, the perfect is ordinarily used to indicate events in the past, where English uses the simple past:

Sie **sind** gestern nach Berlin **geflogen.**	*They **flew** to Berlin yesterday.*
Er **hat** die Zeitung um sieben **gelesen.**	*He **read** the newspaper at seven.*

There are no progressive or emphatic forms in the German perfect:

$$\text{Ich habe gesprochen.} \begin{cases} \text{I spoke.} \\ \text{I have spoken.} \\ \text{I was speaking.} \\ \text{I did speak.} \end{cases}$$

2 ◆ The Question Words *wohin* and *woher*

1. **Wohin?** (where to?) asks for the destination of a verb's motion:

Wohin gehst du? or: **Wo** gehst du **hin?**	*Where are you going?*

The directional particle **hin** may be separated from the **wo** and placed at the end of the question.

2. **Woher?** (from where?) asks for the origin of a verb's motion.

Woher kommen Sie? or: **Wo** kommen Sie **her?**	*Where do you come from?*

Woher can also mean "from what source":

Woher hast du so viel Geld?	*Where did you get so much money?*
Woher kennst du sie?	*Where do you know her from?*
Woher wissen Sie das?	*How do you know that?*

■ Note that English **where** is used to ask about location, destination, *and* origin. German has *three separate* question words:

Where are you?	**Wo** bist du?
Where are you going?	**Wohin** gehst du?
Where do you come from?	**Woher** kommst du?

Üben wir!

A. Your teacher will give you some information. Your friend doesn't quite hear it, and you repeat it.

> EXAMPLE: Teacher: Ich komme aus der Schweiz.
> Student A: Woher kommt er?
> Student B: Er kommt aus der Schweiz.

1. Ich wohne in Dortmund.
2. Ich fliege in die Schweiz.
3. Meine Familie kommt aus dem Norden.
4. Ich gehe jetzt ins Kino.
5. Mein Sohn studiert in Freiburg.
6. Meine Tochter fährt nach Rom.
7. John kommt aus Kanada.
8. Carla bleibt in Deutschland.

3 ♦ Two-Way Prepositions

You know that some prepositions in German always take the accusative, while others always take the dative case. A third group, the two-way prepositions, are followed by the accusative when they signal *destination*, and by the dative when they signal *location*. The verb determines whether the sentence indicates destination or location:

Destination	Location
Answers the question **Wohin?**	Answers the question **Wo?**
in	
into, to	in
Wir **gehen in die Mensa.**	Wir **sitzen in der** Mensa.
We're going to the cafeteria.	*We're sitting in the cafeteria.*
auf	
onto	on, upon, on top of
Inge **legt** das Buch **auf den Tisch.**	Das Buch **liegt auf dem** Tisch.
Inge is putting the book on the table.	*The book is lying on the table.*

Üben wir!

A. Answer the questions with *in die Mensa* or *in der Mensa* as appropriate.

1. Wo ist Karin?
2. Wo geht ihr jetzt hin?
3. Wohin läuft er so schnell?
4. Wo sollen wir Wolf treffen?

B. Answer the questions with *auf den Tisch* or *auf dem Tisch* as appropriate.

1. Wo liegt meine Zeitung?
2. Wo soll ich das Geld hinlegen?
3. Wo liegen die Karten für heute abend?
4. Wohin hast du das Buch gelegt?

Here are the other two-way prepositions:

Destination Answers the question **Wohin?**	**Location** Answers the question **Wo?**
an	
to, toward Hans **geht an das** Fenster. *Hans walks toward the window.*	at, alongside of Hans **steht an dem** Fenster. *Hans is standing at the window.*
hinter	
behind Der Wagen **fährt hinter das** Haus. *The car drives behind the house.*	behind Der Wagen **steht hinter dem** Haus. *The car stands behind the house.*
neben	
beside, next to **Leg** dein Buch **neben die** Zeitung! *Put your book next to the newspaper.*	beside, next to Dein Buch **liegt neben der** Zeitung. *Your book is lying next to the newspaper.*
über	
over; across Wir **fliegen über das** Meer. *We're flying across the ocean.*	above Die Sonne **scheint über dem** Meer. *The sun shines over the ocean.*
unter[1]	
under Das Kind **geht unter den** Tisch. *The child goes under the table.*	under Das Kind **ist unter dem** Tisch. *The child is under the table.*
vor	
in front of Der Wagen **fährt vor das** Hotel. *The car drives in front of the hotel.*	in front of Der Wagen **wartet vor dem** Hotel. *The car is waiting in front of the hotel.*
zwischen	
between Er **läuft zwischen die** Bäume. *He's running between the trees.*	between Er **steht zwischen den** Bäumen. *He's standing between the trees.*

[1]When **unter** means "among," it always takes the dative: **unter den Studenten**—*among the students.*

Mit der
Bahn
in den
Schnee...

The prepositions **an** and **in** are usually contracted with the articles **das** and **dem:**

an das → ans	Hans geht **ans** Fenster.
an dem → am	Hans steht **am** Fenster.
in das → ins	Ich gehe jetzt **ins** Hotel.
in dem → im	Wir wohnen **im** Hotel.

Üben wir!

A. Substitute the new verb you will hear and change the article accordingly.

EXAMPLE: Georg wartet vor der Mensa. (fahren)
Georg fährt vor **die** Mensa.

1. Wir fahren in die Stadt. (wohnen, arbeiten, laufen)
2. Jutta steht hinter dem Haus. (laufen, fahren, arbeiten)
3. Das Kind läuft unter den Tisch. (liegen, gehen, warten)
4. Hans steht am Fenster. (gehen, warten, lesen, laufen)

German **an** and **auf** do not correspond exactly to any English prepositions.

1. **an** signals motion toward or location at a border, edge, or vertical surface:

Sie steht **am** Tisch.	*She's standing **at** the table.*
Wir fahren **an** das Meer.	*We're driving **to** the sea.*

2. **auf** signals motion onto or location upon a horizontal surface:

Das Buch liegt **auf dem** Tisch.	*The book is (lying) **on** the table.*
Leg das Buch **auf den** Tisch.	*Put the book **on** the table.*

Üben wir!

A. (Books open) Read these sentences aloud, filling in each blank with either **an** or **auf** and the article.

Destination: article in the accusative

1. Karl geht _____ Tafel.
2. Legen Sie Ihren Mantel _____Stuhl.
3. Marga fährt im Sommer _____ Meer.
4. Ich habe das Vorlesungsverzeichnis _____ Schreibtisch gelegt.

Location: article in the dative

1. Das Kind sitzt _____ Stuhl.
2. Karl steht _____ Tür.
3. Unser Haus liegt _____ Meer.
4. Das Essen ist schon _____ Tisch.

Üben wir!

Say where Hans is going or where he is located in these pictures. Use **auf** or **an.**

4 ♦ Masculine N-Nouns

A few masculine nouns referring to persons take the ending **-en** or **-n** in all cases except the nominative singular:

	singular	*plural*
nom.	der Student	die Studenten
acc.	den Studenten	die Studenten
dat.	dem Studenten	den Studenten

Der Student kennt München sehr gut.

The student knows Munich very well.

Kennst du **den Studenten?**

Do you know the student?

Gib **dem Studenten** das Wörterbuch.

Give the dictionary to the student.

Here are the N-nouns you already know:

der **Herr, -n, -en**[1]
der **Journalist, -en, -en**
der **Student, -en, -en**
der **Tourist, -en, -en**

[1]N-nouns will be marked in the vocabulary by the inclusion of the singular ending as well as the plural.

The title **Herr** (*Mr.*) also has these endings:

> Das ist **Herr** Weiß.
> Kennen Sie **Herrn** Weiß?

A. Substitute the new nouns you will hear.

> EXAMPLE: Kennen Sie *den Herrn*? (der Tourist)
> Kennen Sie den Touristen?

1. Ich verkaufe *dem Studenten* eine Postkarte.
   (der Herr, Herr Weiß, der Tourist)
2. Fragen wir *den Lehrer*!
   (der Student, der Journalist, ihr Mann, Herr Weiß)
3. Wollen Sie *meinen Freund* kennenlernen?
   (sein Bruder, der Tourist, der Student, der Lehrling)

5 ◆ Expanding Your Vocabulary

Verbal Nouns

In principle, any German infinitive may act as a noun. It is then capitalized and is always neuter:

> einkaufen → **das Einkaufen** (*shopping*)

> **Das Einkaufen** hat uns müde   *Shopping made us tired.*
> gemacht.

These verbal nouns often correspond to English gerunds (**-ing** forms) but also to other nouns. Here are some examples:

das Fahren	driving
das Lernen	learning; studying
das Wohnen	living
das Essen	food
das Leben	life
das Sein	being, existence
das Wissen	knowledge

The Noun Prefix Haupt-

The prefix **Haupt-** is attached to nouns and adds the meaning *main, chief, primary, most important*:

das **Hauptfach**	academic major
das **Fach**	area of study
die **Hauptfrage**	the main question
das **Hauptgericht**	main course, entrée
das **Gericht**	course
die **Hauptstadt**	capital city

Leicht zu merken

die **Philosophie**	Philosophie

Wortschatz 2

Verben

an·kommen, ist angekommen to arrive
aus·geben (gibt aus), hat ausgegeben to spend (money)
bauen to build
beginnen, hat begonnen to begin
belegen to register for, to take (a university course)
schicken to send
sitzen, hat gesessen to sit

Substantive

der **Ausweis, -e** I.D. card
  der **Studentenausweis** student I.D.
der **Brief, -e** letter
der **Film, -e** film, movie
der **Fuß, ̈e** foot
  zu Fuß on foot
der **Stadtplan, ̈e** city map

das **Ende, -n** end
  Ende Februar (at) the end of February

das **Glück** happiness; luck
  Glück haben to be lucky
das **Hauptfach, ̈er** major field
das **Kino, -s** movie theater
  ins Kino to the movies
das **Konzert, -e** concert
das **Nebenfach, ̈er** minor field
das **Theater, -** theater

die **Antwort, -en** answer
die **Bibliothek, -en** library
die **Geschichte, -n** story; history
die **Kirche, -n** church
die **Minute, -n** minute
die **Mitte** middle
  Mitte Februar (in) the middle of February
die **Wohnung, -en** apartment

die **Ferien** (*pl.*) (school or university) vacation
  die **Semesterferien** semester break

Andere Vokabeln

billig inexpensive, cheap
ein paar a couple (of); a few
furchtbar terrible
ganz entire, whole
gerade just, (at) this moment
kostenlos free of charge
lieb dear, nice, sweet
  Lieber Mike! Dear Mike, . . .
  Das ist lieb von dir! That's sweet of you.
links to the left; on the left
rechts to the right; on the right
sofort immediately, right away

Gegensätze

billig ≠ teuer	cheap ≠ expensive
lang ≠ kurz	long ≠ short
rechts ≠ links	right ≠ left
Glück haben ≠ Pech haben	to be lucky ≠ to be unlucky

Freiburg im Breisgau

A Note on Letter Writing

Here are some conventions of informal letters in German:

1. The salutation is:

> Lieber Klaus, (*masc. addressee*)
> Liebe Anna, (*fem. addressee*)
> Liebe Schmidts, Liebe Freunde! (*plural*)

Some Germans use an exclamation point rather than a comma after the salutation.

2. All forms of the pronouns **du** and **ihr,** including the possessive adjectives **dein** and **euer** are capitalized in a letter (Du, Ihr, Dein, Euer)

3. The most usual closing is:

> Viele (herzliche) Grüße, many cordial greetings (= warmest regards)
>
> Dein Heinz (*masc. writer*)
> Deine Anna (*fem. writer*)
>
> Euer Stefan
> Eure Karin
>
> Ihr Karl Pohl
> Ihre Angelika Klein

Ein Brief aus Freiburg

Klaus Martens aus Freiburg hat gerade einen Brief von seinem amerikanischen Freund Michael Hayward bekommen. Klaus schickt ihm sofort eine Antwort:

Freiburg, den 20.2.88

Lieber Mike,

Dein Brief ist gestern angekommen, und ich möchte Dir sofort eine Antwort schicken. Du hast geschrieben, Du willst zwei Semester an der Uni in Freiburg Geschichte studieren. Das finde ich ganz toll! Ich studiere auch Ge-
5 schichte, aber nur im Nebenfach. Mein Hauptfach ist Philo-   *last*
sophie. Letztes° Semester habe ich ein sehr interessantes Seminar über Bismarck[1] belegt. Vielleicht können wir im Herbst zusammen in die Vorlesung über deutsche Geschichte von 1870 bis 1919 gehen.

10 Jetzt willst Du sicher etwas mehr über die Unis in Deutschland hören. Unsere Semesterferien haben gerade be-
gonnen; also habe ich endlich ein bißchen Freizeit. Übrigens sind diese Ferien zwischen dem Winter- und dem Som-   ***länger als*** = *longer than*
mersemester viel länger als° in Amerika—von Mitte Fe-
15 bruar bis Ende April.

Wie Du vielleicht schon weißt, sind alle deutschen Universitäten staatlich;° das bedeutet, sie sind für die Stu-   *state-run*
denten fast kostenlos. Man muß nur für Wohnung, Essen, Bücher und Kleidung Geld ausgeben. In der Mensa kann
20 man immer billig essen, aber mit dem Wohnen ist es nicht so einfach. Man hat nicht genug Studentenwohnheime gebaut, und Studentenbuden° sind furchtbar teuer geworden.   *student rooms in private dwellings*
Du hast aber Glück! Bei uns in der WG wird nächstes Jahr ein Zimmer frei, und Du kannst selbstverständlich hier
25 wohnen.

Jeder Student bekommt übrigens einen Studen-
tenausweis. Mit diesem Ausweis kann man die Bibliothek benutzen° und auch überall billige Karten für Filme und   *use*
Konzerte kaufen. Ich schicke Dir auch ein paar Postkarten
30 und einen Stadtplan von Freiburg. Auf dem Stadtplan siehst Du links die Universität und rechts davon° die Stadtmitte.   *of it*
Wir wohnen in der Altstadt zwischen der Universitäts-
kirche und dem Rathaus. Von unserem Haus bis zur Uni

---

[1] Otto von Bismarck (1815–1898), German statesman, Prussian Chancellor under whose leadership the German states were united to found the German Empire in 1871.

In einer Studentenkneipe (*pub*) (Karlsruhe, BRD)

35 sind es nur fünfzehn Minuten zu Fuß. Man kann auch leicht ins Kino oder ins Theater gehen. Die Geschäfte sind auch nicht weit.

Also, Schluß° für heute. Seit dem Semesterende habe ich nicht mehr so lange am Schreibtisch gesessen! Viele herzliche Grüße an° Dich und die ganze Familie.

that's all

herzliche . . . an = warmest regards to

Dein

Klaus

Fragen zum Lesestück

1. Von wem hat Klaus Martens einen Brief bekommen?
2. Was will sein Freund aus Amerika tun?
3. Warum hat Klaus jetzt etwas mehr Zeit?
4. Was studiert Klaus in Freiburg? Was ist sein Nebenfach?
5. Ist das Studentenleben in Freiburg sehr teuer?
6. Wo kann Mike wohnen?
7. Was schickt Klaus seinem Freund?

Vom Lesen zum Sprechen

Das Studium   University Studies

studieren an (+ *dat.*)	to study at
Ich studiere an der Universität Konstanz.	I'm studying at the university of Konstanz.
die **Vorlesung, -en**	lecture course
das **Seminar, -e**	seminar
das **Fach, ⁼er**	area of study; subject
das **Hauptfach, ⁼er**	major field of study
das **Nebenfach, ⁼er**	minor field of study
das **Wintersemester**	fall term (usually October-February)
das **Sommersemester**	spring term (usually May-July)
die **Bibliothek, -en**	library
die **Klausur, -en**	test (*during the semester*)
die **Prüfung, -en**	exam (*at the end of the semester*)
das **Referat, -e**	oral report; written term paper
ein Referat halten	to give a report
ein Referat schreiben	to write a paper

Einige Studienfächer   Some Areas of Study

die **Anglistik**	English studies
die **Biologie**	biology
die **Chemie**	chemistry
die **Elektrotechnik**	electrical engineering
die **Frauenstudien** (*plural*)	Women's studies
die **Germanistik**	German studies
die **Geschichte**	history
die **Informatik**	computer science
Jura (used without article)	law
die **Kunstgeschichte**	art history
die **Landwirtschaft**	agriculture
die **Linguistik**	linguistics
die **Mathematik**	mathematics
die **Medizin**	medicine
die **Musikwissenschaft**	musicology
die **Pädagogik**	education
die **Philosophie**	philosophy
die **Physik**	physics
die **Politikwissenschaft**	political science
die **Psychologie**	psychology
die **Soziologie**	sociology
die **Wirtschaftswissenschaft**	economics

A. Sprechen Sie mit Ihrem Professor und den anderen Studenten über Ihr Studium!

1. Was studieren Sie?
2. Was ist Ihr Hauptfach? Ihr Nebenfach?
3. Was wollen Sie nach dem Studium machen?
4. Müssen Sie oft Referate schreiben oder halten? Tun Sie das gern?
5. Wie viele Vorlesungen oder Seminare belegen Sie dieses Semester?
6. Müssen Sie oft in der Bibliothek arbeiten?
7. Brauchen Sie Deutsch für Ihr Studium oder für Ihren Beruf?
8. Was kostet das Studium bei Ihnen?

Das Studentenzimmer

1. das Telefon, -e	8. das Radio, -s
2. das Bett, -en	9. das Bücherregal, -e
3. die Lampe, -n	10. das Plakat, -e
4. der Teppich, -e	11. der Spiegel, -
5. die Schreibmaschine, -n	12. der Wecker, -
6. der Plattenspieler, -	13. der Kleiderschrank, ¨e
7. die Schallplatten	14. der Schlüssel, -

B. Beschreiben Sie dieses Studentenzimmer.

1. Kann man hier gut wohnen? Warum?
2. Ist dieses Zimmer Ihrem Zimmer ähnlich? Was gibt es zum Beispiel *nicht* bei Ihnen?
3. Beschreiben Sie Ihr Studentenzimmer.

Mündliche Übungen

A. Persönliche Fragen

1. Muß man an Ihrer Universität ein Zimmer suchen?
2. Gibt es genug Studentenwohnheime an Ihrer Uni?
3. Wohnen Sie auf dem Campus oder bei einer Familie?
4. Müssen Sie jedes Semester ein Vorlesungsverzeichnis kaufen?
5. Was liegt auf Ihrem Schreibtisch?
6. Haben Sie gestern am Schreibtisch gesessen? Wie lange?
7. Wann haben Sie hier mit dem Studium angefangen?

B. Place the following situation in the past by changing the tense from present to perfect.

> EXAMPLE: Mike studiert ein Jahr in Freiburg.
> Mike hat ein Jahr in Freiburg studiert.

1. Er kommt im September in Freiburg an.
2. Er hat keinen Wintermantel.
3. Er geht sofort mit Klaus einkaufen.
4. Für seine Bücher gibt er viel Geld aus. *geben*
5. Sein Zimmer in der WG findet er schön.
6. Klaus kauft ihm ein Vorlesungsverzeichnis.
7. Er geht mit der Familie ins Konzert.
8. Das Konzert beginnt schon um sieben.
9. Die Musik ist sehr schön.
10. Er schreibt eine Postkarte nach Hause.

C. Was hat Inge gemacht? *Seminararbeit*

Montag	Seminararbeit endlich anfangen!
Dienstag	Stadtplan kaufen; durch die Altstadt laufen
Mittwoch	In der Bibliothek arbeiten; am Abend Freunde besuchen
Donnerstag	Briefe schreiben; dann Musik hören
Freitag	schwimmen gehen; Englisch lernen
Samstag	1 Stunde im Wald laufen; Uli anrufen, zusammen Wein trinken
Sonntag	am Abend ins Konzert

Look at Inge's date book and tell what she did on the various days of the week.

> EXAMPLE: Am Sonntag abend ist sie ins Konzert gegangen.

D. Ask other students what they still have to do. They respond according to the example, saying that they have already done it.

> EXAMPLE: Student 1: Mußt du noch einkaufen?
> Student 2: Nein, ich habe schon eingekauft.

1. Mußt du noch essen?
2. Mußt du noch arbeiten?
3. Mußt du den Brief noch schreiben?
4. Willst du noch die Zeitung lesen?
5. Sollst du mit deiner Professorin sprechen?
6. Möchtest du Karl kennenlernen?

E. Here is a classroom. Answer the questions about where the people and things are located, using the prepositions suggested.

> EXAMPLE: Wo sitzt der Lehrer? (auf)
> Er sitzt auf dem Tisch.

1. Wo sitzt Marie? (vor)
2. Wo steht Jutta? (hinter)
3. Wo steht Karl? (an)
4. Wo steht Gertrud? (zwischen)
5. Wo sitzt der Lehrer? (auf)
6. Wo steht Emil? (neben/Freund)
7. Wo liegt die Zeitung? (unter)
8. Wo sind diese Leute? (in)

Now describe the locations of other people and objects. (*For example*: Wo steht der Tisch?)

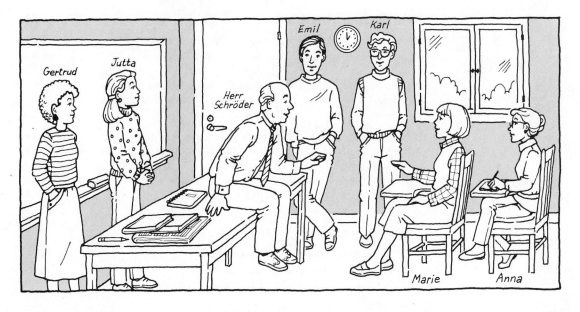

F. Here is another picture of the same classroom, but now everyone is moving around and doing things. Tell where they are going and what they are doing.

1. Wohin legt Gertrud ihr Buch? (neben)
2. Wo geht Karl hin? (an)
3. Wohin legt der Lehrer das Buch? (auf)
4. Wo geht Emil hin? (in)
5. Wo geht Anna hin? (an)

Describe any other actions you can.

Schriftliche Übungen

G. Maria is a philosophy student at the University of Tübingen. She is well organized, as is apparent from the page in her appointment calendar shown on page 175.
Write a paragraph in German using the perfect tense to describe her activities on April 1st. Begin with: „Am Freitag ist Maria früh aufgestanden . . . "

H. You have read Klaus Marten's „Brief aus Freiburg" in which he prepares Mike Hayward for his studies at a German university. Now pretend you are a student writing home after the first week in Freiburg. Describe to your family or friends your first impressions and activities. (Exercises A and B above may give you some ideas.)

I. Wie sagt man das auf deutsch?

1. I've bought you a university catalogue.
2. I hope it did not cost much.
3. No, it was cheap. Shall I put it on your desk?

4. The lecture began at ten o'clock.
5. Unfortunately, I arrived too late.
6. I stood behind my friends and I didn't hear anything.

7. What did you study in Konstanz?
8. History was my major but I also studied German.
9. Did you have a room in the old city?
10. Yes, I lived between the church and the theater.

FREITAG, den 1. April

7 Uhr	besonders früh aufstehen
8 Uhr	mit Regine Kaffee trinken
9 Uhr	in Prof. Schmalzreiths Vorlesung
10 Uhr	10:15 Rolf ~~treffen~~ mit, zusammen einkaufen gehen
11 Uhr	mit Kirsten und Trude in der Mensa
12 Uhr	
13 Uhr	Heinz kommt vorbei; Referat besprechen

14 Uhr	Seminar bei Prof. Denker
15 Uhr	
16 Uhr	16.30 mit Toni zur Buchhandlung
17 Uhr	Rolf und Erika kommen zu mir
Abend:	zusammen kochen
21 Uhr	PARTY

Gäste nach Hause schicken
— ins Bett — „Faust" lesen.

Almanach

Mark Twain Visits Heidelberg

This picture of student life in 19th-century Heidelberg is condensed from Mark Twain's account in *A Tramp Abroad,* published in 1879.

The summer semester was in full tide; consequently the most frequent figure in and about Heidelberg was the student. One sees so many students abroad at all hours, that he presently begins to wonder if they ever have any working hours. Each can choose for himself whether he will work or play; for German university life is a very free life; it seems to have no restraints. The student does not live in college buildings but hires his own lodgings and takes his meals when and where he pleases. He goes to bed when it suits him and does not get up at all unless he wants to. He passes no examination upon entering college. He merely

Zeichnung von (drawing by) Ludwig Richter.

Heidelberg: Schloßhof (*palace courtyard*)

pays a trifling fee of five or ten dollars, receives a card entitling him to the privileges of the university, and that is the end of it. He is now ready for business, —or play, as he shall prefer. If he elects to work, he finds a large list of courses to choose from but he can skip attendance.

The result of this is that lecture-courses are often delivered to very slim audiences. I heard of one case where, day after day, the lecturer's audience consisted of three students, —and always the same three. But one day two of them remained away. The lecturer began as usual: "Gentlemen," then, without a smile, he corrected himself, saying, "Sir," and went on with his discourse.

The German student has been in the rigid bondage of the gymnasium for so long that the large liberty of university life is just what he needs and appreciates; as it cannot last forever he makes the most of it and lays up a good rest against the day that must see him put on the chains once more and enter the slavery of official or professional life.

Auf Reisen

Dialoge
Am Bahnhof ♦ Vor der Reise ♦
Nach dem Mittagessen

Wortschatz 1

Grammatik
1. Perfect Tense of Irregular Weak
   Verbs
2. Perfect Tense of Modal Verbs
3. Coordinating Conjunctions
   aber versus **sondern** ♦
   Position of **nicht** before
   sondern
4. Verbs with Dative Objects
5. Personal Dative
6. More on Two-Way Prepositions
7. Expanding Your Vocabulary
   Identifying Noun Gender ♦
   Leicht zu merken

Wortschatz 2

Lesestück
Unterwegs per Autostop oder mit
der Bahn.

Vom Lesen zum Sprechen
Reisen und Verkehr

Almanach
Youth Hostels

Am Bahnhof

GEPÄCKTRÄGER: Darf ich Ihnen helfen?
TOURISTIN: Ja, bitte! Können Sie mir den Koffer tragen?
GEPÄCKTRÄGER: Gerne. Wohin müssen Sie?
TOURISTIN: Gleis drei. Mein Zug fährt gleich ab.

Vor der Reise

MARION: Suchst du die Kamera?
JOST: Nein, nicht die Kamera, sondern den Reiseführer.
MARION: Wohin hast du ihn denn gelegt?
JOST: Auf den Tisch, glaube ich.
MARION: Ja, hier liegt er unter der Weinflasche.
JOST: Kannst du die Flasche auf den Boden stellen? Wir müssen noch Campingplätze in der Schweiz suchen.

Nach dem Mittagessen

FRAU KÖNIG: Heinz? Ach, *da* bist du. Warum hast du mir nicht geantwortet?
HERR KÖNIG: Ich habe auf dem Bett gelegen und bin dann einfach eingeschlafen.
FRAU KÖNIG: Ach, es tut mir leid. Das habe ich nicht gewußt.
HERR KÖNIG: Das macht nichts. Ich habe sowieso aufstehen wollen.

„Auf Wiedersehen!"

Wortschatz 1

At the Train Station

PORTER: May I help you?
TOURIST: Yes, please! Can you carry the suitcase for me?
PORTER: Gladly. Where do you have to go?
TOURIST: Track three. My train is leaving right away.

Before the Trip

MARION: Are you looking for the camera?
JOST: No, not the camera, but the guidebook.
MARION: Where did you put it?
JOST: On the table, I think.
MARION: Yes, here it is, under the wine bottle.
JOST: Can you put the bottle on the floor? We still have to look for campgrounds in Switzerland.

After Lunch

MRS. KÖNIG: Heinz? Oh, *there* you are. Why didn't you answer me?
MR. KÖNIG: I was lying on the bed and then simply fell asleep.
MRS. KÖNIG: Oh, I'm sorry. I didn't know that.
MR. KÖNIG: It doesn't matter. I intended to get up anyway.

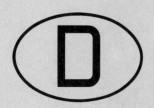

Verben

ab · fahren (fährt ab), ist abgefahren to depart, leave (by vehicle)
antworten (+ *dat.*) to answer (a person)
danken (+ *dat.*) to thank
ein · schlafen (schläft ein), ist eingeschlafen to fall asleep
gefallen (gefällt), hat gefallen (+ *dat. of person*) to please, appeal to
gehören (+ *dat. of person*) to belong to (a person)
hängen (*trans.*) to hang up
hängen, hat gehangen (*intrans.*) to be hanging
helfen, hat geholfen (+ *dat.*) to help
setzen to set (down), put
stellen to put, place

Substantive

der **Bahnhof, ⸚e** train station
der **Boden, ⸚** ground; floor

Gegensätze

abfahren ≠ ankommen	to depart ≠ to arrive
einschlafen ≠ aufwachen	to fall asleep ≠ to wake up
fragen ≠ antworten	to ask ≠ to answer[1]

der **Campingplatz, ⸚e** campground
der **Gepäckträger, -** porter, redcap
der **Koffer, -** suitcase
der **Reiseführer, -** guide book
der **Zug, ⸚e** train
das **Bett, -en** bed
  ins Bett gehen to go to bed
das **Gepäck** luggage
das **Gleis, -e** track
die **Flasche, -n** bottle
die **Kamera, -s** camera

Andere Vokabeln

gleich right away, immediately
sondern but rather
sowieso anyway

Nützliche Ausdrücke

Es (das) tut mir leid. I'm sorry (about that).
Es (das) macht nichts. It (that) doesn't matter.
Das ist mir egal. It's all the same to me. I don't care (about that).

[1] Note that **fragen** takes an accusative object but **antworten** takes a dative object: **Er fragt mich.** but **Er antwortet mir.** Note also that **antworten** can only have a person as its object. You will learn the German equivalent of "to answer a question" later.

Neue Kombinationen

A. Substitute the new elements you will hear.

1. Können Sie mir *den Koffer* tragen?
   (die Bücher, diese Flaschen, mein Gepäck)
2. Wohin hast du *den Reiseführer* gelegt?
   (den Stadtplan, meinen Pullover, meine Jacke)
3. Ich suche etwas *auf der Karte.*
   (im Zimmer, draußen, im Wald, unter dem Bett)
4. Ich habe nicht *aufstehen wollen.*
   (aufhören sollen, aufwachen wollen, anfangen können)

B. (books open) Match each question on the left with an appropriate response (or responses) on the right.

Ich kann den Koffer nicht tragen.	Das macht nichts.
Wohin hast du die Flasche gestellt?	Auf Gleis drei.
Wo liegt denn unser Stadtplan?	Auf den Boden.
Hast du das nicht gewußt?	Oh, das tut mir leid.
Wo fährt denn dein Zug ab?	Auf dem Tisch.
	Doch!

Übung zur Aussprache

See the Introduction, p. 5, for the pronunciation of the sound represented by **ü** (and occasionally by **y**).

long u	*long* ü	*long* i	*long* ü	*long* ü	*short* ü
fuhr	für	vier	für	Hüte	Hütte
Schnur	Schnüre	Tier	Tür	Mühle	Müller
Hut	Hüte	Mieder	müder	Mythe	Mütter
Mut	Mythe	sieden	Süden	Düne	dünner
gut	Güte	Kiel	kühl		

Now read the following sentences aloud:

1. Günter kommt aus Lübeck und kennt den Süden nicht.
2. Müssen wir schnell machen?
3. Ja, wir müssen früh da sein. Später gibt es keine Züge nach München.

Grammatik

1 ◆ Perfect Tense of Irregular Weak Verbs

There are a handful of irregular weak verbs in German. While they have the weak participle form **ge——t**, they change their stem vowel, and in some cases stem consonants. The ones you have learned so far are:

bringen	hat **gebracht**
mitbringen	hat **mitgebracht**
kennen	hat **gekannt**
wissen	hat **gewußt**

Üben wir!

A. Change the following sentences to the perfect tense.

1. Kennst du diesen Film schon?
2. Sie bringen mir eine Flasche Wein.
3. Kennen Sie Herrn Schneider?
4. Das wissen wir schon.
5. Wir bringen die Kinder mit.
6. Sie weiß viel über Deutschland.

2 ◆ Perfect Tense of Modal Verbs

You know that modal verbs are usually used with a dependent infinitive:

Ich **muß**	viel	**schreiben.**	*I have to write a lot.*
Wir **wollen**	nach Hause	**gehen.**	*We want to go home.*

Here are the same sentences in the perfect tense:

Ich **habe**	viel	**schreiben müssen.**	*I had to write a lot.*
Wir **haben**	nach Hause	**gehen wollen.**	*We wanted to go home.*

A modal verb with a dependent infinitive uses its own *infinitive* form instead of a past participle to form the perfect tense.[1] The infinitive of the modal verb *follows* the dependent infinitive. This construction is called a *double infinitive.*

---

[1] All the modal verbs are irregular weak verbs and have past participles on the pattern **ge——t** (dürfen—**gedurft**, können—**gekonnt**, mögen—**gemocht**, müssen—**gemußt**, sollen—**gesollt**, wollen—**gewollt**). These past participles, however, are used *only* when there is no dependent infinitive:

Das hat er nicht **gekonnt.**	*He wasn't able to do that.*
Sie hat mich nicht **gemocht.**	*She didn't like me.*
Das habe ich nicht **gewollt.**	*I didn't want that to happen.*

■ Note: The modal verbs always use **haben** as their auxiliary in the perfect tense, regardless of the dependent infinitive:

Wir **sind** nach Hause gegangen.   *We went home.*
but
Wir **haben** nach Hause gehen wollen.   *We wanted to go home.*

 Üben wir!

A. Substitute the new modal you will hear for the one in the double infinitive.

1. Leider haben unsere Freunde nicht bleiben *können*. (wollen, dürfen)
2. Kurt hat die Vorlesung hören *dürfen*. (können, wollen, müssen)

B. Substitute the new infinitive you will hear for the one in the double infinitive:

1. Das habe ich leider nicht *machen* können.
   (hören, sehen, sagen, essen, schreiben)
2. Was haben Sie *antworten* müssen?
   (schreiben, kaufen, lernen, einkaufen)

C. Change the following sentences from present to perfect tense, using the double infinitive.

        EXAMPLE: Wir müssen schnell machen.
                     Wir haben schnell machen müssen.

1. Ich will in der Stadt bleiben.
2. Ich muß manchmal weinen.
3. Ich muß ihnen eine Flasche Wein kaufen.
4. Ich kann das Weingeschäft nicht finden.
5. Kann Ihnen die Frau helfen?
6. Leider kann sie es mir nicht sagen.

3 ◆ Coordinating Conjunctions

Coordinating conjunctions are words that join clauses of equal rank. Each clause could stand alone as a sentence. The coordinating conjunction joins them without making one subordinate to the other.[1] Two of the most common coordinating conjunctions in English are **and** and **or:**

      Christa is eighteen.   Her brother is sixteen.
      Christa is eighteen **and** her brother is sixteen.

      Can you open the window?   Should I do it?
      Can you open the window, **or** should I do it?

---

[1] A subordinating conjunction, on the other hand, introduces a clause that is *subordinate* to the main clause. The subordinate clause modifies or elucidates the thought in the main clause. You will learn about subordinating conjunctions in Chapter 8.

The most common coordinating conjunctions in German are:

und	and
oder	or
aber	but, however
sondern	but rather
denn	for, because

Coordinating conjunctions are *not* counted when determining first position and second position in the clause. This means that the word order of the following clause is *not* affected by the conjunction:

Christa ist achtzehn.   Ihr Bruder ist sechzehn.

$$0 \qquad 1 \qquad 2$$

Christa ist achtzehn, **und** ihr Bruder ist sechzehn.

Kannst du das Fenster aufmachen?   Soll ich es machen?
Kannst du das Fenster aufmachen, **oder** soll ich es machen?

Klaus muß bis drei arbeiten.   Dann kann er nach Hause.
Klaus muß bis drei arbeiten, **aber** dann kann er nach Hause.

Ute kommt nicht zu Fuß.   Sie fährt mit dem Auto.
Ute kommt nicht zu Fuß, **sondern** sie fährt mit dem Auto.

Helmut ißt erst um sieben.   Er arbeitet bis sechs.
Helmut ißt erst um sieben, **denn** er arbeitet bis sechs.

The coordinating conjunctions are also used to join units smaller than a clause:

Ich habe einen Bruder **und** eine Schwester.
Möchtest du Wein **oder** Bier?
Dieser Laden ist gut, **aber** sehr teuer.
Barbara ist nicht hier, **sondern** in Italien.

Note on punctuation: There is always a comma before **aber, sondern** and **denn.** Before **und** and **oder,** there is only a comma if a complete clause (with subject) follows:

Jens geht in die Stadt und kauft Lebensmittel ein.
Jens geht in die Stadt, und Maria kauft Lebensmittel ein.

Üben wir!

A. Join the following sentences together with the coordinating conjunction indicated.

EXAMPLE: Ich schlafe gern. Ich muß immer früh aufstehen. (aber)
Ich schlafe gern, aber ich muß immer früh aufstehen.

1. Meine Eltern kommen morgen. Wir fahren zusammen nach München. (und)
2. Ich bringe das Buch mit. Ich möchte dir etwas zeigen. (denn)

Mädchen in Tracht unterwegs zum Volksfest (die Tracht - *folk costume*)

3. Willst du allein wohnen? Willst du in einer WG wohnen? (oder)
4. Willst du in der Mensa essen? Wollen wir bei mir etwas kochen? (oder)
5. Ich wohne in der Stadt. Mein Bruder wohnt auf dem Land. (aber)
6. Wir müssen jetzt gehen. Unser Zug fährt gleich ab. (denn)
7. Gisela studiert in Freiburg. Ich möchte sie dort besuchen. (und)
8. Ich habe sie gefragt. Sie hat mir nicht geantwortet. (aber)

aber *vs.* sondern

Aber and **sondern** are both coordinating conjunctions translated with English **but**. Both express a contrast, but they are *not* interchangeable. **Sondern** *must* be used when **but** means **but rather.** Compare the following sentences:

Er bleibt zu Hause, **aber** sie geht einkaufen.	*He's staying at home but she's going shopping.*
Er bleibt heute nicht zu Hause, **sondern** geht einkaufen.	*He's not staying home today, but (rather) is going shopping.*

Sondern always follows a *negative* statement and expresses an alternative:

Das ist kein Wein, **sondern** Wasser.	*That's not wine, it's water.*
Käthe hat es nicht getan, **sondern** die Kinder.	*Käthe didn't do it, the children did.*

Note that the clause following **sondern** may leave out elements it has in common with the first clause. Such deletion is called *ellipsis*:

> Er bleibt nicht zu Hause, sondern (er) geht einkaufen.
> Das ist kein Wein, sondern (das ist) Wasser.
> Käthe hat es nicht getan, sondern die Kinder (haben es getan).

Position of nicht *before* sondern

You have learned that in negations, **nicht** *follows* the direct object and expressions of definite time (see p. 71). However, if these elements are followed by an alternative introduced by **sondern, nicht** will *precede* them. This is because when **nicht** negates only a single element, rather than the whole sentence, it immediately *precedes* that element:

> Ich kaufe den Mantel nicht.
> *but*
> Ich kaufe **nicht den Mantel,** sondern die Jacke.

> Johanna arbeitet heute nicht.
> *but*
> Johanna arbeitet **nicht heute,** sondern morgen.[1]

Üben wir!

A. Listen to each pair of sentences and then connect them with **aber** or **sondern.** Make use of ellipsis if you can.

> EXAMPLE: Ich lese das Buch nicht. Ich lese die Zeitung.
> Ich lese nicht das Buch, sondern die Zeitung.

1. Sie fliegt nach Italien. Ihr Mann fährt mit dem Zug.
2. Sie haßt mich nicht. Sie liebt mich.
3. Es ist noch nicht sieben Uhr. Er ist schon zu Hause.
4. Ich fahre nicht mit dem Auto. Ich komme zu Fuß.
5. Ich trage meinen Mantel nicht. Ich trage meine Jacke.
6. Bernd mag dieses Bier nicht. Lutz trinkt es gern.

Tyrolean Airways, A-6020 Innsbruck
Fürstenweg 180, Telefon 81 7 77

Frankfurt

Zürich   Wien

INNSBRUCK

---

[1] When the contrast expressed by **sondern** is especially strong, the sentence can even begin with **nicht**: Nicht den Mantel kaufe ich, sondern die Jacke. *It's not the coat I'm buying, but the jacket.*

4 ◆ Verbs with Dative Objects

A few German verbs require an object in the dative case rather than the accusative. Two of these are **helfen** and **antworten:**

Ich sehe den Mann
but
Ich helfe **dem Mann.**

I see the man.

I'm helping the man.

Du kennst die Frau.
but
Du antwortest **der Frau.**

You know the woman.

You answer the woman.

This chapter introduces the following verbs with dative objects:

antworten	*to answer (someone)*
danken	*to thank*
gefallen	*to please*
gehören	*to belong to*
glauben	*to believe (someone)*[1]
helfen	*to help*

The dative object is usually a person:

Marie dankt dem Lehrer.

Marie thanks the teacher.

Wem gehört der Wagen?

Who owns the car? (Literally: To whom does the car belong?)

Diese Stadt gefällt **mir.**

I like this city. (Literally: This city pleases me.)

■ Note the translation of the last example above. **Gefallen** is the German equivalent of "to like something," but subject and object are the reverse of English. Remember that the verb must agree in number with the subject:

Die Städte **gefallen** mir.

I like the cities.

Üben wir!

A. Substitute the new dative objects cued in English.

EXAMPLE: Bernd soll uns helfen. (me)
Bernd soll mir helfen.

1. Die Kinder helfen *ihrem Vater* gern.
   (me, you, their aunt, the teacher)
2. Dieser Pulli gehört *dir.*
   (you ⟨polite form⟩, them, her, the child, Frau Braun, Herr Braun)
3. Das Zimmer gefällt *mir* sehr gut.
   (us, her, my cousin, his brother)

[1] **Glauben** takes an accusative inanimate object, but a dative personal object: **Ich glaube das.** but **Ich glaube dir.** One can thus say: **Ich glaube dir das.** = I believe you when you say that.

„Unser Zug fährt auf Gleis 8 ab."

Now substitute the new subjects you will hear.

4. *Das Kleid* gefällt mir sehr.
   (die Stadt, diese Musik, diese Leute, dieser Beruf, diese Kleider)

B. Wie sagt man das auf deutsch? (Use *gefallen*)

> EXAMPLE: I like these fairy-tales.
> Diese Märchen gefallen mir.

1. She likes this church.
2. I like this weather.
3. They like the work.
4. He likes your letters.
5. We like the lectures.
6. Do you like this book?

C. Now ask each other how you like certain things and people, for example:

Beethoven	Mozart	das Deutschbuch
die Uni	diese Stadt	das Essen in der Mensa

EXAMPLE: Wie gefällt dir Mozart?
Mozart gefällt mir gut.

5 ♦ Personal Dative

The dative case is used to indicate a person's involvement in or reaction to a situation. This dative usually comes immediately after the subject and verb is often translated by English **to** or **for**:

Ist es **Ihnen** zu kalt?	*Is it too cold for you?*
Es wird **mir** zu dunkel.	*It's getting too dark for me.*
Wie geht es **dir?**	*How are you?* (**Literally:** *How goes it for you?*)
Wie geht es **Ihrer Mutter?**	*How is your mother?*
Das ist **mir** egal.	*It's all the same to me.*

This dative may often be omitted without changing the basic meaning of the sentence:

Ist es zu kalt?   Es wird zu dunkel.   Wie geht es?

But it may *not* be omitted in the expression

Das tut **mir** leid.   *I'm sorry.*

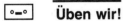

Üben wir!

A. Answer the following questions positively. Substitute dative pronouns for proper names.

EXAMPLE: Geht es Luise besser?
Ja, es geht ihr besser.

1. Ist es dir warm genug?
2. Tut es Robert leid?
3. Ist es Ihnen egal?
4. Das Buch ist Anna zu langweilig, nicht wahr?
5. Geht es deinem Vater besser?
6. Ist euch das Zimmer zu kalt?
7. Ist Ihnen sieben Uhr zu früh?
8. Ist dir die Hose zu teuer?

There is an important group of verb pairs that is used with the two-way prepositions. One verb of each pair is always used with the accusative case and the other with the dative case. They show respectively destination and location:

Destination (accusative)	Location (dative)
weak transitive verbs	strong intransitive verbs
hängen, hat gehängt: to hang (up)	**hängen, hat gehangen:** to be hanging
Er hat die Karte **an die Wand** gehängt. He hung the map on the wall.	Die Karte hat **an der Wand** gehangen. The map hung on the wall.
legen, hat gelegt: to lay (down), put	**liegen, hat gelegen:** to lie, be lying
Ich lege das Buch **auf den Tisch.** I'm putting the book on the table.	Das Buch liegt **auf dem Tisch.** The book is (lying) on the table.
setzen, hat gesetzt: to set (down), put	**sitzen, hat gesessen:** to sit, be sitting
Sie setzt das Kind **auf den Stuhl.** She's putting the child on the chair.	Das Kind sitzt **auf dem Stuhl.** The child is (sitting) on the chair.
stellen, hat gestellt: to place (down), put	**stehen, hat gestanden:** to stand, be standing
Ich stelle die Flasche **neben die Uhr.** I'll put the bottle next to the clock.	Die Flasche steht **neben der Uhr.** The bottle's standing next to the clock.

■ Note that **hängen** has one infinitive form but a weak and strong participle.
■ **Legen** and **liegen** are used when objects are *laid* down or are *lying* in a horizontal position. **Stellen** and **stehen** are used when objects are *stood up* or are *standing* in a vertical position, thus:

Ich **lege** das Buch auf den Tisch.

I'm putting the book (down flat) on the table.

but
Ich **stelle** das Buch ins Regal.

I'm putting the book (upright) in the bookcase.

Üben wir!

A. (books open.) Insert the correct forms of the verbs above to show location or destination.

1. Soll ich die Straßenkarte an die Wand _____ ?

2. Nein, du kannst sie einfach auf den Tisch _____ .

3. Wohin hast du mein Vorlesungsverzeichnis _____ ?

4. Wieso? _____ es nicht auf deinem Schreibtisch?

5. _____ Sie bitte die Weinflaschen auf den Boden.

6. Aber sie _____ schon dort!

Im Speisewagen (*dining car*)

7. Wo _____ denn mein Koffer?

8. Hast du ihn nicht hinter die Tür _____ ?

9. Ich habe das Kind auf den Stuhl _____ .

10. Hoffentlich _____ es noch dort.

B. Describe what Peter did, then the resulting situation.

     EXAMPLE: stellen / Weinflasche / Tisch
                Peter hat die Weinflasche auf den Tisch gestellt.
                Jetzt steht sie auf dem Tisch.

1. legen / Buch / Boden

2. setzen / Kind / Stuhl

3. hängen / Bild / über / Tafel

4. stellen / Stuhl / in / Zimmer

Identifying Noun Gender

Now that you have acquired a vocabulary of several hundred words in German, you can begin to recognize some patterns in the gender of nouns. You have learned that verbal nouns like **das Essen** and **das Einkaufen** are always neuter. You already know that agent nouns and nouns of nationality ending in **-er** or **-erin** are masculine and feminine, respectively (**Lehrer/in**, **Amerikaner/in**).

Nouns ending in the following suffixes are *always feminine* and *always* add **-en** in the plural:

-ung (forms nouns on verb stems)	die Buchhandlung, -en die Entschuldigung, -en die Vorlesung, -en
-heit and **-keit** (form nouns on adjective stems and from other nouns)	die Freiheit, -en (freedom) die Freundlichkeit, -en (friendliness)
-schaft (forms abstract nouns from more concrete nouns, often equals English **-hood** or **-ship**)	die Landschaft, -en die Freundschaft, -en (friendship)
-ion and **-tät** (words borrowed from French or Latin)	die Diskussion, -en die Universität, -en die Solidarität

Üben wir!

A. Guess the meanings of these words:

1. die Möglichkeit
2. die Wanderung
3. die Ähnlichkeit
4. die Mehrheit
5. die Meinung
6. die Lehrerschaft
7. die Menschheit
8. die Wohnung
9. die Schönheit
10. die Stellung

Leicht zu merken

der **Horizont**   Horizont
packen
die **Wanderlust**

Wortschatz 2

Verben

aus·steigen, ist ausgestiegen to get out (of a vehicle)
erlauben (+ *dat. of person*) to permit, allow
erlaubt permitted
erzählen to tell, recount
hoffen to hope
mit·nehmen (nimmt mit), hat mitgenommen to take along
reden to speak, talk
reisen, ist gereist to travel
sparen to save (money)
trampen (*pronounced „trämpen"*), **ist getrampt** to hitchhike
übernachten to spend the night
verbieten, hat verboten (+ *dat. of person*) to forbid, prohibit
verboten prohibited

Substantive

der **Abend, -e** evening
am **Abend** in the evening
der **Bus, -se** bus
der **Rucksack, ⁻e** rucksack, backpack

das **Abteil, -e** railway compartment
das **Ausland** (*sing.*) foreign countries
im **Ausland** abroad
das **Beispiel, -e** example
zum **Beispiel (z. B.)** for example (e. g.)
das **Flugzeug, -e** airplane
das **Foto, -s** photograph
ein **Foto machen** to take a picture
das **Gefühl, -e** feeling
das **Gespräch, -e** conversation
(das) **Italien** Italy

die **Bahn** railroad; railway system
die **Fahrkarte, -n** ticket (for bus, train, streetcar, etc.)

die **Fahrt, -en** trip, ride
die **Freiheit, -en** freedom
die **Jugendherberge, -n** Youth Hostel
die **Straßenbahn, -en** streetcar

Andere Vokabeln

bequem comfortable
heutzutage nowadays
pünktlich punctual, on time
schlimm bad
so so
sympathisch friendly, congenial, likeable
unterwegs en route; on the go
verrückt (*slang*) crazy

Nützliche Ausdrücke

per Autostop reisen = trampen
Das macht (mir) Spaß. That is fun (for me).

Gegensätze

aussteigen ≠ einsteigen	to get out ≠ to get in (a vehicle)
erlaubt ≠ verboten	permitted ≠ prohibited

Unterwegs per Autostop oder mit der Bahn

Mit dem Sommer kommt wieder die Wanderlust. Dann packt man den Koffer oder den Rucksack und macht eine Reise. Viele Menschen fahren mit dem eigenen° Wagen oder mit dem Flugzeug. Aber junge Leute besitzen oft keinen Wagen oder wollen ihr Geld sparen. Darum fahren sie mit der Bahn oder reisen per Autostop. Ein paar junge Leute haben uns von ihren Reiseerfahrungen° erzählt.

„Trampen erweitert° den Horizont. Ich bin zum Beispiel dieses Jahr nicht nur in der BRD, sondern auch im Ausland getrampt, und ich habe überall sympathische Menschen kennengelernt. In Italien ist es besonders schön gewesen. Ein Autofahrer hat mich und meinen Freund von Florenz nach Rom mitgenommen. Er hat ein bißchen Deutsch verstanden, und wir haben dann drei Tage bei seiner Familie gewohnt. Ich habe ein paar schöne Fotos von seinen Kindern gemacht. Das hat uns Spaß gemacht, und ich hoffe, wir können sie nächstes Jahr wieder besuchen. Ja, im Zug kann man die Menschen einfach nicht so gut kennenlernen."
(Adrienne, 20, aus Kaisersaschern)

„Ich habe ein Gefühl von Freiheit, wenn ich trampe, aber es gibt auch immer ein bißchen Unsicherheit.° Ich komme gern am Abend in einer Stadt mit einer Jugendherberge an. Ein paar Mal° bin ich zu früh aus einem Auto

own

travel experiences

broadens

insecurity

ein . . . Mal = *a couple of times*

Auf der Autobahn

„Müssen wir im Bahnhof übernachten?"

ausgestiegen und habe darum mit dem Bus oder mit der
25 Straßenbahn zur Jugendherberge fahren müssen. Einmal
war° die Jugendherberge schon geschlossen, und ich habe im
Bahnhof übernachten müssen. Gott sei Dank ist das erlaubt,
und es ist eigentlich nicht so schlimm gewesen."

was

(Thomas, 21, aus Tübingen)

30   „Heutzutage fahre ich meistens mit der Bahn, denn das
Trampen gefällt mir nicht mehr und ich habe nicht so viel
Zeit wie früher.° Ich finde, die Bahn macht das Reisen sehr
einfach und bequem. Man braucht nicht—wie beim Autostop—am Straßenrand° zu stehen, sondern man geht einfach
35 zum Bahnhof, kauft eine Fahrkarte und steigt in den Zug
ein. Und man weiß, man kommt pünktlich an.

so . . . früher = *as much time as I
used to*
side of the road

     Im Abteil kommt man oft mit anderen° Menschen ins
Gespräch.° Am Wochenende habe ich zum Beispiel nach
Hannover fahren müssen. Während der Fahrt habe ich mit
40 einem Musikstudenten geredet. Ich habe ihm mit seinem
Gepäck geholfen, denn er hatte nicht nur einen Rucksack
und einen Koffer mit, sondern auch eine Baßgeige.° Verrückt, nicht?

other
kommt . . . Gespräch = *starts a
conversation*

bass fiddle

(Herbert Zimmermann, 30, aus Heidelberg)

Fragen zum Lesestück

1. Warum reist man gern im Sommer?
2. Wie kann man im Urlaub Geld sparen?
3. Wie kann man Menschen im Ausland kennenlernen?
4. Wo kann man oft billig übernachten?
5. Warum muß man als Tramper manchmal im Bahnhof übernachten?
6. Finden Sie das so schlimm?
7. Macht Ihnen das Trampen Spaß? Warum oder warum nicht?
8. Warum ist das Reisen mit der Bahn einfach und bequem?
9. Warum gefällt es Herbert Zimmermann im Zugabteil?

Vom Lesen zum Sprechen

Reisen und Verkehr   Travel and Traffic

You already know some of these words.

Verben

ab·fahren ≠ an·kommen
ein·steigen ≠ aus·steigen
um·steigen   to transfer,
   change (trains, buses, etc.)

Substantive

der **Bus, -se**
der **Bahnhof, ⁻e**
der **Flughafen, ⁻** airport
der **Zug, ⁻e**
der **Wagen, -**
der **Verkehr**   traffic

das **Flugzeug, -e**
das **Auto, -s**
das **Fahrrad, ⁻er**   bicycle
das **Moped, -s**

die **Autobahn, -en**
   expressway, high-speed
   highway
die **Haltestelle, -n**
   streetcar or bus stop
die **Bahn**
   die **U-Bahn**   subway
   train
   die **Straßenbahn**
die **Fahrkarte, -n**

Andere Vokabeln

geradeaus   straight ahead

Gegensätze

rechts ≠ links

Pattern Sentences

Repeat these expressions aloud.

Man fährt **mit** dem Wagen.   One goes **by** car.
          mit der Bahn.   by train.
          mit dem Bus.   by bus.
Ich warte **auf** den Zug.   I am waiting **for** the train.
          auf den Bus.   for the bus
          auf die Straßenbahn.   for the street-car.
Sie warten **am** Bahnhof.   They are waiting **at the** station.
          an der Haltestelle.   at the bus (or
                                              streetcar) stop.
Wir fahren **zum** Bahnhof.   We're driving **to the** train station.
          zum Flughafen.   to the airport.

A. Gruppenarbeit: Sprechen Sie in Gruppen von zwei oder drei Studenten.

1. Beschreiben Sie die Fahrt zu einem Freund oder einer Freundin. Wohin müssen Sie fahren? Wie fährt man? Wo muß man warten? Wo steigt man ein und aus? Muß man umsteigen?

2. Ihre Gruppe macht eine Reise ins Ausland. Beschreiben Sie diese Reise. Wohin wollen Sie fahren? Wie fahren Sie? Wie lange wollen Sie dort bleiben? Was müssen Sie mitnehmen?

3. (Prepare this dialogue with a friend.) Sie stehen seit einer Stunde an der Straße. Endlich hält ein Auto, und Sie steigen ein. Sprechen Sie mit dem Autofahrer über das Trampen und Ihre Ferien.

Mündliche Übungen

A. Persönliche Fragen

1. Besitzen Sie einen Wagen oder ein Fahrrad?
2. Gibt es eine Straßenbahn in Ihrer Stadt?
3. Wie ist der Verkehr in Ihrer Stadt?
4. Reisen Sie manchmal mit der Bahn? Wohin?
5. Sind Sie schon einmal getrampt? Wie ist das gewesen?
6. Haben Sie schon einmal in einer Jugendherberge übernachtet? Wo?
7. Fahren Sie oft mit dem Bus? Was machen Sie während der Fahrt?
8. Reden Sie gern mit Menschen im Zug?

B. Complete the sentence with any clause after the coordinating conjunction.

EXAMPLE: Philosophie ist mein Hauptfach, aber . . .
Philosophie ist mein Hauptfach, aber ich studiere auch Geschichte.

1. Ich muß jetzt gehen, denn . . .
2. Leider habe ich jetzt keine Zeit, aber . . .
3. Ich will heute abend nicht ins Kino, sondern . . .
4. Am Meer kann man in der Sonne liegen oder . . .
5. Morgen habe ich etwas mehr Zeit, denn . . .
6. Das Vorlesungsverzeichnis liegt nicht auf dem Tisch, sondern . . .
7. Das Übernachten im Bahnhof ist nicht verboten, sondern . . .

C. (books open) Using the cues below and the conjunction **sondern,** say you're not going to do one thing, but rather another.

EXAMPLE: kaufen / den Mantel / die Jacke
Ich kaufe nicht den Mantel, sondern die Jacke.

1. gehen / ins Theater / ins Kino
2. besuchen / meine Schwester / meinen Bruder
3. lesen / Buch / Brief
4. gehen / spazieren / schwimmen
5. werden / Journalist / Professor

D. Your teacher asks the class a general question. Student A turns to a neighbor and directs the question specifically to him or her. Student B answers with anything that makes sense.

> EXAMPLE: Teacher: Wer kann mir morgen helfen?
> Student A: Kannst *du* ihm/ihr morgen helfen?
> Student B: Nein, leider kann ich ihm/ihr nicht helfen.

1. Wer glaubt mir?
2. Wer kann mir antworten?
3. Wem gehört denn dieses Buch?
4. Wem gefällt das Wetter heute?
5. Wem sollen wir für den Wein danken?
6. Wer kann mir heute helfen?

E. Frau Schneider is working around the house. Describe what she is doing in the pictures in the left columns, then describe the result of her efforts pictured on the right.

Schriftliche Übungen

F. In den Semesterferien sind Sie viel gereist. Beschreiben Sie Ihre Reise. (*Write a paragraph in perfect tense, describing either a real or imaginary journey.*)

G. Schreiben Sie das Gespräch zwischen Herbert Zimmermann und dem Musikstudenten im Zugabteil (see reading, p. 195).

H. Wie sagt man das auf deutsch?

1. Were you able to take a trip this year?
2. Yes, we went to Italy.
3. Did you bring the children along?
4. Yes, they like Italy very much. (use *gefallen*)

5. Does this suitcase belong to you?
6. No, it doesn't belong to me, but to my brother.
7. Should I put it here on the floor?
8. Yes, please. Thank you. ("I thank you.")

9. How is your husband?
10. He's not very well.
11. Oh, I'm sorry.

12. Nowadays the trains are very comfortable.
13. You can sit in the compartment and read or sleep.

Almanach

Youth Hostels

There are about 560 Youth Hostels in West Germany, 100 in Austria, and 85 in Switzerland. They are meeting places for young travellers from all over the world. In addition to providing inexpensive food and lodging, they offer a variety of courses and organized trips.

Opposite is a copy of a page from the Youth Hostel handbook for West Germany as well as a key explaining the symbols used.

Membership in the AYH (American Youth Hostels) entitles the cardholder to privileges in hostels all over the world. To apply for membership, write to:

American Youth Hostels, Inc.
National Administrative Offices
1332 "I" Street, N.W., 8th Floor
Washington, D.C. 20005

Postleitzahl	Jugendherberge / Adresse / Herbergseltern	Lvb	Telefon	Betten	Tagesräume	Hobby- und Sporträume	Warmwasser	Dusche	Familienzimmer	Kochgelegenheit	Vollverpflegung	für Behinderte geeignet	Freibad	Hallenbad	Wintersport-Möglichkeiten	ev. Kirche	kath. Kirche	Bahnhof	Bus	Straßenbahn	Besondere Bedingungen	mehr über die JH / Seite
2720	Rotenburg/Wümme, Verdener Str. 104, Gästehaus	Unt.-Ems	04261 4051	152	3	1	x	x	—	—	x	—	20	20	—	x	x	30	—	—	—	S. 332
8803	Rothenburg o.d.T., Roßmühle, Doris u. Eduard Schmitz	Bayern	09861 4510	141	1	x	x	x	4	x	x	—	15	15	x	x	x	20	x	—	—	S. 178
8803	Rothenburg o.d.T., „Spitalhof" Pf. 1206, Klaus u. Beate Moll	Bayern	09861 889	90	3	—	x	x	—	—	x	—	15	15	x	x	x	20	x	—	—	S. 178
8774	Rothenfels „Burg", Verwaltung, Burg Rothenfels	Bayern	09393 1015	200	4	1	x	x	—	—	x	○	—	—	—	—	x	15	—	—	—	S. 178
7210	Rottweil a. Neckar, Lorenzgasse 8, Elisabeth u. Hans-Peter Schobel	Schwab.	0741 6274	78	2	—	x	x	—	—	x	—	15	15	x	x	x	20	—	—	—	S. 309
7820	Rudenberg-Neustadt, Titisee Neustadt, Rudenberg 6, Irene und Horst Brömel	Baden	07651 7360	138	5	2	x	x	2	—	x	○	30	—	x	x	x	30	—	—	⊙	S. 137
6220	Rüdesheim, Am Kreuzberg, Hella u. Manfred Alt	Hessen	06722 2711	222	4	1	x	x	2	—	x	—	—	20	—	x	x	20	20	—	* ⊙	S. 226
6090	Rüsselsheim, Hauptm.-Scheuermann-Weg 6, Gisela u. Konrad Merz	Hessen	06142 42346	116	6	1	x	x	—	—	x	—	10	15	—	x	x	15	5	—	* ⊙	S. 226
4784	Rüthen, Am Rabenknapp 5, Cläre und Herbert Gillert	Westf.-L.	02952 483	108	4	1	—	x	1	—	x	○	1	—	—	x	x	—	15	—	—	S. 363
5107	Rurberg, Simmerath-Rurberg, Aloisia u. Gerhard Lis	Rheinl.	02473 2200	176	7	3	x	x	3	x	x	○	2 km	6,5 km	x	—	x	14 km	20	—	⊙	S. 269
2932	Ruttelerfeld/Zetel 1-Neuenburg, Zollweg 27, Ingeborg u. Rolf Flenker	Unt.-Ems	04452 416	136	4	2	x	x	—	—	x	—	60	—	—	x	x	—	45	—	—	S. 332
6600	Saarbrücken, Meerwiesertalweg 31, Marga u. Albert Dumont	Saarl.	0681 33040	181	5	3	x	x	—	—	x	○	20	15	—	x	x	20	2	—	● *	S. 295
5510	Saarburg, Bottelter Str. 8, Renate u. Willi Guth	Rhl.-Pf.	06581 2555	134	3	—	—	x	—	—	x	—	5	—	—	x	x	15	10	—	—	S. 289
8391	Saldenburg „Waldlaterne", In der Burg, Ingeborg u. Hans Leischer	Bayern	08504 1655	166	3	4	x	x	—	—	x	○	10	30	x	—	x	—	20	—	—	S. 178
2904	Sandhatten/Hatten, Wöschenweg 28, Uwe u. Anke Möller	Unt.-Ems	04482 330	130	6	—	x	x	—	—	x	○	25	120	—	30	60	105 75	10	—	—	S. 332
6541	Sargenroth, Kirchweg 1, Gudrun u. Hermann Weiß	Rhl.-Pf.	06761 2500	148	4	1	x	x	3	—	x	x	90	im Haus	—	x	x	90	5	—	⊙ *	S. 289

Zeichenerklärung/Key/Legende   Seite/Page   25/26 und 50/51

Kurzinformationen über alle Jugendherbergen
Short informations of all Youth Hostels
Informations brèves sur les Auberges de Jeunesse

Legende: Postleitzahl · Jugendherberge Adresse Herbergseltern · Lvb · Telefon · Betten · Tagesräume · Hobby- und Sporträume · Warmwasser · Dusche · Familienzimmer · Kochgelegenheit · Vollverpflegung · für Behinderte geeignet Erläuterungen s. Seite 25/26 · Freibad Minuten · Hallenbad Minuten · Wintersport-Möglichkeiten · ev. Kirche · kath. Kirche · Bahnhof Minuten · Bus Minuten · Straßenbahn Minuten · Besondere Bedingungen · mehr über die JH Seite

Kapitel 8

Das Leben in der Stadt

Dialoge

„Brauchen wir noch etwas?" ◆ Der Stadtbummel ◆ „Zahlen bitte!"

Wortschatz 1

Grammatik

1. Subordinating Conjunctions
   Verb Last Word Order in the Subordinate Clause ◆ Question Words as Subordinating Conjunctions ◆ Verbs with Separable Prefixes in Subordinate Clauses ◆ Order of Clauses in the Sentence
2. Infinitive Constructions with **zu**
   Infinitives with **um . . . zu** and **ohne . . . zu**
3. Genitive Case
   Formation ◆ Use of the Genitive ◆ Prepositions with the Genitive
4. Telling Time
   Asking for the Time ◆ Official Time-Telling
5. Nouns of Measure, Weight, and Number
6. Translating English *to:*
   nach, zu, in
7. Expanding Your Vocabulary
   Leicht zu merken

Wortschatz 2

Lesestück

Aspekte der Großstadt

Vom Lesen zum Sprechen

In der Stadt ◆ Essen im Restaurant

Almanach

Das Kulturleben einer Stadt

Dialoge

„Brauchen wir noch etwas?"

DORA: Weißt du, ob Max zum Abendessen kommt?

FRANZ: Ja, ich habe ihm gesagt, daß wir um halb sieben essen. Komisch, daß er noch nicht hier ist.

DORA: Soll ich schnell zum Supermarkt, um noch etwas einzukaufen?

FRANZ: Ja. Wir brauchen ein Kilo Kartoffeln, 500 Gramm Leberwurst, Brot, Käse und einen Liter Milch.

DORA: Ist das alles?

FRANZ: Ich glaube ja.

Der Stadtbummel

HELMUT: Da es nicht mehr regnet, können wir jetzt unseren Stadtbummel machen. Hast du immer noch Lust mitzukommen?

MARIANNE: Gerne. Was gibt es denn hier zu sehen?

HELMUT: Die Gebäude der Altstadt sind besonders interessant, und bist du je in unserem Kunstmuseum gewesen?

MARIANNE: Nein, noch nie. Weißt du, wo wir später billig essen können?

HELMUT: Ja, wenn wir nachher Hunger haben, ist es nicht weit zu einem Restaurant in der Nähe des Rathauses.

„Zahlen bitte!"

KELLNERIN: So, hat es Ihnen geschmeckt?

GAST: Ausgezeichnet!

KELLNERIN: Möchten Sie noch etwas bestellen?

GAST: Danke,[1] ich möchte zahlen, bitte.

KELLNERIN: Sie haben Schnitzel, Pommes frites, einen Salat und ein Bier gehabt, nicht wahr?

GAST: Ja, und auch eine Tasse Kaffee.

KELLNERIN: Das macht DM 25,80, bitte sehr.

[1] **Danke** = "No thanks."

Wortschatz 1

"What else do we need?"

DORA: Do you know if Max is coming to dinner?

FRANZ: Yes, I told him we were eating at 6:30. Funny that he's not here yet.

DORA: Shall I go to the super-market quickly to buy anything else?

FRANZ: Yes, we need a kilogram of potatoes, 500 grams of liverwurst, bread, cheese and a liter of milk.

DORA: Is that everything?

FRANZ: I think so.

A Stroll Through Town

HELMUT: Since it isn't raining any more, we can take a stroll through town. Want to come along?

MARIANNE: Gladly. What is there to see here?

HELMUT: The buildings of the old city center are especially interesting, and have you ever been in our art museum?

MARIANNE: No, never. Do you know where we can eat cheaply later on?

HELMUT: Yes, if we're hungry later, it isn't far to a restaurant near the town hall.

"Check please!"

WAITRESS: Well, did it taste good?[1]

PATRON: Excellent!

WAITRESS: Would you like to order anything else?

PATRON: No thank you. I'd like the check, please.

WAITRESS: You had a cutlet, French fries, a salad, and a beer, right?

PATRON: Yes, and a cup of coffee, too.

WAITRESS: That comes to twenty-five marks eighty, please.

[1] Equivalent phrase in the same situation in an American restaurant might be, "Was everything all right?"

Verben

bestellen to order

schmecken to taste (*trans. and intrans.*); taste good

Wie schmeckt es dir? How does it taste? How do you like it?

zahlen to pay

Substantive

der **Bummel, -** stroll, walk

der **Stadtbummel** stroll through the city

der **Gast, ⁻e** guest; patron

der **Hunger** hunger

der **Kaffee** coffee

der **Käse** cheese

der **Kellner, -** waiter

der **Liter** liter

der **Salat, -e** salad; lettuce

der **Supermarkt, ⁻e** supermarket

das **Abendessen, -** supper, evening meal

zum Abendessen for supper

das **Brot, -e** bread

das **Gebäude, -** building

das **Glas, ⁻er** glass

das **Gramm** gram

das **Kilo** (*short for* das **Kilogramm**)

das **Kilogramm** kilogram

das **Museum, Museen** museum

das **Rathaus, ⁻er** town hall

das **Restaurant, -s** restaurant

das **Schnitzel, -** cutlet, chop

die **Kartoffel, -n** potato

die **Kellnerin, -nen** waitress

die **Kunst, ⁻e** art

die **Milch** milk

die **Tasse, -n** cup

die **Wurst, ⁻e** sausage

die **Leberwurst** liverwurst

Andere Vokabeln

alles (*sing.*) everything

ausgezeichnet excellent

da (*sub. conj.*) since (*causal*)

daß (*sub. conj.*) that

halb half

halb sieben 6:30 (see grammar, p. 217)

je ever

komisch funny; strange

nachher later on, after that

noch etwas something else, anything more

ob (*sub. conj.*) if, whether

später later

um . . . zu in order to

weil (*sub. conj.*) because

weit far, far away

wenn (*sub. conj.*) if

wieviel how much

Nützliche Ausdrücke

bitte sehr you're welcome (*intensification of* **bitte**)

Ich glaube ja. I think so.

Hunger haben to be hungry

Sie hat Hunger. She's hungry.

Lust haben (etwas zu tun) to want (to do something)

in der Nähe (+ *gen.*) near, nearby

Zahlen bitte! (May I have the) check please!

Gegensätze

je ≠ (noch) nie	ever ≠ never (yet)

Neue Kombinationen

A. Replace the words in italics with the cue you will hear.

1. Ich wohne in der Nähe *des Rathauses.*
   (des Museums, des Kinos, der Uni, der Kirche)
2. Max kommt heute *zum Abendessen.*   (zum Mittagessen, zum Kaffee)
3. Wir essen *um halb sieben.*   (um vier Uhr, um halb acht, um neun)
4. Was gibt es hier zu *sehen?*   (tun, kaufen, lesen, trinken)
5. Ich muß nach Hause, *um das Essen zu kochen.*   (um Hausaufgaben zu machen, um meinem Vater zu helfen, um etwas zu essen)

B. *Warum gehen Sie in die Stadt?* Tell why you are going into town. Repeat the cue you will hear.

EXAMPLE: Teacher: . . . . um einen Film zu sehen.
Student: Ich gehe in die Stadt, um einen Film zu sehen.

1. um das Museum zu besuchen.
2. um ein Restaurant zu finden.
3. um Kaffee zu trinken.
4. um meine Freunde zu treffen.
5. um Lebensmittel einzukaufen.
6. um eine Kamera zu kaufen.
7. um mit Annette einen Stadtbummel zu machen.
8. um die Gebäude der Altstadt zu sehen.
9. um meinem Bruder einen Stadtplan zu kaufen.
10. um meinen Verwandten die Kirchen zu zeigen.

Übung zur Aussprache

Review the differences in pronunciation between final **-e** and final **-er** in the Introduction, p. 5, then practice with this list of contrastive pairs:

final -e	*final* -er	*final* -e	*final* -er
schaue	Schauer	bitte	bitter
eine	einer	lose	loser
fahre	Fahrer	Wunde	Wunder
rede	Räder	gönne	Gönner
Liebe	lieber	müde	müder

Now say the following sentences aloud:

1. Ist Walther Fabrikarbeiter?
2. Ja, er arbeitet in einer Fabrik in Hannover. Seine Freundin heißt Susanne Müller.
3. Ich glaube, ich kenne sie. Sie wohnt in einer Stadt in der Nähe von Hannover.

Grammatik

1 ♦ Subordinating Conjunctions

Subordinating conjunctions, like coordinating conjunctions (see p. 183 ff.), join two clauses together. But the clause beginning with a subordinating conjunction becomes subordinate to, or dependent on, the other clause (the main clause). A subordinate clause cannot stand alone in speech or writing.

main clause	*subordinate clause*
I know	that they still remember me.
	("that they still remember me" is not a complete sentence.)

In this chapter you will learn the following subordinating conjunctions:

da	since (causal, *not* temporal)
daß	that
ob	whether, if (= whether)
weil	because
wenn	if

Verb Last Word Order in the Subordinate Clause

Unlike coordinating conjunctions, which do not affect word order, subordinating conjunctions move the inflected verb to the end of the subordinate clause:

Wir essen um halb sieben.

Ich glaube, **daß** wir um halb sieben essen.
I think that we're eating at 6:30.

Brauchen wir noch etwas?

Weißt du, **ob** wir noch etwas brauchen?
Do you know whether we need anything else?

Ich habe gerade gegessen.

Ich habe keinen Hunger, **weil** ich gerade gegessen habe.
I'm not hungry because I've just eaten.

Ich habe Zeit.

Ich helfe dir, **wenn** ich Zeit habe.
I'll help you if I have time.

„Möchten Sie jetzt zahlen?"

A. Expand the statements you will hear as in the example.

> EXAMPLE: Die Wurst ist teuer.
> Ich weiß, daß die Wurst teuer ist.

1. Wir essen um sieben.
2. Sie brauchen eine Flasche Wein.
3. Diese Gebäude sind interessant.
4. Der Tourist will essen.
5. Marie sucht ein Restaurant.
6. Sie haben einen Salat gegessen.
7. Erich hat Bier getrunken.
8. Es hat ihnen geschmeckt.

B. You don't know the answers to the following questions. Begin with **Ich weiß nicht, ob . . .**

> EXAMPLE: Ist das Essen teuer?
> Ich weiß nicht, ob das Essen teuer ist.

1. Wohnt sie in Berlin?
2. Ist das Abendessen schon fertig?
3. Müssen wir jetzt gehen?
4. Spielt er gern Fußball?
5. Hat sie je in Freiburg studiert?
6. Arbeitet man abends?
7. Ist er je nach Italien gereist?
8. Können wir die Altstadt sehen?

C. Explain why you're staying home today. Change the sentence you will hear to a **weil**-clause, moving the verb to the end.

> EXAMPLE: Das Wetter ist nicht schön.
> Ich bleibe zu Hause, weil das Wetter nicht schön ist.

1. Meine Freunde besuchen mich.
2. Ich muß etwas schreiben.
3. Ich habe gestern zu viel gearbeitet.
4. Ich muß das Abendessen kochen.
5. Ich bin gern allein.
6. Ich will nicht ins Kino.
7. Die Kinder brauchen mich.
8. Die Läden sind geschlossen.

Question Words as Subordinating Conjunctions

The question words (**wann, warum, was, wer, wen, wem, wie, wo,** etc.) act as subordinating conjunctions when they introduce an indirect question (i.e., a question restated as a subordinate clause):

> Was brauchen wir zum Abendessen?
>
> Weißt du, **was** wir zum Abendessen brauchen?
> *Do you know what we need for supper?*
>
> Wer ist das?
>
> Ich kann Ihnen nicht sagen, **wer** das ist.
> *I can't tell you who that is.*

Üben wir!

A. You don't know the answers to these questions about a hitchhiking trip.

> EXAMPLE: Wer steht da?
> Ich weiß nicht, wer da steht.

1. Wohin wollen sie reisen?
2. Warum packen sie die Rucksäcke?
3. Wann wollen sie in Italien sein?
4. Wie ist das Wetter in Italien?
5. Wo wollen sie übernachten?
6. Was kostet das Essen in der Jugendherberge?
7. Warum fahren sie nicht mit dem Zug?
8. Wen wollen sie besuchen?

Verbs with Separable Prefixes in Subordinate Clauses

You know that when a verb with a separable prefix is used in a main clause, the prefix is separated from the verb and placed at the end of the clause:

Dort **kaufe** ich immer **ein.**

In a subordinate clause, the verb moves to the end of the clause and the prefix is attached to it.

Weißt du, warum ich ▭▭▭▭ immer dort ⌐einkaufe?⌐

Üben wir!

A. Tell the rest of the class what your teacher has asked you.

EXAMPLE: Teacher: Wann stehen Sie auf?
Student: Sie hat gefragt, wann ich aufstehe.

Teacher: Sind Sie müde?
Student: Sie hat gefragt, ob ich müde bin.

1. Wann fängt das Semester an?
2. Kommt Bernd vorbei?
3. Warum fährt Regine ab?
4. Bringt Maria die Kinder mit?
5. Hört die Musik bald auf?
6. Mit wem geht Hans abends spazieren?
7. Wo steigt man in die Straßenbahn ein?
8. Wo steigen wir aus?
9. Kommen Ihre Gäste morgen zurück?
10. Wer macht das Fenster zu?

Order of Clauses in the Sentence

Subordinate clauses may either follow or precede the main clause:

    1   **2**
Ich spreche langsam, da ich nicht viel Deutsch gelernt habe.
            1   **2**
Da ich nicht viel Deutsch gelernt habe, spreche ich langsam.

In the latter case, the *entire* subordinate clause occupies the first position. The verb of the main clause follows it immediately in second position. The two inflected verbs are thus directly adjacent to each other, separated by a comma:

subordinate clause	*main clause*
Wenn ich Zeit **habe,**	**gehe** ich ins Museum.
Ob er sympathisch **ist,**	**weiß** ich nicht.

A. Reverse the order of the clauses in the sentences you will hear.

EXAMPLE: Sie kann mir nicht sagen, wo sie wohnt.
Wo sie wohnt, kann sie mir nicht sagen.

1. Ich weiß nicht, was wir brauchen.
2. Ich glaube nicht, daß ich etwas vergessen habe.
3. Ich kaufe dir das Buch, da ich sowieso zur Buchhandlung muß.
4. Ich komme später vorbei, wenn du willst.
5. Ich habe nicht gewußt, daß er mich nicht verstanden hat.
6. Ich komme mit, wenn du in die Stadt gehst.

2 ♦ Infinitive Constructions with *zu*

The German infinitive is sometimes preceded by **zu**. For the most part, this construction parallels the use of the English infinitive with **to**:

Was gibt es hier **zu sehen**?   *What is there to see here?*
Hast du Zeit, diesen Brief **zu lesen**?   *Do you have time to read this letter?*

Like the inflected verb in a subordinate clause, the infinitive with **zu** comes *at the end* of its phrase. In English, the infinitive comes *at the beginning* of its phrase.
   When the verb has a separable prefix, the **zu** is inserted between the prefix and the verb stem:

   abzufahren   spazierenzugehen

Ich hoffe, bald **abzufahren**.   *I hope to leave soon.*
Wer hat Lust, mit mir   *Who wants to go for a walk with*
   spazierenzugehen?   *me?*

Here are some cases in which the infinitive with **zu** is used:

■ as the complement of certain verbs such as **anfangen, aufhören, hoffen** and **vergessen**; and with constructions like **Lust haben, Zeit haben**, and **Spaß machen**:

Fangen wir an **zu essen**.[1]   *Let's begin to eat.*
Sie hat aufgehört, Geschichte **zu**   *She stopped studying history.*
   studieren.
Ich habe vergessen, dir von meiner   *I forgot to tell you about my trip.*
   Reise **zu erzählen**.
Ich habe keine Lust, heute   *I don't want to go swimming*
   schwimmen zu gehen.   *today.*
Es macht Spaß, einen Stadtbummel   *It's fun to take a stroll through the*
   zu machen.   *city.*

[1] Note on punctuation: The infinitive with **zu** is not set off by a comma if it has no complements of its own. If it has complements it must be set off by a comma:
   Ich fange an zu essen.   Ich fange an, Brot zu essen.

■ as the complement of certain adjectives such as **schön, erlaubt,** and **verboten:**

Es ist verboten, während der Vorlesung **zu essen.**	*Eating is prohibited during the lecture.*
Ich finde es schön, im Restaurant **zu essen.**	*I find it nice to eat in a restaurant.*

Üben wir!

A. Restate the sentences you will hear as infinitive phrases. Begin with the cued phrase, as in the example.

> EXAMPLE: Er schreibt den Brief. Er hat begonnen, . . .
> Er hat begonnen, den Brief zu schreiben.

1. Wir sehen die Altstadt. Wir haben Zeit, . . .
2. Ich gehe schwimmen. Es macht mir Spaß, . . .
3. Sie hat nicht mit ihrem Freund gesprochen. Sie hat vergessen, . . .
4. Willst du ins Museum gehen? Hast du Lust, . . . ?
5. Am Samstag bleibt man im Bett. Am Samstag ist es schön, . . .
6. Du machst das Abitur nicht. Es ist Unsinn, . . .
7. Hier dürfen wir nicht tanzen. Es ist verboten, . . .
8. Sie macht keine Reisen mehr. Sie hat aufgehört, . . .

Stehimbiß (*stand-up snack bar*)

B. Your teacher asks if certain things are permitted here. Use **erlaubt** or **verboten** plus infinitive phrases to respond.

EXAMPLE: Darf man hier schnell fahren?
Ja, es ist erlaubt, schnell zu fahren.
or: Nein, es ist verboten, schnell zu fahren.

1. Darf man hier ein Foto machen?
2. Darf man hier aussteigen?
3. Darf man hier per Autostop reisen?
4. Darf man hier sitzen?
5. Darf man im Bahnhof übernachten?
6. Darf man in der Bibliothek essen?
7. Darf man hier Fußball spielen?
8. Darf man während der Deutschstunde einschlafen?

Infinitives with um . . . zu and ohne . . . zu

1. **um . . . zu** = in order to

Ich muß in die Stadt, **um** Lebensmittel **einzukaufen.**	*I have to go to town in order to buy groceries.*
Ich fahre nach Deutschland, **um** Deutsch **zu lernen.**	*I'm going to Germany in order to learn German.*

2. **ohne . . . zu** = without . . . -ing

Sie hat die Stadt verlassen, **ohne** mich **zu besuchen.**	*She left the city without visiting me.*
Ich habe das Buch gelesen, **ohne** es **zu verstehen.**	*I read the book without understanding it.*

Üben wir!

A. Change the **weil**-clause to an **um . . . zu** phrase, eliminating the modal verbs.

EXAMPLE: Ich gehe in die Stadt, weil ich einkaufen will.
Ich gehe in die Stadt, um einzukaufen.

1. Ich gehe ins Restaurant, weil ich etwas essen will.
2. Sie sitzt am Fenster, weil sie die Straße sehen möchte.
3. Oft trampen Studenten, weil sie Geld sparen wollen.
4. Manchmal fährt man ins Ausland, weil man mehr lernen möchte.
5. Ich gehe in diesen Laden, weil ich einen Pulli kaufen will.

B. Combine these sentences, changing the second one to an **ohne . . . zu** phrase.

EXAMPLE: Er hat den Koffer genommen. Er hat mich nicht gefragt.
Er hat den Koffer genommen, ohne mich zu fragen.

1. Sie sind abgefahren. Sie haben nicht „auf Wiedersehen" gesagt.
2. Ich arbeite in einem Geschäft. Ich kenne den Chef nicht.
3. Karin hat ein Zimmer gefunden. Sie hat nicht lange gesucht.
4. Geh nicht spazieren. Du trägst keinen Mantel.
5. Sie dürfen nicht ins Konzert. Sie haben keine Karten gekauft.

3 ◆ Genitive Case

The genitive case expresses possession (**John's** books) or a relationship between two nouns marked in English by the preposition **of** (the color **of your eyes**):

der Wagen **meiner Mutter**	*my mother's* car
die Freunde **der Kinder**	*the children's* friends
das Haus **meines Bruders**	*my brother's* house
Macs Freundin	*Mac's* girlfriend
das Ende **des Filmes**	*the end of the movie*
die Häuser **der Stadt**	*the houses of the city*

Formation

1. **der**-words and **ein**-words in the genitive

	masc.	neut.	fem.	plural
nom.	der Mann	das Kind	die Frau	die Leute
acc.	den Mann	das Kind	die Frau	die Leute
dat.	dem Mann	dem Kind	der Frau	den Leuten
gen.	**des Mannes**	**des Kindes**	**der Frau**	**der Leute**
	eines Mannes	eines Kindes	einer Frau	keiner Leute
	meines Mannes	eures Kindes	Ihrer Frau	unserer Leute
	dieses Mannes	jedes Kindes	welcher Frau	dieser Leute

■ The genitive endings of **der**-words and **ein**-words are identical:

masc.	neut.	fem.	plural
-es	**-es**	**-er**	**-er**

■ In addition, singular masculine and neuter *nouns* add the ending **-es** if the
■ noun has one syllable, **-s** if it has more than one syllable.
Feminine singular and all plural nouns have *no* ending in the genitive.

German does *not* use an apostrophe with the genitive ending (my husband's
car = der Wagen meines **Mannes**).

Ist das der Vater des Kind**es**?	*Is that the child's father?*
Wo ist das Buch des Professor**s**?	*Where is the professor's book?*

Obst– und Gemüsehändler: „Was darf's heute sein, Frau Bronski?"

Masculine N-nouns have the same **-en** or **-n** ending in the genitive as in the accusative and dative. They do *not* add an **-es** in the genitive singular:

Kennen Sie die Frau dieses Herr**n**?	*Do you know this gentleman's wife?*
Kennen Sie die Frau meines Studen**ten**?	*Do you know my student's wife?*
Kennen Sie die Frau des Journalis**ten**?	*Do you know the journalist's wife?*

2. Genitive of Interrogative Pronoun: **wessen.** The genitive form of the question word **wer** is **wessen** (whose?)

Wessen Buch ist das?   *Whose book is this?*

 Üben wir!

A. Change these noun phrases from nominative to genitive.

EXAMPLE: der Zug   des Zuges

1. ein Arzt
2. mein Freund
3. unser Vater
4. die Lehrerin
5. das Kind
6. die Leute
7. jede Uni
8. eine Mutter
9. der Student
10. dieser Herr
11. das Essen
12. diese Zimmer
13. die Züge
14. unsere Uhr

Use of the Genitive

German uses the genitive case for both persons and things, whereas English usually reserves **'s** for people and animals and uses **of** for things:

das Haus **meines Bruders**   *my brother's* house
die Häuser **der Stadt**   the houses *of the city*

In German, the genitive generally *follows* the noun it modifies. In English, the possessive *precedes* the noun:

der Wagen **meiner Mutter**   *my mother's* car
die Freunde **der Kinder**   the *children's* friends

Proper names and kinship titles used as names, however, usually *precede* the noun as in English:

Karls Freundin   *Karl's* girlfriend
Mutters Wagen   *Mother's* car

Proper names simply add **-s** without an apostrophe in the genitive (**Karl's** girlfriend = **Karls** Freundin).

Spoken German frequently substitutes **von** plus dative case for the genitive in phrases corresponding to English phrases such as "a friend of my brother's," "a cousin of mine":

Er ist ein Freund **von meinem Bruder.**   He's a friend *of my brother's.*
Michael ist ein Vetter **von mir.**   Michael is a cousin *of mine.*

Üben wir!

A. Provide German equivalents for the following phrases. Make one noun genitive and the other nominative.

EXAMPLE: your girlfriend's sister
die Schwester deiner Freundin

1. the walls of my room
2. the end of the week
3. Karl's major
4. the children's pictures
5. the history of the war
6. his brother's house
7. her sister's boyfriend
8. the cities of Switzerland
9. a student's letter
10. the rooms of the house
11. the students of Germany
12. the cities of Europe
13. the windows of this room
14. your mother's car
15. the history of these countries
16. a friend of yours
17. a student of Michael's
18. Grandmother's clock

B. Whom do these things belong to? Use the genitive case in your answer.

> EXAMPLE: Gehört diese Uhr Ihrer Schwester?
> Ja, das ist die Uhr meiner Schwester.

1. Gehört dieser Koffer dem Gast?
2. Gehört dieser Stadtplan deiner Lehrerin?
3. Gehört dieses Zimmer einem Amerikaner?
4. Gehört der Ausweis deinem Freund?
5. Gehört dieses Haus seinen Eltern?
6. Gehören diese Bücher Ihrem Sohn?

Prepositions With the Genitive

There is a small group of prepositions which take the genitive case:

(an)statt	instead of	Schreib eine Karte **statt eines Briefes.**
trotz[1]	in spite of, despite	**Trotz des Wetters** sind wir ans Meer gefahren.
während	during	**Während der Woche** fährt er oft in die Stadt.
wegen	because of, on account of	**Wegen seiner Arbeit** kann er nicht kommen.

Üben wir!

A. Form prepositional phrases with the elements provided.

> EXAMPLE: während / Sommer
> während des Sommers

1. trotz / Wetter
2. während / Ferien
3. statt / Straßenkarte
4. wegen / mein / Mutter
5. trotz / unser / Problem
6. wegen / mein / Beruf
7. trotz / Arbeit
8. während / Tag
9. anstatt / Hotel
10. während / Woche

B. Give German equivalents for these prepositional phrases.

1. because of her friend
2. during the year
3. despite his money
4. during a film
5. instead of the boss
6. instead of a postcard
7. in spite of my friends
8. because of my German class
9. due to her profession
10. instead of a road map

---

[1] In spoken German **trotz** is frequently used with the dative case, but the genitive is preferred.

Asking For the Time

There are two ways to ask the time in German:

Wie spät ist es?
Wieviel Uhr ist es?   *What time is it?*

Here are some possible responses:

Es ist drei Uhr.

Es ist Viertel nach sieben.

Es ist Viertel vor zehn.

Es ist ein Uhr. or: Es ist eins.[1]

Es ist elf (Minuten) nach zehn.

Es ist vierzehn vor acht.

The half hour is counted in relation to the following full hour, not the preceding hour as in English:

Es ist halb acht.
(literally: "It's half way to eight.")

[1]Note that when you drop the word **Uhr, ein** becomes **eins.**

Üben wir!

A. Wie spät ist es bitte?

1   2   3   4

5   6   7   8

Asking What Time Something Occurred or Will Occur

There are two ways to ask when something occurred or will occur: **um wieviel Uhr?** or **wann?**

Um wieviel Uhr/Wann hat das Konzert begonnen?	*At what time/When did the concert begin?*
Es hat um halb neun begonnen.	*It began at eight-thirty.*

Üben wir!

A. Ask the questions which elicit these answers.

> EXAMPLE: Wir haben um sechs gegessen.
> **Wann / Um wieviel Uhr** habt ihr gegessen?

1. Der Film fängt um halb acht an.
2. Sein Zug fährt um elf ab.
3. Wir haben ihn gestern besucht.
4. Ich bin um elf Uhr noch im Seminar gewesen.

B. Now give the answers indicated by the clocks.

1. Um wieviel Uhr wollt ihr abfahren?

2. Wann kommt denn Barbara an?

3. Um wieviel Uhr können wir Sie besuchen?

4. Wann beginnt die Deutschstunde?

5. Um wieviel Uhr gehen wir ins Kino?

Official Time-Telling

German has another way of telling time: in this system, one gives the full hour and the number of minutes past it:

written	*spoken*	
1.40 Uhr	Es ist ein Uhr vierzig.	*It's 1:40 A.M.*
7.55 Uhr	Es ist sieben Uhr fünfundfünfzig.	*It's 7:55 A.M.*

Instead of using A.M. and P.M., German uses this formal system on a twenty-four hour basis. This is the way the time is given in the media, in train schedules, etc. Subtract 12 to get the P.M. time as used in English.

20.00 Uhr	**Es ist zwanzig Uhr.** Sie hören unser Abendkonzert.	*It's eight o'clock. And now our evening concert.*
13.25 Uhr	Der Zug nach Hamburg fährt um **dreizehn Uhr fünfundzwanzig** ab.	*The train to Hamburg departs at 1:25 P.M.*

Bern, Schweiz

| | | **Üben wir!** | **A.** Give these times in the twenty-four hour German system. |

EXAMPLE: 11:20 P.M.   Es ist 23.20 Uhr.

1. 1:55 P.M.   3. 6:47 P.M.   5. 11:30 A.M.

2. 6:02 P.M.   4. 10:52 P.M.   6. 8:16 P.M.

5 ◆ Nouns of Measure, Weight, and Number

Nouns indicating measure and weight are *not* followed by a prepositional phrase, as they are in English:

ein Glas Bier	a glass *of* beer
eine Flasche Wein	a bottle *of* wine
eine Tasse Kaffee	a cup *of* coffee
ein Kilogramm Leberwurst	a kilogram *of* liverwurst
ein Liter Milch	a liter *of* milk

Masculine and neuter nouns of measure remain in the singular even after numerals greater than one:

drei **Glas** Bier	three glass*es* of beer
300 **Gramm**	300 grams

Feminine nouns of measure, however, *do* use their plural forms:

zwei Tass**en** Kaffee	two cups of coffee
drei Flasch**en** Wein	three bottles of wine

Üben wir!

A. Pass on the orders of your friends who can't speak German to the waiter in a restaurant. Begin with „Bringen Sie uns bitte . . ."

EXAMPLE: . . . a cup of coffee.
Bringen Sie uns bitte eine Tasse Kaffee.

1. . . . a glass of wine and two cups of coffee.
2. . . . five glasses of beer.
3. . . . a bottle of wine and three cups of coffee.
4. . . . three glasses of beer, two glasses of wine, and a cup of coffee.

6 ♦ Translating English *to*

The all-purpose English preposition indicating destination is **to**: We're going **to Germany, to the ocean, to the train station, to the movies, to Grandmother's.** German has several equivalents for English **to**, depending on the destination:

1. **nach** with cities, states, and most countries:

Wir fahren **nach Wien.**
          nach Kalifornien.
          nach Deutschland.
          nach Italien.
          nach Europa.

and in the idiom **nach Hause:**

Wir fahren **nach Hause.**

2. **zu** with people and some locations:

Ich gehe **zu meinen Freunden.**
          zu meiner Großmutter.

          zum Bahnhof.
          zur Buchhandlung.
          zur Post. (post office)

3. **in** with countries whose names are feminine or plural, and with some locations:

Ich fahre **in die Schweiz.**
          in die DDR. (= Deutsche Demokratische Republik)
          in die USA.

Wir gehen **ins Kino.**
          in die Kirche.
          ins Konzert.
          in die Mensa.
          ins Museum.
          ins Restaurant.
          ins Theater.
          in die Stadt. (= downtown)
          ins Bett.

Here is a rough rule of thumb for deciding whether to use **zu** or **in** with a destination within a city: **in** is usually used with destinations where one will spend a relatively long time (**ins Kino, ins Restaurant, in die Kirche, ins Bett**); **zu** is usually used with destinations involving a briefer visit (**zum Bahnhof, zur Post**).

7 ♦ Expanding Your Vocabulary

Leicht zu merken

der **Aspekt -e**	A*spekt*
die **Metropole, -n**	Metro*pole*
der **Streß**	

Wortschatz 2

Verben

ärgern to annoy; offend
**Schi laufen (läuft Schi), ist
Schi gelaufen** to ski
steigen, ist gestiegen to
climb
**verbringen, hat
verbracht** to spend
(time)

Substantive

der **Eindruck, ⸚e**
impression
der **Fußgänger, -** pedestrian
der **Preis, -e** price

(das) **England** England
das **Jahrhundert, -e**
century
(das) **München** Munich
das **Rad, ⸚er** wheel; bicycle
das **Fahrrad, ⸚er** bicycle
(das) **Rußland** Russia
(das) **Skandinavien**
Scandinavia

die **Ecke, -n** corner
an der Ecke at the
corner
um die Ecke around
the corner
die **Fußgängerzone, -n**
pedestrian mall
die **Großstadt, ⸚e** large
city (over 500,000 inhab-
itants)
die **Kleinstadt, ⸚e** town
(5,000 to 20,000 inhab-
itants)
die **Tour, -en** tour
die **Alpen** (pl.) the Alps

Andere Vokabeln

geradeaus straight ahead
obwohl (sub. conj.) although
trotzdem in spite of that,
nevertheless
zuerst first, at first

Nützliche Ausdrücke

aufs Land to the country
auf dem Land in the
country

Mit dem Auto

Köln

nach Köln und in Köln

Dom. Altstadt. Hohe Straße. Messe.
Kongresse. Museen. Tanzbrunnen.
Rheinschiffahrt.

Es macht Spaß, in Köln zu sein.
Und es ist kein Problem, hinzukommen. Zehn Autobahnen
führen in die Stadt.

Und Parkplätze gibt es mehr als in den meisten
Großstädten.

Wir zeigen Ihnen, wie Sie am einfachsten hinkommen
und wo Sie am besten parken.

(Die Zahlen 1 bis 18 in den Innentexten stehen für die entsprechenden numerierten Fotos.)

Aspekte der Großstadt

Eindrücke eines Amerikaners

Mark Walker, Student: „Dieses Jahr verbringe ich zwei Semester als Austauschstudent° an der Universität Hamburg. Ich komme aus einer Kleinstadt in Colorado, wo es viel Platz und wenig Menschen gibt. Darum war es für mich zuerst schwer zu verstehen, wie die Deutschen so dicht zusammengedrängt° leben können. Manchmal habe ich das Gefühl, daß ich nie allein sein kann.

    Aber das bedeutet nicht, daß Hamburg mir nicht gefällt. Im Gegenteil!° Ich finde es phantastisch, daß es in der Stadt so viel zu tun gibt. Wenn ich Lust habe, kann ich jeden Tag ins Konzert, ins Kino oder ins Museum gehen. Hamburg ist die zweitgrößte° Stadt der Bundesrepublik und eine internationale Metropole. Weil es eine Hafenstadt° ist, hat es seit Jahrhunderten Verbindungen° mit England, Skandinavien, Rußland und vielen anderen° Ländern.

    Wenn das Stadtleben mir zu viel wird, dann ist es sehr leicht, mein Fahrrad zu nehmen, in die Bahn zu steigen und aufs Land zu fahren. In der Lüneburger Heide[1] im Süden kann man schöne Radtouren machen. Dieser Kontrast zwischen Stadt und Land scheint mir besonders typisch für Deutschland. Das Land ist den Stadtbewohnern° sehr wichtig als Erholung° vom Streß des Alltags.°

„Ich wohne gern hier"

Beate Kreuz, Sozialarbeiterin° in München: „Ich arbeite mit jungen Leuten aus Gastarbeiterfamilien.[2] Sie haben oft keinen Schulabschluß° und können keine Arbeit finden. Ich sehe also jeden Tag die Probleme einer Großstadt wie München. Trotz dieser Probleme wohne ich sehr gern hier. Obwohl die Wohnungsnot° in München schlimm ist, haben ein paar Freunde und ich eine Wohnung in einem alten Gebäude finden können. Ich kann mit der S-Bahn° überall hinfahren° und brauche überhaupt kein Auto. Im Sommer gehen wir in der Isar[3] schwimmen, und im Winter laufen

---

exchange student

dicht zusammengedrängt = *crowded together*

im Gegenteil = *on the contrary*

second-largest
port city
ties
other

city dwellers
rest / everyday life

social worker

diploma

housing shortage

Stadtbahn = *commuter rail service*
überall hin- . . . = *everywhere*

---

[1] The Lüneburg Heath, an extensive nature preserve on the North German plain, south of Hamburg, north of Hannover.

[2] Families of foreign, or "guest" workers. These are workers from Turkey, Italy, Yugoslavia, and other southern European countries, principally employed in heavy industry and construction.

[3] Munich is located on the Isar, a 160-mile long tributary of the Danube River originating in the Austrian alps.

Eisdiele (*ice-cream parlor*) in der Fußgängerzone

wir in den Alpen Schi. In der Kaufinger Straße⁴ gibt es eine
große Fußgängerzone, wo viele Leute gern einen Ein-
kaufsbummel machen. Aber in meinem Beruf sehe ich so
viel Arbeitslosigkeit,° daß mich der Konsumzwang° und die
hohen° Preise ärgern. Trotzdem kann man auch ohne viel
Geld in München gut leben.

*unemployment / pressure to buy /
high*

⁴Formerly a major traffic thoroughfare in central Munich.

Fragen zum Lesestück

1. Woher kommt Mark Walker?
2. Wie gefällt ihm Hamburg?
3. Welches Gefühl hat er manchmal?
4. Was kann er jeden Tag tun, wenn er Lust hat?
5. Warum gibt es soviel Streß in der Stadt?
6. Was ist Beate Kreuz von Beruf?
7. Warum braucht sie kein Auto?
8. Was macht sie im Sommer? im Winter?
9. Erklären Sie, warum die hohen Preise Beate ärgen.

Vom Lesen zum Sprechen

In der Stadt

die **Brücke, -n**	bridge
die **Post**	post office
das **Café, -s**	café
das **Kaufhaus, ̈er**	department store
das **Taxi, -s**	taxicab

Patterns
(useful phrases with familiar vocabulary)

1. Asking directions

> Entschuldigen Sie, wie komme ich zur Post?
> Können Sie mir sagen, wo die Brücke ist?
> wann der Zug abfährt?

2. Giving directions

> Das ist gleich in der Nähe.
> Das ist nicht weit von hier.
> Gehen Sie geradeaus, und dann nach links.
> nach rechts.
> um die Ecke.

Finding Your Way Around

A. Use the map on the facing page to ask each other directions.

1. You are standing in front of the post office and want to find your way to the market square.
2. You are in the museum and have to return to your hotel to meet somebody.
3. You are in the pedestrian zone and are suddenly hungry. You need help finding a restaurant.

B. *Gruppenarbeit* Mit einer Studentengruppe machen Sie eine Reise durch Deutschland. Heute abend sind Sie in einer Großstadt angekommen und übernachten in der Altstadt im Hotel Sommerhof (siehe Stadtplan).

Wohin wollen Sie gehen?

Was möchten Sie besonders gerne tun oder sehen?

Wo wollen Sie essen?

Was machen Sie am Abend?

Wie kommen Sie überall hin—zu Fuß, mit einem Taxi oder mit der Straßenbahn?

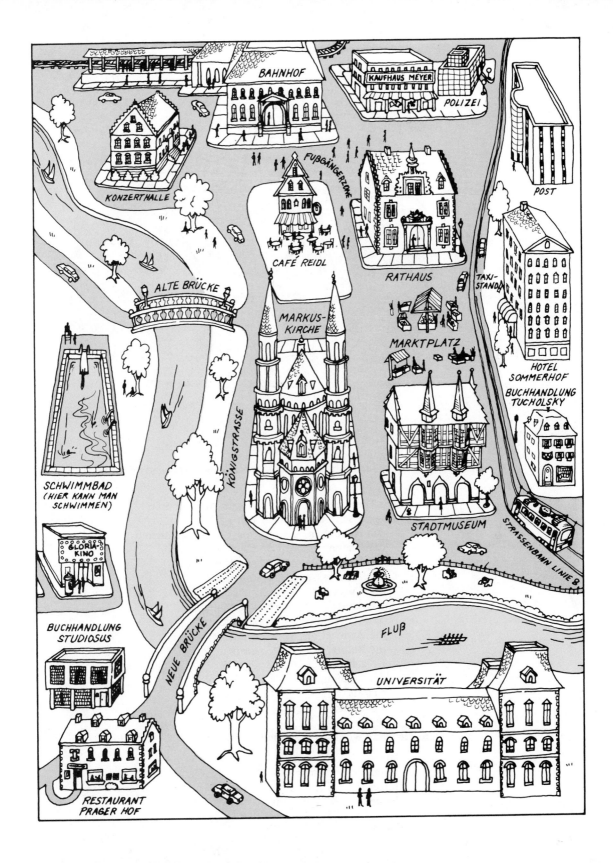

Essen im Restaurant

1. die **Serviette, -n**

2. die **Gabel, -n**

3. der **Teller, -**

4. das **Messer, -**

5. der **Löffel, -**

6. das **Glas, ̈er**

Was gibt's zum Essen?

You already know the words for several things to eat and drink. Here are some more:

das **Hauptgericht**	entrée, main course
der **Fisch, -e**	fish
das **Hähnchen, -**	(roast or fried) chicken
der **Braten**	roast
der **Salat**	salad; lettuce
die **Tomate, -n**	tomato
die **Gurke, -n**	cucumber
das **Gemüse**	vegetables
das **Sauerkraut**	sauerkraut
die **Zwiebel, -n**	onion
die **Bohne, -n**	bean
der **Nachtisch**	dessert
der **Kuchen, -**	cake
das **Eis**	ice cream
das **Obst**	fruit

Here are some words to describe how food tastes:

süß	sweet
sauer	sour
bitter	bitter
lecker	delicious

You already know the phrase „Haben Sie Hunger?" Also useful is „Haben Sie Durst?" ("Are you thirsty?") Before a meal Germans wish each other „Guten Appetit!"

A. Reden wir über das Essen.

1. Fragen Sie die anderen Studenten, was sie gern essen.
2. Fragen Sie sie, was ihnen schmeckt oder nicht schmeckt.

B. *Rollenspiel.* Form groups of three or four. One student plays the waiter or waitress, the others order a meal. Use the vocabulary on this page and a menu if your instructor provides one.

Mündliche Übungen

A. Persönliche Fragen

1. Kommen Sie aus einer Großstadt? aus einer Kleinstadt?
2. Was gibt es in Ihrer Stadt zu sehen?
3. Wie oft essen Sie im Restaurant?
4. Wo fahren Sie in den Ferien hin?
5. Wo haben Sie als Kind die Ferien verbracht? Auf dem Land? In den Bergen? Am Meer?
6. Besitzen Sie ein Fahrrad?
7. Machen Sie gern Radtouren? Wohin?
8. Was oder wer ärgert Sie besonders?

B. Answer the question you will hear, using an **um . . . zu** phrase.

> EXAMPLE: Warum gehen Sie in die Altstadt?
> Um Lebensmittel zu kaufen.

1. Warum gehst du ins Wasser?
2. Warum lernst du Deutsch?
3. Warum fahren Studenten per Autostop?
4. Warum bist du nach Österreich gefahren?
5. Warum geht man ins Kino?
6. Warum geht man denn ins Museum?

C. Complete the sentences you will hear cued, using verb-last word order. Tell about your own plans, likes, dislikes, etc.

> EXAMPLE: Es ist möglich, daß . . .
> Es ist möglich, daß ich heute abend mit Freunden Karten spiele.

1. Es ist möglich, daß . . .
2. Ich weiß, daß . . .
3. Ich weiß nicht, ob . . .
4. Ich weiß nicht, warum . . .
5. Es tut mir leid, daß . . .
6. Es scheint mir interessant, daß . . .
7. Ich finde es schön, wenn . . .
8. Es gefällt mir sehr, daß . . .

D. The car in which you and some friends are riding has been stopped by police looking for contraband. Answer their questions about what belongs to whom, following the English cues.

> EXAMPLE: Wessen Koffer ist das? (my girlfriend's)
> Das ist der Koffer meiner Freundin.

1. Wessen Rucksack ist das? (my brother's)
2. Wem gehören diese Bücher? (to me)
3. Wessen Bierflasche ist das? (Georg's)
4. Wessen Briefe sind das? (mine)
5. Wessen Pullover ist das? (my father's)
6. Wem gehört diese Straßenkarte? (to my friends)
7. Wessen Ausweis ist das? (this hitchhiker's)
8. Wessen Geld ist das? (my friends')

E. Ask your classmates when they do certain things. Your teacher will cue the activity.

> EXAMPLE: Teacher: aufstehen
> Student A: Um wieviel Uhr stehst du auf?
> Student B: Ich stehe um halb acht auf.

1. aufstehen
2. in der Mensa essen
3. zur Deutschstunde gehen
4. einkaufen gehen
5. nach Hause gehen
6. Hausaufgaben machen
7. ins Bett gehen
8. einschlafen

„Ich habe ein Hähnchen für das Wochenende gekauft."

F. Ask each other questions about the trains arriving at and departing from Mannheim. Use the schedule below and state times in the 24-hour system.

EXAMPLE: Wann kommt der Zug aus Hamburg an?
Er kommt um 14.22 Uhr in Mannheim an.

Um wieviel Uhr fährt er in Hamburg ab?
Um 9.33 Uhr.

Mannheim Hbf (Hauptbahnhof)

| | Ankunft (arrivals) | | | Abfahrt (departures) | |
Zug-Nr.	ab[1]	an[1]	Zug-Nr.	ab	an
6342	Hamburg 9.33 Uhr	Mannheim 14.22 Uhr	1338	Mannheim 5.42 Uhr	Zürich 8.12 Uhr
7422	München 10.03 Uhr	Mannheim 13.10 Uhr	2472	Mannheim 6.06 Uhr	Nürnberg 9.33 Uhr
1387	Frankfurt 11.20 Uhr	Mannheim 12.01 Uhr	6606	Mannheim 7.55 Uhr	Straßburg 8.40 Uhr
7703	Wien 10.10 Uhr	Mannheim 17.56 Uhr	2203	Mannheim 10.12 Uhr	Innsbruck 15.46 Uhr
9311	Berlin 11.05 Uhr	Mannheim 19.16 Uhr	3679	Mannheim 13.23 Uhr	Prag 20.09 Uhr

[1] *ab:* time and place of departure; *an:* time and place of arrival.

Schriftliche Übungen

G. Fantasize that you are an urban planner with the opportunity to create an ideal human environment. Describe this city in a paragraph or two. What does it have or not have?

H. You have spent the day exploring the *Altstadt* on p. 227. It is now evening and you have returned to your hotel to write to a German friend. Describe your day and give your impressions of the people and their way of life. To remind yourself of the letter-writing conventions, see p. 167.

I. Wie sagt man das auf deutsch?

1. Can you please tell us where the town hall is?
2. It isn't far from here. If you go around the corner you'll see it.
3. Thanks very much.

4. What time is it?
5. It is ten past four. Why do you ask?
6. Do I still have time to go shopping?
7. Yes, of course. If you go right away, I'll come with you.

Almanach

Cultural Life in the City

German city life is rich in cultural opportunities. Even relatively small cities often have excellent theaters, museums, and symphony orchestras. Nowadays cultural life is heavily subsidised by government monies, which makes artistic innovation financially possible and opens "high culture" to a broad public. The images collected here hint at the richness of these opportunities.

3. September

20 Uhr/Philharmonie
Festakademie
zur Eröffnung der 35. Berliner Festwochen
Dietrich Fischer-Dieskau Bariton
Ensemble Modern der Jungen Deutschen Philharmonie
Leitung **Ernest Bour**
Ruzicka, Celan-Gesänge (Uraufführung)
Auftragswerk der Berliner Festwochen
Schönberg, Kammersymphonie op. 9

4. September

20 Uhr/Philharmonie
Pittsburgh Symphony Orchestra
Leitung **Lorin Maazel**
Britten, Sinfonia da Requiem
Strawinsky, Symphonie in drei Sätzen
Dvořák, Symphonie Nr. 9 »Aus der Neuen Welt«

5. September

20 Uhr/Philharmonie
Berliner Philharmonisches Orchester
Leitung **Riccardo Muti**
Claudio Arrau Klavier
Beethoven, Klavierkonzert Nr. 3
Bruckner, Symphonie Nr. 4

7. September

18 Uhr/Staatsbibliothek
Dang Thai Son Klavier
Werke von Chopin, Debussy und Prokofieff

20 Uhr/Kaiser-Wilhelm-Gedächtniskirche
Gerd Zacher Orgel
Werke von Schönberg, Juan Allende-Blin (Uraufführung),
Mauricio Kagel und Bach

20 Uhr/Philharmonie
Symphonieorchester des Bayerischen Rundfunks
Leitung **Sir Colin Davis**
Karl Amadeus Hartmann, Symphonie Nr. 6
Beethoven, Symphonie Nr. 3 »Eroica«

8. September

18 Uhr/Staatsbibliothek
Saschko Gawriloff Violine
Siegfried Palm Cello
Bruno Canino Klavier
Werke von Mauricio Kagel

20 Uhr/Philharmonie
Berliner Philharmonisches Orchester
Leitung **Charles Dutoit**
Männerchor der St. Hedwigs-Kathedrale/
Männerchor des Städtischen Musikvereins Düsseldorf
Händel, Concerto grosso op. 6/7
Bernd Alois Zimmermann, »Stille und V...

Where is German spoken?

◄ Thun See (Schweiz)

Salzburg bei Nacht (Österreich) ▲

◄ Hochzeit im Rathaus (Wenigerode, DDR)

▲ Blumenmarkt (Aachen, BRD)

Auf der Straße: ein Schornsteinfeger (chimney sweep)
(Rothenburg ob der Tauber, BRD)

Innsbruck. Blick nach Norden auf die Nordkette
(Österreich)

Bankgebäude (Frankfurt, BRD)

Schistation im Berner Oberland. Im Hintergrund,
die Jungfrau (Schweiz)

Touristen in der DDR

Karlskirche in Wien   (18. Jahrhundert)

Sankt Jakob in Tirol   (Österreich)

Der Opernball in Wien   (Österreich)

Summary
and
Review

FORMS

1 ♦ Verbs

A. Separable Prefix Verbs (prefix is stressed)

anfangen	**kennen**lernen
aufstehen	**mit**kommen
anrufen	

The prefix separates in the present tense:

	inflected stem		*prefix*
Wir	**fangen**	bald	**an.**
Sie	**steht**	um sieben	**auf.**
Wann	**kommst**	du denn	**mit?**

The prefix separates in the imperative:

inflected stem		*prefix*
Fangen	Sie bald	**an!**
Steht	um sieben	**auf!**
Komm	bitte	**mit!**

The infinitive (prefix attached to stem) is used with the modal verb:

	modal		*infinitive*
Sie	**müssen**	bald	**anfangen.**
Du	**sollst**	jetzt endlich	**aufstehen.**

B. Inseparable Prefix Verbs (prefix is not stressed)
The following prefixes are inseparable: **be-, ent-, er-, ge-, ver-, zer-.**

EXAMPLES: bedeuten, gefallen, vergessen
Er vergißt alles.
Er hat seine Freunde vergessen.
Vergeßt eure Hausaufgaben nicht!

C. Perfect Tense

1. Inflected Auxiliary (**haben** or **sein**) + Past Participle

	auxiliary		*part participle*
Ich	**habe**	einen Wagen	**gekauft.**
Sie	**ist**	nach Wien	**geflogen.**

2. **sein** as Auxiliary in the Perfect

The verb must be *intransitive* and show *change of location or condition.*

Wir	**sind**	nach Hause gegangen.	*(change of location)*
Ich	**bin**	schnell gelaufen.	*(change of location)*
Hans	**ist**	groß geworden.	*(change of condition)*

■ Exceptions are **bleiben** and **sein.**

Sie	**sind**	zehn Tage geblieben.
Er	**ist**	oft in Berlin gewesen.

3. Weak vs. Strong Past Participles

Weak Participles

ge + STEM + (e)t

sagen:	Was hat er dir	**gesagt?**
kaufen:	Wo haben Sie das	**gekauft?**
arbeiten:	Ich habe heute nicht	**gearbeitet.**
kosten:	Das hat viel	**gekostet.**

Verbs ending in **-ieren** do *not* add the prefix **ge-** in the past participle:

studieren:	Sie hat in Freiburg	**studiert.**
telefonieren:	Ich habe mit Erika	**telefoniert.**

Strong Participles

ge + PERFECT STEM + en

geben:	Vater hat mir Geld	**gegeben.**
helfen:	Sie haben uns	**geholfen.**
fahren:	Ich bin nach Deutschland	**gefahren.**
trinken:	Was habt ihr denn	**getrunken?**

■ The perfect stem is not predictable from the infinitive form. Past participles must be memorized.

4. Past Participles of Verbs with Separable (Stressed) Prefixes:

PREFIX + ge + STEM and ENDING

anfangen:	Wann hat der Film	**angefangen?**
aufhören:	Hat er schon	**aufgehört?**

5. Past Participles of Verbs with Inseparable (Unstressed) Prefixes:

PREFIX + STEM and ENDING (no *-ge-*)		
beschreiben:	Er hat sein Haus	beschrieben.
vergessen:	Sie hat mich	vergessen.

6. Perfect Tense of Modal Verbs

	auxiliary **haben**		*double* *infinitive*
Wir	**haben**	das nicht	**verstehen können.**
Sie	**hat**		**mitgehen dürfen.**

D. Verbs with Dative Objects:

The following verbs require a dative object.

antworten	Antworten Sie **mir**, bitte.
danken	Er hat **mir** für den Roman gedankt.
gefallen	Das gefällt **mir** sehr.
gehören	**Wem** gehört das?
glauben	Ich kann **Ihnen** nicht glauben.
helfen	Hilf **mir**, bitte!

2 ◆ Noun Phrases

A. der-words

Here is the complete paradigm:

Definite Article + Noun			
		Singular	*Plural*
masculine	**nom.**	der Mann	die Männer
	acc.	den Mann	die Männer
	dat.	dem Mann	den Männern
	gen.	des Mannes	der Männer
neuter	**nom.**	das Kind	die Kinder
	acc.	das Kind	die Kinder
	dat.	dem Kind	den Kindern
	gen.	des Kindes	der Kinder
feminine	**nom.**	die Frau	die Frauen
	acc.	die Frau	die Frauen
	dat.	der Frau	den Frauen
	gen.	der Frau	der Frauen

■ Dative plural of all nouns ends in **-n** (except when the plural form is **-s**: den Hotels, den Kinos).
■ The masculine and neuter genitive takes **-es** only when the noun is one syllable. Otherwise, add **-s**: des Vaters, des Problems.

B. ein-words

Here is the complete paradigm:

		Singular	Plural
ein-Word + Noun			
masculine			
	nom.	kein Mann	keine Männer
	acc.	keinen Mann	keine Männer
	dat.	keinem Mann	keinen Männern
	gen.	keines Mannes	keiner Männer
neuter			
	nom.	kein Kind	keine Kinder
	acc.	kein Kind	keine Kinder
	dat.	keinem Kind	keinen Kindern
	gen.	keines Kindes	keiner Kinder
feminine			
	nom.	keine Frau	keine Frauen
	acc.	keine Frau	keine Frauen
	dat.	keiner Frau	keinen Frauen
	gen.	keiner Frau	keiner Frauen

3 ◆ Genitive Phrases

Genitive case follows the noun it modifies:

genitive

der Wagen	meines Freundes
die Kinder	seiner Schwester
die Häuser	dieser Stadt

Exception: Proper names in the genitive precede the noun they modify:

Beethovens	Symphonien
Utes	Freundin
Kurts	Großmutter

4 ◆ Masculine N-nouns

	singular	*plural*
nom.	der Student	die Studenten
acc.	den Studenten	die Studenten
dat.	dem Studenten	den Studenten
gen.	des Studenten	der Studenten

Similarly:

der Herr, -n, -en	gentleman; Mr.
der Mensch, -en, -en	person, human being
der Journalist, -en, -en	journalist
der Tourist, -en, -en	tourist

5 ♦ Prepositions

A. Prepositions with Dative

aus	out of; from (country or city)
außer	except for; in addition to
bei	near; at; in the home of
mit	with
nach	after
seit	since (temporal)
von	from; of; by
zu	to

B. Two-Way Prepositions (with accusative or dative)

	Destination **Wohin?** with accusative	*Location* **Wo?** with dative
an	to, toward	at, alongside of
auf	onto	on top of, on
hinter	behind	behind
in	into	in
neben	beside	beside
über	over; across	above
unter	under	under
vor	in front of	in front of
zwischen	between	between

C. Prepositions with genitive:

(an)statt	instead of
trotz	in spite of
während	during
wegen	because of, on account of

D. Translating English "to"

1. **nach**—with cities and most countries

   Wir fahren **nach** Berlin.
   Wann reist ihr **nach** Italien?

2. **zu**—with people and some locations

   Ich gehe heute abend **zu** Inge.
   Gehen wir jetzt **zum** Bahnhof.

3. **in**—with countries whose names are preceded by an article

   Wir wollen im Sommer **in die** Schweiz.
   Wir machen eine Reise **in die** DDR.

   and with some locations:

   Kommst du mit **ins** Konzert?
   Ich gehe gern **ins** Kino.

WORD ORDER

1 ♦ Joining Clauses

A. Coordinating conjunctions: **aber, denn, oder, sondern, und**

Coordinating conjunctions do *not* affect word order.

Clause 1 (verb second)	*Coordinating Conjunction*	*Clause 2* (verb second)
Ich bleibe nicht.		Ich gehe nach Hause.
Ich **bleibe** nicht,	**sondern**	ich **gehe** nach Hause.

B. Subordinating conjunctions: **da, daß, ob, obwohl, weil, wenn** and question words introducing subordinate clauses: **wann, warum, was, wem, wen, wer, wessen, wie, wo, woher, wohin**

Subordinating conjunctions require verb-last word-order.

Main Clause (verb second)	*Subordinating Conjunction*	*Subordinate Clause* (verb last)
Ich weiß nicht,	**ob**	sie in München **wohnt.**

or

Subordinating Conjunction	*Subordinate Clause* (verb last)	*Main Clause* (verb first, i.e., in second position)
Ob	sie in München **wohnt,**	**weiß** ich nicht.

2 ♦ Infinitive Phrases

1. The infinitive with **zu** comes at the end of its phrase:

   Es war schön.   Ich habe Sie endlich kennengelernt.
   Es war schön, Sie endlich **kennenzulernen.**

   Haben Sie morgen Zeit?   Ich möchte mit Ihnen sprechen.
   Haben Sie morgen Zeit, mit mir **zu sprechen?**

2. **um . . . zu** = in order to

   Ich reise nach Deutschland.   Ich möchte dort studieren.
   Ich reise nach Deutschland, **um** dort **zu studieren.**

3. **ohne . . . zu** = without (doing something)

   Ich habe ein Jahr dort gelebt.   Ich habe Ihren Sohn nicht kennengelernt.
   Ich habe ein Jahr dort gelebt, **ohne** Ihren Sohn **kennenzulernen.**

3 ♦ Order of Direct and Indirect Objects

When both objects are nouns, their usual order is:

	dative	*accusative*
Geben wir	**unserem** Lehrer	**ein** Buch.

When the direct object is a pronoun, however, the order must be:

	accusative	*dative*
Geben wir	**es**	**unserem** Lehrer.
Geben wir	**es**	**ihm.**

4 ♦ Pronoun Word Order

Personal pronouns come either in first position:

> **Er** ist gern allein.

or immediately after the inflected verb in the order nominative, accusative, dative.

> Heute gebe **ich es ihm.**

FUNCTIONS

1 ♦ Telling Time

Wieviel Uhr ist es?
Wie spät ist es?

Es ist halb elf.
Es ist 10.30 Uhr.

Es ist zwanzig nach zwei.
Es ist 2.20 Uhr.

Es ist ein Uhr.
Es ist *eins*.

Es ist Viertel vor sieben.
Es ist 6.45 Uhr.

Remember the official 24-hour time keeping system:

Es ist 22.15 Uhr.   *It's 10:15 P.M.*

2 ◆ Review of Useful Expressions

A. Time and Place

Woher kommen Sie?
Wohin gehst du nach der Stunde?
Ich gehe vor elf Uhr ins Bett.
Gehen wir zu Fuß oder fahren wir mit der Straßenbahn?

B. Requesting and Giving Information

Was kostet das, bitte?   Hast du Lust, etwas zu tun?
Das kostet DM 4,50.   Warum siehst du heute so müde
Gefällt dir die Musik?   aus?

C. Reactions and Opinions

Quatsch!   Du hast Glück gehabt.
Sei nicht so dumm!   Wir haben Pech gehabt.
Es tut mir leid.   Das schmeckt mir gut.
Es macht nichts.   Ich glaube ja.
Das macht mir Spaß.

Test Your Progress

A. Fill in the blank with the correct preposition or contraction (preposition + article).

1. Ich bin _____ vier Semestern _____ dieser Uni.
2. _____ Professor Beißner möchte ich eine Dissertation _____ Kafka schreiben.
3. Ich habe seinen Namen nicht _____ Vorlesungsverzeichnis gefunden.
4. Jeden Tag fahre ich _____ meiner Freundin _____ meinem Moped _____ Universität.
5. _____ dem Semesterende wollen wir _____ den Ferien zusammen nach Österreich fahren.
6. _____ dem Schreibtisch _____ mir zu Hause liegen alle meine Bücher _____ (except for) dem Geschichtsbuch.

B. Form questions to which these are the answers.

1. Er fliegt nach Wien.
2. Sie kommt aus Berlin.
3. Doch, das stimmt.
4. Doch, natürlich habe ich Zeit für dich.
5. Das hat mein Großvater immer gesagt.
6. Die Landkarte gehört meinem Freund.
7. Am Dienstag sollen wir das machen.
8. Die Kinder sind heute bei ihrer Tante.

C. Fill in the blank with the correct prepositional phrase. Each one will contain a German equivalent of "to".

1. Kommst du mit _____ Kino?
2. Nein, leider nicht. Ich fahre heute abend _____ meiner Kusine.
3. Mußt du also _____ die Schweiz?
4. Ja, ich muß zuerst _____ Basel und dann mit dem Zug _____ Zürich fahren.
5. Warte, ich komme mit dir _____ Bahnhof und gehe später _____ Hause.

D. Complete the sentence according to the English cue. In the second sentence, substitute pronouns for objects.

1. Die Großmutter erzählt (*the children a fairy-tale*) _____.
   Sie erzählt _____ _____ am Abend.
2. Ich habe (*my friend the article*) _____ gezeigt. Bitte, zeigen Sie (*it to me*) _____ _____ bald.
3. Der Professor gibt (*the students an example*) _____.
   Dann erklärt er _____ _____ .

E. Restate the following sentences in the perfect tense.

1. Karin bleibt heute zu Hause.
2. Meine Freunde wohnen nicht in München.
3. Um wieviel Uhr stehst du denn auf?
4. Ich schreibe einen Brief an meine Familie.
5. Sie vergißt meinen Namen immer.
6. Ich muß eine Stunde bleiben.
7. Die Schüler sind oft müde.
8. Ich habe leider keine Zeit.
9. Sie wird Lehrerin.
10. Wir fahren am Freitag nach Salzburg.

F. Combine the sentences with the conjunctions cued in English.

1. Kommst du mit? (or) Bleibst du hier?
2. (because) Ich habe keine Zeit. Ich kann Ihnen nicht helfen.
3. Hamburg liegt nicht im Süden Deutschlands. (but rather) Es liegt im Norden.
4. Ich weiß nicht. (whether) Ist er hier?
5. (since) Wir haben wenig Geld. Wir müssen trampen.
6. (if) Du kannst mir helfen. Ich bin bald fertig.
7. Jan hat nicht studiert. (but) Er weiß viel über Geschichte.
8. Hast du gehört? (that) Tante Lina besucht uns morgen.
9. (although) Sie ist nie in Europa gewesen. Sie spricht gut Deutsch.
10. Ich besuche euch. (if) Wir können im Sommer nach Europa.

G. Complete these sentences, using the genitive phrase cued in English.

1. Wir nehmen (*my friends' car*).
2. Kennen Sie schon (*the end of this film*)?
3. Nein, aber (*Karl's brother*) sagte, daß es gut ist.
4. (*My teacher's house*) liegt gleich um die Ecke.
5. (*Barbara's house*) ist auch nicht weit von hier.
6. Mir gefällt (*the language of these people*) sehr.
7. Mir gefällt mein Studium (*in spite of the work*).
8. (*Because of my work*) kann ich leider nicht mitkommen.
9. Ist denn (*the life of a student*) so schwer?

H. Give the German for these sentences with time expressions.

1. What time is it, please?
2. It is almost seven-thirty.
3. When is the train supposed to arrive?
4. It arrives at eight fifty-nine P.M.
5. What are you doing at quarter to eight?

I. Look at the English verb cued at the beginning of each sentence. Insert its correct German form in the blank. Supply also the preposition (or contraction) needed.

1. (*to lie*) Manchmal _____ ich bis neun _____ Bett.
2. (*to lay*) Du kannst deine Tasche _____ den Stuhl _____ .
3. (*to put*) Sollen wir Ihren Schreibtisch _____ Büro _____ , Herr Doktor?
4. (*to stand*) Ja bitte, aber er soll nicht direkt _____ Fenster _____ .
5. (*to sit*) Darf ich ein paar Minuten hier _____ Tisch _____ ?

J. Combine these sentences by changing the one in italics into an infinitive phrase.

> EXAMPLE: Es ist sehr schön. *Wir gehen im Sommer hier schwimmen.*
> Es ist sehr schön, im Sommer hier schwimmen zu gehen.

1. Wir haben keine Lust. *Wir sollen Onkel Georg besuchen.*
2. *Sie wollten etwas über Kunst lernen.* (um . . . zu) Sie gingen ins Museum.
3. Es war sehr lieb von ihr. *Sie hat mir eine Karte aus Köln geschickt.*
4. Du gehst schon? *Du hast Julia nicht auf Wiedersehen gesagt.*
(ohne . . . zu)

Der Sport

Dialoge
Das neue Fahrrad ♦ „Treibst du Sport?" ♦ „Wo warst du?"

Wortschatz 1

Grammatik
1. Attributive Adjectives
   Predicate Adjectives vs. Attributive Adjectives ♦ The Noun Phrase ♦ Attributive Adjectives after **der**-Words ♦ Attributive Adjectives after **ein**-Words
2. Simple Past of **sein** and **haben**
3. Word Order: Time-Manner-Place
4. Expanding Your Vocabulary
   Ordinal Numbers and Dates ♦ Leicht zu merken

Wortschatz 2

Lesestück
Sport für alle

Vom Lesen zum Sprechen
Der Sport

Almanach
Sport Culture in the Two Germanies

Das neue Fahrrad

MÄDCHEN: Wie gefällt dir mein neues Fahrrad?

JUNGE: Toll! Wo hast du das denn her?

MÄDCHEN: Es war[1] ein Geburtstagsgeschenk von meinem reichen Onkel Leo.

JUNGE: War[1] dein altes Rad denn schon kaputt?

MÄDCHEN: Nein, aber ich brauche ein leichtes Rad, damit ich in den Ferien eine lange Radtour machen kann.

„Treibst du Sport?"

UDO: Sag mal, Hannes, treibst du eigentlich Sport?

HANNES: Klar. Ich verbringe alle freien Stunden auf dem Tennisplatz. Du spielst auch gern Tennis, nicht?

UDO: Ja, aber ich bin kein sehr guter Spieler.

HANNES: Da kann ich dir einen guten Tennislehrer empfehlen.

„Wo warst du?"

MARIANNE: Ich habe dich gestern überall gesucht. Wo warst du denn?

FRANK: Ach, ich hatte[2] Lust, schwimmen zu gehen, und da bin ich mit dem Rad zum neuen Schwimmbad gefahren.

MARIANNE: Wie kommt man denn dahin?

FRANK: Es ist gar nicht schwer zu finden. Man fährt zuerst über die alte Brücke, dann sofort links in die nächste Straße. Es liegt hinter dem großen Sportplatz.

Fahrrad am Bahnhof

Naturerlebnis ohne Streß

---

[1] **war-**: simple past tense of **sein**. See p. 255.

[2] **hatte**: simple past tense of **haben**. See p. 255.

Wortschatz 1

The New Bicycle

GIRL: How do you like my new bicycle?

BOY: Great! Where did you get it?

GIRL: It was a birthday present from my rich Uncle Leo.

BOY: Was your old bike already worn out?

GIRL: No, but I need a light-weight bike, so that I can take a long bike trip during vacation.

Do You Play Sports?

UDO: Hey, Hannes, do you play sports?

HANNES: Sure. I spend all my free hours on the tennis court. You like to play tennis too, don't you?

UDO: Yes I do, but I'm not a very good player.

HANNES: Then I can recommend a good tennis teacher to you.

Where Were You?

MARIANNE: I was looking all over for you yesterday. Where were you anyway?

FRANK: Oh, I felt like going swimming, and so I rode my bike to the new swimming pool.

MARIANNE: How do you get there?

FRANK: It isn't at all hard to find. First you ride over the old bridge, then immediately left at the next street. It's behind the big athletic field.

Verben

empfehlen (emfiehlt), hat empfohlen to recommend

treiben, hat getrieben to drive, force, propel

Sport treiben to play sports

Substantive

der **Geburtstag, -e** birthday

Wann hast du Geburtstag? When is your birthday?

zum Geburtstag for one's birthday

der **Junge, -n, -n** boy

der **Sport** sport

der **Sportplatz, ⁻e** playing field

der **Tennisplatz, ⁻e** tennis court

das **Geschenk, -e** gift, present

das **Mädchen, -** girl

das **Schwimmbad, ⁻er** swimming pool

das **Tennis** tennis

Gegensätze

die **Brücke, -n** bridge

die **Farbe, -n** color

Andere Vokabeln

blau blue

braun brown

dahin there (as goal of motion)

Wie komme ich dahin? = How do I get there?

damit (*sub. conj.*) so that

gelb yellow

gestern nachmittag yesterday afternoon

grau gray

grün green

kaputt broken, wrecked; exhausted

klar clear; *colloq.*: sure, of course

nächst-[1] next; nearest

reich rich

rot red

schwarz black

weiß white

reich ≠ arm	rich ≠ poor

[1] The hyphen indicates that this adjective cannot be used without an ending. For adjective endings, see below, pp. 249–254.

Neue Kombinationen

A. Replace the words in italics with the ones you will hear. Notice that the adjectives all have endings.

1. Wo ist mein *neues Fahrrad*?
   (neues Auto; altes Buch; blaues Hemd; kleines Moped)

2. Es ist ein Geschenk von meinem *reichen Onkel*.
   (kleinen Bruder, alten Freund, freundlichen Professor, deutschen Großvater)

3. Leider habe ich keine *große Lust*.
   (freie Stunde, neue Hose, gute Freundin, braune Jacke)

4. Bist du ein *guter Spieler*?
   (guter Schwimmer, schlechter Fahrer, höflicher Tramper, moderner Mensch, typischer Amerikaner)

5. War *dein altes Rad* schon kaputt?
   (dein alter Koffer, dein schönes Geschenk, dein roter Wagen, deine teure Uhr)

6. Ich kann dir *einen guten Lehrer* empfehlen.
   (ein gutes Restaurant, einen guten Wein, ein interessantes Buch, eine schöne Reise, einen komischen Roman)

Fußballfans

B. Say why you need money. Use the English cue and introduce your answer with **damit.**

Ich brauche Geld . . .

1. . . . so that I can buy a city map.
2. . . . so that I can buy a ticket.
3. . . . so that I can take a trip.
4. . . . so that I can go shopping.
5. . . . so that I can spend the night here.

Now use **um . . . zu:**

Ich brauche Geld . . .

6. . . . in order to buy a city map.
7. . . . in order to buy a ticket.
8. . . . in order to take a trip.
9. . . . in order to go shopping.
10. . . . in order to spend the night here.

C. Say what colors certain things are.

> EXAMPLE: Welche Farbe hat Georgs Hemd?
> Sein Hemd ist rot.

Welche Farbe hat / haben . . . ?

> der Kaffee?
>
> der Wald?
>
> das Meer?
>
> die Tafel?
>
> die Wände dieses Zimmers?
>
> seine Hose?
>
> diese Bäume im Sommer?
>
> euer Wagen?
>
> der Pulli dieses Mädchens?
>
> der Wein?
>
> das Hemd dieses Jungen?

⟦cassette icon⟧

Übung zur Aussprache

Starting with this chapter, the *Übung zur Aussprache* section will contain a German poem for you to read aloud. We'll begin with an anonymous twelfth-century love poem in modern translation.

Du bist mein, ich bin dein,	
Des° sollst du gewiß° sein.	*of that / certain*
Du bist verschlossen°	*locked up*
In meinem Herzen,°	*heart*
Verloren° ist das Schlüsselein:°	*lost / little key*
Du mußt immer drinnen° sein.	*inside*

Grammatik

1 ◆ Attributive Adjectives

Predicate Adjectives vs. Attributive Adjectives

Adjectives in English and German may appear in either of two positions in a sentence.

1. They may follow the verbs *to be, to become, to remain* and *to seem* (**sein, werden, bleiben, scheinen**), in which case they are called *predicate adjectives* because they constitute the second part of the predicate.

	predicate adjectives	
Das Rad ist	**leicht.**	*The bicycle is light.*
Meine Großeltern werden	**alt.**	*My grandparents are getting old.*
Das Wetter bleibt	**sonnig.**	*The weather remains sunny.*

Predicate adjectives have *no endings*.

2. Adjectives may also occur *before* a noun. In this position they are called *attributive adjectives.*

	attributive adjectives		
das	**leichte**	Rad	*the light-weight bicycle*
meine	**alten**	Großeltern	*my old grandparents*
das	**sonnige**	Wetter	*the sunny weather*

German attributive adjectives *always* have endings.

The Noun Phrase

Attributive adjectives occur in noun phrases. A noun phrase consists of a noun and the words directly associated with it. English and German noun phrases have similar structures. They consist typically of three types of words: **limiting words, descriptive adjectives,** and **nouns:**

limiting word	descriptive adjective	noun
die	gute	Spielerin
mein	neues	Fahrrad
ein	junger	Lehrer
alle	freien	Stunden

In German, the limiting words are divided into two categories with which you are already familiar; **der**-words and **ein**-words:

der-words	*ein*-words	
der	ein	
dieser	kein	
jeder	mein	
welcher	dein	
alle[1]	sein	
	ihr	possessive
	unser	adjectives
	euer	
	ihr, Ihr	

Some of the endings of attributive adjectives change depending on whether the preceding limiting word is a **der**-word or an **ein**-word.

Attributive Adjectives After **der**-words

When the limiting word in a noun phrase is a **der**-word, the attributive adjective ends in **-en** except in the nominative singular of all three genders and in the neuter and feminine accusative. In these cases, the adjective ends in **-e**.

	masc.	*neut.*	*fem.*	*plural*
nom.	der gute Mann	das gute Kind	die gute Frau	die guten Leute
acc.	den guten Mann	das gute Kind	die gute Frau	die guten Leute
dat.	dem guten Mann	dem guten Kind	der guten Frau	den guten Leuten
gen.	des guten Mannes	des guten Kindes	der guten Frau	der guten Leute

Abstracting the endings, we get:

Adjective Endings Following **der**-words				
	masc.	*neut.*	*fem.*	*plural*
nom.	-e	-e	-e	-en
acc.	-en	-e	-e	-en
dat.	-en	-en	-en	-en
gen.	-en	-en	-en	-en

Note that if more than one adjective occurs in a noun phrase, they all take the same ending:

der gute alte Mann
die guten alten Zeiten

---

[1] **Alle** is usually used in the plural and takes the regular plural endings, i.e.: **alle** (nom. and acc.), **allen** (dat.), **aller** (genitive). **Alle** is often followed by a second limiting word. They will both have the same ending: **alle meine Freunde, alle diese Leute.**

Adjectives with base forms ending in **-er (teuer)** or **-el (dunkel)** drop the penultimate **-e-** before adding endings:

teuer   das **teure** Buch
dunkel   das **dunkle** Haus

◻▬◻ **Üben wir!**

A. Substitute the new noun you will hear, making the necessary changes.

1. Dieses schöne *Geschenk* gefällt mir.
   (Mensch, Mädchen, Kind, Uhr, Gebäude, Haus, Sonne, Junge, Kirche, Kirchen, Berg, Berge)
2. Helfen Sie dieser alten *Frau!*
   (Mann, Leute, Arbeiterin, Professor)
3. Ich brauche das neue *Auto.*
   (Buch, Arbeiter, Karte, Zeitungen, Wagen, Brot, Jacke, Bücher)
4. Das ist das Foto des jungen *Amerikaners.*
   (Freund, Kind, Frau, Leute, Lehrerin, Lehrer, Mädchen)
5. Jede moderne *Frau* weiß das.
   (Mensch, Arbeiterin, Junge, Mädchen, Kind, Schülerin, Schüler)
6. Kennen Sie alle großen *Städte?*
   (Bilder, Universitäten, Kirchen, Tennisspieler)
7. Sie wohnt neben dem alten *Gebäude.*
   (Kirche, Laden, Sportplatz)
8. Er kennt jeden neuen *Studenten.*
   (Studentin, Kind, Mitarbeiter, Buch, Straße)
9. Das ist der Wagen des neuen *Chefs.*
   (Arbeiter, Arbeiterin, Student, Kellner, Familie)
10. Sie geht mit dem kleinen *Jungen* spazieren.
    (Kind, Kinder, Schülerin, Mädchen, Mann)

B. Add each new word you will hear to the sentence.

EXAMPLE: Mir gefällt das Haus. (schön)
Mir gefällt das schöne Haus. (alt)
Mir gefällt das schöne alte Haus.

1. Dort wohnt der Student. (klug, deutsch)
2. Er wohnt in diesem Haus. (groß, dunkel)
3. Er wohnt bei der Familie. (nett, amerikanisch)
4. Möchten Sie diese Gebäude sehen? (typisch, modern)
5. Alle Gebäude gefallen mir. (neu, schön)
6. Ich zeige Ihnen das Rathaus (interessant, alt)
7. Kennst du diesen Mann? (langweilig, jung)
8. Er spricht gern mit jedem Menschen. (reich, wichtig)
9. Die Studentin ist vorbeigekommen. (sympathisch, deutsch)
10. Sie hat diesen Artikel geschrieben. (dumm, lang)
11. Sie ist die Tochter der Professorin. (freundlich, deutsch)

C. (books open) Make a statement. Another student asks you what kind of thing you're talking about. Use adjectives from the list to give more information.

schön	alt	furchtbar
teuer	klein	hell
blau	gelb	lang
warm	schwer	neu
leicht	deutsch	einfach
grün	bunt	interessant
braun	dunkel	schwarz
häßlich	langweilig	

EXAMPLE: Student A: Endlich habe ich das Buch gelesen.
Student B: Welches Buch?
Student A: Das neue, interessante Buch.

1. Gestern habe ich mir das Moped gekauft.
2. Ich glaube, der Rucksack gehört Susanna.
3. Er liest jeden Tag die Zeitung.
4. Hoffentlich wartet er im Zimmer. (In welchem . . . ?)
5. Sie sitzen zusammen unter der Brücke. (Unter welcher . . . ?)
6. Ich habe mir endlich die Schuhe gekauft.
7. Ich glaube, ich kaufe mir das Bild.
8. Wir waren gestern abend in einem Film. (In . . . ?)
9. Sie kam schnell aus dem Laden. (Aus . . . ?)

Geländelauf (*cross-country run*)

D. Answer your teacher's question with a complete sentence.

> EXAMPLE: Dieser Zug fährt langsam, aber dieser fährt schnell.
> Mit welchem Zug fahren Sie?
> Ich fahre mit dem schnellen (langsamen) Zug.

1. Dieser Kaffee ist heiß, aber dieser ist kalt. Welchen trinken Sie?
2. Dieses Hemd ist billig, aber dieses ist teuer. Welches gefällt Ihnen?
3. Diese Kartoffeln sind groß, aber diese sind klein. Welche nehmen Sie?
4. Dieser Tag ist warm gewesen, aber dieser ist kühl gewesen. Welcher Tag hat dir gefallen?
5. Dieser Kurs ist schwer, aber dieser ist leicht. Welchen wollen Sie belegen?
6. Diese Stadt ist schön, aber diese ist häßlich. In welcher Stadt möchten Sie wohnen?
7. Dieses Zimmer ist hell, aber dieses ist dunkel. Welches Zimmer gefällt Ihnen?
8. Dieses Hotel ist alt, aber dieses ist neu. In welchem möchten Sie übernachten?

E. Now repeat the above sentences, this time with two students answering as follows:

> EXAMPLE: Teacher: Dieser Zug fährt langsam, aber dieser fährt schnell. Mit welchem Zug fahren Sie?
> Student A: Ich fahre mit dem schnellen Zug.
> Student B: Dann fährst du nicht mit dem langsamen Zug.

Attributive Adjectives after ein-words

When the limiting word in a noun phrase is an **ein**-word (**ein, kein** or the possessive adjectives **mein, dein,** etc.), the following attributive adjective has the same ending as it would after a **der**-word (**-e** or **-en**), with three exceptions.

In the masculine nominative singular the ending is **-er** (**ein gut*er* Mann** versus **der gute Mann**). In the neuter nominative and accusative singular the ending is **-es** (**ein gut*es* Kind** versus **das gute Kind**). Note that these are precisely the cases in which the **ein**-word has no ending of its own.

The following tables highlight the three cases in which **ein**-words are followed by a different ending than the **der**-words. Compare them with the tables on page 250.

	masc.			*neut.*		
nom.	ein	junger	Mann	ein	junges	Kind
acc.	einen	jungen	Mann	ein	junges	Kind
dat.	einem	jungen	Mann	einem	jungen	Kind
gen.	eines	jungen	Mannes	eines	jungen	Kindes

	fem.			*plural*		
nom.	eine	junge	Frau	meine[1]	jungen	Freunde
acc.	eine	junge	Frau	meine	jungen	Freunde
dat.	einer	jungen	Frau	meinen	jungen	Freunden
gen.	einer	jungen	Frau	meiner	jungen	Freunde

[1] We use **meine** here because **ein** has no plural form.

Abstracting the endings, we get:

	masc.	neut	fem.	plural
Adjective Endings Following *ein*-words				
nom.	-er	-es	-e	-en
acc.	-en	-es	-e	-en
dat.	-en	-en	-en	-en
gen.	-en	-en	-en	-en

Üben wir!

A. Substitute the new noun you will hear, making the necessary changes.

1. Ich kenne einen interessanten *Mann*.
   (Professor, Mädchen, Frau, Studentin, Buch, Student)
2. Ihr neues *Rad* hat viel gekostet.
   (Uhr, Koffer, Bücher, Hemd, Jacke, Kleider, Haus, Mantel)
3. Wir haben in einem schönen *Hotel* übernachtet.
   (Gebäude, Wohnung, Haus, Jugendherberge, Stadt, Wald)
4. Das ist das Rad meines kleinen *Freundes*.
   (Tochter, Kind, Kinder, Schwester, Freundin, Schüler)
5. Hier gibt es keine gute *Buchhandlung*.
   (Restaurant, Schule, Theater, Bücher, Pommes frites, Bier, Zeitungen)
6. Wir gehen mit unserem deutschen *Freund* ins Kino.
   (Freundin, Freunde, Tante, Onkel, Tanten)
7. Unsere kleine *Schwester* sagt das immer.
   (Bruder, Kind, Schülerinnen, Kinder, Tochter, Sohn)
8. Trotz des schlechten *Wetters* ist er gefahren. (Straßen, Wagen, Fahrrad)

B. Answer the questions according to the example.

> EXAMPLE: Das Haus ist schön, nicht wahr?
> Ja, das ist ein schönes Haus.

1. Die Brücke ist alt, nicht?
2. Der Mann ist reich, nicht wahr?
3. Das Hotel ist teuer, nicht wahr?
4. Der Automechaniker ist gut, nicht?
5. Das Kind ist müde, nicht wahr?
6. Die Buchhandlung ist groß, nicht?

C. Answer the questions according to the example.

> EXAMPLE: Ist der Wagen neu?
> Nein, wir haben keinen neuen Wagen.

1. Ist das Zimmer frei?
2. Ist die Wurst billig?
3. Sind diese Bücher langweilig?
4. Sind die Städte alt?

5. Ist der Schreibtisch modern?
6. Ist das Haus groß?

7. Ist die Straße steil?
8. Ist das Gebäude alt?

D. Substitute each word you will hear for the appropriate word in the sentence.

> EXAMPLE: Er hat dein altes Haus gekauft. (Wagen)
> Er hat deinen alten Wagen gekauft. (gesehen)
> Er hat deinen alten Wagen gesehen.

1. Sie saß in meinem kleinen Zimmer. (ein)(groß)(Wohnung)(Wagen)
2. Die neue Woche hat begonnen. (ein)(Tag)(Semester)(unser)(Leben)
3. Kannst du keine guten Bücher finden? (Buch)(Zug)(Züge)(Beispiel)(leicht)
4. Suchen Sie eine bessere Wohnung? (Haus)(Mantel)(neu)(Ihr)(Zimmer)

E. Answer according to the example.

> EXAMPLE: Hier ist eine kleine Flasche und eine große Flasche.
> Welche brauchst du?
> Ich brauche die große Flasche.

1. Wir haben ein billiges Zimmer und ein teures Zimmer. Welches möchten Sie haben?
2. Gestern ist ein warmer Tag gewesen. Heute ist ein kühler Tag. Welcher gefällt dir besser?
3. In der Fußgängerzone gibt es ein großes und ein kleines Restaurant. In welches sollen wir gehen?
4. Das ist ein langweiliger Professor. Das ist ein interessanter Professor. Welcher ist dein Professor?

2 ◆ Simple Past of *sein* and *haben*

In Chapter 6, you learned to use the perfect tense to talk about the past. German verbs also have a one-word past form, called the *simple past tense*. You will learn how to form the simple past of all German verbs in Chapter 10. For now, learn the simple past forms of **sein** and **haben,** since they occur frequently in conversation.

ich **war**	I was	wir **waren**	we were
du **warst**	you were	ihr **wart**	you were
er, es, sie **war**	he, it, she was	sie, Sie **waren**	they, you were
ich **hatte**	I had	wir **hatten**	we had
du **hattest**	you had	ihr **hattet**	you had
er, es, sie **hatte**	he, it, she had	sie, Sie **hatten**	they, you had

A. Substitute the new subjects you will hear.

1. *Wir* waren gestern im Museum.
   (ich, ihr, meine Schwester, die müden Touristen)
2. *Ich* hatte Angst.
   (das Kind, die Kinder, die Mädchen, mein reicher Onkel)
3. Hatte *er* Hunger?
   (du, ihr, die ganze Familie, die Klasse, die jungen Schüler)

B. Wie sagt man das auf deutsch? (Use simple past tense.)

1. His question was not dumb.
2. Did he have a wife?
3. My aunt was very rich.
4. Were they hungry?
5. Weren't you in the lecture?
6. I was afraid.
7. They had my books.
8. My friends were on the tennis court.

3 ♦ Word Order: Time-Manner-Place

In German statements, adverbs or adverbial phrases following the verb must come in the sequence: time, manner, place. The usual sequence in English is the reverse: place, manner, time.

	time	*manner*	*place*
Er fährt	**morgen**	**mit dem Auto**	**nach Bremen.**

	place	*manner*	*time*
He's going	**to Bremen**	**by car**	**tomorrow.**

A good mnemonic device is that the adverbs answer the following questions in alphabetical order:

Wann? (morgen)   **Wie?** (mit dem Auto)   **Wo(hin)?** (nach Bremen)

A. Your neighbor asks you when you're going to various places. Answer according to the example:

EXAMPLE: Wann fliegen Sie nach Kopenhagen? (morgen)
   Ich fliege morgen nach Kopenhagen.

1. Wann sind Sie in die Schweiz gefahren?
   (im Frühling, im September, im Sommer, am Montag)
2. Wann gehen Sie zu Ostendorffs?
   (morgen, im April, heute, jetzt, bald)

„Es sind noch 2 Stunden bis zum Gipfel."
(der Gipfel = *summit*)

Wanderweg

B. Your neighbor asks you where you are going at certain times. Answer according to the example.

> EXAMPLE: Wohin fahren Sie heute? (nach Basel)
> Ich fahre heute nach Basel.

1. Wohin fliegen Sie im September? (in die Schweiz, nach Berlin, wieder nach Hause, zurück nach Amerika)
2. Wohin willst du heute? (in die Stadt, zu Carola, in den Wald)

C. Add to the sentences the expression of manner you will hear.

> EXAMPLE: Ich fahre morgen nach Salzburg. (mit dem Auto.)
> Ich fahre morgen mit dem Auto nach Salzburg.

1. Wir sind gestern nach Hause gefahren. (mit den Kindern, mit dem Auto)
2. Er geht abends ins Kino. (mit seinen Freunden, gern, ohne mich)

Ordinal Numbers and Dates

The ordinal numbers (first, second, third, etc.) are adjectives and take the usual adjective endings.

From one to nineteen, add **-t-** and the appropriate adjective ending to the cardinal number. Note the irregular forms.

der, das, die **erste**	1st	elfte	11th
zweite	2nd	zwölfte	12th
dritte	3rd	dreizehnte	13th
vierte	4th	vierzehnte	14th
fünfte	5th	fünfzehnte	15th
sechste	6th	sechzehnte	16th
siebte	7th	siebzehnte	17th
achte	8th	achtzehnte	18th
neunte	9th	neunzehnte	19th
zehnte	10th		

From twenty on up, add **-st-** and the adjective ending to the cardinal number:

der, das, die zwanzigste	20th
einundzwanzigste	21st
zweiundzwanzigste	22nd
dreiundzwanzigste	23rd
usw.	etc.
dreißigste	30th
vierzigste	40th
hundertste	100th
tausendste	1000th

In written German, an ordinal number is indicated by a period after the numeral.

der 10. November = der zehn**te** November

Here is how to ask for and give the date:

Den wievielten haben wir heute?   or
Der wievielte ist heute?

What's the date today?
(literally: *"The how manyeth do we have today/is today?"*)

Heute haben wir den dreizehnten.
Heute ist der dreizehnte.

Today is the thirteenth.

Here is how to say on what date something occurs:

am zehnten August	*on the tenth of August*
am ersten Mai	*on the first of May*

In German, the date is given in this order: day, month, year.

den 1.2.1988	*February 1, 1988*

A. (books open) Answer the question with the date given.

Der wievielte ist heute?

1. 3. August (Heute ist . . .)
2. 9. Februar
3. 1. Mai
4. 7. Juli
5. 2. Januar
6. 8. April

Den wievielten haben wir heute?

7. 5. März (Heute haben wir . . .)
8. 13. Juni
9. 11. November
10. 19. September
11. 21. Dezember
12. 28. Oktober

Wann kommt Frank?

13. 4. Januar (Er kommt am . . .)
14. 30. September
15. 6. April
16. 25. Juli
17. 31. Oktober
18. 20. Februar

B. Now talk about Susanne's activities in February. Here's a page from her appointment book:

EXAMPLE: Wann besucht sie Heinz? Sie besucht ihn am ersten Februar.

FEBRUAR	
1 Heinz besuchen	9 im Computerzentrum arbeiten
2	10
3 ins Theater gehen („Mutter Courage")	11 ins Kino („Männer")
4	12
5	13
6 mit Jörg und Katja essen gehen	. . .
7 schwimmen gehen (19 Uhr)	20 Reise nach München
8	21 in die Berge fahren

■ German has two possibilities for telling the year in which something occurred, neither of which is like English:

Man hat die Tennisplätze **im Jahre 1982** gebaut.
Man hat die Tennisplätze **1982** gebaut.

} They built the tennis courts in 1982.

■ You *cannot* say **in 1982** in German.
■ The German sentence can begin with the year alone:

1982 hat man die Tennisplätze gebaut.

In 1982 they built the tennis courts.

Leicht zu merken

der **Amateur, -e**	Amateur
der **Athlet, -en, -en**	Athlet
definieren	
direkt	
der **Fan, -s**	
idealistisch	
das **Idol, -e**	Idol
joggen	
kulturell	kulturell
olympisch	
die **Organisation, -en**	Organisation
organisieren	
zentral	zentral

Hürdenlauf (*hurdle race*) in der Sportstunde

Wortschatz 2

Verben

benutzen to use
erfahren (erfährt), hat erfahren to find out, learn
rad·fahren (fährt Rad), ist radgefahren to bicycle
teil·nehmen (nimmt teil), hat teilgenommen an + *dat.* to take part in, participate in
treffen (trifft), hat getroffen to meet (by appointment)
verlieren, hat verloren to lose

Substantive

der Klub, -s club
der Name, -ns, -n[1] name
der Sportler, - athlete (*m.*)
der Staat, -en state
der Zuschauer, - spectator

das Dorf, ¨er village
das Mitglied, -er member

die Bewegung, -en movement; exercise
die DDR = die Deutsche Demokratische Republik the GDR = German Democratic Republic

die Gesellschaft, -en society
die Gesundheit health
die Jugend youth, young people
die Mannschaft, -en team
die Sportlerin, -nen athlete (*f.*)
die Welt world

Andere Vokabeln

aktiv active
bekannt known; well known
beliebt popular
eigen- own
gesund healthy
mindestens at least
politisch political
viele (*pronoun*) many people

Nützliche Ausdrücke

nicht nur . . . sondern auch not only . . . but also
usw. = und so weiter etc. = etcetera

Gegensätze

aktiv ≠ passiv	active ≠ passive
gesund ≠ krank	healthy ≠ sick

[1] The noun **Name** is irregular: singular: **der Name, den Namen, dem Namen, des Namens**; plural: **die Namen, die Namen, den Namen, der Namen.**

Sport für alle

In Deutschland, Österreich und der Schweiz spielt der Sport eine sehr wichtige Rolle im modernen Leben. Die olympischen Athleten aus der DDR, die Schiläufer aus Österreich, Liechtenstein[1] und der Schweiz, und die großen Fußballspieler aus der Bundesrepublik sind in der ganzen Welt bekannt. Und welcher Tennisfan kennt heutzutage den Namen des „Wunderkinds"° Boris Becker nicht? Seit seinem ersten Wimbledon-Sieg° 1985 im Alter von° 17 Jahren ist er zu einem Idol aller jungen Tennisspieler geworden.

Aber nicht nur die Berufssportler, sondern auch Menschen aus allen Berufen und allen Schichten° der Gesellschaft treiben Sport. Viele haben erfahren, daß es gesund ist und auch Spaß macht, in der Freizeit zu joggen, radzufahren oder Tennis zu spielen. Der Amateursport ist in den deutschsprachigen° Ländern besser organisiert als in den

prodigy
*Wimbledon victory / **im ... von** = at the age of*

levels

German-speaking

Radrennen (das Rennen = *race*)

[1] A small independent principality located between Austria and Switzerland.

USA. Mindestens jeder fünfte Bundesbürger° ist zum Beispiel Mitglied in einem Sportklub, wo man Tennis, Tischtennis, Volleyball, Fußball usw. spielen kann. Natürlich ist der Sportklub auch ein Ort,° wo man alte Freunde trifft und neue Menschen kennenlernt. Seit dem Zweiten Weltkrieg ist der Fußball in Deutschland sehr beliebt geworden, und heutzutage hat fast jedes kleine Dorf seine eigene Fußballmannschaft. Der Sportklub ist deshalb° sehr wichtig geworden, weil man im Alltag° wenig Bewegung hat. Statt zu Fuß zu gehen, benutzt man heute den Wagen, und so braucht man den Sport, um aktiv und fit zu bleiben.

In der DDR wird der Sport direkt vom Staat unterstützt.° Man treibt Sport überall: in den Schulen und Universitäten, in den Fabriken und in der Freien Deutschen Jugend (FDJ), der politischen Organisation für junge Menschen. Die Verfassung° der DDR definiert den Sport als ein Bürgerrecht° und als zentral für das kulturelle Leben des Landes.

Wenn der Sport seinen idealistischen Zweck° nicht verlieren soll, dann darf man nicht nur Zuschauer bleiben, sondern muß aktiv am Sport teilnehmen. Erst dann macht er jedem Menschen Spaß und fördert° die Gesundheit.

citizen of the FRG

place

for that reason
daily life

wird . . . unterstützt = is supported

constitution
citizen's right

purpose

promotes

Fragen zum Lesestück

1. Ist Ihnen Boris Becker bekannt? Wer ist er?
2. Aus welchen Ländern kommen die großen Schiläufer?
3. Was hat fast jedes kleine Dorf in der BRD?
4. Warum ist es heutzutage besonders wichtig, Sport zu treiben?
5. Warum geht man heutzutage nicht mehr viel zu Fuß?
6. Welcher Sport ist seit dem Zweiten Weltkrieg in Deutschland beliebt geworden?
7. Welche Rolle spielt der Sport im Leben der DDR?
8. Warum soll man beim Sport nicht nur Zuschauer bleiben?

Vom Lesen zum Sprechen

You already know some of this vocabulary useful for talking about sports.

Nouns	Verbs
der **Zuschauer,** -	**verlieren**
das **Spiel, -e** game	**gewinnen, hat gewonnen**
	to win
der **Amateur, -e** amateur	**schlagen, hat geschlagen**
	to hit; beat
die **Mannschaft, -en**	**trainieren** to train

die **Sportart, -en:** type of sport

laufen
der **Läufer,** -
die **Läuferin, -nen**

schwimmen
der **Schwimmer,** -
die **Schwimmerin, -nen**

schilaufen
der **Schiläufer,** -
die **Schiläuferin, -nen**

radfahren
der **Radfahrer,** -
die **Radfahrerin, -nen**

boxen
der **Boxer,** -

Fußball spielen
der **Fußballspieler,** -

Volleyball spielen
der **Volleyballspieler,** -
die **Volleyballspielerin, -nen**

(Eis)hockey spielen
der **Hockeyspieler,** -

A. Klassendiskussion: Sprechen Sie mit den anderen Studenten.

1. Welchen Sport treiben Sie?
2. Warum gefällt Ihnen dieser Sport?
3. Sind Sie in einer Universitätsmannschaft?
4. Sind Sie Mitglied eines Sportklubs?

B. Topics for class debates:

1. Man soll in Amerika mehr Sport treiben. Ja oder nein?
2. Man kann fit bleiben, ohne Sport zu treiben. Ja oder nein?
3. In Deutschland gibt es keine Universitätsmannschaften. Finden Sie solche Mannschaften an amerikanischen Unis gut, oder nicht gut? Warum?

Mündliche Übungen

A. Persönliche Fragen

1. Besitzen Sie ein Fahrrad? Beschreiben Sie es.
2. Haben Sie je eine lange Radtour gemacht? Wann war das? Wohin sind Sie gefahren?
3. Spielen Sie gern Tennis? Sind Sie ein guter oder ein schlechter Spieler?
4. Wo waren Sie gestern?
5. Was haben Sie dort gemacht?
6. Was machen Sie gern in Ihrer Freizeit?

B. Beschreiben Sie Ihr Klassenzimmer.

> z.B. Dort hängt ein großes Bild an der Wand.
> Dort steht ein kleiner Tisch.

C. Beschreiben Sie die Kleider eines Studenten oder einer Studentin im Zimmer. Ihre Freunde müssen dann sagen, wen Sie beschrieben haben.

> z.B. a. Wer trägt heute eine alte Hose und ein häßliches Hemd?
> b. Meinst du Rick?

D. Prepare before class. Find a picture in a magazine or book and prepare a description of it for class presentation. Use as many attributive adjectives as you can. Your description could sound something like this:

„Ich habe ein schönes Bild in einem alten Buch gefunden. Hier sieht man viele Häuser in einem kleinen Dorf. In der Mitte des Bildes steht eine alte Kirche und vor dieser schönen Kirche geht ein alter Mann mit einem jungen Kind spazieren. Hinter dem Dorf sieht man auch einen dunklen Wald."

E. You have misplaced your clothes and need help. A classmate helps identify the lost items by using adjectives cued from the list provided.

schön	grün	dunkel
weiß	braun	furchtbar
rot	häßlich	hell
teuer	grau	lang
blau	alt	neu
warm	gelb	einfach
leicht	bunt	schwarz

EXAMPLE: Student 1: Wo ist mein neuer Pulli?
Student 2: Meinst du den schönen roten Pulli?

1. Wo ist denn mein Hemd?
2. Ich suche meine neue Bluse.
3. Wo ist meine Jacke?
4. Ich weiß nicht, wo mein Mantel ist.
5. Jetzt habe ich meine Schuhe verloren.
6. Ist meine Hose hier im Zimmer?
7. Liegt mein Pullover noch bei dir im Zimmer?

Schriftliche Übungen

F. Rewrite this narrative filling in each blank with an appropriate adjective. Don't forget to include the adjective endings where they are needed!

Heute ist der _____ Mai und es ist ein _____ Tag. Ich gehe im _____ _____ Wald mit meiner _____ Freundin Gabriele spazieren. Die Sonne ist _____ , aber im Wald ist es _____ . Wir haben ein Mittagessen mitgebracht. Um ein Uhr bekommen wir Hunger. Aber wir haben vergessen, Wein mitzubringen. Wir wissen, daß es im Wald ein _____ Restaurant gibt, und nach einer Stunde finden wir es. Wir kaufen eine _____ Flasche Wein. Die Kellnerin ist eine sehr _____ Frau. Wir sprechen mit ihr über das _____ Wetter. Sie hat auch ein _____ Kind, und wir spielen ein bißchen mit diesem _____ Mädchen. Später treffen wir meinen _____ Freund Hannes. Er zeigt uns sein _____ Fahrrad. Am Ende dieses _____ Tages fahren wir mit der Straßenbahn in die _____ Stadt zurück.

G. Construct sentences from the elements provided. Be able to translate the sentences accurately.

1. Die/neu/Filme/aus/Italien/gefallen/den/deutsch/Studenten.
2. Mein/reich/Onkel/wohnen/in/dies-/alt/Haus.
3. Nach/unser/lang/Wanderung/können/wir/in/ein/billig/Restaurant/ein/kalt/Bier/trinken.
4. Ihr/klein/Kind/tragen/immer/ein/lang/bunt/Hemd.
5. Mein/neu/Wohnung/ist/sonnig/und/haben/ein/groß/Schreibtisch.
6. Der/sympathisch/Tramper/vergessen/sein/interessant/Bücher/in/mein/neu/Auto. (perfect tense)

Schiläufer auf der Piste
(die Piste = *ski course*)

7. Wir/waren/in/ein/phantastisch/Jugendherberge/in/die Schweiz//wo/
   wir/in/ein/groß/Zimmer/übernachten. (second clause, perfect tense)
8. Vor/groß/Hotel/stehen/mein/teuer/grün/Wagen.
9. Um/ein/lang/und/gesund/Leben/haben//sollen/jed-/Mensch/aktiv/
   bleiben.
10. Bei/dies-/schön/Wetter/wollen/ich/in/neu/Schwimmbad/gehen.

H. Wie sagt man das auf deutsch?

1. Have you seen my new blue sweater?
2. Didn't you put it on the big table in your room?
3. Unfortunately not. I think I've lost it.

4. What is the date today?
5. It's April 5th. Why do you ask?
6. I forgot to telephone my old friend Markus.

7. Where are you studying next year?
8. I'm staying here in the fall but I'm spending the second semester at a
   German university.
9. Really? At which university?
10. At the University of Konstanz. It is a beautiful old town with a well-
    known new university.

Almanach

Sport Culture in the Two Germanies

For over a century prior to the division of Germany after World War II, sport played an important role in the life of the nation. Organized gymnastics, for example, originated in 1811 as part of the nationalistic fervor directed against the invading armies of Napoleon. By the end of the nineteenth century, a workers' sport movement (*Arbeitersportbewegung*) had been founded. This group eventually counted two million members and was to become an important ally of the Social Democratic Party (SPD) shortly before both were suppressed by Hitler in 1933. Both postwar Germanies, therefore, could look back upon a rich tradition of sport as they formulated their respective programs for encouraging mass participation in athletics and success in international competition.

Since about 1950, both the Federal Republic of Germany (FRG) and the German Democratic Republic (GDR) have viewed their sport rivalry as a symbol of a larger political competition. Although the FRG maintained its competitive supremacy at the international level during the 1950's, the GDR has since developed the world's most successful—and controversial—sport program. At the Montreal Olympic Games in 1976 East Germany's unofficial point total was second only to that of the Soviet Union, and actually greater than that of the United States—an unusual feat for a nation of only 18 million that was not permitted its own Olympic team until 1968. Sport officials in West Germany responded to this success by forming their own committees of inquiry to reorganize both mass sport (*i.e.,* „*Trimm Dich*"—"Get Fit") and high performance (*Hochleistung*) sport. There are good reasons, however, why East Germany will probably continue to prevail in international competition. The government conducts classified research in sport medicine and searches nationwide for talented athletes who are then trained in special sport schools and supported by the state.

Deutschland im 20. Jahrhundert

Dialoge
- „Was ist los?"
- Damals
- Schlimme Zeiten

Wortschatz 1

Grammatik
1. Unpreceded Adjectives
2. Simple Past Tense
   - Formation
   - Use
3. German Equivalents for English "when": **als, wenn, wann**
4. Past Perfect Tense Formation • Use
5. Some Time Expressions **vor** + dative = ago • Expressing Duration
6. Expanding Your Vocabulary The Noun Suffix **-ismus**
   - City Names as Adjectives
   - Leicht zu merken

Wortschatz 2

Lesestück
Besuch einer Ausstellung historischer Plakate

Vom Lesen zum Sprechen
Die Politik

Almanach
Political Parties in West Germany

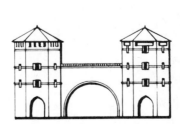

Dialoge

„Was ist los?"

JÜRGEN: Heinz, was ist los? Du siehst so unglücklich aus.

HEINZ: Ach, Barbara hatte gestern Geburtstag, und da wollte ich ihr eine Armbanduhr schenken. Ich hatte sie schon letzte Woche gekauft.

JÜRGEN: Und, was ist denn passiert?

HEINZ: Ja, gestern morgen war die Uhr noch in meiner Tasche, aber als ich sie Barbara geben wollte, konnte ich sie nicht mehr finden.

JÜRGEN: Das tut mir leid. Hoffentlich hat sie dir niemand gestohlen.

Damals

HERR ZIEGLER: Wie lange wohnen Sie schon hier?

HERR PLANCK: Seit letztem Jahr. Vorher habe ich in Wiesbaden gewohnt.

HERR ZIEGLER: Wirklich? Das wußte ich nicht. Als ich ein Kind war, war ich jeden Sommer dort und habe meine Großeltern besucht.

HERR PLANCK: Ja, damals vor dem Krieg war die Stadt ganz anders.

Schlimme Zeiten

STEFFI: Oma, darf ich dir ein paar Fragen über deine Kindheit stellen? Wann bist du eigentlich geboren?

OMA: Im Jahre 1935. Ich bin während des Krieges aufgewachsen. Warum?

STEFFI: Wir lesen gerade in der Schule über diese Zeit. Ich möchte hören, wie es dir damals ging.

OMA: Gott sei Dank lebten wir auf dem Land, und zuerst ging es uns gut. Aber das dauerte nur bis 1943.

STEFFI: Was ist dann passiert?

OMA: Dann ist mein Bruder in Rußland gefallen, und ein Jahr später starb meine Mutter.

Wortschatz 1

"What's Wrong?"

JÜRGEN: Heinz, what's wrong? You look so unhappy.

HEINZ: Oh, yesterday was Barbara's birthday and I wanted to give her a watch. I had already bought it last week.

JÜRGEN: And so what happened?

HEINZ: Well, yesterday morning the watch was still in my pocket, but when I was about to give it to Barbara, I couldn't find it any more.

JÜRGEN: I'm sorry. I hope no one stole it from you.

Back Then

MR. ZIEGLER: How long have you lived here?

MR. PLANCK: Since last year. Before that I lived in Wiesbaden.

MR. ZIEGLER: Really? I didn't know that. When I was a child, I was there every summer and visited my grandparents.

MR. PLANCK: Ah, back then, before the war, the city was very different.

Tough Times

STEFFI: Grandma, may I ask you a few questions about your childhood? When were you born?

GRANDMA: In 1935. I grew up during the war. Why?

STEFFI: We're just reading about that time in school. I'd like to hear what life was like for you back then.

GRANDMA: Thank heavens we lived in the country and at first we made out all right. But that only lasted until 1943.

STEFFI: What happened then?

GRANDMA: Then my brother was killed in action in Russia and my mother died a year later.

Verben

auf·wachsen (wächst auf), wuchs auf, ist aufgewachsen to grow up

dauern to last; take (time)

fallen (fällt), fiel, ist gefallen to fall; die in battle

passieren, passierte, ist passiert to happen

stehlen (stiehlt), stahl, hat gestohlen to steal

sterben (stirbt), starb, ist gestorben to die

Substantive

der **Monat, -e** month

der **Nachmittag, -e** afternoon

  am Nachmittag in the afternoon

der **Opa, -s** grandpa

die **Armbanduhr, -en** wristwatch

die **Kindheit** childhood

die **Oma, -s** grandma

die **Tasche, -n** pocket

Andere Vokabeln

als (*sub. conj.*) when

damals at that time, back then

geboren born

gestern morgen yesterday morning

letzt- last

seit langem for a long time

unglücklich unhappy

vorher before that, earlier

Nützliche Ausdrücke

eine Frage stellen to ask a question

Wann sind Sie geboren? When were you born?

Gegensätze

unglücklich ≠ glücklich	unhappy ≠ happy
vorher ≠ nachher	before that ≠ after that

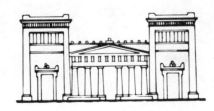

Neue Kombinationen

A. Replace the words in italics with the new word or phrase you will hear.

1. Darf ich dir eine Frage *über deine Kindheit* stellen?
   (über deine Familie, über dein Hauptfach, über unsere Hausaufgaben, über Sport)
2. Er sieht so *unglücklich* aus.
   (sympathisch, interessant, freundlich, gesund)

B. Your teacher asks you if you have lost anything. Say that you have, and then name the object cued.

> EXAMPLE: Haben Sie etwas verloren? (watch)
> Ja, ich habe meine Armbanduhr verloren.

(ID-card, dictionary, gym shoes, sweater, forty Marks, coffee cup)

C. Answer with a prepositional phrase. Use as many 2-way prepositions as possible.

> EXAMPLE: Wo war die neue Uhr? (Tasche)
> Sie war in meiner Tasche.

(Schreibtisch, Bett, Schaufenster, Jacke, Koffer, Zeitungen)
Now expand your answer with an adjective and the noun.

> EXAMPLE: Wo war die neue Uhr? (neue Tasche)
> Sie war in meiner neuen Tasche.

(großer Schreibtisch, altes Bett, buntes Schaufenster, leichte Jacke, schwerer Koffer, deutsche Zeitungen)

D. Answer the question using the English cue.

1. Wann sind Sie geboren?
   (before the war, in January, in the fall)
2. Wo haben Sie damals gewohnt?
   (in town, in the country, nearby, above a bookstore, in the old city)
3. Was wolltest du ihr schenken?
   (a watch, a newspaper, a coat, the city map, a backpack)

Übung zur Aussprache

Bertolt Brecht (1898–1956) fled Germany in 1933 to settle temporarily in Scandinavia. The poem that follows, written in Finland during World War II, is the sixth of the short cycle "1940," the year of its conception. Practice reading the poem aloud.

Mein junger Sohn fragt mich: Soll ich
  Mathematik lernen?
Wozu,° möchte ich sagen. Daß zwei Stück°   *what for? / pieces of*
  Brot mehr ist als eines
Das wirst du auch so merken.°   *you'll notice anyway*
Mein junger Sohn fragt mich: Soll ich
  Französisch° lernen?   *French*
Wozu, möchte ich sagen. Dieses Reich°   *empire*
  geht unter.° Und   *will collapse*
Reibe° du nur mit der Hand den Bauch°   *rub / stomach*
  und stöhne°   *groan*
Und man wird dich schon verstehen.
Mein junger Sohn fragt mich: Soll ich
  Geschichte lernen?
Wozu, möchte ich sagen. Lerne du nur
  deinen Kopf in die Erde stecken°   *to stick your head in the*
Da wirst du vielleicht übrig bleiben.°   *sand / will . . . survive*

Ja, lerne Mathematik, sage ich
Lerne Französisch, lerne Geschichte!

Bertolt Brecht

Grammatik

1 ♦ Unpreceded Adjectives

Many noun phrases have no limiting word (i.e., no **der**-word or **ein**-word, see pp. 249–250):

Deutsche Kinder lernen das früh.
Ich trinke gern **kaltes Bier.**

German children learn that early.
I like to drink cold beer.

We will call the attributive adjectives in such phrases *unpreceded* adjectives. Unpreceded adjectives take the same endings as **dieser,** with two exceptions. In the masculine and neuter genitive singular, the unpreceded adjective takes the ending **-en.** The noun itself has the genitive ending **-es** or **-s.**

	masc.	*neut.*	*fem.*	*plural*
nom.	kalter Wein	kaltes Bier	kalte Milch	kalte Suppen
acc.	kalten Wein	kaltes Bier	kalte Milch	kalte Suppen
dat.	kaltem Wein	kalten Bieres	kalter Milch	kalten Suppen
gen.	kalten Weines	kalten Bieres	kalter Milch	kalter Suppen

Üben wir!

A. Substitute the new noun you will hear, changing the adjective ending and verb as necessary.

1. Alte *Filme* gefallen mir.
   (Bilder, Wein, Kunst, Kirchen, Märchen)
2. Mögen Sie deutsches *Bier*?
   (Wein, Bücher, Wurst, Brot)
3. Wegen schlechten *Wetters* bleiben wir zu Hause.
   (Straßen)

B. In each sentence you will hear, change the noun phrase with **ein** to the plural and make other necessary changes.

> EXAMPLE: Wollen wir einen alten Film sehen?
> Wollen wir alte Filme sehen?

1. Gibt es hier einen interessanten Laden?
2. Das ist ein guter Film.
3. Ich bin mit einem alten Freund ins Theater gegangen.
4. Der Lehrer hat eine kluge Schülerin.
5. Du hast ein schönes Hemd gekauft.
6. Hier gibt es eine dunkle, alte Straße.

C. Fill in the blanks with the appropriate endings.

1. Nach schwer _____ Arbeit trinke ich gern kalt _____ Bier.
2. Meine Tante kommt immer mit schwer _____ Gepäck an.
3. Es ist schwierig, lang _____ Reisen mit klein _____ Kindern zu machen.
4. Mein Vater fährt nicht gern auf steil _____ Straßen.
5. Der Chef kommt in wenig _____ Minuten zurück.
6. Welchen deutschen Wein findet man in grün _____ Flaschen?
7. Ich spreche gern mit intelligent _____ Menschen.
8. Diese Studenten kommen aus viel _____ Ländern.

2 ♦ Simple Past Tense

Simple past tense is used in written German to narrate a series of interconnected events in the past. Most novels are written in the simple past. In spoken German, it is most often used with the frequently occurring verbs **sein, haben** (you learned their simple past tense in Chapter 9), and the modal verbs.

Formation

1. Simple Past of Weak Verbs
   The marker for the simple past is **-te.** Regular weak verbs form the simple past by adding the following endings to the verb stem:

ich wohn **te**	I lived	wir wohn **ten**	we lived
du wohn **test**	you lived	ihr wohn **tet**	you lived
er, es, sie wohn **te**	he, it, she lived	sie, Sie wohn **ten**	they, you lived

Verbs whose stems end in **-d** or **-t** add an **-e-** between the stem and these endings:

ich arbeit **ete**	I worked	wir arbeit **eten**	we worked
du arbeit **etest**	you worked	ihr arbeit **etet**	you worked
er, es, sie arbeit **ete**	he, it, she worked	sie, Sie arbeit **eten**	they, you worked

For regular weak verbs, the only form you need to know to generate all other possible forms is the infinitive: **wohnen (wohnte, gewohnt).**

Üben wir! **A.** Substitute the new subjects you will hear.

1. *Ich* wohnte damals in Wien. (du, Anna, wir, ihr, die Brüder)
2. *Inge* wartete an der Ecke. (Leo, wir, ich, die Männer, du)
3. *Wir* lernten Richard in Berlin kennen. (du, ich, die Frauen, er, ihr)
4. *Sie* übernachteten im Hotel. (wir, er, ich, meine Schwester, du)

B. In this account of Dora's day in town, change the sentences from present to simple past tense.

1. Dora braucht Lebensmittel.
2. Sie wartet an der Ecke.
3. Sie kauft in einem kleinen Laden ein.
4. Sie dankt der Frau im Laden.
5. Sie hört Musik auf der Straße.
6. Draußen schneit es.
7. Sie sucht ein Restaurant.
8. Sie fragt zwei Studenten.
9. Die Studenten zeigen ihr ein gutes Restaurant.

2. Simple Past of Strong Verbs

The strong verbs do *not* have the marker **-te.** Instead, the verb stem is changed and takes the following endings:

nehmen		*nahm*		*hat genommen*
ich nahm	I took	wir nahm **en**		we took
du nahm **st**	you took	ihr nahm **t**		you took
er, es, sie nahm	he, it, she took	sie, Sie nahm **en**		they, you took

■ Note that the **ich-** and the **er-**form of strong verbs take *no* endings in the simple past.

The simple past stem is the last of the "principal parts" of a German verb you must learn. The principal parts are the forms you must know in order to generate all other forms of a given verb:

Infinitive	*3rd person singular present* [1]	*Simple past stem*	*Auxiliary + past participle*
nehmen	nimmt	nahm	hat genommen

The following table contains the principal parts of all the strong verbs you have learned so far. As an aid to memorization, they have been arranged into groups according to the way their stem-vowels change in the past tenses. Memorize their simple past stems and review your knowledge of the other principal parts.[1]

---

[1] All verbs which umlaut their stem vowel in the present tense **du-** and **er-** forms are strong. The principal parts of all strong verbs used in the book will be found in Appendix 1. Neither list includes verbs formed by adding prefixes to stems you know, e.g. **abfahren, beschreiben,** etc.

Principal Parts of Strong Verbs

Infinitive	3rd sing. present	Simple past	Perfect	English
anfangen	fängt an	**fing an**	hat angefangen	to begin
fallen	fällt	**fiel**	ist gefallen	to fall
halten	hält	**hielt**	hat gehalten	to hold; stop
schlafen	schläft	**schlief**	hat geschlafen	to sleep
verlassen	verläßt	**verließ**	hat verlassen	to leave
fahren	fährt	**fuhr**	ist gefahren	to drive
tragen	trägt	**trug**	hat getragen	to carry; wear
aufwachsen	wächst auf	**wuchs auf**	ist aufgewachsen	to grow up
essen	ißt	**aß**	hat gegessen	to eat
geben	gibt	**gab**	hat gegeben	to give
lesen	liest	**las**	hat gelesen	to read
sehen	sieht	**sah**	hat gesehen	to see
vergessen	vergißt	**vergaß**	hat vergessen	to forget
empfehlen	empfiehlt	**empfahl**	hat empfohlen	to recommend
helfen	hilft	**half**	hat geholfen	to help
nehmen	nimmt	**nahm**	hat genommen	to take
sprechen	spricht	**sprach**	hat gesprochen	to speak
stehlen	stiehlt	**stahl**	hat gestohlen	to steal
sterben	stirbt	**starb**	ist gestorben	to die
treffen	trifft	**traf**	hat getroffen	to meet
bleiben		**blieb**	ist geblieben	to stay
scheinen		**schien**	hat geschienen	to shine, seem
schreiben		**schrieb**	hat geschrieben	to write
steigen		**stieg**	ist gestiegen	to climb
treiben		**trieb**	hat getrieben	to drive, propel
beginnen		**begann**	hat begonnen	to begin
schwimmen		**schwamm**	ist geschwommen	to swim
finden		**fand**	hat gefunden	to find
trinken		**trank**	hat getrunken	to drink
singen		**sang**	hat gesungen	to sing
liegen		**lag**	hat gelegen	to lie
sitzen		**saß**	hat gesessen	to sit
fliegen		**flog**	ist geflogen	to fly
schließen		**schloß**	hat geschlossen	to close
verbieten		**verbot**	hat verboten	to forbid
verlieren		**verlor**	hat verloren	to lose
anrufen		**rief an**	hat angerufen	to call up
gehen		**ging**	ist gegangen	to go
hängen		**hing**	hat gehangen	to be hanging
heißen		**hieß**	hat geheißen	to be called
kommen		**kam**	ist gekommen	to come
laufen	läuft	**lief**	ist gelaufen	to run
sein	ist	**war**	ist gewesen	to be
stehen		**stand**	hat gestanden	to stand
tun		**tat**	hat getan	to do

A. Substitute the new subjects you will hear and change the verb accordingly.

1. Wir schliefen bis halb zehn. (ich, Annette, die Sportler, mein Großvater)
2. Meine Mutter rief mich gestern an. (mein Vater, meine Freunde, du)
3. Der Film begann um 8 Uhr. (wir, das Konzert, ich)
4. Hans trank ein Bier und ging. (ich, wir, die Männer, du, Emil)
5. Die Amerikaner blieben zwei Stunden. (ich, wir, mein Freund, die Besucher)
6. Herr Schwarz fuhr nach Wien. (wir, die Schüler, ich, der Zug)
7. Der Professor sprach über die Weimarer Republik. (die Lehrerin, meine Großmutter, wir, die Studenten, ich)
8. Er sah damals noch jung aus. (die Mädchen, du, wir, ich, Tante Margret)
9. Sie schloß die Tür und stand vor dem Haus. (der Tourist, die Kinder, ich)
10. Ich vergaß seinen Namen. (wir, meine Eltern, Astrid)
11. Der Zug kam spät an. (meine Freunde, du, ich, wir, Hans)
12. Das Kind lief schnell ins Haus. (wir, die Kinder, ich, du)
13. Sie saß am Tisch und tat nichts. (ich, mein Onkel, wir, die Frauen)

B. Change these sentences from present to simple past tense.

1. Mir gefällt sein neues Fahrrad.
2. Barbara ruft um halb fünf an.
3. Sie schwimmt sehr oft, um fit zu bleiben.
4. Ich finde das Buch interessant.
5. Jede Woche schreibt sie mir eine Postkarte.
6. In der Schule trägt Frau Brandt ein Kleid.
7. Sehr oft hilft sie mir bei den Hausaufgaben.
8. Wir essen in einem bekannten Restaurant.
9. Am Donnerstag fliegt Robert nach New York.
10. Um acht gehen die Kinder zur Schule.
11. Sie heißt Dora Schilling.
12. Am Montag kommt Bertolt zurück.
13. Er liegt gern im Bett und liest die Zeitung.
14. Was tun die Touristen, wenn ein Hotel zu teuer ist?

Köln am Rhein

3. Simple Past of Modal Verbs

The modal verbs form their simple past with the **-te** marker, like the weak verbs. But those modals that have an umlaut in the infinitive *drop* it in the past tense:

	können, **konnte**			
ich konn **te**	I was able	wir konn **ten**	we were able
du konn **test**	you were able	ihr konn **tet**	you were able
er, es, sie konn **te**	he, it, she was able	sie, Sie konn **ten**	they, you were able

Similarly:

dürfen	**durfte**
mögen	**mochte**[1]
müssen	**mußte**
sollen	**sollte**
wollen	**wollte**

Üben wir!

A. Substitute the new subjects you will hear.

1. *Ich* konnte mein Rad nicht finden. (du, Lisa, wir, ihr, die Schüler)
2. *Karin* mochte den Professor nicht. (wir, die Studenten, ihr, du, ich)
3. *Wir* durften einen Monat bleiben. (ihr, er, die Touristen, du, ich)
4. Mußtest *du* wieder gehen? (wir, Heinrich, die Kinder, ihr)
5. *Ich* wollte etwas sagen. (du, er, wir, ihr, die Mädchen)
6. *Wir* sollten da sein. (er, die Briefe, ich, du, ihr)

B. Jutta is annoyed that people are changing their minds. Complete her sentences according to the example.

EXAMPLE: Warum willst du nicht aufstehen?
Vor fünf Minuten wolltest du aufstehen.

1. Warum magst du die Suppe nicht?
2. Warum will Barbara nicht mitfahren?
3. Warum dürfen die Kinder nicht mehr spielen?
4. Warum wollt ihr nicht ins Museum mitkommen?
5. Warum sollen wir nicht lachen?
6. Warum darf ich nicht schwimmen?
7. Warum kannst du nicht mehr lesen?
8. Warum darf er nicht sprechen?

[1]Note that **mögen**, in addition to dropping the umlaut, has a consonant change in the simple past.

4. Simple Past of Irregular Weak Verbs

The irregular weak verbs (see p. 182) change their stems in the simple past, but also use the **-te** marker.

wissen, **wußte**, hat gewußt			
ich wuß **te**	I knew	wir wuß **ten**	we knew
du wuß **test**	you knew	ihr wuß **tet**	you knew
er, es, sie wuß **te**	he, it, she knew	sie, Sie wuß **ten**	they, you knew

Similarly:

bringen **brachte** hat gebracht
kennen **kannte** hat gekannt

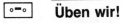

Üben wir!

A. Substitute the new subjects you will hear.

1. *Ich* kannte Hans sehr gut. (du, wir, unsere Freunde, er, ihr)
2. *Er* brachte Wein mit. (ihr, du, die Studenten, Anna, ich, wir)
3. *Ich* wußte das nicht. (wir, du, Hanna, ihr, unsere Freunde)

B. Now change the sentences you will hear from present to simple past.

1. Andreas kennt Wiesbaden sehr gut.
2. Dort besucht er oft seine Großeltern.
3. Sie wissen alles über die Stadt.
4. Er bringt ihnen immer Geschenke mit.

5. Simple Past of *werden*

The verb **werden** is irregular in the simple past:

ich **wurde**	I became	wir **wurden**	we became
du **wurdest**	you became	ihr **wurdet**	you became
er, es, sie **wurde**	he, it, she became	sie, Sie **wurden**	they, you became

Gestern **wurde** es sehr kalt.   *Yesterday it got very cold.*

Üben wir!

A. Substitute the new subjects you will hear.

Gestern wurden wir schnell müde.   (ich, ihr, er, die Kinder, du)

B. Now change the sentences you will hear from present to simple past tense.

1. Wird Irmtraud Journalistin?
2. Meine Töchter werden Lehrerinnen.
3. Wann wirst du 18?
4. Im Sommer wird es erst um 10 dunkel.

Use of Simple Past Tense

In English, there is a difference in meaning between past tense and perfect tense. Compare these sentences:

> I saw her in the restaurant.
> I have seen her in the restaurant.

The first sentence refers to a unique event in the past, while the second implies that "she" is often in the restaurant and may be there again. In German, there is *no* difference in meaning between simple past and perfect tense. They both simply label the sentence as "past:"

> Ich sah sie im Restaurant. } *I saw her in the*
> Ich habe sie im Restaurant gesehen. } *restaurant.*

The difference between German simple past and perfet tense is mainly one of usage: they are used under different circumstances. Here are some cases in which simple past is used:

1. In written German, simple past is the standard tense used to narrate a series of connected events in the past (e.g., in letters, newspaper reports, and in fiction):

Vor einem Wald **wohnte** ein Holzhacker mit seinen zwei Kindern. Sie **hießen** Hänsel und Gretel. She **hatten** wenig zu essen, und ihre Stiefmutter **wollte** sie los werden.

At the edge of a forest lived a woodcutter with his two children. Their names were Hansel and Gretel. They had little to eat, and their stepmother wanted to get rid of them.

Kleinstadt mit alten Stadtmauerresten (*remains of old city wall*)

2. In the spoken language, with the frequently used verbs **sein, haben,** and the modals, most Germans prefer simple past to perfect (but perfect is also correct!):

Wo **warst** du denn gestern?	*Where were you yesterday?*
Ich habe auf dich gewartet.	*I waited for you.*
Ich **hatte** kein Geld mehr und **mußte** nach Hause.	*I had no more money and had to go home.*

3. After the subordinating conjunction **als** ("when," referring to a point or stretch of time in the past), simple past tense is required:

Als wir aus dem Haus **kamen,** haben wir Andreas gesehen.	*When we came out of the house, we saw Andreas.*
Hans hat uns oft besucht, **als** er in New York **wohnte.**	*Hans often visited us when he lived in New York.*

Üben wir!

A. Change the following telephone conversation from present to simple past.

1. Wo bist du denn?
2. Ich bin bei Stefan.
3. Ich muß in die Stadt und komme erst um drei wieder nach Hause.
4. Ich darf bei Stefan essen.
5. Ich habe Hunger und kann nicht warten.

B. Say that it was already late when the following things happened. Use **als** and simple past tense.

> EXAMPLE: Ich sah sie.
> Es war schon spät, als ich sie sah.

1. Ich fand den Laden.
2. Er ging endlich.
3. Wir kamen in München an.
4. Er kaufte die dritte Flasche.
5. Sie fuhr mit dem Zug ab.
6. Er begann die Arbeit.
7. Sie besuchten mich.
8. Ich versuchte, dich anzurufen.

C. (books open) Complete the following sentences with an **als**-clause.

1. Jürgen konnte die Armbanduhr nicht finden, als . . .
2. Herr Ziegler hat jeden Sommer seine Großeltern besucht, als . . .
3. Es ging der Großmutter nicht gut, als . . .
4. Sie lief schnell in das Haus, als . . .
5. Das Kind fiel vom Stuhl, als . . .
6. Alle Schüler lachten, als . . .

3 ♦ German Equivalents for English "when": *als, wenn, wann*

It is important to distinguish among three German subordinating conjunctions, each of which may be translated by English *when:*

1. **als** = when (in the past)
   Als is a subordinating conjunction referring to an event or state in the past and requires the simple past tense:

Als wir in Wien waren, haben wir Andreas besucht.	*When we were in Vienna, we visited Andreas.*

2. **wenn** = when, whenever, if
   a. **Wenn** is a subordinating conjunction. It means "when" in reference to an event in the *present* or *future*. Since it can also mean "if," clauses with **wenn** can be ambiguous:

Wenn wir in Wien sind, besuchen wir Andreas.	*When (If) we're in Vienna, we'll visit Andreas.*

   b. **Wenn** also means "whenever" in reference to habitual or repeated action *in the past or present*. It is often used in conjunction with an adverb like **immer** to avoid ambiguity between "whenever" and "if":

Wenn Hans nach Wien kommt, geht er **immer** ins Kaffeehaus.	*Whenever Hans comes to Vienna, he always goes to a coffee house.*

   Note carefully the difference in meaning between **als** and **wenn** used with simple past tense:

Als sie das sagte, wurde er rot.	*When she said that he turned red.*
Wenn sie das sagte, wurde er immer rot.	*Whenever she said that he always turned red.*

3. **wann** = when?
   Wann is always a question word, used both in direct and indirect questions:

Wann kommt der Zug an?	*When does the train arrive?*
Ich weiß nicht, **wann** der Zug ankommt.	*I don't know when the train arrives.*

Üben wir!

A. (books open) Supply **als, wenn,** or **wann** as appropriate.

1. _____ darf ich spielen?
2. _____ du deine Hausaufgaben gemacht hast.
3. _____ fängt der Film an?
4. Ich weiß nicht, _____ der Film anfängt.
5. Karl kann es uns sagen, _____ er zurückkommt.
6. Wir haben viele Filme gesehen, _____ wir in Berlin waren.

7. Das möchte ich auch tun, _____ ich nach Berlin fahre.
8. _____ ich gestern an der Uni war, habe ich Angelika getroffen. Sie hat gesagt, sie kommt heute abend mit.
9. Gut! _____ Angelika mitkommt, macht es mehr Spaß.

B. Wie sagt man das auf deutsch?

1. When did you meet Claudia?
2. I met her when I studied in Vienna.
3. Whenever I'm in Vienna, I always write her a postcard.
4. I don't know when I'll go to Vienna again.

5. When I was young I hitchhiked a lot.
6. When I go to Europe, I'll do that too.
7. When are you going to Europe?
8. When I have enough money.

4 ♦ Past Perfect Tense

Formation

The past perfect tense is formed with the simple past tense of the auxiliary verb (**hatte** or **war**) and the past participle in final position:

ich	**hatte gegessen**	I had eaten
du	**hattest gegessen**	you had eaten
er, es, sie	**hatte gegessen**	he, it, she had eaten
wir	**hatten gegessen**	we had eaten
ihr	**hattet gegessen**	you had eaten
sie, Sie	**hatten gegessen**	they, you had eaten
ich	**war aufgestanden**	I had gotten up
du	**warst aufgestanden**	you had gotten up
er, es, sie	**war aufgestanden**	he, it, she had gotten up
wir	**waren aufgestanden**	we had gotten up
ihr	**wart aufgestanden**	you had gotten up
sie, Sie	**waren aufgestanden**	they, you had gotten up

800 JAHRE MÜNCHEN 20
DEUTSCHE BUNDESPOST

Use

The past perfect tense refers to an event in the past which *precedes* another event in the past. Look at the following timetable of events, then at how they are combined in the sentences that follow:

8.00 Uhr	Ulla hat gegessen.	10.00 Uhr	Ulla ist zur Uni gegangen.
9.00 Uhr	Hans ist aufgestanden.	11.00 Uhr	Hans hat gegessen.

Time ⟶

event 1   *event 2*

Ulla hatte schon **gegessen** . . . . als Hans aufstand.
Ulla had already eaten . . . . *when Hans got up.*

The order of clauses may be reversed:

⟵ Time

event 2   *event 1*

Als Hans aufstand, ... hatte Ulla schon gegessen.
When Hans got up . . . . *Ulla had already eaten.*

The subordinating conjunction **nachdem** (after) is often used with the past perfect tense:

Nachdem Ulla gegessen hatte, ging sie zur Uni.	*After Ulla had eaten she went to the university.*

Üben wir!

A. Say what you had already done when Inge came home.

> EXAMPLE: Obst eingekauft
> Als Inge nach Hause kam, hatte ich schon Obst ein-gekauft.

1. Kartoffeln gekocht
2. zur Uni gegangen
3. ins Restaurant gegangen

4. die Kinder ins Bett gebracht
5. alles gefunden
6. abgefahren

---

5 ♦ Some Time Expressions

vor + dative = *ago.*

vor fünf Minuten	five minutes ago
vor einer Stunde	an hour ago
vor drei Tagen	three days ago
vor einem Monat	a month ago
vor hundert Jahren	a hundred years ago
usw.	etc.

Baukräne (*construction cranes*) mit Kölner Dom im Hintergrund

A. Tell when Karl left according to the cues in English.

> EXAMPLE: two days ago
> Karl ist vor zwei Tagen abgefahren.

1. a minute ago
2. an hour ago
3. three years ago
4. five hours ago
5. ten days ago

6. a week ago
7. two weeks ago
8. a year ago
9. six months ago
10. a month ago

B. Answer these questions with **vor** + dative.

> EXAMPLE: Wann haben Sie die Hausaufgaben angefangen?
> Ich habe sie vor zwanzig Minuten angefangen.

1. Wann sind Sie aufgestanden?
2. Wann haben Sie gegessen?
3. Wann haben Sie angefangen, Deutsch zu lernen?
4. Wann haben Sie zuerst von dieser Universität gehört?
5. Wann haben Sie angefangen, hier zu studieren?

Expressing Duration

1. Accusative Case for Duration

German uses the accusative case alone to express how long an action or state continues, while English often uses the preposition *for*:

Wir sind **einen Tag** geblieben.	*We stayed **for a day.***
Wir haben **ein Jahr** in Berlin gewohnt.	*We lived in Berlin **for a year.***
Der Sprachkurs dauerte **einen Monat.**	*The language course lasted **a month.***

Üben wir!

A. Tell how long you stayed in Mannheim, according to the cues in English.

EXAMPLE: for an hour
Ich bin eine Stunde in Mannheim geblieben.

1. for two days
2. for a day
3. for a week
4. for three weeks
5. for a year
6. for four years

B. Tell how long the ride lasted.

EXAMPLE: for a day
Die Fahrt dauerte einen Tag.

1. for an hour
2. for two hours
3. for a minute
4. for ten minutes
5. for two days
6. for a day

2. Duration Ending in the Past or Continuing in the Present

There is a difference between German and English in the way they show whether an action or state ended in the past, or whether it is continuing at the moment of speaking.

English makes this distinction by using different verb tenses:

We **lived** in Berlin for three years.	*past tense* for a state ending in the past
We **have lived** in Berlin for three years.	*perfect tense* for a state continuing at the moment of speaking

German uses simple past *or* perfect for a state ending in the past:

Wir **wohnten** drei Jahre in Berlin.	
Wir **haben** drei Jahre in Berlin gewohnt.	*We **lived** three years in Berlin.*

For a state continuing at the moment of speaking, German uses *present* tense and one of these adverbial phrases:

schon + accusative: **schon drei Jahre**
(schon) seit + dative: **seit drei Jahren**
schon seit drei Jahren

	present tense	*adverbial phrase*		
Wir	**wohnen**	**schon drei Jahre**	in Berlin.	We **have lived** for three years in Berlin
Wir	**wohnen**	**seit drei Jahren**	in Berlin.	
Wir	**wohnen**	**schon seit drei Jahren**	in Berlin.	

■ These sentences are the most foreign to English speakers. Note carefully the difference between verb tenses in the two languages.
■ Note also the phrases:

schon lange
seit langem } for a long time

Üben wir!

A. You will hear a question about how long something has been continuing. Answer in each case that it has been continuing for two years. Use **schon, seit,** or **schon seit** as directed.

EXAMPLE: (use **schon**) Wie lange arbeiten Sie schon hier?
Ich arbeite schon zwei Jahre hier.

(use **schon**)
1. Wie lange studieren Sie schon hier?
2. Wie lange wohnt er schon in Wien?
3. Wie lange hilft er euch schon?
4. Wie lange spricht man schon über das Problem?

(use **seit**)
5. Seit wann ist das erlaubt?
6. Seit wann kaufst du hier ein?
7. Seit wann gibt es hier eine Fußgängerzone?
8. Seit wann habt ihr das Auto?

(use **schon seit**)
9. Wie lange seid ihr schon Freunde?
10. Wie lange kennst du ihn schon?
11. Wie lange ist er schon Kellner?
12. Wie lange wohnt sie schon in New York?

B. Answer these questions about how long you have been doing things.

1. Wie lange studieren Sie schon hier?
2. Seit wann lernen Sie Deutsch?
3. Wie lange studieren Sie schon Fremdsprachen?
4. Seit wann tragen Sie diese Hose?
5. Wie lange kennen Sie schon meinen Namen?
6. Seit wann gibt es hier eine Uni?

C. Now give German equivalents for the following sentences. Remember to use present tense!

1. We have known him for a year.
2. He has lived here for two weeks.
3. We have been shopping here for a long time.
4. Barbara has already been here five days.
5. She has studied in Boston for two semesters.
6. For ten years there's been a restaurant here.
7. Michael has been reading this book for a long time.
8. I've been hungry for two days.

6 ◆ Expanding Your Vocabulary

The Noun Suffix -ismus

English words ending in *-ism* usually denote a system of belief, a doctrine, or a characteristic. Most have German equivalents ending in the suffix **-ismus**. These words are all *masculine* in German.

der **Antisemitismus**	anti-Semitism
der **Extremismus**	extremism
der **Idealismus**	idealism
der **Kapitalismus**	capitalism
der **Kommunismus**	communism
der **Optimismus**	optimism
der **Pessimismus**	pessimism

What others can you guess?

City Names as Adjectives

Names of cities used as attributive adjectives are capitalized and simply add **-er** in *all* cases:

Bist du in einem **New Yorker** Taxi gefahren?	*Did you ride in a New York taxicab?*
Haben Sie die **Wiener** Museen gesehen?	*Have you seen the Viennese museums?*
Wir lesen eine Geschichte der **Weimarer** Republik.	*We're reading a history of the Weimar Republic.*

A. Answer as in the example:

EXAMPLE: Kennen Sie die Restaurants in Berlin?
Ja, ich kenne die Berliner Restaurants sehr gut!

1. Kennen Sie die Studenten in Bonn?
2. Kennen Sie die Buchhandlungen in Köln?
3. Kennen Sie die Straßen von Paris?
4. Kennen Sie die Museen in Boston?

Leicht zu merken

demokratisch	
der **Direktor, -en**	Di*rek*tor, Di*rekt*oren
die **Epoche, -n**	E*poch*e
extrem	
historisch	
ideologisch	
illegal	*il*legal
die **Inflation**	Inflati*on*
legal	le*gal*
manipulieren	manipu*lie*ren
die **Methode, -n**	Me*th*ode
die **Opposition, -en**	Oppositi*on*
die **Republik, -en**	Repub*lik*
die **Situation, -en**	Situati*on*
symbolisch	
terroristisch	terro*ris*tisch

Neue Wohnhäuser und im
Krieg zerstörtes Gebäude
(Ost-Berlin)

Wortschatz 2

Verben

erklären to explain
führen to lead
gewinnen, gewann, hat gewonnen to win
nennen, nannte, hat genannt to name, call
retten save, rescue
stören to disturb
unterbrechen (unterbricht), unterbrach, hat unterbrochen to interrupt
versuchen to try, attempt
wachsen (wächst), wuchs, ist gewachsen to grow
zählen to count

Substantive

der **Anfang, ¨e** beginning
  am Anfang at the beginning
der **Arm, -e** arm
der **Besuch, -e** visit
der **Politiker, -** politician (*m.*)
der **Schriftsteller, -** writer (*m.*)

das **Plakat, -e** poster
das **Volk ¨er** people, nation, folk
das **Wort**
  die **Worte** words (*in a context*)
  die **Wörter** words (*unconnected, as in a list, cf.* **Wörterbuch**)

die **Ausstellung, -en** exhibition
die **Dame, -n** lady
die **Demokratie, -n** democracy
die **Gefahr, -en** danger
die **Hauptstadt, ¨e** capital
die **Idee, -n** idea
die **Industrie, -n** industry
die **Partei, -en** political party
die **Politik** politics
die **Politikerin, -nen** politician (*f.*)
die **Schriftstellerin, -nen** writer (*f.*)

Andere Vokabeln

arbeitslos unemployed
bevor (*sub. conj.*) before
hart hard; tough; harsh
nachdem (*sub. conj.*) after
stark strong
unruhig restless, troubled

Nützliche Ausdrücke

mehr als more than
meine Damen und Herren ladies and gentlemen

Gegensätze

unruhig ≠ ruhig	restless ≠ calm, peaceful
stark ≠ schwach	strong ≠ weak

Besuch einer Ausstellung historischer Plakate

Im Hessischen Landesmuseum° in Darmstadt[1] gab es vor ein paar Monaten eine Ausstellung politischer Plakate aus der Weimarer Republik (1919–1933). Der Museumsdirektor führte eine Gruppe amerikanischer Studenten durch die Austellung.

5 „Meine Damen und Herren, herzlich willkommen° im Landesmuseum! Bevor wir in die Ausstellung gehen, möchte ich Ihnen ein paar Worte über die Geschichte der Weimarer Republik sagen. Wenn Sie Fragen haben, dürfen Sie

10 sie jederzeit° stellen—das stört mich gar nicht.

Was war das eigentlich, die Weimarer Republik? So nennen wir den deutschen Staat in der Zeit zwischen dem Ende des ersten Weltkrieges 1918 und dem Anfang des Dritten Reiches[2] im Januar 1933. Es war Deutschlands erster

15 Versuch,° eine demokratische Staatsform zu entwickeln.° Unsere Plakate zeigen die extremen ideologischen Gegensätze° dieser Epoche. Aber sie zeigen auch, wie man gegensätzliche Ideen oft mit ähnlichen Bildern darstellen° konnte."

20 Hier unterbrach ein Student mit einer Frage: „Entschuldigung, aber können Sie uns erklären, warum es die 'Weimarer' Republik hieß? War Berlin nicht die Hauptstadt?"

Hessian State Museum

herzlich willkommen = *May I welcome you cordially*

at any time

attempt / develop

polarities
represent

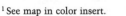

[1] See map in color insert.
[2] The Third Reich: the Nazis' own name for their regime (1933–1945)

"Sicher. Berlin blieb auch die Hauptstadt, aber die Politiker kamen 1919 in der Stadt Weimar zusammen, um die neue demokratische Verfassung zu beschließen.° In Berlin war die politische Situation damals sehr unruhig, und außerdem° hat Weimar wichtige symbolische Bedeutung als die Stadt, wo die großen Schriftsteller Goethe und Schiller[3] gelebt und gearbeitet haben.

Die ersten Jahre der Republik waren eine Zeit der Arbeitslosigkeit und Inflation. Unter dem harten Versailler Friedensvertrag[4] sollte Deutschland 20 Milliarden° Goldmark an die Siegermächte° zahlen. Unser erstes Plakat, aus

Verfassung . . . beschließen = *ratify the constitution*
moreover

billion
victors

---

[3] Johannn Wolfgang von Goethe (1749–1832); Friedrich von Schiller (1759–1805).
[4] The Peace Treaty of Versailles. This treaty officially ended the First World War in 1919.

35	der Zeit vor 1925, zeigt den deutschen Reichsadler° durch den Versailler Vertrag gefesselt.°	imperial eagle fettered

der Zeit vor 1925, zeigt den deutschen Reichsadler° durch den Versailler Vertrag gefesselt.°

Als die New Yorker Börse° 1929 stürzte,° wurde die Wirtschaftskrise° in den Industrieländern Europas katastrophal.° Man zählte im Februar 1930 schon mehr als 3,5 Millionen arbeitslose Menschen in Deutschland.

Diese Wirtschaftskrise brachte die junge deutsche Demokratie in politische Gefahr, denn schon 1932 waren sechs Millionen Menschen arbeitslos. Es gab damals mehr als dreißig politische Parteien, und besonders die antidemokratischen konnten schnell wachsen. Auf diesem zweiten Plakat sieht man, wie die 'starke Hand' der katholischen Zentrumspartei[5] die extremen Parteien erwürgt.° 1933 siegte° aber die Nationalsozialistische Deutsche Arbeiterpartei (NSDAP)—die Nazis—über alle anderen Parteien und wurde die stärkste° im Reichstag.[6] Ihr Führer Adolf Hitler benutzte den Antisemitismus und Antikommunismus, um die Ängste des Volkes zu manipulieren. Ein Plakat der Nazis zeigt den symbolischen 'starken Mann', der° Deutschland retten soll. Die Opposition sehen Sie noch auf diesem Plakat von 1931, wo starke Arme versuchen, das Hakenkreuz° der Nazis zu zerreißen.“°

Eine Studentin stellte eine Frage: „Ist denn Hitler nicht illegal an die Macht gekommen?“°

„Eigentlich nicht,“ antwortete der Museumsdirektor. „Nachdem seine Partei die Mehrheit° gewann, hat man ihn auf legale Weise zum Kanzler ernannt.° Erst als er Kanzler geworden war, konnte er mit terroristischen Methoden die Republik in eine Diktatur verwandeln.° Deutschland ist also ein gutes Beispiel für die Zerstörung° einer schwachen Demokratie durch wirtschaftliche Not° und politischen Extremismus.“

imperial eagle
fettered
stock market / crashed
economic crisis
catastrophic

strangles / triumphed

strongest

who

swastika / rip apart

***an . . . gekommen** = came to power*

majority
***zum . . . ernannt** = appointed chancellor*
***in . . . verwandeln** = transform into a dictatorship / destruction*
***wirtschaftliche Not** = economic hardship*

[5] The conservative Center Party, consisting mainly of Catholic voters.
[6] The German Parliament until 1945.

Fragen zum Lesestück

1. Warum besuchen die Studenten das Museum?
2. Aus welcher Zeit sind die Plakate in dieser Ausstellung?
3. Wer führt die Studenten durch die Ausstellung?
4. Was erklärt der Direktor, bevor die Gruppe die Ausstellung besucht?
5. Wann dürfen die Studenten den Museumsdirektor unterbrechen?
6. Welche Zeit meint man mit der Weimarer Republik?
7. Was war damals die Hauptstadt Deutschlands?
8. Was waren die Probleme in den ersten Jahren der Weimarer Republik?
9. Warum war die junge deutsche Demokratie in Gefahr?
10. Wann wurde Hitler Reichskanzler?

Vom Lesen zum Sprechen

Die Politik   Politics

Here is some vocabulary for talking about politics. You already know some of these words.

die **Freiheit**	
der **Frieden**	peace
der **Krieg, -e**	
die **Politik**	politics; policy
der **Politiker, -**	
die **Politikerin, -nen**	
der **Präsident, -en, -en**	president
die **Regierung**	government in power, administration
der **Staat**	
das **Volk**	
die **Wahl, -en**	choice; election
wählen	to choose; elect; vote

Gruppenarbeit auf deutsch:

A. Found and name a new political party.

B. Briefly list what your party is for and against.

C. The posters in this chapter show that animals are often used as political symbols. Design an election poster using one of the animals below and a slogan of your invention:

der **Adler, -**	eagle
der **Bär, -en, -en**	bear
der **Elefant, -en, -en**	elephant
der **Esel, -**	donkey
der **Löwe, -n, -n**	lion
die **Schlange, -n**	snake
die **Taube, -n**	dove

D. Each party presents its platform and poster to the others. Here are some useful phrases:

> Unser Plakat zeigt . . . .
> Wir sind für . . . .
> Wir sind gegen . . . .
> Ihr sollt unsere Partei wählen, weil . . . .
> Wählt die _____ Partei, weil . . . .

E. Zur Diskussion:

1. Ist es wichtig für Politiker, die Geschichte ihres Landes zu kennen? Was meinen Sie?
2. Können wir aus der Geschichte der Weimarer Republik etwas für unser Land lernen? Können Sie Beispiele geben?

Mündliche Übungen

A. Persönliche Fragen

1. Wann sind Sie geboren?
2. Wissen Sie, wann Ihre Eltern geboren sind?
3. Was haben Sie Ihrer Mutter zum Geburtstag geschenkt?
4. Wo sind Sie aufgewachsen?
5. Haben Sie in der Schule etwas über moderne Geschichte gelernt?
6. Haben Sie schon eine historische Ausstellung gesehen? Welche?
7. Wie lange sind Sie schon an dieser Uni?
8. Wie lange wohnen Sie schon hier in dieser Stadt?
9. Was haben Sie im Sommer gemacht, als Sie ein Kind waren?

B. (books open) Say what you are looking for. Use an adjective from column one and a noun from column two. Your neighbor responds that they don't have any.

EXAMPLE: Ich suche amerikanische Zeitungen.
Leider haben wir keine amerikanischen Zeitungen.

amerikanisch	Romane
kurz	Politiker
bekannt	Pullis
gesund	Geschenke
toll	Lebensmittel
lang	Zeitungen
billig	Plakate
ehrlich	Rucksäcke
schnell	Restaurants
besser	Bücher
rot	Professoren
interessant	Ideen
bunt	Fahrräder

C. Use the cues below to ask each other questions about your grandparents when they were young. Then invent your own questions. Use simple past tense.

> EXAMPLE: in Europa wohnen?
> Wohnte deine Großmutter in Europa, als sie jung war?
> Ja, sie wohnte in Italien.

1. aus einer großen Familie kommen?
2. Auto fahren können?
3. zur Universität gehen?
4. arbeiten müssen?
5. eine Fremdsprache können?
6. nach Amerika kommen?

D. Gruppenarbeit. (books open) Work together in groups of four or five to write a short story in the simple past tense. Each member of the group takes a turn choosing a verb from the list and adding a sentence to the story, until all the verbs have been used. One person is the secretary and writes down what the others say. Begin with this sentence: „Vor vielen Jahren lebte ein armer Student in einem alten Haus."

aufstehen	helfen	heißen
arbeiten	sterben	kochen
fahren	gehen	stehlen
essen	sagen	sein
vergessen	(ein)schlafen	übernachten
sprechen	trinken	zeigen
versuchen	geben	

Read your stories aloud in class.

E. (books open) Sentences with indirect and direct objects. Create sentences with a verb from column 1, an indirect object from column 2, and a direct object from column 3. Make the necessary changes in adjective endings.

> EXAMPLE: Ich schreibe meinem reichen Onkel einen langen Brief.
> *or*
> Geben Sie den Kindern ein Geburtstagsgeschenk!

1.	*2.*	*3.*
geben	mein reicher Onkel	ein langer Brief
schenken	meine junge Tante	dieser neue Roman
kaufen	die Kinder	unsere schöne Altstadt
zeigen	unsere neuen Freunde	das alte Märchen
erzählen	meine Großeltern	ein Geburtstags-geschenk
schreiben	das nette Mädchen	neue Turnschuhe

F. Work in pairs and find out the birthdays of your partner and his or her family and friends; write them down.

EXAMPLE: In welchem Jahr bist du geboren?
Wann hast du denn Geburtstag?
Possible answers:
Ich bin 1970 geboren. *or* Ich bin im Jahr 1970 geboren.
Ich habe am 1. Februar Geburtstag.

Person	Geburtsjahr	Tag und Monat
Gesprächspartner/-in		
Mutter		
Vater		
Schwester		
Bruder		
Freundin		
Freund		
Tante		
Zimmerkamerad/-in		

Alte Kapelle (*chapel*) und Erdfunkstation (*ground radio station*) in Bayern

Schriftliche Übungen

G. Tell what you did yesterday by creating sentences from the elements provided. Use simple past and past perfect tenses.

1. nachdem/ich/essen//ich/treffen/mein/Freunde/vor/Museum
2. dort/es/geben/interessant/Ausstellung/von/politisch/Plakate
3. wir/wollen/sehen/Ausstellung//um . . . zu/etwas/lernen/über/modern/Geschichte
4. wir/unterbrechen//um . . . zu/der Museumsdirektor/Fragen/stellen
5. Plakate/zeigen/die/viel/Partei/während/dies-/Zeit

H. Essay. Take the story you composed orally with your classmates in exercise D above, and polish it as a written assignment.

I. Wie sagt man das auf deutsch?

1. How long have you lived in this house?
2. We've been here for two years, and we like it a lot.
3. When my husband worked in Bonn we only had a small apartment.
4. You look unhappy. Did something happen to you?
5. I think somebody stole my new knapsack from me.
6. I was in the Mensa two hours ago, and after I had eaten I couldn't find it any more.
7. I hope you can find it again.
8. Can one buy American newspapers here?
9. I'm sorry, we don't have any American newspapers, but only German newspapers.

Hamburg: Blick auf die Alster und Innenstadt (der Blick - *view*)

Almanach

Political Parties in West Germany

Five parties are currently represented in the West German Parliament, or *Bundestag*. These are the *CDU* (*Christlich-Demokratische Union*) with its Bavarian sister party the *CSU* (*Christlich-Soziale Union*); the *SPD* (*Sozialdemokratische Partei Deutschlands*); the *FDP* (*Freie Demokratische Partei*); and *Die Grünen*.

The *CDU* and *CSU* form the conservative end of the political spectrum, receiving consistently 45–50% of the popular vote. The *SPD* is, for the most part, a mildly reformist party dedicated to the welfare state, with only a minority supporting a program of true socialism. The *SPD* receives its 40–50% of the popular vote from industrial workers, students, and young professionals. The *FDP* is a small party receiving around 5–10% of the popular vote that has never been able to reach a majority on its own and has therefore shifted its support back and forth between the *CDU* and *SPD*. In 1983 the *CDU-CSU* and the *FDP* together formed a ruling coalition.

The present political parties represent ideologies that existed before 1933. But the authors of the constitution of the Federal Republic wanted to avoid the factionalism of the many parties that competed for power during the Weimar Republic. Thus, the constitution stipulates that a party must receive at least 5% of the vote to be represented in the *Bundestag*. As a result the political spectrum has been narrowed and fringe parties have been all but eliminated from representation in parliament.

A completely new development on the political scene is the group called *Die Grünen*, a loose federation of voters from all segments of the populace devoted to the preservation of the environment. They are outspokenly radical in their opposition to nuclear power, to Germany's role in the NATO alliance, and in their support of feminist issues. During the 1983 election, they obtained somewhat more than 5% of the vote and for the first time gained representation in the *Bundestag*.

Die Deutsche Demokratische Republik

Dialoge
Die Abiturientenreise ♦ Ein Unfall

Wortschatz 1

Grammatik
1. Adjectival Nouns
   Adjectival Nouns Referring to
   People ♦ Adjectival Nouns
   Referring to Concepts
2. Adjectives of Indefinite Number
3. Reflexive Verbs
   Reflexive Verbs and Pronouns
   ♦ Verbs with Accusative
   Reflexive Pronouns ♦ Verbs
   with Dative Reflexive Pronouns
4. Dative Pronouns with Parts of
   the Body and Clothing
5. More on **bei**
6. Expanding Your Vocabulary
   Country Names, Nouns and
   Adjectives of Nationality
   ♦ Leicht zu merken

Wortschatz 2

Lesestück
Die Deutsche Demokratische
Republik

Vom Lesen zum Sprechen
An der Grenze

Almanach
Profile of the German Democratic
Republic

Dialoge

Die Abiturientenreise

TANTE ELISE: Tag, Inge! Was gibt's Neues?

INGE: Unsere Klasse hat eine DDR-Reise gemacht.

TANTE ELISE: Wirklich? Wie war es denn? Ich kann mir vorstellen, daß ihr viel Interessantes gesehen habt.

INGE: Ja, besonders in Dresden.[1] Dort haben wir auch einige nette Schüler kennengelernt.

TANTE ELISE: Dresden . . . . Hast du eigentlich gewußt, daß wir dort Verwandte haben? Ich habe sie seit dreißig Jahren nicht mehr gesehen, aber wir schreiben uns noch regelmäßig.

Ein Unfall
(Stefan bricht sich das Bein)

MUTTER: Markus, zieh dich schnell an und komm mit!

VATER: Warum? Ist etwas Schlimmes passiert?

MUTTER: Ja, Stefan hatte einen Unfall mit dem Moped und hat sich verletzt!

VATER: Um Gottes Willen! Beeilen wir uns! Hast du den Arzt schon angerufen?

MUTTER: Ja, vor einigen Minuten. Ich fürchte, Stefan hat sich das Bein gebrochen.

(Anna besucht Stefan im Krankenhaus)

STEFAN: Ich freue mich, daß du mich besuchst.

ANNA: Fühlst du dich heute besser, oder tut dir das Bein noch weh?

STEFAN: Ach, es geht. Ich kann mich schon selber waschen, aber ich darf noch nicht aufstehen.

ANNA: Schade. Komm, ich habe dir Schokolade und Blumen mitgebracht.

STEFAN: Oh, wie hübsch! Das ist lieb von dir!

---

[1] City in the southeast GDR, pop. ca. 524,000.

Wortschatz 1

The Senior Class Trip.

AUNT ELISE: Hello, Inge. What's new?

INGE: Our class took a trip to the GDR.

AUNT ELISE: Really? How was it? I can imagine that you saw a lot of interesting things.

INGE: Yes, especially in Dresden. We also met some nice (high-school) students there.

AUNT ELISE: Dresden . . . Did you actually know that we have relatives there? We haven't seen each other for thirty years but we write each other regularly.

An Accident
(Stefan breaks his leg)

MOTHER: Markus, get dressed and come along!

FATHER: Why? Has something bad happened?

MOTHER: Yes, Stefan had an accident with the moped and has injured himself.

VATER: For heaven's sake! Let's hurry! Have you already called the doctor?

MUTTER: Yes, a couple of minutes ago. I'm afraid Stefan has broken his leg.

(Anna is visiting Stefan in the hospital)

STEFAN: I am glad that you're visiting me.

ANNA: Do you feel better today or does your leg still hurt?

STEFAN: Oh, it's all right. I can wash myself but I can't get up yet.

ANNA: That's too bad. Come on, I've brought you chocolate and flowers.

STEFAN: Oh, how pretty! That's nice of you!

Verben

sich etwas ansehen (sieht an), sah an, hat angesehen (+ *dat.*) to take a look at something

sich anziehen, zog an, hat angezogen to get dressed

sich beeilen to hurry

brechen (bricht), brach, hat gebrochen to break

sich erkälten to catch a cold

freuen to please
  Das freut mich. That pleases me; makes me happy.

sich freuen to be happy, be glad

sich fühlen to feel (*intrans.*)

sich die Haare kämmen to comb one's hair

sich etwas leisten können to be able to afford something
  Das kann ich mir nicht leisten. I can't afford that.

putzen to clean

sich setzen to sit down

sich verletzen to injure oneself, get hurt

sich etwas vorstellen to imagine something

waschen (wäscht), wusch, hat gewaschen to wash

weh tun, tat weh, hat weh getan (+ *dat. of person*) to hurt
  Das tut (mir) weh. That hurts (me).

der **Arzt, -̈e** doctor (*m.*)

der **Beamte, -n** (*adj. noun*) official, civil servant (*m.*)

der **Finger, -** finger

der **Kopf, -̈e** head

der **Mund, -̈er** mouth

der **Unfall, -̈e** accident

der/die **Verwandte, -n** (*adj. noun*) relative

der **Zahn, -̈e** tooth

das **Auge, -n** eye

das **Bein, -e** leg

das **Gesicht, -er** face

das **Haar, -e** hair

das **Krankenhaus, -̈er** hospital

das **Ohr, -en** ear

die **Ärztin, -nen** doctor (*f.*)

die **Beamtin, -nen** official, civil servant (*f.*)

die **Blume, -n** flower

die **Nase, -n** nose

die **Schokolade** chocolate

Andere Vokabeln

ander- other, different

einige some

hübsch pretty, handsome

mehrere several, a few

nett nice

regelmäßig regular

schade too bad
  Das ist schade! That's a shame! Too bad! What a pity!

selber, selbst by myself, yourself, ourselves, etc.

sich (*third person reflexive pronoun, see below, pp. 311–317*)

wenige few

Nützliche Ausdrücke

Es geht. It's all right. Not bad.

Um Gottes Willen! For heaven's sake!

Was gibt's Neues? What's new?

Gegensätze

sich anziehen ≠ sich ausziehen
to get dressed ≠ to get undressed

Neue Kombinationen

A. Replace the word in italics with the cue you will hear.

1. Er hatte einen Unfall *mit dem Moped.*
   (mit dem Fahrrad, auf der Straße, vor unserem Haus, in der Stadt)

2. Ich freue mich, daß du mich *besuchst.*
   (magst, brauchst, mitnimmst, fragst, verstehst)

3. Ist etwas *Schlimmes* passiert?
   (Neues, Gutes, Schönes, Interessantes, Tolles)

4. Wir haben einige *nette Schüler* kennengelernt.
   (sympathische Menschen, amerikanische Touristen, freundliche Studenten)

5. Ich fürchte, er hat sich *das Bein* gebrochen.
   (den Fuß, die Hand, den Arm)

B. Answer the following questions. Begin your answer with „Es gibt . . . "

EXAMPLE: Was gibt's zum Abendessen?
Es gibt Schnitzel und Pommes frites.

1. Was gibt's heute abend im Kino?

2. Was gibt's diese Woche im Museum?

3. Was gibt's heute in der Mensa zu essen?

4. Was gibt's in der Fußgängerzone zu kaufen?

5. Was gibt's in der Altstadt zu sehen?

6. Was gibt's heute zum Mittagessen?

C. *Antonyms.* Use the cue you will hear to ask for your neighbors' opinions. They reply that they think the opposite is true.

EXAMPLE: Teacher: diese Diskussion / langweilig
Student A: Findest du diese Diskussion langweilig?
Student B: Nein, ich finde sie interessant.

1. die deutsche Sprache / häßlich

2. das Problem / leicht

3. einen Stadtbummel / eine gute Idee

4. das Wetter / zu kalt

5. diesen Mantel / sehr teuer

6. die Geschichte / interessant

7. diesen Kaffee / zu stark

8. meine Haare / zu lang

Wolf Biermann

Übung zur Aussprache

Here is the text of a song by Wolf Biermann, who was born in Hamburg in 1936. His father, a dock worker and Communist, was murdered by the Nazis in the Auschwitz concentration camp. In 1953, Biermann moved to the German Democratic Republic, where he soon came into conflict with the regime. He was forbidden to perform in the GDR. In 1976, on a concert tour in the Federal Republic, Biermann was deprived of his GDR citizenship. He now lives in the West. Biermann performs his own songs, accompanying himself on the guitar. This song dates from 1968.

Es senkt das deutsche Dunkel

Es senkt das deutsche Dunkel°	*darkness*
sich° über mein Gemüt.°	**senkt . . . sich:** *descends / spirit*
Es dunkelt übermächtig°	*becomes overwhelmingly dark*
In meinem Lied.°	*song*
Das kommt, weil ich mein Deutschland	
So tief zerrissen° seh	*deeply split*
Ich lieg in der bess'ren Hälfte°	*better half*
Und habe doppelt Weh.°	*twice the pain*

Grammatik

1 ◆ Adjectival Nouns

Adjectival Nouns Referring to People

In English, adjectives by themselves occasionally function as nouns, but only as collective designations with the definite article:

The rich are different.　　　　　　　**Die Reichen** sind anders.

In German, adjectival nouns are more frequent and their use is less restricted than in English. They can refer to individuals as well as to collective groups. Masculine adjectival nouns denote men, feminine denote women, while plural adjectival nouns simply denote "people." Adjectival nouns are capitalized and *receive adjective endings as though they were followed by the nouns „Mann," „Frau," or „Menschen."*

Here are some examples which include these nouns in parentheses to make the structure clear. Note the adjective endings!

Die Reichen (Menschen) **sind anders.**	*The rich are different.*
Der Reiche (Mann) **wohnt hier.**	*The rich man lives here.*
Ein Reicher (Mann) **wohnt hier.**	*A rich man lives here.*
Kennst du diesen Reichen (Mann)?	*Do you know this rich man?*
Die Reiche (Frau) **kennt mich.**	*The rich woman knows me.*
Das Haus gehört einer Reichen (Frau).	*The house belongs to a rich woman.*

In principle, any adjective can be used as an adjectival noun. Here are some frequently occurring ones you should learn:

der/die[1] **Alte, -n**	old man, old woman
der/die **Arme, -n**	poor man, poor woman
der **Beamte, -n**	official, civil servant (m.)[2]
der/die **Bekannte, -n**	acquaintance, friend
der/die **Deutsche, -n**[3]	German man, German woman
der/die **Grüne, -n**	member of the "Greens," the environmental political party
der/die **Kleine, -n**	little boy, little girl (or: short man, short woman)
der/die **Kranke, -n**	sick man, sick woman
der/die **Tote, -n**	dead man, dead woman
der/die **Verwandte, -n** (*from* **verwandt,** *related*)	relative

[1] From now on, we will list adjectival nouns in the *Wortschatz* in this way.
[2] Note that only the masculine form is an adjectival noun. The feminine form ends in **-in: die Beamtin.**
[3] This is the *only* noun of nationality that is adjectival.

A. Complete the sentence you will hear with the appropriate form of **mein Bekannter** (my friend—masculine).

> EXAMPLE: Das ist _____ .
> Das ist mein Bekannter.

1. Heute zum Mittagessen treffe ich _____ .
2. Ich gehe oft mit _____ Volleyball spielen.
3. Das ist die Frau _____ .
4. _____ heißt Robert.

B. Now use a form of **meine Bekannten** (my friends).

1. Das sind _____ .
2. Kennen Sie _____ ?
3. Helfen Sie bitte _____ !
4. Das sind die Kinder _____ .

C. Now use a form of **die Deutsche** (the German woman).

1. Wie heißt denn _____ ?
2. Meinst du _____ ?
4. Ich trampe mit _____ nach Italien.
5. Ist das der Rucksack _____ ?

D. Now use a form of **die Deutschen** (the Germans).

1. Wir sind alle hier, außer _____ .
2. Da kommen _____ !
3. Wer trägt denn die Koffer _____ ?
4. Wir machen das für _____ .

E. Now use a form of **unser Verwandter** (our relative—masculine)

1. Helmut ist _____ .
2. Kennt sie _____ ?
3. Du sollst mit _____ sprechen.
4. Die Tochter _____ besucht uns morgen.

Adjectival Nouns Referring to Concepts

Adjectival nouns in the neuter occur only in the singular. They are abstract nouns signaling the *quality* designated by the adjective. There are several English equivalents for this:

Das Neue gefällt mir.   *I like new things.*
I like what is new.

Ich suche **das Gute**.   *I seek the good.*
I seek that which is good.
I'm looking for the good part.

■ Do not confuse adjectival nouns with noun phrases which have omitted the noun. The noun may be omitted when it has already been used in the immediately preceding noun phrase:

Das alte Haus gefällt dir,
aber **das neue** gefällt mir.

*You like the old house
but I like the new one.*

In English, this deleted noun must be replaced by "one."

Neuter adjectival nouns occur most frequently after the indefinite pronouns **etwas** (something), **nichts** (nothing), **viel** (much, a lot of), and **wenig** (not much, little):

etwas Neues
nichts Schönes
viel Gutes
wenig Interessantes

something new
nothing beautiful
much that is good
little of interest

Since these pronouns are *not* limiting words, the adjectival noun gets the full neuter endings of **dieses:**

nominative
Etwas Interessantes ist mir gestern
    passiert.

*Something interesting
    happened to me yesterday.*

accusative
Hier gibt es **etwas Interessantes.**

*There's something interesting
    here.*

dative
Fangen wir mit **etwas Interessantem** an.

*Let's begin with something
    interesting.*

Zeichnung: Valerry

Üben wir!	**A.** Answer according to the example, using **neu** with **nichts** and **etwas**.

EXAMPLE: Teacher: Was hat der Professor gesagt?
                    Student A: Er hat nichts Neues gesagt.
                    Student B: Doch, er hat etwas Neues gesagt.

1. Was hat euch der Lehrer erzählt?
2. Was habt ihr in der Sportstunde gespielt?
3. Was haben euch eure Eltern geschrieben?
4. Was hatte die Buchhandlung?
5. Was habt ihr in der Altstadt gefunden?

B. Now answer with **viel** and **wenig** and the cue in parentheses.

EXAMPLE: Teacher: Was gibt's im Museum? (schön)
                    Student A: Es gibt viel Schönes.
                    Student B: Nein, es gibt wenig Schönes.

1. Was kann man in der Fußgängerzone sehen? (interessant)
2. Was hast du in der Zeitung gelesen? (wichtig)
3. Was hast du über diese Politikerin gehört? (gut)
4. Was gibt's im Museum? (neu)

2 ◆ Adjectives of Indefinite Number

These adjectives are used with nouns in the plural to indicate indefinite amounts:

wenige	*few*	**andere**	*other(s)*
einige	*some*	**viele**	*many*
mehrere	*several*		

The adjectives of indefinite number are *not* limiting words, and therefore take the same endings as attributive adjectives. This means that an adjective of indefinite number and any descriptive adjectives that follow it will have the *same ending*.

without a limiting word:
Wenige alte Leute waren da.   *Few old people were there.*

with a limiting word:
Die **wenigen alten** Leute haben   *The few old people had fun.*
   Spaß gehabt.

Used by themselves, without a following noun, these indefinite adjectives become indefinite pronouns referring to human beings:

Viele sagen, der Film ist   *Many (people) say the film is*
  interessant.   *interesting.*
Wenige sagen, er ist gut.   *Few (people) say it's good.*
Einige gehen ins Kino, **andere** *Some (people) go to the movies,*
  gehen ins Theater.   *others go to the theater.*

A. Add each new word you will hear to the sentence, giving it the correct ending.

> EXAMPLE: Darf ich Postkarten haben? (einige)
> Darf ich einige Postkarten haben? (schön)
> Darf ich einige schöne Postkarten haben?

1. Sie hat schon Filme gesehen. (mehrere, deutsch)
2. Haben Sie die Mitglieder gekannt? (andere, neu)
3. Schüler verstehen das nicht. (viele, jung, amerikanisch)
4. Er hat mit Menschen gesprochen. (wenige, interessant)
5. Filme gefallen mir sehr. (einige, neu, deutsch)
6. Das sind die Probleme der Journalisten. (andere, jung)
7. Ich kenne Restaurants in Hamburg. (einige, gut)

B. Respond to each question as in the example, replacing **Leute** with **einige** and **andere**.

> EXAMPLE: Teacher: Gehen diese Leute ins Kino?
> Student A: Einige gehen ins Kino.
> Student B: Andere gehen nicht ins Kino.

1. Kennen diese Leute den Film?
2. Kennst du diese Leute?
3. Gehst du mit diesen Leuten ins Kino?
4. Hat der Film diesen Leuten gefallen?

3 ◆ Reflexive Verbs

Reflexive Verbs and Pronouns

In most sentences with objects, the subject and the object are two different people or things:

subj.   obj.

Ich habe **ihn** verletzt.   *I hurt him.*
Ich habe **ihm** geholfen.   *I helped him.*

When a verb's object refers to the *same* person or thing as its subject, the verb is called *reflexive*. The object of a *reflexive verb* is always a pronoun called a *reflexive pronoun*.

subj.   obj.

Ich habe **mich** verletzt.   *I hurt myself.*
Ich habe **mir** selbst[1] geholfen.   *I helped myself.*

---

[1] The words **selbst** and **selber** are adverbs meaning *by myself, yourself, himself, ourselves,* etc.:
Ich kann das **selber** machen.   *I can do it by myself.*
Used after reflexive pronouns, they emphasize the reflexive:
Wir müssen ihn noch waschen.   *We still have to wash him.*
Nein, er hat sich schon **selbst**   *No, he has already washed himself.*
gewaschen.

The reflexive pronouns in English all end in **-self** or **-selves**, e.g., **myself, himself, herself, themselves.** In German, there are both accusative and dative reflexive pronouns. As you can see in the following table, they are identical in form to the personal pronouns except in the third person and the formal second person, where the reflexive pronoun is **sich.**[1]

Reflexive Pronouns

| | *singular* | | *plural* | |
	acc.	*dat.*	*acc.*	*dat.*
1st person	mich	mir	uns	uns
2nd person	dich	dir	euch	euch
3rd person	sich	sich	sich	sich
(and formal 2nd pers.)				

■ In the plural, the reflexive pronouns often denote reciprocity and are the equivalent of English *each other:*

Wir treffen **uns** morgen.	*We'll meet **each other** tomorrow.*
Kennt ihr **euch?**	*Do you know **each other?***
Wir kennen **uns** seit langem.	*We've known **each other** for a long time.*

Verbs With Accusative Reflexive Pronouns

Any transitive verb may be used reflexively. Here is a sample conjugation using **sich verletzen:**

Ich habe **mich** verletzt.	*I hurt **myself.***
Du hast **dich** verletzt.	*You hurt **yourself.***
Er (es, sie) hat **sich** verletzt.	*He (it, she) hurt **himself (itself, herself).***
Wir haben **uns** verletzt.	*We hurt **ourselves.***
Ihr habt **euch** verletzt.	*You hurt **yourselves.***
Sie haben **sich** verletzt.	*They (you) hurt **themselves (yourself, yourselves).***

Üben wir!

A. Substitute the new subject you will hear and make other necessary changes:

1. Ich kenne mich gut.
   (du, Monika, Georg, Sie)
2. Du hast dich verletzt!
   (Jens, ich, Anna, ihr, wir, diese Jungen, Sie)
3. Wir kennen uns seit Jahren.
   (ihr, diese Menschen, Karla und ich)
4. Wo treffen wir uns morgen? (sie—*plural*, ihr, Sie)
5. Sie haben sich in Bonn kennengelernt.
   (ihr, wir, Sie, diese Freunde)

---

[1] Note on spelling: **sich** is not capitalized even when it refers to the polite pronoun **Sie.**

B. Respond as in the example.

> EXAMPLE: Ich mag dich und du magst mich.
> Ja, wir mögen uns.

1. Anna versteht Stefan und er versteht sie.
2. Ich sehe dich morgen, und du siehst mich morgen.
3. Herr Mohn trifft Frau Riedel vor der Bibliothek, und sie trifft ihn auch dort.

C. Answer each question according to the example.

> EXAMPLE: Wen kennt er denn?
> Er kennt nur sich selbst.

1. Wen verstehst du denn?
2. Wen mag sie denn?
3. Wen hat er verletzt?

Dresden: Lenin-Denkmal am Leninplatz

German Reflexive Verbs That Are Intransitive in English

Many German reflexive verbs have English equivalents that are intransitive:

German: reflexive	English: intransitive
sich anziehen	to get dressed
sich setzen	to sit down
sich waschen	to get washed

German transitive verbs *require* an accusative object even when that object is identical with the subject. Many English transitive verbs become *intransitive* when their subject performs an action on itself:

German transitive ⟶ reflexive		English transitive ⟶ intransitive	
Sie wäscht **ihren Sohn**.	Sie wäscht **sich**.	*She's washing her son.*	*She's washing.*
Er zog **das Kind** an.	Er zog **sich** an.	*He dressed the child.*	*He got dressed.*

Üben wir!

A. Here is an account of Stefan's first morning home from the hospital. Repeat it sentence by sentence after your teacher.

1. Um sieben hat sich Stefan gewaschen.
2. Um halb acht hat er sich angezogen.
3. Dann hat er sich an den Tisch gesetzt.
4. Endlich konnte er wieder alles selber machen.

Now retell the story about each of the following: the students, yourself, Jens, you and a friend, me.

Verbs Requiring the Accusative Reflexive

Verbs like **anziehen** and **waschen** may be used either reflexively (**Sie wäscht sich.**) or non-reflexively (**Sie wäscht den Wagen.**). Some German verbs, however, must *always* be used with an accusative reflexive pronoun. Their English equivalents are intransitive:

German: reflexive	English: intransitive
sich beeilen	to hurry
sich erkälten	to catch cold
sich freuen	to be happy
sich fühlen	to feel

Üben wir!

A. Respond as in the example.

    EXAMPLE: Soll ich mich beeilen?
             Ja, beeile dich!

(use **du**-form)

1. Soll ich mich waschen?
2. Soll ich mich freuen?
3. Darf ich mich setzen?
4. Muß ich mich anziehen?

(use **ihr**-form)

5. Sollen wir uns freuen?
6. Sollen wir uns schön anziehen?
7. Müssen wir uns beeilen?
8. Dürfen wir uns setzen?

(use **Sie**-form)

9. Soll ich mich anziehen?
10. Darf ich mich setzen?
11. Müssen wir uns beeilen?
12. Sollen wir uns morgen treffen?

B. Answer the questions either positively or negatively.

> EXAMPLE: Fühlen Sie sich besser?
> Ja, ich fühle mich besser.
> *or:* Nein, ich fühle mich nicht besser.

1. Haben Sie sich erholt?
2. Freuen Sie sich?
3. Müssen Sie sich beeilen?
4. Wollen Sie sich anziehen?
5. Können Sie sich setzen?
6. Können Sie sich waschen?
7. Haben Sie sich verletzt?
8. Haben Sie sich die Zähne geputzt?
9. Haben Sie sich erkältet?

Verbs With Dative Reflexive Pronouns

1. Verbs With Dative Objects
   You have already seen that a verb like **helfen,** which requires a dative object, must be used with a reflexive pronoun when the subject and object are identical:

   Ich kann **mir selber** helfen.   *I can help myself.*

2. Reflexive Indirect Object
   The subject and *indirect* object can be identical. In this case the indirect object is a *dative* reflexive pronoun:

Ich kaufe **mir** Blumen.	*I'm buying **myself** flowers.*
Du kaufst **dir** Blumen.	*You're buying **yourself** flowers.*
Sie kauft **sich** Blumen.	*She's buying **herself** flowers.*
Wir kaufen **uns** Blumen.	*We're buying **ourselves** flowers.*
Ihr kauft **euch** Blumen.	*You're buying **yourselves** flowers.*
Sie kaufen **sich** Blumen.	*They're buying **themselves** flowers.*

   ■ Notice that except for **mir** and **dir,** the dative reflexive pronouns are identical in form to the accusative reflexive pronouns.
   ■ The dative reflexive makes explicit the fact that the subject is the beneficiary of its own action. It may be omitted without changing the basic meaning of the sentence:

Ich kaufe mir eine Jacke.	*I'm buying myself a jacket.*
Ich kaufe eine Jacke.	*I'm buying a jacket.*

Üben wir!

A. Show that the subject is doing something for himself or herself by adding the dative reflexive pronoun to these sentences:

> EXAMPLE: Er kauft einen Pulli.
> Er kauft sich einen Pulli.

1. Ich nehme eine Zeitung mit.
2. Hast du etwas Schönes gekauft?
3. Ich habe nur Wein gekauft.
4. Wir kochen etwas zu Hause.
5. Marga kocht eine Suppe.
6. Helmut kauft eine Fahrkarte nach Köln.

Verbs Requiring the Dative Reflexive

There are some German verbs that must *always* be used with the dative reflexive pronoun. They all require a (non-reflexive) direct object. Their English equivalents are *not* reflexive:

German: dative reflexive	English: not reflexive
sich etwas ansehen	to take a look at, look over
Ich wollte **mir** den Wagen ansehen.	*I wanted to take a look at the car.*
sich etwas leisten können	to be able to afford
Kannst du **dir** ein neues Fahrrad leisten?	*Can you afford a new bicycle?*
sich etwas vorstellen	to imagine
Das kann ich **mir** nicht vorstellen.	*I can't imagine that.*

■ Verbs *requiring* the accusative or dative reflexive are conventionally indicated in vocabularies and dictionaries by the third-person **sich**. Since **sich** can be either accusative or dative, the inclusion of the direct object **etwas** indicates that the **sich** is a *dative* reflexive: **sich** (dative) **etwas** (accusative) **ansehen.**

`○━○` **Üben wir!**

A. Substitute the new objects you will hear and make all other necessary changes.

1. Was will er sich ansehen?
   (wir, ihr, du, sie, die Touristen, ich, Sie)
2. Er möchte sich diese alte Kirche ansehen.
   (die Touristen, ich, wir, Sie, du, ihr)
3. Er konnte sich nichts Besseres vorstellen.
   (ich, du, wir, die Amerikaner, ihr, sie)
4. Wie konnte er sich eine Reise leisten?
   (du, ihr, wir, ich, Sie)

4 ◆ Dative Pronouns with Parts of the Body and Clothing

In contrast to English, German does not usually use the genitive or possessive adjective (**mein, dein, sein,** etc). with parts of the body or with articles of clothing when they are being put on or taken off. Instead, it uses the personal dative:

Die Mutter wäscht **dem Kind** die Hände.	*The mother washes the child's hands.*
Sie zog **ihm** den Mantel an.	*She put his coat on for him.*

If the subject is performing the action on itself, the dative pronoun is reflexive:

Ich habe **mir** die Hände gewaschen.	*I washed my hands.*
Er zog **sich** den Mantel an.	*He put on his coat.*
Stefan hat **sich** das Bein gebrochen.	*Stefan broke his leg.*

Üben wir!

A. Review your knowledge of parts of the body by identifying them in the accompanying picture.

cat: die **Katze, -n**   *dog:* der **Hund, -e**

B. Substitute the new subjects you will hear and make other necessary changes.

1. Wie hat er sich das Bein gebrochen? (ich, sie, du, Sie)
2. Ich möchte mir die Hände waschen. (er, die Kinder, du, ihr, wir)
3. Du hast dir den Fuß verletzt. (er, Inge, ich)
4. Ich soll mir die Schuhe anziehen. (du, Robert, wir, ihr, die Kinder)

C. Say that people are putting on various articles of clothing, using the cue you will hear.

> EXAMPLE: du/Jacke
> Du ziehst dir die Jacke an.

1. ich/die Schuhe
2. Anton/Pulli
3. du/Hose
4. Vater/Jacke

5. ich/Hemd
6. wir/Mantel
7. du/Kleid
8. du/Bluse

D. Tell four-year-old Jonas that he is a big boy now and can take care of himself.

> EXAMPLE: A. Wer zieht mich an?
> B. Du kannst dich schon selbst anziehen.
> A. Wer wäscht mir die Hände?
> B. Du kannst dir schon selbst die Hände waschen.

1. Wer wäscht mich?
2. Wer zieht mir die Schuhe an?
3. Wer kämmt mir die Haare?
4. Wer wäscht mir die Hände?

5. Wer zieht mich an?
6. Wer putzt mir die Zähne?
7. Wer wäscht mir das Gesicht?
8. Wer putzt mir die Nase?

5 ◆ More on *bei*

In Chapter 5 you learned that the dative preposition **bei** has the spatial meanings "in the home of," "near," or "at."

However, **bei** more frequently is used to set a scene. It then has the meanings "during," "while . . . ing," "at" (an activity or someone's home or business):

Er hat sich **beim Schilaufen** verletzt.	*He hurt himself while skiing.*
Marion ist jetzt **bei der Arbeit.**	*Marion's at work now.*
Ich lese oft **beim Essen.**	*I often read during meals.*
Ich war gestern **beim Arzt.**	*I was at the doctor's yesterday.*

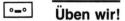 **Üben wir!**

A. Restate the subordinate clauses as phrases with **bei.**

> EXAMPLE: Ich falle nie, wenn ich Schi laufe.
> Ich falle nie beim Schilaufen.

1. Störe mich nicht, wenn ich lese.
2. Wir treffen uns oft, wenn wir radfahren.
3. Sprich bitte nicht, wenn du ißt!
4. Wenn wir spazieren gehen, können wir zusammen reden.
5. Ich höre gern Musik, wenn ich Auto fahre.
6. Ich ziehe mir die Schuhe aus, wenn ich arbeite.

B. (books open) Answer the question with the **bei**-phrase cued in English.

> EXAMPLE: Wie hat er sich denn verletzt? (while skiing)
> Beim Schilaufen.

1. Wo sind Sie morgen um zehn? (at work)
2. Wie lernt man viele Menschen kennen? (while hitchhiking)
3. Wann reden Sie nicht viel? (when driving a car)
4. Wo ist denn Ihre Frau? (at the doctor's)
5. Wie hast du so viel·Geld verloren? (playing cards)
6. Wo hast du Hilde kennengelernt? (at the first lecture)

6 ♦ Expanding Your Vocabulary

Country Names, Nouns and Adjectives of Nationality

The only designation of nationality that is an adjectival noun is:

die Deutsche	the German (woman)
eine Deutsche	a German (woman)
der Deutsche	the German (man)
ein Deutscher	a German (man)
die Deutschen	the Germans
Deutsche	Germans

Of the other nouns of nationality, some have a masculine form ending in **-er** and a feminine in **-erin**:

Country	*Adjective*	*Male Native*	*Female Native*
Amerika	amerikanisch	der **Amerikaner**, -	die **Amerikanerin**, -nen
England	englisch	der **Engländer**, -	die **Engländerin**, -nen
Italien	italienisch	der **Italiener**, -	die **Italienerin**, -nen
Österreich	österreichisch	der **Österreicher**, -	die **Österreicherin**, -nen
die **Schweiz**	schweizerisch	der **Schweizer**, -	die **Schweizerin**, -nen

Other nouns of nationality are N-nouns in the masculine and add **-in** (and sometimes an umlaut) in the feminine:

Frankreich	französisch	der **Franzose**, -n, -n	die **Französin**, -nen
Jugoslawien	jugoslawisch	der **Jugoslawe**, -n, -n	die **Jugoslawin**, -nen
Rußland	russisch	der **Russe**, -n, -n	die **Russin**, -nen

■ Remember that when stating a person's nationality, German does not use the indefinite article (see page 139):

Sind Sie Deutsche?	*Are you a German?*
Nein, ich bin Französin.	*No, I'm French.*

<table>
<tr><td>**Üben wir!**</td><td>**A.** Your teacher will hand you a slip of paper telling what country you are from (**Deutschland, Frankreich, Rußland, Italien, Amerika, England, Österreich, die Schweiz**). Now mingle with your fellow students and find out where they're from.</td></tr>
</table>

EXAMPLE: A. Wo kommst du denn her?
B. Ich komme aus England.
A. Ach, du bist Engländer(in)!

Leicht zu merken

demokratisch	
finanziell	finanzi*ell*
die **Form, -en**	
die **Generation, -en**	Generati*on*
das **Großbritannien**	
das **Ideal -e**	Ide*al*
illegitim	*il*legitim
der/die **Intellektuelle, -n**	Intellektu*elle*
kapitalistisch	kapita*lis*tisch
kommunistisch	kommun*is*tisch
der **Marxist, -en, -en**	Marx*ist*
die **Million, -en**	Milli*on*
das **Moskau**	
die **Reparation, -en**	Reparati*on*
der **Satellit, -en, -en**	Satel*lit*
die **Sowjets**	Sow*jets*
die **Sowjetunion**	Sow*jet*union
sozialistisch	
das **Symbol -e**	Symb*ol*
transportieren	transpor*tie*ren
die **Zone, -n**	

Wortschatz 2

Verben

aus · wandern to emigrate
erscheinen, erschien, ist erschienen to appear
kritisieren to criticize
leisten to achieve, accomplish
verlangen to demand

Substantive

der **Bürger, -** citizen
der **Dichter, -** poet
der **Grund, ̈e** ground; reason
der **Russe, -n, -n** Russian *m.*
der **Spiegel, -** mirror
der **Zweck, -e** purpose

das **Frankreich** France
das **Lied, -er** song
die **Grenze, -n** border
die **Hälfte, -n** half
die **Hilfe** help, aid
die **Mauer, -n** wall (*freestanding or outside*)
die **Reaktion, -en** reaction
die **Russin, -nen** Russian (*f.*)
die **Seite, -n** side; page

die **Situation, -en** situation
die **Tatsache, -n** fact
die **Wirtschaft** economy
die **Zukunft** future

Andere Vokabeln

beid- both
berühmt famous
europäisch European
hoch (*predicte adj.*), **hoh-** (*attributive adj.*) high
  Das Gebäude ist hoch. *But:* **das hohe Gebäude**
kaum hardly, barely
mancher, -es, -e many a
  manche (*plur.*) some
offen open
tot dead
verschieden different, various
wahr true

Nützliche Ausdrücke

am Ende at/in the end
auf der einen Seite on the one hand
auf der anderen Seite on the other hand
ohne Zweifel without doubt, doubtless

Gegensätze

auswandern ≠ **einwandern**	to emigrate ≠ to immigrate
offen ≠ **geschlossen**	open ≠ closed
verschieden ≠ **ähnlich**	different ≠ similar
am Ende ≠ **am Anfang**	at the end ≠ at the beginning

Die Deutsche Demokratische Republik

Über die Deutsche Demokratische Republik (DDR) wissen wir im Westen wahrscheinlich weniger als° über die anderen deutschsprachigen Länder. Der Grund liegt im „Kalten Krieg"—in der weltpolitischen Spannung° zwi-
5   schen den kapitalistischen Ländern im Westen und den kommunistischen Ländern im Osten seit dem Zweiten Weltkrieg. Die DDR ist ein sozialistisches Land, und sie gehört zum Warschauer Pakt.[1] Viele nennen sie einfach einen Satellitenstaat Moskaus. Daß es aber seit vierzig Jah-
10   ren zwei verschiedene deutsche Staaten gibt, ist eine politische Tatsache.

Die Geschichte der Teilung° Deutschlands ist ein Spiegel der europäischen Geschichte in der zweiten Hälfte des zwanzigsten Jahrhunderts. Am Ende des Zweiten Welt-
15   kriegs im Jahre 1945 teilten die vier Alliierten° Amerika, England, Frankreich und die Sowjetunion das besiegte°

weniger als = *less than*

tension

division

allies
defeated

[1] Warsaw Pact: the mutual defense pact among the eastern European countries allied with the Soviet Union.

Dresden an der Elbe

Deutschland in vier Zonen auf.° Diese Zonen sollten nur so
lange bestehen,° bis man eine neue, entnazifizierte° deutsche Regierung bilden° konnte.

20   Schon bald aber wurde es klar, daß die Alliierten sich
über die Zukunft Deutschlands nicht einig waren.° Man darf
nicht vergessen, daß der Zweite Weltkrieg die Sowjetunion
20 Millionen Tote gekostet hatte. Die Russen fühlten sich
also berechtigt,° in ihrer Zone hohe Reparationen zu ver-
25 langen. Ganze Fabriken transportierte man nach Rußland,
um dort einen neuen Anfang in der Industrie möglich zu
machen. Auf der anderen Seite konnten die Westdeutschen
mit der großen finanziellen Hilfe des Marshallplans[2] ihre
Industrie und Wirtschaft schnell wiederaufbauen.° Das ver-
30 standen die Sowjets als die Wiedereinführung° des Ka-
pitalismus statt der Entnazifizierung Deutschlands. Die
ideologischen Konflikte wurden immer schlimmer,° bis
man im Mai 1949 aus den Westzonen die BRD gründete.°
Die russische Reaktion darauf° war die Gründung der DDR
35 im Oktober 1949. Jeder Staat sah sich als das „wahre
Deutschland" und den anderen als illegitim.

    Am Anfang blieb die Grenze zwischen den beiden deut-
schen Staaten relativ offen, besonders in der Hauptstadt
Berlin. Darum konnten zwischen 1945 und 1961 zirka 2,7
40 Millionen über diese Grenze nach Westen auswandern.
1961 unterbrach die DDR–Regierung den Auswanderer-
strom° durch den Bau der Berliner Mauer. Diese Mauer ist
für den Westen ein berühmtes Symbol für den Bankrott° der
DDR-Regierung. Für die DDR aber hat sie ihren Zweck
45 erfüllt: der Staat verlor seine ausgebildeten° Arbeiter nicht
mehr.

    Ohne Zweifel hat die DDR seit 1949 viel geleistet. So
ist sie heute ein starkes Industrieland, und ihre Bürger leben
in sozialer Sicherheit.° Ohne Zweifel ist aber die DDR ein
50 Staat, wo politische Opposition kaum möglich ist.

    Die Situation mancher Intellektuellen und Schrift-
steller in der DDR ist paradox.° Als Marxisten bejahen° sie
die Ideale des Sozialismus. Aber sie kritisieren das un-
demokratische System. Oft dürfen ihre Bücher nur im
55 Westen erscheinen. Ein berühmtes Beispiel ist der Dichter
und Liedermacher Wolf Biermann. Er ist in Hamburg geboren und 1953 freiwillig° in die DDR eingewandert. 1976, als
er in der BRD auf einer Konzerttour war, hat ihn die
DDR–Regierung ausgebürgert.° Seine Gefühle über
60 Deutschland drückte er schon 1968, als er noch in der DDR
lebte, in einem Lied aus:°
    Ich lieg' in der bess'ren Hälfte
    Und habe doppelt Weh.
In diese „bessere Hälfte" darf er aber nicht mehr zurück.

---

[2] Marshall Plan: European Recovery Program, named for George C. Marshall
(1880–1959) U.S. Secretary of State (1947–49) who instituted the measure to
rebuild the economies of Western Europe destroyed in the war.

teilten . . . auf = divided
exist / de-Nazified
form

sich . . . nicht einig waren = were not in agreement

justified

rebuild
reintroduction

immer schlimmer = worse and worse
founded
to that

stream
of emigrants
bankruptcy

skilled

security

paradoxical / accept

voluntarily

expatriated

drückte . . . aus = expressed

Der Berliner Dom (Ost-Berlin)

Stadtplan für Fußgänger (Berlin-Mitte)

Fragen zum Lesestück

1. Warum kennen wir im Westen die DDR so wenig?
2. Wie viele Zonen gab es in Deutschland nach dem Zweiten Weltkrieg?
3. Nennen Sie die vier Alliierten.
4. Von wem bekamen die Deutschen finanzielle Hilfe?
5. Seit wann gibt es zwei moderne deutsche Staaten?
6. Wann hat die DDR die Mauer gebaut?
7. Was bedeutet die Mauer für den Westen? Und für den Osten?
8. Was kritisieren viele Intellektuelle in der DDR?
9. Was wissen Sie über Wolf Biermann?

Vom Lesen zum Sprechen

An der Grenze

packen	to pack
auspacken	to unpack
der **Paß**, die **Pässe**	passport
schmuggeln	to smuggle
der **Schnaps**	distilled spirits
die **Zigarette, -n**	cigarette
der **Zoll**	customs
Haben Sie etwas zu verzollen?	Do you have anything to declare?
der **Zollbeamte**	customs official

Useful to Recall

der **Ausweis, -e**
der **Beamte, -n** (*adj. noun*)
die **Beamtin, -nen**
die **Grenze, -n**
 an der Grenze
der **Kaffee**
der **Rucksack, ̈-e**
aufmachen

A. Sie machen eine Reise nach Deutschland. Was packen Sie in den Koffer oder den Rucksack? Was wollen Sie dann zurückbringen, wenn Sie nach Hause kommen? Müssen Sie etwas verzollen, wenn Sie zurückkommen?

B. Was sagen diese Leute?

Mündliche Übungen

A. Persönliche Fragen

1. Haben Sie je einen Unfall gehabt?
2. Haben Sie sich je das Bein gebrochen? (die Hand, den Arm, den Finger)
3. Haben sie Verwandte in Europa? Haben Sie sie je besucht?
4. Ist Ihnen diese Woche etwas Schönes passiert? (etwas Schlimmes?)
5. Was kaufen Sie sich am Anfang des Semesters?
6. Wann fühlen Sie sich besonders glücklich? (unglücklich?)
7. Wann putzen Sie sich die Zähne?
8. Ziehen Sie sich an, bevor Sie sich die Zähne putzen?

B. Rollenspiel: You are shopping in Germany with a friend who speaks no German. Relay your friend's comments and questions to a salesperson, who then answers in the negative.

> EXAMPLE: Teacher: Do they have anything new?
> Student A: Mein Freund möchte wissen, ob Sie etwas Neues haben.
> Student B: Nein, wir haben leider nichts Neues.

Do they have anything cheap? (interesting, small, modern, colorful, old, expensive)

C. Rollenspiel: (books open) You are a clerk in a department store. Your teacher is a customer who needs a lot of assistance. Respond to your teacher's queries using an adjective of indefinite number in your answer:

einige	viele
wenige	mehrere
andere	

> EXAMPLE: Teacher: Guten Tag. Ich brauche heute weiße Turnschuhe.
> Student: O, wir haben viele weiße Turnschuhe.
> *or:* Leider haben wir heute nur noch wenige weiße Turnschuhe.

1. Ich suche eine gute Armbanduhr für meine Tochter.
2. Haben Sie einen Stadtplan von Zürich?
3. Die braunen Handschuhe gefallen mir nicht. Haben Sie andere?
4. Verkaufen Sie auch Mopeds?
5. Können Sie mir eine leichte Jacke zeigen?

D. Spiel. Der Lehrer fragt: „Wo tut's Ihnen weh?" Ein Student zeigt z.B. auf seinen Fuß und sagt: „Mein Fuß tut mir weh!" Dann sagt ein anderer Student: „Ja, er hat sich den Fuß verletzt."

E. Here is a description of a conversation between two Germans, one from the East and one from the West. The West German, Helmut, is from Saarbrücken, and is on an *Abiturientenreise* to the GDR. He speaks with Erich, who is from Leipzig. Act out the conversation between the two and try to improvise.

Erich sagt, daß er sich freut, endlich einen Schüler aus der Bundesrepublik kennenzulernen. Er will wissen, wie Helmut und seine Gruppe hergefahren sind, was sie sehen und wissen wollen, ob sie hier Leute kennen oder Verwandte haben.

Helmut antwortet und stellt auch seine eigenen Fragen. Er fragt z.B., ob Erich gern Sport treibt, ob er später studieren möchte, und was er in seiner Freizeit macht.

Schriftliche Übungen

F. Rewrite the following story as a dialogue between Dr. Büchner and his patient, Mr. Lenz, who is in the hospital.

Dr. Büchner kommt morgens sehr früh ins Krankenzimmer und sagt Herrn Lenz guten Morgen. Er möchte wissen, wie es ihm geht und ob er sich besser fühlt. Er fragt, wo es ihm noch weh tut, und was er sonst noch braucht. Der Arzt sagt, daß er sich schon vorstellen kann, wie langweilig es ist, so lange im Bett liegen zu müssen.

Herr Lenz antwortet, daß es ihm nicht so gut geht, daß er noch sehr krank ist, daß es ihm überall weh tut, daß er das Essen im Krankenhaus nicht mag, und daß er einige neue Romane haben will.

Dr. Büchner meint, Herr Lenz hat sich fast erholt. Er soll sich anziehen, denn er darf heute nach Hause.

An der Technischen Schule
für Optik in Jena (DDR)

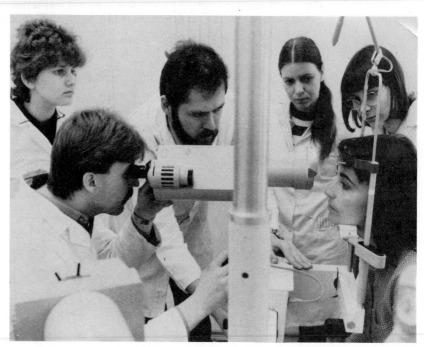

G. Fill in the blanks with appropriate nouns formed from adjectives. Choose from the following list.

gut	schön	verwandt	bekannt
deutsch	alt	grün	interessant
neu	kalt	toll	modern
besonders	schlimm		

1. Hast du etwas _____ zu berichten?
2. Ja, in der Stadt habe ich heute etwas ganz _____ gesehen.
3. Wirklich? In unserer langweiligen Stadt? Das ist schon etwas _____!
4. Kennst du Steffi Hartmann? Sie ist _____ und ist gerade aus Stuttgart angekommen.
5. Wie nett, dich kennenzulernen, Steffi! Eine alte _____ von mir aus der Schulzeit heißt Hartmann und wohnt auch in Stuttgart.
6. Ja, dann ist sie vielleicht sogar eine _____ von mir. Unsere Familie ist ziemlich groß.
7. Das _____ bei uns im Sommer ist nicht nur das Wetter, sondern auch die hohen Berge und die schöne Natur.
8. Für mich ist das etwas _____ . Wie du weißt, bin ich aus dem Norden, wo es im Sommer ziemlich kalt ist.
9. In unserem kleinen alten Dorf auf dem Land gibt es wenig _____ zu sehen.
10. Das macht nichts. Das gibt's in der Großstadt. Ich bin zu euch gekommen, um das _____ zu sehen.

H. Create sentences from the elements provided. You may add words.

1. wegen/dies/Situation/viel/Menschen/auswandern (perfect tense)
2. als/man/Mauer/bauen//können/wenig/Menschen/nach/Westen/reisen
3. ich/können/nicht/glauben//alle/Bürger/dies/Land/unglücklich
4. wenn/über/Land/fliegen//können/man/Grenze/sehen
5. dort/aussehen/Leben/anders/
6. kennen/du/politisch/Lieder/dies-/Dichter?

I. Wie sagt man das auf deutsch?

1. When did your relatives immigrate to America?
2. Some emigrated from Germany fifteen years ago.
3. But others arrived in New York City at the beginning of the twentieth century.
4. Ute told me that you got hurt.
5. Yes, I broke my arm last week.
6. How did that happen?
7. I had an accident with my new bicycle.
8. I've just returned from Dresden.
9. Have you ever been to the German Democratic Republic?
10. I know East Berlin a little bit because I have acquaintances there.

Almanach

Profile of the German Democratic Republic

Area: 108,333 square kilometers; 41,827 square miles
Population: 16.6 million or 154 people per square
kilometer (398 per sq. mi.)

The country is divided into fifteen districts, each named
after its governing town.

Currency: DDR-Mark

Major cities: Berlin (East), capital (pop. 1,196,000); Leipzig;
Dresden; Magdeburg

The GDR is a member of COMECON (Council for Mutual Economic Assistance), the "common market" of the socialist countries. After the Soviet Union it is the most important industrial country in COMECON. It is also a member of the Warsaw Pact, the military alliance among the Soviet Union and Bulgaria, Poland, Romania, Czechoslovakia, Hungary and the GDR. In 1973 the GDR became a member of the United Nations.

Magdeburg (DDR): Fotos von Gewerkschaftsmitgliedern (die Gewerkschaft = trade union; FDGB = Freier Deutscher Gewerkschaftsbund)

12

Erinnerungen

Dialoge
Das Referat ◆ Rita hat sich
verlobt ◆ Vor der Wohnungstür

Wortschatz 1

Grammatik
1. Comparison of Adjectives and
   Adverbs
   Formation of the Comparative ◆
   Formation of the Superlative ◆
   Umlaut in Comparative and
   Superlative ◆ Irregular
   Comparatives and Superlatives
   ◆ Comparisons
2. Relative Clauses
   Relative Pronouns ◆ The
   Relative Pronoun **was** ◆ The
   Indefinite Pronouns **wer** and
   was
3. The Verb **lassen**
4. **Mal** and its Use
5. Questions with **was für**? (What
   kind of?)
6. Parts of the Day
7. Expanding Your Vocabulary
   The Prefix **irgend-**

Wortschatz 2

Lesestück
Zwei Denkmäler

Vom Lesen Zum Sprechen
„Das geht mir nicht aus dem Kopf"

Almanach
Five Modern Women Writers

Dialoge

Das Referat

ANNA: Tag, Karin. Hast du das Buch, das ich dir geliehen habe?

KARIN: Nein, ich habe es zu Hause gelassen. Darf ich es etwas länger behalten?

ANNA: Klar.

KARIN: Ich brauche es noch für mein Referat.

ANNA: Willst du auch meine Schreibmaschine benutzen?

KARIN: Danke, diesmal versuche ich, das Referat auf dem neuen Computer zu schreiben.

Rita hat sich verlobt

PETRA: Sag mal, kennst du den Typ, mit dem Rita gestern weggegangen ist?

URSULA: Meinst du den Mann, der so schick angezogen war?

PETRA: Genau.

URSULA: Das war Rudi. Sie hat sich mit ihm verlobt.

PETRA: Ich muß sagen, er sah besser aus als ihr letzter Freund.

URSULA: Das finde ich auch. Und er ist auch intelligenter.

Vor der Wohnungstür

FRAU SCHWARZER: Guten Abend, Herr Beck!

HERR BECK: Guten Abend, Frau Schwarzer!

FRAU SCHWARZER: Ich wollte Sie etwas fragen. Wo kann ich am billigsten meinen Wagen reparieren lassen?

HERR BECK: Was für einen Wagen haben Sie denn?

FRAU SCHWARZER: Einen alten VW.

HERR BECK: In der nächsten Querstraße gibt es den besten Automechaniker in der Gegend, aber er ist leider auch teuer.

FRAU SCHWARZER: Schade. Dann mache ich das lieber selber.

Wortschatz 1

The Term Paper

ANNA: Hi Karin. Do you have the book that I lent you?

KARIN: No, I left it at home. May I keep it a bit longer?

ANNA: Sure.

KARIN: I still need it for my paper.

ANNA: Do you want to use my typewriter, too?

KARIN: No thanks. This time I'm going to try writing my paper on the new computer.

Rita Has Gotten Engaged

PETRA: Tell me, do you know the guy Rita left with yesterday?

URSULA: Do you mean the man who was dressed so stylishly?

PETRA: Exactly.

URSULA: That was Rudi. They have gotten engaged.

PETRA: I have to say that he looked better than her last boyfriend.

URSULA: I think so too. And he's more intelligent, too.

Outside the Apartment Door

MS. SCHWARZER: Good evening, Mr. Beck.

MR. BECK: Good evening, Ms. Schwarzer.

MS. SCHWARZER: I wanted to ask you something. Where can I get my car repaired most cheaply?

MR. BECK: What kind of car do you have?

MS. SCHWARZER: An old VW.

MR. BECK: The best mechanic in the area is on the next cross street, but he's also very expensive.

MS. SCHWARZER: Too bad. Then I'd rather do it myself.

Verben

behalten (behält), behielt, hat behalten to keep, retain

erinnern an (+ *acc.*) to remind of

sich erinnern an (+ *acc.*) to remember

lassen (läßt), ließ, hat gelassen to leave (something or someone), leave behind; let, allow; cause to be done

leihen, lieh, hat geliehen to lend

reparieren to repair

sich verloben mit to become engaged to

weg·gehen, ging weg, ist weggegangen to go away, leave

Substantive

der Computer, - computer

der Mechaniker, - mechanic

der Typ, -en type; (*slang*) guy

der Zimmerkamerad, -en, -en roommate (*m.*)

das Mal, -e time (*in the sense of "occasion"*)

das Referat, -e oral report; written term paper

die Erinnerung, -en memory

die Gegend, -en area, region

die Maschine, -n machine

die Nacht, ¨e night
in der Nacht at night, in the night
Gute Nacht. Good night.

die Querstraße, -n cross-street

die Schreibmaschine, -n typewriter

die Zimmerkameradin, -nen roommate (*f.*)

Andere Vokabeln

angezogen (*past participle of* **anziehen**) dressed
Er war gut angezogen. He was well-dressed.

diesmal this time

genau exact

intelligent intelligent

nah(e) near

schick chic, fashionable

übermorgen the day after tomorrow

vorgestern the day before yesterday

Nützliche Ausdrücke

Das finde ich auch. I think so too.

Sag mal . . . Tell me . . .

Ich wohne in der Beethovenstraße. I live on Beethoven Street.

was für what kind of

Neue Kombinationen

A. Replace the word in italics with the cue you will hear.

1. Hast du das *Buch*, das ich dir geliehen habe?
   (Hemd, Auto, Vorlesungsverzeichnis, Glas, Bild)
2. Hast du eine *Schreibmaschine*, die ich benutzen darf?
   (Tasse, Fahrkarte, Jacke, Landkarte)
3. Wer war der *Typ*, der so schick aussah?
   (Student, Tourist, Amerikaner, Deutsche, Herr)
4. Sie war *intelligenter* als meine Freundin.
   (interessanter, berühmter, sympathischer, höflicher)
5. Wo kann ich *meinen alten Wagen* reparieren lassen?
   (meine alte Schreibmaschine, diese neue Uhr, ein teures Moped, meinen neuen Computer, mein altes Fahrrad)

B. Answer the questions using the words and phrases cued.

> EXAMPLE: Was brauchst du noch für dein Referat? (deine Schreibmaschine)
> Ich brauche noch deine Schreibmaschine.

1. Wann bringst du mir meine Bücher zurück? (morgen)
2. Wo wohnt der beste Mechaniker für meinen Wagen? (in der Beethovenstraße)
3. Mit wem ist deine Freundin gestern abend weggegangen? (mit einem intelligenten Typ)
4. Was für einen Wagen besitzen Sie? (einen alten VW)
5. Wem hast du deine Jacke geliehen? (einem sympathischen Studenten)

C. Your teacher tells you that certain people are sick or injured. Respond as in the example.

> EXAMPLE: Hast du gehört? Rita hat sich verletzt.
> O wie schade! Hoffentlich geht es ihr bald besser.

1. Hast du gehört? Meine Tante hat sich das Bein gebrochen.
2. Haben Sie gehört? Stefan war krank und darf noch nicht aufstehen.
3. Hast du gehört? Die Studenten haben sich erkältet.
4. Haben Sie gehört? Petra und Ursula fühlten sich gestern krank.
5. Habt ihr gehört? Ich habe mir letzten Monat den Arm gebrochen.

Übung zur Aussprache

Joseph von Eichendorff (1788–1857) was one of the foremost poets of the Romantic movement in Germany. Reverence for nature, longing for one's beloved, nostalgia for one's homeland are all typical themes for the Romantics. The poem "Heimweh" is from Eichendorff's story *Aus dem Leben eines Taugenichts (From the Life of a Good-for-Nothing)*, in which the hero, in Italy, yearns for Germany and his beloved.

Zeichnung (*drawing*) von Ludwig Richter (19. Jhdt.)

Heimweh°	*homesickness*
Wer in die Fremde° will wandern°	= **ins Ausland** / *wander*
Der muß mit der Liebsten° gehn,[1]	*beloved*
Es jubeln° und lassen die andern	*rejoice*
Den Fremden alleine stehn.	
Was wisset ihr, dunkele Wipfel,°	*treetops*
Von der alten, schönen Zeit?	
Ach, die Heimat° hinter den Gipfeln,°	*homeland / peaks*
Wie liegt sie von hier so weit!	
Am liebsten[2] betracht° ich die Sterne,°	*comtemplate / stars*
Die schienen, wie° ich ging zu ihr,	= **als**
Die Nachtigall° hör ich so gerne,	*nightingale*
Sie sang° vor der Liebsten Tür.	*sang*
Der Morgen, das ist meine Freude!°	*joy*
Da steig ich in stiller° Stund'	*quiet*
Auf den höchsten° Berg in die Weite,°	*highest / distance*
Grüß dich,° Deutschland, aus	*greetings to you / from the*
Herzensgrund!°	*bottom of my heart*

[1] Shortened from **gehen.**
[2] **am liebsten** = most of all, I like to (superlative of **gern,** see p. 341).

Grammatik

1 ◆ Comparison of Adjectives and Adverbs

When adjectives or adverbs are used in comparisons, they can occur in three degrees:

Positive Degree *(basic form):*

Jutta läuft **schnell**.
Jörg ist so **intelligent** wie Dieter.

so intelligent wie = as intelligent as.
*Jutta runs **fast**.*
*Jörg is as **intelligent** as Dieter.*

Comparative Degree *(marker: -er):*

Jutta läuft **schneller** als ich.
Jörg ist **intelligenter** als Helmut.

intelligenter als = more intelligent than.
*Jutta runs **faster** than I.*
*Jörg is **more intelligent** than Helmut.*

Superlative Degree *(marker: -st):*

Jutta läuft **am schnellsten**.
In unserer Klasse ist Jörg **am intelligentesten**.

am intelligentesten = most intelligent.
*Jutta runs **fastest**.*
*In our class, Jörg is **most intelligent**.*

Formation of the Comparative

1. To form the comparative degree of any adjective or adverb, add the marker **-er** to the basic form:

   basic form[1] **+ -er = comparative degree**

schnell	**-er**	**schneller**	*faster*
schön	**-er**	**schöner**	*more beautiful*
intelligent	**-er**	**intelligenter**	*more intelligent*

   English adjectives longer than two syllables form their comparative with **more: beautiful → more beautiful**. German has no comparative marker parallel to English *more*. No matter how long a German adjective is, simply add **-er: intelligent—intelligenter**.

2. Attributive adjectives add the regular adjective endings after the comparative **-er** ending, for example:

   basic form + -er- + adjective ending

schnell-	**-er-**	**-en**
intelligent-	**-er-**	**-e**

   Wir fuhren mit dem **schnelleren Zug**.
   Jörg war der **intelligentere** Student.

   *We went by the **faster** train.*
   *Jörg was the **more intelligent** student.*

[1] Note on spelling: adjectives ending in **-el** and **-er** drop the **-e-** in the comparative: **dunkel—dunkler; teuer—teurer**.

3. **als** = *than* when used with the comparative:

Jörg ist intelligenter **als** Helmut.   *Jörg is more intelligent **than** Helmut.*

A. Your teacher is praising Jörg, but you respond that you are *more* everything than he is.

EXAMPLE: Jörg ist intelligent.
Aber ich bin intelligenter als er.

1. Jörg ist hübsch.
2. Er ist ruhig.
3. Er läuft schnell.
4. Er ist ehrlich.
5. Jörg ist interessant.
6. Er ist freundlich.
7. Jörg steht früh auf.
8. Er zieht sich schick an.

B. Pretend you are trying to sell things to choosy customers. Respond to the comments below with a sentence using the adjective in the comparative degree.

EXAMPLE: Diese Blusen sind mir nicht dunkel genug.
Hier haben wir dunklere Blusen.

1. Diese Blumen sind mir nicht schön genug.
2. Diese Taschen sind mir nicht leicht genug.
3. Diese Motorräder sind mir nicht schnell genug.
4. Diese Bücher sind mir nicht billig genug.
5. Diese Häuser sind mir nicht hell genug.
6. Diese Autos sind mir nicht groß genug.

Formation of the Superlative

The superlative is formed in the following ways:

1. Adverbs: **am schnellsten** (most quickly)

   All adverbs form their superlative in the following way:
   am _____ -(e)sten[1]

   Jutta läuft **am schnellsten.**   *Jutta runs **fastest**.*

   German has no superlative marker like English **most**. No matter how long an adverb is, simply add **-sten**:

   am intelligentesten   *most intelligently*

---

[1] Note on spelling: an extra **-e-** is added when the basic form ends in **-d, -t,** or a sibilant: **am mildesten, am heißesten.**

2. Attributive Adjectives: **die intelligenteste Studentin**

In attributive adjectives, add the regular adjective endings after the superlative **-(e)st** ending, for example:

> ***basic form*** + **-(e)st-** + ***adjective ending***
>
> intelligent- **-est-** **-e**
> schnell- **-st-** **-en**

Meine **intelligenteste** Studentin heißt Marianne.	*My **most intelligent** student is named Marianne.*
Wir fuhren mit dem **schnellsten** Zug.	*We took the **fastest** train.*

3. Predicate Adjectives: (a) **am intelligentesten,** (b) **die intelligenteste**

Predicate adjectives in the superlative may occur either in the **am** _____ **-sten** form or with the definite article and regular adjective endings:

Albert ist **am intelligentesten.**	*Albert is **most intelligent.***
Albert ist **der intelligenteste.**	*Albert is **the most intelligent.***
Diese Bücher sind **die interessantesten.**	*These books are **the most interesting ones.***

Üben wir!

A. Your teacher is praising Christa and you respond by praising yourself in the superlative.

> EXAMPLE: Christa läuft schnell.
> Aber ich laufe am schnellsten.

1. Christa ist modern.
2. Sie ist sehr beliebt.
3. Sie singt sehr schön.
4. Christa ist immer ruhig.
5. Sie sieht immer hübsch aus.
6. Sie ist sehr aktiv.

B. In the sentence you will hear, put the attributive adjective into the superlative degree.

> EXAMPLE: Ich sage dir die wichtigen Namen.
> Ich sage dir die wichtigsten Namen.

1. Können Sie mir die billigen Weine zeigen?
2. Er ist das ruhige Mitglied unserer Gruppe.
3. Hier haben Sie unsere neuen Schuhe.
4. Ich schreibe die langweiligen Briefe.
5. Die steile Straße führte nach links.
6. Ich kaufe die teuere Bluse.
7. Sie wohnen in dem schönen Haus.
8. Können wir mit den wichtigen Problemen beginnen?
9. Ich zeige Ihnen unsere neuen Schreibmaschinen.

C. Pretend that you are trying to sell things to choosy customers. Respond to the questions below using the adjective in the superlative degree.

> EXAMPLE: Können Sie mir billige Weine zeigen?
> Selbstverständlich, hier sind unsere billigsten Weine.

1. Können Sie mir Ihre neuen Schuhe zeigen?
2. Können Sie mir ein paar wichtige Zeitungen zeigen?
3. Haben Sie einige interessante Bücher?
4. Können sie mir ein paar teure Blusen zeigen?
5. Ich möchte die neuen Schreibmaschinen sehen.
6. Ich möchte gern moderne Wohnungen sehen.

Umlaut in Comparative and Superlative

Many one-syllable adjectives and adverbs whose stem vowels are **a, o,** or **u** (but *not* **au**) are umlauted in the comparative and superlative degrees. Here is a list of those you are already familiar with. Some occur in easy-to-remember pairs of opposites:

alt	älter	am ältesten	*old*
jung	jünger	am jüngsten	*young*
dumm	dümmer	am dümmsten	*dumb*
klug	klüger	am klügsten	*smart*
kalt	kälter	am kältesten	*cold*
warm	wärmer	am wärmsten	*warm*
kurz	kürzer	am kürzesten	*short*
lang	länger	am längsten	*long*
stark	stärker	am stärksten	*strong*
schwach	schwächer	am schwächsten	*weak*
hart	härter	am härtesten	*hard, harsh*
krank	kränker	am kränksten	*sick*
oft	öfter	am öftesten	*often*
rot	röter	am rötesten	*red*
schwarz	schwärzer	am schwärzesten	*black*

Üben wir! **A.** Respond as in the example.

> EXAMPLE: Teacher: Meine Wohnung ist kalt.
> Student A: Meine Wohnung ist noch kälter.
> Student B: Aber meine Wohnung ist am kältesten.

1. Mein Bruder ist stark.
2. Mein Auto ist alt.
3. Mein Referat ist lang.
4. Mein Freund ist krank.

5. Meine Schwester ist jung.
6. Mein Zimmer ist warm.
7. Mein Besuch war kurz.
8. Mein Beruf ist hart.

Irregular Comparatives and Superlatives

There are only a few adjectives and adverbs in German with irregular forms in the comparative and superlative. Here are the most frequent:

groß	big	**größer**	bigger	**am größten**[1]	biggest
gut	good	**besser**	better	**am besten**	best
hoch, hoh-	high	**höher**	higher	**am höchsten**	highest
nahe	near	**näher**	nearer	**am nächsten**	nearest; next
viel	much, many	**mehr**	more	**am meisten**	most
gern	gladly, like to	**lieber**	preferably, rather	**am liebsten**	most like to, like best of all to

Note how the three degrees of the adverb **gern** are used:

Ich gehe **gern** ins Kino.	*I **like to go** to the movies.*
Barbara geht **lieber** ins Theater.	*Barbara **would rather** go to the theater.*
Wir bleiben **am liebsten** zu Hause.	***Best of all**, we like to stay at home.*

Viel and its opposite **wenig** present special problems:

1. In the positive degree **viel** and **wenig** have no endings when they mean **much** or **not much** (amounts that are *un*countable). They have regular plural endings when they mean **many** or **not many** (of things that *are* countable).

   not countable:

Ich esse **viel** Brot.	*I eat a lot of bread.*
Ich habe nur **wenig** Geld.	*I only have a little money.*

   countable:

Sie hat **viele** Freunde.	*She has many friends.*
Ich habe **wenige** Bekannte hier.	*I have few acquaintances here.*

[1] The irregularity here is that the superlative just adds **-t** rather than **-est.**

2. In the comparative degree (**mehr/weniger,** more/less, fewer) they *never* take adjective endings:

Er hat **weniger** Geld als ich.   *He has less money than I.*
Hat sie **mehr** Freunde als du?   *Does she have more friends than you?*

	no endings	*endings*
positive	**viel** much, a lot of **wenig** not much, not a lot of	**viele** many **wenige** not many
comparative	**mehr** more **weniger** less, fewer	
superlative		**der, das, die meist-** most **der, das, die wenigst-** least, fewest

■ Note that the German equivalents of expressions such as *most people, most houses, most students,* etc. must have the definite article: **die** meisten Menschen; **die** meisten Häuser; **die** meisten Studenten.

Üben wir!

A. Compare the cities Hamburg, Salzburg, and Frankfurt as in the example.

> EXAMPLE: Teacher: Frankfurt ist schön. Und Hamburg?
> Student A: Hamburg ist schöner.
> Teacher: Und Salzburg?
> Student B: Salzburg ist am schönsten.

1. Salzburg ist groß. Und Frankfurt? Und Hamburg?
2. Hamburg liegt nicht hoch. Aber Frankfurt? Und Salzburg?
3. Ich fahre gern nach Frankfurt. Und Hamburg? Und Salzburg?
4. Frankfurt gefällt mir gut. Und Hamburg? Und Salzburg?
5. In Frankfurt trinkt man viel Bier. Und in Salzburg? Und in Hamburg?
6. Das hört man wenig in Salzburg. Und in Frankfurt? Und in Hamburg?

B. Respond to the sentence you will hear with a comparative, as in the example.

> EXAMPLE: Ich bin müde.
> Aber ich bin noch müder.

1. Das kann ich gut verstehen.
2. Ich trinke viel Kaffee.
3. Meine Stadt ist groß.
4. Unsere Berge sind hoch.
5. Ich esse wenig Wurst.

C. Respond to the sentence you will hear with a superlative, as in the example.

> EXAMPLE: Ist sie eine schnelle Läuferin?
> Ja, sie ist sogar die schnellste Läuferin.

1. Hat New York hohe Gebäude?
2. Ist das ein großes Problem?
3. Kennst du ein gutes Restaurant?
4. Kennst du viele Leute in diesem Dorf?
5. Hast du auch wenig Brot gegessen?
6. Gibt es bei euch gute Straßen?

D. Respond to the sentence you hear by saying you would prefer to do something else.

> EXAMPLE: Trinken Sie gern Milch?
> Nein, ich trinke lieber Wasser.

1. Gehen Sie gern ins Theater?
2. Hören Sie gern Rockmusik?
3. Lesen Sie gern Romane?
4. Wohnen Sie gern in der Stadt?
5. Spielen Sie gern Fußball?
6. Trinken Sie gern Wein?
7. Reisen Sie gern ins Ausland?
8. Fahren Sie gern Rad?

E. Tell what you like to do best, as in the example.

> EXAMPLE: Trinkst du gern Milch?
> Ja, aber am liebsten trinke ich Bier.

1. Liest du gern die Zeitung?
2. Wohnst du gern in der Altstadt?
3. Sprichst du gern Englisch?
4. Treibst du gern Sport?
5. Ißt du gern Schokolade?
6. Schwimmst du gern im Winter?

F. Wie sagt man das auf deutsch? Use forms of **viel** and **wenig.**

1. I ate a lot.
2. I didn't say much.
3. I said very little.
4. Few people know that.
5. He didn't write me many letters.
6. Unfortunately, I have little time.
7. Most students live in dormitories.
8. He has fewer friends than his brother.
9. The tourists saw less than I did.
10. She met more people than I did.

Comparisons

1. **genauso . . . wie** = (just, exactly) as . . . as
   nicht so . . . wie = not as . . . as
   The positive degree with **genauso . . . wie** shows equality (or, when negated, lack of equality)

Heute ist es **genauso** kalt **wie** gestern.	*Today is **just as** cold **as** yesterday.*
Stuttgart ist **nicht so** groß **wie** Berlin.	*Stuttgart is **not as** large **as** Berlin.*

2. **immer** + comparative for progressive change
   Instead of repeating the comparative to show progressive change, German generally uses **immer**:

Das Kind wird **immer größer**.	*The child's getting **bigger and bigger**.*
Die Welt wird **immer verrückter**.	*The world's getting **crazier and crazier**.*

3. **je . . . desto** = the . . . the
   The German compound conjunction **je . . . desto** is always used with a pair of comparatives.

Je schneller, desto besser.	*The faster the better.*

   When **je . . . desto** joins two full clauses, the **je**-clause has dependent word order, while **desto** is a coordinating conjunction.

Je länger ich lebe, **desto weniger** weiß ich.	*The longer I live, the less I know.*

A. Respond to each sentence as in the example.

> EXAMPLE: Ist Ihr Referat genauso lang wie Hermanns Referat?
> Nein, mein Referat ist länger als Hermanns Referat.

1. Ist diese Kirche genauso hoch wie die andere?
2. Sind diese Geschichten genauso verrückt wie die anderen?
3. Ist das zweite Buch genauso kurz wie das erste?
4. Ist Deutsch genauso schwer wie Englisch?
5. Fährt ein Zug genauso schnell wie ein Bus?
6. Findest du alte Filme genauso interessant wie neue?

B. Now respond to the question by saying that things are alike.

> EXAMPLE: War die graue Hose billiger als die blaue?
> Nein, sie war genauso billig wie die blaue.

1. Sind die Amerikaner freundlicher als die Deutschen?
2. Kostet das Essen in der Schweiz mehr als in Deutschland?
3. Sind seine Ideen besser als meine?
4. Essen Sie Pommes frites lieber als Brot?
5. Sind die Berge in Colorado höher als die Alpen?
6. Trinken Sie mehr Milch als Wasser?

C. Respond to each sentence with **immer** + comparative to express "more and more."

> EXAMPLE: Die Lebensmittel sind heutzutage so teuer.
> Ja, und sie werden immer teurer.

1. Dieser Politiker ist sehr beliebt.
2. Das Wetter ist heute so warm.
3. Ihre Tochter ist so groß geworden.
4. Die Computer sind heutzutage so schnell.
5. Die Hausaufgaben sind leicht.
6. Ihr Deutsch ist schon so gut.

D. Complete each sentence with an appropriate clause beginning with **desto**.

> EXAMPLE: Je wärmer es wird, . . . (gern/schwimmen gehen)
> Je wärmer es wird, desto lieber gehen wir schwimmen.

1. Je höher der Berg, . . . (steil/Pfad)
2. Je müder ich bin, . . . (viel/schlafen)
3. Je mehr ich lerne, . . . (wenig/wissen)
4. Je schwieriger das Buch, . . . (langsam/lesen)
5. Je berühmter die Sportlerin, . . . (viel Geld/verdienen)

2 ♦ Relative Clauses

A relative clause is a subordinate clause which modifies or further clarifies a noun.

Das ist das neue Buch.

*That is the **new** book.*

    main clause   relative clause
Das ist das Buch, **das du mir geliehen hast.**

That is the book
that you lent me.

The relative clause **das du mir geliehen hast** modifies **Buch** by telling *which* book is being talked about.

Relative clauses begin with a relative pronoun (English: *who(m), whose, that, which*). In German, relative pronouns have the same form as the definite article *except in the dative plural* (**denen** for **den**) *and in the genitive* (**dessen** for **des**, **deren** for **der**). Study the following table. Note especially the forms in boldface, which are different from the definite article.

Relative Pronouns

	masc.	*neut.*	*fem.*	*plur.*
nom.	der	das	die	die
acc.	den	das	die	die
dat.	dem	dem	der	**denen**
gen.	**dessen**	**dessen**	**deren**	**deren**

Sentences having a relative clause can be thought of as a combination of two separate sentences sharing an identical element (either a noun or pronoun). This element in the main clause is called the *antecedent*. In the relative clause, this element is replaced by a relative pronoun that refers back to the antecedent. Here are some examples:

                     masc.
                     sing.
    antecedent   *nom.*
1. Das ist **der Typ.**   **Er** war im Kino.

Das ist der Typ, **der** im Kino war.
That's the guy who was at the movies.

                         fem.
                         sing.
    antecedent   *dative*
2. Kennst du **die Frau?**   Ich arbeite mit **ihr.**

Kennst du die Frau, mit **der** ich arbeite?
Do you know the woman (whom) I work with?

3. Das ist **der Schriftsteller.**   *antecedent*   *masc. sing. genitive*   Die Romane **des Schriftstellers** sind berühmt.

Das ist der Schriftsteller, **dessen** Romane berühmt sind.
That's the writer whose novels are famous.

4. Hast du **die Bücher?**   *antecedent*   *acc. plural*   Ich habe **sie** dir geliehen.

Hast du die Bücher, **die** ich dir geliehen habe?
Do you have the books (that) I lent you?

Notes on relative clauses:

■ The relative pronoun is *never* omitted in German, as it often is in English (examples 2 and 4 above).

■ The relative pronoun agrees in gender and number with its antecedent, but its *case* is determined by its function in the relative clause:

fem. *fem.*
sing. *sing.*
nominative *dative*
Das ist **die Frau,** mit **der** ich arbeite.

■ If the relative pronoun is the object of a preposition, the preposition *precedes* it in the relative clause (example 2 above). Although in English the preposition often comes at the end of the sentence, this is *never* the case in German.

■ The relative clause, like all other subordinate clauses in German, has verb-final word order.[1]

■ The relative clause usually is placed immediately after its antecedent:

Das Buch, das du mir geliehen   *The book you lent me helped me.*
hast, hat mir geholfen.

Üben wir!

A. Repeat the sentence you will hear and give the English equivalent.

EXAMPLE: Das ist der Mann, der uns kennt.
That is the man who knows us.

1. Das ist der Mann, der hier wohnt.
2. Das ist der Mann, den ich kenne.
3. Das ist der Mann, dem wir helfen.
4. Das ist der Mann, dessen Frau ich kenne.

[1] Note on punctuation: in German, the relative clause is *always* preceded by a comma.

5. Das ist das Moped, das sehr schnell fährt.

6. Das ist das Moped, das sie gekauft hat.

7. Das ist das Moped, von dem man spricht.

8. Das ist das Moped, dessen Farbe mir gefällt.

9. Das ist die Frau, die Deutsch kann.

10. Das ist die Frau, die wir brauchen.

11. Das ist die Frau, der wir Geld geben.

12. Das ist die Frau, deren Roman ich kenne.

13. Das sind die Leute, die mich kennen.

14. Das sind die Leute, die ich kenne.

15. Das sind die Leute, denen wir helfen.

16. Das sind die Leute, deren Kinder wir kennen.

B. Give the German equivalents of the English sentences you will hear.

1. That's the student who knows me.

2. That's the student I know.

3. That's the student I'm helping.

4. That's the student whose car I have.

5. That's the child who speaks English.

6. That's the child I met.

7. That's the child I'm giving a present to.

8. That's the child whose parents aren't here.

9. That's the (female) student who is studying in Berlin.

10. That's the (female) student we're looking for.

11. That's the (female) student I'm giving the book to.

12. That's the (female) student whose family comes from France.

13. Those are the friends who eat in the mensa.

14. Those are the friends we visited.

15. Those are the friends who like the film. (use *gefallen*)

16. Those are the friends whose apartment is so large.

C. Respond to each question as in the example.

EXAMPLE: Arbeitest du für diesen Chef?
Ja, das ist der Chef, für den ich arbeite.

1. Sind Sie durch diese Stadt gefahren?

2. Haben Sie in diesem Hotel übernachtet?

3. Haben Sie mit diesen Amerikanern gesprochen?

4. Haben Sie in diesem Restaurant gegessen?

5. Haben Sie an diesem Tisch gesessen?

6. Bereiten Sie sich auf diese Reise vor?

7. Lesen Sie Bücher über dieses Land?

D. Ask a classmate a question about things he or she is wearing. Follow the model. The response will contain a relative clause.

> EXAMPLE: Student A: Hast du einen neuen Mantel?
> Student B: Nein, das ist der Mantel, den ich letztes Jahr gekauft habe.

Hast du eine nèue Jacke? (eine neue Uhr, neue Schuhe, einen neuen Pullover, ein neues Kleid)

E. Say that these are the people you have been talking about.

> EXAMPLE: Max
> Das ist Max, von dem ich schon viel erzählt habe.

(mein Bruder, Helen, meine Eltern, mein Zimmerkamerad, meine Freundinnen)

F. Join together the two sentences you will hear by making the second one a relative clause.

> EXAMPLE: Ich kenne die Frau. Du meinst sie.
> Ich kenne die Frau, die du meinst.

1. Hast du die Schreibmaschine? Sie gehört mir.
2. Nein, ich habe eine Schreibmaschine. Sie gehört Rita.

3. Ist das die Geschichte? Horst hat sie erzählt.
4. Ja, er erzählt Geschichten. Man muß über seine Geschichten lachen.

5. Das ist ein Buch. Sie hat es letztes Jahr geschrieben.
6. Meinst du das Buch? Es ist jetzt sehr berühmt.

7. Ist das der Mann? Sie haben ihm geholfen.
8. Nein, ich habe einem anderen Mann geholfen. Er war viel älter.

9. Kennst du die Studenten? Sie wohnen in der Altstadt.
10. Natürlich, das sind die Studenten. Ich esse in der Mensa mit ihnen.

11. Wie heißt der Junge? Sein Vater ist Professor.
12. Er hat einen englischen Namen. Ich habe ihn vergessen.

13. Ist die Frau nett? Du wohnst bei ihr.
14. Ja, das ist eine Frau. Ihre Kinder sind nicht mehr zu Hause.

The Relative Pronoun was

A relative clause following the antecedents **etwas, nichts, viel, wenig,** and **alles** begins with **was** in German.

Gibt es noch **etwas, was** Sie brauchen?

Is there something else (that) you need?

Nein, Sie haben **nichts, was** ich brauche.

No, you have nothing (that) I need.

Alles, was er sagt, ist falsch.

Everything (that) he says is wrong.

Was must also begin a relative clause whose antecedent is a neuter adjectival noun (see above, pp. 308–309.)

Was war **das Interessante, was** du mir zeigen wolltest?

What was the interesting thing (that) you wanted to show me?

Ist das **das Beste, was** Sie haben?

Is that the best (that) you have?

Was also begins a relative clause whose antecedent is an entire clause (English uses *which*).

Rita ist glücklich, was ich nicht verstehen kann.

Rita is happy, which I can't understand.

Üben wir!

A. Replace the neuter adjectival noun in each sentence with nouns formed from the cued adjectives you will hear. Use the superlative.

> EXAMPLE: Ist das das Beste, was Sie haben? (billig)
> Ist das das Billigste, was Sie haben?

1. Das war das Wichtigste, was er sagte.
   (schwierig, schrecklich, intelligent, langweilig)
2. Ist das das Neueste, was du gesehen hast?
   (wichtig, schön, interessant, nett)

B. Respond to each question as in the example.

> EXAMPLE: Hat er etwas Interessantes?
> Ja, er hat etwas, was ich interessant finde.

1. Sagt er etwas Wichtiges?
2. Hat das Restaurant etwas Gutes?
3. Hat das Museum etwas Modernes?
4. Sagt sie etwas Typisches?
5. Siehst du etwas Schönes?

C. Join the two sentences you will hear into one. The second will become a relative clause beginning with **was** and refer to the entire first clause.

> EXAMPLE: Rita ist glücklich. Ich kann das nicht verstehen.
> Rita ist glücklich, was ich nicht verstehen kann.

1. Er hat sich verletzt. Das ist schade.
2. Sie möchte seit langem Musik studieren. Ich finde das interessant.
3. Er will nächstes Jahr arbeiten. Das ist intelligent.
4. Sie ruft mich nicht an. Ich kann es nicht verstehen.

The Indefinite Pronouns wer and was

The question words **wer** and **was** may begin subordinate clauses and signal indefiniteness (*cf.* English *whoever, anyone who, whatever, anything that*) or an unnamed antecedent (*cf.* English *the one who, the thing that*).

Wer noch keine Karte hat, soll um halb acht kommen.	*Anyone who doesn't have a ticket yet should come at 7:30.*
Nehmen Sie, **was** Sie wollen.	*Take whatever you want.*
Wer das gesagt hat, war intelligent.	*Whoever said that was intelligent.*
Was mich ärgert, sind die hohen Preise.	*The thing that annoys me are the high prices.*

Üben wir!

A. Restate the following sentences for a friend who hasn't understood them, changing them to indefinite statements beginning with **wer**.

> EXAMPLE: Teacher: Wenn Sie Hunger haben, dürfen Sie jetzt essen.
> Student A: Was hat sie gesagt?
> Student B: Wer Hunger hat, darf jetzt essen.

1. Wenn Sie schlafen wollen, können Sie jetzt gehen.
2. Wenn Sie gern Bier trinken, sollen Sie es hier kaufen.
3. Wenn Sie Kunst mögen, können Sie ins Museum gehen.
4. Wenn Sie gute Geschichten kennen, sollen Sie sie erzählen.

B. Respond to the question, using **was** in your answer.

> EXAMPLE: Was trinkst du gern, Wein oder Bier?
> Was ich gern trinke, ist Bier.

1. Was essen Sie gern, Brot oder Kartoffeln?
2. Was baut man hier, eine neue Uni oder ein neues Krankenhaus?
3. Was verstehen Sie nicht, nur dieses Wort oder die ganze Geschichte?
4. Was haben Sie noch nicht gelesen, das Ende der Geschichte oder den Anfang?
5. Was wollten Sie ihm schenken, eine Armbanduhr oder ein Rad?
6. Was hast du vergessen, deinen Mantel oder dein Geld?

3 ◆ The Verb *lassen*

The verb **lassen** has several meanings in German:

1. to leave (something or someone), leave behind

Lassen Sie uns bitte allein.	*Please leave us alone.*
Hast du deinen Mantel im Restaurant **gelassen?**	*Did you leave your coat in the restaurant?*

2. to allow, let: **lassen** + infinitive

Man **läßt** uns **gehen.**	*They're letting us leave.*
Laß doch die Kinder **spielen!**	*Let the children play!*

3. to have or order something done: **lassen** + infinitive

Here **lassen** is used to show that the subject is not performing an action, but having it done by someone else.

Sie **läßt** ihren Wagen **reparieren.**	*She's having her car repaired.*

The performer of the action may be indicated in the *accusative:*

Sie **läßt** den Mechaniker ihren Wagen **reparieren.**	*She's having the mechanic fix her car.*

The person for whom the action is performed may be indicated in the *dative.* If this person is the same as the subject, then a reflexive pronoun is used:

Er läßt **sich** den Koffer tragen.	*He's having **his** suitcase carried.*
Wir lassen **uns** ein Haus bauen.	*We're having a house built (for ourselves).*

When used with an infinitive in final position (meanings 2 and 3 above), **lassen** has a double infinitive construction in the perfect, just like the modal verbs:

double infinitive

Man hat uns	**gehen lassen.**	*They let us leave.*
Ich habe den Wagen	**reparieren lassen.**	*I had my car repaired.*

Üben wir!

A. Say where things or people were left.

> EXAMPLE: Wo ist seine Jacke? (zu Hause)
> Er hat sie zu Hause gelassen.

1. Wo sind eure Kinder? (zu Hause)
2. Wo ist meine Jacke? (im Auto)
3. Wo ist Ihr Referat, Frau Miller? (auf dem Schreibtisch)
4. Wo ist unser Geld? (im Rucksack)
5. Wo ist ihr Wagen? (in der Schweiz)
6. Wo ist seine Tochter? (bei ihrer Großmutter)

„Wir haben das Baby bei den Großeltern gelassen."
(Burgenland, Österreich)

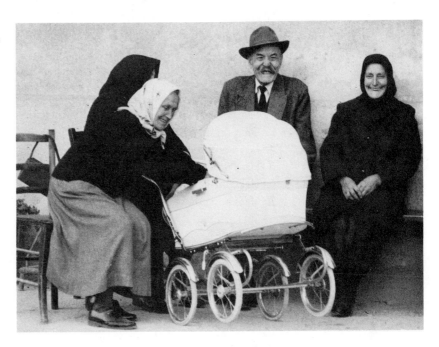

B. Substitute the new subjects you will hear.

1. *Meine Eltern* lassen mich nicht allein gehen.
   (meine Mutter, mein Vater, meine Freunde, mein Freund, meine Freundin)
2. *Er* läßt sich ein neues Haus bauen.
   (wir, Müllers, du, ihr, Herr Schaum)
3. *Wir* haben die Kinder spielen lassen.
   (ich, das Mädchen, die jungen Eltern, der Vater, du, ihr)
4. *Der Professor* hat uns ein langes Referat schreiben lassen.
   (unser Lehrer, diese zwei Lehrerinnen, Herr Lehmann)

C. Tell what you are or were allowed to do. Use the double infinitive construction in the perfect.

> EXAMPLE: Dürft ihr ins Kino?
> Ja, man läßt uns ins Kino gehen.
>
> Habt ihr um sechs gehen dürfen?
> Ja, man hat uns um sechs gehen lassen.

1. Darfst du die Kirche besuchen?
2. Hast du alles sagen dürfen?
3. Dürft ihr draußen spielen?
4. Hast du lange schlafen dürfen?
5. Dürft ihr nach Italien trampen?
6. Habt ihr ohne Jacke ins Konzert gehen dürfen?

D. Say that people had things done rather than doing them for themselves.

> EXAMPLE: Hast du das selber gemacht?
> Nein, ich habe es machen lassen.

1. Hast du den Tisch selber gemacht?
2. Hat er den Laden selbst aufgemacht?
3. Hast du den Wagen selber repariert?
4. Hat Frau Blume den Koffer selbst getragen?
5. Hast du die Bücher selber gekauft?
6. Habt ihr den Brief selber geschickt?
7. Haben Sie dieses Referat selbst geschrieben?

4 ◆ *Mal* and Its Use

The English word *time* has two German equivalents, **die Zeit** and **das Mal.**
Zeit denotes time in general:

Ich habe keine Zeit für Sie.	*I have no time for you.*

Mal denotes an occasion:

Das erste Mal habe ich den Film nicht verstanden.	*I didn't understand the film the first time.*
Wie viele Male hast du ihn gesehen?	*How many times did you see it?*

Learn these idioms with **Mal:**

zum ersten (zweiten, dritten, letzten) Mal	*for the first (second, third, last) time*
diesmal	*this time*
jedes Mal	*every time*

The suffix **-mal** is attached to cardinal numbers to form adverbs indicating repetition:

einmal	*once*
zweimal	*twice*
zwanzigmal	*twenty times*
hundertmal	*a hundred times*
zigmal	*umpteen times*
Das habe ich euch schon zigmal gesagt!	*I've already told you that umpteen times!*

Üben wir!

A. Give German equivalents for these sentences:

1. We don't have enough time.
2. This time we understand better.
3. Please give me more time.
4. He did it every time.
5. Today is my first time.
6. I need time and money.

B. Your teacher holds up a certain number of fingers, seven for example. Use this as a cue to have the following exchange:

> EXAMPLE: Student A: Er hat das siebenmal gemacht.
> Student B: Und jetzt macht er es zum achten Mal.

Now substitute other past participles to say how often various things were done: gelesen, gesehen, versucht, gesagt, angefangen.

5 ◆ Questions with *was für?* (what kind of?)

Was für + noun phrase is used to introduce questions asking "What kind of . . . ?"

The **für** in **was für** is *not* the preposition **für** that requires the accusative. The case of the noun following **was für** depends on its use in the sentence.

nominative

Was für ein Chef ist Herr Motz?   *What kind of boss is Mr. Motz?*

accusative

Was für einen Wagen habt ihr?   *What sort of car do you have?*

In prepositional phrases think of **was für** as being inserted into the phrase without changing the grammar:

Er wohnt **in einem Haus.**

In was für **einem Haus** wohnt er?   *What sort of house does he live in?*

Sie redet gern **mit Menschen.**

Mit was für **Menschen** redet sie gern?   *What kind of people does she like to talk to?*

| ⊙—⊙ | **Üben wir!** | **A.** Use **was für** to ask for more information, as in the example. |

> EXAMPLE: Peter hat sich einen neuen Wagen gekauft.
> Was für einen Wagen hat er denn gekauft?

1. Ich kaufe mir ein Plakat für mein Zimmer.
2. Wir wollen heute einen Film sehen.
3. Tania hat ihre Turnschuhe getragen.
4. Er trinkt gern Wein.
5. Ich war gerade in einem Konzert.
6. Wir gehen morgen in eine Ausstellung.

German uses the following expressions for parts of the day:

gestern { früh / nachmittag / abend } yesterday { morning / afternoon / evening }

heute { früh (or) morgen / nachmittag / abend } this { morning / afternoon / evening }

morgen { früh / nachmittag / abend } tomorrow { morning / afternoon / evening }

In addition, remember:

vorgestern	the day before yesterday
übermorgen	the day after tomorrow
die Nacht, ⁻e	night
in der Nacht	at night

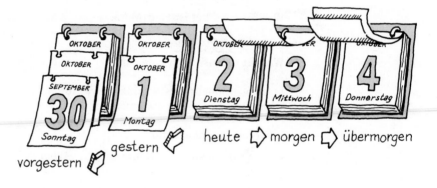

vorgestern gestern heute ⇨ morgen ⇨ übermorgen

Üben wir!

A. Use one of the expressions above to say when you did or will do the following things.

EXAMPLE: Wann haben sie Kaffee getrunken?
Ich habe gestern früh Kaffee getrunken.
or: Ich habe vorgestern Kaffee getrunken.

1. Wann haben Sie Ihre Freunde besucht?
2. Wann sind Sie einkaufen gegangen?
3. Wann haben Sie Ihre Hausaufgaben gemacht?
4. Wann sind Sie ins Kino gegangen?
5. Wann sind Sie zur Uni gefahren?
6. Wann haben Sie geschlafen?
7. Wann gehen Sie wieder nach Hause?

8. Wann besuchen Sie Herrn Hofer?
9. Wann gehen Sie ins Konzert?
10. Wann gehen Sie ins Museum?
11. Wann fahren Sie ans Meer?
12. Wann wollen Sie radfahren?
13. Wann treffen Sie Ihre Freunde?

7 ◆ Expanding Your Vocabulary

The prefix irgend-

When prefixed to question words like **wo, wie** and **wann,** the prefix **irgend-**
creates indefinite adverbs like English **somewhere, somehow, sometime,** etc.

irgendwo	somewhere (or other), anywhere
irgendwie	somehow (or other)
irgendwann	sometime (or other), any time

Hast du meine Zeitung **irgendwo**
  gesehen?
Kommen sie **irgendwann** vorbei?
Das können wir uns schon
  irgendwie leisten.

Have you seen my newspaper
  anywhere?
Will you come by sometime?
We can afford that somehow or
  other.

Wortschatz 2

Verben

holen   to fetch, get
wieder·sehen (sieht wieder), sah wieder, hat wiedergesehen   to see again, meet again
zerstören   to destroy

Substantive

der **Dom, -e**   cathedral
der **Fluß, Flüsse**   river
der **Stein, -e**   stone

das **Denkmal, ̈er**   monument
das **Schiff, -e**   ship

die **Ebene, -n**   plain
die **Erde**   earth
die **Erzählung, -en**   story, narrative
die **Freude, -n**   joy
die **Größe, -n**   size; greatness

die **Heimat**   native place or country, homeland
die **Macht, ̈e**   power, might

Andere Vokabeln

einzig-   single, only
fern   distant, far away
flach   flat
grausam   terrible, gruesome; cruel
jüdisch   Jewish
tief   deep

Nützliche Ausdrücke

Das geht mir nicht aus dem Kopf. =   Das kann ich nicht vergessen.
werden aus   to become of
Was ist aus ihm geworden?   What's become of him?

Gegensätze

fern ≠ nahe	distant ≠ near
tief ≠ hoch	deep ≠ high

Zwei Denkmäler

Anna Seghers is the pseudonym of Netty Reiling, who was born in Mainz in 1900. She studied art history and sinology and married the Hungarian Lászlo Radványi in 1926. Because of her membership in the Communist Party she was forced to flee Germany in 1933. She sought asylum in France and Mexico and much of her writing in exile reflects the turbulent existence of a refugee and committed antifascist. In 1947 she moved to East Germany, where she died in 1983.

The following brief, reflective essay shows her personal involvement with the city of her youth. She focuses on two symbolic "monuments"—one of grand, cultural significance, the other of individual suffering on a human scale.

In der Emigration° begann ich eine Erzählung, die der Krieg unterbrochen hat. Ihr Anfang ist mir noch in Erinnerung. Nicht Wort für Wort, aber dem Sinn nach.° Was mich damals erregt° hat, geht mir auch heute nicht aus dem Kopf. Ich erinnere mich an eine Erinnerung.

In meiner Heimat, in Mainz am Rhein, gab es zwei Denkmäler, die ich niemals° vergessen konnte, in Freude und Angst, auf Schiffen, in fernen Städten. Eins° ist der Dom. Wie ich als Schulkind zu meinem Erstaunen° sah, ist er auf Pfeilern° gebaut, die tief in die Erde hineingehen°—damals kam es mir vor, beinahe° so hoch wie der Dom hochragt.° Ihre Risse sind auszementiert worden,° sagte man, in vergangener° Zeit, da, wo das Grundwasser Unheil stiftete.° Ich weiß nicht, ob das stimmt, was uns ein Lehrer erzählte: Die romanischen° und gotischen° Pfeiler seien haltbarer° als die jüngeren.

Dieser Dom über der Rheinebene wäre mir in all seiner Macht und Größe geblieben,° wenn ich ihn auch nie wieder gesehen hätte.° Aber ebensowenig° kann ich ein anderes Denkmal in meiner Heimtstadt vergessen. Es bestand nur aus° einem einzigen flachen Stein, den man in das Pflaster° einer Straße gesetzt hat. Hieß die Straße Bonifaziusstraße? Hieß sie Frauenlobstraße? Das weiß ich nicht mehr. Ich weiß nur, daß der Stein zum Gedächtnis° einer Frau eingefügt wurde,° die im ersten Weltkrieg durch Bombensplitter umkam,° als sie Milch für ihr Kind holen wollte. Wenn ich mich recht° erinnere, war sie die Frau des jüdischen Weinhändlers° Eppstein. Menschenfresserisch,° grausam war der erste Weltkrieg, man begann aber erst an seinem Ende mit Luftangriffen° auf Städte und Menschen.

(Glossen:)

here: *in exile*

dem . . . nach = the sense of it
excited

niemals = *nie*
one of them
astonishment
pillars / go into
beinahe = *fast* / looms up
Risse . . . worden = cracks have been patched / past / *Grundwasser . . . stiftete* = groundwater caused damage / romanesque / gothic / *seien haltbarer* = were more durable

wäre . . . geblieben = would have remained / *wenn . . . hätte* = even if I had never seen it again / no more easily / *bestand . . . aus* = consisted of / pavement

zum Gedächtnis = in memory
eingefügt wurde = had been set in
durch . . . umkam = was killed by shrapnel / rightly
wine merchant / cannibalistic

air raids

Darum hat man zum Gedächtnis der Frau den Stein ein-
gesetzt, flach wie das Pflaster, und ihren Namen ein-
graviert.°

engraved

35 Der Dom hat die Luftangriffe des zweiten Weltkriegs
irgendwie überstanden,° wie auch° die Stadt zerstört worden
ist.° Er ragt° über Fluß und Ebene. Ob der kleine flache
Gedenkstein° noch da ist, das weiß ich nicht. Bei meinen
Besuchen habe ich ihn nicht mehr gefunden.

*survived / **wie auch** = **obwohl***
***zerstört . . . ist** = was destroyed /
looms / commemorative stone*

40 In der Erzählung, die ich vor dem zweiten Weltkrieg zu
schreiben begann und im Krieg verlor, ist die Rede von° dem
Kind, dem die Mutter Milch holen wollte, aber nicht
heimbringen° konnte. Ich hatte die Absicht,° in dem Buch
zu erzählen, was aus diesem Mädchen geworden ist.

***ist . . . von** = the story is about*

***heimbringen** = **nach Hause bringen** /
intention*

Fragen zum Lesestück

1. Was hat Anna Seghers' Erzählung unterbrochen?
2. Wo ist sie geboren?
3. Was konnte sie nie vergessen?
4. Über welche Denkmäler schreibt sie?
5. Beschreiben Sie diese zwei Denkmäler.
6. An wen sollte der Stein erinnern?
7. Hat Anna Seghers den Stein wieder gefunden?
8. Wann begann sie, die Erzählung zu schreiben?
9. Was wollte sie in dem Buch erzählen?

Vom Lesen zum Sprechen

„Das geht mir nicht aus dem Kopf"

These new words will be useful in talking about your past.

die **Erfahrung, -en**	experience
die **Gegenwart**	present (time)
das **Heimweh**	homesickness
die **Vergangenheit**	past
der **Ort, -e**	place; small town
um·ziehen, zog um,	to move (residence)
ist umgezogen	

Here are some words and phrases you already know that will also be useful:

verlassen	**sich erinnern an**
alte Freunde	**wiedersehen**
anders werden	

Zur Diskussion

1. Erinnern Sie sich besonders gut an etwas aus Ihrer Kindheit? Zum Beispiel an einen Menschen oder einen Ort, ein Gebäude, wo Sie gewohnt haben oder viel Zeit verbracht haben? Warum geht es Ihnen nicht aus dem Kopf? Erzählen Sie den anderen Studenten über diese wichtigen Erinnerungen.
2. Leben sie noch in der Stadt, wo Sie geboren sind, oder sind Sie umgezogen? Gefällt es Ihnen besser in dem Ort, wo Sie jetzt wohnen? Besuchen Sie manchmal Ihren Geburtsort? Was wollen Sie dort wiedersehen? Was ist anders geworden?
3. Für einige Menschen scheint die Vergangenheit immer schöner als die Gegenwart. Wie kann man das erklären?

Mündliche Übungen

A. Persönliche Fragen

1. Schreiben Sie Ihre Referate auf einer Schreibmaschine oder auf einem Computer?
2. Wann haben Sie zum ersten Mal mit einem Computer gearbeitet?
3. Gibt es etwas, was Sie Ihren Freunden nicht gern leihen?
4. Besitzen Sie viele schicke Kleider?
5. Kennen Sie jemand, der sich besonders schick anzieht?
6. Kennen Sie jemand, der sich mehr als einmal verlobt hat?
7. Haben Sie sich je verlobt?
8. Besitzen Sie einen Wagen? Was für einen?
9. Reparieren Sie Ihren Wagen selbst?
10. Lassen Sie Ihren Wagen manchmal reparieren? Von wem?

B. Vergleichen wir! Describe and compare as many people and things in your classroom as you can. Use positive, comparative, and superlative degrees, attributively as well as in the predicate:

> EXAMPLE: Jean ist größer (*taller*) als ich.
> Harry ist hier der größte.
> Nein, ich bin genau so groß wie Harry.
> Rebecca trägt ein schöneres Hemd als ich.
> Deine Schuhe finde ich nicht so schön wie meine.

C. Spiel: Student A sagt seinem Freund (Studenten B), was er tun soll. Student B tut es. Student C sagt, was geschieht.

> EXAMPLE: A: Thomas, steh mal auf!
> B: (steht auf)
> C: Er läßt Thomas aufstehen.

(z.B. Fenster aufmachen, Tür schließen, Buch aufmachen, etwas an die Tafel schreiben, an die Tür gehen, aus dem Zimmer gehen)

D. Answer the following questions using relative clauses.

> EXAMPLE: Gehst du oft in dieses Restaurant?
> Ja, das ist das Restaurant, in das ich oft gehe.

1. Gehen Sie mit diesen Leuten ins Kino?
2. Haben Sie diesen Film gesehen?
3. Läuft dieser Film heute abend?
4. Hat Ihnen dieser Film gefallen?
5. Soll ich dieses Fenster aufmachen?

„Ich kenne eine Buchhandlung, in der man auch Schallplatten kaufen kann."

6. Haben Sie in dieser Stadt gelebt?

7. Gehört Ihnen dieses Auto?

8. Sprichst du von diesem Mädchen?

9. Sind die Kinder dieser Leute schon groß?

10. Werden Sie diese Leute oft besuchen?

11. Möchten Sie den Preis dieser Armbanduhr wissen?

12. Können wir diesem Ausländer noch helfen?

13. Schenken Sie dieser Frau eine Flasche Wein?

14. Arbeiten Sie für diesen Chef?

15. Kennen Sie schon das Ende dieser Erzählung?

E. Use the phrase *was für?* to ask each other questions about various people and things. Here are some vocabulary and examples to get you going:

Armbanduhr	Erinnerungen	Stadt
Arbeit	Diskussion	Hausaufgaben
Ausweis	Frage	Hose
Mensch	Geschenk	Wagen
Lebensmittel	Fahrrad	Maschine

EXAMPLE: Was für ein Mensch ist deine Zimmerkameradin? — Sie ist ein sehr netter Mensch.
Was für eine Stadt war deine Heimtstadt?
Was für Geschenke hast du zum Geburtstag bekommen?

Schriftliche Übungen

F. Answer each question with a sentence containing a relative clause.

EXAMPLE: Mit was für Menschen verbringen Sie gern Ihre Ferien?
Ich verbringe gern meine Ferien mit Menschen, mit denen ich Sport treiben kann.

1. Was für Erzählungen lesen Sie gern?

2. Was für ein Film spielt heute abend?

3. In was für einer Gesellschaft lebt man am besten?

4. Was für Romane finden Sie interessant?

5. Mit was für Menschen leben Sie gern zusammen?

6. Aus was für einer Familie kommen Sie?

7. Was für Städte gefallen Ihnen besonders gut?

8. Was für Erinnerungen an Ihre Kindheit haben Sie?

G. Anna Seghers wollte vor vielen Jahren eine Geschichte über das Kind schreiben, dessen Mutter Milch holen wollte.

1. Schreiben Sie den Anfang dieser Geschichte. *oder*

2. Schreiben Sie das Ende dieser Geschichte. Was ist aus dem Kind geworden? Was für Erinnerungen hat dieser Mensch heute?

H. Wie sagt man das auf deutsch?

1. Can you repair your car yourself or do you prefer to have it repaired?
2. I often have it repaired.
3. I know a nice German (man) who's the best auto mechanic in town.
4. Are German trains really more punctual than American trains?
5. Yes, but the trains in France are the fastest.
6. What kind of trip did you take last year?
7. We went to Switzerland and saw the highest mountains in Europe.
8. I can't imagine anything more beautiful.
9. I've been in Europe twice but I've never been in Switzerland, which is really a shame.
10. Will your parents let you come along next time?

Almanach

Five Modern Women Writers

Ingeborg Bachmann (1926–1973)

Ingeborg Bachmann was born in Klagenfurt, Austria, the country where she also attended university. Though she initially won fame for her lyric poetry, Bachmann also wrote radio plays and short stories as well as an opera libretto and a novel.

Ingeborg Bachmann

Angelika Mechtel (b. 1943)

Angelika Mechtel was born in Dresden, though she now resides near Munich. She has written poetry, short stories, radio plays, and novels critical of modern West German society and the role of women within it.

Angelika Mechtel

Ingeborg Drewitz

Ingeborg Drewitz (1923–1986)

Ingeborg Drewitz was born in Berlin and lived there her entire life. She published dramas, short stories, radio plays, and novels, and also worked extensively as a journalist. Her partly autobiographical novel *Gestern war heute* (Yesterday Was Today - 1978) tells the story of three generations of women whose personal lives reflect political and social developments in 20th-century Berlin.

Christa Wolf (b. 1929)

Christa Wolf was born in Landsberg an der Warthe, in what is now Poland. Her novel *Kindheitsmuster* (Childhood Pattern - 1976) reflects her childhood during the Third Reich. She worked as an editor before publishing her first fiction in 1961, and has travelled and lectured widely in the West. Her latest book, *Störfall* (Disruptive Incident - 1987) concerns the nuclear disaster at Chernobyl.

Sarah Kirsch (b. 1935)

Sarah Kirsch was born in Limlingerode in the Harz region (now GDR). She now lives in the West. She is primarily a lyric poet, whose verse is characterized by intensity of language and precise, pictorial images. Her love poetry is striking for its combination of melancholy and single moments of recollected joy.

Christa Wolf

Sarah Kirsch

Summary and Review

FORMS

1 ♦ Verbs

A. Simple Past Tense

1. Weak Verbs

stem + -(e)te + endings			
ich	**sagte**	wir	**sagten**
du	**sagtest**	ihr	**sagtet**
er, es, sie	**sagte**	sie, Sie	**sagten**
ich	**arbeitete**	wir	**arbeiteten**
du	**arbeitetest**	ihr	**arbeitetet**
er, es, sie	**arbeitete**	sie, Sie	**arbeiteten**

2. Irregular Weak Verbs

changed stem + -te + ending			
wissen, **wußte**			
ich	**wußte**	wir	**wußten**
du	**wußtest**	ihr	**wußtet**
er, es, sie	**wußte**	sie, Sie	**wußten**

Similarly:

bringen	**brachte**
nennen	**nannte**
kennen	**kannte**
verbringen	**verbrachte**

and the modal verbs (no umlaut in past stem):

dürfen	**durfte**	müssen	**mußte**
können	**konnte**	sollen	**sollte**
mögen	**mochte**	wollen	**wollte**

3. **haben** and **werden** (irregular in the simple past):

ich	**hatte**	wir	**hatten**
du	**hattest**	ihr	**hattet**
er, es, sie	**hatte**	sie, Sie	**hatten**

ich	**wurde**	wir	**wurden**
du	**wurdest**	ihr	**wurdet**
er, es, sie	**wurde**	sie, Sie	**wurden**

4. Strong Verbs

changed stem + endings

nehmen, **nahm**

ich	**nahm**	wir	**nahmen**
du	**nahmst**	ihr	**nahmt**
er, es, sie	**nahm**	sie, Sie	**nahmen**

The simple past tense of strong verbs will be found in the table on page 278. In chapters 11 and 12 you learned these additional verbs:

sich an·ziehen	**zog an**	hat **angezogen**	to get dressed
brechen	**brach**	hat **gebrochen**	to break
lassen	**ließ**	hat **gelassen**	to let, leave
leihen	**lieh**	hat **geliehen**	to lend; borrow
waschen	**wusch**	hat **gewaschen**	to wash

B. Past Perfect Tense

Simple past of the auxiliary + Past Participle

Ich **hatte** das schon **gesagt.**	*I **had said** it already.*
Sie **war** fünf Jahre da **gewesen.**	*She **had been** there for five years.*
Nachdem sie sich **umgezogen** **hatten,** gingen sie ins Theater.	*After they **had changed** their clothes, they went to the theater.*

C. Reflexive Verbs

1. Accusative and dative reflexive pronouns

mich / mir	uns
dich / dir	euch
sich	sich

2. Reflexive pronoun is *accusative* when the subject and direct object are the same person or thing:

subject		reflexive direct object	
Ich	habe	**mich**	verletzt.
Wir	haben	**uns**	kennengelernt.
Stefan	muß	**sich**	beeilen.

3. Reflexive pronoun is *dative* when the subject and indirect object are the same person or thing (something *else* is the direct object).

subject		dative reflexive	direct object	
Ich	kaufte	**mir**	einen Hut.	
Du	bestellst	**dir**	ein Bier.	
Wir	sehen	**uns**	die Kirche	an.

The following reflexive verbs have been introduced through Chapter 12.

sich etwas ansehen	*to have a look at something*
sich anziehen	*to get dressed*
sich ausziehen	*to get undressed*
sich beeilen	*to hurry*
sich erkälten	*to catch cold*
sich erinnern an	*to remember*
sich freuen	*to be happy, pleased*
sich fühlen	*to feel*
sich die Haare kämmen	*to comb one's hair*
sich etwas leisten können	*to be able to afford something*
sich setzen	*to sit down*
sich verletzen	*to hurt oneself*
sich verloben mit	*to become engaged to*
sich etwas vorstellen	*to imagine something*

D. The Verb **lassen**

1. "to leave, leave behind" (perfect tense: **hat gelassen**):

> **Lassen** Sie mich allein.
> **Hast** du deine Tasche im Restaurant **gelassen**?

2. "to let, permit, allow" (perfect tense: double infinitive):

> Sie **lassen** uns heute nacht hier **schlafen.**
> Sie **haben** uns bis neun Uhr **schlafen lassen.**

3. "to cause (something to be done), have (something done)" (perfect tense: double infinitive):

> Sie **läßt** den Arzt **kommen.**
> Sie **hat** den Arzt **kommen lassen.**

A noun or pronoun in the *dative* indicates for whom the action is performed:

> Ich lasse **mir** das Essen bringen.

2 ◆ Adjective Endings, Comparisons and Adjectival Nouns

A. Adjective Endings after **der**-words: **-e** and **-en**

	masc.			*neut.*		
nom.	der	junge	Mann	das	junge	Kind
acc.	den	jungen	Mann	das	junge	Kind
dat.	dem	jungen	Mann	dem	jungen	Kind
gen.	des	jungen	Mannes	des	jungen	Kindes

	fem.			*plural*		
nom.	die	junge	Frau	die	jungen	Leute
acc.	die	junge	Frau	die	jungen	Leute
dat.	der	jungen	Frau	den	jungen	Leuten
gen.	der	jungen	Frau	der	jungen	Leute

B. Endings after **ein**-words (boxed endings differ from **der**-word endings):

	masc.			*neut.*		
nom.	ein	junger	Mann	ein	junges	Kind
acc.	einen	jungen	Mann	ein	junges	Kind
dat.	einem	jungen	Mann	einem	jungen	Kind
gen.	eines	jungen	Mannes	eines	jungen	Kindes

	fem.			*plural*		
nom.	eine	junge	Frau	keine	jungen	Leute
acc.	eine	junge	Frau	keine	jungen	Leute
dat.	einer	jungen	Frau	keinen	jungen	Leuten
gen.	einer	jungen	Frau	keiner	jungen	Leute

C. Endings of unpreceded adjectives (= endings of **dieser** except in masculine and neuter genitive singular):

	masc.		neut.		fem.		plural	
nom.	kalter	Wein	kaltes	Bier	kalte	Milch	kalte	Suppen
acc.	kalten	Wein	kaltes	Bier	kalte	Milch	kalte	Suppen
dat.	kaltem	Wein	kaltem	Bier	kalter	Milch	kalten	Suppen
gen.	kalten	Weines	kalten	Bieres	kalter	Milch	kalter	Suppen

D. Comparison of Adjectives and Adverbs

1. Basic Forms:

positive degree	comparative degree (+ -er)	superlative degree (am -(e)sten)
glücklich	glücklicher	am glücklichsten
interessant	interessanter	am interessantesten

2. With Adjective Endings:

eine	**glückliche**	Kindheit	*a happy childhood*
eine	**glücklichere**	Kindheit	*a happier childhood*
die	**glücklichste**	Kindheit	*the happiest childhood*
	interessante	Ideen	*interesting ideas*
	interessantere	Ideen	*more interesting ideas*
die	**interessantesten**	Ideen	*the most interesting ideas*

Note the two possibilities in the superlative:

Diese Ideen sind **am interessantesten.**
Diese Ideen sind **die interessantesten.**

3. Adjectives and Adverbs with Umlaut in the Comparative and Superlative:

old	alt	älter	am ältesten
young	jung	jünger	am jüngsten
cold	kalt	kälter	am kältesten
warm	warm	wärmer	am wärmsten
short	kurz	kürzer	am kürzesten
long	lang	länger	am längsten
strong	stark	stärker	am stärksten
weak	schwach	schwächer	am schwächsten
tough	hart	härter	am härtesten
sick	krank	kränker	am kränksten
often	oft	öfter	am öftesten
red	rot	röter	am rötesten
black	schwarz	schwärzer	am schwärzesten

4. Irregular Comparatives and Superlatives

big	groß	größer	am größten
good	gut	besser	am besten
high	hoch, hoh-	höher	am höchsten
near	nahe	näher	am nächsten
much	viel	mehr	am meisten
gladly	gern	lieber	am liebsten

5. **viel** and **wenig**

positive degree   *without adjective endings*
viel = much, a lot of
wenig = not much, not a lot of
with adjective endings
viele = many
wenige = not many

comparative degree   *no adjective endings*
mehr = more
weniger = less

superlative degree   *with adjective endings*
der, das, die meist- = most
der, das, die wenigst- = least, fewest

E. Adjectival Nouns

Adjectival nouns are capitalized and receive adjective endings.

1. Referring to people: masculine and feminine singular *and* plural:

attributive adjective	vs.	*adjectival noun*
unsere kleine Tochter		**Unsere Kleine** ist heute krank. *Our little girl is sick today.*
ein deutscher Student	vs.	Dieser Student ist **Deutscher.** *This student is a German.*
mit den alten Leuten	vs.	Ich will mit **den Alten** arbeiten. *I want to work with (the) old people.*

Remember that the following words are always adjectival nouns:

der/die **Bekannte**	*acquaintance, friend*
der/die **Deutsche**	*German*
der/die **Verwandte**	*relative*
der **Beamte**	*official (m.)*

2. Referring to concepts: neuter, singular *only:*

Das ist **das Schönste,** was ich je gesehen habe.	*That is the most beautiful thing I've ever seen.*
Haben Sie **etwas Billigeres?**	*Do you have anything cheaper?*
Ich habe **nichts Interessantes** gehört.	*I have not heard anything interesting.*

3 ◆ Relative Pronouns

A. Basic Forms

	masculine	*neuter*	*feminine*	*plural*
nominative	der	das	die	die
accusative	den	das	die	die
dative	dem	dem	der	denen
genitive	dessen	dessen	deren	deren

B. Rules for Use

a. The relative pronoun refers to an antecedent that precedes it.

b. The relative pronoun agrees with its antecedent in *number* and *gender*.

c. The *case* of the relative pronoun is determined by its use in the relative clause.

d. Only a preposition may precede the relative pronoun in the relative clause.

e. The relative clause has verb-final word order.

antecedent	relative pronoun	
Das ist **der Film,**	**der**	jetzt läuft.
	an **den**	ich mich nicht erinnern konnte.
	von **dem**	sie sprachen.
	dessen	Anfang mir so gut gefällt.

C. **Was** as a Relative Pronoun

Was is the relative pronoun when the antecedent is:

a. **etwas, nichts, viel, wenig, alles**
Das war **alles, was** sie sagte.

b. a neuter adjectival noun
Das war **das Schönste, was** ich je gesehen habe.

c. an entire clause
Sie wollen jetzt schlafen, was ich gut verstehen kann.

FUNCTIONS

1 ◆ Comparing

A. genauso . . . wie = as . . . as (with positive degree):
nicht so . . . wie = not as . . . as

Die zweite Geschichte war **nicht so interessant wie** die erste.

*The second story was **not as interesting as** the first.*

B. als = than (with comparative degree):

Jetzt sind die Preise **höher als** letztes Jahr.	*Now the prices are **higher than** last year.*

C. immer + comparative degree indicates progressive change:

Im Frühling werden die Tage **immer länger**.	*In the spring the days get **longer and longer***

D. je . . . desto = the . . . the (with comparative degree):

Je früher, desto besser.	***The sooner the better.***
Je mehr man lernt, **desto mehr** versteht man.	***The more** one learns **the more** one understands.*

Note that **je** requires verb-last word order, while **desto** requires verb-second word order.

2 ◆ Expressing Time

A. Parts of the Day

gestern abend	*yesterday evening*
heute abend	*this evening*
in der Nacht	*at night*
morgen früh	*tomorrow morning*
vorgestern	*the day before yesterday*
übermorgen	*the day after tomorrow*

B. Dates

1. Today's date

nom. Der wievielte ist heute? Heute ist der erste Februar. *or:*	
acc. Den wievielten haben wir heute? Heute haben wir den ersten Februar.	*What's today's date?* *Today is February first.*

2. On what day of the week? **am . . .**

Wann fährst du ab?	**Am Donnerstag.** Aber **am Montag** komme ich zurück.

3. On what day of the month? **am** . . .

Wann ist sie angekommen?	**Am 5. April.** (Am fünften April)
Wann kommen Sie zurück?	Ich komme **am 22. Oktober** zurück. (am zweiundzwanzigsten Oktober)

4. In what month? **im** . . .

Wann war sie in Rom?	**Im September.** Aber **im Dezember** war sie wieder zu Hause.

5. In what year?

In welchem Jahr ist er gestorben?	Er ist **im Jahre 1955** gestorben. *or:* Er ist **1955** gestorben.

C. Mal

1. **das Mal** = a point in time, an occasion.

Das erste ⎫
  zweite ⎬ Mal.
   dritte ⎭
	The first ⎫
	  second ⎬ *time.*
	   third ⎭

zum ersten/zweiten Mal	*for the first/second time*
Er war **zum ersten Mal** in Kanada.	*He was in Canada for the first time.*

2. cardinal number + **–mal** = "how many times"

Ich bin **einmal** dort gewesen.	*I have been there **once**.*
Den Film habe ich **dreimal** gesehen.	*I've seen the film **three times**.*
Das habe ich dir schon **zigmal** gesagt.	*I've told you that **umpteen times**.*

D. ago = **vor** + dative

Wann war sie in Rom?	Das war **vor drei Monaten.**
Wann ist das passiert?	**Vor vielen Jahren.**
Wann machte er das?	**Vor einer Stunde.**

E. Expressing Duration

1. accusative case = English "for" + time phrase

Ich habe **eine Stunde** gewartet.	*I waited **for one hour**.*

2. Action ending in the past:

Ich **wohnte** fünf Jahre in Berlin. Ich **habe** fünf Jahre in Berlin **gewohnt.** ⎫⎬⎭	*I lived in Berlin for five years.*

If the action has ended, German uses simple past *or* perfect + a time phrase.

3. Action continuing in the present:

Ich wohne **schon ein Jahr** in
   Berlin.
Ich wohne **seit einem Jahr** in   } **I've lived** *in Berlin for a year.*
   Berlin.
Ich wohne **schon seit einem Jahr**
   in Berlin.

If the action is still going on, German uses *present tense* plus **schon** or (**schon**) **seit** plus a time phrase.

F. Equivalents for English "when"

 1. **wann**

   a. Question word = "at what time?"

      Wann ist das passiert?

   b. Conjunction = "at what time"

      Ich weiß nicht, **wann** das passiert ist.

 2. **wenn**

   a. Conjunction = "when" in the present or future

      Wenn Sie uns besuchen, zeigen wir Ihnen die Stadt.

   b. Conjunction = "whenever" in past or present

      Wenn ich nach Berlin kam, haben wir uns immer gesehen.

   c. Conjunction = "if"

      Wenn ich kann, helfe ich dir gerne.

 3. **als** = "when" for a single event or period in the past (almost always used with simple past tense)

      Als ich jung war, durfte ich nicht allein in die Stadt.

3 ◆ Review of Useful Expressions

 1. Time and Place

      Wann sind Sie geboren?
      Wie komme ich dahin?

2. Requesting Information

> Sag mal, . . .
> Was ist los?
> Was gibt's Neues?
> Darf ich eine Frage stellen?
> Wann hast du Geburtstag?
> Was hast du zum Geburtstag bekommen?

3. Reactions and Opinions:

> Ohne Zweifel!
> Das finde ich auch.
> Das ist schade!
> Das tut mir weh.
> Um Gottes Willen!

Test Your Progress 3

A. Complete these sentences using the German reflexive verb cued in English.

1. Ich hörte, dein Vater hat _____ (*got hurt*).
2. Ja, aber Gott sei Dank _____ (*he already feels*) viel besser.
3. Stimmt es, daß Rita _____ (*has gotten engaged*)?
4. Richtig, darum _____ (*she's happy*) so sehr.
5. Komm doch, wir müssen _____ (*hurry up*).
6. Ich komme schon, aber ich muß _____ (*to comb my hair*).
7. Hast du _____ (*already gotten dressed*)?
8. Noch nicht, die Zeitung möchte ich _____ (*have a look at*).

B. Complete this paragraph, using the appropriate word cued in English. Don't forget the adjective endings!

Wenn man (*this*) Monat ins (*old*) Landesmuseum geht, sieht man (*a new*) Ausstellung über (*German*) Geschichte in (*our*) Jahrhundert. Dort kann man sich (*various interesting*) Plakate ansehen und (*the political*) Kunst in der Zeit der (*first German*) Republik studieren. Man sieht auf (*these old*) Plakaten, wie die (*many*) Parteien versucht haben, die Ängste (*of the German people*) zu manipulieren. Das (*first*) Bild ist ein (*good*) Beispiel für (*such political*) Plakate während (*this important*) Epoche. Es zeigt (*a „strong*) Mann". Natürlich sollte der (*unemployed German*) an einen „Führer" denken.

C. Fill in the blanks with **wenn, wann,** or **als** as appropriate.

_____ ich jung war, wollte ich Fußballspieler werden. _____ mein Vater mich samstags zum Spiel mitnahm, habe ich mich immer gefreut. „_____ darf ich einen Fußball haben?" fragte ich immer. Vater sagte: „_____ du sechs bist." _____ ich aber sechs wurde, wollte ich Cowboy werden. Ich kann mich nicht mehr erinnern, _____ ich dann Arzt werden wollte. _____ ich Ihnen jetzt sage, was ich bin, glauben Sie es mir nicht: ich bin Fußballspieler geworden!

D. Use the verb **lassen** in the German equivalents of these sentences.

1. Please let me stay!
2. Did you leave your luggage in the car?
3. She's having the meal brought to her.
4. Did you have the doctor come?
5. Leave your coat on the chair.
6. Can we let the children play for another hour?

E. Restate each sentence, putting the adjective or adverb into the comparative and then into the superlative.

> EXAMPLE: Unsere Schwester ist *eine gute* Schülerin.
> Unsere Schwester ist *eine bessere* Schülerin.
> Unsere Schwester ist *die beste* Schülerin.

1. Ich trinke *gern* deutschen Wein.
2. Die Menschen, die in dieser Gegend wohnen, sind *arm*.
3. Zum Frühstück esse ich *viel* Brot.
4. Das ist ja *ein starkes* Bier.
5. Man baut hier *große* Studentenwohnheime.
6. Schmidts habe *viele* Kinder.
7. Mein Mantel ist *warm*.
8. *Viele* Menschen verstehen mich nicht.
9. Wir fanden diese Geschichte *interessant*.
10. Du bist *ein kluges* Kind.

F. Fill in the blanks with the appropriate relative pronoun.

1. Wie heißt der Chef, für _____ du arbeitest?
2. Er heißt Herr Martens, und sein Sohn, mit _____ ich zur Schule ging, heißt Knut.
3. Ist das nicht der Junge, _____ (whose) Foto in der Zeitung war?
4. Ja, die Fußballmannschaft, für _____ er spielt, hat gerade gewonnen.
5. 1985 war das letzte Jahr, _____ ich in Deutschland verbracht habe.
6. Was war das Schönste, _____ du dort an der Uni gemacht hast?
7. Die Seminare, an _____ ich teilgenommen habe, waren alle besonders interessant.
8. Die Professorin, bei _____ ich ein Seminar über Goethe belegte, hat mir viel geholfen.
9. Die Deutschen, _____ im Studentenwohnheim wohnten, waren auch sehr sympathisch.
10. Ja, das war etwas, _____ ich nie vergessen werde.

G. Insert a phrase with **Mal** or **-mal** into these sentences to express points in time.

1. Das war (*the last time*), daß ich sie gesehen habe.
2. Ich kann ihn (*one more time*) fragen.
3. Bist du mehr als (*three times*) in der Schweiz gewesen?
4. Das (*second time*) war ich erst elf Jahre alt.
5. (*Back then*) konnte ich noch nicht so gut Deutsch wie jetzt.

H. Wie sagt man das auf deutsch?

1. What kind of a house do you live in?
2. I'm having my roommate bring me my breakfast.
3. Unfortunately, he didn't want to help me this morning.
4. When you came in at 7:30 you disturbed me.
5. How long have you been learning German?
6. Some professors, whose names I've forgotten, were excellent.
7. I went to the station with them the day before yesterday.
8. Actually I find the blue shirt most beautiful.
9. After I had eaten, I went to the movies. (*second clause: simple past*)
10. Back then we lived in a small apartment. (*use simple past*)
11. That is my new acquaintance, Paul.
12. My sister is just as old as I am.

Die Schweiz

Dialoge
Schilaufen in der Schweiz ◆ Am Informationsschalter im Bahnhof ◆ In einer Wohngemeinschaft

Wortschatz 1

Grammatik
1. Verbs with Prepositional Complements
2. Pronouns as Objects of Prepositions
   da-Compounds ◆ **wo**-Compounds
3. Future Tense
4. Wanting X to Do Y
5. Past Participles as Adjectives
6. Expanding Your Vocabulary
   Leicht zu merken

Wortschatz 2

Lesestück
Zwei Schweizer stellen ihre Heimat vor

Vom Lesen zum Sprechen
Klischees

Almanach
Profile of Switzerland

Schilaufen in der Schweiz

BRIGITTE: Ich freue mich sehr auf die Semesterferien.

JOHANNA: Hast du vor, wieder Schi zu laufen?

BRIGITTE: Ja, ich werde zwei Wochen in der Schweiz verbringen. Ich fliege morgen früh nach Zürich.

JOHANNA: Hast du früher nicht Angst vorm Fliegen gehabt?

BRIGITTE: Doch, aber ich habe mich mehr oder weniger daran gewöhnt, und mit dem Auto dauert die Fahrt einfach zu lang.

Am Informationsschalter im Bahnhof

TOURIST: Entschuldigung, darf ich Sie um Auskunft bitten?

BEAMTIN: Gerne. Wie kann ich Ihnen helfen?

TOURIST: Ich bin zum ersten Mal in Basel und kenne mich nicht aus. Ich interessiere mich besonders für moderne Kunst und möchte gern ein Museum besuchen.

BEAMTIN: Dann lohnt es sich, in unser Kunstmuseum zu gehen. Gleich vor dem Bahnhof ist eine Haltestelle. Dort müssen Sie auf die Straßenbahn, Linie 2, warten. Steigen Sie am Kunstmuseum aus.

TOURIST: Ich danke Ihnen für die Hilfe.

BEAMTIN: Bitte sehr.

In einer Wohngemeinschaft

UTE: Nina, du hast schon wieder deine Sachen nicht aufgeräumt.

NINA: Oh, seid mir bitte nicht böse. Ich mußte mich heute morgen sehr beeilen.

LUTZ: In letzter Zeit geschieht es aber zu oft, daß du alles einfach liegen läßt. Wir können diese Unordnung nicht mehr ausstehen.

NINA: Ihr habt schon recht. In den letzten Wochen hatte ich sehr viel zu tun. Ich werde mich von jetzt an mehr um die Wohnung kümmern.

Wortschatz 1

Skiing in Switzerland

BRIGITTE: I'm really looking forward to the semester break.

JOHANNA: Do you plan to go skiing again?

BRIGITTE: Yes, I'm going to spend two weeks in Switzerland. I'm flying to Zürich tomorrow morning.

JOHANNA: Didn't you used to be afraid of flying?

BRIGITTE: Yes I was, but I've more or less gotten used to it, and the trip just takes too long by car.

At the Information Window in the Train Station

TOURIST: Excuse me, may I ask you for information?

OFFICIAL: Gladly. How can I help you?

TOURIST: I'm in Basel for the first time and don't know my way around. I'm especially interested in modern art and would like to visit a museum.

OFFICIAL: Then it's really worthwhile to go to our Art Museum. There's a streetcar stop right in front of the train station. Wait there for the number 2. Get out at the Art Museum.

TOURIST: Thanks for the help.

OFFICIAL: You're welcome.

In a Communal Living Group

UTE: Nina, you didn't clean up your things again.

NINA: Oh, please don't be mad at me. I was really in a hurry this morning.

LUTZ: But lately it's happened too often that you just leave everything lying around. We can't stand this mess any more.

NINA: You're right. I've had a lot to do the last few weeks. I'll take more care of the apartment from now on.

Verben

Angst haben vor (+ *dat.*) to be afraid of

auf·räumen to tidy up, straighten up

sich aus·kennen to know one's way around
Hier kenne ich mich nicht aus. I don't know my way around here.

etwas aus·stehen können to be able to stand something
Ich kann ihn nicht ausstehen. I can't stand him.

bitten, bat, hat gebeten um to ask for, request
Er bittet mich um das Geld. He's asking me for the money.

danken für to thank for

sich freuen auf (+ *acc.*) to look forward to

geschehen (geschieht), geschah, ist geschehen to happen

sich gewöhnen an (+ *acc.*) to get used to

sich interessieren für to be interested in

sich kümmern um to look after, take care of, deal with

sich lohnen to be worthwhile, worth the trouble

recht haben to be right

sich vor·bereiten auf (+ *acc.*) to prepare for

vor·haben to plan, have in mind

warten auf (+ *acc.*) to wait for

Substantive

der **Schalter, -** counter, window

die **Auskunft** information

die **Haltestelle, -n** (streetcar or bus) stop

die **Linie, -n** (streetcar or bus) line

die **Sache, -n** thing, object; matter, affair
deine Sachen your belongings
Kümmern Sie sich bitte um diese Sache. Please take care of this matter.

die **Unordnung** disorder, mess

Andere Vokabeln

böse (+ *dat.*) angry (at)
Seid mir nicht böse. Don't be mad at me.

wohl probably

Nützliche Ausdrücke

in letzter Zeit lately

mehr oder weniger more or less

von jetzt an from now on

Gegensätze

die **Unordnung** ≠ die **Ordnung**   disorder ≠ order

Neue Kombinationen

A. Replace the word in italics with the cue you will hear.

1. Ich freue mich auf *die Semesterferien.*
   (das Wochenende, den Film, die Bahnreise, unser Gespräch, deinen Besuch)
2. Hast du nicht Angst vor *dem Fliegen* gehabt?
   (dem Abitur, der Schule, diesem Typ)
3. Ich kann mich nicht an *das Klima* gewöhnen.
   (das Stadtleben, diese Wohngemeinschaft, meinen Zimmerkameraden, das deutsche Essen)
4. Darf ich Sie um *Auskunft* bitten?
   (Hilfe, ein Foto, Ihre Fahrkarte, Ihre Hausaufgaben)
5. Ich interessiere mich besonders für *moderne Kunst.*
   (französischen Wein, alte Gebäude, schnelle Autos, alte Filme)

B. Your teacher asks you what you plan to do. Your response will be cued in English. Use an infinitive phrase with **zu** in your answer.

> EXAMPLE: Was hast du vor? (go to the movies)
> Ich habe vor, ins Kino zu gehen.

1. go skiing
2. play sports
3. wear a sweater
4. go to the museum
5. go swimming
6. talk to Rita
7. work this evening
8. call up Martin

C. Tell whether or not you know your way around in various places, as in the example.

> EXAMPLE: Kennen sie Basel?
> Ja, in Basel kenne ich mich gut aus.
> or: Nein, in Basel kenne ich mich nicht aus.

1. Kennen Sie München?
2. Kennen Sie die Altstadt?
3. Kennen Sie das Kunstmuseum?
4. Kennen Sie die Städte am Rhein?
5. Kennen Sie diese alte Kirche?
6. Kennen Sie diese Gegend?
7. Kennen Sie die Alpen?

Übung zur Aussprache

Eugen Gomringer was born in Bolivia, to Swiss parents, in 1925. His typically polyglot Swiss background is reflected in the fact that he has written poems in German, Swiss German dialect, French, English, and Spanish. Gomringer is a leading exponent of concrete poetry (**konkrete Poesie**), which rejects metaphor, radically simplifies syntax, and considers the printed page a visual as much as a linguistic experience. The following poem consists entirely of nouns followed by relative clauses in strict parallelism. The reader is required to work out their interrelationships for himself. Pay particular attention to the verb tenses as you read this poem aloud.

nachwort°		*afterword*
das dorf, das ich nachts° hörte		*in the night*
der wald, in dem ich schlief		
das land, das ich überflog°		*flew across*
die stadt, in der ich wohnte		
das haus, das den freunden gehörte		
die frau, die ich kannte		
das bild, das mich wach hielt°		*kept awake*
der klang,° der mir gefiel		*sound*
das buch, in dem ich las		
der stein, den ich fand		
der mann, den ich verstand		
das kind, das ich lehrte°		*taught*
der baum, den ich blühen° sah		*blooming*
das tier,° das ich fürchtete		*animal*
die sprache, die ich spreche		
die schrift,° die ich schreibe		*writing*

Erstbesteigung (*first ascent*) des Matterhorns (4 478 m) im Jahre 1865

Grammatik

1 ◆ Verbs With Prepositional Complements

Many verbs need a prepositional phrase to complement them in certain meanings:

Ich spreche **mit ihm.**	*I'm talking **with him.***
Ich spreche **gegen ihn.**	*I'm speaking **against him.***

In the examples above, English and German happen to use parallel prepositions. In many cases, however, they do not. For example:

Er wartet **auf** seinen Bruder.	*He's waiting **for** his brother.*

For this reason, you must learn the verb and the preposition used with it *together.* Don't just learn **bitten—to ask, request,** but rather **bitten um—to ask *for.***

Here is a list of the verbs with prepositional complements you already know from this and previous chapters (note that sometimes the complete verbal idea also involves a noun, as in **Angst haben vor**).

1. **Angst haben vor** (+ *dat.*) *to be afraid of*

Hast du Angst vorm Fliegen?	*Are you afraid of flying?*

2. **bitten um** *to ask for, request*

Sie bat mich gestern um Hilfe.	*She asked me for help yesterday.*

3. **danken für** *to thank for*

Ich möchte Ihnen für die schönen Blumen danken.	*I would like to thank you for the beautiful flowers.*

4. **erinnern an** (+ *acc.*) *to remind of*

Das erinnert mich an etwas Wichtiges.	*That reminds me of something important.*

5. **sich erinnern an** (+ *acc.*) *to remember*

Sie hat sich an meinen Geburtstag erinnert.	*She remembered my birthday.*

6. **sich freuen auf** (+ *acc.*) *to look forward to*

Ich freue mich auf die Ferien!	*I'm looking forward to the vacation!*

7. **sich gewöhnen an** (+ *acc.*)   *to get used to*

Sie konnte sich nicht an das kalte Wetter gewöhnen.

She couldn't get used to the cold weather.

8. **sich interessieren für**   *to be interested in*

Interessieren Sie sich für moderne Kunst?

Are you interested in modern art?

9. **sich kümmern um**   *to look after, take care of, deal with*

Ich werde mich mehr um die Wohnung kümmern.

I'll take more care of the apartment.

10. **teil·nehmen an** (+ *dat.*)   *to take part in, participate in*

Nimmst du aktiv am Sport teil?

Do you participate actively in sports?

11. **sich verloben mit**   *to get engaged to*

Rita hat sich mit Rudi verlobt.

Rita got engaged to Rudi.

12. **sich vor·bereiten auf** (+ *acc.*)   *to prepare for*

Wir bereiten uns auf seinen Besuch vor.

We're preparing for his visit.

13. **warten auf** (+ *acc.*)   *to wait for*

Auf wen warten Sie denn?

Whom are you waiting for?

The prepositional phrase is a verbal complement (see p. 67) and constitutes the second part of the predicate. This means that it will come at the end of the sentence or phrase:

Sie kümmert sich seit Wochen nicht mehr um ihre Arbeit.

For weeks she hasn't been taking care of her work.

Note that when the preposition used with a verb is a two-way preposition, you must also learn whether it is followed by dative or accusative when used with this verb. Don't just learn **warten auf—to wait for,** but rather **warten auf +** *accusative*—**to wait for.** It is useful to know that the two-way prepositions **auf** and **über** almost always take accusative case when used as verbal complements in a non-spatial sense:

Spatial	*Non-spatial*
Er wartet auf der Straße.	Er wartet auf die Lehrerin.
He's waiting on the street.	*He's waiting for the teacher.*

Note that some verbs can take both an accusative or dative object *and* a prepositional complement:

	d. o.	*prep. compl.*	
Er bittet	**die Beamtin**	**um Auskunft.**	*He asks the official for information.*

	dat. o.	*prep. compl.*	
Ich danke	**dir**	**für das Geschenk.**	*I thank you for the present.*

	d. o.	*prep. compl.*	
Das erinnert	**mich**	**an meine Heimat.**	*That reminds me of my home.*

Be careful not to confuse prepositional complements (**erinnern an**) and separable prefixes (**ankommen**). Although the latter sometimes look like prepositions, they are not, because they have no object:

Verb + Preposition

object
Er erinnert mich **an meinen Bruder.**

BUT:

Separable Prefix
Der Zug kommt um 9 Uhr **an.**

Üben wir!

A. Substitute the new prepositional objects cued in English.

1. Wir warten auf unseren Freund.
   (the train, the streetcar, our friends, the wine)
2. Sie dankten uns für unsere Hilfe.
   (the present, the weekend, the information, our visit, everything)
3. Hast du Angst vor dem Fliegen?
   (the long trip, a political discussion, these friendly people)
4. Ich möchte Sie um die Schreibmaschine bitten.
   (a glass of water, your help, the course catalogue, a better room)
5. Er hat an der Diskussion teilgenommen.
   (the seminar, the last war, the conversation)

B. Now practice the verbs + prepositions that are also reflexive.

1. Interessieren Sie sich für deutsche Filme?
   (modern art, old books, French wine)

2. Ich habe mich noch nicht an das Klima gewöhnt.
   (the language, the food, the weather, the winter)

3. Kannst du dich ein bißchen mehr um die Wohnung kümmern?
   (the children, the house, our relatives, this matter)

4. Ich muß mich auf meine Vorlesung vorbereiten.
   (the weekend, the vacation, our trip to Switzerland)

5. Freut ihr euch auf den Besuch?
   (dinner, German class, her letter)

6. Erinnerst du dich an meine Tante?
   (my uncle, your homeland, last summer)

2 ♦ Pronouns as Objects of Prepositions: *da*-Compounds and *wo*-Compounds

da-*Compounds*

When noun objects of prepositions are replaced by pronouns, a distinction is made in German between nouns referring to people and nouns referring to inanimate objects.

1. Nouns referring to people are replaced by personal pronouns following the preposition, as you would expect:

Steht Christof hinter Gabriele?	*Is Christof standing behind Gabriele?*
Ja, er steht **hinter ihr.**	*Yes, he's standing **behind her.***
Sprichst du oft mit den Kindern?	*Do you often talk with the children?*
Ja, ich spreche oft **mit ihnen.**	*Yes, I often speak **with them.***
Wartet ihr auf Manfred?	*Are you waiting for Manfred?*
Ja, wir warten **auf ihn.**	*Yes, we're waiting **for him.***

2. Nouns referring to inanimate objects are all replaced by the prefix **da-** plus the preposition. Note that if the preposition begins with a vowel, **da-** becomes **dar-: da + auf = darauf, da + über = darüber:**

Steht dein Auto vor oder hinter dem Haus?	*Is your car in front of the house or behind it?*
Es steht **dahinter.**	*It's **behind it.***
Was machen wir mit diesem Schreibtisch?	*What will we do with this desk?*
Ich weiß nicht, was wir **damit** machen.	*I don't know what we'll do **with it.***
Wie lange warten Sie schon auf den Zug?	*How long have you been waiting for the train?*
Ich warte schon 10 Minuten **darauf.**	*I've been waiting **for it** for ten minutes.*

Üben wir!

A. Respond as in the example.

> EXAMPLE: Stand er neben dem Fenster?
> Ja, er stand daneben.

1. Fangt ihr mit der Arbeit an?
2. Hast du nach dem Film gegessen?
3. Interessieren Sie sich für Romane?
4. Hat er lange auf die Straßenbahn gewartet?
5. Habt ihr an der Diskussion teilgenommen?
6. Hat sie sich an das Wetter gewöhnt?
7. Hat sie wieder um Geld gebeten?
8. Bereitest du dich auf die Deutschstunde vor?
9. Liegt meine Zeitung unter deinem Rucksack?
10. Erinnerst du dich an den Urlaub?
11. Hat sie vor der Mensa gewartet?

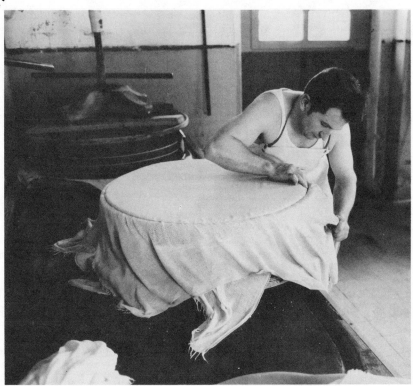

Käsezubereitung in der Nähe von Bern (die Zubereitung = *preparation*)

B. Respond as in the example. How you answer will depend on whether the prepositional object is animate or inanimate.

> EXAMPLES: Sitzt Ingrid hinter Hans?
> Ja, sie sitzt hinter ihm.
>
> Sitzt Ingrid hinter dem Schreibtisch?
> Ja, sie sitzt dahinter.

1. Hast du dich an das Wetter gewöhnt?
2. Bist du mit Ursula gegangen?
3. Erinnern Sie sich an die guten alten Zeiten?
4. Können wir über diese Fragen sprechen?
5. Wohnst du bei Frau Lindner?
6. Sind Sie gegen diesen Politiker?
7. Waren Sie gegen seine Ideen?
8. Interessieren Sie sich für Sport?
9. Fährst du mit Karin?
10. Hat er dir für das Geschenk gedankt?

wo-Compounds

The same animate-inanimate distinction is made with question words when a preposition is involved. to ask a question about a person, Germans use the preposition + **wen** or **wem:**

Auf wen warten Sie?	***Whom*** *are you waiting for!*
Mit wem spielen die Kinder?	***Whom*** *are the children playing with!*

However, when asking about a thing, **wen** and **wem** are replaced by **wo-** + the preposition involved:

Worauf warten Sie?	***What*** *are you waiting for!*
Womit spielt das Kind?	***What*** *is the child playing with!*

Note that **wo-** changes to **wor-** if the preposition begins with a vowel: **wo + auf = worauf; wo + unter = worunter.**

Üben wir!

A. You're in a noisy room and can't hear very well. Ask your friend to repeat what has been said. (Use a **wo-**compound or preposition + pronoun as appropriate).

> EXAMPLES: Teacher: Er hat auf den Brief gewartet.
> Student A: Worauf hat er gewartet?
> Student B: Auf den Brief.
>
> Teacher: Sie hat auf Robert gewartet.
> Student A: Auf wen hat sie gewartet?
> Student B: Auf Robert.

1. Wir freuen uns auf Ritas Geburtstag.
2. Wir haben mit Professor Hansen gearbeitet.
3. Rita hat sich mit Rudi verlobt.
4. Wir müssen uns um die Wohnung kümmern.
5. Heinz interessiert sich für deutschen Wein.
6. Wir sind sehr stolz auf unsere Sportlerinnen.
7. Wir haben Angst vor diesem Typ.
8. Luise kann sich nicht an die Arbeit gewöhnen.

B. Respond to the following questions with your own answers.

1. Wofür interessieren Sie sich?
2. Wovor haben Sie manchmal Angst?
3. Worauf warten Sie?
4. Woran möchten Sie teilnehmen?
5. Worum müssen Sie sich kümmern?
6. Worauf freuen Sie sich?
7. Worauf sollen Sie sich vorbereiten?
8. Woran können Sie sich nicht gewöhnen?

3 ♦ Future Tense

Formation: **werden** + *infinitive*

The future is a compound tense, consisting of an inflected form of the auxiliary **werden** plus a dependent infinitive in final position.

ich **werde schlafen**	I will sleep	wir **werden schlafen**	we will sleep
du **wirst schlafen**	you will sleep	ihr **werdet schlafen**	you will sleep
er, es, sie **wird schlafen**	he, it, she will sleep	sie, Sie **werden schlafen**	they, you will sleep

■ **Werden** as the future auxiliary corresponds to **shall** or **will** in English. Do not confuse it with the modal **wollen:**

Er **wird** schlafen. He **will** *sleep.*
Er **will** schlafen. He **wants to** *sleep.*

The infinitive of a modal verb in the future *follows* its own dependent infinitive, exactly the reverse of English:

Wir werden es **tun müssen.**

We will **have to do** it.

Use

1. To show future time
   German usually uses *present tense* to express future meaning, especially when a time expression makes the future meaning clear:

   Er kommt morgen.   *He's coming tomorrow.*

   Future tense makes the future meaning explicit and is more frequent in the absence of an expression showing future time:

   Er wird sicher zurückkommen.   *He will surely return.*

2. To show probability
   The future tense, often with an adverb like **wohl** (probably) or **sicher** (surely), is frequently used to express *present* probability or likelihood:

   Sie werden sicher schon im   *They're surely at the office by*
     Büro sein.   *now.*
   Das wird wohl so sein.   *That's probably the way it is.*

Üben wir!

A. Respond in the future tense, as in the example.

> EXAMPLE: Hat er schon gegessen?
>   Nein, aber er wird bald essen.

1. Hat es schon geregnet?
2. Hast du das schon versucht?
3. Seid ihr schon Schi gelaufen?
4. Hat er Zeit in der Schweiz verbracht?
5. Haben Sie Deutsch lernen müssen?
6. Haben Sie mit ihm reden können?
7. Hat euch Susi schon besucht?
8. Hast du schon am Gespräch teilgenommen?

B. Answer the following questions by giving a likely reason. Use the cues to help you.

> EXAMPLE: Warum ist Jürgen nicht zum Seminar gekommen?
>   Er wird wohl krank sein.

(in den Ferien sein, keinen Spielplatz haben, bei der Arbeit sein, viel zu tun haben, für seine Arbeit brauchen, in ihrem Wochenendhaus sein)

1. Wo ist denn Franziska?
2. Warum lernt Michael Italienisch?
3. Wo sind denn Müllers dieses Wochenende? Ihr Haus ist dunkel.
4. Warum spielen die Kinder immer auf der Straße?
5. Warum hat Nikki nicht aufgeräumt?

4 ♦ Wanting X to Do Y

To express the idea that a person wants something to happen or be done, English uses a direct object and an infinitive phrase.[1]

	Direct Object	*Infinitive Phrase*
She would like	*the music*	*to stop.*
I don't want	*him*	*to think that.*

German uses a **daß**-clause following **wollen** or **möchte** to say the same thing:

Sie möchte,	**daß die Musik aufhört.**
Ich will nicht,	**daß er das glaubt.**

Üben wir!

A. You have a strict boss. Answer a new employee's questions about his regulations. Begin your answer with **Der Chef will, daß . . .**

EXAMPLE: Müssen wir um acht im Büro sein?
Ja, der Chef will, daß wir um acht im Büro sind.

1. Müssen wir den ganzen Tag hier bleiben?
2. Müssen wir immer pünktlich sein?
3. Dürfen wir erst um zehn Kaffee trinken?
4. Müssen wir diese Schreibmaschinen benutzen?
5. Müssen wir am Samstag arbeiten?
6. Sollen wir uns schick anziehen?

Schweizer
Bauernhäuser (der
Bauer = *farmer,
peasant*)

[1] Note that in English, the direct object of the main verb is also the subject of the infinitive. In German, the entire **daß**-clause is the direct object.

B. Now say what you would like to happen. Begin with **Ich möchte, daß . . .**

> EXAMPLE: Die Musik soll aufhören.
> Ich möchte, daß die Musik aufhört.

1. Die Sonne soll scheinen.
2. Ihr sollt alle ruhig sein.
3. Paul soll jetzt reden.
4. Du sollst nicht zu viel trinken.
5. Ihr sollt das nicht vergessen.
6. Man soll mehr Studentenwohnheime bauen.

5 ♦ Past Participles as Adjectives

Past participles of verbs are often used as attributive adjectives. They take regular adjective endings:

$$verkaufen \longrightarrow \textbf{verkauft}$$

Welche Bücher haben Sie schon verkauft?	*Which books have you already sold?*
Das sind die **verkauften** Bücher.	*Those are the sold books.*

$$bauen \longrightarrow \textbf{gebaut}$$

Hast du den neu **gebauten** Sportplatz schon gesehen?	*Have you seen the newly built playing field yet?*

6 ♦ Expanding Your Vocabulary

Leicht zu merken

automatisch	
die **Barriere, -n**	Barrie re
der **Dialekt, -e**	Dialekt
konservativ	konservativ
neutral	neutral
die **Neutralität**	Neutralität
offiziell	offiziell
praktisch	
das **Prozent**	
romantisch	
stabil	stabil
die **Stabilität**	Stabilität

Wortschatz 2

Verben

antworten auf (+ *acc.*) to answer (something)
   Antworten Sie bitte auf die Frage! Please answer the question!
sich ärgern (über + *acc.*) to get annoyed (at), be annoyed (about)
denken, dachte, hat gedacht to think
   denken an (+ *acc.*) to think of
sich erholen (von) to recover (from), get well; have a rest
gebrauchen to use
gehören zu to be a part of, be one of
klingen, klang, hat geklungen sound
   Das klingt gut. That sounds good.
sich etwas überlegen to consider, ponder, think something over
   Das muß ich mir überlegen. I have to think it over.
vor·stellen to introduce; to present
   Darf ich meine Tante vorstellen? May I introduce my aunt?

Substantive

der **Ort, -e** place; small town
der **Rechtsanwalt, ⸚e** lawyer (*m.*)
der **Schweizer, -** Swiss (*m.*)

das **Werk, -e** work; composition

die **Firma, die Firmen** firm, company
die **Rechtsanwältin, -nen** lawyer (*f.*)
die **Schweizerin, -nen** Swiss (*f.*)
die **Schwierigkeit, -en** difficulty

Andere Vokabeln

beides (*sing.*) both things
froh happy, glad
miteinander with each other, together
sauber clean
stolz auf (+ *acc.*) proud of
verantwortlich für responsible for

Nützlicher Ausdruck

in Zukunft in the future

Gegensätze

froh ≠ **traurig**	happy ≠ sad
sauber ≠ **schmutzig**	clean ≠ dirty

Zwei Schweizer stellen ihre Heimat vor

Dr. Anton Vischer, Rechtsanwalt aus Basel, 45 Jahre alt.

„In meinem Beruf bin ich für die Investitionen° aus-
ländischer Firmen verantwortlich und reise deshalb viel ins
Ausland. Dort höre ich oft die alten Klischees über meine
Heimat. Wenn man sagt, daß man aus der Schweiz kommt,
denken viele Menschen automatisch an saubere Straßen,
Schokolade, Uhren, Käse und an die Schweizergarde° im
Vatikan. Darüber ärgere ich mich immer ein bißchen. Ich
möchte lieber, daß andere wissen, was für eine politische
Ausnahme° die Schweiz in Europa bildet.° Davon werde ich
Ihnen erzählen.

Schon seit dem 13. Jahrhundert hat sie eine demokratische Verfassung.° Sie gehört also zu den ältesten und
stabilsten Demokratien der Welt. In beiden Weltkriegen ist
die Schweiz neutral geblieben, und sie hat sich ihre Neutralität und ihre politische Stabilität bis heute bewahrt.°

investments

Swiss Guard

exception / constitutes

constitution

preserved

Rheinufer in Basel
(das Ufer = *riverbank*)

«Mi Wält!»

Einige werden unsere Gesellschaft wohl zu konservativ finden. In einem Kanton[1] haben die Frauen z.B. immer noch kein Wahlrecht° bekommen. Aber man darf nicht vergessen, daß es in der Schweiz durchaus° einen Platz für soziale Kritik° gibt. Das zeigen die Werke unserer bekanntesten Schriftsteller wie Max Frisch und Friedrich Dürrenmatt.[2]

Jemand fragte mich einmal, ob ich stolz bin, Schweizer zu sein. Darauf habe ich sofort ‚ja‘ geantwortet, aber in Zukunft werde ich mir die Antwort genauer überlegen. Ich werde einfach sagen, ich bin froh, Schweizer zu sein, denn meine Heimat ist das schönste Land, das ich kenne. Da ich meine Freizeit immer auf Bergtouren verbringe, ist mein Leben mit der Alpenlandschaft eng verbunden.° Für mich sind die Alpen ein Ort, wo ich mich körperlich und seelisch° erholen kann. Das klingt vielleicht romantisch, aber eigentlich bin ich ein ganz praktischer Mensch."

suffrage
by all means
criticism

eng verbunden = *closely connected*
körperlich . . . seelisch = *physically and emotionally*

[1] Switzerland is composed of twenty-three cantons, each with considerable autonomy. All women vote in national elections, but in the canton of Appenzell, women may not vote in local elections.
[2] Max Frisch (b. 1911) and Friedrich Dürrenmatt (b. 1921). Each has written novels and plays.

Nicole Wehrli, Dolmetscherin° aus Biel, 24 Jahre alt

„Ich bin in der zweisprachigen° Stadt Biel—auf französisch Bienne—aufgewachsen, direkt an der Sprachgrenze zwischen der französischen und der deutschen Schweiz. Bei uns
35 können Sie manchmal auf der Straße Gespräche hören, in denen die Menschen beides—Französisch *und* Deutsch— miteinander reden. In der Schule habe ich dann Latein,° Englisch und Italienisch gelernt. Sie werden sich also nicht wundern,° daß ich mich für Fremdsprachen interessiere.
40   Die Eidgenossenschaft[3] ist wohl ein Unikum° in Europa, denn sie ist viersprachig. Die Sprachbarrieren waren lange Zeit ein Hindernis° für die politische Vereinigung der Kantone und machen uns heute noch manchmal Schwierigkeiten. Achtzehn Prozent der Bevölkerung° hat Französisch
45 als Muttersprache, zwölf Prozent sprechen Italienisch und etwa° ein Prozent Rätoromanisch.[4] Unser ‚Schwyzerdütsch‘[5] können die meisten Deutschen nicht verstehen. Da unsere Kinder das Hochdeutsch° erst in der Schule lernen müssen, ist es oft so schwer wie eine Fremdsprache. Die
50 geschriebene und offizielle Sprache in den Schulen bleibt Hochdeutsch, aber nach dem Unterricht° gebrauchen Lehrer und Schüler den Dialekt, wenn sie miteinander reden."

interpreter

bilingual

Latin

sich wundern = *be surprised*
something unique

obstacle

population

approximately

High German

nach . . . Unterricht = *after class*

Glista d'hotels
Hotelliste – Liste des hôtels

Winter / Hiver / Inverno   Sommer / Eté / Estate

SAMEDAN
1720 m
im Herzen des Oberengadins

---

[3] Confederation, i.e., *Confoederatio Helvetica:* official designation for the Swiss republic.
[4] Rhaetoromansh, or simply Romansh, is a Romance language—a remnant of the original Roman occupation in the alpine territories—spoken by c. 40,000 rural Swiss in the canton of Grisons (Graubünden). Long under threat of extinction, it was declared one of the four national languages in 1938.
[5] Swiss-German dialect.

Bergwanderer, Kühe und Berglandschaft (die Kuh, ¨e)

Fragen zum Lesestück

1. Was ist Dr. Vischer von Beruf?
2. Wofür ist er verantwortlich?
3. Welche Klischees hört er über die Schweiz, wenn er im Ausland ist?
4. Wie reagiert er auf die Klischees, die er manchmal hört?
5. Seit wann hat die Schweiz eine demokratische Verfassung?
6. Was macht Herr Vischer in seiner Freizeit?
7. Was wissen Sie über die Stadt, in der Nicole Wehrli aufgewachsen ist?
8. Welche Sprachen hört man dort auf der Straße?
9. Wieviele Schweizer sind deutschsprachig?
10. Warum haben manche Deutsche Schwierigkeiten, die Schweizer zu verstehen?
11. Was für Schwierigkeiten haben die Kinder in der Schule?

Vom Lesen zum Sprechen

Klischees

Dr. Anton Vischer sprach von den Klischees, die er oft im Ausland über seine Heimat hört. Sie kennen wohl auch Klischees über Ihr eigenes Land und auch über andere Länder. Hier sind einige Wörter, die Sie in einer Diskussion über Klischees gebrauchen können.

das **Klischee, -s**	
der **Ausländer, -**	foreigner
klischeehaft (*adj.*)	cliché, stereotyped
eine **klischeehafte Meinung**	stereotyped opinion
objektiv	objective
subjektiv	subjective
das **Vorurteil, -e**	prejudice
die **Wahrheit, -en**	truth

Zur Diskussion

1. Welche Klischees haben Sie schon über Ihre Heimat gehört? Was finden Ausländer z.B. „typisch amerikanisch"?

POSSIBLE RESPONSE: „Alle Amerikaner trinken Coca-Cola."

2. Nennen Sie einige Klischees über die deutschsprachigen Länder (BRD, DDR, Österreich, die Schweiz). Woher kommen diese Klischees?

POSSIBLE RESPONSE: „Alle Deutschen trinken Bier und essen Wurst."

Mündliche Übungen

A. Persönliche Fragen

1. Was hast du in den Ferien vor?
2. Wovor hast du Angst?
3. Woran können Sie sich nicht gewöhnen?
4. Was machen Sie, wenn Sie sich in einer fremden Stadt nicht auskennen?
5. Wofür interessieren Sie sich besonders?
6. Räumen Sie oft Ihr Zimmer auf?
7. Was geschieht, wenn Sie Ihre Sachen einfach liegen lassen?
8. Sind Sie in letzter Zeit sehr beschäftigt gewesen? Warum?
9. Lohnt es sich, in das Kunstmuseum zu gehen?
10. Worauf freuen Sie sich besonders?

B. Use the verbs listed below to ask each other questions beginning with a **wo**-compound.

> EXAMPLE: Teacher: denken an
> Student A: Woran denkst du denn?
> Student B: Ich denke an die Semesterferien.

1. sich freuen auf
2. sich interessieren für
3. sich ärgern über
4. sich erinnern an
5. sich kümmern um

6. sich vorbereiten auf
7. warten auf
8. antworten auf
9. sich gewöhnen an
10. Angst haben vor

C. Guided responses with **da-**compounds. Your teacher asks a question and you respond affirmatively. Then another student comments that everybody does that. Here is how it goes:

> EXAMPLE: Teacher: Freuen Sie sich auf die Ferien?
> Student A: Ja, ich freue mich darauf.
> Student B: Darauf freuen wir uns alle.

1. Interessierst du dich für Fremdsprachen?
2. Freuen Sie sich auf das Wochenende?
3. Wartest du auf die Straßenbahn?
4. Bittest du ihn um Geld?
5. Helfen Sie ihr mit den Hausaufgaben?
6. Kümmern Sie sich um diese Sachen?
7. Gewöhnen Sie sich an unser Klima?
8. Erinnerst du dich an Barbaras Besuch?
9. Antworten Sie sofort auf meine Briefe?
10. Bist du stolz auf diese Arbeit?
11. Sind Sie für diese Sachen verantwortlich?
12. Denkst du an die Zukunft?

D. Wie wird es sein?

1. Use the future tense to read your neighbor's palm.

> EXAMPLE: Du wirst lange leben.
> Du wirst viermal heiraten und zehn Kinder haben.

2. Sind Sie Optimist oder Pessimist? Speculate about life fifty years from now. Use future tense.

> EXAMPLE: In fünfzig Jahren werden wir (nicht) besser leben.
> Die Welt wird vielleicht freier sein.
> Die Menschen werden (nicht) glücklicher sein.
> Doch, wir werden alle . . . .

E. Rollenspiel. Act out these situations with each other.

1. „Darf ich um Auskunft bitten?" (Tourist und Beamter)
   Sie sind in dieser Stadt fremd. Sie müssen also um Auskunft bitten. Sie
   möchten wissen, was man hier alles machen und sehen kann. Der Beamte
   (oder die Beamtin) am Schalter sagt Ihnen, was man hier machen kann
   und wie man dahin kommt.

2. „Wer hat diese Unordnung gemacht?" (Drei Zimmerkameraden)
   Ihre Zimmerkameraden ärgern sich über Sie und sagen Ihnen, Sie kümmern sich nicht genug um Ihre Sachen. Sie finden aber, daß das nicht
   stimmt und antworten, daß Sie letzte Woche alles selber aufgeräumt
   haben. Darüber ägern sich Ihre Zimmerkameraden, weil sie Ihnen nicht
   glauben.

F. You are in charge of the apartment this week. Tell your roommates what
you'd like them to do. They respond with the future tense, saying they will
do as you instruct. Here is how the exchange can start.

EXAMPLE: Student A: Richard, ich möchte, daß du die Wohnung aufräumst.
Student B: Gut. Ich werde heute die Wohnung aufräumen.

die Wohnung aufräumen
Lebensmittel einkaufen
das Auto reparieren lassen
Konzertkarten kaufen
die Fenster putzen
Bücher zur Bibliothek
  zurückbringen

Robert am Dienstag zum
  Bahnhof bringen
die Betten machen
Blumen für morgen abend
  kaufen
ein neues Vorlesungsverzeichnis holen

Luzern: Blick von der Kapellbrücke auf die Jesuitenkirche (der Blick = *view*)

Schriftliche Übungen

G. Fill in the past participles cued in English. When they are used as attributive adjectives, do not forget the correct endings.

> EXAMPLE: Die Tür war _____. (closed)
> Die Tür war geschlossen.
> Ich stand vor einer _____ Tür.
> Ich stand vor einer geschlossenen Tür.

1. Wer hat im Zimmer _____? (cleaned up)
   Es ist schön, in einem _____ Zimmer zu sitzen.
2. Letztes Jahr habe ich sehr viel Geld _____. (saved)
   Mit meinem _____ Geld will ich eine Reise ins Ausland machen.
3. Hast du vielleicht deinen Rucksack _____? (lost)
   Eine neue Kamera war in meinem _____ Rucksack.
4. Ich habe meine Hemden _____. (washed)
   Die _____ Hemden hängen draußen hinter dem Haus.
5. Der Mann, mit dem sie sich verlobt hat, ist immer schick _____. (dressed)
   Nur schick _____ Männer gehen mit ihr aus.
6. Ich habe meine Sachen zu Hause _____. (forgotten)
   Aber die _____ Sachen sind Gott sei Dank nicht sehr wichtig.
7. Frau Schwarzer hat ihren Wagen selber _____. (repaired)
   Ihr _____ Wagen läuft jetzt gut.
8. Alle Studenten waren auf die Deutschstunde gut _____. (prepared)
   Der Professor ist stolz auf die gut _____ Studenten.

H. Schreiben Sie eine Seite über eine der beiden Fragen.

1. Gibt es Sprachbarrieren in Ihrer Heimat? Beschreiben Sie einige.
2. Kennen Sie Ausländer, die in Amerika leben, und deren Muttersprache nicht Englisch ist? Was für Schwierigkeiten haben sie?

I. Wie sagt man das auf deutsch?

1. Are you looking forward to the end of the semester?
2. Yes, I'm planning to go skiing in Switzerland.
3. That sounds good. Have a good trip.

4. What do you think of when you hear the word "Switzerland"?
5. I remember my old grandmother, who ate a lot of chocolate.

6. Excuse me, do you know your way around in the library?
7. A bit. How can I help you?
8. I'm interested in modern writers.
9. I'll have to think about that.

10. What are you so annoyed about?
11. My roommate asked me for money again this morning.
12. Will you give it to him?

Almanach

Profile of Switzerland

Area: 41,293 square kilometers; 15,943 square miles
Population: 6.5 million, or 158 people per square kilometer (411 per sq. mi.)
Currency: Swiss franc; 1 sfr. = 100 Rappen or Centimes
Major cities: Berne (*Bern*), capital (pop. 162,000), Zürich (largest city, pop. 420,000), Basel, Geneva (*Genf*), Lausanne

Switzerland has one of the highest per capita incomes in the world as well as one of the highest standards of living. The rivers of the Alps provide inexpensive hydroelectric power. The mountains also attract countless tourists, thus creating Switzerland's main service industry.

Switzerland has not sent its troops into foreign wars since 1515. It adheres to its neutrality even to the extent of staying out of the United Nations and the Common Market. It is, however, a member of several special UN agencies. The second headquarters of the UN are in Geneva which is also the seat of the Red Cross and of the World Council of Churches.

Reiter (*horseman*) aus dem Historischen Museum (Bern)

Lausanne

Weinbau in der Schweiz (der Weinbau = *viniculture*)

Schloßturm (Rapperswil)

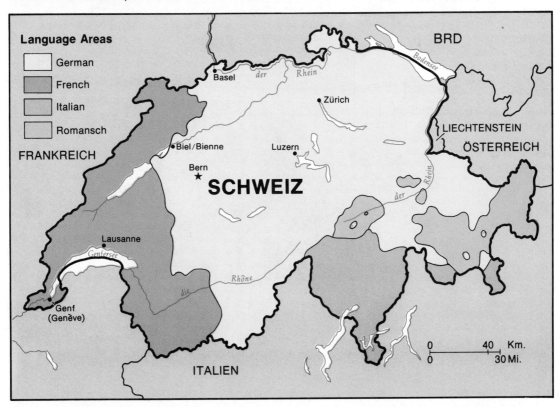

Language Areas

German
French
Italian
Romansch

BRD

Basel
der Rhein
Bodensee

Zürich

LIECHTENSTEIN
ÖSTERREICH

FRANKREICH

Biel/Bienne
Luzern

Bern
SCHWEIZ

der Rhein

Lausanne
Genfersee
die Rhône

Genf
(Genève)

ITALIEN

0   40 Km.
0   30 Mi.

Österreich

Dialoge
An der Rezeption ♦ Zwei
Studentinnen in Wien ♦ Auf
Urlaub in Österreich

Wortschatz 1

Grammatik
1. Present Tense of the General
   Subjunctive
2. More Time Expressions
3. Expanding Your Vocabulary:
   The Suffix **-lang** and the
   Adverbs **montags, dienstags,**
   etc.

Wortschatz 2

Lesestück
Zwei Österreicher stellen sich vor

Vom Lesen zum Sprechen
Wie stellt man sich vor?

Almanach
Profile of Austria

Dialoge

An der Rezeption

TOURIST: Grüß Gott! Hätten Sie noch ein Zimmer frei für heute nacht?

HOTELANGESTELLTER: Wünschen Sie ein Einzelzimmer oder ein Doppelzimmer?

TOURIST: Am liebsten hätte ich ein Einzelzimmer mit Bad.

ANGESTELLTER: Das könnte ich Ihnen erst morgen geben. Im Moment ist nur ein Doppelzimmer mit Dusche frei.

TOURIST: Was würde das denn kosten?

ANGESTELLER: 500 Schilling mit Frühstück.

TOURIST: Dürfte ich mir das Zimmer ansehen?

ANGESTELLTER: Selbstverständlich. Das wäre Zimmer Nummer 14 im ersten Stock.

Zwei Studentinnen in Wien

CLAUDIA: Was machen wir denn heute abend?

ESTHER: Könnten wir nicht nach Grinzing zum Heurigen[1] fahren?

CLAUDIA: Ja, das wäre schön! Laden wir doch Max und Tobias auch ein.

ESTHER: Gute Idee! Wir könnten sie entweder jetzt oder erst nach dem Abendessen abholen.

Auf Urlaub in Österreich

RICHARD: Ursula, hättest du vielleicht noch österreichisches Geld?

URSULA: Nein, warum fragst du?

RICHARD: Weil ich auch keine Schillinge mehr habe.

URSULA: Wenn es nicht so spät wäre, könnten wir noch bei der Bank Geld wechseln.

RICHARD: Das macht nichts, man kann auch an der Hotelkasse Geld wechseln, oder wir zahlen im Restaurant mit Kreditkarte oder Reiseschecks.

WEINGUT   HEURIGER
WELSER
1190 WIEN-HEILIGENSTADT
PROBUSGASSE 12

---

[1] **Heurige** are taverns in the neighborhood of Vienna, each one originally belonging to a vineyard and serving wine (called **Heuriger**) pressed the previous October (**heuer** = "this year"). Grinzing is a suburb of Vienna.

Wortschatz 1

At the Reception Desk

TOURIST: Hello, would you still have a room free for tonight?

HOTEL CLERK: Do you want a single or a double room?

TOURIST: I'd prefer a single room with bath.

HOTEL CLERK: I couldn't give you that until tomorrow. At the moment there is only a double room with shower available.

TOURIST: What would that cost?

HOTEL CLERK: 500 Schillings with breakfast.

TOURIST: May I please have a look at the room?

HOTEL CLERK: Of course. That would be room number 14 on the second floor.

Two Students in Vienna

CLAUDIA: What shall we do tonight?

ESTHER: Couldn't we go to a *Heuriger* in Grinzing?

CLAUDIA: Yes, that would be great. Let's invite Max and Tobias too.

ESTHER: Good idea! We could either pick them up now or after dinner.

On Vacation in Austria

RICHARD: Ursula, would you possibly still have some Austrian money?

URSULA: No, why do you ask?

RICHARD: Because I don't have any Schillings left either.

URSULA: If it weren't so late we could change money at the bank.

RICHARD: That doesn't matter, we can change money here at the hotel cashier or pay with a credit card or traveler's checks in the restaurant.

Verben

ab · holen to pick up, fetch, get

aus · gehen, ging aus, ist ausgegangen to go out

ein · laden (lädt ein), lud ein, hat eingeladen to invite

wechseln to change (money)

wünschen to wish

Sustantive

der/die **Angestellte, -n** employee

der **Scheck, -s** check
der **Reisescheck, -s** traveler's check

der **Schilling, -e** Austrian shilling

der **Stock** floor (of a building)
der erste Stock the second floor
im ersten Stock on the second floor

das **Bad, ⁻er** bath
ein Bad nehmen to take a bath
das **Badezimmer, -** bath room

das **Doppelzimmer, -** double room

das **Einzelzimmer, -** single room

das **Erdgeschoß** first floor, ground floor

das **Frühstück** breakfast

die **Bank, -en** bank

die **Dusche, -n** shower

die **Kasse, -n** cash register; cashier's office

die **Rezeption** (hotel) reception desk

Andere Vokabeln

entweder . . . oder either . . . or

österreichisch Austrian

Nützlicher Ausdruck

Grüß Gott! Hello! (in southern Germany and Austria)

Gegensätze

---
entweder . . . oder ≠ weder . . . noch
either . . . or ≠ neither . . . nor

Neue Kombinationen

A. Replace the words in italics with the cue you will hear.

1. Das könnte ich Ihnen *geben*.
   (sagen, zeigen, erzählen, bringen, kaufen)
2. Am liebsten hätte der Gast *ein Einzelzimmer*.
   (ein Doppelzimmer, ein großes Frühstück, eine Tasse Kaffee, ein Zimmer mit Dusche)
3. Was würde *das kosten*?
   (sie sagen, Herr Lehmann meinen, er denken, deine Mutter antworten)
4. *Könnten* sie bald nach Wien fahren?
   (dürften, sollten, müßten, möchten)
5. Hätten Sie noch *österreichisches Geld*?
   (ein bißchen Zeit, ein Zimmer frei, andere Zeitungen, eine Frage)

B. Respond either positively or negatively to the suggestions you will hear, as in the example. Here are some adjectives you can use:

toll	phantastisch	langweilig
schön	nett	schrecklich
gut	interessant	schlimm

EXAMPLE: Fahren wir doch heute abend nach Grinzing!
        Ja, das wäre schön! *or:* Nein, das wäre langweilig!

1. Gehen wir doch heute abend aus!
2. Laden wir doch Hans ein!
3. Fliegen wir in die Schweiz zum Schilaufen!
4. Gehen wir morgen abend ins Konzert!
5. Besuchen wir heute die alte Kirche!
6. Fahren wir zusammen in die Berge!

Alte Ladenschilder (Salzburg) (das Schild, -er = *sign*)

The Austrian poet Ernst Jandl was born in Vienna in 1925. He has been a *Gymnasium* teacher since 1949. In the following poem, he shows that it is possible to tell a whole story using only one vowel. Reading it aloud will be a good review of the German long and short **o**!

ottos mops°	*mutt*
ottos mops trotzt°	*won't obey*
otto: fort° mops fort	*go away*
ottos mops hopst° fort	*hops*
otto: soso	
otto holt koks°	*coal briquettes*
otto holt obst°	*fruit*
otto horcht°	*listens*
otto: mops mops	
otto hofft	
ottos mops klopft°	*knocks*
otto: komm mops komm	
ottos mops kommt	
ottos mops kotzt°	*pukes*
otto: ogottogott	

Bibliothek in der Hofburg (Wien) (die Hofburg = *Imperial Residence*)

Grammatik

1 ◆ Present Tense of the General Subjunctive[1]

A speaker may have various attitudes toward what he is saying. On the one hand, he can present something as fact. On the other, he can present it as merely hypothetical, conjectural, or as contrary to fact. There are two different sets of verb forms in German and English for these two possibilities, called the *indicative* and the *subjunctive* "moods" (from Latin *modus:* manner, mode, way).

Up to now, you have been using the *indicative* to talk about what is definite, certain, and real:

Barbara **ist** nicht hier.	*Barbara **isn't** here.*
Ich **glaube** das.	*I **believe** that.*

The *subjunctive* is used to talk about hypothetical, uncertain, or unreal situations, and also to make polite statements and requests:

Wenn Barbara nur hier **wäre**!	*If only Barbara **were** here!*
Wenn ich das nicht **glaubte** . . .	*If I **didn't believe** that . . .*

English *present* subjunctive is signalled by what looks like *past-tense* forms or by *would* + a verb[2]:

If they *lived* nearby, we *would visit* them.	(condition contrary to fact)
If only I *had* more time!	(wish contrary to fact)
I *would like* to have a room.	(polite request)

Note that the words *lived* and *had* in the above examples are identical to the past in *form*, but present in *meaning*:

If he *lived* nearby . . .	(right now)
If only I *had* more time!	(right now)

Formation of the Present Subjunctive

The present tense of the general subjunctive in German is also based on past indicative forms.

1. Weak Verbs

The present subjunctive of weak verbs is identical with their simple past indicative:

wenn ich wohn **te**	if I lived	wenn wir wohn **ten**	if we lived
wenn du wohn **test**	if you lived	wenn ihr wohn·**tet**	if you lived
wenn er wohn **te**	if he lived	wenn sie wohn **ten**	if they lived

---

[1] There is also a special subjunctive in German which we will introduce in Chapter 16.
[2] The only separate subjunctive form in English is *were* in *I were* and *he were.*

■ A wish contrary to fact is expressed in German by a **wenn**-clause in the subjunctive (verb last) with an added **nur**:

Wenn er nur näher wohnte!   *If only he lived closer!*

Üben wir!

A. Make wishes contrary to the facts you will hear. Use **nur**, put the verb at the end, and eliminate **nicht**.

EXAMPLE: Er wohnt nicht hier.   *He doesn't live here.*
          Wenn er nur hier wohnte!   *If only he lived here!*

1. Sie kauft das nicht.
2. Er beeilt sich nicht.
3. Das dauert nicht länger.
4. Ich erhole mich nicht.
5. Sie setzen sich nicht.
6. Maria macht die Tür nicht zu.
7. Hans bestellt nicht genug Bier.
8. Sie besuchen mich nicht.
9. Meine Großeltern wohnen nicht bei uns.
10. Inge wechselt ihr Geld nicht.

2. Strong Verbs

The present subjunctive of strong verbs is also based on their past indicative forms, but these forms are changed according to the following three-step procedure:

a. Take the simple past stem of the verb:

   fahren **fuhr-**   gehen **ging-**   laufen **lief-**   sein **war-**

b. Add an umlaut to the stem vowel whenever possible:

   führ-   **ging-**   **lief-**   **wär-**

c. Add the following personal endings:

ich **wär e**	I would be	wir **wär en**	we would be
du **wär est**	you would be	ihr **wär et**	you would be
er, es, sie **wär e**	he, it, she would be	sie, Sie **wär en**	they, you would be

Note the difference between the present subjunctive endings and the past indicative endings of strong verbs:

present subjunctive	*past indicative*
ich ging **e**	ich ging
du ging **est**	du ging **st**
er ging **e**	er ging
wir ging **en**	wir ging **en**
ihr ging **et**	ihr ging **t**
sie ging **en**	sie ging **en**

■ Only the **wir** and the plural **sie** endings are the same.

For the next exercise, review your knowledge of these past stems:

laufen	**lief**	finden	**fand**
scheinen	**schien**	gehen	**ging**
kommen	**kam**	fahren	**fuhr**
anfangen	**fing an**	sein	**war**
gefallen	**gefiel**	schlafen	**schlief**
tun	**tat**	bekommen	**bekam**
aussteigen	**stieg aus**		

Üben wir!

A. Make wishes contrary to the facts you hear. You may substitute pronouns for nouns and names.

EXAMPLE: Meine Gäste gehen nicht nach Hause.
Wenn sie nur nach Hause gingen!

1. Mein Sohn läuft nicht schnell.
2. Die Sonne scheint nicht.
3. Robert kommt nicht um zwölf.
4. Sie geht nicht mit mir spazieren.
5. Ich bin nicht alt genug.
6. Das Kind schläft nicht länger.
7. Wir bekommen kein Doppelzimmer.
8. Laura findet ihre Kreditkarte nicht.
9. Meine Uhr geht nicht.
10. Sie fahren nicht nach Amerika.
11. Er fängt nicht an.
12. Die Wohnung gefällt mir nicht.
13. Das tut sie nicht gern.
14. Hier steigen sie nicht aus.

3. Modal Verbs

To form the present subjunctive of modal verbs, take the past indicative, *including endings*, and add an umlaut to the stem vowel of only those verbs that have an umlaut in their infinitive:

infinitive		*past indicative*	
dürfen	to be allowed	**ich durfte**	I was allowed

		present subjunctive			
ich	**dürfte**	I would be allowed	wir	**dürften**	we would be allowed
du	**dürftest**	you would be allowed	ihr	**dürftet**	you would be allowed
er, es, sie	**dürfte**	he, it, she would be allowed	sie, Sie	**dürften**	they, you would be allowed

past indicative		*present subjunctive*	
ich konnte	I was able to	ich **könnte**	I could, would be able to
ich mochte	I liked	ich **möchte**	I would like to
ich mußte	I had to	ich **müßte**	I would have to

Note that the present subjunctive of **sollen** and **wollen** is *not* umlauted, and so looks just like the past indicative:

		past indicative	present subjunctive
ich	**sollte**	I was supposed to	I ought to
ich	**wollte**	I wanted to	I would want to

Üben wir!

A. Make wishes contrary to the facts you will hear.

> EXAMPLE: Sie kann kein Englisch.
> Wenn sie nur Englisch könnte!

1. Ich kann kein Französisch.
2. Die Gäste müssen nach Hause.
3. Wir dürfen nicht länger bleiben.
4. Du willst nicht nach Grinzing.
5. Ihr könnt nicht mitfahren.
6. Unsere Freunde müssen bald abfahren.
7. Ich darf nicht alles sagen.
8. Sie wollen nicht helfen.

B. Listen to your teacher say each sentence, then say whether it is past indicative or present subjunctive.

1. Durfte er das machen?
2. Dürfte er das machen?
3. Wir könnten ihn heute abholen.
4. Wir konnten ihn heute abholen.
5. Sie müßte das wissen.
6. Sie mußte das wissen.
7. Mochte er das Frühstück?
8. Möchte er das Frühstück?

Now, with open books, repeat each sentence aloud and give the English equivalent.

C. Listen closely to the question your teacher asks. When it is in the past tense, answer with „Ja, gestern . . .". When it is in the subjunctive mood, answer with „Ja, ich glaube . . .".

> EXAMPLE: Durfte er das machen?
> Ja, gestern durfte er das machen.
> Dürfte er das machen?
> Ja, ich glaube, er dürfte das machen.

1. Mußte sie anfangen?
2. Konnten wir die Frage besprechen?
3. Könnten wir allein in die Stadt?
4. Müßte ich dort übernachten?
5. Mochte er das Essen im Hotel?
6. Möchten Sie im Hotel essen?

4. Irregular Verbs: *haben, werden, wissen*

To form the present subjunctive of the irregular verbs **haben, werden,** and **wissen,** take the past indicative, *including endings,* and add an umlaut to the stem vowel:

past indicative		*present subjunctive*	
ich hatte	I had	ich **hätte**	I would have
ich wurde	I became	ich **würde**	I would become
ich wußte	I knew	ich **wüßte**	I would know

Mozarts Geburtshaus
(Salzburg)

A. Make wishes contrary to the facts you will hear.

1. Ich weiß das nicht.
2. Paul hat keine guten Freunde.
3. Du wirst wieder krank.
4. Wir wissen seinen Namen nicht.
5. Ich habe keine Zeit.
6. Wir haben Hunger.
7. Er weiß es nicht.
8. Du hast kein Geld.
9. Ich weiß nicht, wie spät es ist.
10. Ich habe keine Reiseschecks.

5. Present subjunctive with *würde*

Present subjunctive can also be formed by using the present subjunctive of the auxiliary verb **werden** plus an infinitive in final position:

ich **würde kommen**	I would come
du **würdest kommen**	you would come
er, es, sie **würde kommen**	he, it, she would come
wir **würden kommen**	we would come
ihr **würdet kommen**	you would come
sie, Sie **würden kommen**	they, you would come

There is no difference in meaning between between the following clauses:

Wenn er **käme** . . .
Wenn er **kommen würde** . . .   *If he would come . . .*

The **würde** subjunctive replaces the present subjunctive especially in the weak verbs where these look just like the past indicative:

Ich sagte das nicht.
     becomes
Ich würde das nicht sagen.   *I wouldn't say that.*

Spoken German also avoids using the present subjunctive of many strong verbs by replacing it with the **würde** subjunctive (but not in the frequently used verbs **sein, haben, wissen** and the modals):

Wenn du Wein tränkest . . .
     becomes
Wenn du Wein trinken würdest . . .   *If you drank wine . . .*

Üben wir!

A. Substitute the new subjects you will hear.

1. Wenn er nur bald kommen würde!
   (du, ihr, die Kinder, sein Brief)
2. Ich würde lieber hier bleiben.
   (wir, die Arbeiter, Marie, du, Sie, Leo, ihr)
3. Was würden Sie machen?
   (er, du, ihr, ich, die Politiker, wir)
4. Ich würde warten.
   (wir, Paul, die Kinder, Angelika)

Use of the General Subjunctive

1. Conditions Contrary to Fact

If x were true, then y would be true. A dependent **wenn**-clause states the condition contrary to fact:

Wenn wir jetzt in Deutschland wären, . . .	*If we were in Germany now . . .*
Wenn ich mehr Geld hätte, . . .	*If I had more money . . .*

The main clause draws the unreal conclusion:

Wenn wir jetzt in Deutschland wären, würden wir sehr schnell Deutsch lernen.
If we were in Germany now we would learn German very quickly.

Wenn ich mehr Geld hätte, brauchte ich nicht so viel zu arbeiten.
If I had more money I wouldn't need to work so much.

Conditions may begin with either the **wenn**-clause or the conclusion:[1]

Wenn wir in Deutschland wären, würden wir sehr schnell Deutsch lernen.

Wir würden sehr schnell Deutsch lernen, wenn wir in Deutschland wären.

It is important to keep in mind that not all conditions are contrary to fact. When they are not, use the indicative rather than the subjunctive. Notice the different implications:

indicative

Wenn der Junge schon achtzehn **ist, darf** er den Film sehen.	*If the boy is already eighteen he may see the movie.*

(*Implication:* I don't know whether he is eighteen or not. He may be.)

subjunctive

Wenn der Junge schon achtzehn **wäre, dürfte** er den Film sehen.	*If the boy were already eighteen he would be allowed to see the movie.*

(*Implication:* I known he's not eighteen so he may not see the movie.)

`[o–o]` **Üben wir!**

A. *(books open)* Here are the facts. Restate the information, saying what would happen if the facts were otherwise.

> EXAMPLE: Weil es so kalt ist, können wir nicht schwimmen.
> Wenn es nicht so kalt wäre, könnten wir schwimmen.

1. Weil es so weit ist, können wir nicht zu Fuß gehen.
2. Weil ich keine Lust habe, mache ich es nicht.
3. Weil dieses Buch langweilig ist, lesen wir es nicht.

---

[1] In formal written German, the **wenn** is sometimes omitted from the **wenn**-clause. Its verb is then placed at the beginning of the clause. Compare the similar structure in English:
Hätte er das Geld, würde er mehr kaufen.   *Had he the money, he would buy more.*

Fiaker vor der
Petruskirche (Wien) (der
Fiaker = *horse-drawn
cab*)

4. Weil der Dom geschlossen ist, können Sie ihn nicht besuchen.
5. Weil ich keine Zeit habe, kann ich keine Dusche nehmen.
6. Weil sie nicht aus Österreich kommt, sagt sie nicht „Grüß Gott."
7. Weil ich keinen Hunger habe, bestelle ich nichts.
8. Weil sie sich nicht für diesen Film interessiert, geht sie nicht mit.

B. *(books open)* Here are the facts. Restate the information, saying what would happen if the facts were otherwise. Begin with the conclusion clause.

EXAMPLE: Wir kommen zu spät, weil du nicht schneller fährst.
Wir würden nicht zu spät kommen, wenn du schneller fahren würdest.

1. Wir bleiben hier, weil er uns braucht.
2. Ich muß jetzt wechseln, weil ich kein österreichisches Geld habe.
3. Wir gehen spazieren, weil die Sonne scheint.
4. Wir trampen nach Italien, weil wir keinen Wagen haben.
5. Ich lese die Zeitung nicht, weil ich so müde bin.
6. Er kann mir nicht danken, weil er meinen Namen nicht weiß.
7. Wir sehen uns nicht, weil er nicht mehr vorbeikommt.
8. Wir können nicht mit euch essen, weil ihr nicht bei uns übernachtet.

2. Wishes Contrary to Fact

You have already learned how to form sentences like **Wenn sie nur hier wäre!** Another way to express a wish contrary to fact is to use the following expressions:

> Ich wollte, sie wäre hier.
> Ich wünschte, sie wäre hier.

Both clauses are in the subjunctive. This construction *never* uses a clause beginning with **daß.**

Üben wir!

A. You will hear the facts. Wish that they were otherwise. Begin with „Ich wollte, . . ." or „Ich wünschte, . . ."

1. Sie kann mich leider nicht besuchen.
2. Ich habe keine Reiseschecks.
3. Das Schwimmen im See ist verboten.
4. Leider darf er nicht mit mir ausgehen.
5. Leider wohnst du nicht in der Nähe.
6. Ich darf mir das Zimmer nicht ansehen.
7. Es kostet so viel.
8. Hier ist leider kein Zimmer frei.

B. Now use „Ich wollte, . . ." or „Ich wünschte, . . ." to express your own wishes.

> EXAMPLE: Ich wollte, ich dürfte diesen Sommer nach Europa.
> Ich wünschte, es wäre draußen wärmer.

3. Hypothetical Statements and Questions

German uses subjunctive to make hypothetical utterances, where English uses *would, could,* or *ought to.*

Du **solltest** daran denken.	*You **ought to** think of that.*
Könnten wir nach Grinzing fahren?	***Could** we drive to Grinzing?*
Das **wäre** schön.	*That **would be** great.*
Ich **würde** das machen.	*I **would** do that.*
Was **würde** das kosten?	*What **would** that cost?*

Üben wir!

A. Change the statements of fact to hypothetical statements what *would, could,* or *ought to* be the case on an outing in Grinzing. Use present subjunctive with **sein, haben,** and the modals and the **würde**-form with other verbs.

> EXAMPLE: Wir sollen zusammen ein Glas Wein trinken.
> Wir sollten zusammen ein Glas Wein trinken.

1. Wir sollen nach Grinzing fahren.
2. Ich habe den ganzen Nachmittag frei.

3. Du kannst dein Buch mitbringen.
4. Wir müssen erst um fünf wieder nach Hause.
5. Es ist so schön, draußen zu sitzen.
6. Wir haben Zeit, über alles zu reden.
7. Wir trinken Wein und essen Brot and Käse.
8. Wir treffen dort viele Bekannte.

4. Polite Requests

German uses the subjunctive to make polite requests. These are sometimes in the form of questions (**Could** you help me please?) and sometimes in the form of statements (I **would** like a beer.). German adds **gern** to such statements.

Könnten Sie mir helfen?	*Could you help me?*
Würden Sie mir bitte die Koffer tragen?	*Would you please carry my bags?*
Ich **hätte gern** ein Bier.	*I would like a beer.*
Ich **wüßte gern,** wo man das findet.	*I'd like to know where you find that.*

Üben wir!

A. Make these questions more polite by changing them to subjunctive.

> EXAMPLE: Können Sie mir bitte ein Kleid zeigen?
> Könnten Sie mir bitte ein Kleid zeigen?

1. Können Sie mir bitte sagen, wann der Zug nach Berlin abfährt?
2. Haben Sie Zeit, eine Tasse Kaffee mit mir zu trinken?
3. Darf ich mich hier setzen?

Wiltener Pfarrkirche
(Innsbruck) (*parish church
of Wilten, a district of
Innsbruck*)

4. Tragen Sie mir bitte die Koffer? (*use* **würde**)

5. Ist es möglich, eine Zeitung zu kaufen?

6. Können Sie mir meinen Platz zeigen?

B. Make these direct questions more polite by changing them into subjunctive statements with **gern.** Begin with „Ich . . .“

> EXAMPLE: Wissen Sie, wie spät es ist?
> Ich wüßte gern, wie spät es ist.

1. Haben Sie ein Einzelzimmer mit Dusche?

2. Haben Sie einen französischen Rotwein?

3. Wissen Sie, wann das Museum zumacht?

4. Wissen Sie, wo man Karten kaufen kann?

2 ◆ More Time Expressions

When no preposition is involved, time phrases telling when, how long, and how often something happens are in the accusative (see p. 288, accusative for duration). Here are some frequently used ones:

jeden Tag (Morgen, Nachmittag, Abend, Montag, Dienstag, Monat, Sommer, usw.)	every day (morning, afternoon, evening, Monday, Tuesday, month, summer, etc.)
jede Stunde (Woche)	every hour (week)
jedes Jahr (Semester)	every year (semester)

Ich gehe **jeden Tag** spazieren.
Jede Woche besuchen wir unsere Großmutter.

I go for a walk every day.
Every week we visit our grandmother.

den ganzen Tag (Morgen, Nachmittag, Abend, Monat, Sommer, usw.)	the whole day (morning, afternoon, evening, month, summer, etc.)
die ganze Stunde (Woche)	the whole hour (week)
das ganze Jahr (Semester)	the whole year (semester)

Horst war **den ganzen Monat** krank.
Er hat **das ganze Jahr** nicht gearbeitet.

Horst was sick the whole month.
He didn't work for the whole year.

nächsten/letzten Montag (Monat/Sommer, usw.)	next/last Monday (month, summer, etc.)
nächste/letzte Woche	next/last week
nächstes/letztes Jahr (Semester)	next/last year (semester)

Wir treffen uns **nächsten Sommer** in Wien.
Letztes Semester habe ich in Innsbruck studiert.

We're meeting in Vienna next summer.
Last semester I studied in Innsbruck.

A. Use a time expression with **jeder** to tell how often you do things.

> EXAMPLE: Wie oft essen Sie Wurst?
> Ich esse jeden Freitag Wurst.

1. Wie oft putzen Sie sich die Zähne?
2. Wie oft fahren Sie in die Berge?
3. Wie oft besuchen Sie Ihre Großmutter?

B. Use a time expression with **ganz** to tell how long things lasted.

> EXAMPLE: Wie lange haben Sie gelesen?
> Ich habe den ganzen Tag gelesen.

1. Wie lange war Barbara krank?
2. Wie lange waren Sie in Wien?
3. Wie lange sind Sie in München geblieben?
4. Wie lange haben Sie mit Frau Krämer gesprochen?

C. Use a time expression with **nächst-** to tell when things will happen.

> EXAMPLE: Wann kommt Herr Peters zurück?
> Er kommt nächsten Freitag zurück.

1. Wann kommt Barbara zurück?
2. Wann wirst du in Konstanz studieren?
3. Wann triffst du Friedrich?
4. Wann fahrt ihr wieder in die Schweiz?

D. Use a time expression with **letzt-** to tell when things happened.

1. Wann hast du ihn kennengelernt?
2. Wann warst du in Konstanz?
3. Wann sind die Studenten zurückgekommen?
4. Wann hast du deine Freunde eingeladen?

3 ♦ Expanding Your Vocabulary:
The Suffix -*lang* and the Adverbs *montags, dienstags,* etc.

To make the German equivalents of the English adverbial phrases **for days, for hours,** etc., add the suffix **-lang** to the plural of the noun:

stunden**lang**	for hours
tage**lang**	for days
wochen**lang**	for weeks
monate**lang**	for months
jahre**lang**	for years

■ These words are adverbs and are *not* captalized. Also learn the adverbial phrase

eine Zeitlang   for a time, for a while

Sie hat **stundenlang** auf mich gewartet.	*She waited for me for hours.*
Wir haben **eine Zeitlang** in der Schweiz gewohnt.	*We lived for a time in Switzerland.*

Üben wir!

A. Say how long you did things, using an adverb ending in **-lang.**

EXAMPLE: Wie lange haben Sie Französisch gelernt?
Ich habe jahrelang Französisch gelernt.

1. Wie lange haben Sie mit Herrn Braun gesprochen?
2. Wie lange haben Sie im Restaurant gesessen?
3. Wie lange hat er nichts gesagt?
4. Wie lange waren Sie krank?
5. Wie lange hat Brigitte in Wien studiert?
6. Wie lange haben Sie auf mich gewartet?

By adding an **-s** to the names of the days or parts of the day, German forms adverbs showing regular or habitual occurrence.

montags	Mondays, every Monday
dienstags	Tuesdays, every Tuesday
usw.	etc.
morgens	in the morning
nachmittags	in the afternoon
abends	in the evening
nachts	at night

These words are adverbs, *not* nouns, and therefore not capitalized.

Üben wir!

A. Tell when certain things occur.

EXAMPLE: Wann joggen Sie am liebsten?
POSSIBLE RESPONSE: Am liebsten jogge ich morgens.

1. Wann habt ihr die Deutschstunde?
2. Wann putzen Sie sich die Zähne?
3. Wann hören Sie am liebsten Musik?
4. Wann ist das Museum geschlossen?
5. Wann könnten wir uns in der Bibliothek treffen?

Leicht zu merken

analysieren	analy*sie*ren
die **Dynastie, -n**	Dynas*tie*
existieren	exis*tie*ren
der **Humor**	Hu*mor*
die **Ironie**	Iro*nie*
der **Kontakt**	Kon*takt*
kreativ	krea*tiv*
literarisch	lite*rarisch*
die **Melancholie**	Melancho*lie*
der **Patient, -en, -en**	Pati*ent*
philosophieren	philoso*phie*ren
produktiv	produk*tiv*
die **Psychoanalyse**	Psychoana*ly*se
die **Tradition, -en**	Tradi*tion*

Wortschatz 2

Verben

erwarten to expect
sich konzentrieren auf
  (+acc.) to concentrate
  on
schauen auf *(+acc.)* to
  look (at)
statt·finden, fand statt,
  hat stattgefunden to
  take place
tanzen to dance
träumen to dream

Substantive

der **Künstler, -** artist *(m.)*
der **Unterschied, -e**
  difference

das **Klavier, -e** piano
das **Reich, -e** empire;
  realm

die **Gegenwart** present
  (time)
die **Gelegenheit, -en**
  opportunity, chance
die **Hochschule, -en**
  university, institution of
  higher learning
die **Künstlerin, -nen**
  artist *(f.)*
die **Vergangenheit** past
  (time)

Andere Vokabeln

außerdem besides, in
  addition
beide *(pl.)* both
ernst serious
  etwas ernst nehmen to
  take something
  seriously

etwas some, a little;
  somewhat
  Ich kann schon etwas
  Deutsch. I already
  speak a little German.
  Ich bin etwas
  müde. I'm somewhat
  tired.
fleißig industrious, hard-
  working
gemütlich cozy, com-
  fortable; quiet, relaxed
zunächst first (of all), to
  begin with
zwar . . . aber it is
  true . . . but

Nützlicher Ausdruck

eine Zeitlang for a time,
  for a while

Gegensätze

fleißig ≠ **faul**   hard-working ≠ lazy

Meine Ski gehören mir

Zwei Österreicher stellen sich vor

Marie-Therese Werdenberg, Musikstudentin in Salzburg

„Ich heiße Marie-Therese Werdenberg und bin Musik-
studentin. Ich komme aus Wien und könnte freilich° dort   *freilich=natürlich*
bei meinen Eltern wohnen, wenn ich an der Musik-
hochschule in Wien studierte. Aber ich studiere lieber in
5   Salzburg, weil ich mich hier besser auf das Klavierspielen
konzentrieren kann. In Wien gäbe es zwar mehr Konzerte,
in die ich gehen könnte, aber hier ist es ruhiger und ge-
mütlicher. Außerdem finden hier im Sommer die be-
rühmten Festspiele[1] statt, und da habe ich die Gelegenheit,   *musicians*
10   mit vielen Musikern° in Kontakt zu kommen.

Die Gärten von Schloß Mirabell (Salzburg) (das Schloß, Schlösser = *castle*)

[1] The **Salzburger Festspiele,** an annual summer festival of drama and classical
music.

Johann Strauß-Denkmal (Wien)

Ja, was wäre die Musikgeschichte ohne Österreich? Salzburg ist Mozarts Geburtsort,° und Haydn, Schubert, Bruckner, Mahler und Schoenberg sind auch alle in Österreich geboren. Beethoven und Brahms—beide deutsche Komponisten°—haben in Wien ihre wichtigsten Werke geschrieben. Und ohne Johann Strauß würde die Welt wohl keinen Walzer° tanzen.

Aber ich sollte nicht nur über Musik sprechen. In Wien gab es um 1900 ein besonders produktives und faszinierendes° kulturelles Leben. Die literarischen Werke von Hugo von Hofmannsthal und Arthur Schnitzler sind ein Spiegel dieser sehr kreativen Zeit. In der Malerei° arbeiteten Künstler wie Oskar Kokoschka und Gustav Klimt. Um diese Zeit begründete° Sigmund Freud die Psychoanalyse. Ich könnte noch viele Namen nennen, aber dann müßten wir fast den ganzen Tag hier sitzen."

birthplace

composers

waltz

fascinating

painting

founded

Hofburg (Wien)

Dr. Ulrich Kraus, Psychologe° aus Wien

psychologist

„Mein Name ist Kraus, und ich bin Psychologe. Mit meinen Patienten und ihren Problemen habe ich mehr als genug zu tun; erwarten Sie also nicht von mir, daß ich den Durchschnittsösterreicher° analysiere. Ich könnte aber mindestens° versuchen, diesen Menschen—den *homo austriacus*—ein bißchen zu beschreiben."

average Austrian
mindestens=wenigstens

Zunächst etwas Geschichte: ich möchte Sie daran erinnern, daß wir Österreicher auf eine sehr alte und große Tradition zurückschauen. Die Habsburger Dynastie regierte° jahrhundertelang über Deutsche, Ungarn, Tschechen, Polen, Italiener, Serben und eine Zeitlang sogar über

ruled

Mexikaner.[2] Was man vom englischen Weltreich sagt, könnte man auch von Österreich sagen: Die Sonne ging nicht unter° über diesem Reich.

ging . . . unter = *set*

Heute spielt unser kleines Land eine viel bescheidenere° politische Rolle. Aber der Kontrast zwischen Vergangenheit und Gegenwart hat zu unserem Humor und unserer Selbstironie beigetragen.° Manchmal habe ich das Gefühl, wir Österreicher sind unglücklich über unsere verlorene Größe, aber wir sind wenigstens glücklich, daß wir unglücklich sind. Verstehen Sie diese Melancholie, die sich selbst nicht ganz ernst nimmt?

more modest

contributed

Viele Österreicher würden den Unterschied zwischen sich und den Deutschen so ausdrücken:° Die Deutschen sind fleißig, aber die Österreicher gemütlich. Die Wiener Kaffeehäuser könnten nicht existieren, wenn der Österreicher nicht gern studenlang vor seinem Mokka[3] säße und träumte. Er philosophiert gern darüber, wie die Welt sein könnte. Darum nennt man Österreich manchmal das Land des Konjunktivs:° „Alles würde hier besser gehen, wenn wir nur . . .“ oder „Das wäre möglich, wenn . . .“

express

subjunctive

Schloß Belvedere (Wien), nach einem alten Stich, zirka 1850 (der Stich, -e = *engraving*)

[2] The Habsburgs ruled the Austrian Empire from 1278 to 1918. The empire included Germans, Hungarians, Czechs, Poles, Italians and Serbs. In 1864 Archduke Maximilian, brother of the Austrian emperor, was made Emperor of Mexico. He was executed in 1867 by republican troops.
[3] A strong, aromatic coffee served in demitasse cups, named after a city in Arabia. The drink was introduced into Vienna during the Turkish siege of the city in 1683. Viennese cafés serve dozens of different styles of coffee, each with its own name.

Fragen zum Lesestück

1. Was studiert Marie-Therese Werdenberg in Salzburg?
2. Warum studiert sie lieber in Salzburg als in Wien?
3. Was könnte sie öfter machen, wenn sie in Wien wohnte?
4. Nennen Sie einen berühmten Mann, der in Salzburg geboren ist.
5. Kennen Sie andere berühmte Namen aus der Musikgeschichte Österreichs?
6. Warum war Wien um 1900 besonders interessant?
7. Erzählen Sie etwas von der Geschichte Österreichs.
8. Was ist der größte Unterschied zwischen Vergangenheit und Gegenwart für die Österreicher?
9. Welche Unterschiede findet Dr. Kraus zwischen den Deutschen und Österreichern?
10. Warum nennt man Österreich manchmal das Land des Konjunktivs?

Vom Lesen zum Sprechen

Wie stellt man sich vor?

You already know that the verb **vorstellen** means "to imagine" when used with a dative reflexive pronoun:

Ich kann **mir** das gut vorstellen.	*I can well imagine that.*
Stell **dir** mal vor!	*Just imagine!*

Vorstellen also means "to introduce" and requires an *accusative* reflexive if one is introducing oneself:

Darf ich **mich** vorstellen?	*May I introduce myself?*
Ich möchte Ihnen meine Frau vorstellen.	*I would like to introduce my wife to you.*

As you have learned, German students use the **du**-form with each other. Older Germans, however, use the **Sie**-form. When meeting a German adult who is not a student, you should use the **Sie**-form unless the German offers the **du**-form.

Here is how two German businessmen might introduce themselves to each other. First names are often avoided altogether.

—Darf ich mich vorstellen? Ich heiße Kindler.	*May I introduce myself? I'm Mr. (Mrs. / Ms.) Kindler.*
—Mein Name is Wegener. Guten Tag, Herr (Frau) Kindler.	*I'm Mr. Wegener. How do you do, Mr. Kindler.*

(They shake hands)

—Es freut mich, Sie kennenzulernen.	*Pleased to meet you.*
or:	
—Nett, Sie kennenzulernen.	*Nice to meet you.*
—Angenehm.	*A pleasure.*

Pretend that you are all business people at a convention. Introduce yourselves to each other. Don't forget to shake hands! Germans shake hands both when they meet and when they part.

Mündliche Übungen

A. Persönliche Fragen

1. Würden Sie lieber in Jugendherbergen oder in Hotels übernachten, wenn Sie nach Österreich reisten? Warum?
2. Was würden Sie machen, wenn das Hotel kein Zimmer frei hätte?
3. Wäre Ihnen 500 Schilling zu teuer für ein Einzelzimmer ohne Bad?
4. Sollte man sich ein Zimmer ansehen, bevor man es nimmt? Warum?
5. Wohin gehen Sie, wenn Sie eine Tasse Kaffee trinken wollen?
6. Wo würden Sie gern Ihren Urlaub verbringen?
7. Haben Sie je Geld wechseln müssen? Wo war das?
8. Zahlen Sie lieber mit Kreditkarte oder Reisescheck?

B. Work in pairs. Your teacher will cue a situation with an infinitive phrase. Ask your neighbor what he or she would do in that situation. Keep asking and see how far you can go, then reverse roles for the next situation.

> EXAMPLE: Teacher: (krank sein)
> Student A: Was würdest du tun, wenn du krank wärest?
> Student B: Ich würde zunächst nach Hause gehen.
> Student A: Und dann?
> Student B: Dann würde ich ins Bett gehen.

1. reich sein
2. in Europa sein
3. kein Student sein
4. wenig Geld haben

5. viel Zeit haben
6. jetzt Ferien haben
7. Hunger haben
8. Politiker sein

C. *Gruppenarbeit.* Discuss the following topics in groups. Use the questions below to guide you. Use subjunctive whenever possible.

1. Sie reisen nächstes Jahr mit einer Studentengruppe nach Österreich. Sie können sich schon ein bißchen darauf vorbereiten.
   a. Was sollte man mitbringen?
   b. Was für Bücher könnte man über Österreich lesen?
   c. Was sollte man dort sehen?
   d. Was wäre das Wichtigste für Sie bei dieser Reise?
2. Sprechen Sie über Berufe, für die Sie sich interessieren würden, z.B. Journalist, Lehrer, Arzt, Politiker, Psychologe.
   a. Wie könnte man sich am besten auf diesen Beruf vorbereiten?
   b. Müßte man an einer Hochschule studieren, um in diesem Beruf zu arbeiten?
   c. Wo könnte man nachher Arbeit finden?
   d. Was wäre das Schönste an diesem Beruf?

D. *Rollenspiel.* Read the description of each situation, then act it out with a partner, using the subjunctive whenever possible to be polite.

1. Kellner und Gast im Restaurant
   The waiter asks what the customer would like to order. The customer asks if they have various things and finally just orders a glass of beer.

2. Hotelangestellter und Tourist
   A tourist arrives at the hotel and inquires about the rooms available. The clerk asks what kind of room the tourist needs. The tourist is not alone but has the family waiting in the car.

3. Psychologin und Patientin
   The psychologist asks her patient if they shouldn't get started. She says yes, but first she would like to ask a question. The psychologist asks what kind of question that would be. The patient asks if they would have the time to have a cup of coffee together. The psychologist says that she's sorry, but she can't do that. When she (the patient) is well again—perhaps in a couple of years—maybe they could go eat together.

Schriftliche Übungen

E. Provide the word or phrase cued in English.

(*Many years ago*), (*when*) noch relativ wenige Touristen nach Österreich kamen, hat man eine Anekdote über eine reiche Amerikanerin erzählt, die (*one month*) in den Bergen verbrachte. Sie wohnte in einem gemütlichen Hotel in einem kleinen Dorf, wo die Menschen sie sehr interessant fanden. (*Each morning*), (*when*) sie Frühstück aß, bestellte sie nur wenig zu essen: ein weich gekochtes Ei [soft-boiled egg] und eine Tasse Kaffee. (*whenever*) das Wetter gut war, verbrachte sie (*the whole day*) draußen, und aß Brot und Käse aus ihrem Rucksack, (*when*) sie Hunger hatte. (*When*) die Dame endlich wieder nach Hause wollte, sagte sie dem Wirt [innkeeper] (*on Sunday*), sie würde (*day after tomorrow*) abfahren. (*On Tuesday*) bestellte sie nach dem Frühstück die Rechnung [bill]. Zunächst las sie die Rechnung und sagte (*for a while*) nichts. Darauf stand „300 Schillinge für 28 Eier". Es stimmte, sie hatte (*for weeks every morning*) ein weiches Ei gegessen, aber sie konnte sich nicht erinnern, (*when*) sie je in ihrem Leben so teure Eier gegessen hatte. Sie ließ sofort den Wirt kommen und bat ihn um eine Erklärung. „(*When*) ich (*every morning*) mein Ei bestellte," sagte sie, „wußte ich nicht, daß sie bei Ihnen so selten [rare] sind. Der Wirt antwortete: „Ja, wissen Sie, gnädige Frau [Madame], die Eier sind bei uns nicht so selten, aber *Amerikanerinnen* sehr." Sie lachte, bezahlte die Rechnung und sagte, sie würde (*next year*) wiederkommen. „Hoffentlich sind (*then*) Amerikanerinnen (*no longer*) so selten."

F. You will read the facts in the indicative. Write conditional sentences about what would be the case if they were not true. Begin with the **wenn**-clause.

> EXAMPLE: Ich wohne leider nicht in Wien. Ich kann keinen guten Kaffee finden.
> Wenn ich in Wien wohnte, könnte ich guten Kaffee finden.

1. Das Konzert fängt jetzt an. Ich kann mein Bier nicht trinken.
2. Harald Petersen kommt leider nicht aus Österreich. Er hat nicht viel Selbstironie.
3. Die Musik gefällt mir. Ich kaufe mir eine Karte fürs Konzert.
4. Meine Freundin kommt heute an. Ich muß sie abholen.
5. Ich habe keinen Hunger. Ich bestelle mir nichts.
6. Fritz geht nicht gern tanzen. Er kommt heute abend nicht mit.
7. Ich habe noch österreichisches Geld. Wir brauchen kein Geld zu wechseln.
8. Regina fühlt sich schlecht. Sie ißt heute nichts.

Now write each sentence again beginning with the conclusion:

> EXAMPLE: Ich wohne nicht in Wien. Ich kann keinen guten Kaffee finden.
> Ich könnte guten Kaffee finden, wenn ich in Wien wohnte.

G. Stellen Sie sich vor, Sie könnten eine Woche lang die Welt regieren. Was würden Sie für die Völker der Erde tun? Was würden Sie von den Menschen verlangen? Schreiben Sie eine Seite darüber.

H. Was würden Sie sich wünschen, wenn Sie drei Wünsche (*wishes*) frei hätten? Warum?

> EXAMPLE: Ich würde mir einen Porsche wünschen, weil ich gern schneller fahren möchte.
> *Oder*: Ich würde mir eine Weltreise wünschen, denn ich möchte die Welt besser kennenlernen.

I. Wie sagt man das auf deutsch?

1. Would you like to go dancing with us tomorrow night?
2. That would be great, but unfortunately I have broken my leg.
3. What a pity! You could come along anyway.
4. My brother, whom you haven't seen for years, will be there.

5. I haven't heard anything from Max for weeks.
6. It would be nice to send him a card. Could you please tell me where he lives.
7. If I knew that, I would write a letter to him myself.

8. Why haven't you written your paper yet? Can't you concentrate on it?
9. No, my roommate always disturbs me at night with her loud music.
10. If you didn't have a piano in your room, you wouldn't have that problem.

Almanach

Profile of Austria

Area: 83,855 square kilometers; 32,376 square miles
Population: 7.5 million or 88 people per square kilometer (233 per sq. mi.)
Austria consists of nine states (Bundesländer).
Currency: Schilling. 1 Schilling = 100 Groschen
Major cities: Vienna (*Wien*), capital (pop. 1,500,000); Graz, Linz, Salzburg, Innsbruck.

Austria is officially neutral though its economic ties are primarily with the West. Aside from basic industries such as machinery, iron and steel, textiles and chemicals, tourism provides an important source of income.

Austria plays a vital role in the United Nations and Vienna has become a center of communication between East and West. With the opening of the "UN-City" in 1979, Vienna became the third seat of the UN. It is also the headquarters for OPEC (Organization of Petroleum Exporting Countries).

Die Gärten von Schloß Schönbrunn (Wien)

TIROL

SALZBURG

OBERÖSTERREICH

NIEDERÖSTERREICH

VORARLBERG

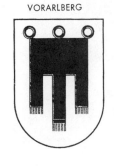

KÄRNTEN

STEIERMARK

BURGENLAND

WIEN

Gastarbeiter in Deutschland

Dialoge
Wo liegt die Heimat? ◆ Die verpaßte Geburtstagsfeier ◆ Vor der Post

Wortschatz 1

Grammatik
1. Past Tense of the General Subjunctive
   Formation ◆ Use
2. Passive Voice
   Formation ◆ Use
3. The Present Participle
   Formation ◆ Use
4. Equivalents for English "think"
5. Directional Prefixes: **hin-** and **her-**
6. Expanding Your Vocabulary
   Leicht zu merken

Wortschatz 2

Lesestück
Leben im gelobten Land

Vom Lesen zum Sprechen
Wohnen und Wohnungen

Almanach
Foreign Workers in Germany

Dialoge

Wo liegt die Heimat?

Carlotta, Schülerin aus einer Gastarbeiterfamilie, wird für die Schülerzeitung interviewt.

INTERVIEWER: Es überrascht mich, daß du als Ausländerin so perfekt Deutsch sprichst.

CARLOTTA: Kein Wunder. Ich bin schließlich in der BRD geboren. Ich werde fast überall für eine Deutsche gehalten.

INTERVIEWER: Aber deine Familie ist doch aus Spanien, nicht wahr? Wo fühlst du dich eigentlich zu Hause?

CARLOTTA: Ich denke oft darüber nach. Deutschland kenne ich zwar besser als Spanien, aber manchmal habe ich das Gefühl, daß ich nicht von allen hier akzeptiert werde.

Die verpaßte Geburtstagsfeier

LILLI: Warum warst du gestern nicht bei Sonjas Geburtstagsfeier? Bist du nicht eingeladen worden?

FELIX: Doch, und ich wünschte, ich wäre dabei gewesen. Aber ich mußte arbeiten.

LILLI: Du hättest wenigstens anrufen können, um ihr zu gratulieren. Sonja war ziemlich enttäuscht.

FELIX: Ja, du hast recht, ich hätte daran denken sollen. Aber wenigstens habe ich ihr heute ein Geburtstagsgeschenk mitgebracht.

Vor der Post

FRAU KÖNIG: Hier ist die Hauptpost. Du könntest deinen Brief dort in den Briefkasten einwerfen.

HERR KÖNIG: Nein, ich glaube, ich habe nicht genug Briefmarken darauf. Ich sollte eigentlich hineingehen, um ihn wiegen zu lassen.

FRAU KÖNIG: Zeig mal her. . . . Aber sind Hartmanns nicht neulich umgezogen? Das ist doch ihre alte Adresse!

HERR KÖNIG: Richtig! Das hätte ich nicht vergessen sollen.

DEUTSCHE BUNDESPOST

Where is Your Home?

Carlotta, school pupil from a family of foreign workers, is being interviewed for the school newspaper.

INTERVIEWER: I'm surprised that you, as a foreigner, speak such perfect German.

CARLOTTA: No wonder! After all, I was born in the FRG. I'm taken for a German almost everywhere.

INTERVIEWER: But your family is from Spain, aren't they? Where do you actually feel at home?

CARLOTTA: I often think about that. On the one hand, I know Germany better than Spain, but sometimes I have the feeling that I'm not accepted by everybody here.

The Missed Birthday Party

LILLI: Why weren't you at Sonja's birthday party yesterday? Weren't you invited?

FELIX: Yes I was, and I wish I had been there, but I had to work.

LILLI: You could at least have phoned to congratulate her. Sonja was pretty disappointed.

FELIX: You're right. I should have thought of it. At least I've brought her a birthday present today.

In Front of the Post Office

MRS. KÖNIG: Here's the Main Post Office. You could put your letter into the mailbox there.

MR. KÖNIG: No, I don't think I have enough stamps on it. I really ought to go inside to have it weighed.

MRS. KÖNIG: Let me see . . . . But didn't the Hartmanns move recently? That's their old address.

MR. KÖNIG: Right! I shouldn't have forgotten that.

akzeptieren to accept
enttäuschen to disappoint
feiern to celebrate
gratulieren (+ *dat.*) to congratulate
Ich gratuliere Ihnen zum Geburtstag! Happy birthday!
halten (hält), hielt, hat gehalten für to take for, regard as, think X is
Ich halte es für möglich. I think it's possible.
interviewen, hat interviewt to interview
nach·denken, dachte nach, hat nachgedacht über (+ *acc.*) to think about; ponder
überraschen to surprise
verpassen to miss (an event or opportunity)
Ich habe meinen Zug verpaßt! I missed my train!
werfen (wirft), warf, hat geworfen to throw
ein·werfen to mail (*a letter*)
wiegen, wog, hat gewogen to weigh (*trans. and intrans.*)
ziehen, zog, hat gezogen to pull
ziehen, zog, ist gezogen to move (to a new town or area: *must include directional*)
Er ist letztes Jahr nach München gezogen. He moved to Munich last year.
um·ziehen to move, change residence

der **Ausländer, -** foreigner (*m.*)
der **Briefkasten, ⸚** mailbox
der **Gastarbeiter, -** foreign worker, guest worker (*m.*)

(das) **Spanien** Spain

die **Adresse, -n** address
die **Ausländerin, -nen** foreigner (*f.*)
die **Briefmarke, -n** postage stamp
die **Feier, -n** celebration, party
die **Gastarbeiterin, -nen** foreign worker, guest worker (*f.*)
die **Post** post office; postal service; mail

Andere Vokabeln

hinein- (*prefix*) in, into (see below, p. 452)
perfekt perfect
schließlich after all, finally

Nützliche Ausdrücke

Kein Wunder! No wonder!
Zeig mal her. Let's see. Show it to me.

Neue Kombinationen

🔲 **A.** Replace the italicized words with the ones you will hear.

1. Ich werde oft für *eine Deutsche* gehalten.
   (eine Amerikanerin, einen Amerikaner, eine Studentin, einen Studenten, einen Deutschen)
2. Hoffentlich werde ich überall *akzeptiert*.
   (verstanden, gebraucht, erwartet, gesehen)
3. Ich hätte das nicht *vergessen* sollen.
   (machen, sagen, mitbringen, erlauben, stehlen, verlieren)
4. Ich wäre gern *dabei gewesen*.
   (zu Hause geblieben, ins Ausland gereist, schneller gefahren, mitgegangen, an der Ecke ausgestiegen)
5. Wo fühlst du dich eigentlich *zu Hause?*
   (frei, am sichersten, am glücklichsten)

🔲 **B.** Say what you're thinking about, as in the example.

> EXAMPLE: Worüber denken Sie nach? (diesen Brief)
> Ich denke über diesen Brief nach.

1. letztes Wochenende
2. meine Familie
3. dein Geburtstagsgeschenk
4. meine Hausaufgaben
5. mein Referat
6. die Vergangenheit

Now invent your own responses.

C. Using the cue from your teacher, ask for your neighbors' opinions. They reply that they think the opposite is true. Use **halten für** + an adjective.

> EXAMPLE: Teacher: Diese Diskussion ist langweilig.
> Student A: Hältst du diese Diskussion für langweilig?
> Student B: Nein, ich halte sie für interessant.

1. Die Idee ist gut.
2. Der Roman ist schwer.
3. Robert ist fleißig.
4. Das Wetter ist kalt.
5. Die Antwort ist richtig.
6. Diese Gegend ist häßlich.
7. Diese Menschen sind glücklich.
8. Dieser Politiker ist unsympathisch.

Übung zur Aussprache

The Turkish writer and poet Aras Ören was born in Istanbul in 1939. Since 1969 he has lived in West Berlin. "Emines Los" (Emine's Destiny) is part of a long verse narrative, "Die Fremde ist auch ein Haus" (Abroad is Also a House, 1980, translated by Gisela Kraft), about a Turkish **Gastarbeiter** family in West Berlin. Here fifteen-year-old Emine ponders her probable future.

Emines Los

Bald tagt° es,	*dawns*
in Berlin wird es früh hell	
zu dieser Jahreszeit, etwa um° drei Uhr.	**etwa um** = *about*
Was war los mit Emine?	
Daß sie eben° noch fünfzehn und fast schon	*just*
sechzehn ist? Ach, ihr habt keine Ahnung°	*idea*
(ihr gleichaltrigen° Deutschen in der Schule),	*of the same age*
die ihr° mit eurem Geküsse° angebt,°	*you who / necking / show off*
euch mal kindisch benehmt, mal hemmungslos,	
mal neugierig, mal mit allen Wassern gewaschen.°	**euch . . . gewaschen** = *sometimes act childish, sometimes uninhibited, sometimes inquisitive, sometimes worldly wise.*
In mir wuchs ein Berg	
zwischen Haus und Straße.	
Auf der Straße war das Haus weit fort,°	*away*
im Haus war die Straße weit fort.	
Das Haus, das sind drei Zimmer	
aus vier Wänden.	
Im Kissen°, das ich sticken° mußte,	*cushion / embroider*
steckt meine Geduld, mein Traum, meine Hoffnung.°	**steckt . . . Hoffnung** = *my patience is contained, my dream, my hope*
Wenn ich groß bin, kann ich nicht Ärztin werden,	
nicht Beamtin, nur ein Kissen,	
und auf dem Kissen eine Stickerei,°	*embroidery*
während ich in den Gebäuden der Fremde°	*of the foreign country*
Fußböden wische° wie meine Mutter.	**Fußböden wische** = *mop floors*

Grammatik

1 ♦ Past Tense of the General Subjunctive

Formation

1. The German subjunctive, unlike the indicative, has only one past tense. It consists of the present tense of the subjunctive of the auxiliary verb (a form of **hätten** or **wären**) plus the past participle:

ich	**hätte**	gewartet	I would have waited
du	**hättest**	gewartet	you would have waited
er, es, sie	**hätte**	gewartet	he, it, she would have waited
wir	**hätten**	gewartet	we would have waited
ihr	**hättet**	gewartet	you would have waited
sie, Sie	**hätten**	gewartet	they, you would have waited
ich	**wäre**	gekommen	I would have come
du	**wärest**	gekommen	you would have come
er, es, sie	**wäre**	gekommen	he, it, she would have come
wir	**wären**	gekommen	we would have come
ihr	**wäret**	gekommen	you would have come
sie, Sie	**wären**	gekommen	they, you would have come

■English uses the word **would** in both the present and past subjunctive. German uses **würden** *only* in the present subjunctive, *not* in the past:

Present: Er **würde** mitkommen.   He *would* come along.
Past: Er **wäre** mitgekommen.   He *would have* come along.

Üben wir!

[cassette icon]

A. Substitute the new subjects you will hear.

1. Er hätte nichts gesagt.
   (ich, wir, Herr Schaf, du, ihr)
2. Alles wäre anders geworden.
   (ich, die Gesellschaft, alle Menschen, du, wir)
3. Wenn die Vorlesung nur nicht so langweilig gewesen wäre!
   (die Diskussion, der Film, die Ferien, das Semester)
4. Dann hätte ich nichts verpaßt.
   (wir, ihr, die Studentèn, du)

B. Change the sentences you will hear from perfect indicative to past subjunctive, then give the English equivalent.

1. Hans hat sie geliebt.
2. Ich bin Schi gelaufen.
3. Wir haben gerne geholfen.
4. Diese Studenten haben das gewußt.
5. Ihr habt es früher gesehen.
6. Du bist nicht lange geblieben.
7. Die Feier hat nicht stattgefunden.
8. Der Chef ist verrückt geworden.

C. Give German equivalents for these sentences.

1. I would have hated it.
2. Bernd wouldn't have waited.
3. You would have known that, Prof. Berger.
4. You probably would not have stayed, Frank.
5. We wouldn't have bothered you.
6. That would have cost too much.
7. You wouldn't have been happy, children.
8. They would have showed us the house.
9. I would have stood there for hours.
10. That would have been excellent.

2. Modal verbs form their past subjunctive with **hätten** plus a double infinitive:

Ich **hätte** 30 Mark **wechseln sollen.**	*I should have changed 30 marks.*
Das **hättest** du nicht **wissen können.**	*You couldn't have known that.*

English equivalents begin with *would have, could have,* or *should have:*

Ich hätte kommen dürfen.	*I **would have** been allowed to come.*
Ich hätte kommen können.	*I **could have** come.*
Ich hätte kommen müssen.	*I **would have** had to come.*
Ich hätte kommen sollen.	*I **should have** come.*
Ich hätte kommen wollen.	*I **would have** wanted to come.*

In subordinate clauses containing a double infinitive, the inflected auxiliary must come *before* the double infinitive. This is the only case in German where the inflected verb is not in final position in a subordinate clause:

Er sagte mir, daß ich 30 Mark **hätte** wechseln sollen.

Ich fragte, wie ich das **hätte** wissen sollen.

A. Substitute the new subjects you will hear.

1. Ich hätte 30 Mark wechseln sollen.
   (du, Markus, wir, ihr, die Studenten)
2. Wie hätten wir die Antwort wissen können?
   (die Studenten, du, ich, Mechthild, ihr)
3. Ihr hättet fragen sollen.
   (ich, wir, die Studenten, Markus, du)
4. Du hättest nicht aufhören sollen.
   (Markus, die Arbeiter, Hanna, wir, ihr, ich)

B. Tell your friends what they should have done.

> EXAMPLE: Wir haben die Reise nicht gemacht.
> Ihr hättet die Reise machen sollen!

1. Wir sind nicht in die Schweiz gefahren.
2. Wir sind nicht in der Stadt geblieben.
3. Wir haben nicht gefragt.
4. Wir haben keine Pause gemacht.

C. Now give German equivalents for the sentences you will hear.

1. We could have flown.
2. We would have had to buy tickets.
3. Frank should have come along.
4. He wouldn't have wanted to come along.
5. He wouldn't have been allowed to come along.

Use

Past subjunctive is used to represent hypothetical, uncertain or contrary-to-fact situations in the past and to make unfulfillable wishes about the past:

Indicative Fact	*Subjunctive Condition Contrary to Fact*
Er **hatte** keine Zeit. Er **ist** nicht **mitgekommen.**	Wenn er Zeit **gehabt hätte, wäre** er **mitgekommen.** *If he had had time, he would have come along.*

Indicative Fact	*Subjunctive Unfulfillable Wish*
Ich **habe** das leider nicht **gesagt.**	Wenn ich das nur **gesagt hätte!** *If only I had said that!*

Indicative Fact	*Subjunctive Hypothetical Statement*
Ich **wußte** das nicht.	Ich **hätte** es aber **wissen sollen.** *But I should have known it.*

A. Here are the facts. Make wishes contrary to the facts in the past subjunctive.

> EXAMPLE: Ich bin nicht ausgestiegen.
> Ich wünschte, ich wäre ausgestiegen.

1. Ich habe die interessante Frau nicht kennengelernt.
2. Ich habe mich nicht vorgestellt.
3. Zu viele Leute waren da.
4. Ich hatte nicht genug Zeit.

Now express your wish using **Wenn...nur...**

> EXAMPLE: Horst war krank.
> Wenn er nur nicht krank gewesen wäre!

5. Der Professor sprach schnell.
6. Ich habe ihn nicht verstanden.
7. Mein Zimmer war nicht aufgeräumt.
8. Ich habe das Buch nicht gelesen.

B. Your friends all had an interesting summer. Say that you would have liked to do what they did. Use **gern** and past subjunctive.

> EXAMPLE: Klaus ist nach Frankfurt gefahren.
> Ich wäre auch gern nach Frankfurt gefahren.

1. Jutta hat in England gearbeitet.
2. Georg ist in die DDR gereist.
3. Max hat eine Bergtour gemacht.
4. Hannes ging jeden Tag schwimmen.
5. Thomas ist oft ins Theater gegangen.

C. Here are the facts. Make a hypothetical statement about what *would*, *could*, or *should* have happened, using the modal verb you will hear.

> EXAMPLE: Er hat keinen Brief geschrieben (sollen)
> Er hätte einen Brief schreiben sollen.

1. Er hat keinen Wein gekauft. (sollen)
2. Wir haben kein Bier bestellt. (können)
3. Sie haben nicht viel verdient. (müssen)
4. Sie hat sich nicht gesetzt. (dürfen)
5. Er hat sich nicht angezogen. (sollen)

D. (books open) Here are the facts. Make conditions contrary to the facts in the past subjunctive.

> EXAMPLE: Er ist nicht mitgekommen. Er hatte keine Zeit.
> Er wäre mitgekommen, wenn er Zeit gehabt hätte.

1. Ich habe keinen Mantel getragen. Es war nicht kalt.
2. Wir haben kein Geld gewechselt. Die Bank war geschlossen.
3. Ich habe sie nicht kennengelernt. Sie wohnte nicht im ersten Stock.
4. Ich habe den Brief nicht eingeworfen. Es gab keinen Briefkasten in der Nähe.
5. Sie hat mich nicht interviewt. Ich war nicht berühmt.

2 ◆ Passive Voice

Compare the following sentences:

Die meisten Studenten lesen diese Zeitung.

Most students read this newspaper.

Diese Zeitung wird von den meisten Studenten gelesen.

This newspaper is read by most students.

Both sentences say essentially the same thing, but the first is in the *active voice* while the second is in the *passive voice*.

Pakistaner, Italiener, Deutscher und Spanier in einem Aluminiumwerk (Lüdenscheid, BRD)

In active sentences, the grammatical subject and the agent or the performer of the action are the same:

Die Studenten lesen.   *The students read.*

In passive sentences, the grammatical subject is the object of the action:

Die Zeitung wird gelesen.   *The newspaper is read.*

A passive sentence is the transformation of an active sentence with a transitive verb. Note how the direct object of the active sentence becomes the subject of the passive sentence.

agent   *direct object*
Active: **Die meisten Studenten** lesen **diese Zeitung.**

subject   *agent*
Passive: **Diese Zeitung** wird **von den meisten Studenten** gelesen.

Formation

1. The passive voice in English consists of the verb *to be* plus a past participle:

Active	*Passive*	
	Aux.	*Part.*
He sees.	He *is*	*seen.*
We never do that.	That *is* never *done.*

The German passive uses the auxiliary **werden** plus a past participle located at the end of the clause:

Active	*Passive*	
	Aux.	*Part.*
Er sieht.	Er **wird**	**gesehen.**
Wir machen das nie.	Das **wird** nie **gemacht.**

Passive Voice

passive infinitive		**gesehen**	werden	to be	*seen.*
present	Er wird	**gesehen.**		He is	*seen.*
past	Er wurde	**gesehen.**		He was	*seen.*
future	Er wird	**gesehen**	werden.	He will be	*seen.*
perfect	Er ist	**gesehen**	**worden.**	He has been	*seen.*
			or	He was	*seen.*
past perfect	Er war	**gesehen**	**worden.**	He had been	*seen.*

▪ The normal past participle of **werden, geworden,** is contracted to **worden** in the perfect tenses of the passive.
▪ Remember the auxiliary for **werden,** is **sein** (er **ist** gesehen worden).
▪ In both English and German, it is the auxiliary that is conjugated (**werden**/*be*). The past participle is invariable through all tenses (**gesehen**/*seen*).

Be careful not to confuse the three uses of **werden:**

> **werden** as main verb = become; get
> Sie **wird** alt. _She's **getting** old._

> **werden** + infinitive = future tense
> Sie **wird** sehen. _She **will** see._

> **werden** + past participle = passive voice
> Sie **wird** gesehen. _She **is** seen._

Üben wir!

A. Substitute the new subjects you will hear.

1. Hanna wird eingeladen. (ich, wir, du, die neuen Schüler, ihr, Herr Braun)
2. Seine Ideen wurden kritisiert. (wir, der Staat, ihr, ich, du, seine Werke)
3. Sind Sie überall akzeptiert worden? (du, der neue Chef, ihr, ich, wir)
4. Ich wurde nicht verstanden. (wir, ihr, die Gastarbeiter, du, dieser Mensch)

B. Say that these things will be done immediately.

> EXAMPLE: Können Sie bitte die Uhr reparieren?
> Ja, die Uhr wird sofort repariert!

1. Können Sie bitte den Brief schreiben?
2. Können Sie bitte die Schuhe putzen?
3. Können Sie bitte Frau Meyer anrufen?
4. Können Sie bitte das Zimmer aufräumen?
5. Können Sie bitte den Brief einwerfen?

C. Change the sentences you will hear from active to passive, being careful to use the same tense as in the active sentence.

(simple past tense)
1. Man schrieb damals viele Briefe.
2. Man las diesen Roman überall.
3. Man zeigte den Film in Europa.
4. Man verkaufte billige Lebensmittel.

(future tense)
5. Was wird man sagen?
6. Man wird das Plakat nicht sehen.
7. Man wird neue Wohnungen bauen.
8. Man wird das Zimmer aufräumen.

(perfect tense)
9. Man hat die alte Wohnung verkauft.
10. Man hat Lebensmittel eingekauft.
11. Man hat den Brief eingeworfen.
12. Man hat Onkel Kurt eingeladen.

2. Modal verbs are followed by a passive infinitive.

Passive with a Modal Verb

present	Das muß	**getan werden.**	That has	*to be done.*
past	Das mußte	**getan werden.**	That had	*to be done.*
future	Das wird	**getan werden** müssen.	That will have	*to be done.*
perfect	Das hat	**getan werden** müssen.	That had	*to be done.*
past perfect	Das hatte	**getan werden** müssen.	That had had	*to be done.*

Remember that the modals take the double infinitive construction in the perfect tenses. In the passive voice, this double infinitive includes the *passive* infinitive. Compare:

double infinitive

Sie hat gestern	**arbeiten** müssen.	*She had to work yesterday.*
Es hat gestern	**getan werden** müssen.	*It had to be done yesterday.*

■ The auxiliary for all modals is **haben.** Note the difference from the passive without a modal:

Das **ist** getan worden.	*That has been done.*
Das **hat** getan werden müssen.	*That had to be done.*

Üben wir!

A. Substitute the new subjects you will hear.

1. Die Schülerin soll interviewt werden. (die Schüler, der Gastarbeiter, ich, wir, mein Freund)

2. Mein Auto mußte verkauft werden. (unsere Wohnung, alle seine Bücher, das alte Haus, die Maschinen)

B. Change the sentences you will hear from active to passive, being careful to use the same tense as in the active sentence.

(*present*)

1. Wir müssen die Wohnung aufräumen.
2. Wir sollen mehr Wein kaufen.
3. Du darfst deine Freunde nicht einladen.
4. Man muß Oma nach Hause bringen.
5. Du darfst das Wort nicht sagen!

(*past*)

6. Man mußte die Läden schließen.
7. Man mußte die Kinder abholen.
8. Man konnte das Mädchen nicht interviewen.
9. Man mußte das Fenster zumachen.
10. Man durfte nichts kochen.

Use of Passive Voice

The passive voice is used to emphasize that something is being acted upon. Most passive sentences make no mention of the agent performing the action.

Diese Häuser wurden sehr schnell gebaut.	*These houses were built very quickly.*
Das wird oft gesagt.	*That's often said.*

When an animate agent *is* expressed, **von** + dative is used.[1]

Diese Häuser wurden **von Gastarbeitern** gebaut.	*These houses were built by foreign workers.*
Das wird **von vielen Menschen** gesagt.	*That is said by many people.*

`◦━◦` **Üben wir!**	**A.** Restate the following sentences in the passive. Express the agent with **von**.

> EXAMPLE: Meine Freundin liest jetzt den Roman.
> Der Roman wird jetzt von meiner Freundin gelesen.

1. Fast alle Studenten belegen dieses Seminar.
2. Am Samstag feiert meine Familie Omas Geburtstag.
3. Deutsche Schüler tragen gern Turnschuhe.
4. Unser Professor empfiehlt dieses Buch.
5. Alle Schüler in der Schweiz müssen Fremdsprachen lernen.
6. Michael hat mich eingeladen.
7. Die Kinder haben das Lied gesungen.
8. Der Staat verbietet das.

3 ◆ The Present Participle

Formation

To form the present participle (English: **-ing**) of a German verb, add **-d** to the infinitive:

schlafend	sleeping
feiernd	celebrating
denkend	thinking
lesend	reading

---

[1] When the agent is some impersonal force, **durch** + accusative is used. See Lesestück, p. 456, line 21.

feuerwehr-Zufahrt

Arbeiter—
Deutsche & Türken
gemeinsam gegen die
KRIEGSVERBRECHER!

Verhindert die
Abschiebung von
70 000 türkischen
Kollegen!

Sgraffiti (West-Berlin)

Use

The German present participle is *not* used as a verbal noun. German uses the infinitive for this purpose: No Parking = **Parken verboten** (see p. 165).

The present participle *is* used:

1. as an attributive adjective with the standard adjective endings.

   Wir wollen das **schlafende** Kind nicht stören.

   We don't want to disturb the sleeping child.

2. occasionally as an adverb.

   Sie sah mich **fragend** an.

   She looked at me questioningly.

Üben wir!

A. Add the present participle of the verb cued as an adjective to the sentence you will hear.

EXAMPLE: Wir können die Preise nicht mehr zahlen. (steigend)
Wir können die steigenden Preise nicht mehr zahlen.

1. Jeder Mensch weiß das. (denkend)
2. Was meinen die Politiker? (führend)
3. Die Arbeitslosigkeit ist ein Problem. (wachsend)
4. Sie hörte die Kinder. (lachend)
5. Bitte stören Sie meinen Zimmerkameraden nicht. (schlafend)

4 ♦ Equivalents for English "think"

Here is a group of verbs whose English equivalents all contain some meaning of the verb "to think:"

1. **meinen**   *to think; have an opinion*

   Was meinst du, sollen wir das   *What do you think? Should we*
   Auto kaufen?   *buy the car?*

2. **denken an** (+ *acc.*)   *to think of, have in mind*

   Er dachte an seine Jugend.   *He was thinking of his youth.*

3. **halten für**   *to take for, regard as, think X is . . . .*

   Ich halte ihn für einen   *I think he is an intelligent pupil.*
   intelligenten Schüler.

4. **halten von**   *to think of; have an opinion about*

   Was halten Sie von ihm?   *What do you think of him?*

5. **nach·denken über** (+ *acc.*)   *to think about; ponder*

   Ich muß über dieses Problem   *I have to think about this*
   nachdenken.   *problem.*

■ Note carefully the distinction between **denken an** and **nachdenken über**. **Denken an** means to have someone or something in mind, and often has the force of "to remember." **Nachdenken über** means to ponder something:

—Vergiß nicht, Milch zu kaufen.   *Don't forget to buy milk.*
—Gut, ich werde **daran denken.**   *O.K., I'll remember it.*

—Was schenken wir Lise zum   *What shall we give Lise for her*
  Geburtstag?   *birthday?*
—Wir sollten **darüber nachdenken.** *We ought to think about that.*

Üben wir!   **A.** Respond either positively or negatively to these questions containing "think" verbs.

> EXAMPLE: Halten Sie die Kamera für zu teuer?
>   Ja, ich halte sie für zu teuer.
>   *or:* Nein, ich halte sie für billig.

1. Meinst du, ich sollte langsamer sprechen?
2. Halten Sie viel von meiner Idee?
3. Wird sie immer an dich denken?
4. Denken Sie oft über die Zukunft nach?
5. Halten Sie dieses Klima für gut?

B. Supply the correct German equivalent of "think."

1. Daran hätte ich nie _____ .
2. Der Professor für Psychologie _____ , kleine Kinder brauchen Märchen.
3. Für mein Referat _____ ich über die Weimarer Republik nach.
4. Er ist zwar sympathisch, aber ich _____ ihn für verrückt.
5. Was _____ Sie von dem Leben in der Großstadt?

C. Wie sagt man das auf deutsch?

1. I often think of Karin.
2. I think she's a good professor.
3. What do *you* think?
4. Have you thought about the lecture?
5. What do you think of the new film?
6. Do you think I'm crazy?

5 ♦ Directional Prefixes: *hin-* and *her-*

Look at the following English sentences:

> May we go out?
> He came out.
> Come in!
> Let's go in.

The German equivalents of these sentences employ the verbs **gehen** and **kommen** with separable prefixes that include the directional indicators **hin-** (motion away from speaker) and **her-** (motion toward the speaker):

Separable Prefixes

motion away from speaker	hin-	+	-ein-[1] -aus-	+	-gehen	= to go in / to go out
motion toward speaker	her-	+	-ein- -aus-	+	-kommen	= to come in / to come out

When someone knocks at the door, Germans simply say: **Herein!** = *Come in!* The prefixes **hin-** and **her-** *must* be used when the direction of motion is not indicated by a prepositional phrase like **ins Haus** or **aus dem Haus.**

Even when a prepositional phrase is used, the directional prefixes may also be used:

> Er ist aus dem Haus **herausgekommen.**
> Sie ging in die Kirche **hinein.**

---

[1] The preposition **in** is replaced by **ein** in these prefixes.

Üben wir!

A. (books open) Complete these sentences according to the English cues.

You're standing outside the house:

1. Gehen wir (*in*)!
2. Karl, komm doch (*out*)!
3. Anna ist vor einer Minute (*gone in*).
4. Bald kommen die Kinder aus dem Haus (*out*).

You're standing inside the house:

5. Kommt Grete bald (*in*)?
6. Es ist so schön, ich möchte jetzt (*go out*).
7. Wir sollten alle (*go out*).
8. (*Come in*)!

6 ◆ Expanding Your Vocabulary

Leicht zu merken

der **Kilometer, -**	Kilometer
die **Mentalität**	Mentalität
der **Ozean, -e**	Ozean
die **Religion, -en**	Religion
renovieren	renovieren

Wortschatz 2

Verben
berichten   to report
klagen   to complain
mieten   to rent (from somebody)
planen   to plan, make plans

Substantive
der **Europäer, -**   European
der **Teil, -e**   part
der **Türke, -n, -n**   Turk (*m.*)

das **Heimweh**   homesickness

die **Kälte**   cold
die **Krankheit, -en**   illness, sickness

die **Million, -en**   million
die **Möglichkeit, -en**   possibility
die **Türkei**   Turkey
die **Türkin, -nen**   Turk (*f.*)

Andere Vokabeln
menschlich   human, like a human being; humane
türkisch   Turkish
verwandt (mit)   related (to)

Nützlicher Ausdruck
nach und nach   gradually, little by little

Türkinnen in Kreuzberg, einem Stadtteil von West-Berlin

Leben im gelobten Land°

gelobten Land = Promised Land

Straßenkehrer *(street sweeper)*

Max von der Grün

Im Jahre 1985 arbeiteten fast 1,6 Millionen Gastarbeiter in der Bundesrepublik. Diese Arbeiter stellen ein ernstes soziales Problem dar.° Sie wurden zwar für die deutsche Wirtschaft gebraucht, die Deutschen haben sie aber nie wirklich akzeptiert. Max von der Grün, 1926 in Bayreuth geboren, von 1951 bis 1963 Bergmann,° jetzt freier° Schriftsteller in Dortmund, berichtete 1975 über das Leben eines türkischen Gastarbeiters in seinem Buch Leben im gelobten Land, aus dem wir einige Stellen hier abdrucken.° Zunächst spricht der Arbeiter Osman Gürlük selbst:

„Diese Kälte° hier in Deutschland macht mich krank; ich habe immer noch Heimweh, heute manchmal noch stärker als vor fünf Jahren; Heimweh ist eine Krankheit, und diese Krankheit ist nur in der Türkei zu heilen;° aber in
5 Anatolien[1] gibt es für mich keine Arbeit, keinen Verdienst,° keine Möglichkeit, irgendwann einmal nach oben zu kommen,° wie ein Mensch zu leben, mit Haus und geregeltem Einkommen:° ich muß vorerst° in Deutschland bleiben, muß mit dieser Krankheit leben; in dieser Kälte; die Kälte
10 hier in Deutschland, das sind die Menschen."

stellen . . . dar = to present

miner / free-lance

reprint

cold

ist nur . . . zu heilen = can only be cured / wages

nach . . . kommen = to get ahead
geregeltem Einkommen = regular income / for the time being

---

[1] Anatolia, the eastern part of Turkey.

Osman Gürlük lebt heute mit seiner Frau und der dreijährigen° Tochter Ißek in einer Zweieinhalbzimmerwohnung im Dortmunder Norden, in einem Viertel,° das ausschließlich° von Türken bewohnt° wird. Die Deutschen sagen: Türkenviertel. Die deutschen Mieter sind nach und nach, als immer mehr Türken in das Viertel kamen, in andere Stadtteile gezogen, in Neubauten.° Das „Türkenviertel" besteht ausschließlich aus° Altbauten, die von den Eignern° heute nur noch notdürftig° renoviert werden, weil die Häuser irgendwann einmal abgerissen° werden durch die geplante Stadtsanierung° . . .

Die Türken in der Bundesrepublik haben es von allen Gastarbeitern am schwersten: sie sind weder Europäer, noch gehören sie einer christlichen° Religion an° und ihre Mentalität ist nicht mit der unseren° verwandt. Um einigermaßen° menschlich leben zu können, müssen sie dreitausend Kilometer entfernt° von ihrer Heimat arbeiten.

Dazu sagt Osman Gürlük: „Ich will nicht klagen, ich bin nur immer wieder darüber erstaunt,° daß dreitausend Kilometer mehr sind als nur dreitausend Kilometer; wahrscheinlich ist es leichter, den Ozean zu durchschwimmen, als deutschen Arbeitern klar zu machen, daß wir Türken nichts anderes wollen als sie auch, nämlich° arbeiten, um anständig° leben zu können; wir sind geduldet,° und das auch nur, so lange wir gebraucht werden; das müssen meine Landsleute° begreifen° lernen."

three-year old
quarter, district
exclusively / inhabited

new buildings
besteht . . . aus = *consists of*
owners / minimally
torn down
urban renewal

Christian / **gehören . . . an** = *are members of* / **der unseren** = *ours*
to some extent
away, removed

astonished

namely
decently / **wir . . . geduldet** = *they put up with us*
compatriots / **begreifen** = **verstehen**

Fragen zum Lesestück

1. Wie viele Gastarbeiter arbeiteten 1985 in der Bundesrepublik?
2. Warum sind diese Arbeiter ein schwieriges Problem für die deutsche Gesellschaft?
3. Wo kommt der Gastarbeiter Osman Gürlük her?
4. Wie beschreibt er sein Heimweh?
5. Wo wäre er nicht krank?
6. Was gibt es in der Türkei nicht für ihn?
7. Meint er das Wetter, wenn er von Kälte spricht?
8. Wo wohnt Osman Gürlük heute? Wie groß ist seine Familie?
9. Wie sieht der Stadtteil aus, in dem er wohnt?
10. Warum haben es die Türken am schwersten von allen Gastarbeitern?
11. Was möchte Osman Gürlük den deutschen Arbeitern klarmachen?

Vom Lesen zum Sprechen

Zur Diskussion

1. Wie wohnen Sie zu Hause? Beschreiben Sie das Haus oder die Wohnung Ihrer Familie.
2. Wie würde Ihr Traumhaus (dream house) aussehen? Beschreiben Sie es.

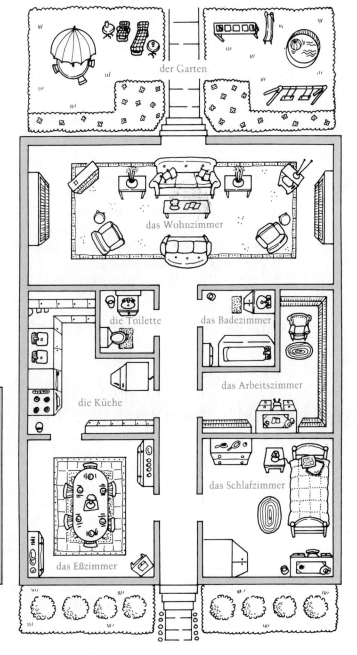

der Garten

das Wohnzimmer

die Toilette

das Badezimmer

die Küche

das Arbeitszimmer

das Schlafzimmer

das Eßzimmer

die Garage

Mündliche Übungen

A. Persönliche Fragen

1. Kennen Sie Ausländer, die perfekt Englisch sprechen?
2. Wie lernt man eine Sprache am schnellsten?
3. Worüber denken Sie oft nach?
4. Haben Sie je einen Zug oder ein Flugzeug verpaßt?
5. In welchem Jahrhundert hätten Sie gern gelebt? Warum?
6. Wann ist Ihre Familie zum letzten Mal umgezogen? Von wo nach wo?
7. Schreiben Sie viele Briefe? An wen?
8. Was planen Sie für das Wochenende?

B. Say who does or did the following things.

> EXAMPLE: Von wem wurde das Fußballspiel gewonnen?
> Es wurde von unserer Mannschaft gewonnen.

1. Von wem wird das Essen im Restaurant gebracht?
2. Von wem werden Autos repariert?
3. Von wem werden Romane geschrieben?
4. Von wem wird das Gepäck getragen?
5. Von wem wurde "Hamlet" geschrieben?
6. Von wem wurde Beethovens Neunte Symphonie geschrieben?
7. Von wem wurde das Referat gehalten?
8. Von wem werden Zeitungsartikel geschrieben?

C. Tell the "life story" of the following objects in the passive voice, using the cues as an aid.

1. die Zeitung:
   Journalisten / geschrieben
   am Morgen auf der Straße / gekauft
   zwischen sieben und halb acht / gelesen
   im Zug / gelassen
   von einem alten Mann / gefunden und gelesen

2. der Roman:
   Schriftsteller / geschrieben
   Buchhandlung / gekauft
   zu Hause / gelesen
   einem Freund / geliehen
   vom Freund / verloren

3. die Wurst:
   Metzger (*butcher*) / gemacht
   Hausfrau / gekauft
   im Wasser / gekocht
   zum Mittagessen / gegessen

4. die Postkarte: in Italien / gekauft
Barbara / geschrieben
zur Post / gebracht
in den Briefkasten / eingeworfen
Familie / gelesen

5. der Tisch: Schreiner (*carpenter*) / gemacht
im Möbelgeschäft / gekauft
nach Hause / gebracht
neben das Bett / gestellt

D. Use the past subjunctive to say what you would have liked to do.

EXAMPLE: Was hätten Sie gestern gern gemacht?
Ich wäre gern im Bett geblieben.
Ich hätte gern Schokolade gegessen.

1. Was hätten Sie gestern gern gemacht?
2. Was hätten Sie letzten Sommer gern gemacht?
3. Was hätten Sie als Kind gern getan?
4. Wohin wären Sie letztes Jahr gern gereist?

E. Say what you *would* have done, if . . . .
Was hätten Sie gemacht, wenn . . . .

1. . . . Sie dieses Semester nicht studiert hätten?
2. . . . Sie letztes Jahr eine Million Dollar gewonnen hätten?
3. . . . Sie vor 500 Jahren gelebt hätten?
4. . . . Sie Beethoven gewesen wären?
5. . . . Sie gestern einen Autounfall gehabt hätten?
6. . . . Sie vorgestern krank gewesen wären?

Schriftliche Übungen

F. Rewrite these sentences in the passive voice. Keep the same tense as in the original active sentence. If the subject of the active sentence is *man*, the passive sentence will not have an agent.

1. Man akzeptiert mich fast überall.
2. Robert interviewt eine spanische Schülerin.
3. Man warf den Brief in den Briefkasten ein.
4. Die Studenten haben die Europareise geplant.
5. Hat Klaus die Wohnung im ersten Stock gemietet?
6. Dort sprach man nur Türkisch.
7. Man muß dieses Problem verstehen.
8. Man konnte die Musik gut hören.

G. People are often annoyed because they should, could, or ought to have done something differently. Use the modal verb cued in parentheses in the past subjunctive.

> EXAMPLE: Ich ärgere mich, daß ich nicht an deinen Geburtstag gedacht habe. (sollen)
> Ich hätte daran denken sollen.

1. Er ärgert sich, daß er seinen Zug verpaßt hat. (dürfen)
2. Ich ärgere mich, daß wir letztes Jahr nicht umgezogen sind. (können)
3. Eva ärgert sich, daß sie nicht Psychologie studiert hat. (können)
4. Ich ärgere mich, daß ich ihr nicht zum Geburtstag gratuliert habe. (sollen)
5. Sie ärgert sich, daß sie ihre Sachen nicht aufgeräumt hat. (müssen)
6. Wir ärgern uns, daß wir gestern kein Geld gewechselt haben. (sollen)
7. Thomas ärgert sich, daß er keine Briefmarken gekauft hat. (können)

H. Schreiben Sie mal darüber!

1. Was für Schwierigkeiten hätten Sie in einem Land, wo kein Englisch gesprochen wird? Beschreiben Sie die Situation.
2. Beschreiben Sie in Ihren eigenen Worten Osman Gürlüks Gefühle als Gastarbeiter in der BRD.
3. Gibt es Gastarbeiter in Nordamerika? Wie ist die Situation anders als in Europa?

I. Wie sagt man das auf deutsch?

1. Would you like to have lived in the 19th century?
2. I have to think about that. (use *nachdenken*)
3. How would life have been different back then?
4. You would not have been able to work with a computer.
5. My paper has to be written soon.
6. When do you need my new typewriter?
7. Either today or the day after tomorrow.
8. What are you writing about?
9. I am writing about foreign workers in Austria and Switzerland.
10. A lot of books have been written about that. (use perfect tense)
11. There is the post office. Didn't you want to mail your letter?
12. Yes, let's go in. I could also buy some stamps.

Almanach

Foreign Workers in Germany

Almost 4 million foreign workers (about 7% of the total population) live in West Germany. They come largely from Turkey, Yugoslavia, Italy, Greece, Spain, and Portugal. Germany has the largest number of "guest" workers in Western Europe. Although immigration has been greatly reduced, this population is still growing at a faster rate than the ethnic Germans due to the influx of illegal workers (*Schwarzarbeiter*) and because families have joined working fathers. The immigrants have a higher birth rate than Northern Europeans, so the proportion of people under 25 is higher among foreigners than nationals. In Kreuzberg, a section of West Berlin, up to 50% of the school children are Turkish.

Türkische Ladeninhaber (Gelsenkirchen, BRD) (der Inhaber, = *owner*)

Die Frau

Dialoge
Goldene Hochzeit ♦ Kind oder
Beruf?

Wortschatz 1

Grammatik
1. Impersonal Passive
2. Subjective Use of Modal Verbs
3. Indirect Quotation and Special
   Subjunctive
   Direct Versus Indirect Quotation ♦ Special Subjunctive
   ♦ Tenses in Indirect Quotation
   ♦ Questions and Commands
   in Indirect Quotation
4. Subjunctive with **als ob** (as if,
   as though)
5. Extended Modifiers
6. Expanding Your Vocabulary
   Leicht zu merken

Wortschatz 2

Lesestück
Gedanken über die Emanzipation
der Frau

Vom Lesen zum Sprechen
Unterschiede

Almanach
The Women's Movement

Dialoge

Goldene Hochzeit

HEINRICH: Liese, du siehst aus, als ob du kaum geschlafen
hättest.

LIESE: Stimmt schon. Bei uns wurde bis halb vier gefeiert.

HEINRICH: Was wurde denn gefeiert?

LIESE: Die goldene Hochzeit meiner Großeltern.

Kind oder Beruf?

MARTHA: Wie macht ihr das eigentlich, wenn euer
Kind da ist? Hast du vor, deine Stelle aufzugeben?

MARGARETHE: Natürlich nicht! Eine so gut bezahlte Stelle
finde ich nicht so schnell wieder. Rolf kann
nachmittags auf das Baby aufpassen, weil er
noch studiert.

MARTHA: Und vormittags?

MARGARETHE: Vormittags bin ich da. Ich habe schon meine
Chefin gefragt, ob es möglich sei, halbtags zu
arbeiten.

MARTHA: Was sagte sie dazu?

MARGARETHE: Sie meinte, das ginge.

Einkaufen am Gemüse– und Blumenmarkt

Wortschatz 1

Golden Wedding Anniversary

HEINRICH: Liese, you look as if you had hardly slept.

LIESE: That's right. Our party went on until 3:30.

HEINRICH: What were you celebrating?

LIESE: My grandparents' golden wedding anniversary.

Child or Career?

MARTHA: How are you going to manage once your child is born? Do you intend to give up your job?

MARGARETHE: Of course not. I won't find such a well-paid job so soon again. Rolf can look after the baby in the afternoons because he's still a student.

MARTHA: And in the mornings?

MARGARETHE: In the mornings I'll be here. I've already asked my boss if it's possible to work part-time.

MARTHA: What did she say to that?

MARGARETHE: She said it would work.

Verben

auf·geben (gibt auf), gab auf, hat aufgegeben to give up (*trans. and intrans.*)

auf·passen (*intrans.*) to pay attention; look out

auf·passen auf (+ *acc.*) to look after

bezahlen to pay

heiraten to marry, get married

Substantive

das **Baby, -s** baby

die **Hochzeit, -en** wedding

die goldene Hochzeit golden wedding anniversary

Andere Vokabeln

als ob (+ *subjunctive*) as if

golden golden

halbtags (*adv.*) half days

halbtags arbeiten to work part time

vormittags (in the) mornings

Nützliche Ausdrücke

Was sagen (meinen) Sie dazu? What do you say to that? What do you think of that?

Stimmt schon. That's right.

Eine Aktion des Bundesministers für Jugend, Familie und Gesundheit

Mit machen macht Mut

FRAUEN KÖNNEN MEHR

Neue Kombinationen

A. Replace the italicized words with the cues you will hear.

1. Du siehst aus, als ob du nicht *geschlafen* hättest.
   (gegessen, begonnen, verstanden, viel verdient, daran gedacht)
2. Bei uns wurde bis halb vier *gefeiert*.
   (getanzt, geredet, getrunken, gesungen, gearbeitet)
3. Meine Chefin sagt, das sei *schwierig*.
   (typisch, ausgezeichnet, unmöglich, phantastisch)
4. Sie fragte, *ob das möglich sei*.
   (ob er Geld habe, ob es noch Kaffee gebe, ob der Film interessant sei, ob Hans kommen könne)

B. (books open) Respond to the sentences on the left with an appropriate answer from the right hand column.

Heute habe ich Geburtstag.	Das wäre nett!
Du sprichst perfekt Deutsch.	Gott sei Dank!
Gehen wir zusammen Schi laufen?	Doch.
Möchten Sie etwas trinken?	Natürlich.
Morgen früh wasche ich mir die Haare.	Kein Wunder!
Stefan hat sich das Bein gebrochen.	Lieber nicht.
Wir bekommen einen neuen Lehrer!	Das überrascht mich.
Wollt ihr viele Kinder haben?	Ich gratuliere!
Ich war bis halb vier auf.	Gerne!
Kannst du mich nicht verstehen?	Gute Idee!
	Wie schade!
	Warum denn?
	Das ist mir egal.

C. Your teacher will say something and ask you what you think of it. Give an appropriate reaction.

> EXAMPLE: Teacher: Rolf und Margarethe haben ein neues Baby.
> Was sagen Sie dazu?
> Possible response: Das finde ich toll.
> *or:* Toll!
> *or:* Sie freuen sich sicher.

1. Bei uns wurde bis halb vier gefeiert! Was sagen Sie dazu?
2. Meine Großeltern feiern ihre goldene Hochzeit.
3. Anna hat eine gut bezahlte Stelle bekommen.
4. Ich würde gern halbtags arbeiten.
5. Ich habe vor, meine Stelle aufzugeben.

Here is part of a poem by a young German woman who expresses her wish to receive equal treatment in job training, especially in areas which have been traditionally reserved for men.

Ich bin, wenn es gestattet° ist, ein Mädchen	*permitted*
Normal im Kopf, und denken kann ich auch	
Will lernen, was mir Spaß macht, genau wie du	
Und nicht, was grade Sitte° ist und Brauch°	*custom / fashion*
Wofür ich mich interessiere, darauf kommt es an°	***darauf . . . an*** = *that's*
Das ist genauso, wie beim Mann	*what's important*
Ich möchte Schreinerin° werden	*cabinet maker*
Doch du sagst, das wäre nichts für mich	
Die Arbeit, die wär viel zu schwer	
Für Mädchen, so körperlich°	*physical*
An's Fließband° kann ich gehen	*assembly line*
Doch° Hobeln,° das ist zu schwer	***doch*** = ***aber*** / *planing*
Da stell mir doch mal einer°	***einer*** = ***jemand***
Diese Logik her°	***stell . . . her:*** (here)
	explain

—Uschi Flacke

Infostand in der Fußgängerzone

Grammatik

1 ♦ Impersonal Passive

One German passive construction has no precise English equivalent. It is used to say that some human activity is going on, without mentioning who performs it.

There is no expressed subject at all, and the verb is *always* in the third person singular:

Bis halb vier **wurde gefeiert.**	*The party went on until 3:30.*
Hier **wird** bis zwei Uhr morgens **getanzt und gesungen.**	*There's dancing and singing here until 2:00 A.M.*

If no other element occupies first position in the sentence, an impersonal **es** is used to fill it. This **es** is not a real subject and disappears if any other element occupies first position:

> **Es** wurde bis halb vier gefeiert.
> **Es** wird hier bis zwei Uhr morgens getanzt.

Similarly, when verbs with dative objects (see p. 187) are used in the passive voice, their objects *remain* in the dative case, and the passive is *always* in the third person singular. An impersonal **es** is in the first position if no other element occupies it.

active:	
Man hilft mir oft.	*They often help me.*

passive:	
Mir wird oft geholfen. ⎫ **Es wird mir oft geholfen.** ⎭	*I'm often helped.*

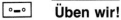

Üben wir!

A. Replace **man** with an impersonal passive construction. Begin with **Es . . .**

> EXAMPLE: Man ißt hier viel.
> Es wird hier viel gegessen.

1. Man singt hier zu laut.
2. Man fängt früh an.
3. Man arbeitete damals schwer.
4. Man fragte nicht viel.

B. Now begin the personal passive with something other than **es.**

> EXAMPLE: Hier ißt man viel.
> Hier wird viel gegessen.

1. Morgen liest und schreibt man viel.
2. Jetzt kauft man ein.
3. Gestern tanzte man bis zwei Uhr.
4. In unserer Stadt baut man immer mehr.

◻━◻ **C.** Change these sentences containing dative objects from active to passive. Begin your sentence with the dative object.

> EXAMPLE: Man gratuliert mir zum Geburtstag.
> Mir wird zum Geburtstag gratuliert.

1. Man hilft mir oft.
2. Man gratuliert dem Chef zum Geburtstag.
3. Man dankt den Arbeiterinnen für die Hilfe.
4. Man glaubte dem Politiker nicht.
5. Man antwortete dem Professor sofort.

2 ◆ Subjective Use of Modal Verbs

The modal verbs are sometimes used to show speakers' subjective attitudes toward what they are saying. By and large, this subjective use parallels English:

1. **mögen** expresses possibility:

   Das **mag** sein.   *That may be.*

2. **müssen** expresses strong probability:

   Diese Menschen **müssen** Touristen sein.   *These people must be tourists.*

3. **sollen** expresses hearsay:

   Sie **soll** eine gute Lehrerin sein.   *She's supposed to be a good teacher.*

   Sie **sollen** so glücklich sein.   *They are said to be so happy.*

4. **können** expresses fairly strong possibility (sometimes = English **may**):

Sie **kann** morgen schon hier sein.   *She may be here as early as tomorrow.*

Kann das Richard sein?   *Can that be Richard?*

5. **wollen** casts doubt on someone else's claim (no parallel in English):

Er will viel über Musik wissen.   *He claims to know a lot about music.*[1]

Üben wir!

A. Give English equivalents for the following sentences and say whether the modal verb is used subjectively or objectively.

1. Kann das Utes Wagen sein?
2. Nein, das muß Richards Wagen sein.
3. Wieso? Sie wollte sich einen roten Wagen kaufen, nicht?
4. Mag sein. Wir müssen Ute fragen.
5. Ja, sie soll um drei wieder da sein.
6. Dann müssen wir zusammen in die Vorlesung.
7. Willst du ein Glas Bier trinken? Drüben wartet Rudi auf uns.
8. Was für eine Jacke trägt er denn da! Und *das* will ein schicker Mann sein!

B. Wie sagt man das auf deutsch?

1. She is supposed to be very famous.
2. That may be.
3. Roland must know a lot about music.
4. He claims to know everything about music.
5. It may be that they don't love each other any more.
6. But they are supposed to be so happy together!

---

[1] The subjective modals also parallel English in the way they form their past tense. Note the difference between objective and subjective.

Objective: Er **mußte** am Montag in Wien **sein.**   *He had to be in Vienna on Monday.*

Subjective: Er **muß** am Montag in Wien **gewesen sein.**   *He must have been in Vienna on Monday.*

Demonstration am Internationalen Frauentag (Hamburg) (die Bundeswehr = *West German army;*
der Bund = *colloq. for* Bundeswehr)

3 ◆ Indirect Quotation and Special Subjunctive

Direct vs. Indirect Quotation

There are two basic ways to report what someone has said: directly or indirectly. You can quote directly, repeating the original speaker's exact words.[1]

Bernd sagt: „Ich muß heute in die Bibliothek."	*Bernd says, "I have to go to the library."*

It is much more common, however, to report speech in *indirect* quotation:

Bernd sagt, er muß heute in die Bibliothek.	*Bernd says he has to go to the library.*
ODER:	*OR:*
Bernd sagt, daß er heute in die Bibliothek muß.	*Bernd says that he has to go to the library.*

A statement in indirect quotation may either be introduced by the conjunction **daß** (**Er sagt, daß . . .**) or by no conjunction (**Er sagt, . . .**).

In the spoken language, many Germans simply use the indicative for indirect quotation, as in the previous examples. In spoken German, it is also acceptable to use general subjunctive for indirect quotation:

Bernd sagte, er **müßte** in die Bibliothek.	*Bernd said he had to go to the library.*
Meine Chefin meint, das **ginge.**	*My boss says that will work.*

[1] Note on punctuation: German usually uses a colon before a direct quotation, while English uses a comma.

However, in formal written and spoken German (for example, in a term paper, newspaper article, or television news report), indirect quotation *must* be expressed with forms called the **special subjunctive:**

> Bernd sagt, er **müsse** heute in die Bibliothek.
> Die Chefin meinte, das **gehe.**

Formation of Special Subjunctive

1. Present Tense

   The present-tense endings of the special subjunctive are the same as those of the general subjunctive: **-e, -est, -e; -en, -et, -en.** But they are attached to the *unchanged infinitive stem* of the verb. In some cases, this procedure results in forms that are identical with the indicative. When this happens, *general* subjunctive must be used for indirect discourse. In the following paradigms, the inadmissible forms are crossed out and replaced by the general subjunctive in parentheses.

---

laufen

ich	~~laufe~~ (liefe)	wir	~~laufen~~ (liefen)
du	laufest	ihr	laufet
er	laufe	sie	~~laufen~~ (liefen)

---

können

ich	könne	wir	~~können~~ (könnten)
du	könnest	ihr	könnet
er	könne	sie	~~können~~ (könnten)

---

wissen

ich	wisse	wir	~~wissen~~ (wüßten)
du	wissest	ihr	wisset
er	wisse	sie	~~wissen~~ (wüßten)

The only German verb with an irregular special subjunctive is **sein:**

---

ich	sei	wir	seien
du	seiest	ihr	seiet
er	sei	sie	seien

■ The preceding tables show that there is *no* special subjunctive in the first and third persons plural, except for the verb **sein.**

2. The future special subjunctive is formed thus:

<table>
<tr><td></td><td colspan="2">**Special Subjunctive**
of **werden**</td><td></td><td>**Infinitive**</td></tr>
<tr><td>Sie</td><td>**werde**</td><td></td><td>morgen</td><td>**wiederkommen.**</td></tr>
</table>

3. The past special subjunctive is formed thus:

<table>
<tr><td></td><td colspan="2">**Special Subjunctive**
of **Auxiliary**</td><td>**Past Participle**</td></tr>
<tr><td>Sie</td><td>**habe**</td><td>das</td><td>**gewußt.**</td></tr>
<tr><td>Er</td><td>**sei**</td><td>dort</td><td>**gewesen.**</td></tr>
</table>

Use of Special Subjunctive

You will encounter special subjunctive most often in the third person singular, introduced by a verb of saying or asking in the indicative:

Frau Donatz sagt, sie **müsse** leider gehen. Sie **fahre** morgen früh ab und **wisse** nicht, wann sie zurückkommen **werde.**	*Ms. Donatz says that unfortunately, she has to go. She's leaving tomorrow and doesn't know when she'll be back.*

In spoken German, special subjunctive is most often used with high-frequency verbs like **sein, haben,** and the modals.

Tenses in Indirect Quotation

In English, the tense of the introductory verb of saying influences the tense of the indirect quotation:

Direct Quotation

"I have to go to the library"

Indirect Quotations

introductory verb in the present } She **says** she **has** to go to the library.

introductory verb in the past } She **said** she **had** to go to the library.

In German, the tense of the introductory verb of saying has *no influence* on the tense of the indirect quotation. The tense of the indirect quotation is *always the same as the tense of the direct quotation* from which it derives. If the tense of the direct quotation was *present,* use *present subjunctive* for the indirect quotation. If it was *future,* use *future subjunctive.* If it was *any past tense,* use *past subjunctive:*

Direct Quotation: *present indicative*

Sabine: „Ich muß in die Bibliothek."

Indirect Quotation: *present subjunctive*

Sabine sagt,
Sabine sagte, } sie müsse in die Bibliothek.

Direct Quotation: *future indicative*

Barbara: „Ich werde das machen."

Indirect Quotation: *future subjunctive*

Barbara sagt,
Barbara sagte, } sie werde das machen.

Direct Quotation: *past or perfect indicative*

Karl: „Ich war nicht da."
Karl: „Ich habe das nicht gewußt."

Indirect Quotation: *past subjunctive*

Karl sagt,
Karl sagte, } er sei nicht da gewesen.

Karl sagt,
Karl sagte, } er habe das nicht gewußt.

If the original quotation is *already* in the subjunctive, the indirect quotation simply *remains* in the subjunctive.

Udo: „Ich möchte ein Glas Wasser."
Udo sagt, er möchte ein Glas Wasser.

Üben wir!

A. Grete said the following things to you. Tell someone else what she said. Use special subjunctive (general subjunctive when necessary).

EXAMPLE: „Ich habe viel zu erzählen."
Sie sagte, sie habe viel zu erzählen.

1. „Ich bin diese Woche sehr glücklich."
2. „Hans und ich werden heiraten."
3. „Ich möchte gern nach England ziehen."
4. „Hans will das auch."
5. „Im Juni sind wir zusammen nach Spanien getrampt."
6. „Es hat wirklich Spaß gemacht."
7. „Wir haben viel Schönes gesehen."
8. „Jetzt ist das Leben wieder langweilig geworden."

B. Now report what Holger said to you, using special subjunctive.

> EXAMPLE: „Ich kann keine Stelle finden."
> Er sagte, er könne keine Stelle finden.

1. „Ich habe überall gesucht."
2. „Vielleicht gibt es Arbeit in der Stadt."
3. „Ich will aber nicht umziehen."
4. „Barbara hat mir geholfen."
5. „Sie hat eine gute Stelle gefunden."
6. „Sie wollte eigentlich Lehrerin werden."
7. „Aber man ist glücklich, Arbeit zu haben."
8. „Ich werde schon etwas finden."

Questions and Commands in Indirect Quotation

1. A yes/no question becomes an **ob**-clause in indirect quotation:

Karin: „Hat Hans genug Geld?"

Karin möchte wissen, **ob** Hans genug Geld habe.	*Karin would like to know if Hans has enough money.*

2. Information questions become subordinate clauses introduced by the question word:

Tourist: „Wo ist der Bahnhof, bitte?"

Der Tourist fragte, **wo** der Bahnhof sei.	*The tourist asked where the train station was.*

3. Commands become statements with the verb **sollen,** with or without **daß:**

Frau Henning: „Kauf das nicht, Heinz!"

Frau Henning sagte zu ihrem Mann, er **solle** das nicht kaufen (. . . daß er das nicht kaufen **solle**).	*Mrs. Henning told her husband not to buy that (that he shouldn't buy that).*

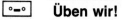 **Üben wir!**

A. Report these conversations in indirect quotation, using special subjunctive.

1. Karla: „Gibt es noch Bier?"
2. Rita: „Natürlich, aber trink doch nicht so viel!"
3. Karla: „Warum soll ich nicht trinken?"
4. Rita: „Es ist nicht gesund."

5. Vater: „Hast du genug Geld?"
6. Tochter: „Nein, gib mir doch mehr!"
7. Vater: „Wofür brauchst du denn so viel?"
8. Tochter: „Ich möchte mir eine neue Jacke kaufen."

Frauen erzählen

Ingeborg Bachmann:
Der Fall Franza
Requiem für
Fanny Goldmann

dtv

1705 / DM 5,80

Fania Fénelon:
Das
Mädchenorchester
in Auschwitz

dtv

1706 / DM 9,80

Füruzan:
Frau ohne Schleier
Türkische
Erzählungen

dtv

1655 / DM 5,80

Gertrud Fussenegger:
Die Pulvermühle¹
Roman

dtv

1507 / DM 9,80

Katherine Mansfield:
Seligkeit und
andere Erzählungen

dtv

1664 / DM 6,80

Joyce Carol Oates:
Grenz-
überschreitungen
Erzählungen

dtv

1643 / DM 8,80

Edna O'Brien:
Mrs. Reinhardt
träumt von No. 10
Erzählungen

dtv

1739 / DM 5,80

Barbara Frischmuth:
Kai und die Liebe
zu den Modellen
Roman

dtv
neue reihe

6313 / DM 6,80

Iris Murdoch:
Der schwarze Prinz
Roman

dtv

1501 / DM 12,80

Mehr Information über
Frauenliteratur im
Taschenbuch bietet das
neue dtv-Gesamtver-
zeichnis. Sie erhalten es
in Ihrer Buchhandlung
oder direkt vom dtv,
Postfach 40 04 22,
8000 München 40.

dtv

4 ◆ Subjunctive with *als ob* (as if, as though)

The subordinating conjunction **als ob** (as if, as though) must be followed by a verb in the subjunctive.[1] **Als ob** clauses are preceded by introductory phrases such as the following:

Du siehst aus, als ob . . .
Es war, als ob . . .
Du tust, als ob . . .

You look as if . . .
It was as if . . .
You act as though . . .

Du siehst aus, **als ob** du krank
  wärest.
Es war, **als ob** wir uns immer
  gekannt hätten.
Er tut, **als ob** er nichts **wüßte.**

You look as though you're sick.

*It was as if we had always known
  each other.*
*He acts as if he didn't know
  anything.*

[1] Either general or special subjunctive may be used, but general subjunctive is more frequent.

A. Your teacher tells you certain things about himself or herself. Say that the teacher *looks* as though the opposite were true.

> EXAMPLE: Ich bin nicht krank!
> Aber Sie sehen aus, als ob Sie krank wären.

1. Ich bin unglücklich.
2. Ich brauche kein Geld!
3. Ich komme nicht aus Österreich.
4. Ich arbeite nicht zu viel.
5. Ich bin kein netter Mensch.
6. Ich habe keinen Hunger.

B. Here are some facts about what you did yesterday. Say that it was *as if* the opposite had been true.

> EXAMPLE: Sie haben ihn nicht gekannt.
> Aber es war, als ob ich ihn gekannt hätte.

1. Sie haben nicht 24 Stunden gearbeitet.
2. Sie haben nicht 12 Stunden geschlafen.
3. Sie waren nicht lange unterwegs.
4. Sie haben diese Gegend nicht gekannt.
5. Sie haben Ihre Sachen nicht vergessen.
6. Sie sind nicht lange in der Stadt geblieben.

C. Your teacher asks you if certain things about Robert are really true. You say he only *acts* as if they were true.

> EXAMPLE: Ist Robert wirklich krank?
> Nein, er tut nur, als ob er krank wäre.

1. Ist Robert wirklich faul?
2. Hat Robert wirklich Probleme?
3. Will er wirklich die Schule verlassen?
4. Gibt er wirklich seine Stelle auf?
5. Hat er wirklich bis zehn geschlafen?
6. Kommt er wirklich nicht zur Geburtstagsfeier?

5 ♦ Extended Modifiers

Look at the following phrases:

diese neue Schriftstellerin	*this new writer*
diese beliebte neue Schriftstellerin	*this propular new writer*
diese sehr beliebte neue Schriftstellerin	*this very popular new writer*

Both German and English can extend noun phrases by inserting a series of adjectives and adverbs between a limiting word (**diese,** this) and its noun (**Schriftstellerin,** writer). In German, however, such a series can be much longer than in English:

diese bei jungen Menschen sehr beliebte neue Schriftstellerin	*this new writer, very popular with young people*
diese bei jungen Menschen in Deutschland sehr beliebte neue Schriftstellerin	*this new writer, very popular with young people in Germany*
diese heute bei vielen jungen Menschen in Deutschland sehr beliebte neue Schriftstellerin	*this new writer, very popular with many young people in German today*

Such extended modifiers are encountered primarily in written German and their use or avoidance is a matter of stylistic preference.

The extended modifier is basically a substitute for a relative clause:

diese bei jungen Menschen beliebte Schriftstellerin =
diese Schriftstellerin, die bei jungen Menschen beliebt ist

Extended modifiers often contain a present or past participle functioning as an adjective (see pp. 394 and 449):

beginnend *(beginning)*	
die in zwei Tagen **beginnenden** Ferien	*the vacation that begins in two days*
bezahlt *(paid)*	
eine so gut **bezahlte** Stelle	*such a well paid job*

Studentinnen in einem Bergwerk (DDR) (das Bergwerk = *mine*)

Üben wir!

A. (books open) Read the sentences aloud and change the extended modifiers to relative clauses, as in the example.

> EXAMPLE: Die in Hamburg geborene Schriftstellerin wohnt heute in Berlin.
> Die Schriftstellerin, die in Hamburg geboren ist, wohnt heute in Berlin.

1. Ihr erstes, im Ausland kaum gelesenes Buch machte sie in Deutschland berühmt.
2. Ihre zwei Jahre jüngere Schwester ist Lehrerin in Düsseldorf.
3. In Berlin wohnt sie in einem alten, von Touristen kaum besuchten Stadtteil.
4. Aus allen Teilen Deutschlands bekommt sie Briefe von ihren oft sehr jungen Lesern.
5. Von ihr erwartet man Antworten auf viele für die Jugend immer ernster werdende Probleme.

6 ◆ Expanding Your Vocabulary

Leicht zu merken

akut	
die **Emanzipation**	Emanzipation
ideal	ideal
industriell	industriell
parallel	parallel
psychologisch	
stereotyp	stereotyp

Wortschatz 2

Verben

ändern to change (*trans.*)
  Sie hat ihr Leben geändert. She changed her life.
sich ändern to change (*intrans.*)
  Ihr Leben hat sich geändert. Her life changed.
  Hier hat sich nichts geändert. Nothing has changed here.
bieten, bot, hat geboten to offer; provide
diskutieren to discuss; debate
erledigen to attend to, take care of, finish

Substantive

der **Erfolg, -e** success
der **Gedanke, -ns, -n** thought
der **Gott, ̈er** god
der **Weg, -e** way, path

das **Geschlecht, -er** sex, gender
das **Gesetz, -e** law
  vor dem Gesetz under the law, in the eyes of the law
das **Thema, Themen** topic, subject, theme
das **Ziel, -e** goal

die **Aufgabe, -n** task, assignment
die **Chance, -n** chance
die **Gleichberechtigung** (*sing.*) equal rights
die **Küche, -n** kitchen
die **Verbesserung, -en** improvement

Andere Vokabeln

berufstätig employed
deutlich clear
gebildet educated
gefährlich dangerous
gleich equal
gleichberechtigt enjoying equal rights

kritisch critical
niedrig low
öffentlich public
ordentlich tidy, orderly
staatlich government(al), state

Nützliche Ausdrücke

eines Tages some day (*in the future*); one day (*in the past*)
es geht um (*must have impersonal* **es** *as subject*) it's a question of . . . ; what's at issue is . . . ; it's about . . .
  Es geht um unseren Lohn. Our wages are at issue.
  In diesem Buch geht es um den Zweiten Weltkrieg. This book is about the Second World War.

Gegensätze

gebildet ≠ ungebildet	educated ≠ uneducated
ordentlich ≠ unordentlich	tidy, orderly ≠ messy, disorderly

Gedanken über die
Emanzipation der Frau

Die Rolle der Frau in der Gesellschaft ist in Deutschland wie fast überall in der Welt zum heißen Diskussionsthema geworden. Es wird sowohl über soziale als auch° über psychologische Fragen diskutiert. Es geht um gleichen Lohn für gleiche Arbeit, aber auch um das Selbstbewußtsein° der Frau und um die Beziehungen° zwischen den Geschlechtern.

    Ein altes Klischee sagt, die Frau solle sich nur um „Kinder, Kirche und Küche" kümmern. Für manche Frauen mag das noch stimmen, aber für die meisten jungen Frauen nicht mehr. Es ist das Ziel der Frauenbewegung, solche Klischees zu bekämpfen° und allen Frauen neue Wege zu eröffnen.° Heutzutage versuchen viele Frauen, aus der traditionellen gesellschaftlichen Rolle auszubrechen.

    In früheren Zeiten wurden fast alle jungen Mädchen auf eine Zukunft als Mutter und Hausfrau vorbereitet. Sie mußten früh lernen, wie die „ideale" Frau sein sollte: bescheiden,° ordentlich und kinderlieb.° Dieses traditionelle Bild hatte sich nach und nach als selbstverständlich und normal etabliert.°

    Im industriellen Zeitalter° aber wurde es immer deutlicher, daß die Industrie die Arbeitskraft° der Frau brauchte. Es waren die ungebildeten und armen Frauen, die in gefährlichen, ungesunden Fabriken arbeiten mußten, weil ihre Familien sonst verhungert° wären. Die Damen der Oberschicht° aber durften zu Hause Herrin° sein, wo es ihre Aufgabe war, den Haushalt° zu führen und gesellschaftliche Unterhaltung° zu bieten. Natürlich gab es schon im 18. und 19. Jahrhundert gebildete und aktive Frauen, wie z.B. Bettina von Arnim, die einen Berliner Salon führte.[1] Heutige° Frauen haben auch gelernt, die trotz aller Schwierigkeiten errungenen Leistungen° dieser früheren Frauengenerationen zu schätzen.°

    Und wie ist es heute? Im Grundgesetz[2] der BRD (Artikel 3) steht zwar, daß alle Menschen vor dem Gesetz gleich seien. Männer und Frauen seien gleichberechtigt. Die

---

sowohl . . . als auch = both . . . and

self-esteem
relationships

combat
open up

modest / fond of children

hatte sich . . . etabliert = had
established itself / era
labor

starved
upper class / mistress
household
entertainment

contemporary

errungenen Leistungen = gained
achievements / appreciate

---

[1] Bettina von Arnim (1785–1859), novelist and essayist, presided over an
  influential literary salon in Berlin.
[2] The "basic law" or Constitution of the FRG.

Verfassung° der DDR (Artikel 20) fügt noch hinzu,° daß die
berufliche Qualifizierung° der Frau eine gesellschaftliche
und staatliche Aufgabe sei. Aber ist diese offizielle Gleichberechtigung schon verwirklicht?° Manche berufstätigen
40 Frauen müssen noch die ganze Hausarbeit erledigen, obwohl sie den gleichen Arbeitstag haben wie ihre Männer. In
solchen Fällen° hat die Frau eine neue Rolle übernommen,°
ohne die alte ganz aufzugeben. In der DDR, wo 80% der
Frauen arbeiten, ist dieses Problem besonders akut.

45   Trotzdem hat sich viel im Leben der Frauen geändert.
Jungen Frauen in beiden deutschen Staaten stehen heute
viel mehr Türen offen als vor einer Generation. Immer mehr
Frauen nehmen aktiv und kritisch am öffentlichen Leben
ihres Landes teil. In der BRD, z.B., spielen Frauen führende
50 Rollen bei den Grünen.[3] Solche Frauen wollen die von den

*constitution / **fügt . . . hinzu** = adds*
berufliche Qualifizierung =
professional training
achieved

cases / taken on

---

[3] The Greens, the environmentalist and anti-nuclear political party (see p. 301 above).

Männern geschaffene° Politik und Kultur nicht einfach mit-   *created*
machen,° sondern ändern. Die auch in Amerika bekannte   *participate in*
DDR-Schriftstellerin Christa Wolf schrieb darüber: „Die
Möglichkeit, die unsere Gesellschaft [den Frauen] gab: zu
55   tun, was die Männer tun, hat sie . . . zu der Frage gebracht:
Was *tun* die Männer überhaupt?° Und will ich das eigent-   *anyway*
lich?"

    Aber parallel zu den Verbesserungen im Leben der Frau
ändert sich auch die Rolle des Mannes. Heutzutage wollen
60   viele Männer mehr Zeit mit ihren Familien verbringen und
sich weniger um Erfolg und Beruf kümmern. Die Frauenemanzipation bringt also viel mehr als nur bessere Berufs-
chancen für Frauen. Sie könnte auch eines Tages beide
Geschlechter von ihren alten stereotypen Rollen befreien.°   *liberate*

Fragen zum Lesestück

1. Was sind die wichtigsten Fragen in der Diskussion über die Frauenemanzipation?
2. Was ist das Ziel der Frauenbewegung?
3. Beschreiben Sie die traditionelle Rolle der Frau.
4. Wie heißt das alte Klischee über die Rolle der Frau?
5. Wie hat die Industrie das Leben der Frau geändert?
6. Was für Frauen arbeiteten in den Fabriken?
7. Sind deutsche Frauen heutzutage gleichberechtigt?
8. Welche Möglichkeiten haben junge Frauen von heute, die die Frauen vor
fünfzig Jahren nicht hatten?
9. Wie hat die Frauenbewegung auch das Leben mancher Männer geändert?
10. Wie könnte die Gesellschaft eines Tages aussehen?

Vom Lesen zum Sprechen

Unterschiede und Ähnlichkeiten

Here is some familiar vocabulary:

ähnlich (+ *dative*)

Sie ist ihren Eltern ähnlich.   *She is similar to her parents.*
                                   or: She is like her parents.

anders als

> Heutzutage ist es ganz anders als vor dreißig Jahren.

gleich

> Wir haben das gleiche Problem.
> Vor dem Gesetz sind alle Menschen gleich.

gleichberechtigt

Zur Diskussion

A. Besprechen Sie einige Unterschiede und Ähnlichkeiten . . .

1. in der Erziehung (*upbringing*) von Mädchen und Jungen.
2. im Leben von Studenten und Studentinnen.

B. Wie haben sich die Rollen der Geschlechter in den letzten Jahren geändert?

Mündliche Übungen

A. Persönliche Fragen

1. Sagen Sie, wie die Studenten rechts und links von Ihnen heute aussehen.
2. Wann haben Sie das letzte Mal bis halb vier gefeiert?
3. Was wurde damals gefeiert?
4. Nach wievielen Jahren feiert man goldene Hochzeit?
5. Was verdient man heutzutage in einer gut bezahlten Stelle?
6. Sie kennen sicher berufstätige Frauen. Was wissen Sie über das Leben dieser Frauen? (Berufsleben, Familienleben, Freizeit)
7. Wollen Sie eines Tages Kinder haben? Wie stellen Sie sich Ihr Familienleben vor?
8. Würden Sie halbtags arbeiten, wenn Ihr Kind noch klein ist?

B. „Worum geht es?" What's it about? Describe the themes and subjects of books and movies you like. Begin your statements with „Es geht um . . ."

EXAMPLE: Teacher: Welche Filme haben Sie in letzter Zeit gesehen?
Student: Letzte Woche habe ich „Casablanca" gesehen.
Teacher: Worum geht es denn in dem Film?
Student: Es geht um Liebe, aber auch um Politik.

C. Use the passive voice to tell what people do in the places pictured. Your sentences may either have a subject or use the impersonal passive.

EXAMPLE: Hier werden Bücher gelesen. or
Hier wird gelesen.

D. *Interviewen und berichten.* Students work in pairs. One student talks for one or two minutes about his or her current activities and interests. The other asks questions, listens, and takes notes. The interviewer then uses special subjunctive to report back to the class what the first student has said.

> EXAMPLE: Student A: Ich spiele viel Tennis und interessiere mich
> auch für Musik (usw.).
> Student B: Jane erzählte mir, sie spiele viel Tennis und
> interessiere sich auch für Musik. Sie sagt
> auch, . . . (usw.).

E. *Rollenspiel.* Spielen Sie diese Situationen mit anderen Studenten.

1. Abends um 6.00 Uhr.
   Frau Berger ist berufstätig. Herr Berger bleibt bei den Kindern zu Hause. Frau Berger kommt nach einem harten Arbeitstag nach Hause.

2. Umziehen oder hierbleiben?
   Monika und Harald sind Studenten in ihrem letzten Semester an der Uni in München. Sie haben vor, bald zu heiraten. Harald hat gerade eine gut bezahlte Stelle in Frankfurt bekommen. Monika hat noch keine Stelle gefunden, aber sie möchte München nicht verlassen.

3. Mutter und Tochter
   Anita (20 Jahre alt) fragt ihre Mutter (50), wie es damals war, als sie jung war. Frau Baumann erzählt ihrer Tochter, was sie als junge Frau gern gemacht hätte, oder was sie anders machen würde.

FRAUEN UND BILDUNG

Was ist. Was sich geändert hat.
Was sich ändern muß.

Schriftliche Übungen

F. Im Fernsehen (*television*) gab es ein Gespräch zwischen einem Interviewer und der bekannten Feministin Elisabeth Schmidt-Dengler. Lesen Sie diesen Bericht über das Interview und schreiben Sie das Gespräch, das die beiden gehabt haben, als Dialog.

Der Interviewer fragte Frau Schmidt-Dengler, wir lange sie wohl noch für die Emanzipation der Frau kämpfen müsse. Das sei schwer zu sagen, meinte sie. Sie werde einfach nicht aufgeben, bis alle Frauen gleichberechtigt seien. Der Interviewer unterbrach und sagte, daß die Gleichberechtigung schon seit Jahren im Grundgesetz stehe. Frau Schmidt-Dengler lachte und sagte, ja, das stimme schon, und das sei auch wichtig. Auf der anderen Seite seien das Grundgesetz und die Wirklichkeit leider oft zwei verschiedene Sachen. Die Frauenemanzipation dürfe nicht nur im Gesetz stehen. Man müsse auch das traditionelle Denken über die Rollen von Mann und Frau ändern. Der Interviewer dankte Frau Schmidt-Dengler für das Gespräch.

Virginia
FRAUENBUCHKRITIK

LITERATUR ÜBER FRAUEN
Bücher für Frauen
Frauen in Gesellschaft

G. Schreiben Sie eine Seite darüber.

Was würde sich in Ihrem Leben ändern, wenn Sie eine Frau/ein Mann wären?

H. Wie sagt man das auf deutsch?

1. Max told me that there was a new restaurant around the corner.
2. Yes, the food is supposed to be very good.
3. But the prices could be lower.
4. Max claims to know a lot about it and he recommended it to me.
5. Did you ask Mimi whether she is coming to the wedding?
6. Yes, but she acted as if she had never heard of it.
7. But Brigitte says she had already invited her last month.
8. Hello, Mr. Lehmann. I haven't seen you for three years.
9. That's right. I just returned. I don't know my way around here anymore.
10. Yes, in the last three years there has been a lot of building. (use impersonal passive)
11. I hope the old city won't be destroyed.

Almanach

Women, Pregnancy, and West German Law

Working women in West Germany enjoy wide coverage under the *Mutterschutzgesetz,* the law protecting mothers.

Gefahrenschutz: a woman may not undertake work that endangers her or her child.

Kündigungsgesetz: a woman cannot be fired during her pregnancy or up to 4 months after the birth of the child (8 months if she has taken a maternity leave).

Beschäftigungsverbot: she may not work 6 weeks prior to delivery date or until 8–12 weeks after the birth.

Mutterschaftshilfe

Mutterschaftsvorsorge: she receives all expenses covering prenatal care, delivery, and related costs.

Mutterschaftsgeld: the full amount of her previous pay (or disability pay or a lump sum).

Mutterschaftsurlaub: maternity leave is usually 4 months after the birth. 93% of women take maternity leaves to care for their newborn children.

	Gefahrenschutz Keine Arbeiten, die die Gesundheit von Mutter und Kind gefährden	**Mutterschutz**
Kündigungsschutz während der Schwangerschaft bis 4 Monate (bei Mutterschaftsurlaub bis 8 Monate) nach der Entbindung		**Beschäftigungsverbot** 6 Wochen vor der Entbindung bis 8 bzw. 12 Wochen nach der Entbindung
Mutterschaftshilfe **Mutterschaftsvorsorge:** Arztliche Betreuung, Hebammenhilfe, Entbindungspauschale **Mutterschaftsgeld:** in Höhe des bisherigen Nettoentgelts oder des Krankengeldes oder einmalig 150 DM		**Mutterschaftsurlaub** bis zu 4 Monaten nach Ablauf der Schutzfrist Mutterschaftsurlaubsgeld (510 DM im Monat)

ZAHLENBILDER
282 501

© Erich Schmidt Verlag GmbH

Wer spricht Deutsch?

Gärtnerin (gardener) in den Schweizer Alpen

Junge Arbeiter in der DDR

Schwäne am Neckar   (Heidelberg, BRD)

Schwarzwaldbauer (Black Forest
farmer)   (BRD)

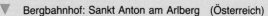
Bergbahnhof: Sankt Anton am Arlberg   (Österreich)

Almabtrieb (festival of driving cattle home in the fall)   (Schweiz)

Kellner in einer Eisdiele (ice-cream parlor)   (BRD)

Delikatessen- und Feinkostladen   (Kassel, BRD)

Frauen in Trachten (folk costumes) (Rothenburg o.d. Tauber, BRD)

Bäckerlehrling mit frischen Brezeln
(fresh soft pretzels)   (BRD)

Zifferblattmaler (clock face painter)   (BRD)

An der Börse (stock market)   (BRD)

Zwei junge Menschen auf einem Mofa (motorcycle)
(Trier, BRD)

▲ Friedensdemonstration der Frauen   (Berlin-West)

▼ Vater und Sohn am Oktoberfest
(München, BRD)

▲ Türkisches Ehepaar (married couple)   (BRD)

▼ Textilindustrie: Design mit dem Computer   (Lörrach, BRD)

Summary and Review

FORMS

1 ◆ Verbs

A. Future Tense: inflected form of **werden** + infinitive

	auxiliary		*infinitive*
Ich	**werde**	das am Montag	**erledigen.**
Sie	**wird**	dich nicht	**verstehen.**

B. General Subjunctive

1. Present tense of general subjunctive

   a. Weak verbs: present subjunctive has the same form as past indicative:

wenn ich **wohnte**	if I lived	wenn wir **wohnten**	if we lived
wenn du **wohntest**	if you lived	wenn ihr **wohntet**	if you lived
wenn sie **wohnte**	if she lived	wenn sie **wohnten**	if they lived

   b. Strong verbs:

   present subjunctive = simple past stem (**fuhr-**)
   +
   umlaut whenever possible (**führ-**)
   +
   subjunctive endings:

wenn ich **führe**	if I drove	wenn wir **führen**	if we drove
wenn du **führest**	if you drove	wenn ihr **führet**	if you drove
wenn er **führe**	if he drove	wenn sie **führen**	if they drove

c. Modal verbs:

present subjunctive = past indicative (**ich sollte, ich durfte**)

\+

umlaut when infinitive has umlaut
(**ich sollte, ich dürfte**):

ich **dürfte**	I would be allowed	ich **müßte**	I would have to
ich **könnte**	I could	ich **sollte**	I ought to
ich **möchte**	I would like to	ich **wollte**	I would want to

d. **haben, werden, wissen:**

present subjunctive = past indicative (**ich hatte, wurde, wußte**)

\+

umlaut (**ich hätte, würde, wüßte**):

wenn ich	**hätte**	if I had	wenn wir	**hätten**	if we had
wenn du	**hättest**	if you had	wenn ihr	**hättet**	if you had
wenn sie	**hätte**	if she had	wenn sie	**hätten**	if they had
wenn ich	**würde**	if I became	wenn wir	**würden**	if we became
wenn du	**würdest**	if you became	wenn ihr	**würdet**	if you became
wenn er	**würde**	if he became	wenn sie	**würden**	if they became
wenn ich	**wüßte**	if I knew	wenn wir	**wüßten**	if we knew
wenn du	**wüßtest**	if you knew	wenn ihr	**wüßtet**	if you knew
wenn sie	**wüßte**	if she knew	wenn sie	**wüßten**	if they knew

e. Present subjunctive with **würde:**

present subjunctive of **werden** + infinitive

ich **würde kommen**	I would come	wir **würden kommen**	we would come
du **würdest kommen**	you would come	ihr **würdet kommen**	you would come
er **würde kommen**	he would come	sie **würden kommen**	they would come

2. Past tense of general subjunctive:

present subjunctive of **sein** *or* **haben** + *past participle*

Ich **hätte** auf dich **gewartet.**   *I **would have waited** for you.*
Wir **wären** gestern abend   *We **would have come***
gekommen.   *yesterday evening.*

3. Past subjunctive with a modal verb:

present subjunctive of haben + **double infinitive**

Ihr **hättet** länger **warten sollen.**	You **should have waited** longer.
Sie **hätten** auch **mitkommen dürfen.**	They **would have been allowed** to come along too.

C. Special Subjunctive (for indirect quotation)

1. Present tense of special subjunctive:

infinitive stem + subjunctive endings

Hans sagte, er **wisse** das schon.	Hans said he already **knew** that.
Marie meint, daß sie das verstehen **könne.**	Marie says she **can** understand that.

2. Future tense of special subjunctive:

present special subjunctive of werden + **infinitive**

Laura fragte, ob er bald **zurückkommen werde.**	Laura asked if he **would come back** soon.

3. Past tense of special subjunctive:

present special subjunctive of haben or sein + **past participle**

Richard sagt, er **habe** das nicht **getan.**	Richard says he **didn't do** that.
Marie fragte, ob er schon **angekommen sei.**	Marie asked if he **had** already **arrived.**

D. Passive Voice

1. Basic conjugation:

---

inflected form of **werden** + past participle

passive infinitive:		gesehen werden	to be seen
present:	Er wird	gesehen.	He is seen.
past:	Er wurde	gesehen.	He was seen.
future	Er wird	gesehen werden.	He will be seen.
perfect:	Er ist	gesehen worden.	He has been seen. or He was seen.
past perfect:	Er war	gesehen worden.	He had been seen.

2. Passive with a modal verb:

---

inflected modal + passive infinitive

---

present:	Das muß	geändert werden.	That must be changed.
past	Das mußte	geändert werden.	That had to be changed.
future:	Das wird	geändert werden müssen.	That will have to be changed.
perfect:	Das hat	geändert werden müssen.	That had to be changed.
past perfect:	Das hatte	geändert werden müssen.	That had had to be changed.

---

3. Impersonal passive construction (for human activities):

The verb is *always* third person singular. There is no expressed subject.

   Hier wird oft getanzt.   *There's often **dancing** here.*

Impersonal **es** begins the sentence if no other element occupies first position:

   Es wird hier oft getanzt.

4. Passive of verbs with dative objects

The dative object remains in the dative case. There is no expressed subject.

   active:

   Man glaubt diesem Politiker nicht mehr.

   passive:

   Diesem Politiker wird nicht   *This politician is no longer*
      mehr geglaubt.   *believed.*

E. Verbs Used With Prepositions

Angst haben vor (+ *dat.*)	to be afraid of
antworten auf (+ *acc.*)	to answer something
sich ärgern über (+ *acc.*)	to be annoyed at
bitten um	to ask for, request
danken für	to thank for
denken an (+ *acc.*)	to think of
sich erholen von	to recover (or recuperate) from
erinnern an (+ *acc.*)	to remind of
sich erinnern an (+ *acc.*)	to remember
sich freuen auf (+ *acc.*)	to look forward to
gehören zu	to be a part of, be one of
sich gewöhnen an (+ *acc.*)	to get used to
glauben an (+ *acc.*)	to believe in
halten für	to take for, regard as, think X is

halten von	to think of, have an opinion about
sich interessieren für	to be interested in
sich konzentrieren auf (+ *acc.*)	to concentrate on
sich kümmern um	to take care of, be concerned with
nach·denken über (+ *acc.*)	to think about; ponder
teil·nehmen an (+ *dat.*)	to take part in
sich verloben mit	to become engaged to
sich vor·bereiten auf (+ *acc.*)	to prepare for
warten auf (+ *acc.*)	to wait for

F. Participles

1. Present participles as adjective and adverbs

   infinitive + **d**

schlafen	+ **d** ⟶ **schlafend**	*sleeping*
spielen	+ **d** ⟶ **spielend**	*playing*

   As an adjective, the present participle takes the usual adjective endings:

Stört das **schlafende** Mädchen nicht!	*Don't disturb the **sleeping** girl.*
Spielende Kinder sind oft laut.	***Playing** children are often loud.*

2. Past participles as adjectives

   Past participles may also be used with the usual endings:

Gut **vorbereitete** Studenten lernen am meisten.	*Well **prepared** students learn the most.*
Ich muß meinen **reparierten** Wagen heute abholen.	*I have to pick up my **repaired** car today.*

2 ◆ Pronouns

da- and **wo**-compounds

Used instead of **preposition + pronoun** when the prepositional object is an inanimate noun:

animate noun object ⟶	*pronoun object*
Er dachte **an seine Freundin.**	Er dachte **an sie.**
Sie interessiert sich **für Goethe.**	**Für wen** interessiert sie sich?

inanimate noun object ⟶	*da-* or *wo-compound*
Er dachte an **die Deutschstunde.**	Er dachte **daran.**
Sie interessiert sich **für Geschichte.**	**Wofür** interessiert sie sich?

FUNCTIONS

1 ♦ Making Wishes and Conditions Contrary to Fact: Subjunctive Mood

A. Conditions contrary to fact:

$$\overbrace{\textbf{Wenn} \ldots (subjunctive\ verb),}^{condition} \qquad \overbrace{(subjunctive\ verb) \ldots}^{conclusion}$$

or:

$$\overbrace{\ldots (subjunctive\ verb) \ldots,}^{conclusion} \qquad \overbrace{\textbf{wenn} \ldots (subjunctive\ verb).}^{condition}$$

Wenn Sie es mir beschreiben könnten, würde ich es verstehen.	*If you could describe it to me I would understand it.*
Natürlich würde ich euch helfen, wenn ich Zeit hätte.	*Of course I would help you if I had time to.*

B. Wishes contrary to fact:

1. **Wenn ... nur ...** (*subjunctive verb*)!

Wenn ich nur mehr Geld hätte!	*If only I had more money!*

2. **Ich wünschte,**
   Ich wollte, } ... (*subjunctive verb*) ....

Ich wünschte, ich könnte etwas Besseres berichten.	*I wish I could report something better.*
Sie wollte, sie hätte das früher gewußt.	*She wishes she had known that earlier.*

2 ♦ Describing with *als ob* (as though) + subjunctive:

Es war,
Er tut, } **als ob** ... (*subjunctive verb*).
Sie sah aus,

Sie sehen aus, als ob sie wenig geschlafen hätten.	*They look as though they hadn't slept much.*
Sie spricht Deutsch, als ob es ihre Muttersprache wäre.	*She speaks German as though it were her native language.*

3 ◆ Polite Requests: Subjunctive Mood

German uses present subjunctive for polite requests. Note the difference in tone between indicative and subjective:

Können Sie nicht aufhören?
Könnten Sie bitte aufhören?

Can't you stop!
Could you please stop!

Haben Sie ein Zimmer frei?
Hätten Sie ein Zimmer frei?

Do you have a room free!
Would you have a room free!

4 ◆ Indirect Quotation

A. German uses special subjunctive for indirect quotation.

introductory clause	*indirect quotation*
Erich sagte,	daß er sehr glücklich sei.

B. The tense of the indirect quote is the same as the tense of the direct quote from which it derives:

	Direct Quotation	Indirect Quotation	
present	„Ich **bin** müde."	Luise sagte, sie **sei** müde.	*present*
past	„Ich **war** müde."		
perfect	„Ich **bin** müde **gewesen.**" }	Luise sagte, sie **sei** müde **gewesen.**	*past*
future	„Ich **werde** müde **sein.**"	Luise sagte, sie **werde** müde **sein.**	*future*

C. Yes/no questions in indirect quotation begin with **ob:**

„Hast du Zeit?" ⟶ Sie fragte, **ob** ich Zeit hätte.

D. Commands in indirect quotation use the verb **sollen:**

„Denk nicht daran!" ⟶ Johann sagte, ich **solle** nicht daran denken.

5 ◆ Indicating Direction

A. Away from the speaker: **hin**

B. Toward the speaker: **her**

6 ◆ Subjective Use of Modal Verbs

A. Possibility: **mögen**

Die Arbeit mag hart sein, aber sie muß trotzdem gemacht werden.

The work may be hard but it has to be done anyway.

B. Strong probability: **müssen**

Sie muß schon in Europa sein.

She must be in Europe already.

C. Hearsay: **sollen**

Sie sollen glücklich sein.

They are supposed to be happy. Word has it they are happy.

D. Fairly strong possibility: **können**

Er kann noch berühmt werden.

He may yet become famous.

E. Doubting a claim: **wollen**

Was? Dieser Politiker will ehrlich sein?

What? This politician claims to be honest?

7 ◆ Time Expressions

A. Accusative for definite time.

The accusative case is used in expressions of definite time when no prepositions are involved.

jeden Tag	*every day*
die ganze Woche	*all week*
den ganzen Monat	*all month*
letztes Semester	*last semester*
nächsten Herbst	*next autumn*

(*but:* genitive for indefinite time:

eines Tages	*some day, one day*)

B. Adverbs of time

montags/dienstags, usw.	*Mondays/Tuesdays, etc.*
nachts	*at night*
abends	*evenings; in the evenings*
morgens	*mornings; in the mornings*
nachmittags	*afternoons; in the afternoons*
vormittags	*mornings; in the mornings*

C. Time phrases with -lang

stundenlang	*for hours*
tagelang	*for days*
jahrelang	*for years*
but: eine Zeitlang	*for a time*

Ich mußte **stundenlang** warten, bevor ein Bus endlich hielt.

I had to wait for hours before a bus finally stopped.

8 ◆ Wanting X to do Y

German uses **möchte** or **wollen** followed by a **daß**-clause:

Wollen Sie, daß ich später vorbeikomme?

Do you want me to come by later?

Nein, ich möchte, daß wir jetzt kurz zusammen reden.

No, I'd like us to talk briefly together right now.

9 ◆ Review of Useful Expressions

1. Time
   In letzter Zeit ist das Leben immer teurer geworden.
   In Zukunft werde ich mehr Geld brauchen.
   Von jetzt an muß ich sparen.

2. Traveling
   Kennen Sie sich hier aus?
   Darf ich Sie um Auskunft bitten?
   Haben Sie ein Zimmer frei?
   Kann ich hier Geld wechseln?
   Danke für die Hilfe.

3. Reactions and Opinions
   Das kann ich nicht ernst nehmen.
   Kein Wunder!
   Sie haben recht.
   Das mag sein.
   Stimmt schon.
   Was halten Sie davon?
   Das halte ich für zu teuer.
   Ich gratuliere Ihnen.
   Sei mir bitte nicht böse!
   Was sagen (meinen) Sie dazu?

TEST YOUR PROGRESS 4

A. Provide the German prepositional phrase cued in English. Note that in some cases the English equivalent may not contain a preposition.

1. Wie lange warten Sie schon (*for something new*)?
2. Glauben Sie noch (*in this government*)?
3. Nein, ich kann mich noch zu gut (*the old government*) erinnern.

4. Wir müssen uns (*for the test*) vorbereiten.
5. Kannst du dich bei diesem Wetter (*on your work*) konzentrieren?
6. Ich kümmere mich gar nicht (*with the test*).

7. Willst du (*in the discussion*) teilnehmen?
8. Nein, ich interessiere mich nicht (*in such problems*).
9. Ich kann mich nicht (*to your friends*) gewöhnen.

10. Denkt Rolf noch (*of me*)?
11. Natürlich. Er bat mich (*for your address*).

12 Was halten Sie (*of him*)?
13. Ich halte ihn (*to be a very good student*).
14. Er erinnert mich (*of his parents*).

15. (*About studying*) an einer Universität habe ich lange nachgedacht.
16. Ich weiß jetzt, ich interessiere mich sehr (*in foreign languages*).
17. Dann sollst du dich (*for the Abitur*) gut vorbereiten.

B. Answer the following questions affirmatively. Replace the prepositional phrase with a **da**-compound or the personal object with a pronoun.

> EXAMPLE: Bereiten Sie sich auf Ihre Reise vor?
> Ja, wir bereiten uns darauf vor.
> *or:* Erinnern Sie sich noch an meine ältere Schwester?
> Ja, ich erinnere mich noch an sie.

1. Haben Sie auf seinen Brief geantwortet?
2. Glaubst du noch an den Erfolg unserer Arbeit?
3. Kannst du dich an diesen Menschen gewöhnen?
4. Hat Sabrina sich um ihren Bruder gekümmert?
5. Halten Sie viel von diesem neuen Gesetz?
6. Habt ihr auch an die anderen Studenten gedacht?

C. You will read the facts. Use subjunctive to write conditional sentences contrary to these facts (changing negations to positive statements). Begin each sentence with the **wenn**-clause or the conclusion clause as indicated. Watch tenses.

EXAMPLE: Er trank nicht viel. Es war nicht ungesund. (*begin with* **wenn**)

Wenn er viel getrunken hätte, wäre es ungesund gewesen.

1. Du kannst nicht halbtags arbeiten. Wir haben nicht genug Geld. (*begin with* **wenn**)
2. Sie hat den Laden nicht früh genug aufgemacht. Wir haben nichts gekauft. (*begin with conclusion*)
3. Er ist nicht freundlich. Man kann nicht gut mit ihm sprechen. (*begin with* **wenn**)
4. Die Straßenbahn hat noch nicht gehalten. Wir können nicht aussteigen. (*begin with conclusion*)
5. Ich habe ihr nicht gratuliert. Ich wußte nicht, daß sie Geburtstag hat. (*begin with* **wenn**)

D. You will read the facts. Use subjunctive to write wishes contrary to these facts. Use **Wenn . . . nur . . .** , **ich wünschte . . .** , or **ich wollte . . .** as indicated. Watch tenses!

EXAMPLE: Wir haben nicht genug Zeit. (wenn . . . nur . . .)

Wenn wir nur genug Zeit hätten!

1. Wir sind noch nicht angekommen. (wenn . . . nur)
2. Heute morgen haben wir die Wohnung nicht aufgeräumt. (ich wünschte)
3. Hier gibt es kein Café. (ich wollte)
4. Leider habe ich meine Reiseschecks vergessen. (wenn . . . nur)
5. Die Preise sind gestiegen. (wenn . . . nur)

E. Respond to each sentence by saying that the persons under discussion only *look* as though something were the case.

EXAMPLE: Ist Rolf wirklich so optimistisch?

Nein, er sieht nur aus, als ob er optimistisch wäre.

1. Sind diese Menschen wirklich so ordentlich?
2. Haben deine Freunde wirklich so viel Geld?
3. Ist Jutta wirklich so konservativ geworden?
4. Kommt Frank wirklich gerade aus den Ferien zurück?

F. Make these requests more polite by putting them into the subjunctive.

1. Können Sie mir helfen?
2. Darf ich eine Frage stellen?
3. Werden Sie morgen vorbeikommen?
4. Haben Sie ein Zimmer mit Bad?
5. Wann soll ich das für Sie machen?

G. Restate the following sentences in the passive. Keep the same tense as the active sentence.

> EXAMPLE: Max baut sich dieses Haus.
> Dieses Haus wird von Max gebaut.

1. Karl hat diesen Brief geschrieben.
2. Die Stadt baut hier eine neue Schule.
3. Professor Müller hält die Vorlesung.
4. Die Studenten mußten die Bücher selber kaufen.
5. Mein Freund sollte die Aufgabe machen.

H. Restate the sentences in the passive.

> EXAMPLE: Wer soll diese Arbeit machen?
> Von wem soll diese Arbeit gemacht werden?

1. Das kann der Chef eines Tages erledigen.
2. Das ganze Buch muß man bis Donnerstag lesen.
3. Diese Arbeit können Sie leicht machen.
4. Ein solches Klischee kann man nicht ernst nehmen.
5. Können alle die Frage verstehen?

I. Replace the verb in parentheses with an adjective formed from its present or past participle. Don't forget the adjective endings!

> EXAMPLE: Wann werden die (bestellen) Bücher endlich ankommen?
> Wann werden die bestellten Bücher endlich ankommen?

1. Ich kann bei (schließen) Fenstern nicht schlafen.
2. Gott sei Dank habe ich das (verlieren) Geld wieder gefunden.
3. Der (übersetzen) Roman kann hoffentlich leichter gelesen werden.
4. Dieser Politiker hat viele (überraschen) Namen genannt.
5. Ein (abfahren) Zug fährt nach und nach schneller.

J. Wie sagt man das auf deutsch?

1. What did you think of her brother?
2. I thought he was very likeable.
3. Do you often think of your childhood?
4. Of course, sometimes I think about it for hours.
5. I think that is no longer correct. What do you think? (i.e., what is your opinion)

K. Restate the following sentences using the appropriate subjective modal.

> EXAMPLE: Es ist unglaublich, daß sie Ausländer sind.
> Sie können keine Ausländer sein.

1. Ich bin sicher, daß die Regierung in dem Land repressiv ist.
2. Man sagt, die Preise seien dort niedriger.
3. Es ist möglich, daß das stimmt.
4. Vielleicht ist er schon dreißig.
5. Sie sagt, sie sei eine gute Künstlerin, aber ich glaube ihr nicht.

L. Report what Gabi said to you, using special subjunctive.

1. Ich war gestern in der Mensa. (Gabi sagte, sie . . .)
2. Das Essen hat mir gut geschmeckt.
3. Ich bereite mich jetzt auf eine Klausur vor.
4. Hat dich Heinz angerufen?
5. Ich bin jetzt ziemlich müde.
6. Zeig mir dein Referat über Thomas Mann.

Answer Key

Test Your Progress 1 *page 118*

A.
1. Barbara möchte schon nach Berlin.
2. Die Studenten wollen noch ein bißchen bleiben.
3. Was trägst du am Freitag?
4. Nimmt Karin die Suppe?
5. Liest du die Zeitung?
6. Schläft er bis neun?
7. Weiß Gisela, wie er heißt?
8. Wartet er bis zehn?

B.
1. scheint; to shine; seem
2. spielen; to play
3. geht; to go
4. bedeutet; to mean
5. meine; to be of the opinion; to think; to mean
6. läuft; to run; to go on foot; to walk
7. stimmt, to be correct
8. schläfst; to sleep
9. fahren; to drive, go (by vehicle)
10. besucht; to visit
11. will; to want to, to intend to
12. darf; to be permitted to
13. wirst; to become
14. schneit, to snow
15. bekommen; to get, receive
16. liest; to read
17. tragt; to carry, wear
18. kann; to be able
19. warte; to wait
20. soll; to be supposed to

C.
1. die/ Schulen
2. das/ Hemden
3. die/ Mütter
4. der/ Schuhe
5. die/ Sprachen
6. der/ Freunde
7. die/ Freundinnen
8. der/ Brüder
9. die/ Schwestern
10. das/ Klischees
11. der/ Söhne
12. die/ Töchter
13. das/ Häuser
14. die/ Zeitungen
15. der/ Berufe
16. das/ Länder
17. der/ Stühle
18. die/ Frauen
19. der/ Lehrer
20. die/ Lehrerin

D.
1. ist nicht langweilig.
2. brauche ich nicht zu arbeiten.
3. will die Zeitung nicht kaufen.
4. brauche ich nicht zu Hause zu sein.
5. hat er kein Geld mehr.
6. habe ich keine Freunde.

E.
1. Nein, ich bin noch nicht müde.
2. Nein, wir wohnen nicht mehr zu Hause.
3. Nein, sie ist nicht mehr Studentin. *or:* keine Studentin mehr.
4. Nein, ich kenne deine Schwester noch nicht. *or:* ich kenne sie noch nicht.
5. Nein, wir haben noch keine Kinder.
6. Nein, ich schreibe keine Briefe mehr.
7. Nein, Sie brauchen nicht mehr hier zu bleiben.
8. Nein, ich habe keine Angst mehr.

F.
1. meine; keine
2. das or ein; kein
3. Ihren
4. meinen
5. unser
6. meine
7. die
8. Ihre
9. Mein; meine
10. Das; keine

G.
1. ihr
2. sie
3. ihr
4. seine
5. ihr
6. Ihren
7. euch
8. eure
9. Ihr
10. sie

H.
1. Ich mag dich sehr.
2. Magst du meine Freunde nicht?

3. Ich möchte allein sein.
4. Ich bin gern allein.
5. Möchtest du (gern) schwimmen gehen?
6. Ich wandere gern.
7. Das Klima hier gefällt mir nicht.

Test Your Progress 2 *page 241*

A. 1. seit; an
2. Bei; über
3. im
4. mit; auf; zur
5. Nach; in
6. Auf; bei; außer

B. 1. Wohin fliegt er (denn)?
2. Woher kommt sie (denn)?
3. Stimmt das nicht?
4. Hast du keine Zeit für mich?
5. Wer hat das immer gesagt?
6. Wem gehört die Landkarte?
7. Wann sollen wir (*or* Sie, *or* sollt ihr) das machen?
8. Wo sind (denn) die Kinder heute?

C. 1. ins
2. zu
3. in
4. nach; nach
5. zum; nach

D. 1. a. den Kindern ein Märchen
   b. es ihnen
2. a. meinem Freund den Artikel
   b. ihn mir
3. a. den Studenten ein Beispiel
   b. es ihnen

E. 1. Karin ist heute zu Hause geblieben.
2. Meine Freunde haben nicht in München gewohnt.
3. Um wieviel Uhr bist du denn aufgestanden?
4. Ich habe einen Brief an meine Familie geschrieben.
5. Sie hat meinen Namen immer vergessen.
6. Ich habe eine Stunde bleiben müssen.

7. Die Schüler sind oft müde gewesen.
8. Ich habe leider keine Zeit gehabt.
9. Sie ist Lehrerin geworden.
10. Wir sind am Freitag nach Salzburg gefahren.

F. 1. Kommst du mit oder bleibst du hier?
2. Weil ich keine Zeit habe, kann ich Ihnen nicht helfen.
3. Hamburg liegt nicht im Süden Deutschlands, sondern (es liegt) im Norden.
4. Ich weiß nicht, ob er hier ist.
5. Da wir wenig Geld haben, müssen wir trampen.
6. Wenn du mir helfen kannst, bin ich bald fertig.
7. Jan hat nicht studiert, aber er weiß viel über Geschichte.
8. Hast du gehört, daß Tante Lina uns morgen besucht?
9. Obwohl sie nie in Europa gewesen ist, spricht sie gut Deutsch.
10. Wir sparen Geld, damit wir im Sommer nach Europa können.

G. 1. den Wagen meines Freundes
2. das Ende dieses Filmes
3. Karls Bruder
4. Das Haus meines Lehrers *or* meiner Lehrerin
5. Barbaras Haus
6. die Sprache dieser Menschen
7. trotz der Arbeit
8. Wegen meiner Arbeit
9. das Leben eines Studenten

H. 1. Wieviel Uhr ist es, bitte? *or:* Wie spät ist es, bitte?
2. Es ist fast halb acht.
3. Wann soll der Zug ankommen?
4. Er kommt um 20.59 Uhr.
5. Was machen Sie heute abend um Viertel vor acht?

I. 1. liege; im
2. auf; legen
3. ins; stellen
4. am *or* vorm; stehen
5. am; sitzen

J. 1. Wir haben keine Lust, Onkel Georg zu besuchen.
2. Um etwas über Kunst zu lernen, gingen sie ins Museum. *or:* Sie gingen ins Museum, um etwas über Kunst zu lernen.
3. Es war sehr lieb von ihr, mir eine Karte aus Köln zu schicken.
4. Du gehst schon, ohne Julia auf Wiedersehen zu sagen?

Test Your Progress 3 *page 377*

A. 1. sich verletzt
2. fühlt er sich schon
3. sich verlobt hat
4. freut sie sich
5. uns beeilen
6. mir die Haare kämmen
7. dich schon angezogen
8. mir ansehen

B. a. diesen
b. alte
c. eine neue
d. deutsche
e. unserem
f. verschiedene interessante
g. die politische
h. ersten deutschen
i. diesen alten
j. vielen
k. des deutschen Volkes
l. erste
m. gutes
n. solche politische
o. dieser wichtigen
p. einen starken
q. arbeitslose Deutsche

C. a. als
b. Wenn
c. Wann
d. Wenn
e. Als
f. wann
g. Wenn

D. 1. Lassen Sie (*or* Laß, *or* Laßt) mich bitte bleiben!
2. Haben Sie Ihr Gepäck im Auto gelassen?
3. Sie läßt sich das Essen bringen.
4. Haben Sie den Arzt kommen lassen?
5. Lassen Sie Ihren Mantel auf dem Stuhl.
6. Können wir die Kinder noch eine Stunde spielen lassen?

E. 1. lieber; am liebsten
2. ärmer; am ärmsten (*or* die ärmsten)
3. mehr; das meiste
4. ein stärkeres; das stärkste
5. größere; die größten
6. mehr; die meisten
7. wärmer; am wärmsten (*or* der wärmste)
8. mehr; die meisten
9. interessanter; am interessantesten (*or* die interessanteste)
10. ein klügeres, das klügste

F. 1. den
2. dem
3. dessen
4. die
5. das
6. was
7. denen
8. der
9. die
10. was

G. 1. das letzte Mal
2. noch einmal
3. dreimal
4. zweite Mal
5. damals

H. 1. In was für einem Haus wohnen Sie?
2. Ich lasse meinen Zimmerkameraden mir mein Frühstück bringen.
3. Leider wollte er mir heute morgen nicht helfen.
4. Als du um halb acht hereingekommen bist, hast du mich gestört.
5. Seit wann lernen Sie Deutsch?
6. Einige Professoren, deren Namen ich vergessen habe, waren besonders sympathisch.
7. Vorgestern bin ich mit ihnen zum Bahnhof gegangen.
8. Eigentlich finde ich das blaue Hemd am schönsten.
9. Nachdem ich gegessen hatte, ging ich ins Kino.
10. Damals wohnten wir in einer kleinen Wohnung.

11. Das ist mein neuer Bekannter, Paul.
12. Meine Schwester ist genauso alt wie ich.

Test Your Progress 4 *page 498*

A.
1. auf etwas Neues
2. an diese Regierung
3. an die alte Regierung
4. auf die Prüfung
5. auf deine Arbeit
6. um die Prüfung, *or* um die Klausur
7. an der Diskussion
8. für solche Probleme
9. an Ihre Freunde
10. an mich
11. um deine Adresse
12. von ihm
13. für einen sehr guten Studenten
14. an seine Eltern
15. über das Studium
16. für Fremdsprachen
17. auf das Abitur

B.
1. Ja, ich habe darauf geantwortet.
2. Ja, ich glaube noch daran.
3. Ja, ich kann mich an ihn (*or* sie) gewöhnen.
4. Ja, sie hat sich um ihn gekümmert.
5. Ja, ich halte viel davon.
6. Ja, wir haben auch an sie gedacht.

C.
1. Wenn du halbtags arbeiten könntest, hätten wir genug Geld.
2. Wir hätten etwas gekauft, wenn sie den Laden früh genug aufgemacht hätte.
3. Wenn er (nur) freundlich wäre, könnte man gut mit ihm sprechen.
4. Wir könnten aussteigen, wenn die Straßenbahn schon gehalten hätte.
5. Wenn ich gewußt hätte, daß sie Geburtstag hat, hätte ich ihr gratuliert.

D.
1. Wenn wir doch nur schon angekommen wären!
2. Ich wünschte, wir hätten die Wohnung heute morgen aufgeräumt.
3. Ich wollte, es gäbe hier ein Café.

4. Wenn ich meine Reiseschecks doch nur nicht vergessen hätte!
5. Wenn die Preise nur nicht gestiegen wären!

E.
1. Nein, sie sehen nur aus, als ob sie so ordentlich wären.
2. Nein, sie sehen nur aus, als ob sie so viel Geld hätten.
3. Nein, sie sieht nur aus, als ob sie konservativ geworden wäre.
4. Nein, er sieht nur aus, als ob er gerade aus den Ferien zurückkäme.

F.
1. Könnten Sie mir helfen?
2. Dürfte ich eine Frage stellen?
3. Würden Sie morgen vorbeikommen?
4. Hätten Sie ein Zimmer mit Bad?
5. Wann sollte ich das für Sie machen?

G.
1. Dieser Brief ist von Karl geschrieben worden.
2. Eine neue Schule wird hier von der Stadt gebaut.
3. Die Vorlesung wird von Professor Müller gehalten.
4. Die Bücher mußten von den Studenten selber gekauft werden.
5. Die Aufgabe sollte von meinem Freund gemacht werden.

H.
1. Das kann eines Tages von dem Chef erledigt werden.
2. Das ganze Buch muß bis Donnerstag gelesen werden.
3. Diese Arbeit kann leicht gemacht werden.
4. Ein solches Klischee kann nicht ernst genommen werden.
5. Kann die Frage von allen verstanden werden?

I.
1. geschlossenen
2. verlorene
3. übersetzte
4. überraschende
5. abfahrender

J.
1. Was hast du von ihrem Bruder gehalten?
2. Ich hielt ihn für sehr sympathisch. *or* ich fand ihn . . . .
3. Denken Sie oft an Ihre Kindheit?
4. Selbstverständlich. Manchmal denke ich stundenlang darüber nach.
5. Ich glaube (meine), das stimmt nicht mehr. Was meinen Sie?

K.
1. Die Regierung in dem Land muß repressiv sein.
2. Die Preise sollen dort niedriger sein.
3. Das kann stimmen. *or* Das mag stimmen.

4. Er kann (*or* mag) schon dreißig sein.
5. Sie will eine gute Künstlerin sein.

L.
1. Gabi sagte, sie sei gestern in der Mensa gewesen.
2. Sie sagte, das Essen habe ihr gut geschmeckt.
3. Sie sagte, sie bereite sich jetzt auf eine Klausur vor.
4. Sie fragte, ob Heinz mich angerufen habe.
5. Sie sagte, sie sei jetzt ziemlich müde.
6. Sie sagte mir, ich solle ihr mein Referat über Thomas Mann zeigen.

Appendix 1

Strong and Irregular Verbs

The following list contains the principal parts of all the strong and irregular verbs in *Neue Horizonte*. With a few exceptions, only the basic stem verbs are listed, e.g., **fahren, bringen, kommen.** Verbs formed by adding a prefix, e.g., **radfahren, verbringen, ankommen,** change their stems in the same way as the basic verb.

infinitive	3rd person sing. present	simple past	perfect	English
anfangen	fängt an	fing an	hat angefangen	begin
anrufen		rief an	hat angerufen	call up
bieten		bot	hat geboten	offer
beginnen		begann	hat begonnen	begin
bitten		bat	hat gebeten	ask for, request
bleiben		blieb	ist geblieben	remain, stay
brechen	bricht	brach	hat gebrochen	break
bringen		brachte	hat gebracht	bring
denken		dachte	hat gedacht	think
dürfen	darf	durfte	hat gedurft	may, be allowed
einladen	lädt ein	lud ein	hat eingeladen	invite
empfehlen	empfiehlt	empfahl	hat empfohlen	recommend
essen	ißt	aß	hat gegessen	eat
fahren	fährt	fuhr	ist gefahren	drive; go (by vehicle)
fallen	fällt	fiel	ist gefallen	fall
finden		fand	hat gefunden	find
fliegen		flog	ist geflogen	fly
geben	gibt	gab	hat gegeben	give
gehen		ging	ist gegangen	go; walk
geschehen	geschieht	geschah	ist geschehen	happen
gewinnen		gewann	hat gewonnen	win
haben	hat	hatte	hat gehabt	have
halten	hält	hielt	hat gehalten	stop; hold
hängen[1]		hing	hat gehangen	hang
heißen		hieß	hat geheißen	be called; mean
helfen	hilft	half	hat geholfen	help
kennen		kannte	hat gekannt	know, be acquainted with

---

[1] When it is transitive, **hängen** is weak: **hängte, hat gehängt.**

infinitive	3rd person sing. present	simple past	perfect	English
klingen		klang	hat geklungen	sound
kommen		kam	ist gekommen	come
können	kann	konnte	hat gekonnt	be able, can
lassen	läßt	ließ	hat gelassen	leave; let; allow to
laufen	läuft	lief	ist gelaufen	run
leihen		lieh	hat geliehen	lend
lesen	liest	las	hat gelesen	read
liegen		lag	hat gelegen	lie
mögen	mag	mochte	hat gemocht	like
müssen	muß	mußte	hat gemußt	must, have to
nehmen	nimmt	nahm	hat genommen	take
nennen		nannte	hat genannt	name
scheinen		schien	hat geschienen	shine; seem
schlafen	schläft	schlief	hat geschlafen	sleep
schlagen	schlägt	schlug	hat geschlagen	hit
schließen		schloß	hat geschlossen	close
schreiben		schrieb	hat geschrieben	write
schwimmen		schwamm	ist geschwommen	swim
sehen	sieht	sah	hat gesehen	see
sein	ist	war	ist gewesen	be
singen		sang	hat gesungen	sing
sitzen		saß	hat gesessen	sit
sollen	soll	sollte	hat gesollt	should
sprechen	spricht	sprach	hat gesprochen	speak
stehen		stand	hat gestanden	stand
stehlen	stiehlt	stahl	hat gestohlen	steal
steigen		stieg	ist gestiegen	climb; rise
sterben	stirbt	starb	ist gestorben	die
tragen	trägt	trug	hat getragen	carry; wear
treffen	trifft	traf	hat getroffen	meet
treiben		trieb	hat getrieben	drive, propel
trinken		trank	hat getrunken	drink
tun		tat	hat getan	do
vergessen	vergißt	vergaß	hat vergessen	forget
verlieren		verlor	hat verloren	lose
wachsen	wächst	wuchs	ist gewachsen	grow
waschen	wäscht	wusch	hat gewaschen	wash
werden	wird	wurde	ist geworden	become
werfen	wirft	warf	hat geworfen	throw
wiegen		wog	hat gewogen	weigh
wissen	weiß	wußte	hat gewußt	know (a fact)
wollen	will	wollte	hat gewollt	want to
ziehen		zog	hat/ist gezogen	pull; move

Appendix 2

Table of Equivalent Weights and Measures

Weight

1 Gramm	= 0.03 ounces
1 Pfund (500 Gramm)	= 1.1 pounds
1 Kilogramm *oder* Kilo (1000 Gramm)	= 2.2 pounds

1 ounce	= 28 Gramm
1 pound	= 0,45 Kilo
1 U. S. ton (2,000 lbs)	= 900 Kilo

Liquid Measure

¼ Liter = 0.53 pints
½ Liter = 1.06 pints
1 Liter = 1.06 quarts

1 pint = 0,47 Liter
1 quart = 0,95 Liter
1 gallon = 3,8 Liter

Distance

1 Zentimeter (10 Millimeter)	= 0.4 inches
1 Meter (100 Zentimeter)	= 39.5 inches *or* 1.1 yards
1 Kilometer (1000 Meter)	= 0.62 miles

1 inch	= 2,5 Zentimeter
1 foot	= 0,3 Meter
1 yard	= 0,9 Meter
1 mile	= 1,6 Kilometer

Temperature

0° Celsius (Centigrade) = −32° Fahrenheit
100° Celsius = 212° Fahrenheit

$$°C = \frac{10(°F - 32)}{18} \qquad °F = \frac{18\ °C}{10} + 32$$

German-English Vocabulary

The following list contains all the words introduced for active use in *Neue Horizonte* except for the personal and relative pronouns, the possessive adjectives, the months of the year, and the cardinal and ordinal numbers (except when the latter are irregular). The first active occurrence of a word is shown by the chapter number followed either by a 1 or 2 (12–1 = introduced in Chapter 12, *Wortschatz 1*) or by the letter G (12G = introduced in Chapter 12, *Grammatik*). Also included is the following non-active vocabulary: 1) the easily-recognized cognates from the *Leicht zu merken* section of each chapter, followed by their chapter number and a G (e.g., **manipulieren** to manipulate, 10G), and 2) the optional vocabulary from the *Vom Lesen zum Sprechen* section of each chapter, followed by chapter number and the letters VLS (e.g., die **Informatik** computer science, 6–VLS).

Strong and irregular verbs are listed with their principal parts. Present-tense stem-vowel change is shown by the inclusion of the third-person singular form in parentheses following the infinitive: **nehmen (nimmt), nahm, hat genommen.** Weak verbs using **sein** as their auxiliary in the perfect tenses are shown by inclusion of the perfect: **reisen, ist gereist.**

Separable prefixes are indicated by a raised dot between prefix and verb stem (**ab·fahren**). This dot is *not* used in German spelling.

A preposition used with a verb follows all its principal parts: **bitten, bat, hat gebeten um.**

Adjectival nouns are indicated thus: der/die **Verwandte, -n.**

Masculine N-nouns and irregular nouns like **Name** are indicated by inclusion of the genitive singular ending preceding the plural ending: **der Student, -en, -en;** der **Name, -ns, -n.**

Adjectives followed by a hyphen may only be used attributively: **eigen-.**

Umlauted and irregular comparative and superlative forms of adjectives and adverbs are indicated in parentheses after the positive form: **arm (ärmer).**

The following abbreviations are used here and in the entire book:

acc.	accusative	*intrans.*	intransitive
adj.	adjective	*m.*	masculine
adj. noun	adjectival noun	*neut.*	neuter
adv.	adverb	*pers.*	person
colloq.	colloquial	*pl.*	plural
dat.	dative	*prep.*	preposition
f.	feminine	*sing.*	singular
fam.	familiar	*sub. conj.*	subordinating conjunction
gen.	genitive	*trans.*	transitive

A

der **Abend, -e** evening, 7–2
  am Abend in the evening, 7–2
das **Abendessen, -** supper, evening meal, 8–1
  zum Abendessen for supper, 8–1
abends (in the) evenings, 5–2
aber but, 1–1
ab·fahren (fährt ab), fuhr ab, ist abgefahren to depart, leave (by vehicle), 7–1
ab·holen to pick up, fetch, get, 14–1
das **Abitur** final secondary school examination, 5–1
das **Abteil, -e** railway compartment, 7–2
ach oh; ah, 2–1
die **Adresse, -n** address, 15–1
der **Adler, -** eagle, 10–VLS
ähnlich (+ *dat.*) similar (to), 3–2
  Sie ist ihrer Mutter ähnlich.
    She's like her mother.
aktiv active, 9–2
akut acute, 16G
akzeptieren to accept, 15–1
alle (*pl.*) all; everybody, 2–1
allein alone, 4–1
alles everything, 8–1
die **Alpen** (*pl.*) the Alps, 8–2
als (*sub. conj.*) when (with *simple past tense*), 10–1; than (with *comparative degree*), 12G
  als ob (+ *subjunctive*) as if, 16–1
also well . . . , 1–1; thus, 4–2
alt (älter) old, 2–2
die **Alternative, -n** alternative, 2G
der **Amateur, -e** amateur, 9G
(das) **Amerika** America, 3–2
der **Amerikaner, -** American (*m.*), 1–2
die **Amerikanerin, -nen** American (*f.*), 1–2
amerikanisch American, 3–2
an (+*acc. or dat.*) to, toward; at, alongside of, 6G
analysieren to analyze, 14G
ander- other, different, 11–1
ändern to change (*trans.*), 16–2
sich ändern to change (*intrans.*), 16–2
anders different, 2–2
der **Anfang, ¨-e** beginning 10–2

am Anfang at the beginning, 10–2
an·fangen (fängt an), fing an, hat angefangen to begin, start, 5–1
angenehm pleasant; "pleasure to meet you," 14–VLS
der/die **Angestellte, -n** employee, 14–1
angezogen dressed (*see* **anziehen**), 12–1
die **Anglistik** English studies, 6–VLS
die **Angst, ¨-e** fear, 3–2
  Angst haben to be afraid, 3–2
  Angst haben vor (+ *dat.*) to be afraid of, 13–1
an·kommen, kam an, ist angekommen to arrive, 6–2
an·rufen, rief an, hat angerufen to call up, 5–1
sich etwas an·sehen (sieht an), sah an, hat angesehen to take a look at something, 11–1
anstatt (+ *gen.*) instead of, 8G
die **Antwort, -en** answer, 6–2
antworten (+ *dat.*) to answer (a person), 7–1
  antworten auf (+ *acc.*) to answer (something), 13–2
an·ziehen, zog an, hat angezogen to dress, 11–1
  sich anziehen to get dressed, 11–1
der **Anzug, ¨-e** suit, 3–VLS
die **Arbeit** work, 2–2
arbeiten to work; study (for a class), 1–1
der **Arbeiter, -** worker (*m.*), 5–2
die **Arbeiterin, -nen** worker (*f.*)
arbeitslos unemployed, 10–2
das **Arbeitszimmer, -** study, 15–VLS
ärgern to annoy; offend, 8–2
  sich ärgern (über + *acc.*) to get annoyed (at), be annoyed (about), 13–2
der **Arm, -e** arm, 10–2
arm poor, 9–1
die **Armbanduhr, -en** wristwatch, 10–1
der **Artikel, -** article, 2–1
der **Arzt, ¨-e** doctor (*m.*) 11–1
die **Ärztin, -nen** doctor (*f.*), 11–1
der **Aspekt, -e** aspect, 8G
der **Athlet, -en, -en** athlete, 9G
auch also, too, 1–1

auf (+*acc. or dat.*) onto; on, upon, on top of, 6G
die **Aufgabe, -n** task, assignment, 16–2
auf·geben (gibt auf), gab auf, hat aufgegeben to give up, 16–1
auf·hören (mit) to cease, stop (doing something), 5–1
auf·machen to open, 5–1
auf·passen to pay attention; look out, 16–1
  auf·passen auf (+ *acc.*) to look after, 16–1
auf·räumen to tidy up, straighten up, 13–1
auf·stehen, stand auf, ist aufgestanden to stand up; get out of bed, 5–1
auf·wachen, ist aufgewacht to wake up (*intrans.*), 7–1
auf·wachsen (wächst auf), wuchs auf, ist aufgewachsen to grow up, 10–2
das **Auge, -n** eye, 11–1
aus (+ *dat.*) out of; from , 5G
aus·brechen (bricht aus), brach aus, ist ausgebrochen to break out
aus·geben (gibt aus), gab aus, hat ausgegeben to spend (money), 6–2
aus·gehen, ging aus, ist ausgegangen to go out, 14–1
ausgezeichnet excellent, 8–1
sich aus·kennen, kannte aus, hat ausgekannt to know one's way around, 13–1
die **Auskunft** information, 13–1
das **Ausland** (*sing.*) foreign countries, 7–2
  im Ausland abroad, 7–2
der **Ausländer, -** foreigner (*m.*), 15–1
die **Ausländerin, -nen** foreigner (*f.*), 15–1
aus·packen to unpack, 11–VLS
aus·schließen, schloß aus, hat ausgeschlossen to close out
aus·sehen (sieht aus), sah aus, hat ausgesehen to appear, look (like), 5–2
außer (+ *dat.*) besides; in addition to, 5G
außerdem (*adverb*) besides, in addition, 14–2
etwas nicht ausstehen können to not be able to stand something *or* someone, 13–1

aus·steigen, stieg aus, ist ausgestiegen to get out (of a vehicle) 7–2
die **Ausstellung, -en** exhibition,
10–2
aus·wandern, ist ausgewandert to
emigrate, 11–2
der **Ausweis, -e** I.D. card, 6–2
sich aus·ziehen, zog aus, hat ausgezogen to get undressed,
11–1
das **Auto, -s** car, 2–2
die **Autobahn, -en** expressway,
high-speed highway, 7–VLS
automatisch automatic, 13G
der **Automechaniker, -** auto mechanic, 5–1
der **Autostop** hitchhiking
per Autostop reisen to hitchhike, 7–2

B

das **Baby, -s** baby, 16–1
das **Bad** bath, 14–1
ein Bad nehmen to take a
bath, 14–1
das **Badezimmer, -** bath room,
14–1
die **Bahn** railroad; railway system, 7–2
der **Bahnhof, ⸚e** train station, 7–1
bald soon, 3–1
die **Bank, -en** bank, 14–1
der **Bär, -en, -en** bear, 10–VLS
barbarisch barbaric, 4G
die **Barriere, -n** barrier, 13G
bauen to build, 6–2
der **Baum, ⸚e** tree, 4–1
der **Beamte, -n** (adj. noun)
official, civil servant (m.),
11–1
die **Beamtin, -nen** official, civil
servant (f.), 11–1
bedeuten to mean, signify, 1–2
sich **beeilen** to hurry, 11–1
**beginnen, begann, hat be-
gonnen** to begin, 6–2
**behalten (behält), behielt, hat be-
halten** to keep, retain, 12–1
bei (+ dat.) in the home of; near;
at, 5–1; during, while —ing,
11G
beid- (adj.) both, 11–2
beide (pl. pronoun) both, 14–2
beides (sing. pronoun) both
things, 13–2

das **Bein, -e** leg, 11–1
das **Beispiel, -e** example, 7–2
zum Beispiel for example,
1–2
bekannt known; well known,
9–2
der/die **Bekannte, -n** acquaintance, friend, 11G
**bekommen, bekam, hat bekom-
men** to receive, get, 4–1
belegen to register for, take (a
university course), 6–2
beliebt popular, 9–2
benutzen to use, 9–2
bequem comfortable, 7–2
der **Berg, -e** mountain, 3–1
berichten to report, 5–2
der **Beruf, -e** profession, vocation,
2–2
Was sind Sie von Beruf?
What is your profession?
5–VLS
berufstätig employed, 16–2
berühmt famous, 11–2
**beschreiben, beschrieb, hat
beschrieben** to describe, 4–2
besitzen, besaß, hat besessen to
own, 2–2
besonders especially, 5–2
**besprechen (bespricht), besprach,
hat besprochen** to discuss,
3–2
besser better, 3–2
best- see gut
bestellen to order, 8–1
der **Besuch, -e** visit, 10–2
besuchen to visit, 3–1
das **Bett, -en** bed, 7–1
ins Bett gehen to go to bed,
7–1
bevor (sub. conj.) before, 10–2
die **Bewegung, -en** movement;
exercise, 9–2
bezahlen to pay, 16–1
die **Bibliothek, -en** library, 6–2
das **Bier, -e** beer, 4–2
bieten, bot, hat geboten to offer;
provide, 16–2
das **Bild, -er** picture; image, 5–2
billig inexpensive, cheap, 6–2
die **Biologie** biology, 6–VLS
bis (+ acc.) until; by, 1–1
bis dann until then, 1–1
bis zu (+ dat.) until, up to,
5–1
ein bißchen a little; a little bit; a
little while, 3–2
bitte you're welcome, 2–1;
please, 3–2

bitte sehr you're welcome,
8–1
bitten, bat, hat gebeten um
(+ acc.) to ask for, request,
13–1
Er bittet mich um das Geld.
He's asking me for the
money.
bitter bitter, 8–VLS
blau blue, 9–1
bleiben, blieb, ist geblieben to
stay, remain, 2–2
der **Bleistift, -e** pencil, intro.
die **Blume, -n** flower, 11–1
die **Bluse, -n** blouse, 3–2
der **Boden, ⸚** ground; floor, 7–1
die **Bohne, -n** bean, 8–VLS
böse (+ dat.) angry (at), 13–1
der **Braten, -** roast, 8–VLS
brauchen to need, 2–1
braun brown, 9–1
die **BRD** (= **Bundesrepublik
Deutschland**) the FRG
(= Federal Republic of
Germany), 2–2
**brechen (bricht), brach, hat ge-
brochen** to break, 11–1
der **Brief, -e** letter, 6–2
der **Briefkasten, ⸚** mailbox, 15–1
die **Briefmarke, -n** postage stamp,
15–1
die **Brille** (sing.) (eye) glasses,
3–VLS
bringen, brachte, hat gebracht to
bring, 6–1
das **Brot, -e** bread, 8–1
die **Brücke, -n** bridge, 9–1
der **Bruder, ⸚** brother, 2–1
das **Buch, ⸚er** book, intro.
das **Bücherregal, -e** bookcase,
6–VLS
die **Buchhandlung, -en** bookstore,
5–2
der **Bummel, -** stroll, walk, 8–1
die **Bundesrepublik Deutschland** The Federal Republic of
Germany, 2–2
bunt colorful, 5–2
der **Bürger, -** citizen, 11–2
das **Büro, -s** office, 1–1
der **Bus, -se** bus, 7–2

C

das **Café, -s** cafe, 8–VLS
der **Campingplatz, ⸚e**
campground, 7–1

die **Chance, -n** chance, 16–2
der **Chef, -s** boss (m.), 5–1
die **Chefin, -nen** boss (f.), 5–1
die **Chemie** chemistry, 6–VLS
der **Computer, -** computer, 12–1

D

da there; here; then, 2–1; since (sub. conj., causal), 8–1
  da drüben over there, 2–1
dahin there (as goal of motion), 9–1
  Wie komme ich dahin? How do I get there?
damals at that time, back then, 10–1
die **Dame, -n** lady, 10–2
  meine Damen und Herren ladies and gentlemen, 10–2
damit (sub. conj.) so that, 9–1
der **Dank** thanks
  vielen Dank many thanks, 2–1
danke thanks, thank you, 1–1
danken (+ dat.) to thank, 7–1
  Nichts zu danken! Don't mention it! 2–1
  danken für (+ acc.) to thank for, 13–1
dann then, 1–1
darum therefore, for that reason, 3–2
das sind (pl. of **das ist**) those are, 2–2
daß that (sub. conj.), 8–1
dauern to last; take (time), 10–1
die **DDR (Deutsche Demokratische Republik)** the GDR (German Democratic Republic), 9–2
definieren to define, 9G
die **Demokratie, -n** democracy, 10–2
demokratisch democratic, 10G
denken, dachte, hat gedacht to think, 13–2
  denken an (+ acc.) to think of, 13–2
das **Denkmal, -̈er** monument, 12–2
denn (untranslatable flavoring particle added to questions), 2–1; for, because, 7G
deutlich clear, 16–2
deutsch German, 2–2
  auf deutsch in German, 1–2

(das) **Deutsch** German language, 3–2
der/die **Deutsche, -n** German, 1–2
desto see **je . . . desto**
die **Deutsche Demokratische Republik** German Democratic Republic (GDR), 9–2
die **Deutsche Mark** (DM) the German Mark, 6–1
(das) **Deutschland** Germany, 1–2
die **Deutschstunde, -n** German class, 3–1
der **Dialekt, -e** dialect, 13G
der **Dichter, -** poet, 11–2
der **Dienstag, -e** Tuesday, intro.
dieser, -es, -e this; these, 5–1
diesmal this time, 12–1
direkt direct, 9G
der **Direktor, -en** director, 10G
die **Diskussion, -en** discussion, 2–2
diskutieren to discuss; debate, 16–2
DM see **Mark**
doch (stressed) yes I do, yes I am, yes he is, etc. (contradictory), 3–1; (unstressed) flavoring particle with commands, 4–1
der **Dom, -e** cathedral, 12–2
der **Donnerstag, -e** Thursday, intro.
das **Doppelzimmer, -** double room, 14–1
das **Dorf, -̈er** village, 9–2
dort there, 2–2
draußen outside, 1–1
dritt- third, 9G
drüben over there, 2–1
dumm (dümmer) dumb, 5–1
dunkel dark, 4–1
durch (+ acc.) through, 4–1
dürfen (darf), durfte, hat gedurft to be allowed to, 3G
der **Durst** thirst
  Haben Sie Durst? Are you thirsty? 8–VLS
die **Dusche, -n** shower, 14–1
die **Dynastie, -n** dynasty, 14G

E

die **Ebene, -n** plain, 12–2
die **Ecke, -n** corner, 8–2
  an der Ecke at the corner, 8–2

  um die Ecke around the corner, 8–2
egal
  Das ist mir egal. It's all the same to me. I don't care (about that). 7–1
ehrlich honest, 3–2
eigen- own, 9–2
eigentlich actually, in fact, 3–2
die **Eile** hurry
  in Eile in a hurry, 1–1
der **Eindruck, -̈e** impression, 8–2
einfach simple, easy, 5–1
einige some, 11–1
ein·kaufen to shop for; go shopping, 5–2
ein·laden (lädt ein), lud ein, hat eingeladen to invite, 14–1
einmal once, 4–1
  noch einmal once again, once more, 4–1
eins one, 1–2
ein·schlafen (schläft ein), schlief ein, ist eingeschlafen to fall asleep, 7–1
ein·steigen, stieg ein, ist eingestiegen to get in (a vehicle), 7–2
ein·wandern, ist eingewandert to immigrate, 11–2
ein·werfen (wirft ein), warf ein, hat eingeworfen to mail (a letter), 15–1
das **Einzelzimmer, -** single room, 14–1
einzig- single, only, 12–2
das **Eis** ice cream, 8–VLS
der **Elefant, -en, -en** elephant, 10–VLS
die **Elektrotechnik** electrical engineering, 6–VLS
der **Elektrotechniker, -** electrician; electrical engineer (m.), 5–VLS
die **Elektrotechnikerin, -nen** electrician; electrical engineer (f.), 5–VLS
die **Eltern** (pl.) parents, 2–1
die **Emanzipation** emancipation, 16G
empfehlen (empfiehlt), empfahl, hat empfohlen to recommend, 9–1
das **Ende, -n** end, 6–2
  Ende Februar at the end of February, 6–2
  am Ende at the end, 11–2
endlich finally, 1–1
(das) **England** England, 8–2

der **Engländer, -** Englishman, 11G
die **Engländerin, -nen** Englishwoman, 11G
englisch English, 11G
(das) **Englisch** English language, 3–2
Entschuldigung! Pardon me! Excuse me! 1–1
enttäuschen to disappoint, 15–1
entweder . . . oder either . . . or, 14–1
die **Epoche, -n** epoch, 10G
die **Erde** earth, 12–2
das **Erdgeschoß** ground floor, first floor, 14–2 (*see* **Stock**)
erfahren (erfährt), erfuhr, hat erfahren to find out, learn, 9–2
die **Erfahrung, -en** experience, 12–VLS
der **Erfolg, -e** success, 16–2
sich **erholen** (**von** + *dat.*) to recover (from), get well; have a rest, 13–2
erinnern an (+ *acc.*) to remind of, 12–1
  sich **erinnern an** (+ *acc.*) to remember, 12–1
die **Erinnerung, -en** memory, 12–1
sich **erkälten** to catch a cold, 11–1
erklären to explain, 10–2
erlauben (+ *dat. of person*) to permit, allow, 7–2
  erlaubt permitted, 7–2
erledigen to attend to, take care of, finish, 16–2
ernst serious, 14–2
  etwas ernst nehmen to take something seriously, 14–2
erscheinen, erschien, ist erschienen to appear, 11–2
erst not until; only, 5–1
erst- first, 9G
erwarten to expect, 14–2
erzählen to tell, recount, 7–2
die **Erzählung, -en** story, narrative, 12–2
der **Esel, -** donkey, 10–VLS
essen (ißt), aß, hat gegessen to eat, 2–1
das **Essen** food, 2–2
das **Eßzimmer, -** dining room, 15–VLS
etwas something, 3–1; some, a little; somewhat, 14–2
(das) **Europa** Europe, 4–2
der **Europäer, -** European, 15–2
europäisch European, 11–2

existieren to exist, 14G
extrem extreme, 10G

F

die **Fabrik, -en** factory, 5–2
das **Fach, ⸚er** area of study; subject, 6–VLS
fahren (fährt), fuhr, ist gefahren to drive, go (by vehicle), 3–1
die **Fahrkarte, -n** ticket (for bus, train, streetcar, etc.), 7–2
das **Fahrrad, ⸚er** bicycle, 8–2
die **Fahrt, -en** trip, ride, 7–2
fallen (fällt), fiel, ist gefallen to fall; die in battle, 10–1
falsch false, incorrect, intro.
die **Familie, -n** family, 2–2
die **Familiendiskussion, -en** family discussion, 2–2
der **Fan, -s** (sports) fan, 9G
die **Farbe, -n** color, 9–1
fast almost, 2–2
faul lazy, 14–2
die **Feier, -n** celebration, party, 15–1
feiern to celebrate, 15–1
das **Fenster, -** window, intro.
die **Ferien** (*pl.*) (university and school) vacation, 6–2
fern distant, far away, 12–2
fertig (mit) done, finished (with); ready, 5–1
der **Film, -e** film, movie, 6–2
finanziell financial, 11G
finden, fand, hat gefunden to find, 2–2
  Das finde ich auch. I think so too. 12–1
der **Finger, -** finger, 11–1
die **Firma, die Firmen** firm, company, 13–2
der **Fisch, -e** fish, 8–VLS
fit in shape, 3–1
flach flat, 12–2
die **Flasche, -n** bottle, 7–1
fleißig industrious, hard-working, 14–2
fliegen, flog, ist geflogen to fly, 1–1
der **Flughafen, ⸚** airport, 7–VLS
das **Flugzeug, -e** airplane, 7–2
der **Fluß, die Flüsse** river, 12–2
die **Form, -en** form, 11G
formell formal, 1G
das **Foto, -s** photograph, 7–2

  ein Foto machen to take a picture, 7–2
die **Frage, -n** question, 2–1
  eine Frage stellen to ask a question, 10–1
fragen to ask, 1–2
(das) **Frankreich** France, 11–2
der **Franzose, -n, -n** Frenchman, 11G
die **Französin, -nen** Frenchwoman, 11G
französisch French, 11G
die **Frau, -en** woman, 1–1
  Frau Kuhn Mrs./Ms. Kuhn
(die) **Frauenstudien** (*plur.*) women's studies, 6–VLS
frei free; unoccupied, 2–1
die **Freiheit, -en** freedom, 7–2
der **Freitag, -e** Friday, intro.
die **Freizeit** free time, leisure time, 5–1
fremd strange; foreign, 3–2
die **Fremdsprache, -n** foreign language, 3–2
die **Freude, -n** joy, 12–2
freuen to please, make happy, 11–1
  sich **freuen** to be happy, be glad, 11–1
  sich **freuen auf** (+ *acc.*) to look forward to, 13–1
der **Freund, -e** friend, 2–1
die **Freundin, -nen** friend (*f.*), 3–1
freundlich friendly, 1–2
der **Frieden** peace, 10–VLS
froh happy, glad, 13–2
früh early, 3–1
der **Frühling** spring, 4–2
das **Frühstück** breakfast, 14–1
sich **fühlen** to feel (*intrans.*), 11–1
führen to lead, 10–2
für (+ *acc.*) for, 1–1
furchtbar terrible, 6–2
fürchten to fear, 3–2
der **Fuß, ⸚e** foot, 6–2
  zu Fuß on foot, 6–2
der **Fußball** soccer; soccer ball, 5–2
  Fußball spielen to play soccer, 5–2
der **Fußgänger, -** pedestrian, 8–2
die **Fußgängerzone, -n** pedestrian mall, 8–2

G

die **Gabel, -n** fork, 8–VLS
ganz entire, whole, 6–2
  ganz gut pretty good, 1–1*

gar nicht   not at all, 3– 2

die Garage, -n   garage, 15–VLS

der Garten, ∵   garden, 15–VLS

der Gast, ¨e   guest; patron, 8–1

der Gastarbeiter, -   foreign worker, (*m.*), 15–1

die Gastarbeiterin, -nen   foreign worker (*f.*), 15–1

das Gebäude, -   building, 8–1

geben (gibt), gab, hat gegeben   to give, 2–2

   es gibt (+ *acc.*)   there is, there are, 2–2

   Was gibt's Neues?   What's new? 11–1

gebildet   educated, 16–2

geboren   born, 10–1

   Wann sind Sie geboren? When were you born? 10–1

gebrauchen   to use, 13–2

der Geburtstag, -e   birthday, 9–1

   Wann hast du Geburtstag? When is your birthday? 9–1

   zum Geburtstag   for (your) birthday, 9–1

der Gedanke, -ns, -n   thought, 16–2

die Gefahr, -en   danger, 10–2

gefährlich   dangerous, 16–2

gefallen (gefällt), gefiel, hat gefallen (+ *dat. of person*)   to please, appeal to, 7–1

das Gefühl, -e   feeling, 7–2

gegen (+ *acc.*)   against, 4G

die Gegend, -en   area, region, 12–1

die Gegenwart   present (time), 14–2

gehen, ging, ist gegangen   to go; walk, 1–1

   Wie geht es Ihnen?   How are you? intro.

   Wie geht es dir?   How are you? 1–2

   Wie geht's?   How are you? 1–1

   Es geht.   It's all right. Not bad. 11–1

   Es geht um (+ *acc., must have impersonal* **es** *as subject*)   it's a question of, what's at issue is, it's about, 16–2

gehören (+ *dat. of person*)   to belong to (a person), 7–1

   gehören zu (+ *dat.*)   to be a part of, be one of, 13–2

gelb   yellow, 9–1

das Geld   money, 2–2

die Gelegenheit, -en   opportunity, chance, 14–2

das Gemüse   vegetables, 8–VLS

gemütlich   cozy, comfortable; quiet, relaxed, 14–2

genau   exact, 12–1

genauso . . . wie   just as . . . as, 12G

die Generation, -en   generation, 11G

genug   enough, 3–1

die Geographie   geography, 4G

das Gepäck   luggage, 7–1

der Gepäckträger, -   porter, redcap, 7–1

gerade   just, at this moment, 6–2

geradeaus   straight ahead, 8–2

die Germanistik   German studies, 6–VLS

gern (lieber, am liebsten)   gladly, with pleasure, 4–1

   gern + *verb* = like to

das Geschäft, -e   business; store, 5–2

die Geschäftsfrau, -en   businesswoman, 5–VLS

der Geschäftsmann, die Geschäftsleute   businessman, 5–VLS

geschehen (geschieht), geschah, ist geschehen   to happen, 13–1

das Geschenk, -e   gift, present, 9–1

die Geschichte, -n   story; history, 6–2

das Geschlecht, -er   sex, gender, 16–2

geschlossen   closed (*see* **schließen**), 11–2

die Geschwister (*pl.*)   siblings, 2–VLS

die Gesellschaft, -en   society, 9–2

gesellschaftlich   social

das Gesetz, -e   law, 16–2

   vor dem Gesetz   under the law, in the eyes of the law, 16–2

das Gesicht, -er   face, 11–1

das Gespräch, -e   conversation, 7–2

gestern   yesterday, 6–1

   gestern früh   yesterday morning, 12G

   gestern morgen   yesterday morning, 10–1

   gestern nachmittag   yesterday afternoon, 9–1

   gestern abend   yesterday evening, 12G

gesund   healthy, 9–2

die Gesundheit   health, 9–2

gewinnen, gewann, hat gewonnen   to win, 10–2

sich gewöhnen an (+ *acc.*)   to get used to, 13–1

das Glas, ¨er   glass, 8–1

glauben (+ *dat. of person*)   to believe; think, 6–1

   Ich glaube ja.   I think so. 8–1

gleich   right away, immediately, 7–1; equal, 16–2

gleichberechtigt   enjoying equal rights, 16–2

die Gleichberechtigung (*sing.*)   equal rights, 16–2

das Gleis, -e   track, 7–1

das Glück   happiness; luck, 6–2

   Glück haben   to be lucky, 6–2

glücklich   happy, 10–1

golden   golden, 16–1

   die goldene Hochzeit   golden wedding anniversary, 16–1

der Gott, ¨er   god, 16–2

   Gott sei Dank   thank goodness, 4G

   Grüß Gott   hello (*in southern Germany and Austria*), 14–1

   Um Gottes Willen!   For heaven's sake! 11–1

das Gramm   gram, 8–1

gratulieren (+ *dat. of person*)   to congratulate, 15–1

grau   gray, 9–1

grausam   terrible, gruesome; cruel, 12–2

die Grenze, -n   border, 11–2

groß (größer, am größten)   big, 2–1

(das) Großbritannien   Great Britain, 11G

die Größe, -n   size; greatness, 12–2

die Großeltern (*pl.*)   grandparents, 2–2

die Großmutter, ¨   grandmother, 2–2

die Großstadt, ¨e   large city (*over 500,000 inhabitants*), 8–2

der Großvater, ¨   grandfather, 2–2

grün   green, 9–1

der Grund, ¨e   ground, reason, 11–2

die Gruppe, -n   group, 1–2

grüßen   to greet, say hello to, 1–2

   Grüß Gott   hello (*in southern Germany and Austria*), 14–1

die Gurke, -n   cucumber, 8–VLS

gut (besser, am besten) good, well, 1–1

    ganz gut pretty good, 1–1
    guten Morgen! good morning! intro.
    guten Tag! hello! intro.
    gute Reise! Have a good trip! 1–1

das **Gymnasium, die Gymnasien** secondary school (*prepares pupils for university*), 3–2

H

das **Haar, -e** hair, 11–1
    sich die Haare kämmen to comb one's hair, 11–1
haben (hat), hatte, hat gehabt to have, 2–1
das **Hähnchen, -** (roast or fried) chicken, 8–VLS
halb half, 8–1
    halb sieben 6:30, 8–1
halbtags half days, 16–1
    halbtags arbeiten to work part time, 16–1
die **Hälfte, -n** half, 11–2
halten (hält), hielt, hat gehalten to stop (*intrans.*); hold, 3–1
    halten für (+ *acc.*) to take for, regard as, think X is, 15–1
    halten von (+ *dat.*) to think of, have an opinion about, 15G
die **Haltestelle, -n** (streetcar or bus) stop, 13–1
die **Hand, ⁻e** hand, 5–1
der **Handschuh, -e** glove, 3–VLS
hängen (*trans.*) to hang (up), 7–1
hängen, hing, hat gehangen (*intrans.*) to be hanging, 7–1
hart (härter) hard; tough; harsh, 10–2
hassen to hate, 3–2
häßlich ugly, 1–1
Haupt- (*prefix*) main, chief, primary, most important, 6G
das **Hauptfach, ⁻er** major field, 6–2
das **Hauptgericht, -e** entree, main course, 8–VLS
die **Hauptstadt, ⁻e** capital, 10–2
das **Haus, ⁻er** house, 1–2
    nach Hause home (*as destination of motion*), 3–1

zu Hause at home, 2–2
die **Hausarbeit** housework, 2–2
die **Hausaufgabe, -n** homework assignment, 3–2
die **Hausfrau, -en** housewife, 2–2
das **Heft, -e** notebook, intro.
die **Heimat** native place or country, homeland, 12–2
das **Heimweh** homesickness, 15–2
heiraten to marry, get married, 16–1
heiß hot, 4–1
heißen, hieß, hat geheißen to be called, 2–1
    Ich heiße . . . My name is . . . , intro.
    Wie heißen Sie? What's your name?, intro.
helfen (hilft), half, hat geholfen (+ *dat.*) to help, 7–1
hell bright, light, 4–1
das **Hemd, -en** shirt, 3–2
her- (*prefix*) *indicates motion toward the speaker*, 15G
der **Herbst** fall, autumn, 4–2
der **Herd, -e** stove, kitchen range, 15–VLS
der **Herr, -n, -en** gentleman, 1–1
    Herr Lehmann Mr. Lehmann, 1–1
    meine Damen und Herren ladies and gentlemen, 10–2
heute today, intro.
    heute abend this evening, tonight, 1–1
    heute früh/heute morgen this morning, 12G
    heute nachmittag this afternoon, 12G
heutzutage nowadays, 7–2
hier here, 1–2
die **Hilfe** help, aid, 11–2
hin- (*prefix*) *indicates motion away from speaker*, 15G
hinein- (*prefix*) in, into, 15–1
hinter (+ *acc.* or *dat.*) behind, 6G
historisch historic, 10G
hoch (*predicative adjective*), **hoh-** (*attributive adjective*) (**höher, am höchsten**) high, 11–2
die **Hochschule, -n** university, institute of higher learning, 14–2
die **Hochzeit, -en** wedding, 16–1
    die goldene Hochzeit golden wedding anniversary, 16–1

hoffen to hope, 7–2
hoffentlich I hope, 4–1
höflich polite, 1–2
holen to fetch, get, 12–2
hören to hear, 3–2
der **Horizont, -e** horizon, 7G
die **Hose, -n** trousers, pants, 3–2
das **Hotel, -s** hotel, 4–1
hübsch pretty, handsome, 11–1
der **Humor** humor, 14G
der **Hund, -e** dog, 11G
der **Hunger** hunger, 8–1
    Hunger haben to be hungry, 8–1
der **Hut, ⁻e** hat, 3–VLS

I

das **Ideal, -e** ideal, 11G
ideal ideal, 16G
idealistisch idealistic, 9G
die **Idee, -n** idea, 10–2
ideologisch ideological, 10G
das **Idol, -e** idol, 9G
illegal illegal, 10G
illegitim illegitimate, 11G
immer always, 1–2
    immer noch still, 4–2
    immer größer bigger and bigger, 12G
in (+ *acc.* or *dat.*) in, 1–1; into, 6G
die **Industrie, -n** industry, 10–2
industriell industrial, 16G
die **Inflation** inflation, 10G
der **Ingenieur, -e** engineer (*m.*), 5–VLS
die **Ingenieurin, -nen** engineer (*f.*), 5–VLS
die **Informatik** computer science, 6–VLS
der/die **Intellektuelle, -n** intellectual, 11G
intelligent intelligent, 12–1
interessant interesting, 3–1
sich interessieren für (+ *acc.*) to be interested in, 13–1
international international, 3G
interviewen to interview, 15–1
irgend- (*prefix*)
    irgendwann sometime or other, any time, 12G
    irgendwie somehow or other, 12G
    irgendwo somewhere or other, anywhere, 12G

die **Ironie** irony, 14G
(das) **Italien** Italy, 7–2
der **Italiener, -** Italian (m.), 11G
die **Italienerin, -nen** Italian (f.), 11G
italienisch Italian, 11G

J

ja yes, 1–1
die **Jacke, -n** jacket, 3–2
das **Jahr, -e** year, 5–1
die **Jahreszeit, -en** season (of the year), 4–VLS
das **Jahrhundert, -e** century, 8–2
je ever, 8–1
    je größer, desto besser the bigger, the better, 12G
die **Jeans** (pl.) (blue) jeans, 3G
jeder, -es, -e each, every, 5G
jemand somebody, someone, 2–2
jetzt now, 3–1
    von jetzt an from now on, 13–1
joggen to jog, 9G
der **Journalist, -en, -en** journalist, 5–2
jüdisch Jewish, 12–2
die **Jugend** (sing.) youth, young people, 9–2
die **Jugendherberge, -n** Youth Hostel, 7–2
(das) **Jugoslawien** Yugoslavia, 5–2
der **Jugoslawe, -n, -n** Yugoslavian (m.), 11G
die **Jugoslawin, -nen** Yugoslavian (f.), 11G
jugoslawisch Yugoslavian, 11G
jung (jünger) young, 2–2
der **Junge, -n, -n** boy, 9–1
Jura (study of) law, 6–VLS

K

der **Kaffee** coffee, 8–1
kalt (kälter) cold, 4–1
die **Kälte** cold, 15–2
die **Kamera, -s** camera, 7–1
kämmen to comb
    sich die Haare kämmen to comb one's hair, 11–1
(das) **Kanada** Canada, 6–1
kapitalistisch capitalistic, 11G
kaputt broken, wrecked; exhausted, 9–1

die **Karte, -n** card; ticket; map, 4–1
die **Kartoffel, -n** potato, 8–1
der **Käse** cheese, 8–1
die **Kasse, -n** cashier; cashier's office, 14–1
die **Katze, -n** cat, 11G
kaufen to buy, 5–1
das **Kaufhaus, ¨er** department store, 8–VLS
kaum hardly, barely, 11–2
kein not a, not any, no, 3–1
    kein . . . mehr no more . . . , not a . . . any longer, 4G
der **Kellner, -** waiter, 8–1
die **Kellnerin, -nen** waitress, 8–1
kennen, kannte, hat gekannt to know, be acquainted with, 2–1
kennen · lernen to get to know; meet, 5–1
das **Kilo** (short for **das Kilogramm**), 8–1
das **Kilogramm** kilogram, 8–1
der **Kilometer, -** kilometer, 15G
das **Kind, -er** child, 1–1
die **Kindheit, -en** childhood, 10–1
das **Kino, -s** movie theater, 6–2
    ins Kino to the movies, 6–2
die **Kirche, -n** church, 6–2
klagen to complain, 15–2
klar clear; (colloq.) sure, of course, 9–1
die **Klasse, -n** class; grade, 1–2
die **Klausur, -en** test (during the semester), 6–VLS
das **Klavier, -e** piano, 14–2
das **Kleid, -er** dress (pl. = dresses or clothes), 3–2
der **Kleiderschrank, ¨e** clothes cupboard, wardrobe, 6–VLS
die **Kleidung** clothing, 3–VLS
klein little, small, 2–1
die **Kleinstadt, ¨e** town (5,000 to 20,000 inhabitants), 8–2
das **Klima** climate, 4–2
klingen, klang, hat geklungen sound, 13–2
das **Klischee -s** cliché, 2–2
klischeehaft cliché, stereotyped, 13–VLS
der **Klub, -s** club, 9–2
klug (klüger) smart, bright, 5–1
kochen to cook, 2–2
der **Koffer, -** suitcase, 7–1
die **Kolonie, -n** colony, 4G
komisch funny; strange, 8–1

kommen, kam, ist gekommen to come, 1–1
kommunistisch Communist, 11G
der **Konflikt, -e** conflict, 2G
können (kann), konnte, hat gekonnt can, be able to, 3–1
    Ich kann Deutsch. I can speak German. 3G
konservativ conservative, 13G
der **Kontakt, -e** contact, 14G
der **Kontrast, -e** contrast, 4G
sich konzentrieren auf (+ acc.) to concentrate on, 14–2
das **Konzert, -e** concert, 6–2
der **Kopf, ¨e** head, 11–1
    Das geht mir nicht aus dem Kopf. I can't forget that. 12–2
der **Korrespondent, -en, -en** correspondent, 5G
kosten to cost, 6–1
kostenlos free of charge, 6–2
krank (kränker) sick, 9–2
das **Krankenhaus, ¨er** hospital, 11–1
die **Krankheit, -en** sickness, 15–2
die **Krawatte, -n** tie, 3–VLS
kreativ creative, 14G
der **Krieg, -e** war, 3–2
kritisch critical, 16–2
kritisieren to criticize, 11–2
die **Küche, -n** kitchen, 16–2
der **Kuchen, -** cake, 8–VLS
der **Kugelschreiber, -** ball-point pen, intro.
kühl cool, 4–2
der **Kühlschrank, ¨e** refrigerator, 15–VLS
die **Kultur, -en** culture, 4G
kulturell cultural, 9G
sich kümmern um (+ acc.) to look after, take care of, deal with, 13–1
die **Kunst, ¨e** art, 8–1
die **Kunstgeschichte** art history, 6–VLS
der **Künstler, -** artist (m.), 14–2
die **Künstlerin, -nen** artist (f.), 14–2
kurz (kürzer) short, 6–2
die **Kusine, -n** cousin (f.), 2–VLS

L

lachen to laugh, 3–2
    lachen über (+ acc.) to laugh about

der **Laden, ⁻** shop, store, 5–1
die **Lampe, -n** lamp, 6–VLS
das **Land, ⁻er** country, 4–2
    auf dem Land in the country, 8–2
    aufs Land to the country, 8–2
die **Landkarte, -n** map, intro.
die **Landschaft, -en** landscape, 4–2
der **Landwirt, -e** farmer (*m.*), 5–VLS
die **Landwirtin, -nen** farmer (*f.*), 5–VLS
die **Landwirtschaft** agriculture, 6–VLS
lang(e) (länger) long; for a long time, 4–1
langsam slow, 3–2
langweilig boring, 3–1
lassen (läßt), ließ, hat gelassen to leave (something *or* someone), leave behind; let, allow; cause to be done, 12–1
laufen (läuft), lief, ist gelaufen to run; to go on foot, walk (*colloq.*), 3–1
laut loud, intro.
leben to live, be alive, 5–2
das **Leben** life, 4–2
die **Lebensmittel** (*pl.*) groceries, 5–2
die **Leberwurst, ⁻e** liverwurst, 8–1
lecker delicious, 8–VLS
legal legal, 10G
legen to lay, put down, 6–1
der **Lehrer, -** teacher (*m.*), intro.
die **Lehrerin, -nen** teacher (*f.*), intro.
der **Lehrling, -e** apprentice, 5–1
leicht light (in weight); easy, 5–2
leid
    Das tut mir leid. I'm sorry about that, 7–1
leider unfortunately, 3–1
leihen, lieh, hat geliehen to lend, 12–1
leise quiet, soft, intro.
leisten to achieve, accomplish, 11–2
    sich etwas leisten können to be able to afford something, 11–1
lernen to learn, 3–2
lesen (liest), las, hat gelesen to read, 2–1
    lesen über (+ *acc.*) to read about, 2–1

letzt- last, 10–1
    in letzter Zeit lately, 13–1
die **Leute** (*pl.*) people, 2–1
lieb dear; nice, sweet, 6–2
    Lieber Fritz! Dear Fritz, (*salutation in letter*), 6–2
lieben to love, 3–2
lieber preferably, rather (*see* **gern**)
am liebsten most like to, like best of all to (*see* **gern**)
das **Lied, -er** song, 11–2
liegen, lag, hat gelegen to lie; be situated, 4–2
die **Linguistik** linguistics, 6–VLS
die **Linie, -n** (streetcar or bus) line, 13–1
links to the left; on the left, 6–2
der **Liter** liter, 8–1
literarisch literary, 14G
der **Löffel, -** spoon, 8–VLS
der **Lohn, ⁻e** wages, 5–2
sich lohnen to be worthwhile, worth the trouble, 13–1
los
    Was ist los? What's the matter? What's going on? 3–1
der **Löwe, -n, -n** lion, 10–VLS
die **Luft** air, 4–VLS
die **Lust** desire
    Lust haben (etwas zu tun) to want to (do something), 8–1

M

machen to make; do, 1–1
    Es macht nichts. It doesn't matter, 7–1
    Das macht (mir) Spaß. That is fun (for me). 7–2
die **Macht, ⁻e** power, might, 12–2
das **Mädchen, -** girl, 9–1
das **Mal, -e** time (*in the sense of occasion*), 12–1
    zum ersten Mal for the first time, 12G
    zum x-ten Mal for the umpteenth time, 12G
mag (*see* **mögen**)
man one (*impersonal pronoun*), 1–2
mancher, -es, -e many a, 11–2
    manche (*plur.*) some
manchmal sometimes, 2–2
manipulieren to manipulate, 10G
der **Mann, ⁻er** man; husband, 2–1
die **Mannschaft, -en** team, 9–2
der **Mantel, ⁻** coat, 3–2

das **Märchen, -** fairy tale, 4–2
die **Mark (die Deutsche Mark— DM)** mark (the German mark), 3G
der **Marxist, -en, -en** Marxist, 11G
die **Maschine, -n** machine, 12–1
die **Mathematik** mathematics, 6–VLS
die **Mauer, -n** (free standing *or* outside) wall, 11–2
der **Mechaniker, -** mechanic, 12–1
die **Medizin** (field of) medicine, 6–VLS
das **Meer, -e** sea, 4–2
mehr more, 2–2
    mehr als more than, 10–2
    mehr oder weniger more or less, 13–1
    nicht mehr no longer, not any more, 2–2
mehrere several, 11–1
meinen to be of the opinion, think, 1–2; to mean 2–1
    Was meinen Sie dazu? What do you say to that? What do you think of that? 16–1
meist- most (*see* **viel**)
meistens mostly, usually, 5–2
die **Melancholie** melancholy, 14G
die **Mensa** university cafeteria, 1–1
der **Mensch, -en, -en** person, human being, 6–1
menschlich human, like a human being; humane, 15–2
die **Mentalität, -en** mentality, 15G
das **Messer, -** knife, 8–VLS
die **Methode, -n** method, 10G
die **Metropole, -n** metropolis, 8G
mieten to rent (from), 15–2
die **Milch** milk, 8–1
mild mild, 4G
die **Million, -en** million, 15–2
mindestens at least, 9–2
die **Minute, -n** minute, 6–1
mit (+ *dat.*) with, 2–1
mit·bringen, brachte mit, hat mitgebracht to bring along, take along, 6–1
miteinander with each other, together, 13–2
das **Mitglied, -er** member, 9–2
mit·kommen, kam mit, ist mitgekommen to come along, 5–1

mit·nehmen (nimmt mit), nahm mit, hat mitgenommen to take along, 7–2

das Mittagessen midday meal, lunch, 5–2

die Mitte middle, 6–2
    Mitte Februar in the middle of February, 6–2

der Mittwoch, -e Wednesday, intro.

modern modern, 4–2

mögen (mag), mochte, hat gemocht to like, 4–1
    möchten would like to, 3–1
    Das mag sein. That may be. 16G

möglich possible, 6–1

die Möglichkeit, -en possibility, 15–2

der Moment, -e moment
    im Moment at the moment, 1–1

der Monat, -e month, 10–1

der Montag, -e Monday, intro.

das Moped, -s moped, 5–1

der Morgen, - morning, 1–1
    Guten Morgen! Good morning! 1–1

morgen tomorrow, intro.
    morgen abend tomorrow evening, 12G
    morgen früh tomorrow morning, 12G
    morgen nachmittag tomorrow afternoon, 12G

morgens (in the) mornings, 14G

(das) Moskau Moscow, 11G

müde tired, weary, 4–1

(das) München Munich, 8–2

der Mund, ¨er mouth, 11–1

das Museum, die Museen museum, 8–1

die Musik music, 3–2

die Musikwissenschaft musicology, 6–VLS

müssen (muß), mußte, hat gemußt must, have to, 3–1

die Mutter, ¨ mother, 2–2

die Muttersprache, -n native language, 5–2

die Mutti, -s mama, mom, 2–VLS

N

nach (+ *dat.*) after, 5G; to (*with cities and countries*), 1–1

nach Hause home (*as destination of motion*), 3–1

nach und nach gradually, little by little, 15–2

nachdem (*sub. conj.*) after, 10–2

nach·denken, dachte nach, hat nachgedacht über (+ *acc.*) to think about, ponder, 15–1

nachher later on, after that, 8–1

der Nachmittag, -e afternoon, 10–1
    am Nachmittag in the afternoon, 10–1

nachmittags (in the) afternoons, 14G

nächst- next; nearest, 9–1
    nächstes Semester next semester, 2–1

die Nacht, ¨e night, 12–1
    Gute Nacht. Good night. 12–1
    in der Nacht in the night, at night, 12–1

der Nachtisch, -e dessert, 8–VLS

nachts at night, 14G

nahe (näher, am nächsten) near, 12–1

die Nähe nearness; vicinity
    in der Nähe (+ *gen.*) near, nearby, 8–1

der Name, -ns, -n name, 9–2

die Nase, -n nose, 11–1

naß wet, damp, 4–2

natürlich natural, 1–1

der Nebel fog, mist, 4–VLS

neben (+ *acc. or dat.*) beside, 6G

das Nebenfach, ¨er minor field, 6–2

neblig foggy, misty, 4–VLS

nehmen (nimmt), nahm, hat genommen to take, 2–1

nein no, 1–1

nennen, nannte, hat genannt to name, call, 10–2

nett nice, 11–1

neu new, 3–2
    Was gibt's Neues? What's new? 11–1

neutral neutral, 13G

die Neutralität neutrality, 13G

nicht not, 1–1
    gar nicht not at all, 3–2
    nicht mehr no longer, not any more, 2–2
    nicht nur ... sondern auch not only ... but also, 9–2
    nicht wahr? isn't it? can't

you? doesn't she? etc., 3–1

nichts nothing, 3–1
    Nichts zu danken! Don't mention it! 2–1
    Es macht nichts. It doesn't matter, 7–1

nie never, 1–2

niedrig low, 16–2

niemand nobody, no one, 2–2

noch still, 2–2
    noch ein another, an additional, 2–2
    noch einmal once again, once more, 4–1
    noch etwas something else, anything more, 8–1
    noch immer still, 4–2
    noch kein- not a ... yet; not any ... yet, 4G
    noch nicht not yet, 4–1
    noch nie never yet, 8–1

(das) Nordamerika North America, 2G

der Norden the North, 4–2

normal normal, 2–2

die Nummer, -n number, intro.

nur only, 2–1

O

ob (*sub. conj.*) if, whether, 8–1

objektiv objective, 13–VLS

das Obst fruit, 8–VLS

obwohl (*sub. conj.*) although, 8–2

oder or, 1–2

offen open, 11–2

öffentlich public, 16–2

offiziell official, 13G

oft (öfter) often, 1–2

ohne (+ *acc.*) without, 4–1
    ohne ... zu without —ing, 8G

das Ohr, -en ear, 11–1

olympisch Olympic, 9G

die Oma, -s grandma, 10–1

der Onkel, - uncle, 2–2

der Opa, -s grandpa, 10–1

die Opposition, -en opposition, 10G

optimistisch optimistic, 3G

die Ordnung order, 13–1

ordentlich tidy, orderly, 16–2

die Organisation, -en organisation, 9G

organisieren to organize, 9G

der Ort, -e place; small town, 13–2

der **Osten** the East, 4–2
(das) **Österreich** Austria, 4–1
der **Österreicher, -** Austrian (*m.*), 11G
die **Österreicherin, -nen** Austrian (*f.*), 11G
österreichisch Austrian, 14–1
der **Ozean, -e** ocean, 15G

P

ein paar a couple (of), a few, 6–2
packen to pack, 7G
die **Pädagogik** (field of) education, 6–VLS
das **Papier** paper, intro.
parallel parallel, 16G
parken to park, 3–1
die **Partei, -en** political party, 10–2
der **Paß, die Pässe** passport, 11–VLS
passieren, ist passiert to happen, 10–1
passiv passive, 9–2
der **Patient, -en, -en** patient, 14G
die **Pause, -n** break; intermission, 3–1
   eine Pause machen to take a break, 3–1
Pech haben to have bad luck, be unlucky, 6–2
per by
   per Autostop reisen to hitchhike, 7–2
perfekt perfect, 15–1
pessimistisch pessimistic, 3G
phantastisch fantastic, 2–1
die **Philosophie** philosophy, 6G
philosophieren to philosophize, 14G
die **Physik** physics, 6–VLS
das **Plakat, -e** poster, 10–2
planen to plan, make plans, 15–2
der **Plattenspieler, -** record player, 6–VLS
der **Platz, ̈e** place; space; city square, 6–1
die **Politik** politics; policy, 10–2
der **Politiker, -** politician (*m.*), 10–2
die **Politikerin, -nen** politician (*f.*), 10–2
die **Politikwissenschaft** political science, 6–VLS
politisch political, 9–2

die **Polizei** (*sing.*) police, 8–VLS
die **Pommes frites** (*pl.*) French fries, 3–2
die **Post** post office; postal service; mail, 15–1
die **Postkarte, -n** postcard, 5–2
praktisch practical, 13G
der **Präsident, -en, -en** president, 10–VLS
der **Preis, -e** price, 8–2
das **Problem, -e** problem, 2–2
produktiv productive, 14G
der **Professor, -en** professor (*m.*), intro.
die **Professorin, -nen** professor (*f.*), intro.
der **Programmierer, -** programmer (*m.*), 5–VLS
die **Programmiererin, -nen** programmer (*f.*), 5–VLS
das **Prozent** percent, 13G
die **Prüfung, -en** examination, 6–VLS
die **Psychoanalyse** psychoanalysis, 14G
die **Psychologie** psychology, 6–VLS
psychologisch psychological, 16G
der **Pulli, -s** (*short for* **Pullover**), 3–2
der **Pullover, -** pullover, jersey, 3–2
pünktlich punctual, on time, 7–2
putzen to clean, 11–1

Q

Quatsch! rubbish! baloney! nonsense! 5–1
die **Querstraße, -n** cross street, 12–1

R

das **Rad, ̈er** wheel; bicycle, 8–2
rad·fahren (fährt Rad), fuhr Rad, ist radgefahren to bicycle, 9–2
der **Radiergummi** eraser, intro.
das **Radio, -s** radio, 6–VLS
das **Rathaus, ̈er** town hall, 8–1
die **Reaktion, -en** reaction, 11–2
recht
recht haben (hat recht), hatte recht, hat recht gehabt to be right, 13–1

rechts to the right; on the right, 6–2
der **Rechtsanwalt, ̈e** lawyer (*m.*), 13–2
die **Rechtsanwältin, -nen** lawyer (*f.*), 13–2
reden to speak, talk, 7–2
das **Referat, -e** oral report; written term paper, 12–1
   ein Referat halten to give a report, 6–VLS
   ein Referat schreiben to write a paper, 6–VLS
regelmäßig regular, 11–1
der **Regen** rain, 4–VLS
die **Regierung** government in power, administration (*U.S.*), 10–VLS
regnen to rain, 1–1
das **Reich, -e** empire; realm, 14–2
reich rich, 9–1
die **Reise, -n** trip, journey, 3–2
   eine Reise machen to take a trip, 3–2
   Gute Reise! Have a good trip! 1–1
der **Reiseführer, -** guide book, 7–1
reisen, ist gereist to travel, 7–2
   per Autostop reisen to hitchhike, 7–2
der **Reisescheck, -s** traveller's check, 14–1
relativ relative, 2G
die **Religion, -en** religion, 15G
renovieren to renovate, 15G
die **Reparation, -en** reparation, 11G
reparieren to repair, 12–1
die **Republik, -en** republic, 10G
das **Restaurant, -s** restaurant, 8–1
retten to save, rescue, 10–2
die **Rezeption** hotel reception desk, 14–1
der **Rhein** the Rhine River, 4G
richtig right, correct, intro.
der **Rock, ̈e** skirt, 3–VLS
die **Rolle, -n** role, 4–2
   eine Rolle spielen to play a part; be of importance, 4–2
der **Roman, -e** novel, 5–2
romantisch romantic, 13G
rot (röter) red, 9–1
der **Rucksack, ̈e** rucksack, backpack, 7–2
ruhig calm, peaceful, 10–2
der **Russe, -n, -n** Russian (*m.*), 11–2

die **Russin, -nen** Russian (f.), 11–2

russisch Russian, 11G

(das) **Rußland** Russia, 8–2

S

die **Sache, -n** thing, object; matter, affair, 13–1

   deine Sachen your belongings, 13–1

sagen to say; tell, 1–2

   sag mal tell me, 12–1

   Was sagen Sie dazu? What do you say to that? What do you think of that? 16–1

der **Salat, -e** salad; lettuce, 8–1

der **Samstag, -e** Saturday, intro.

der **Satellit, -en, -en** satellite, 11G

sauber clean, 13–2

saŭer sour, 8–VLS

das **Sauerkraut** sauerkraut, 8–VLS

schade too bad, 11–1

   Das ist schade! That's a shame! Too bad! What a pity! 11–1

die **Schallplatte, -n** (phonograph) record, 6–VLS

der **Schalter, -** counter, window, 13–1

schauen (auf + *acc.*) to look (at), 14–2

das **Schaufenster, -** store window, 5–2

der **Scheck, -s** check, 14–1

scheinen, schien, hat geschienen to shine; seem, 1–1

schenken to give (as a gift), 5–1

schick chic, fashionable, 12–1

schicken to send, 6–2

das **Schiff, -e** ship, 12–2

Schi laufen (läuft Schi), lief Schi, ist Schi gelaufen to ski, 8–2

der **Schilling, -e** Austrian shilling, 14–1

schlafen (schläft), schlief, hat geschlafen to sleep, 3–1

das **Schlafzimmer, -** bedroom, 15–VLS

schlagen (schlägt), schlug, hat geschlagen to hit; beat, 9–VLS

die **Schlange, -n** snake, 10–VLS

schlecht bad, 1–1

schließen, schloß, hat geschlossen to close, 5–2

schließlich after all, finally, 15–1

schlimm bad, 7–2

der **Schlüssel, -** key, 6–VLS

schmecken to taste (*trans. and intrans.*); taste good, 8–1

schmuggeln to smuggle, 11–VLS

schmutzig dirty, 13–2

der **Schnaps, ¨e** distilled spirits, schnapps, 11–VLS

der **Schnee** snow, 4–2

schneien to snow, 4–2

schnell fast, 3–2

das **Schnitzel, -** cutlet, chop, 8–1

die **Schokolade** chocolate, 11–1

schon already, 3–1

schön beautiful, 1–1

schrecklich terrible, 4–2

schreiben, schrieb, hat geschrieben to write, 3–2

   schreiben über (+ *acc.*) to write about, 3–2

die **Schreibmaschine, -n** typewriter, 6–VLS, 12–1

der **Schreibtisch, -e** desk, 6–1

der **Schriftsteller, -** writer (*m.*), 10–2

die **Schriftstellerin, -nen** writer (f.), 10–2

der **Schuh, -e** shoe, 3–2

die **Schule, -n** school, 2–1

der **Schüler, -** secondary school pupil (*m.*), intro.

die **Schülerin, -nen** secondary school pupil (f.), intro.

das **Schulsystem, -e** school system, 3G

schwach (schwächer) weak, 10–2

schwarz (schwärzer) black, 9–1

die **Schweiz** Switzerland, 4–2

der **Schweizer, -** Swiss (*m.*), 13–2

die **Schweizerin, -nen** Swiss (f.), 13–2

schweizerisch Swiss, 11G

schwer heavy; hard, difficult, 5–2

die **Schwester, -n** sister, 2–1

schwierig difficult, 5–1

die **Schwierigkeit, -en** difficulty, 13–2

das **Schwimmbad, ¨er** swimming pool, 9–1

schwimmen, schwamm, ist geschwommen to swim, 4–1

der **See, -n** lake, 4–1

   am See at the lake

sehen (sieht), sah, hat gesehen to see, 2–1

sehr very, 1–1

sein (ist), war, ist gewesen to be, 1–1

seit (+ *dat.*) since, 5–1

   seit 5 Jahren for (the past) 5 years, 5-1

   seit langem for a long time, 10–1

die **Seite, -n** side; page, 11–2

   auf der einen Seite/auf der anderen Seite on the one hand/on the other hand, 11–2

der **Sekretär, -e** secretary (*m.*), 5–VLS

die **Sekretärin, -nen** secretary (f.), 5–VLS

selber/selbst by myself, yourself, ourselves, etc., 11–1

selbstverständlich "It goes without saying that . . ." , 4G

selten seldom, 1–2

das **Semester, -** semester, 2–1

   nächstes Semester next semester, 2–1

die **Semesterferien** (*pl.*) semester break, 6–2

das **Seminar, -e** (university) seminar, 4–1

die **Serviette, -n** napkin, 8–VLS

setzen to set (down), put, 7–1

   sich setzen to sit down, 11–1

sich (3rd person reflexive pronoun) himself; herself; themselves; yourself, yourselves (formal second person), 11–1

sicher certain, sure, 2–1

siebt- seventh, 9G

singen, sang, hat gesungen to sing, 3–2

die **Situation, -en** situation, 11–2

sitzen, saß, hat gesessen to sit, 6–2

(das) **Skandinavien** Scandinavia, 8–2

so like this, 1–2; so, 7–2

das **Sofa, -s** sofa, 15–VLS

sofort immediately, right away, 6–2

sogar even, in fact, 1–2

der **Sohn, ¨e** son, 2–1

solcher, -es, -e such, 5G

die **Solidarität** solidarity, 1G

sollen (soll), sollte, hat gesollt should, be supposed to, 3–1

der **Sommer** summer, 4–2

das **Sommersemester** spring term (usually May–July), 6–VLS

sondern but rather, 7–1

der **Sonnabend, -e** Saturday, intro.
die **Sonne** sun, 1–1
sonnig sunny, 4–2
der **Sonntag, -e** Sunday, intro.
sowieso anyway, 7–1
die **Sowjets** the Soviets, 11G
die **Sowjetunion** the Soviet
  Union, 11G
sozial social, 2G
sozialistisch Socialist, 11G
die **Soziologie** sociology, 6–VLS
(das) **Spanien** Spain, 15–1
sparen to save (money), 7–2
der **Spaß** fun
  Das macht (mir) Spaß. That
  is fun (for me). 7–2
spät late, 3–1
  Wie spät ist es? What time
  is it? 8G
später later, 8–1
spazieren · gehen, ging spazieren,
  ist spazierengegangen to go
  for a walk, 5–2
der **Spiegel, -** mirror, 11–2
das **Spiel, -e** game, 9–VLS
spielen to play, 1–1
der **Sport** sport, 9–1
  Sport treiben to play sports,
  9–1
der **Sportler, -** athlete (m.), 9–2
die **Sportlerin, -nen** athlete (f.),
  9–2
der **Sportplatz, ̈e** playing field,
  9–1
die **Sprache, -n** language, 3–2
sprechen (spricht), sprach, hat
  gesprochen to speak, talk,
  2–1
  sprechen über (+ acc.) to
  talk about, 2–1
der **Staat, -en** state, 9–2
staatlich government(al), state,
  16–2
stabil stabile, 13G
die **Stabilität** stability, 13G
die **Stadt, ̈e** city, 4–1
der **Stadtbummel, -** stroll through
  the city, 8–1
der **Stadtplan, ̈e** city map, 6–2
stark (stärker) strong, 10–2
statt (+ gen.) instead of, 8G
statt · finden, fand statt, hat stattge-
  funden to take place, 14–2
stehen, stand, hat gestanden to
  stand, 5–1
stehlen (stiehlt), stahl, hat
  gestohlen to steal, 10–1
steigen, stieg, ist gestiegen to
  climb, 8–2

steil steep, 3–1
der **Stein, -e** stone, 12–2
die **Stelle, -n** job, position, 2–2
stellen to put, place, 7–1
  eine Frage stellen to ask a
  question, 10–1
sterben (stirbt), starb, ist gestor-
  ben to die, 10–1
stereotyp stereotyped, 16G
die **Stimme, -n** voice, 5–2
stimmen to be right (impersonal
  only), 1–2
  das stimmt that's right,
  that's true
  Stimmt schon. That's right.
  16–1
der **Stock** floor (of a building),
  14–2
  der erste Stock the second
  floor (see **Erdgeschoß**)
  im ersten Stock on the second floor
stolz auf (+ acc.) proud of, 13–2
stören to disturb, 10–2
die **Straße, -n** street; road, 1–1
  in der X-straße on X Street,
  12–1
die **Straßenbahn, -en** streetcar,
  7–2
der **Streß, die Stresse** stress, 8G
der **Student, -en, -en** university
  student (m.), intro.
die **Studentin, -nen** university
  student (f.), intro.
der **Studentenausweis, -e** student
  I.D., 6–2
das **Studentenwohnheim, -e**
  student dormitory, 6–1
studieren to attend a university,
  1–2
  studieren an (+ dat.) to
  study at, 6–VLS
das **Studium** university studies,
  6–VLS
der **Stuhl, ̈e** chair, intro.
die **Stunde, -n** hour; class hour,
  3–1
subjektiv subjective, 13–VLS
suchen to look for, seek, 2–1
der **Süden** the South, 4–2
der **Supermarkt, ̈e** supermarket,
  8–1
die **Suppe, -n** soup, 1–1
süß sweet, 8–VLS
das **Symbol, -e** symbol, 11G
symbolisch symbolic, 10G
sympathisch friendly, congenial,
  likeable, 7–2
das **System, -e** system, 3G

T

die **Tafel, -n** blackboard, intro.
der **Tag, -e** day, 1–1
  eines Tages some day (in the
  future); one day (in the past),
  16–2
  Guten Tag! Hello! intro.
  jeden Tag every day, 5–2
die **Tante, -n** aunt, 2–2
tanzen to dance, 14–2
die **Tasche, -n** pocket, 10–1
die **Tasse, -n** cup, 8–1
die **Tatsache, -n** fact, 11–2
die **Taube, -n** dove, 10–VLS
das **Taxi, -s** taxicab, 8–VLS
der **Teil, -e** part, 15–2
teil · nehmen (nimmt teil), nahm
  teil, hat teilgenommen an
  (+ dat.) to take part in, participate in, 9–2
das **Telefon, -e** telephone, 6–VLS
der **Teller, -** plate, 8–VLS
das **Tennis** tennis, 9–1
der **Tennisplatz, ̈e** tennis court,
  9–1
der **Teppich, -e** rug, 6–VLS
terroristisch terrorist (adj.), 10G
teuer expensive, 6–2
das **Theater, -** theater, 6–2
das **Thema, die Themen** topic,
  subject, theme, 16–2
tief deep, 12–2
der **Tisch, -e** table, intro.
die **Tochter, ̈** daughter, 2–2
die **Toilette, -n** lavatory, 15–VLS
toll (colloq.) great; terrific, 3–2
die **Tomate, -n** tomato, 8–VLS
tot dead, 11–2
die **Tour, -en** tour, 8–2
der **Tourist, -en, -en** tourist (m.),
  1–2
die **Touristin, -nen** tourist (f.)
die **Tradition, -en** tradition, 14G
traditionell traditional, 2G
tragen (trägt), trug, hat getra-
  gen to carry; wear, 3–2
trainieren to train, 9–VLS
trampen, ist getrampt to hitchhike, 7–2
transportieren to transport, 11G
träumen to dream, 14–2
traurig sad, 13–2
treffen (trifft), traf, hat getroffen
  to meet (by appointment), 9–2
treiben, trieb, hat getrieben to
  drive, force, propel, 9–1
  Sport treiben to play sports,
  9–1

trinken, trank, hat getrunken to drink, 4–2

trocken dry, 4–2

trotz (+ *gen.*) in spite of, despite, 8G

trotzdem in spite of that, nevertheless, 8–2

Tschüs! So long! 1–1

das **T-Shirt, -s** T-shirt, 3–VLS

tun, tat, hat getan to do, 3–1

    Es tut mir leid. I'm sorry (about that), 7–1

    Das tut mir weh. That hurts (me). 11–1

    Er tut, als ob . . . (+ *subjunctive*) He acts as if . . . , 16G

die **Tür, -en** door, intro.

der **Türke, -n, -n** Turk (*m.*), 15–2

die **Türkin, -nen** Turk (*f.*), 15–2

die **Türkei** Turkey, 15–2

türkisch Turkish, 15–2

der **Turnschuh, -e** sneaker, gym shoe, 3–2

der **Typ, -en** type; (*slang*) guy, 12–1

typisch typical, 1–1

U

die **U-Bahn** (= **Untergrundbahn**) subway train, 7–VLS

üben to practice, intro.

über (+ *acc.*) about, 2–1; (+ *acc. or dat.*) over, across; above, 6G

überall everywhere, 2–2

sich etwas überlegen to consider, ponder, think something over, 13–2

übermorgen the day after tomorrow, 12–1

übernachten to spend the night, 7–2

überraschen to surprise, 15–1

übersetzen to translate, intro.

übrigens by the way, 1–1

die **Uhr, -en** clock, intro.

    9 Uhr 9 o'clock, 5–1

    Wieviel Uhr ist es? What time is it? 8G

um (+ *acc.*) at (*with times*), 1–1; around (the outside of), 4G

um . . . zu in order to, 8–1

um·steigen, stieg um, ist umgestiegen to transfer, change (*trains, buses, etc.*), 7–VLS

um·ziehen, zog um, ist umgezogen to move, change residence, 15–1

und and, 1–1

der **Unfall, ̈e** accident, 11–1

ungebildet uneducated, 16–2

unglücklich unhappy, 10–1

die **Uni, -s** (*colloq.*) university, 6–1

    an der Uni at the university, 6–1

die **Universität, -en** university, 6–1

    an der Universität at the university, 6–1

unmöglich impossible, 6–1

unordentlich messy, disorderly, 16–2

die **Unordnung** disorder, mess, 13–1

unruhig restless, troubled, 10–2

der **Unsinn** nonsense, foolishness, 5–1

unter (+ *acc. or dat.*) under, beneath; among, 6–1

unterbrechen (unterbricht), unterbrach, hat unterbrochen to interrupt, 10–2

der **Unterschied, -e** difference, 14–2

unterwegs en route; on the go, 7–2

unwichtig unimportant, 2–2

der **Urlaub** vacation (from a job), 4–1

    Urlaub machen to take a vacation (from a job), 5–2

die **USA** (*pl.*) the USA, 5–2

usw. (= **und so weiter**) etc., 9–2

V

der **Vater, ̈** father, 2–1

der **Vati, -s** papa, dad, 2–VLS

verantwortlich für (+ *acc.*) responsible for, 13–2

verbieten, verbot, hat verboten (+ *dat. of person*) to forbid, prohibit, 7–2

    verboten forbidden, prohibited, 7–2

die **Verbesserung, -en** improvement, 16–2

verbringen, verbrachte, hat verbracht to spend (time), 8–2

verdienen to earn, 2–2

die **Vergangenheit** past (time), 14–2

vergessen (vergißt), vergaß, hat vergessen to forget, 5–2

verkaufen to sell, 5–2

der **Verkehr** traffic, 7–VLS

verlangen to demand, 11–2

verlassen (verläßt), verließ, hat verlassen to leave (a person or place), 5–1

sich verletzen to injure oneself, get hurt, 11–1

verlieren, verlor, hat verloren to lose, 9–2

sich verloben mit (+ *dat.*) to become engaged to, 12–1

verpassen to miss (an event *or* opportunity), 15–1

verrückt (*slang*) crazy, 7–2

verschieden different, various, 11–2

verstehen, verstand, hat verstanden to understand, 3–1

versuchen to try, attempt, 10–2

verwandt (mit + *dat.*) related (to), 15–2

der/die **Verwandte, -n** relative, 11–1

verzollen to pay duty on, declare, 11–VLS

    Haben Sie etwas zu verzollen? Do you have anything to declare?

der **Vetter, -n** cousin (*m.*), 2–VLS

viel (mehr, am meisten) much, a lot, 1–1

viele many, 1–2; (*pronoun*) many people, 9–2

    vielen Dank many thanks, 2–1

vielleicht maybe, perhaps, 1–1

das **Volk, ̈er** people, nation, folk, 10–2

von (+ *dat.*) from, 4–2; of; by, 5G

vor (+ *acc. or dat.*) in front of, 6G

    vor einem Jahr a year ago, 10G

vorbei·kommen, kam vorbei, ist vorbeigekommen to come by, drop by, 5–2

sich vor·bereiten auf (+ *acc.*) to prepare for, 13–1

vorgestern the day before yesterday, 12–1

vor·haben (hat vor), hatte vor, hat vorgehabt to plan, have in mind, 13–1

vorher before that, earlier, 10–1

die **Vorlesung, -en** university lecture, 6–1

das **Vorlesungsverzeichnis, -se** university catalogue, list of lectures and courses, 6–1

vormittags (in the) mornings, 16–1

vor·stellen to introduce, present, 13–2

sich vor·stellen to introduce oneself, 13–2

sich etwas vor·stellen to imagine something, 11–1

das **Vorurteil, -e** prejudice, 13–VLS

W

wachsen (wächst), wuchs, ist gewachsen to grow, 10–2

der **Wagen, -** car, 3–1

die **Wahl, -en** choice; election, 10–VLS

wählen to choose; elect, 10–VLS

wahr true, 11–2

nicht wahr? isn't it? can't you? doesn't she? etc., 3–1

während (+ gen.) during, 8G

die **Wahrheit, -en** truth, 13–VLS

wahrscheinlich probably, 1–2

der **Wald, ̈er** forest, 4–2

die **Wand, ̈e** (interior) wall, intro.

die **Wanderlust** wanderlust, 7G

wandern, ist gewandert to hike, 4–2

wann? when? 1–1

warm (wärmer) warm, 4–2

warten to wait, 4–1

warten auf (+ acc.) to wait for, 13–1

warum? why? 1–1

was? what? 1–1

was für? what kind of? 12–1

Was ist los? What's the matter?; What's going on? 3–1

waschen (wäscht), wusch, hat gewaschen to wash, 11–1

das **Wasser** water, 4–1

wechseln to change (money), 14–1

der **Wecker, -** alarm clock, 6–VLS

weder . . . noch neither . . . nor, 14–1

der **Weg, -e** way, path, 16–2

wegen (+ gen.) because of, on account of, 8G

weg·gehen, ging weg, ist weggegangen to go away, leave, 12–1

weh tun, tat weh, hat weh getan (+ dat. of person) to hurt, 11–1

weil (sub. conj.) because, 8–1

der **Wein, -e** wine, 4–2

weinen to cry, 3–2

weiß white, 9–1

weit far, far away, 8–1

welcher, -es, -e? which? 5G

die **Welt** world, 9–2

wem? (dat.) to whom? for whom?, 5G

wen? (acc.) whom?, 2–1

wenig small amount, little, not much, 5–1

mehr oder weniger more or less, 13–1

wenige few, 11–1

wenigstens at least, 2–2

wenn (sub. conj.) if, 8–1; when, whenever, 10G

wer? (nom.) who?, 1–1

werden (wird), wurde, ist geworden to become, get (in the sense of "become"), 4–1

werden aus (+ dat.) to become of, 12–2

werfen (wirft), warf, hat geworfen to throw, 15–1

das **Werk, -e** work; composition, 13–2

wessen? whose? 8G

der **Westen** the West, 4–2

das **Wetter** weather, 1–1

die **WG** (= **Wohngemeinschaft**) communal living group, 6–1

wichtig important, 2–2

wie? how?; like, as, 1–1

wie viele? how many? 2–1

wieder again, 1–1

wiederholen to repeat, intro.

wieder·sehen (sieht wieder), sah wieder, hat wiedergesehen to see again, meet again, 12–2

Wiedersehen

Auf Wiedersehen! Good-bye! intro.

wiegen, wog, hat gewogen (trans. and intrans.) to weigh, 15–1

(das) **Wien** Vienna, 1–1

wieso? How come? How's that? What do you mean? 2–1

wieviel? how much? 8–1

Wieviel Uhr ist es? What time is it? 8G

wie viele? how many? 2–1

wievielt-

Den wievielten haben wir heute? What's the date today? 9G

Der wievielte ist heute? What's the date today? 9G

wild wild, 4G

der **Winter, -** winter, 4–1

im Winter in the winter, 4–1

das **Wintersemester** fall term (usually October–February), 6–VLS

wirklich real; really, 6–1

die **Wirtschaft** economy, 11–2

die **Wirtschaftswissenschaft** economics, 6–VLS

wissen (weiß), wußte, hat gewußt to know (a fact), 2–1

wo? where? 1–1

die **Woche, -n** week, 5–2

das **Wochenende -n** weekend, 5–2

am Wochenende on the weekend, 5–2

woher? from where? 6–1

wohin? to where? 6–1

wohl probably, 13–1

wohnen to live, dwell, 1–2

die **Wohngemeinschaft, -en** communal living group, 6–1

die **Wohnung, -en** apartment, 6–2

das **Wohnzimmer, -** living room, 15–VLS

die **Wolke, -n** cloud, 4–VLS

wolkig cloudy, 4–VLS

wollen (will), wollte, hat gewollt to want to, intend to, 3–1; to claim to, 16G

worden special form of the past participle of **werden** used in the perfect tenses of the passive voice

das **Wort** word, 10–2 (2 plural forms: **die Worte**—words in context, **die Wörter**—unconnected words, as in a dictionary)

das **Wörterbuch, ̈er** dictionary, 5–2

das **Wunder, -** miracle

Kein Wunder! No wonder! 15–1

wünschen to wish, 14–1

die **Wurst, ̈e** sausage, 8–1

Z

zahlen to pay, 8–1
    Zahlen bitte! Check please!
    8–1
zählen to count, 10–2
der **Zahn, ̈-e** tooth, 11–1
zeigen to show, 5–1
    Zeig mal her. Let's see.
    Show it to me. 15–1
die **Zeit, -en** time, 5–1
    in letzter Zeit lately, 13–1
Zeitlang
    eine Zeitlang for a time, for
    a while, 14–2
die **Zeitung, -en** newspaper, 2–1
zentral central, 9G
zerstören to destroy, 12–2
ziehen, zog, hat gezogen to pull,
    15–1; **ist gezogen** to move
    (to a new town or area: *must
    include directional*), 15–1
das **Ziel, -e** goal, 16–2

ziemlich fairly, quite, 1–2
die **Zigarette, -n** cigarette,
    11–VLS
zigmal umpteen times, 12G
das **Zimmer, -** room, 2–1
der **Zimmerkamerad, -en, -en**
    roommate (*m.*), 12–1
die **Zimmerkameradin, -nen**
    roommate (*f.*), 12–1
zirka circa, 4G
der **Zoll** customs, 11–VLS
die **Zone, -n** zone, 11G
zu to; too, 1–1
    zu Fuß on foot, 6–2
    zu Hause at home, 2–2
zuerst first, at first, 8-2
der **Zug, ̈-e** train, 7–1
zu·hören (+ *dat.*) to listen (to)
    Hören sie mir zu!
    Listen to me.
die **Zukunft** future, 11–2
    in Zukunft in the future,
    13–2

zu·machen to close, 5–2
zunächst first (of all), to begin
    with, 14–2
zurück back, 1–1
**zurück·bringen, brachte zurück,
    hat zurückgebracht** to bring
    back
**zurück·kommen, kam zurück, ist
    zurückgekommen** to come
    back, 1–1
zusammen together, 4–1
der **Zuschauer, -** spectator, 9–2
zwar . . . aber it is true, to be
    sure . . . but, 14–2
der **Zweck, -e** purpose, 11–2
der **Zweifel, -** doubt
    ohne Zweifel without doubt,
    doubtless, 11–2
die **Zwiebel, -n** onion, 8–VLS
zwischen (+ *acc. or dat.*)
    between, 2–2

English-German Vocabulary

A

a lot, much viel (mehr, am meisten)
about über (+ *acc.*)
above über (+ *acc. or dat.*)
abroad im Ausland
accept akzeptieren
accident der Unfall, ⸚e
achieve, accomplish leisten
acquaintance, friend der/die Bekannte, -n
acquainted: be acquainted with, know kennen, kannte, hat gekannt
across, over über (+ *acc. or dat.*)
act tun als ob (+ *subjunctive*) **He acts as if . . .** Er tut, als ob . . .
active aktiv
actually, in fact eigentlich
acute akut
address die Adresse, -n
affair, matter die Sache, -n
afford: to be able to afford something sich etwas leisten können
afraid: to be afraid Angst haben **to be afraid of** Angst haben vor (+ *dat.*)
after nach (+ *dat., preposition*); nachdem (*sub. conj.*)
after all, finally schließlich
afternoon der Nachmittag, -e; **in the afternoon** am Nachmittag; **(in the) afternoons** nachmittags
again wieder
against gegen (+ *acc.*)
ago vor (+ *dat.*); **a year ago** vor einem Jahr
agriculture die Landwirtschaft
aid die Hilfe
air die Luft
airplane das Flugzeug, -e
airport der Flughafen, ⸚
alarm clock der Wecker, -
allow, permit erlauben (+ *dat. of person*) **be allowed to** dürfen (darf), durfte, hat gedurft

almost fast
alone allein
the Alps die Alpen (*pl.*)
already schon
also auch
alternative die Alternative, -n
although obwohl (*sub. conj.*)
always immer
amateur der Amateur, -e
America (das) Amerika; **American** amerikanisch; der Amerikaner, - (*m.*); die Amerikanerin, -nen (*f.*)
among unter (+ *acc. or dat.*)
analyze analysieren
and und
angry (at) böse (+ *dat.*)
annoy, offend ärgern
another, an additional noch ein
answer die Antwort, -en
   answer (something) antworten auf (+ *acc.*)
   answer (a person) antworten (+ *dat.*)
any time irgendwann
anyway sowieso
apartment die Wohnung, -en
appeal to gefallen (gefällt), gefiel, hat gefallen (+ *dat. of person*)
appear, look (like) aus·sehen (sieht aus), sah aus, hat ausgesehen
appear erscheinen, erschien, ist erschienen
apprentice der Lehrling, -e
April (der) April
area, region die Gegend, -en
arm der Arm, -e
around (the outside of) um (+ *acc.*)
arrive an·kommen, kam an, ist angekommen
art die Kunst, ⸚e
   art history die Kunstgeschichte
article der Artikel, -
artist der Künstler, - (*m.*); die Künstlerin, -nen (*f.*)
as if als ob (+ *subjunctive*)
ask fragen
   ask a question eine Frage stellen

ask for, request bitten, bat, hat gebeten um (+ *acc.*)
   He's asking me for the money. Er bittet mich um das Geld.
aspect der Aspekt, -e
assignment die Aufgabe, -n
at, alongside of an (+ *acc. or dat.*)
   at that time, back then damals
   at (*with times*) um (+ *acc.*)
   at (*someone's place/home/business*) bei
athlete der Athlet, -en, -en; der Sportler, - (*m.*); die Sportlerin, -nen (*f.*)
attend to, take care of, finish erledigen
   attend a university studieren
August (der) August
aunt die Tante, -n
Austria (das) Österreich
Austrian österreichisch; der Österreicher, - (*m.*); die Österreicherin, -nen (*f.*)
auto mechanic der Automechaniker, -
automatic automatisch
autumn, fall der Herbst

B

baby das Baby, -s
back zurück
backpack der Rucksack, ⸚e
bad schlimm; schlecht
   too bad schade
   Too bad! That's a shame! What a pity! Das ist schade!
ball-point pen der Kugelschreiber, -
bank die Bank, -en
barbaric barbarisch
barely kaum
barrier die Barriere, -n
bath das Bad; **to take a bath** ein Bad nehmen
bathroom das Badezimmer, -
be sein (ist), war, ist gewesen
bean die Bohne, -n
bear der Bär, -en, -en

beautiful schön

because weil (*sub. conj.*)

because of, on account of wegen (+ *gen.*)

become, get werden (wird), wurde, ist geworden

to become of werden aus (+ *dat.*)

bed das Bett, -en

to go to bed ins Bett gehen

bedroom das Schlafzimmer, -

beer das Bier, -e

before bevor (*sub. conj.*)

before that, earlier vorher

begin, start an·fangen (fängt an), fing an, hat angefangen; beginnen, begann, hat begonnen

beginning der Anfang, ⸚e;

at the beginning am Anfang

behind hinter (+ *acc.* or *dat.*)

believe; think glauben (+ *dat. of person*)

belong to (*a person*) gehören (+ *dat. of person*)

belongings: your belongings deine Sachen

beside neben (+ *acc.* or *dat.*)

besides außer (+ *dat.*)

better besser

between zwischen (+ *acc.* or *dat.*)

bicycle das Fahrrad, ⸚er; rad·fahren (fährt Rad), fuhr Rad, ist radgefahren

bicycle; wheel das Rad, ⸚er

big groß (größer, am größten)

biology die Biologie

birthday der Geburtstag, -e

When is your birthday? Wann hast du Geburtstag?

for (your) birthday zum Geburtstag

bit, a little bit ein bißchen

bitter bitter

black schwarz (schwärzer)

blackboard die Tafel, -n

blouse die Bluse, -n

blue blau

book das Buch, ⸚er

bookcase das Bücherregal, -e

bookstore die Buchhandlung, -en

border die Grenze, -n

boring langweilig

born geboren; **When were you born?** Wann sind Sie geboren?

boss der Chef, -s (*m.*); die Chefin, -nen (*f.*)

both beid-; beide (*pl.*); **both things** beides (*sing.*)

bottle · die Flasche, -n

boy der Junge, -n, -n

bread das Brot, -e

break brechen (bricht), brach, hat gebrochen

break; intermission die Pause, -n;

to take a break eine Pause machen

break out aus·brechen (bricht aus), brach aus, ist ausgebrochen

breakfast das Frühstück

bridge die Brücke, -n

bright, smart klug (klüger)

bright, light hell

bring bringen, brachte, hat gebracht

bring along, take along mit·bringen, brachte mit, hat mitgebracht

bring back zurück·bringen, brachte zurück, hat zurückgebracht

broken, wrecked kaputt

brother der Bruder, ⸚

brown braun

build bauen

building das Gebäude, -

bus der Bus, -se

business; store das Geschäft, -e

businessman der Geschäftsmann, die Geschäftsleute

businesswoman die Geschäftsfrau, -en

but aber

but rather sondern

buy kaufen

by von (+ *dat.*)

by; until bis (+ *acc.*)

by myself, yourself, ourselves (etc.) selber/selbst

by the way übrigens

C

café das Café, -s

cafeteria (*in a university*) die Mensa

cake der Kuchen, -

call up an·rufen, rief an, hat angerufen

call, to be called heißen, hieß, hat geheißen

calm, peaceful ruhig

camera die Kamera, -s

campground der Campingplatz, ⸚e

can, be able to können (kann), konnte, hat gekonnt

Canada (das) Kanada

capital die Hauptstadt, ⸚e

capitalistic kapitalistisch

car das Auto, -s; der Wagen, -

card; ticket; map die Karte, -n

care; I don't care (about that). Das ist mir egal.

take care of, deal with sich kümmern um (+ *acc.*)

carry; wear tragen (trägt), trug, hat getragen

cashier; cashier's office die Kasse, -n

catalogue, list of courses das Vorlesungsverzeichnis, -se

catch a cold sich erkälten

cathedral der Dom, -e

cease (*doing something*) auf·hören (mit)

celebrate feiern

celebration, party die Feier, -n

central zentral

century das Jahrhundert, -e

certain, sure sicher

chair der Stuhl, ⸚e

easy chair der Sessel, -

chance, opportunity die Gelegenheit, -en; die Chance, -n

change (*intrans.*) sich ändern; (*trans.*) ändern

change residence um·ziehen, zog um, ist umgezogen

change (*money*) wechseln

change (*trains, buses, etc.*) um·steigen, stieg um, ist umgestiegen

cheap billig

check der Scheck, -s

Check please! Zahlen bitte!

cheese der Käse

chemistry die Chemie

chic, fashionable schick

chicken (*roast or fried*) das Hähnchen, -

chief Haupt- (*prefix*)

child das Kind, -er

childhood die Kindheit, -en

chocolate die Schokolade

choice; election die Wahl, -en

choose; elect wählen

chop, cutlet das Schnitzel, -

church die Kirche, -n

cigarette die Zigarette, -n

circa zirka

citizen der Bürger, -

city die Stadt, ⸚e
large city (*over 500,000 inhabitants*) die Großstadt, ⸚e
city map der Stadtplan, ⸚e
civil servant, official der Beamte, -n (*m.*), (*adj. noun*); die Beamtin, -nen (*f.*)
claim to wollen (will), wollte, hat gewollt
class; grade die Klasse, -n
class hour die Stunde, -n
clean sauber (*adj.*); putzen (*verb*)
clear klar, deutlich
cliché das Klischee -s; **cliché, stereotyped** klischeehaft
climate das Klima
climb steigen, stieg, ist gestiegen
clock die Uhr, -en; **9 o'clock** 9 Uhr
close schließen, schloß, hat geschlossen; zu·machen
closed geschlossen
close out; exclude aus·schließen, schloß aus, hat ausgeschlossen
clothes cupboard, wardrobe der Kleiderschrank, ⸚e
clothing die Kleidung
cloud die Wolke, -n
cloudy wolkig
club der Klub, -s
coat der Mantel, ⸚
coffee der Kaffee
cold kalt (kälter);
cold (*noun*) die Kälte
colony die Kolonie, -n
color die Farbe, -n
colorful bunt
comb kämmen
to comb one's hair sich die Haare kämmen
come kommen, kam, ist gekommen
come along mit·kommen, kam mit, ist mitgekommen
come by, drop by vorbei·kommen, kam vorbei, ist vorbeigekommen
come back zurück·kommen, kam zurück, ist zurückgekommen
comfortable bequem; gemütlich
communal living group die WG (= Wohngemeinschaft)
Communist kommunistisch
company, firm die Firma, die Firmen
complain klagen

computer der Computer, -
computer science die Informatik
concentrate on sich konzentrieren auf (+ *acc.*)
concert das Konzert, -e
conflict der Konflikt, -e
congratulate gratulieren (+ *dat. of person*)
conservative konservativ
consider, ponder, think something over sich etwas überlegen
contact der Kontakt, -e
contrast der Kontrast, -e
conversation das Gespräch, -e
cook kochen
cool kühl
corner die Ecke, -n
at the corner an der Ecke;
around the corner um die Ecke
correct richtig
correspondent der Korrespondent, -en, -en
cost kosten
count zählen
counter, window der Schalter, -
country das Land, ⸚er
in the country auf dem Land
to the country aufs Land
a couple (of), a few ein paar
cousin die Kusine, -n (*f.*); der Vetter, -n (*m.*)
cozy, comfortable; quiet, relaxed gemütlich
crazy verrückt (*slang*)
creative kreativ
critical kritisch
criticize kritisieren
cross street die Querstraße, -n
cruel grausam
cry weinen
cucumber die Gurke, -n
cultural kulturell
culture die Kultur, -en
cup die Tasse, -n
customs der Zoll
cutlet, chop das Schnitzel, -

D

dance tanzen
danger die Gefahr, -en
dangerous gefährlich
dark dunkel
daughter die Tochter, ⸚

day der Tag, -e
every day jeden Tag
some day (*in the future*) eines Tages
the day before yesterday vorgestern
the day after tomorrow übermorgen
dead tot
dear; nice, sweet lieb
Dear Fritz, (*salutation in letter*) Lieber Fritz!
December (der) Dezember
declare, pay duty on verzollen
Do you have anything to declare? Haben Sie etwas zu verzollen?
deep tief
define definieren
delicious lecker
demand verlangen
democracy die Demokratie, -n
democratic demokratisch
department store das Kaufhaus, ⸚er
pullover, jersey der Pullover, -; der Pulli, -s
describe beschreiben, beschrieb, hat beschrieben
desire die Lust
desk der Schreibtisch, -e
despite, in spite of trotz (+ *gen.*)
dessert der Nachtisch, -e
destroy zerstören
dialect der Dialekt, -e
dictionary das Wörterbuch, ⸚er
die sterben (stirbt), starb, ist gestorben
die in battle fallen (fällt), fiel, ist gefallen
difference der Unterschied, -e
different anders; **different, various** verschieden
difficult, hard schwer, schwierig
difficulty die Schwierigkeit, -en
dining room das Eßzimmer, -
dinner, evening meal das Abendessen
for dinner zum Abendessen
direct direkt
director der Direktor, -en
dirty schmutzig
disappoint enttäuschen
discuss besprechen (bespricht), besprach, hat besprochen; **discuss; debate** diskutieren
discussion die Diskussion, -en
disorder, mess die Unordnung

disorderly unordentlich

distant, far away fern

distilled spirits, schnapps der Schnaps, ⁻e

disturb stören

DM- *see* **mark**

do tun, tat, hat getan; machen

doctor der Arzt, ⁻e (*m.*); die Ärztin, -nen (*f.*)

done, finished (with); ready fertig (mit)

donkey der Esel, -

door die Tür, -en

double room das Doppelzimmer

doubt der Zweifel, -

  without doubt, doubtless ohne Zweifel

dove die Taube, -n

dream träumen

dress das Kleid, -er (*plural,* Kleider, *means* **dresses** *or* **clothes**)

  to dress (sich) an·ziehen, zog an, hat angezogen

  dressed angezogen

drink trinken, trank, hat getrunken

drive, go (*by vehicle*) fahren (fährt), fuhr, ist gefahren

drive, force, propel treiben, trieb, hat getrieben

dry trocken

dumb dumm (dümmer)

during während (+ *gen.*)

dynasty die Dynastie, -n

E

each, every jeder, -es, -e

eagle der Adler, -

ear das Ohr, -en

earlier, before that vorher

early früh

earn verdienen

earth die Erde

the East der Osten

easy, simple leicht, einfach

eat essen (ißt) aß, hat gegessen

economics die Wirtschaftswissenschaft

economy die Wirtschaft

educated gebildet

education (*the academic study*) die Pädagogik

either . . . or entweder . . . oder

elect wählen

election die Wahl, -en

electrical engineering die Elektrotechnik

electrician; electrical engineer der Elektrotechniker, -(*m.*); die Elektrotechnikerin, -nen (*f.*)

elephant der Elefant, -en, -en

emancipation die Emanzipation

emigrate aus·wandern, ist ausgewandert

empire; realm das Reich, -e

employed berufstätig

employee der/die Angestellte, -n

en route; on the go unterwegs

end das Ende, -n

  at the end of February Ende Februar

  at the end am Ende

engaged, become engaged to sich verloben mit (+ *dat.*)

engineer der Ingenieur, -e (*m.*); die Ingenieurin, -nen (*f.*)

England (das) England

English englisch (*adj.*)

English language (das) Englisch

English studies die Anglistik

Englishman der Engländer, -; **Englishwoman** die Engländerin, -nen

enough genug

entire, whole ganz

entrée das Hauptgericht, -e

epoch die Epoche, -n

equal gleich; **enjoying equal rights** gleichberechtigt

  equal rights die Gleichberechtigung (*sing.*)

eraser der Radiergummi

especially besonders

etc. usw. (= und so weiter)

Europe (das) Europa

  European europäisch; der Europäer, -

even, in fact sogar

evening der Abend, -e

  in the evening am Abend

  (in the) evenings abends

  Good evening. Guten Abend.

ever je

every jeder, -es, -e

everybody, all alle (*pl.*)

everything alles

everywhere überall

exact genau

examination die Prüfung, -en

  oral exam mündliche Prüfung

written exam schriftliche Prüfung; die Klausur, -en

final secondary school examination das Abitur

exam, written test (*of more importance than a* Prüfung) die Klausur, -en

  to take an exam eine Klausur/eine Prüfung schreiben

example das Beispiel, -e; **for example** zum Beispiel

excellent ausgezeichnet

Excuse me! Entschuldigung!

exhausted kaputt (*slang*)

exhibition die Ausstellung, -en

exist existieren

expect erwarten

expensive teuer

experience die Erfahrung, -en

explain erklären

expressway die Autobahn, -en

extreme extrem

eye das Auge, -n

F

face das Gesicht, -er

fact die Tatsache, -n

factory die Fabrik, -en

fairly, quite ziemlich

fairy tale das Märchen, -

fall asleep ein·schlafen (schläft ein), schlief ein, ist eingeschlafen

fall, autumn der Herbst

fall term das Wintersemester (*usually October-February*)

fall; die in battle fallen (fällt), fiel, ist gefallen

false, incorrect falsch

family die Familie, -n

  family discussion die Familiendiskussion, -en

famous berühmt

fan der Fan, -s

fantastic phantastisch

far away, distant fern; weit

farmer der Landwirt, -e (*m.*); die Landwirtin, -nen (*f.*)

fashionable schick

fast schnell

father der Vater, ⁻

  papa, dad der Vati, -s

fear fürchten (*verb*); die Angst, ⁻e (*noun*)

February (der) Februar

Federal Republic of Germany (FRG) die Bundesrepublik Deutschland (BRD)

feel (*intrans.*) sich fühlen

feeling das Gefühl, -e

fetch, get holen; ab·holen

few wenige

film, movie der Film, -e

finally endlich, schließlich

financial finanziell

find out, learn erfahren (erfährt), erfuhr, hat erfahren

find finden, fand, hat gefunden

finger der Finger, -

finished (with); done, ready fertig (mit)

firm, company die Firma, die Firmen

first erst-

first (of all), to begin with zunächst

first, at first zuerst

fish der Fisch, -e

flat flach

floor (*of a building*) der Stock

   first floor das Erdgeschoß

   the second floor der erste Stock

   on the second floor im ersten Stock

floor (*of a room*); **ground; soil** der Boden, ⁼

flower die Blume, -n

fly fliegen, flog, ist geflogen

fog, mist der Nebel

foggy, misty neblig

food das Essen

foolishness der Unsinn

foot der Fuß, ⁼e; **on foot** zu Fuß

for, because denn (*coord. conj.*)

for für (+ *acc.*)

for a while eine Zeitlang

For heaven's sake! Um Gottes Willen!

forbid, prohibit verbieten, verbot, hat verboten (+ *dat. of person*)

   forbidden, prohibited verboten

force, propel treiben, trieb, hat getrieben

foreign fremd

foreign language die Fremdsprache, -n

foreign countries das Ausland (*sing.*)

foreigner der Ausländer, - (*m.*); die Ausländerin, -nen (*f.*)

foreign worker, guest worker der Gastarbeiter, - (*m.*); die Gastarbeiterin, -nen (*f.*)

forest der Wald, ⁼er

forget vergessen (vergißt), vergaß, hat vergessen

   I can't forget that. Das geht mir nicht aus dem Kopf.

fork die Gabel, -n

form die Form, -en

formal formell

France (das) Frankreich

free time, leisure time die Freizeit

free, unoccupied frei

free of charge kostenlos

freedom die Freiheit, -en

French fries die Pommes frites (*pl.*)

French französisch

Frenchman der Franzose, -n, -n

Frenchwoman die Französin, -nen

FRG (= Federal Republic of Germany) BRD (= Bundesrepublik Deutschland)

Friday (der) Freitag, -e

friend der Freund, -e (*m.*); die Freundin, -nen (*f.*)

   friendly freundlich; sympathisch

from von (+ *dat.*)

   from; out of aus (+ *dat.*)

front: in front of vor (+ *acc. or dat.*)

fruit das Obst

fun der Spaß

   That is fun (for me). Das macht (mir) Spaß.

funny; strange komisch

furniture die Möbel (*pl.*)

future die Zukunft

   in the future in Zukunft

G

game das Spiel, -e

   soccer game das Fußballspiel

garage die Garage, -n

garden der Garten, ⁼

GDR (German Democratic Republic) die DDR (Deutsche Demokratische Republik)

gender, sex das Geschlecht, -er

generation die Generation, -en

gentleman der Herr, -n, -en

geography die Geographie

German deutsch

   German language (das) Deutsch

   in German auf deutsch

   German der/die Deutsche, -n

German class die Deutschstunde, -n

German studies die Germanistik

German Mark (currency) die Deutsche Mark (DM)

German Democratic Republic (GDR) die Deutsche Demokratische Republik (DDR)

Germany (das) Deutschland

get annoyed (at), be annoyed (about) sich ärgern (über + *acc.*)

   get out of bed auf·stehen, stand auf, ist aufgestanden

   get out (of a vehicle) aus·steigen, stieg aus, ist ausgestiegen

   get to know; meet kennen·lernen

   get, How do I get there? Wie komme ich dahin?

   get well sich erholen (von)

   get, fetch holen, ab·holen

   get in (*a vehicle*) ein·steigen, stieg ein, ist eingestiegen

   get dressed sich anziehen

   get, receive bekommen, bekam, hat bekommen

   get used to sich gewöhnen an (+ *acc.*)

   get undressed sich aus·ziehen, zog aus, hat ausgezogen

gift, present das Geschenk, -e

girl das Mädchen, -

give geben (gibt), gab, hat gegeben

   give (*as a gift*) schenken

   give up auf·geben (gibt auf), gab auf, hat aufgegeben

glad, happy froh

gladly, with pleasure gern (lieber, am liebsten)

glass das Glas, ⁼er

   (eye)glasses die Brille (*sing.*)

glove der Handschuh, -e

go; walk gehen, ging, ist gegangen

   go (by vehicle), drive fahren (fährt), fuhr, ist gefahren

   go away, leave weg·gehen, ging weg, ist weggegangen

   go out aus·gehen, ging aus, ist ausgegangen

   "It goes without saying that . . ." selbstverständlich

goal das Ziel, -e

god der Gott, ⁼er

golden golden

good, well gut (besser, am besten)

    pretty good ganz gut

Good-bye! Auf Wiedersehen!

goodness: thank goodness Gott sei Dank.

government in power; administration (U.S.) die Regierung

    government(al), state staatlich

gradually, little by little nach und nach

gram das Gramm

grandfather der Großvater, ¨

grandma die Oma, -s

grandmother die Großmutter, ¨

grandpa der Opa, -s

grandparents die Großeltern (*pl.*)

gray grau

Great Britain (das) Großbritannien

great; terrific toll (*colloq.*)

greatness die Größe, -n

green grün

greet, say hello to grüßen

groceries die Lebensmittel (*pl.*)

ground, reason der Grund, ¨e

ground floor, first floor das Erdgeschoß

    ground, soil; floor (of a room) der Boden, ¨

group die Gruppe, -n

grow wachsen (wächst), wuchs, ist gewachsen

grow up auf·wachsen (wächst auf), wuchs auf, ist aufgewachsen

gruesome grausam

guest; patron der Gast, ¨e

guide book der Reiseführer, -

guy der Typ, -en (*slang*)

H

hair das Haar, -e

    comb one's hair sich die Haare kämmen

half halb; die Hälfte, -n

    half days halbtags

hand die Hand, ¨e

    on the one hand/on the other hand auf der einen Seite/auf der anderen Seite

handsome hübsch, schön

hang, to be hanging hängen, hing, hat gehangen (*intrans.*)

hang (up) hängen (*trans.*)

happen passieren, ist passiert; geschehen (geschieht), geschah, ist geschehen

happiness das Glück

happy glücklich; froh

to be happy glücklich sein; sich freuen (über + *acc.*)

hard, difficult schwer, schwierig

hard, tough; harsh hart (härter)

hard-working, industrious fleißig

hardly, barely kaum

hat der Hut, ¨e

hate hassen

have haben (hat), hatte, hat gehabt

    have an opinion about halten von (+ *dat.*)

    have in mind vor·haben (hat vor), hatte vor, hat vorgehabt

head der Kopf, ¨e

health die Gesundheit

healthy gesund

hear hören

heavy schwer

hello: say hello to grüßen

    Hello! Guten Tag!; Grüß Gott! (*in southern Germany and Austria*)

help helfen (hilft), half, hat geholfen (+ *dat.*); die Hilfe

here hier

high hoch (höher, am höchsten)

highway die Autobahn, -en

hike wandern, ist gewandert

historic historisch

history, story die Geschichte, -n

hit; beat schlagen (schlägt), schlug, hat geschlagen

hitchhike per Autostop reisen; trampen, ist getrampt

    hitchhiking der Autostop

hold halten (hält), hielt, hat gehalten

home (*as destination of motion*) nach Hause

    at home, in the home zu Hause

    at the home of bei (+ *dat.*)

homeland die Heimat

homesickness das Heimweh

homework assignment die Hausaufgabe, -n

honest ehrlich

hope hoffen

    I hope, let's hope hoffentlich

horizon der Horizont, -e

hospital das Krankenhaus, ¨er

hot heiß

hotel das Hotel, -s

hour; class hour die Stunde, -n

house das Haus, ¨er

housewife die Hausfrau, -en

housework die Hausarbeit

how wie

    how much? wieviel?

    how many? wie viele?

    How come? How's that? What do you mean? wieso?

human; humane menschlich

humor der Humor

hunger der Hunger

    to be hungry Hunger haben

hurry die Eile; sich beeilen

    in a hurry in Eile

hurt weh tun, tat weh, hat weh getan (+ *dat. of person*)

    That hurts (me). Das tut mir weh.

I

I.D. card der Ausweis, -e

ice cream das Eis

idea die Idee, -n

ideal das Ideal, -e; ideal

idealistic idealistisch

ideological ideologisch

idol das Idol, -e

if wenn (*sub. conj.*)

if, whether ob (*sub. conj.*)

illegal illegal

illegitimate illegitim

image; picture das Bild, -er

imagine something sich etwas vor·stellen

immediately, right away sofort

immigrate ein·wandern, ist eingewandert

important wichtig

    be of importance, to be a factor eine Rolle spielen

    most important Haupt- (*prefix*)

impossible unmöglich

impression der Eindruck, ¨e

improvement die Verbesserung, -en

in; into in (+ *acc. or dat.*)

    in, into hinein- (*prefix*)

    in fact, actually eigentlich

    in addition, besides außerdem

    in addition to außer (+ *dat.*);

    in shape fit

    in spite of, despite trotz (+ *gen.*)

in spite of that, nevertheless trotzdem
in order to um . . . zu
incorrect falsch
industrial industriell
industrious, hard-working fleißig
industry die Industrie, -n
inexpensive billig
inflation die Inflation
information die Auskunft
injure oneself, get hurt sich verletzen
instead of anstatt (+ gen.); statt
(+ gen.)
institution of higher learning, university die Hochschule, -n
intellectual der/die Intellektuelle, -n
intelligent intelligent
interested, to be interested
in sich interessieren für
(+ acc.)
interesting interessant
intermission die Pause, -n
international international
interrupt unterbrechen (unterbricht), unterbrach, hat unterbrochen
interview interviewen
introduce, present vor·stellen
introduce oneself sich
vor·stellen
invite ein·laden (lädt ein), lud
ein, hat eingeladen
irony die Ironie
issue: What's at issue is . . . Es
geht um . . . (+ acc.)
Italian italienisch; der Italiener, -
(m.); die Italienerin, -nen (f.)
Italy (das) Italien

J

jacket die Jacke, -n
January (der) Januar
jeans, bluejeans die Jeans (pl.)
Jewish jüdisch
job, position die Stelle, -n
jog joggen
journalist der Journalist, -en, -en
journey die Reise, -n
joy die Freude, -n
July (der) Juli
June (der) Juni
just as . . . as genauso . . . wie
just, at this moment gerade

K

keep, retain behalten (behält), behielt, hat behalten
key der Schlüssel, -
kilogram das Kilogramm; das
Kilo
kilometer der Kilometer, -
kitchen die Küche, -n
knife das Messer, -
know (a fact) wissen (weiß),
wußte, hat gewußt
know, be acquainted with
kennen, kannte, hat gekannt
to know one's way around
sich aus·kennen, kannte s.
aus, hat s. ausgekannt
well known bekannt

L

lady die Dame, -n
Ladies and gentlemen.
Meine Damen und Herren.
lake der See, -n
at the lake am See
lamp die Lampe, -n
landscape die Landschaft, -en
language die Sprache, -n
last letzt-
last; take (time) dauern
late spät
lately in letzter Zeit
later on, after that nachher
laugh lachen
to laugh about lachen über
(+ acc.)
lavatory die Toilette, -n
law das Gesetz, -e
under the law, in the eyes of
the law vor dem Gesetz
(study of) law Jura (used
without article)
lawyer der Rechtsanwalt, ⁐e (m.);
die Rechtsanwältin, -nen (f.)
lay, put down legen
lazy faul
lead führen
learn lernen
least, at least wenigstens
leave (something or someone);
leave behind lassen (läßt),
ließ, hat gelassen
leave, depart (by vehicle)
ab·fahren (fährt ab), fuhr ab,
ist abgefahren

leave (a person or
place) verlassen (verläßt),
verließ, hat verlassen
lecture (at a university) die Vorlesung, -en
left, to the left, on the left links
leg das Bein, -e
legal legal
lend leihen, lieh, hat geliehen
let, allow; cause to be done
lassen (läßt), ließ, hat gelassen
letter der Brief, -e
lettuce; salad der Salat, -e
library die Bibliothek, -en
lie; be situated liegen, lag, hat
gelegen
life das Leben
light (in weight) leicht
light, bright hell
like mögen (mag), mochte, hat
gemocht
would like to möchten
likeable, friendly sympathisch
like this, so so
like, as wie
line (streetcar or bus) die
Linie, - n
linguistics die Linguistik
lion der Löwe, -n, -n
listen zu·hören (+ dat.)
liter der Liter
literary literarisch
little, small klein
a little, not much wenig
a little bit; a little while ein
bißchen
live, be alive leben
live, dwell wohnen
liverwurst die Leberwurst, ⁐e
living room das Wohnzimmer, -
long; for a long time lang(e),
(länger)
look (at) schauen (auf + acc.)
look (like), appear aus·sehen
(sieht aus), sah aus, hat ausgesehen
look forward to sich freuen
auf (+ acc.)
look after, take care of, deal
with sich kümmern um
(+ acc.)
look after auf·passen auf
(+ acc.)
look out auf·passen
look for, seek suchen
lose verlieren, verlor, hat verloren
loud laut

love   lieben
low   niedrig
luck   das Glück
    to be lucky   Glück haben
    to have bad luck, be un-
    lucky   Pech haben
lunch   das Mittagessen
luggage   das Gepäck

M

machine   die Maschine, -n
mail (a letter)   (einen Brief)
    ein·werfen (wirft ein), warf
    ein, hat eingeworfen
mail   die Post
mailbox   der Briefkasten, -
main   Haupt- (*prefix*)
    main course   das Haupt-
    gericht, -e
    major field   das Hauptfach,
    ¨er
make; do   machen
mama, mom   die Mutti, -s
man; husband   der Mann, ¨er
manipulate   manipulieren
many, many people   viele
    (*pronoun*);
    many thanks   vielen Dank
map   die Landkarte, -n
March   (der) März
mark (the German mark)   die
    Mark (die Deutsche Mark,
    DM)
marry, get married   heiraten
Marxist   der Marxist, -en, -en
mathematics   die Mathematik
matter, affair   die Sache, -n
    It doesn't matter.   Es macht
    nichts.
    What's the matter? What's go-
    ing on?   Was ist los?
May   (der) Mai
may: That may be.   Das mag sein.
maybe, perhaps   vielleicht
mean   meinen
    mean, signify   bedeuten
mechanic   der Mechaniker, -
medicine   die Medizin
meet; get to know
    kennen·lernen
    meet (by appointment)
    treffen (trifft), traf, hat getrof-
    fen
melancholy   die Melancholie
member   das Mitglied, -er

memory   die Erinnerung, -en
mentality   die Mentalität, -en
mention: Don't mention
    it!   Nichts zu danken!
mess   die Unordnung
method   die Methode, -n
metropolis   die Metropole, -n
middle   die Mitte
    in the middle of Febru-
    ary   Mitte Februar
mild   mild
milk   die Milch
million   die Million, -en
minor field   das Nebenfach, ¨er
minute   die Minute, -n
miracle   das Wunder, -
mirror   der Spiegel, -
miss (*an event or opportu-*
    nity)   verpassen
mister: Mr. Lehmann   Herr Leh-
    mann
modern   modern
moment   der Moment, -e; **at the**
    moment   im Moment
Monday   (der) Montag, -e
money   das Geld
month   der Monat, -e
monument   das Denkmal, ¨er
moped   das Moped, -s
more   mehr
    more than   mehr als
    more or less   mehr oder
    weniger
morning   der Morgen, -
    Good morning!   Guten Mor-
    gen!
    this morning   heute früh;
    heute morgen
    (in the) mornings
    vormittags, morgens
    Morning!   Morgen!
Moscow   (das) Moskau
most   meist-
    mostly, usually   meistens
mother   die Mutter, ¨
mountain   der Berg, -e
mouth   der Mund, ¨er
move, change residence
    um·ziehen, zog um, ist umge-
    zogen
    move   ziehen, zog, ist gezo-
    gen (*to a new town or area:*
    must include destination)
movement; exercise   die Bewe-
    gung, -en
movie   der Film, -e
movie theater   das Kino, -s
    to the movies   ins Kino

Mrs./Ms. Kuhn   Frau Kuhn
much, a lot   viel (mehr, am mei-
    sten)
Munich   (das) München
museum   das Museum, die Mu-
    seen
music   die Musik
musicology   die Musikwis-
    senschaft
must, have to   müssen (muß),
    mußte, hat gemußt

N

name, call   nennen, nannte, hat
    genannt
name   der Name, -ns, -n
name: My name is . . .   Ich
    heiße . . .
napkin   die Serviette, -n
narrative, story   die Erzählung,
    -en
native country or place, home-
    land   die Heimat
native language   die Mutter-
    sprache, -n
natural   natürlich
near   nahe (näher, am nächsten);
    bei
    nearby   in der Nähe (+ *gen.*)
    nearness; vicinity   die Nähe
need   brauchen
neither . . . nor   weder . . . noch
neutral   neutral
neutrality   die Neutralität
never   nie
nevertheless   trotzdem
new   neu
    What's new?   Was gibt's
    Neues?
newspaper   die Zeitung, -en
next; nearest   nächst-
nice   nett; lieb
night   die Nacht, ¨e
    Good night.   Gute Nacht.
    in the night, at night   in der
    Nacht, nachts
no   nein
No wonder!   Kein Wunder!
nobody, no one   niemand
nonsense   der Unsinn
    Nonsense!   Quatsch!
normal   normal
North America   (das) Nord-
    amerika
(the) North   der Norden

nose die Nase, -n
not nicht
    not at all gar nicht
    not any more, no
    longer nicht mehr
    not much wenig
    not only . . . but also nicht
    nur . . . sondern auch
    not a, not any, no kein
    not until; only erst
notebook das Heft, -e
nothing nichts
novel der Roman, -e
November (der) November
now jetzt; **from now on** von
    jetzt an
nowadays heutzutage
number die Nummer, -n

O

objective objektiv
ocean der Ozean, -e
October (der) Oktober
of von (+ *dat.*)
offer bieten, bot, hat geboten
office das Büro, -s
official der Beamte, -n (*adj. noun*)
    (*m.*); die Beamtin, -nen (*f.*)
    official offiziell
often oft (öfter)
oh; ah ach
old alt (älter)
Olympic olympisch
on (top of) auf (+ *acc. or dat.*)
    onto; upon auf (+ *acc. or
    dat.*)
    on the go unterwegs
once einmal
once again, once more noch ein-
    mal
one eins
one (*impersonal pronoun*) man
onion die Zwiebel, -n
only nur
    only; not until erst
open offen (*adj.*); auf·machen
opinion: to be of the opinion,
    think; mean meinen
opportunity, chance die Gelegen-
    heit, -en
opposition die Opposition, -en
optimistic optimistisch
or oder
order bestellen; die Ordnung
orderly ordentlich

organisation die Organisation, -en
organize organisieren
other, different ander-
outside draußen
over, across über (+ *acc. or dat.*)
    over there da drüben
own eigen- (*adj.*); besitzen, besaß,
    hat besessen

P

pack packen
page die Seite, -n
pants die Hose, -n
paper das Papier
    term paper das
    Referat, -e
parallel parallel
Pardon me! Entschuldigung!
parents die Eltern (*pl.*)
park parken
part der Teil, -e
    to play a part; be impor-
    tant eine Rolle spielen
    be a part of, be one
    of gehören zu (+ *dat.*)
participate in teil·nehmen
    (nimmt teil), nahm teil, hat
    teilgenommen an (+ *dat.*)
party, celebration die Feier, -n
    political party die Partei,
    -en
passive passiv
passport der Paß, die Pässe
past (time) die Vergangenheit
patient der Patient, -en, -en
pay bezahlen; zahlen
    pay duty on, declare
    verzollen
pay attention auf·passen
peace der Frieden
peaceful ruhig
pedestrian der Fußgänger, -
    pedestrian mall die
    Fußgängerzone, -n
pencil der Bleistift, -e
people die Leute (*pl.*)
    people, nation, folk das
    Volk, ⸚er
percent der Prozent
perfect perfekt
permit, allow erlauben (+ *dat. of
    person*)
permitted erlaubt
person, human being der Mensch,
    -en, -en

pessimistic pessimistisch
philosophy die Philosophie
philosophize philosophieren
photograph das Foto, -s
    to take a photograph ein
    Foto machen
physics die Physik
piano das Klavier, -e
pick up ab·holen
picture; image das Bild, -er
place; space der Platz, ⸚e
place; small town der Ort, -e
    to place stellen, legen, setzen
plain die Ebene, -n
plan, have in mind vor·haben
    (hat vor), hatte vor, hat vorge-
    habt
    to make plans planen
plate der Teller, -
play spielen
    play sports Sport treiben
playing field der Sportplatz, ⸚e
pleasant angenehm
please bitte
please, appeal to gefallen (gefällt),
    gefiel, hat gefallen
    (+ *dat. of person*)
please, make happy freuen
pleasure: With pleasure gern
    (lieber, am liebsten)
Pleasure to meet you!
    Angenehm!
pocket die Tasche, -n
poet der Dichter, -
police die Polizei (*sing.*)
polite höflich
political politisch
    political science die Politik-
    wissenschaft
politician der Politiker, -(*m.*); die
    Politikerin, -nen (*f.*)
politics; policy die Politik
ponder, think something
    over sich etwas überlegen
poor arm
popular beliebt
porter, redcap der Gepäckträger, -
possible möglich
possibility die Möglichkeit, -en
post office; postal service;
    mail die Post
postage stamp die Briefmarke, -n
postcard die Postkarte, -n
poster das Plakat, -e
potato die Kartoffel, -n
power, might die Macht, ⸚e
practical praktisch
practice üben

preferably, rather lieber
prejudice das Vorurteil, -e
prepare for sich vor·bereiten auf
    (+ *acc.*)
present (time) die Gegenwart
present das Geschenk, -e
president der Präsident, -en, -en
pretty hübsch
    pretty good ganz gut
price der Preis, -e
primary, most important Haupt-
    (*prefix*)
probably wohl; wahrscheinlich
problem das Problem, -e
productive produktiv
profession, vocation der Beruf, -e
    What is your profession?
    Was sind Sie von Beruf?
professor der Professor, -en (*m.*);
    die Professorin, -nen (*f.*)
programmer der Programmierer, -
    (*m.*); die Programmiererin,
    -nen (*f.*)
proud of stolz auf (+ *acc.*)
psychoanalysis die Psychoanalyse
psychological psychologisch
psychology die Psychologie
public öffentlich
pull ziehen, zog, hat gezogen
punctual, on time pünktlich
pupil (*secondary school*) der
    Schüler, - (*m.*); die Schülerin,
    -nen (*f.*)
purpose der Zweck, -e
put, put down, place stellen,
    legen, setzen

Q

question die Frage, -n
    to ask a question eine Frage
    stellen
    It's a question of . . . Es
    geht um . . . (+ *acc.*)
quiet, soft leise
quiet, relaxed gemütlich
quite ziemlich

R

radio das Radio, -s
railroad, railway system die Bahn
railway compartment das Abteil, -e

rain der Regen; regnen
rather lieber (*comparative of*
    gern)
reaction die Reaktion, -en
read lesen (liest), las, hat gelesen;
    to read about lesen über (+
    acc.)
ready; finished (with) fertig (mit)
real, really wirklich
reason der Grund, ¨e
    for that reason darum
receive, get bekommen, bekam,
    hat bekommen
reception desk (*hotel*) die Rezep-
    tion
recommend empfehlen
    (empfiehlt), empfahl, hat emp-
    fohlen
record (*phonograph*) die
    Schallplatte, -n
record player der Plattenspieler, -
recount, tell erzählen
recover (from), get well; renew
    oneself sich erholen (von)
red rot (röter)
refrigerator der Kühlschrank, ¨e
regard as, think X is halten für
    (+ *acc.*)
register for, take (*a university
    course*) belegen
regular regelmäßig
related (to) verwandt (mit)
relative relativ (*adj.*); der/die Ver-
    wandte, -n
religion die Religion, -en
remember sich erinnern an
    (+ *acc.*)
remind of erinnern an (+ *acc.*)
renovate renovieren
rent (*from*) mieten
repair reparieren
reparation die Reparation, -en
repeat wiederholen
report berichten
    oral report das Referat, -e
    to give a report (*in class*) ein
    Referat halten
republic die Republik, -en
responsible for verantwortlich für
    (+ *acc.*)
restaurant das Restaurant, -s
restless, troubled unruhig
retain, keep behalten (behält), be-
    hielt, hat behalten
the Rhine River der Rhein
rich reich
right, correct richtig
    That's right. Das stimmt.

    That's right. That's true.
    Stimmt schon.
    to be right recht haben
    to be right (*impersonal
    only*) stimmen
    right away gleich, sofort
    It's all right. Not bad. Es
    geht.
right (*direction*) recht-
    **to the right; on the
    right** rechts
river der Fluß, die Flüsse
roast der Braten, -
role die Rolle, -n
romantic romantisch
room das Zimmer, -
roommate der Zimmer-
    kamerad, -en, -en (*m.*); die
    Zimmerkameradin, -nen (*f.*)
Rubbish! Baloney! Quatsch!
rucksack, backpack der Ruck-
    sack, ¨e
rug der Teppich, -e
run laufen (läuft), lief, ist
    gelaufen
Russia (das) Rußland
Russian russisch; der Russe, -n,
    -n (*m.*); die Russin, -nen (*f.*)

S

sad traurig
salad; lettuce der Salat, -e
**same: It's all the same to
    me.** Das ist mir egal.
satellite der Satellit, -en, -en
Saturday (der) Sonnabend, -e;
    (der) Samstag, -e
sauerkraut das Sauerkraut
sausage die Wurst, ¨e
save (*money*) sparen
save, rescue retten
say sagen
    **It goes without saying
    that . . .** selbstverständlich
Scandinavia (das) Skandinavien
schnapps, distilled spirits der
    Schnaps, ¨e
school die Schule, -n
    school system das Schul-
    system, -e
    secondary school (*preparing
    for university*) das Gymna-
    sium, die Gymnasien
sea das Meer, -e
season (*of the year*) die Jahreszeit,
    -en

secretary der Sekretär, -e (*m.*); die Sekretärin, -nen (*f.*)

see sehen (sieht), sah, hat gesehen

see, meet (*one another*) **again** wieder·sehen (sieht wieder), sah wieder, hat wiedergesehen

seem; shine scheinen, schien, hat geschienen

seldom selten

sell verkaufen

semester das Semester, -

semester break die Semesterferien (*pl.*)

seminar (*university*) das Seminar, -e

send schicken

September (der) September

serious ernst

take something seriously etwas ernst nehmen

set (down), put setzen

seventh siebt-

several mehrere

sex, gender das Geschlecht, -er

shilling (*Austrian currency*) der Schilling, -e

shine; seem scheinen, schien, hat geschienen

ship das Schiff, -e

shirt das Hemd, -en

shoe der Schuh, -e

shop, store der Laden, ⸚

go shopping ein·kaufen

short kurz (kürzer)

should, be supposed to sollen (soll), sollte, hat gesollt

show zeigen

Show it to me. Zeig mal her.

shower die Dusche, -n

siblings die Geschwister (*pl.*)

sick krank (kränker)

sickness die Krankheit, -en

side; page die Seite, -n

signify, mean bedeuten

similar ähnlich (+ *dat.*)

simple, easy einfach

since seit (+ *dat.*); da (*sub. conj., causal*)

sing singen, sang, hat gesungen

single, only einzig-

single room das Einzelzimmer, -

sister die Schwester, -n

sit sitzen, saß, hat gesessen

sit down sich setzen

situation die Situation, -en

to be situated liegen, lag, hat gelegen

size die Größe, -n

ski Schi laufen (läuft Schi), lief Schi, ist Schi gelaufen

skirt der Rock, ⸚e

sleep schlafen (schläft), schlief, hat geschlafen

slow langsam

small, little klein

small town der Ort, -e

small amount wenig

smart, bright klug (klüger)

smuggle schmuggeln

snake die Schlange, -n

sneaker, gym shoe der Turnschuh, -e

snow der Schnee; schneien

so that damit (*sub. conj.*)

So long! Tschüs!

soccer (der) Fußball

soccer ball der Fußball, ⸚e

to play soccer Fußball spielen

social gesellschaftlich, sozial

Socialist sozialistisch

society die Gesellschaft, -en

sociology die Soziologie

sofa das Sofa, -s

solidarity die Solidarität

some manche, einige

some, a little etwas

somebody, someone jemand

somehow or other irgendwie

something; some, a little; somewhat etwas

something else, anything more noch etwas

sometime or other, any time irgendwann

sometimes manchmal

somewhat etwas

somewhere or other, anywhere irgendwo

son der Sohn, ⸚e

song das Lied, -er

soon bald

sorry: I'm sorry (about that). Es tut mir leid.

sound klingen, klang, hat geklungen

soup die Suppe, -n

sour sauer

(the) South der Süden

(the) Soviet Union die Sowjetunion

(the) Soviets die Sowjets

space der Platz, ⸚e

Spain (das) Spanien

speak, talk sprechen (spricht), sprach, hat gesprochen; reden

I can speak German. Ich kann Deutsch.

spectator der Zuschauer, -

spend (*money*) aus·geben (gibt aus), gab aus, hat ausgegeben

spend (*time*) verbringen, verbrachte, hat verbracht

spend the night übernachten

spoon der Löffel, -

sport der Sport

to play sports Sport treiben

spring der Frühling

spring term das Sommersemester (*usually May–July*)

stabile stabil

stability die Stabilität

stand stehen, stand, hat gestanden

stand up auf·stehen, stand auf, ist aufgestanden

not be able to stand something or someone etwas nicht ausstehen können

start, begin an·fangen (fängt an), fing an, hat angefangen; beginnen, begann, hat begonnen

state der Staat, -en

station (*railway*) der Bahnhof, ⸚e

stay, remain bleiben, blieb, ist geblieben

steal stehlen (stiehlt), stahl, hat gestohlen

steep steil

stereotyped klischeehaft; stereotyp

still noch, noch immer, immer noch

stone der Stein, -e

stop (*intrans.*) halten (hält), hielt, hat gehalten

streetcar or bus stop die Haltestelle, -n

to stop (doing something) auf·hören (mit)

store, shop der Laden, ⸚

store window das Schaufenster, -

story, narrative die Erzählung, -en

story; history die Geschichte, -n

stove, kitchen range der Herd, -e

straight ahead geradeaus

straighten up   auf·räumen
strange; foreign   fremd
strange; funny   komisch
street; road   die Straße, -n
   cross street   die Querstraße, -n
streetcar   die Straßenbahn, -en
stress   der Streß, die Stresse
stroll, walk   der Bummel, -
   stroll through the city   der
   Stadtbummel, -
strong   stark (stärker)
student (at a university)   der Student, -en, -en (m.); die
   Studentin, -nen (f.)
   student dormitory   das Studentenwohnheim, -e
   student I.D.   der Studentenausweis, -e
study at   studieren an (+ dat.)
   study   das Arbeitszimmer, -
   study (for a class)   arbeiten;
   sich vorbereiten auf (+ acc.)
subject, area of study   das Fach, ̈er
   subject, theme   das Thema,
   die Themen
subjective   subjektiv
subway train   die U-Bahn
   (= Untergrundbahn)
success   der Erfolg, -e
such   solcher, -es, -e
suit   der Anzug, ̈e
suitcase   der Koffer, -
summer   der Sommer
sun   die Sonne
sunny   sonnig
Sunday   (der) Sonntag, -e
supermarket   der Supermarkt, ̈e
supper   das Abendessen, -
   for supper   zum Abendessen
supposed to   sollen (soll), sollte,
   hat gesollt
sure   sicher
sure, of course   klar (colloq.)
surprise   überraschen
sweet   süß
swim   schwimmen, schwamm, ist
   geschwommen
swimming pool   das Schwimmbad, ̈er
Swiss   der Schweizer, - (m.); die
   Schweizerin, -nen (f.);
   schweizerisch
Switzerland   (die) Schweiz
symbol   das Symbol, -e
symbolic   symbolisch
system   das System, -e

T

T-shirt   das T-Shirt, -s
table   der Tisch, -e
take   nehmen (nimmt), nahm, hat
   genommen
   take a look at something
   sich etwas an·sehen (sieht
   an), sah an, hat angesehen
   take along   mit·nehmen
   (nimmt mit), nahm mit, hat
   mitgenommen
   take a picture   ein Foto
   machen
   take care of, deal with   sich
   kümmern um (+ acc.);
   erledigen
   take part in   teil·nehmen
   (nimmt teil), nahm teil, hat
   teilgenommen an (+ dat.)
   take (a university course)
   belegen
   take place   statt·finden,
   fand statt, hat stattgefunden
   take for, regard as, think X
   is   halten für (+ acc.)
   take (time); last   dauern
talk   reden; sprechen (spricht),
   sprach, hat gesprochen
talk about   sprechen über (+ acc.)
task   die Aufgabe, -n
taste (trans. and intrans.); taste
   good   schmecken
taxicab   das Taxi, -s
teacher   der Lehrer, - (m.); die
   Lehrerin, -nen (f.),
team   die Mannschaft, -en
telephone   das Telefon, -e
television set   der Fernseher, -
tell, recount   erzählen
tell; say   sagen;
   Tell me . . .   Sag mal, . . .
tennis   das Tennis,
   tennis court   der Tennisplatz, ̈e
term paper   das Referat, -e
terrible   furchtbar, grausam
terrific   toll (slang)
terrorist (adj.)   terroristisch
test, written examination   die
   Klausur, -en; die Prüfung, -en
   to take a test   eine Klausur
   schreiben
than (with comparative degree)
   als
thank   danken (+ dat)
   thank for   danken für

thank goodness   Gott sei
Dank.
thanks   der Dank
   many thanks   vielen Dank
   thanks, thank you   danke
that (sub. conj.)   daß
theater   das Theater,
theme, subject, topic   das Thema,
   die Themen
then   dann
there   da, dort; dahin (as goal of
   motion)
   How do I get there?   Wie
   komme ich dahin?
there is, there are   es gibt (+ acc.)
therefore, for that reason   darum
thing, object   die Sache, -n
think   denken, dachte, hat
   gedacht
   think of   denken an (+ acc.)
   think about, ponder
   nach·denken über (+ acc.)
   think of, have an opinion
   about   halten von (+ dat.)
   think, believe   glauben
   (+ dat. of person)
   think something over   sich
   etwas überlegen
   I think so too.   Das finde ich
   auch.
   I think so.   Ich glaube ja.
   What do you think of
   that?   Was meinen Sie dazu?
third   dritt-
thirst   der Durst
   Are you thirsty?   Haben Sie
   Durst?
this   dieser, -es, -e
   this afternoon   heute nachmittag
   this time   diesmal
those are   das sind (pl. of das ist)
thought   der Gedanke, -ns, -n
through   durch (+ acc.)
throw   werfen (wirft), warf, hat
   geworfen
Thursday   (der) Donnerstag, -e
thus   also
ticket (for bus, train, streetcar,
   etc.)   die Fahrkarte, -n
tidy up   auf·räumen
tie, necktie   die Krawatte, -n
time   die Zeit, -en
   das Mal, -e (=occasion)
   for the first time   zum ersten
   Mal
   for the umpteenth time

zum x-ten Mal
for a time, for a while eine
Zeitlang
on time pünktlich
What time is it? Wie spät ist
es? Wieviel Uhr ist es?
tired, weary müde
to nach (*with cities and countries*); zu
to, toward; at, alongside of
an (+ *acc. or dat.*)
to be sure . . . but zwar . . .
aber
to begin with zunächst
together zusammen
together, with each other
miteinander
toilet, lavatory die Toilette, -n
tomato die Tomate, -n
tomorrow morgen
tomorrow afternoon morgen
nachmittag
tomorrow evening morgen
abend
tomorrow morning morgen
früh
too auch; zu
tooth der Zahn, ⸚e
topic, subject, theme das Thema,
die Themen
tour die Tour, -en
tourist der Tourist, -en, -en (*m.*);
die Touristin, -nen (*f.*)
town (*5,000 to 20,000 inhabitants*) die Kleinstadt, ⸚e
town hall das Rathaus, ⸚er
track das Gleis, -e
tradition die Tradition, -en
traditional traditionell
traffic der Verkehr
train der Zug, ⸚e
train station der Bahnhof, ⸚e
train trainieren
**transfer, change (trains, buses,
etc.)** um·steigen, stieg um,
ist umgestiegen
translate übersetzen
transport transportieren
travel reisen, ist gereist
traveller's check der Reisescheck, -s
tree der Baum, ⸚e
trip, ride die Fahrt, -en
trip, journey die Reise, -n; **to
take a trip** eine Reise
machen
Have a good trip! Gute
Reise!

trousers, pants die Hose, -n
true wahr
**true: it is true, to be sure . . .
but** zwar . . . aber
truth die Wahrheit, -en
try, attempt versuchen
Tuesday (der) Dienstag, -e
Turk der Türke, -n, -n (*m.*); die
Türkin, -nen (*f.*)
Turkish türkisch
Turkey die Türkei
type der Typ, -en
typewriter die Schreibmaschine, -n
typical typisch

U

ugly häßlich
umpteen times zigmal
uncle der Onkel, -
under, beneath; among unter
(+ *dat. of person*)
understand verstehen, verstand,
hat verstanden
uneducated ungebildet
unemployed arbeitslos
unfortunately leider
unhappy unglücklich
unimportant unwichtig
university die Universität, -en;
die Uni, -s (*colloq.*); die Hochschule, -n
at the university an der Universität; an der Uni
university studies das
Studium
unoccupied, free frei
unpack aus·packen
until, up to bis zu (+ *dat.*)
until; by bis (+ *acc.*)
until then bis dann
(the) USA die USA (*pl.*)
use gebrauchen, benutzen

V

vacation (*university and school*)
die Ferien (*pl.*); (*from a
job*) der Urlaub
to take a vacation Ferien,
Urlaub machen
various, different verschieden
vegetables das Gemüse

very sehr
Vienna (das) Wien
village das Dorf, ⸚er
visit der Besuch, -e; besuchen
voice die Stimme, -n

W

wages der Lohn, ⸚e
wait warten
to wait for warten auf
(+ *acc.*)
waiter der Kellner, -
waitress die Kellnerin, -nen
wake up (*intrans.*) auf·wachen,
ist aufgewacht
walk gehen, ging, ist gegangen;
laufen (läuft), lief, ist gelaufen
(*colloq.*)
to go for a walk spazie-
ren·gehen, ging spazieren, ist
spazierengegangen
wall (*free standing or outside*) die
Mauer, -n; **interior wall** die
Wand, ⸚e
wanderlust die Wanderlust
want to (*do something*)
Lust haben (etwas zu tun)
**want to; intend to; claim
to** wollen (will), wollte, hat
gewollt
war der Krieg, -e
warm warm (wärmer)
wash waschen (wäscht), wusch,
hat gewaschen
water das Wasser
way, path der Weg, -e
weak schwach (schwächer)
weather das Wetter
wedding die Hochzeit, -en
**golden wedding anniver-
sary** die goldene Hochzeit
Wednesday (der) Mittwoch, -e
week die Woche, -n
weekend das Wochenende -n
on the weekend am Wo-
chenende
weigh wiegen, wog, hat gewogen
(*trans. and intrans.*)
welcome: you're welcome bitte,
bitte sehr
well . . . also . . .
(the) West der Westen
wet naß
what was
what kind of was für

when (*with simple past tense*) **als** (*sub. conj.*); **wann** (*question word*); **wenn** (*with present or future tense*)

whenever wenn (*sub. conj.*)

where wo

  to where wohin

  from where woher

which welcher, -es, -e

while, a little while ein bißchen

white weiß

who wer (*nom.*)

whole ganz

whom wem (*dat.*); wen (*acc.*)

whose wessen

why warum

wild wild

win gewinnen, gewann, hat gewonnen

window das Fenster, -

wine der Wein, -e

winter der Winter, -

  in the winter im Winter

wish wünschen

with mit (+ *dat.*)

without ohne (+ *acc.*)

  withou...

woman di...

women's st...

  dien (*p*...

word das Wort (*2 plural forms:* die Worte—*words in context,* die Wörter—*unconnected words, as in a dictionary*)

work die Arbeit; das Werk, -e **work; study** (*for a class*) arbeiten

  work part time halbtags arbeiten

worker der Arbeiter, -

world die Welt

worthwhile: to be worthwhile sich lohnen

wrecked, broken kaputt

wristwatch die Armbanduhr, -en

write schreiben, schrieb, hat geschrieben

  write about schreiben über (+ *acc.*)

  to write a paper ein Referat schreiben

writer der Schriftsteller, -(*m.*); die Schriftstellerin, -nen (*f.*)

yes ja

  yes I do, yes I am, yes he is, etc. doch (*stressed*)

yesterday gestern

  yesterday morning gestern früh, gestern morgen

  yesterday afternoon gestern nachmittag

  yesterday evening gestern abend

yet, already schon

  never yet noch nie

  not yet noch nicht

young jung (jünger)

Youth Hostel die Jugendherberge, -n

youth, young people die Jugend (*sing.*)

Yugoslavia (das) Jugoslawien **Yugoslavian** jugoslawisch; der Jugoslawe, -n, -n (*m.*); die Jugoslawin, -nen (*f.*)

Z

zone die Zone, -n

Index

of Grammatical, Lexical, and Orthographical Topics

Academic fields, 170
Accusative case
  for the direct object, 47
  formation of, 47
  of interrogative pronoun, 48
  of personal pronouns, 48
  prepositions with, 96–97
  in time expressions, 421, 496
Active voice, 445–46
Adjectival nouns, 307–09, 372
Adjectives
  as nouns, 307–09, 372
  attributive, 249–54, 339
  attributive versus predicate, 249
  city names as, 290
  comparison of, 337–44, 371–72
  with complementary infinitive, 211
  endings following **der**-words, 250, 370
  endings following **ein**-words, 253–54, 370
  endings when unpreceded, 275, 371
  of indefinite number, 310
  past participles as, 394
  possessive, 49–50, 114, 250
  predicate, 67, 94, 339
  present participles as, 450
  unpreceded, 275
Adverbs, 18 (note 3)
  comparison of, 337–44, 371–72
  montags, etc., 423, 497
  present participle as, 450
  of repetition with **-mal,** 354
  sentence adverbs, 101
  with the suffix **-lang,** 422–23, 497
  word order of, 256
Agent in passive voice, 449, 449 (note)
Agent nouns, 139–40
Agreement
  in gender, 25
  of possessive adjectives, 49
  of relative pronouns, 347
Alle, 250 (note)

Als
  versus **wann** and **wenn,** 284, 376
  with comparative degree, 338, 374
Als ob, 475, 494
Animal names, 296, 318
Antecedent, 346–47, 350, 351
Article
  definite, 25, 47, 114
  indefinite, 27, 47, 114
  omission of, 139
Attributive adjectives. *See* Adjectives, attributive
Auxiliary verbs, 154
  haben versus **sein** in the perfect tense, 156, 234
  hätten and **wären** in the past subjunctive, 441
  werden in the future tense, 391
  werden in the passive voice, 446–47
  würden in present subjunctive, 416

Bei, 319

Capitalization, 11
  of formal second-person, 21, 49
  of second-person forms in letters, 167
Cardinal numbers. *See* Numbers, cardinal
Case, 27. *See also* Accusative case, Dative case, Genitive case, Nominative case
City vocabulary, 226
Classroom expressions and objects, 12, 13
Clichés, 400
Clothing vocabulary, 80
Colors, 81
Commands, 90–93, 115–16
Comparison of adjectives and adverbs, 337–44, 371–72
  irregular forms, 341, 372
Complements, 67, 71, 210, 211, 385–87

Conditional sentences, indicative versus subjunctive in, 417
Conditions contrary to fact, 417, 443, 494
Conjunctions
  aber versus **sondern,** 185–86
  coordinating, 183–86, 238
  subordinating, 206–9, 238, 475
Countries, names of, 320
Customs vocabulary, 326

Da-compounds, 388, 493
Dates, 258–59, 374
Dative case
  dative pronouns with parts of the body and clothing, 317–18
  for indirect object, 129
  formation of, 130
  of interrogative pronoun, 130
  as object of certain verbs, 187, 235, 467
  of personal pronouns, 131
  personal, 189, 317–18
  prepositions with, 135–36
  with **trotz,** 216 (note)
Day, parts of, 356
Days of the week, 13
Definite article. *See* Article, definite
Der-words, 137
  as limiting words, 250
  declension of, 235
  versus **ein**-words, 137
Direct object, 47
  reflexive, 311–12
Directional prefixes (**hin-** and **her-**), 452, 495–96
Doch
  as contradictory, 74
  as flavoring particle in commands, 90
Double infinitive. *See* Infinitive, double
Duration. *See* Time, expressing duration

Ein-words, 49, 114

declension of, 236
kein, 73
  as limiting words, 250
  versus **der**-words, 137
Ellipsis, 186
Extended modifiers, 476–77

Family members and relatives, 56
Flavoring particles
  denn, 50
  doch with imperative, 90
Food vocabulary, 228–29
Future tense, 391–92, 489
  to express probability, 392

Gehen plus infinitive, 102
Gender. *See* Nouns, gender of
General subjunctive
  past tense of, 441–43, 490–91
  present tense of, 411–16, 489–90
  present tense with **würde,** 416,
    490
  use of, 417–20, 443
Genitive case, 213–16
  formation of, 213–14
  of interrogative pronoun, 214
  prepositions with, 216
  use of, 215, 236
Gern, 98–99
  comparison of, 341
Greetings, 12–13

Haben
  present subjunctive of, 415
  present tense of, 46
  simple past tense of, 255, 368
Haupt-, 165
Hypothetical statements and questions, 419, 443

Immer with comparative degree,
  344, 374
Imperative. *See* Commands
Impersonal pronoun, 100
Indefinite article. *See* Article,
  indefinite
Indefinite pronouns, 351
Indicative mood, 411
Indirect object, 129
  reflexive, 316
Indirect quotation, 470–74, 495
  questions and commands in, 474
  special subjunctive in, 471–72
  tenses in, 472–73
Infinitive
  double, 182, 352, 369, 370, 442,
    448
  formation of, 21, 111

omission of, with a modal verb,
  70
  passive, 446, 448
  phrases with **zu,** 210–12, 238
  as verbal noun, 165
  with **gehen,** 102
  with **lassen,** 352
  with modal verbs, 69
  with **um . . . zu** and **ohne . . . zu,**
    212, 238
Inflection of verbs, 21
Inseparable prefixes, 127, 233
  past participles of verbs with,
    155, 159, 235
Interrogative pronouns. *See* Pronouns, interrogative
Introducing one's self, 430
Irgend-, 357
Irregular verbs. *See* **Haben, Sein,
  Werden, Wissen**
Irregular weak verbs
  perfect tense of, 182
  simple past tense of, 281, 367

Je . . . desto, 344, 374

Kein. *See* **Ein**-words, Negation

Lassen, 352, 369–70
Letter-writing conventions, 167
"Like," German equivalents of,
  98–99, 117–18
Limiting words, 249. *See also* **Der**-words, **Ein**-words

Mal and **-mal,** 354, 375
Man, 100
Modal verbs 67–70, 112–13
  mögen, 98–99
  negating **müssen,** 94
  past participles of, 182 (note)
  past subjunctive of, 442
  perfect tense of, 182–83, 235
  present subjunctive of, 413–14
  present tense of, 69
  simple past tense of, 280, 367
  subjective use of, 468–69, 496
  with passive voice, 448
Months of the year, 31

N-nouns. *See* Nouns, n-nouns.
Nationality, nouns and adjectives
  of, 320
Negation, 71–73, 116–17, 130
  negating **müssen,** 94
  negating **schon** and **noch,** 95–96
  of single element, 186
  with **kein,** 73

with **nicht,** 71–72
Nicht. *See* Negation
Nicht wahr?, 74
Nominative case
  formation of, 27
  for the predicate nominative, 28
  for the subject, 27
  See also Predicate nominative
Nouns
  adjectival, 307–9, 350, 372
  agent, 139–40
  compound, 76
  gender of, 25, 192
  n-nouns, 164, 236
  noun phrase, 114, 235–36, 249,
    477
  of measure, weight, and number,
    221
  plural of, 26
  suffixes of, 192, 290
  verbal, 165
Numbers
  cardinal, 52, 75
  ordinal, 258

Ohne . . . zu. *See* Infinitive
Ordinal numbers, 258

Participles. *See* Past participles,
  Present participles
Passive voice, 445–49, 491–92
  agent in, 449, 449 (note)
  formation of, 446–48
  impersonal (subjectless), 467,
    492
  passive infinitive, 446, 448
  use of, 449
  with modal verbs, 448
Past participles, 154, 234–35
  as adjectives, 394, 493
  in extended modifiers, 477
  in the passive, 446
  of inseparable-prefix verbs, 155,
    159
  of separable-prefix verbs, 158
  of strong verbs, 155, 157
  of weak verbs, 154–55
Past perfect tense, 285–86, 368
Past tense. *See* Past tense of the
  subjunctive, Simple past tense
Past tense of the subjunctive
  general subjunctive, 441–43
  special subjunctive, 472
Perfect tense, 154–60, 182–83,
  233–35
Personal pronouns. *See* Pronouns,
  personal
Plural. *See* Nouns, plural of

Polite requests, 420, 495
Politics vocabulary, 296
Possessive adjectives. *See* Adjectives, possessive
Predicate, 67
  modal verb as first part of, 68
  and position of **nicht,** 71
  two-part structure of, 69
Predicate adjectives. *See* Adjectives, predicate
Predicate nominative, 28, 28 (note), 67, 94
Prefixes. *See* Directional prefixes, **Haupt-,** Inseparable prefixes, **Irgend-,** Separable prefixes
Prepositions
  bei, 319
  complementing verbs, 385–87, 492–93
  replaced by **da-** and **wo-**compounds, 388–90, 493
  two-way, 161–63, 237, 386
  two-way prepositions with certain verbs, 190
  with accusative case, 96–97, 114
  with dative case, 135–36, 237
  with genitive case, 216–237
Present participles, 449–50, 493
  in extended modifiers, 477
Present tense
  of general subjunctive, 411–16
  of **haben,** 46
  of indicative, 21–24, 111–12
  of **sein,** 24
  of special subjunctive, 471
  of **wissen,** 46
  stem-vowel change in, 44–45, 66
  used to express duration, 288–89
  with future meaning, 24
Principal parts of verbs, 277
Professions, 144
Pronouns
  as objects of prepositions, 388–90, 493
  dative pronouns with parts of the body and clothing, 317–18
  gender agreement of, 25
  indefinite, 310, 351
  interrogative, 48, 130, 214
  man, 100
  personal, 21, 48, 113, 131
  reflexive, 311–12, 352, 368–69
  relative, 346–47, 350, 373
  word order of, 132, 134
Punctuation, 11, 101
  of coordinate clauses, 184
  of direct quotation, 470 (note)
  of infinitive phrases, 210 (note)

of numbers, 75
of relative clauses, 347 (note)

Questions
  formation of, 30, 115
  in indirect quotation, 474
  indirect questions, 208
Question words, 30, 48, 115, 130, 160, 214, 355, 390
  as subordinating conjunctions, 208

Reflexive pronouns, 312, 352, 368–69
Reflexive verbs, 311–17, 368–69
Relative clauses, 346–50
  extended modifier as substitute for, 477
Relative pronouns, 346–47, 350, 373
Restaurant vocabulary, 228–29
Rooms of a house, 457

Seasons of the year, 106
Sein
  as auxiliary in the perfect tense, 156, 234
  followed by predicate nominative, 28, 67
  imperative of, 93, 116
  present tense of, 24
  simple past tense of, 255
  special subjunctive of, 471
Sentences
  the predicate of, 67
  word order in, 29–30
Separable prefixes, 126–27, 233
  in infinitive phrases with **zu,** 210
  in subordinate clauses, 209
  past participles of verbs with, 158, 234
  versus prepositional complements, 387
Simple past tense, 255, 276–83, 367–68
  of **haben,** 255, 368
  of irregular weak verbs, 281, 367
  of modal verbs, 280, 367
  of strong verbs, 277–78, 368
  of weak verbs, 276, 367
  of **werden,** 281, 368
  use of, 282–83
Special subjunctive, 471–72, 475 (note), 491
Sports vocabulary, 264
Statements, formation of, 29, 115

Stem
  of a verb, 22, 111
  past stem of strong verbs, 277
Strong verbs, 154
  past participles of, 155, 157, 234
  simple past tense of, 277–78, 368
  present subjunctive of, 412–13
Student's room, vocabulary for, 171
Subject of the sentence, 21, 27
Subjunctive. *See* General subjunctive, Special subjunctive
Subordinate clauses, 206–209, 238
  after indefinite pronouns, 351
  after question words, 208
  after relative pronouns, 346–47
  after subordinating conjunctions, 206
Subordinating conjunctions. *See* Conjunctions, subordinating
Syllabication, 11

Tense, 21
  compound, 154, 391
  See also Future tense, Past perfect tense, Past tense of the subjunctive, Perfect tense, Present tense, Simple past tense
"Think," German equivalents of, 451
Time
  asking for the, 217, 239
  dates, 258–59, 374
  expressing duration, 288–89, 375–76
  expressions in accusative, 421, 496
  expressions in genitive, 496
  parts of the day, 356, 374
  telling, 217–219, 239–40
  vor + dative = ago, 286, 375
  year, as adverb or in adverbial phrase, 260, 375
  See also **Mal**
"To," German equivalents of, 222, 237
Travel vocabulary, 196, 231
Twenty-four hour clock, 219, 240

Um . . . zu. *See* Infinitive
Umlaut in comparative and superlative, 340, 371
University studies, vocabulary for, 170

Verbs
active voice of, 445–46
auxiliary, 154, 156
imperative forms of, 90–93
indicative mood of, 411
infinitive of, 21
inflection of, 21
irregular, 112, 182. *See also*
   Haben, Irregular weak verbs,
   Sein, Werden, Wissen
modal verbs, 67–70, 112–13
passive voice of, 445–49, 491–92
principal parts of, 277
reflexive, 311–17, 368–69
stems of, 22, 111
stem-vowel change in present
   tense of, 44–45, 66, 112
subjunctive mood of. *See* General subjunctive, Special subjunctive
tenses of, *See* Future tense, Past
   perfect tense, Past tense of the
   subjunctive, Perfect tense,
   Present tense, Simple past
   tense, Tense
with complementary infinitive
   phrase, 210
with dative objects, 187, 235,
   315
with inseparable prefixes, 127,
   155, 159, 233
with complementary prepositional phrase, 385–87, 492–93
with separable prefixes, 126–27,
   233
with two-way prepositions, 190

See also Auxiliary verbs, Directional prefixes, **Gehen,**
   Infinitive, Inseparable prefixes,
   Lassen, Modal verbs, Passive
   voice, Past participles, Predicate,
   Present participles, Separable
   prefixes, Strong verbs, Weak
   verbs
Viel, comparison of, 341–42, 372

Wann versus **als** and **wenn,** 284,
   376
Wanting X to do Y, 393, 497
Was as a relative pronoun, 350,
   373
Was für, 355
Weak nouns. *See* Nouns, N-nouns.
Weak verbs, 154
   past participle of, 154–55, 234
   simple past tense of, 276, 367
   present subjunctive of, 411
Weather vocabulary, 106
Wenig, comparison of, 341–42, 372
Wenn versus **als** and **wann,** 284,
   376
Werden
   as auxiliary for future tense,
      391–92, 489
   as auxiliary for passive voice,
      446–47
   as auxiliary for present subjunc-
      tive, 416
   present subjunctive of, 415
   present tense of, 94

simple past tense of, 281, 368
"When," German equivalents of,
   284, 376
Wishes contrary to fact, 412, 419,
   443, 494
Wissen
   present subjunctive of, 415
   present tense of, 46
   versus **kennen,** 46
Wo-compounds, 390, 493
Word order
   after a coordinating conjunction,
      184, 238
   after a subordinating conjunc-
      tion, 206, 238
   in infinitive phrases, 210, 238
   in negations, 71–72, 130
   in questions, 30
   in statements, 29
   of adverbs (time-manner-place),
      256
   of noun in genitive case, 215,
      236
   of noun objects, 129, 239
   of personal pronouns, 134, 239
   of pronoun objects, 132, 239
   when first clause is subordinate,
      209
   with double infinitive in subor-
      dinate clause, 442
Worden, 446

Year, as adverb or in adverbial
   phrase, 260, 375

Credits

Illustrations

Ruth J. Flanigan: 12, 61, 80, 164, 171, 173, 174, 198, 199, 217, 218, 219, 227, 228, 239, 240, 258, 318, 326, 356, 453, 457, 484, 495, 496

Maps

Richard Pusey/Charthouse: 39, 331, 405, 435, color insert